GUIDE TO BRITISH CINEMA

Reference Guides to the World's Cinema

Guide to the Cinema of Spain
Marvin D'Lugo

Guide to American Cinema, 1965–1995
Daniel Curran

Guide to African Cinema
Sharon A. Russell

Guide to American Cinema, 1930–1965
Thomas R. Whissen

Guide to the Silent Years of American Cinema
Donald W. McCaffrey and Christopher P. Jacobs

Guide to the Cinema of Sweden and Finland
Per Olov Qvist and Peter von Bagh

Guide to the Cinema(s) of Canada
Peter Harry Rist, editor

GUIDE TO BRITISH CINEMA

GEOFF MAYER

Reference Guides to the World's Cinema
Pierre L. Horn, Series Adviser

GREENWOOD PRESS
Westport, Connecticut • London

Library of Congress Cataloging-in-Publication Data

Mayer, Geoff.
   Guide to British cinema / Geoff Mayer.
      p. cm—(Reference guides to the world's cinema, ISSN 1090–8234)
   Includes bibliographical references and index.
   ISBN: 0–313–30307–X (alk. paper)
   1. Motion pictures—Great Britain—History. I. Title. II. Series.
   PN1993.5.G7 M327   2003
   791.43′0941—dc21   2002075325

British Library Cataloguing in Publication Data is available.

Library of Congress Catalog Card Number: 2002075325
ISBN: 0–313–30307–X
ISSN: 1090–8234

First published in 2003

Greenwood Press, 88 Post Road West, Westport, CT 06881
An imprint of Greenwood Publishing Group, Inc.
www.greenwood.com

Printed in the United States of America

The paper used in this book complies with the
Permanent Paper Standard issued by the National
Information Standards Organization (Z39.48–1984).

10 9 8 7 6 5 4 3 2 1

CONTENTS

Series Foreword   vii

Acknowledgments   ix

Introduction   xi

Guide to British Cinema   1

Appendix: List of Films, Actors, and Directors, 1929–2000   401

Selected Bibliography   405

Index   411

SERIES FOREWORD

For the first time, on December 28, 1895, at the Grand Café in Paris, France, the inventors of the *Cinématographe,* Auguste and Louis Lumière, showed a series of eleven two-minute silent shorts to a public of thirty-five people each paying the high entry fee of one gold Franc. From that moment, a new era had begun, for the Lumière brothers were not only successful in their commercial venture, but also unknowingly created a new visual medium quickly to become, throughout the world, the half-popular entertainment, half-sophisticated art of the cinema. Eventually, the contribution of each member of the profession, especially that of the director and performers, took on enormous importance. A century later, the situation remains very much the same. The purpose of Greenwood's *Reference Guides to the World's Cinema* is to give a representative idea of what each country or region has to offer to the evolution, development, and richness of film. At the same time, because each volume seeks to present a balance between the interests of the general public and those of students and scholars of the medium, the choices are by necessity selective (although as comprehensive as possible) and often reflect the author's own idiosyncracies.

André Malraux, the French novelist and essayist, wrote about the cinema and filmmakers: "The desire to build up a world apart and self-contained, existing in its own right . . . represents humanization in the deepest, certainly the most enigmatic, sense of the word." On the other hand, then, every *Guide* explores this observation by offering discussions, written in a jargon-free style, of the motion-picture art and its practitioners, and on the other provides much-needed information, seldom available in English, including filmographies, awards and honors, and ad hoc bibliographies.

Pierre L. Horn
Wright State University

ACKNOWLEDGMENTS

I wish to thank Brian McFarlane, who shared his extensive knowledge of the British film industry, especially with regard to the actors and filmmakers of the pre-1960 period. I would also like to thank La Trobe University and postgraduate students, Liz Dance and Susan Johnston, who read the manuscript and made valuable suggestions, and finally Lesley Barbara Mayer for her support and assistance. All mistakes, omissions, and idiosyncratic opinions are, of course, mine.

INTRODUCTION

Interest in the British cinema has never been stronger. Unlike earlier periods, it is no longer confined to a small number of prestigious directors, such as Alfred Hitchcock,* or genres, notably Hammer Studios and the horror film. Today, it is wide-ranging. This was confirmed recently when Manchester University Press announced the directors chosen for a new series of books. The first director was Lance Comfort,* followed by Jack Clayton* and J. Lee Thompson.* Clayton, possibly, but Comfort and Lee Thompson! Why not David Lean,* Carol Reed,* or another book on Hitchcock? The decision to begin with a director who rarely, except for a brief period in the 1940s, worked with major stars in A-level films is symptomatic of a shift or a broadening of parameters. While this change did not take place overnight, it gathered strength throughout the 1990s until we now have reached a stage where one of Comfort's best films, *Great Day** (1945), a strange mixture of melodrama and film noir within a rural wartime setting, can be discussed with the same rigour and intensity as more prestigious films from the same period, such as *Brief Encounter* (1945).*

The British film industry, as opposed to studies of the British cinema, is much more fragile. This has been the case of most of the twentieth century. Despite periodic claims of a "renaissance" and revival, and despite occasional films that enjoy worldwide fame and fortune, the film industry is as insecure as ever. In 1933, Alexander Korda's* production of *The Private Life of Henry VIII** had its world premiere at Radio City Music Hall in New York and grossed, on first release, more than half a million pounds. This precipitated a boom in film production and the construction of Korda's studio at Denham. By 1938, the boom was well and truly over and Korda had lost control of his studio. Sixty years after *The Private Life of Henry VIII*, *Four Weddings and a Funeral** (1994) earned more than $250 million, followed three years later by the worldwide success of *The Full Monty.** Yet, the U.S. cinema has strengthened its hold on the British market, and overseas financing for most major British feature film productions is still necessary.

Studies of the British cinema have, for many years, been affected by the indifference, and sometimes contempt, expressed by critics, filmmakers, and academics in the 1950s and 1960s. It is tedious to repeat claims such as François Truffaut's 1960s infamous judgment that there is a "certain incompatibility between the terms 'cinema' and 'Britain,'"[1] coupled with Indian director Satayit Ray's observation that "I do not think the British are temperamentally equipped to make best use of the movie camera,"[2] and Jean Luc Godard's 1958 dismissal that "one has to really rack one's brains to find anything to say about a British film. One wonders why. But that's the way it is. And there isn't even an exception to prove the rule."[3] Nevertheless, such comments, coupled with the determination of critics in the 1950s and 1960s from *Cahiérs du Cinema,* the British film journal *Movie,* and others, to rehabilitate the reputation of the Hollywood cinema, while ignoring or dismissing the British cinema, came at a crucial stage in the growth of film studies and related academic disciplines. For many years, there was little interest in British cinema, as Alan Lovell implied in the title to a 1969 BFI seminar paper when he described the British cinema as "The Unknown Cinema."

Raymond Durgnat's 1970 publication *A Mirror for England,* followed by Rachel Low's *The History of the British Film* and especially David Pirie's *A Heritage of Horror* and Charles Barr's *Ealing Studio* were important in extending interest beyond the "safe pockets" of the industry. Gradually, it also extended to genres other than the horror film. In the 1940s and early 1960s, what little critical interest there was, especially that shown by newspaper critics, was circumscribed by the virtues of the documentary film. This was reflected in the bias toward films that replicated the conventions of a "realist" presentation located within "significant" subject matter. Conversely, many fine films and directors were underappreciated. The poor treatment of Michael Powell's* films in the 1940s and 1950s, for example, is instructive. More recently, since the 1970s, the elevation of Powell into the pantheon of great directors and the high regard for films such as *Peeping Tom** (1959) is a legacy of this period.

The *Guide* to *the British Cinema* reflects this change. It includes entries not only on Alfred Hitchcock, Laurence Olivier, David Lean, Peter Greenaway, Robert Hamer, Alexander Mackendrick, Dirk Bogarde, Nicholas Roeg, and Carol Reed, but also Lance Comfort, Roy Ward Baker, Cy R. Endfield, Val Guest, Christopher Lee, Peter Cushing, Sally Gray, J. Lee Thompson, John Guillermin, Ray Winstone, and other actors and directors long associated with the less prestigious levels of the industry. Even within the "pantheon" of great films and great directors, there is a need to reevaluate "lesser" or "failed" films. Hence, there are entries on two of Lean's undervalued films: *The Passionate Friends* (1949) and *Madeleine* (1950).

Even in those areas that have received extensive coverage, such as Hammer Films, there are still gaps. For example, interest in Hammer is mostly restricted to their horror films. Yet the studio produced many non-horror films, especially low-budget crime films. While the American B film has been subject to extensive examination for many years, studies of the low-budget British B film is just beginning. Consider *Cash on Demand* (1961),* a Hammer crime film costarring Peter Cushing* with André Morell, another B veteran. While Cushing, because of his association with the horror film, is well known, there is relatively little interest in his non-horror performances. Yet, in *Cash on Demand* he, arguably, gives his greatest film performance (as did Morell). That this film should be ignored by critics was understandable as it was released during the peak years of the British New Wave. *Cash on Demand,* a low-budget genre film, was the antithesis of films such as *Saturday Night and Sunday Morning* (1960) and *A Taste of Honey* (1961). Even if critics were aware that *Cash on Demand* reworked Charles Dickens's *A Christmas Carol,* it would not have made much difference. It was released by Hammer, it was a genre film, and it had a small budget.

The *Guide* includes key films, directors, and actors from 1929, the beginning of the British sound film, until 2000. Box office success, award-winning films, and films that initiated new directions, such as *Room at the Top** (1958) and *The Curse of Frankenstein* (1957),* are included. The *Guide* also includes less well-defined cycles, such as that rich vein of dark British melodramas produced in the immediate postwar period from 1945 to 1950. While the French were first to detect a profound change in the U.S. cinema in the 1940s, similar changes in the postwar British cinema have received little attention. Yet, tough crime films such as *They Made Me a Fugitive** (1947), "morbid" and morally problematic melodramas, often starring Eric Portman,* such as *Daybreak* (1948), *Dear Murderer** (1948), *The Mark of Cain** (1948), *Corridor of Mirrors** (1948), and *The Spider and the Fly** (1949), reiterated the formal and thematic changes evident in prestigious literary adaptations such as *Great Expectations** (1946).

The *Guide* includes only narrative feature films, meaning those films loosely described as the "popular cinema," and hence it excludes documentary, short films, and the avant-garde. The term "popular," however, covers a lot of territory and does not, at least in terms of this book, include just box office successes. There are many entries on films that did not succeed commercially, or existed only on the formal edges of the mainstream cinema, such as *This Sporting Life** (1963) and *Accident** (1967). The period under study extends from the first "talkie," Alfred Hitchcock's *Blackmail** (1929), to Terence Davies's masterpiece *House of Mirth** (2000). The only deviation is a brief entry on Hitchcock's first suspense film *The Lodger** (1926).

The *Guide* is not just a "best of" in terms of award winners, although many such films are included. Hence, subjectivity, critical judgment, or merely a lack of space may mean that a reader's favorite film or filmmaker is missing. There has been a concerted attempt to include examples of the "best," as well as films that were significant at the time of their release, such as *Georgy Girl** in 1966. There are also films from the key directors, selected examples from the major genres, particularly horror (since 1957), crime, and war films, and representative films from specific cycles, such as the Gainsborough melodrama, the Ealing comedy, and the British New Wave. An asterisk beside a film, actor or director indicates that there is an entry on the film/actor/director in the book.

While acknowledging the peaks of creativity, the *Guide* also includes examples from the "middle" and the lower levels of the industry. There is a bias in terms of the most prolific period of British film production: the 1940s and 1950s. Conversely, there are few films from the 1970s when the industry was relatively dormant. After the 1950s, there was also, as in many other countries, a fragmentation of the "general" audience. This resulted in a smaller number of regular moviegoers and a predominantly younger audience. This was accompanied by a reduction of local support for British films. Thus, films such as *Shallow Grave** (1994), *Trainspotting* (1996), *Lock, Stock and Two Smoking Barrels* (1998), and *Snatch** (2000) were not produced for a "general" audience, as were the pre-1950s films, but were marketed to "niche" groups.

Attempts to bolster British film production extend as far back as the 1927 Cinematograph Films Act and the so-called quota quickies. These low-budget films, often with elementary story lines, reflected distinctive regional and cultural attributes, such as the British music hall tradition. Many such films, often produced by subsidiary companies associated with the Hollywood studios, were designed primarily for the British market. Although they often drew on material from popular genres, most were distinctively British. This pattern of shared (Hollywood) conventions and local inflections remained after World War II, even in films with larger budgets produced with one eye on the U.S. market. For example, *Take My Life** (1947), Ronald Neame's* first film as a director, shared a similar story line with Robert Siodmak's 1944 Hollywood film noir *Phantom Lady.* Both films are concerned with women determined to save their (weak) boyfriend/husband from the gallows. Yet, both films are very different.

What constitutes a British film? "British" films often rely on overseas, mostly U.S., money. *Great Day,* for example, was produced by RKO British Productions, an offshoot of the U.S. studio that distributed the film in the United States. Similarly, United Artists provided the financing for *Tom Jones** (1963) after Bryanston, a British company, hesitated when it was decided to make the film in color. Bryanston soon went bankrupt. The extraordinary success of *Tom Jones* encouraged other U.S. studios to invest in the British cinema, especially during the Swinging London cycle of the mid-1960s, and *Georgy Girl* was one of Columbia's most successful films in 1967. Similarly, other "British" award-winning films, such as *Chariots of Fire** (1981) and *The English Patient* (1996), were financed overseas. There is also the complication in the late 1930s, 1940s, and 1950s of the U.S. studios sending a couple of stars, a director, and a screenwriter for filming in England with predominantly British casts and technicians. *So Evil My Love** was filmed in England in 1948 by Paramount Studios and *Night and the City** was made by Twentieth Century Fox in 1950.

Although there are gaps in this guide, a primary aim has been to provide some sense of what Julian Petley describes as the "lost continent." This evocative description refers to the heart of any national cinema—the great body of films

with modest ambitions. In this regard, I have included two Norman Wisdom*
films. Why? Because I wanted to (a) emphasise the popularity of Wisdom in the
1950s and early 1960s and (b) indicate a change in Wisdom's films after John
Paddy Carstairs was replaced in 1959 by Robert Asher as director. I have combined the entry on the last Carstairs-Wisdom film *The Square Peg* (1958) with the
first Asher-Wisdom film *Follow a Star* (1959). Similarly, there are two *Carry On*
films, the first, *Carry on Sergeant* (1958), followed by one of the most successful,
Carry on Cleo (1965).

Throughout the book the terms "New Wave" and "Swinging London films"
appear. The British New Wave refers to a relatively short-lived, but highly influential, cycle of feature films released between January 1959 (*Room at the Top**)
and the early 1960s. The cycle was in serious decline by 1963. There were a number of developments in the 1950s which shaped its characteristic aesthetic (spare,
bleak), recurring themes (such as the depiction of mass culture as essentially
superficial) and dramatic focus (the English working class). Some of these
aspects were evident in the "Free Cinema" documentary film movement found in
screenings at the National Film Theatre between 1956 and 1959. Also, the critical
reception of John Osborne's play *Look Back in Anger* in 1956 and the success of
John Braine's best selling 1957 novel *Room at the Top* were important in providing a transition to feature films by demonstrating the commercial potential of
such works.[4]

While the emphasis in the New Wave was on the young angry working class
male, this cycle was supplanted by different concerns in the "Swinging London"
films in the period from 1964 to 1966. While both cycles showed protagonists
determined to defy traditional social and moral conventions, the "Swinging London" films were characterized by a greater sense of optimism and a stronger interest in the desires and ambitions of young women.[5] These films also represented a
formal shift in the British cinema with their undermining of classical film conventions, especially the use of filmic space and narrative continuity. This may
indicate, as Alan Lovell notes,[6] the influence of an "art school surrealism," an
influence that also permeated music in the 1960s.

The *Guide* includes not only major British films, such as *The Third Man**
(1949), but entries on less ambitious, but nevertheless challenging, idiosyncratic
films such as *The Brothers** (1947), a dark, brooding melodrama, and *Daughter
of Darkness** (1948), another disturbing, morally ambivalent melodrama. The
Guide includes examples from the popular genres, such Victor Saville's remake
of Stanley Houghton's 1912 domestic melodrama *Hindle Wakes** (1931) that, in
terms of cinematic technique or "progressive" social meaning, is equal to the best
that Hollywood produced in 1931. Similarly, J. Lee Thompson's *Ice Cold in
Alex** (1957), a superior, "subversive" war film, and *Brighton Rock** (1947), the
remarkable "psychological" gangster film from the Boulting brothers, matched
anything produced by Hollywood in the these two popular genres. In other words,
the *Guide to the British Cinema* tries to provide a feel for the overall industry, the

great films and filmmakers, as well as those films and artists who have not received sufficient recognition for their contribution to the "lost continent."

NOTES

1. F. Truffaut, *Hitchcock,* London, Paladin, 1978, p. 140.
2. See S. Ray, *Our Films, Their Films,* Bombay, Orient London, 1974, p. 144.
3. Quoted in S. Chibnall, *J. Lee Thompson,* Manchester, Manchester University Press, 2000, p. 1.
4. Adam Lowenstein also notes the significance of "The Movement", a British literary cycle of the early and mid-1950s. This group was, amongst other influences, important in the development of the New Wave. See A. Lowenstein, "Under-the-skin horrors": Social Realism and Classlessness in *Peeping Tom* and the British New Wave," in J. Ashby and A. Higson, *British Cinema, Past and Present,* London, Routledge, 2000, p. 225.
5. See Moya Luckett, "Travel and Mobility: Femininity and National Identity in Swinging London Films," in Ashby and Higson, *British Cinema, Past and Present,* pp. 233–234.
6. See A. Lovell, "The Known Cinema?" in R. Murphy, *The British Cinema Book,* London, BFI Publishing, 1997, p. 242, note 7.

ABOVE US THE WAVES (Rank, 1955)—War. *Director:* Ralph Thomas; *Producer:* William MacQuitty; *Script:* Robin Estridge, based on a novel by Charles Esme Thornton Warren and James Benson; *Cinematography:* Ernest Steward; *Music:* Arthur Benjamin; *Cast:* John Mills (Commander Fraser), John Gregson (Lieutenant Alec Duffy), Donald Sinden (Lieutenant Tom Corbett), James Robertson Justice (Admiral Ryder), Michael Medwin (Smart), James Kenney (Abercrombie), O. E. Hasse (Captain of the *Tirpitz*), Lee Patterson (Cox), Anthony Newley (Engineer), and John Horsley (Lieutenant Anderson).

Near the end of *Above Us the Waves,* the captain of the German battleship *Tirpitz* surveys the extensive damage to his ship caused by explosives planted by the British sailors, who were led by Commodore Fraser. Expecting the worst, the captured sailors brace themselves for a violent reaction from the German who has just lost one of the prized vessels of the German navy. Instead, the German captain congratulates them and salutes their bravery. This scene is typical of the difference between British war films made during World War II and the characteristic presentation of the enemy in the mid-1950s' revival where the Germans were no longer the ruthless sadists of the 1940s films but men, like their British counterparts, sent out to do a job. Simple contrasts in ideology and excessive outpourings of moral outrage were no longer preeminent aspects of the story line, which was much more concerned with celebrating the bravery of the British officer class. A similar structure is evident in *The Colditz Story** (1955), where the German Kommandant is distressed at the prospect of British casualties.

The low-key ending in *Above Us the Waves,* which concludes with a survey of the forlorn faces of the British sailors as they realize that one of their companion midget submarines has been lost in a Norwegian fjord, is typical of the entire film that traces the training of a small group of men. Their mission is to sink the *Tirpitz,* a gigantic German battleship, which has been terrorizing the British navy in the North Atlantic. When their first attempt fails, the men are forced to seek refuge in Sweden. Their second attempt, with the use of the newly developed midget submarines, succeeds although all of the British sailors are either killed or captured. The success of the mission is not celebrated in the film, which is careful to highlight the human cost. Similarly, the film eschews overt heroics in favor of highlighting the inherent dangers of the mission and, by implication, the understated bravery of the men involved as director Ralph Thomas opts for a "realist" presentation of an actual (1943) military mission.

John Mills* reprises his tight-lipped, strict but caring commanding officer persona, popularized in a number of similar films, particularly *Morning Departure* (1950). The rest of the cast, including genre stalwarts such as Donald Sinden and John Gregson, are lightly sketched in with only some minor perfunctory personal details provided. Instead, the film is more concerned with the celebration of a distinctive group of men, the officer class. In this regard, it is typical of the war films produced by Rank in the 1950s, as opposed to similar films in the 1940s that celebrated the contribution of every class (the "People's War"), not just the officer elite.

ACCIDENT (Royal Avenue Chelsea, 1967)—Drama. *Director:* Joseph Losey; *Producers:* Joseph Losey and Norman Priggen; *Script:* Nicolas Mosley (novel) and Harold Pinter; *Photography:* Gerry Fisher; *Music:* John Dankworth; *Cast:* Dirk Bogarde (Stephen), Stanley Baker (Charley), Jacqueline Sassard (Anna), Michael York (William), Vivien Merchant (Rosalind), Delphine Seyrig (Francesca), Alexander Knox (College Provost), and Ann Firbank (Laura).

Accident, the second collaboration between Joseph Losey,* U.S. expatriate director, and Harold Pinter, continues their cold, detached critique of the British class system that they began in 1963 with *The Servant.* The film begins with a car crash near the home of middle-aged Oxford academic Stephen, resulting in the death of William, one of his students. The driver of the car, Anna, another student, is protected by Stephen from the police as she has been drinking. The rest of the film occurs as a flashback to this event.

The basic plot of the film is the stuff of melodrama as the story is primarily concerned with sexual betrayal, lust, and death. Stephen, married to Rosalind, who is about to have another child, covets Anna, while Charley, another Oxford academic and married to Laura, is sleeping with Anna. As a moral contrast to these middle-aged academics, "Innocence" is personified by young William, who only wants to marry Anna. In the hands of Losey and Pinter, the polarized moral dimension so crucial to melodrama is placed within a much more ethically complex structure, leaving only repression and emptiness, and the death of innocence.

This is a cold film as Losey and Pinter remove emotion and feeling from their characterization of Stephen and Charley, complemented by a succession of visual distancing techniques such as a preponderance of static long shots accompanied by long pauses in the dialogue and John Dankworth's minimalist jazz score. Losey refuses to associate any form of passion with his two Oxford academics. Even when Stephen visits London to rekindle a sexual affair with former student

Francesca, Losey eradicates the potential sensuality of their liaison by removing their dialogue and placing it on the soundtrack over cold images of their meal and the aftermath of their sex. Only Rosalind is allowed an emotional response when Stephen tells her Charley is sleeping with Anna. Even here her vehemence against Charley, and sympathy for his wife, is misdirected as her husband only wants to take Charley's place. The remainder of the film, which is fraught with betrayal and lust, retains a surface civility that only masks the repressed emotions.

Dirk Bogarde* and Stanley Baker* are superb in a film that largely depends on the unspoken or the slightest reaction to register meaning. For example, when Stephen returns to Oxford after sleeping with the provost's daughter, he casually tells the father that he saw his daughter Francesca in London. When the provost tells Stephen to give his best wishes to Francesca next time he sees her, Stephen replies that he does not think he will be seeing her for some time. Without a close-up or any other kind of filmic emphasis, the mouth of the provost (Alexander Knox) merely registers the slightest reaction to this comment. In melodrama, the representation of a father's awareness that one of his married staff members has been having sex with his daughter would be signaled by confrontation and conflict. In Losey and Pinter, the reaction of the provost is ambiguous, just sufficient to indicate that the provost is well aware of the affair and the probability that it will not continue. Similarly, *Accident* refuses to resolve moral issues raised throughout the body of the drama. There is no redemption or catharsis at the close—merely a dead man and an expectation that the characters will continue to suffer within the constraints of the institutions (such as marriage and academia) in which they exist.

Losey, for *Accident,* won the Grand Jury Prize at the 1967 Cannes Film Festival and the film was nominated for the 1968 BAFTA Awards for Best British Film and the American Golden Globe as Best English Language Foreign Film. Pinter and Bogarde were also nominated for Best Screenplay and Best Actor at the BAFTA Awards.

ACES HIGH (EMI/Cinema Artists Pictures, 1976)—War. *Director:* Jack Gold; *Producer:* Benjamin S. Fisz; *Script:* Howard Barker, based on the play *Journey's End* by R. C. Sheriff and the novel *Sagittarius Rising* by Cecil Lewis; *Cinematography:* Gerry Fisher; *Music:* Carlo Rustichelli and Richard Hartley; *Cast:* Malcolm McDowell (Gresham), Christopher Plummer (Sinclair), Simon Ward (Crawford), Peter Firth (Croft), David Wood (Thompson), John Gielgud (Headmaster), Trevor Howard (Colonel Silkin), Richard Johnson (Lyle), Ray Milland (Brigadier Whale), Christopher Blake (Roberts), David Daker (Bennett), and Tim Pigott-Smith (Stoppard).

Malcolm McDowell, an icon of youthful rebelliousness and anarchy in films such as *If . . .* (1968) and *A Clockwork Orange* (1971), gives one of his best performances as Gresham, the tormented leader of the 76th Squadron fighting the Germans in the air over France during World War I. After Gresham returns to his old school and rouses the boys with a patriotic speech, a young student (Croft) follows Gresham back to France and joins his squadron. However, unlike the idealized world that Gresham describes to the boys at school, reality at the front is much less civilized as young pilots regularly perish, largely due to the British military decision not to provide parachutes so as to prevent pilots from abandoning their planes.

The film's anti-war message is directed not at the Germans but at the British military hierarchy. This hierarchy is represented by aging military leaders unfamiliar with conditions at the front (personified by Ray Milland, Trevor Howard,* and Richard Johnson). Just as blonde Mark Lee symbolized the sacrifice of an entire generation of young Australian men during World War I in *Gallipoli* (1981), Peter Firth similarly represents the death of 'Innocence' in *Aces High*. Having just brought down his first German plane, and losing his virginity at a French nightclub, Croft dies in a midair collision at the end of the film. The inevitability of Croft's death, and the inevitability of more young men dying, is stressed in the film's final scene as the disillusioned Gresham welcomes three more totally unprepared recruits into his squadron, knowing they will soon follow Croft. *Aces High* reworks the basic futility-of-war theme developed in earlier aviation films, such as *The Dawn Patrol* (both the 1930 and 1938 versions). The film, with strong production values and a powerful message, deserved a wider audience and greater critical recognition. The cinematography by Gerry Fisher and Peter Allwork was nominated at the 1977 BAFTA Film Awards.

AGAINST THE WIND (Ealing, 1948)—Espionage. *Director:* Charles Crichton; *Producers:* Michael Balcon, Sidney Cole (associate), *Script:* T. E. Clarke and Michael Pertwee, additional dialogue by Paul Vincent Carroll, based on a story by J. Elder Wills; Cinematography: Lionel Banes; *Music:* Leslie Bridgewater; *Cast:* Robert Beatty (Father Phillip), Jack Warner (Max Cronk), Simone Signoret (Michele), Gordon Jackson (Johnny Duncan), Paul Dupuis (Jacques Picquart), Peter Illing (Andrew), James Robertson Justice (Ackerman), and John Slater (Emile Meyer).

Against the Wind, a war film produced by Ealing Studios, is a surprisingly tough, non-sentimental espionage drama that follows a group of unlikely people, including a Catholic priest, in their initial training and subsequent mission to rescue an allied agent from occupied Belgium. The tenor of the film is established in the initial scenes. For example, Johnny Duncan explains the types of sabotage activities engaged in by the unit. This includes despatching expensive women's underwear behind the enemy line so that the enemy will believe that their women are collaborating and/or sleeping with the Allies.

The film's theme is expressed by Andrew, an experienced agent, when he warns his trainees that duty must always come first "and friendship a bad second. Once you start mixing duty and affection you start digging graves. Your own and others." As a consequence, most of the group perish after making some form of personal sacrifice—Jacques Picquart has to spurn his fiancée to protect their mission, Emile Meyer is forced to radically change his appearance, and Michele loses her lover when he is exposed as a quisling. The film's major surprise occurs when Max is revealed as a traitor supplying information to an Irish spy in exchange for money. This is a effective piece of casting against type—Jack Warner,* even at this relatively early stage in his film career, was normally a positive character, a quality that is reinforced early in the film when he provides emotional support for Michele. Later, in a tense moment, Michele is forced to execute Max while he is shaving.

Against the Wind was not the commercial success that Ealing had hoped for, and writer T. E. B. Clarke and director Charles Crichton,* after the great success of *Hue and Cry** a year earlier, returned to comedy. Nevertheless, while the timing of *Against the Wind* may have worked against the commercial success of the film, it is a superior espionage drama that avoids most of the cliches found in this genre. While the mission is mostly successful, there is none of the self-congratulatory tone and jingoism that characterized similar British or U.S. films. At the end, the remnants of the group merely walk back into their farmhouse in preparation for their next job. Sentimentality and romance are evident but underplayed although there are some signs of the communal spirit that was to characterize films produced by Ealing.

ALFIE (Sheldrake Films, 1966)—Comedy. *Director:* Lewis Gilbert; *Producers:* Lewis Gilbert and John Gilbert (associate); *Script:* Bill Naughton, based on his play; *Photography:* Otto Heller; *Music:* Sonny Rollins; *Cast:* Michael Caine (Alfie Elkins), Shelley Winters (Ruby), Millicent Martin (Siddie), Julia Foster (Gilda), Jane Asher (Annie), Shirley Ann Field (Carla), Vivian Merchant (Lily), Eleanor Bron (Doctor), Denholm Elliott (Abortionist), Alfie Bass (Harry), and Sidney Taffler (Frank).

Alfie was promoted in the 1960s as a sex comedy, and the film played an enormous part in establishing the career and screen persona of Michael Caine.* Caine was nominated for the 1966 Academy Awards and won the National Society of Film Critics Award in the United States for his performance as the vain, cowardly, working-class Don Juan. Viewing the film thirty years after its release, it no longer seems a jaunty, innovative comedy celebrating an irresistible working-class lad. Instead, it comes across as a sobering portrait of a sad irresponsible male.

The episodic "adventures" of Alfie Elkins began as a radio play in 1962 as *Alfie Elkins and his Little Life,* written by Bill Naughton. This was transformed into a play and Naughton also wrote the screenplay. Alfie's "adventures" include abandoning his girlfriend Gilda and their son, impregnating a friend's wife, walking out on her suffering during a backyard abortion, and then provoking a young girl, Annie, into leaving his flat when she gets to be too much of a habit. The only (minor) setback to Alfie's "adventures" occurs near the end of the film when Alfie learns that the worldly Ruby plays his game of sexual betrayal even better than he does. This rebuff is compounded when Siddie, a married woman he ditched after she wanted him to meet her husband, is hesitant in resuming their affair.

The moral conventions of screen melodrama traditionally demand the redemption of the rake, the realization that marriage or a monogamous relationship is genuinely more satisfying than casual sex. The fact that *Alfie* does not fulfil this convention provides the only real sign of innovation. Alfie's habit of periodically addressing the camera, even during his lovemaking, was hardly a cutting-edge technique, even in 1966. It can be found in many Hollywood comedies well before 1966—see, for example, the Abbot and Costello comedies in the 1940s or Laurel and Hardy films in the 1930s.

Alfie is a conventional 1960s British film expressing a cynical view of the world. At the close of the film, Alfie retains the same attitude to women ("they're all birds") that he expressed at the start. He indicates that this will not change his attitude to commitment—the only difference is his admission that his "adventures" have not provided him with any long-term satisfaction as he is gradually losing his "peace of mind." The film closes with his confused address to the audience, reinforced by the words of Burt Bacharach and Hal David's pop song over the end credits, "So what's the answer? That's what I keep asking myself. What's it all about?" The film provides a clue in the final image of Alfie walking away accompanied by the same stray mongrel shown in the opening scene.

Alfie won the 1966 Golden Globe Award as Best English Language Foreign Film. It was nominated for the 1966 Academy awards and the BAFTA Film Awards, and won the Special Jury Prize at Cannes. Naughton's screenplay was nominated for the Academy Awards. Vivien Merchant won the most Promising Newcomer Award at the 1966 BAFTA Awards. She was also nominated for Best Supporting Actress at the U.S. Academy Awards.

ALL NIGHT LONG (Rank, 1961)—Drama. *Director:* Basil Deaden; *Producers:* Michael Relph and Bob Roberts; *Script:* Nel King and William Shakespeare; *Photography:* Edward Scaife; *Music:* Philip Green; *Cast:* Patrick McGoohan (Johnnie Cousin), Richard Attenborough (Rod Hamilton), Betsy Blair (Emily), Keith Michell (Cass), Paul Harris (Aurelius Rex), Marti Stevens (Delia Lane), and Bernard Braden (Berger).

Although the dramatic structure of the film is clearly borrowed from *Othello,* the film stands by itself largely through the performance of Patrick McGoohan as the Iago-like drummer Johnnie Cousin. The film is set in the apartment of wealthy Rod Hamilton, who gives a first anniversary party for black jazz musician Rex and his white wife, Delia Lane. At the party, Cousin's machinations create tension and violence among the guests.

Cousins makes a deal with agent Berger to form a new jazz group if he can persuade Rex's wife, Delia, to break a promise to her husband not to perform again. When Delia declines Cousins's invitation to join his proposed band, Cousins responds by progressively playing on Rex's fear that Delia has been intimate with their best friend Cass. The bittersweet ending leaves the frustrated Cousins banging away on his drums as everybody, including his loyal wife Emily, abandons him. Basil Dearden's* film cleverly integrates the jazz music by party guests, such as John Dankworth, Charlie Mingus, and Dave Brubeck, into the film at key points so that the music complements the uneasy mood of the overall film.

AND NOW THE SCREAMING STARTS! (Amicus Film, 1973)—Gothic/horror. *Director:* Roy Ward Baker; *Producers:* Max Rosenberg and Milton Subotsky; *Script:* Roger Marshall, based on the novel *Fengriffen* by David Case; *Photography:* Denys Coop; *Music:* Douglas Gamley; *Cast:* Peter Cushing (Dr. Pope), Herbert Lom (Henry Fengriffen), Stephanie Beacham (Catherine Fengriffen), Ian Ogilvy (Charles Fengriffen), Patrick Magee (Dr. Whittle), Rosalie Crutchley (Mrs. Luke), Guy Rolfe (Maitland), and Geoffrey Whitehead (Silas Jr., Silas Sr.).

Utilizing a familiar motif from the horror genre, the sins of the Father revisited on subsequent generations, *And Now the Screaming Starts!* is one of the few British films produced by two U.S. producers Max Rosenberg and Milton Subotsky that does not utilize an omnibus story format (e.g., see *Asylum** [1972] and *Vault of Horror* [1973]). Instead, *And Now the Screaming Starts!* is a careful blending of the conventions of the Gothic and horror genres that eschews the semicomedic flavor that characterized many of the Amicus productions of the early 1970s. A dark, foreboding atmosphere is maintained until the final revelation.

The Gothic basis of the story is established in the film's precredit voice-over from young Catherine as she travels to the Fengriffen castle to be married to Charles Fengriffen: "In my dreams I go back to the year 1795 to a time when I was happy. I was on my way to be married. I was going to the house in which I was to find my days filled with fear, my nights filled with terror." After reaching the castle, Charles provides Catherine with a short family history as they move past portraits of his ancestors. Catherine is drawn to the portrait of Charles's grandfather Sir Henry Fengriffen. A hand seemingly reaches out from the painting toward Catherine and this action becomes a recurring motif in the film.

The middle section of the film is more formulaic as a severed, bloodied hand roams the corridors of the castle killing anybody trying to assist Catherine as she tries to explain that she was violated by a stranger on her wedding night. After the arrival of Dr. Pope, Charles exposes the basis of Catherine's terror as he outlines the grisly family legend involving Sir Henry Fengriffen's amputation of the hand of Silas, a woodsman in Henry's employment. This followed Silas's attempt to prevent the drunken aristocrat from raping Silas's wife and his promise that the first virgin bride to live in the Fengriffen castle estate would be violated by him or his son, Silas Jr. Silas and his son are easily identified by the large birthmark on their faces—this is significant at the end of the film as the traumatized Catherine cradles her son with the same facial markings.

And Now the Screaming Starts!, which was also released under the more Gothic title of *Fengriffen,* dramatizes the response of the working class toward barbaric feudal customs, such as Sir Henry's determination to invoke the sexual rights of the landlord. The film benefits from Roy Ward Baker's* direction and his ability to enhance its formulaic (Gothic) premise through a pervasive sense of violation and injustice.

ANDERSON, LINDSAY (1923–1994). Born Lindsay Gordon Anderson in Bangalore, India, in 1923, Anderson's contribution to the British film industry was as a scholar, polemicist, and a key filmmaker during the "renaissance" of the early 1960s. Anderson was a trenchant critic of the British class system and the way it effected the shape and ethos of the British cinema. Many of his key films, such as *This Sporting Life** (1963) and *If . . .* (1968), were motivated by his desire to expose the inherent inequities of British institutions. Anderson especially objected to the overall "middle-class" tone of the British cinema, particularly in the 1950s. During this period, he wrote his lengthy celebration of U.S. director John Ford for *Sight and Sound,* emphasizing the creativity and poetry of Ford's Westerns—Anderson developed this idea further in a 1981 book that, in turn, was adapted for a television documentary with Anderson as host.

Anderson, Karel Reisz, Tony Richardson,* and Lorenza Mazzeti developed the Free Cinema movement in the mid-1950s so that they could get their films distributed and reviewed and to this end they developed a manifesto critical of the prevailing tone of the British film industry. Anderson and his colleagues were not immediately successful at breaking down the existing barriers to their entry into the industry, or even changing the emphasis of the British documentary cinema toward a more poetic tone. Consequently, Anderson moved into theater direction in 1956 and he was associated with London's Royal Court Theatre, which proved to be significant in the development of the New Wave in the late 1950s.

Anderson's breakthrough in the cinema came with *This Sporting Life.* Actor Richard Harris was also important in shaping the film as he convinced scriptwriter David Storey to return to the flashback structure found in Storey's novel. His next feature film, the groundbreaking *If . . . ,* was financed by Paramount after failing to attract any financial interest from within Britain. This film, with its biting attack on the British educational system, was not a financial success. Anderson's decision to film some sequences in black and white and some in color arose from the hesitancy of Czechoslovakian cinematographer Miroslav Ondricek to shoot a color scene in a school chapel in Cheltenham without more lamps. This decision generated considerable critical discussion as to its meaning. *O Lucky Man!* (1973) was even more innovative in its use of music as a distancing device and the fact that the same actors reappeared in the film in different parts. Again, the financing of this film came from Hollywood where Warner Brothers considered Malcolm McDowell, following his success in Stanley Kubrick's *A Clockwork Orange* (1971), a potential star.

Anderson continued to develop his notion of the "cinema as poetry." He used allegory and satire in *Britannia Hospital* (1982), his second last film, and the last of the "Mick Travis trilogy" with McDowell. His last feature film was the more conventional *Whales of August* (1987), which was shot on Cliff Island near Portland, Maine. With a cast of veteran U.S. actors, including the troublesome Bette Davis, Lillian Gish (in her last feature film), Ann Sothern, Harry Carey Jr., and Vincent Price.

Six feature films and seventeen shorts, including an Oscar-winning documentary on deaf children (*Thursday's Children* [1953]), plus a three-hour miniseries for U.S. television satirizing U.S. televangelism, *Twenty* (*Glory! Glory!* [1989]), was a sparse return for an articulate director with a strong vision for the role of the cinema in society. However, Anderson's distaste for conventional cinema restricted his opportunities in film and he was more prolific as a theater director. Anderson acted occasionally in the cinema (e.g., as the master of Caius in *Chariots of Fire** [1981]). He also narrated television documentaries celebrating the contributions of D. W. Griffiths, Harold Lloyd, Buster Keaton, and Ingmar Bergman to the cinema. Anderson was nominated for Best Direction for *If . . .* at the 1969 BAFTA Film Awards and won a Golden Palm Award at the 1969 Cannes Film Festival. He was also nominated for *O Lucky Man!* and *Britannia Hospital* at the 1973 and 1982 Cannes Film Festival. Anderson died of a heart attack in Angoulême, France, on August 30, 1994.

FILMS: Meet the Pioneers (1948), Idlers That Work (1949), Three Installations (1952), Wakefield Express (1952), Thursday's Children, O Dreamland (1953), Trunk Conveyor (1954), Green and Pleasant Land (1955), The Children Upstairs, a Hundred Thousand Children (1955), Henry (1955), Foot and Mouth (1955), Twenty Pounds a Ton (1955), Energy First (1955), Every Day Except Christmas (1957), The March to Aldermaston (codir., 1957), This Sporting Life (1963), The White Bus (1967), The Singing Lesson (1967), If . . . (1968), O Lucky Man! (1973), In Celebration (1974), Britannia Hospital (1982), The Whales of August (1987), and Is That All There Is? (1993).

ANGELS AND INSECTS (Playhouse International/Samuel Goldwyn, 1995)— Historical melodrama. *Director:* Philip Haas; *Producers:* Belinda Hass, Joyce Herlithy, Kerry Orent, and Lindsay Law (executive); *Script:* Belinda Hass and Philip Hass, based on the novella *Morpho Eugenia* by A. S. Wyatt; *Cinematography:* Bernard Zitzermann; *Music:* Alexander Balanescu; *Cast:* Mark Rylance (William Adamson), Kristin Scott Thomas (Matty Crompton), Patsy Kensit (Eugenia Alabaster), Jeremy Kemp (Sir Harald Alabaster), Douglas Henshall (Edgar Alabaster), Annette Badland (Lady Alabaster), Chris Larkin (Robin), and Anna Massey (Miss Mead).

Angels and Insects, a subversive and perceptive examination of the habits of the British aristocracy, works largely through metaphor and the film draws a clear analogy between the social and sexual mores of the Alabaster family and the survival strategies of an insect colony. The period in which the film is set is crucial in understanding its purpose. The film begins in 1858, the year in which Charles Darwin's *Origin of the Species* was published. Within this context, Lady Alabaster is presented as the equivalent of the queen bee, pampered by her servants, fed to bursting point with no social function beyond producing children to be reared by nannies.

Anthropologist William Adamson loses virtually all of his rare specimens in a shipwreck, while returning from South America to England. He presents the only surviving insect, a rare butterfly, to Sir Harald Alabaster, an aristocrat obsessed with the preservation of insects and the process of natural survival. After Adamson is invited to live in the Alabaster household and to organize Sir Harald's collection, he is intrigued by Sir Harald's oldest daughter Eugenia, a woman troubled by the recent suicide of her fiancé. Adamson courts Eugenia and she, surprisingly, accepts his marriage proposal although he is a poor man from a working-class family. Soon, they have a number of children although Adamson is puzzled by his wife's attitude to him, particularly the rapidity with which her sexual behavior alternates between brief periods of intense cooperation and long periods of disinterest.

Adamson forms a working relationship with the family tutor Matty Crompton. She is fascinated with recording the habits of ant colonies on the estate. The film emphasizes the differences between Matty and William, and the female members of the Alabaster family. This is particularly evident in their clothes. The drab, dark colors worn by Matty contrasts strongly with the rich colors of the Alabaster costumes—bold yellows, blacks, blue, and reds that complement their hair styles and hats employing fruits, animals, and even eggs. However, the Alabaster women are shown to be sickly and decadent and the bright colors mask their illness. These aspects come together at the film's climax when William catches Eugenia in bed with her brutish brother Edgar. It is then that William realizes that Edgar is the father of Eugenia's children, a fact known by others as Matty points out to William—there are "people in the house who know everything, yet remain invisible."

Angels and Insects is concerned with destructive aspects of the British class system. Philip Hass and Belinda Hass, however, are not interested in providing a broad critique, preferring instead to draw out its hypocritical conventions with a measured, seemingly leisurely story that works primarily through metaphor and carefully developed systems of association, visual, and otherwise.

THE ARSENAL STADIUM MYSTERY (General/Rank, 1939)—Crime/police. *Director:* Thorold Dickinson; *Producer:* Josef Somlo; *Script:* Donald Bull and Patrick Kirwan, adaptation by Thorold Dickinson and Alan Hyman, from a novel by Leonard Reginald Gribble; *Cinematography:* Desmond Dickinson; *Cast:* Leslie Banks (Inspector Anthony Slade), Greta Gynt (Gwen Lee), Ian McLean (Sergeant Clinton), Liane Linden (Inga Larsen), Anthony Bushell (John Doyce), Esmond Knight (Raille), Brian Worth (Philip Moring), and Wyndham Goldie (Kindilett).

In *The Arsenal Stadium Mystery,* Thorold Dickinson,* who also adapted the script, has fun with the conventions of the prewar British detective formula. Soccer star and womanizer John Doyce collapses and dies during a charity soccer game between the professional Arsenal Soccer team and an amateur club The Trojans at Highbury Stadium. A number of suspects are uncovered during the investigation by eccentric Scotland Yard inspector Slade and his equally bizarre partner Sergeant Clinton. The suspects include the manager of the Trojans,

Kindilett, fellow players Philip Moring and Raille, together with attractive model Gwen Lee, who was playing Doyce and Moring off against each other.

Ultimately, the mystery merely provides a context for the comedic skills of Leslie Banks* as Inspector Slade, who proceeds to steal every scene that he is in. After Doyce's murder, Slade is introduced to the audience dancing across an auditorium stage as he prepares his fellow policemen, dressed in a ballet costume, for a revue. Slade concludes the film in the same way. In between, Slade investigates the murder and consistent with the formula, indicates quite early that he knows how the murder was committed. Having solved the crime in his own mind, Slade leaves the hapless Clinton to catch the criminal while he returns to producing his police revue. As a detective/mystery film, it is characterized by its lack of seriousness and Slade normally upstages each scene with a gesture or line of dialogue (he accuses a fellow police officer who has lost the man he is following of being too preoccupied with filling out his expense account). Slade changes hats regularly throughout the investigation as an indication of his progress—ranging from a beret to a fisherman's headgear complete with fishing tackle!

The Arsenal Stadium Mystery has an added bonus for English soccer fans (in the late 1930s) by including players from the Arsenal Soccer Club, at practice, relaxing, and playing.

ASQUITH, ANTHONY (1902–1968). Michael Denison, who starred in one of Anthony Asquith's best films, *The Importance of Being Earnest* (1952), considered Asquith a fine director and "interpreter, and that is how I like my directors to be."[1] Stewart Granger,* like Phyllis Calvert,* considered Asquith the best director he worked with on the popular Gainsborough melodramas of the 1940s (Calvert and Granger costarred in Asquith's *Fanny by Gaslight* in 1944), with both actors having little regard for other directors such as Arthur Crabtree, Bernard Knowles, and especially Leslie Arliss (Granger: "A bunch of bloody awful directors at Gainsborough").[2] Producer Anthony Havelock-Allan, on the other hand, considered Asquith a good, but not great director—"perhaps not ruthless enough"—a judgment based on the fact that he was a little "soft" in his treatment of political films such as *The Young Lovers** (1954) and *Orders to Kill* (1958).

Asquith, the son of Lord Herbert Asquith the Liberal prime minister, was educated at Oxford and, in 1925, helped establish the London Film Society. Asquith's early films, beginning in 1927 with *Shooting Stars,* demonstrated visual flair. This was not characteristic of his later films where "taste," fine performances, and craftsman-like qualities were more obvious. Asquith learned his trade on "quota quickies" and he consolidated his reputation with *Pygmalion* in 1938, followed by a series of quality films emanating from his long collaboration with playwright Terence Rattigan—beginning with *French without Tears* (1939), the excellent *The Winslow Boy** (1948), and the even better *The Browning Version* (1951). Rattigan also coscripted, with Anatole de Grunwald, Asquith's *The Way to the Stars* (1945), one of his best films. On the other hand, *The Final Test*

(1953), Asquith's adaptation of a television play by Rattigan, was less successful, although this may have had something to do with its bizarre premise of Jack Warner* as an aging cricketer attempting to hold the English innings together against the Australian bowlers in a test match.

Asquith's output in the 1950s and 1960s was uneven. A planned film on the life of Lawrence of Arabia from his Cambridge days until his death, starring Dirk Bogarde* as Lawrence, was aborted by Rank ten days prior to the start of filming. This cancellation deeply affected Asquith and, after quickly searching for another script, he convinced Bogarde to work with him on George Bernard Shaw's *The Doctor's Dilemma* (1959). The film, however, was not a commercial success. Earlier in the decade, he enjoyed more success with an adaptation of Oscar Wilde's *The Importance of Being Earnest.* He ended the decade with another international success, Shaw's *The Millionairess* (1960), costarring Sophia Loren and Peter Sellers.* His final two films, *The V.I.P.s* (1963), scripted by Rattigan with an all-star class playing rich and privileged people, and the episodic *The Yellow Rolls-Royce* (1964), based on another Rattigan script, were bloated productions that lacked dramatic edge. Asquith was president of the Association of Cine-Technicians from 1937 until his death in 1968.

FILMS: Shooting Stars (codir., 1927), Underground (1928), The Runaway Princess (1929), A Cottage on Dartmoor (1930), Tell England (1931), Dance Pretty Lady (1933), The Lucky Number (1933), Youth Will Be Served (1933), Unfinished Symphony (codir., 1934), Moscow Nights (1936), The Story of Papworth: The Village of Hope (short, 1936), Pygmalion (codir., 1938), French without Tears (1939), Guide Dogs for the Blind (short, 1939), Freedom Radio (1940), Quiet Wedding (1940), Channel Incident (short, 1940), Cottage to Let (1941), Rush Hour (short, 1941), Uncensored (1942), We Dive at Dawn (1943), The Demi-Paradise (1943), Welcome to Britain (short, 1943), Fanny by Gaslight (1944), Two Fathers (short, 1944), The Way to the Stars (1945), While the Sun Shines (1946), The Winslow Boy (1948), The Woman in Question (1950), World without Shadow (1950), The Browning Version (1951), The Importance of Being Earnest (1952), The Net (1953), The Final Test (1953), The Young Lovers (1954), Carrington, V.C. (1954), On Such a Night (short, 1955), Orders to Kill (1958), The Doctor's Dilemma (1959), Libel (1959), The Millionairess (1960), Zero (1960), Two Living, One Dead (1961), Guns of Darkness (1962), An Evening with the Royal Ballet (1963), The V.I.P.s (1963), and The Yellow Rolls-Royce (1964).

ASYLUM (Amicus Film, 1972)—Horror. *Director:* Roy Ward Baker; *Producers:* Max Rosenberg and Milton Subotsky; *Script:* Robert Bloch; *Photography:* Denys Coop; *Music:* Douglas Gamley; *Cast:* Peter Cushing (Smith), Patrick Magee (Dr. Rutherford), Herbert Lom (Dr. Byron), Robert Powell (Dr. Martin), Barbara Parkins (Bonnie), Britt Ekland (Lucy), Megs Jenkins (Miss Higgins), Richard Todd (Walter), Sylvia Syms (Ruth), James Villiers (George), Charlotte Rampling (Barbara), Geoffrey Bayldon (Max Reynolds), Ann Firbank (Anna), and Barry Morse (Bruno).

When Dr. Martin arrives at Dunsmoor, a clinic for the insane, for his interview with Dr. Rutherford, Rutherford tells him that he can have the position if he can ascertain which one of four insane patients is the former head of the clinic (Dr. Star). This challenge provides the necessary linking device for the usual Amicus format of providing four or five episodic stories that normally end with a twist and/or violence.

In the first story, "Frozen Fear," Walter kills his rich wife, Ruth, and after severing each limb and the head from the trunk, he neatly wraps each part in brown paper and places them in the family freezer. Ruth's body, however, refuses to lie down and die and, after killing Walter, her disembodied limbs attack Walter's girlfriend Bonnie. Finally, Bonnie is forced to hack away at her own face with an axe when Ruth's hand grabs hold of her. "The Weird Tailor" brings a body back to life after following the instructions of an ancient book. The third tale, "Lucy Comes to Life," introduces the split personality motif that the screenwriter Robert Bloch used so successfully in his most famous screenplay for Alfred Hitchcock's* *Psycho* (1960). In this episode Barbara murders her husband and nurse under the influence of "Lucy," the homicidal half of her split personality. The final tale, "Mannikins of Horror," brings all of the elements together as a demented doctor makes homunculi that kill Dr. Rutherford. A hospital orderly then reveals that he is the murderous Dr. Star and kills Martin. The film ends with the arrival of a new applicant—hence the story will repeat itself.

The omnibus story format in *Asylum* is, like many of the Amicus films, entirely plot driven, leaving little room for character development, although Roy Ward Baker's* direction supplements the fatalistic atmosphere of the gloomy clinic wherever possible, particularly his stylized use of drawings of madness and suffering early in the film which foreshadows the bizarre nature of each story.

ATTENBOROUGH, RICHARD (b. 1923). Richard Attenborough was born in 1923 in Cambridge. The son of a school administrator, Attenborough has been a major figure in the British cinema since the late 1940s. While studying acting at Royal Academy of Dramatic Art, he appeared in *Ah, Wilderness* in a small theater in London and U.S. agent Al Parker arranged a test for a small role in Noël Coward's *In Which We Serve* (1942). Later in the decade, his startling performance as the psychotic baby-faced gangster Pinkie Brown in *Brighton Rock* (1947) changed both his status in the industry and his screen persona. This role came soon after spending some time with Edward G. Robinson, famous for his gangster performances in the 1930s.

Although Attenborough worked steadily throughout most of the 1940s and 1950s, he became disillusioned with the roles offered to him and the conservative nature of British cinema ("It seemed to us that the same old movies, in some form re-dressed, re-shaped, were being churned out. There were very few people challenging the subject.").[3] As a result, he formed a partnership with actor/writer/director Bryan Forbes* and they wrote, produced, and (Attenborough) starred in *The Angry Silence* (1960), a significant film because of its confrontational subject matter: a union man who refuses to join a wildcat strike. Attenborough convinced everybody in the production to work for scale and take a percentage of the profits. Attenborough, who wanted Kenneth More* for the central role of Tom Curtis, took the part when More pulled out shortly before filming began. He acknowledged later that *The Angry Silence* marked a significant change in his career.

For many years, Attenborough had longed to make a film about the life of Mohandas Gandhi and in 1982 he directed this award-winning film. Prior to this, he honed his directorial skills on *Oh! What A Lovely War* (1969), *Young Winston* (1972), *A Bridge Too Far* (1977), and *Magic* (1978). Receiving £5,000 from Sir John Davis at Rank, who opposed the proposed film on the grounds that Gandhi was not a commercial proposition, Attenborough was able to develop the screenplay into one of the most successful British films. *Gandhi* (1982) won the Oscar for Best Picture and he won Best Director at the 1983 Academy Awards, the BAFTA Awards, and the Golden Globes.

A broad sweeping epic with high moral purpose seemed to suit Attenborough. While *A Chorus Line* (1985) failed, he succeeded with another epic depiction of injustice, *Cry Freedom* (1987), which was nominated for Best Picture and Attenborough Best Director at the 1988 BAFTA Awards. Attenborough won the David Lean Award for Best Director in 1993 for *Shadowlands* (1993), which followed the failure of *Chaplin* (1992), another project that he had nurtured for a long time.

Attenborough's success as a director should not obscure the fact that he is one of the most durable actors in the British cinema. Notable performances include his subdued killer in *10 Rillington Place* (1970). He won the 1965 BAFTA Best Actor Award for *Guns at Batasi* (1964) and both the BAFTA and New York Critics Awards for Best Actor in *Séance on a Wet Afternoon* (1964), plus a Golden Globe in 1967 for Best Supporting Actor in *The Sand Pebbles* (1965). Attenborough not only sang in *Dr. Dolittle* (1967), but also won the Golden Globe for Best Supporting Actor. After mainly directing for some years, he returned to acting as the billionaire entrepreneur who unleashes the dinosaurs in Steven Spielberg's *Jurassic Park* (1993) and the 1997 sequel. He also had a supporting role in the low budget adaptation of Spike Milligan's novel *Puckoon*. As part of the film's promotion at the time of its release in 2002 Attenborough was asked if he has stopped chasing Oscars: Attenborough leans forward and slams the table so hard the tea-cups rattle. "Before we begin," he tells the interviewer, "I never. . . . cried at the Oscars—that's myth" he says, referring to his emotional speech when accepting eight Academy Awards for *Ghandi* in 1982. "In fact, I don't really like the Oscars; it's a commercial promotional event. It helps immeasurably to sell films, but it's hardly the Nobel prize.'"[4] Attenborough was knighted in 1976 and received a life peerage in 1993.

FILMS: In Which We Serve (1942), Schweik's New Adventures (1943), The Hundred Pound Window (1943), Journey Together (1945), A Matter of Life and Death (1946), School for Secrets (1946), The Man Within (1947), Dancing with Crime (1947), Brighton Rock (1947), London Belongs to Me (1948), The Guinea Pig (1948), The Lost People (1949), Boys in Brown (1949), Morning Departure (1950), Hell Is Sold Out (1950), The Magic Box (1951), The Gift Horse (1952), Father's Doing Fine (1952), Eight O'Clock

Walk (1954), The Ship That Died of Shame (1955), Private's Progress (1956), The Baby and the Battleship (1956), Brothers-in-Law (1957), The Scamp (1957), Dunkirk (1958), The Man Upstairs (1958), Sea of Sand (1958), Danger Within (1959), I'm All Right Jack (1959), Jet Storm (1959), SOS Pacific (1959), The Angry Silence (also coprod., 1960), The League of Gentlemen (1960), Whistle Down the Wind (prod., 1961), The L-Shaped Room (prod., 1962), All Night Long (1962), The Dock Brief (1962), The Great Escape (1963), Only Two Can Play (1963), Guns at Batasi (1964), Séance on a Wet Afternoon (also prod., 1964), The Flight of the Phoenix (1965), The Sand Pebbles (1965), Dr. Dolittle (1967), The Bliss of Mrs. Blossom (1968), Only When I Larf (1968), Oh! What a Lovely War (dir. 1969), David Copperfield (1969), The Magic Christian (1969), The Last Grenade (1970), Loot (1970), 10 Rillington Place (1970), A Severed Head (1971), Young Winston (1972), And Then There Were None (1974), Conduct Unbecoming (1975), Rosebud (1975), Brannigan (1975), A Bridge Too Far (dir., 1977), Magic (dir., 1978), The Human Factor (1979), Gandhi (dir., 1982), A Chorus Line (dir., 1985), Cry Freedom (dir., 1987), Chaplin (dir., 1992), Jurassic Park (dir., 1993), Shadowlands (dir., 1993), Miracle on 34th Street (1994), Hamlet (1996), Lost World (1997), In Love and War (dir., 1997), Elizabeth (1998), Grey Owl (dir. and prod., 1999), Jacob and the Amazing Technicolor Dreamcoat (1999), and Puckoon (2002).

NOTES

1. B. McFarlane, *An Autobiography of British Cinema, by the Actors and Filmmakers Who Made It.* London, Methuen, 1997, p. 172.
2. McFarlane, *An Autobiography of British Cinema,* p. 230.
3. McFarlane, *An Autobiography of British Cinema,* p. 35.
4. Quoted in the *The Age,* July 26, 2002, p. 3 (The Culture section).

B

BACK ROOM BOY (Gainsborough, 1942)—Comedy. *Director:* Herbert Mason; *Producer:* Edward Black; *Script:* Marriott Edgar, Val Guest, and J. O. C. Orton; *Photography:* Jack E. Cox; *Music:* Hans May; *Cast:* Arthur Askey (Arthur Pilbeam), Moore Marriott (Jerry), Graham Moffatt (Albert), Googie Withers (Bobbie), Vera Francis (Jane), and Joyce Howard (Betty).

When Will Hay* moved from Gainsborough to Ealing Studios just before the outbreak of World War II, popular radio comedian Arthur Askey was chosen to replace him. Askey's first film, *Band Waggon* (1939), was based on his successful BBC radio program. In *Band Waggon,* Askey, forced to leave his living quarters on the roof of Broadcasting House, moves into a castle that is supposedly haunted. The ghost is exposed as Moore Marriott, who is working with a gang of spies to scare away any outsiders. Askey followed with a new version of Arnold Ridley's play *Ghost Train* (1941), with German spies replacing smugglers.

In *Back Room Boy,* Arthur Pilbeam loses his girlfriend Jane when their romantic moments are interrupted every hour because of his vocation as the man responsible for pushing the button for the BBC's "six pips" time signal. Determined to get away from all women, Pilbeam moves to an isolated lighthouse off the Scottish coast where he finds himself surrounded by females—first, a young independent girl who lives nearby and then by a group of chorus girls forced into the lighthouse when their boat sinks.

The film balances a clever mix of music hall comedy, with a leering Marriott perpetually trying to peek at the girls while they undress, with the thrills of a suspense film. The inhabitants of the lighthouse mysteriously disappear one by one, leaving Pilbeam to combat the Nazi spies who are utilizing the lighthouse while planting sea mines. Small, with huge horn-rimmed glasses, Askey milks every possible situation in this film, which was one of his best.

BAKER, ROY WARD (b. 1916). After the success of *Morning Departure* (1950), Roy Baker's fourth film, Twentieth Century Fox invited him to Hollywood (he changed his name to Roy Ward Baker in 1957 when he discovered that there was a sound editor with the name of Roy Baker). After meeting Darryl F. Zanuck, the head of the studio, Baker was sent back to Denham Studios in Britain to direct a remake of *Berkeley Square,* which was renamed *The House on the Square* (1951), starring Tyrone Power and Ann Blyth. Baker then returned to Hollywood for three Hollywood films. The most famous was the first, *Don't Bother to Knock* (1952), which costarred Marilyn Monroe with Richard Widmark. The second film, a relatively low-budget film noir, *Night without Sleep* (1952), costarring Gary Merrill and Linda Darnell, is instructive in establishing the dark, pessimistic undercurrent that characterizes many of Baker's pre-1962 films. *Night without Sleep* was concerned with twenty-four hours in the life of Richard Morton. He drinks, romances Darnell, and fights with his mistress Hildegarde Knef. At the end of this period, he discovers that he murdered his wife twenty-four hours ago, a fact he had forgotten in his drunken stupor.

Baker began with Gainsborough Studios in 1934 and stayed with this company until the outbreak of World War II. He gained valuable experience working at a variety of activities, including location manager. During the war, he was seconded to the Army Kinematograph Service Film Production Unit at the old Fox-British Studios at Wembley Park where he worked on training films. During this period, Baker met novelist and scriptwriter Eric Ambler. In 1945, Ambler invited Baker to direct his script of J. Sheridan Le Fanu's Gothic melodrama *Uncle Silas.* However, Two Cities cancelled the project (it was later filmed with Charles Frank directing) and asked Ambler to write an original story that became *The October Man* (1947).* This bleak, psychological drama concerns Jim Ackland, a young chemist who suffers a mental collapse after the death of a child in a bus accident. Later, following the death of a woman in his boarding house, he contemplates suicide.

After limited success with *The Weaker Sex* (1948), a drama of the home front during the war, and the crime film, *Paper Orchid* (1948), Baker's most successful film prior to *A Night to Remember* (1958) was *Morning Departure.* While the film purported to celebrate the sacrifices made by British servicemen, the tone of the film is bleak as it focuses on a small group of men trapped when their submarine hits a mine. When sixty-four sailors perished in the HMS *Truculent* after it sank in the Thames just prior to the release of *Morning Departure,* Baker's film received a lot of publicity and its success proved a great boost to his career, including a Hollywood contract.

After Baker's other Hollywood film, the—outdoor drama *Inferno* (1953), starring Robert Ryan, he returned to Britain (and Rank) for *Passage Home* (1954), an intense melodrama set on a cargo ship traveling from South America to England. The confined nature of the setting intensified the film's fervid atmosphere of sexual repression, emanating from the desire of the ship's captain (Peter Finch*) for Diane Cilento. Finch's feelings eventually erupt into attempted rape. The film's final image, with Cilento and Finch exchanging glances many years later, is typical of Baker as he challenges the film's perfunctory "happy" ending. *Jacqueline* (1955), a sentimental Irish tale, was a slight film, followed by *Tiger in* *the Smoke* (1956), a crime melodrama, based on the Margery Allingham novel. Although the film benefited from a strong, atmospheric opening, the sense of tension and anxiety dissipated after the appearance of Tony Wright, who was fatally miscast as the film's psychotic villain. *The One That Got Away* (1957) was a rare British film in that it focused on the successful escape of a German fighter pilot (Hardy Kruger) after his capture by the British. Then came Baker's most widely known film, *A Night to Remember,* still the best film account of the sinking of the *Titanic,* which projected both a sense of drama and historical veracity.

Baker, in 1958–1959, was at the peak of his success. His fall was equally dramatic. His next film *The Singer Not the Song* (1960), a film that he did not want to make, was a bizarre melodrama set in Mexico. The production was beset by hostilities on the set and the film was weakened by the casting of Dirk Bogarde* as a Mexican bandit in conflict with a priest (John Mills*). The casting of young Mylene Demongeot, who is involved with both the priest and the bandit, exposed the substantial age difference between Mills and Demongeot. Baker's strength, an ability to bring the best out of a genre film, was not sufficient to save this film as it required a more excessive, surreal approach. Baker admitted that this failure set his career back many years. His next film, the racial drama *Flame in the Streets* (1961), was a solid film with social relevance. However, it failed to attract a substantial audience and, together with the lack of box office success with *The Singer Not the Song* and *Two Left Feet* (1962) (co-written by Baker), meant that he was relegated to television production for much of the 1960s. This was also due to changes in the British film industry, especially the decline of the middle-budget genre film at which Baker excelled.

Baker returned to feature films with the superior science fiction film *Quatermass and the Pit* (1967), the third Quatermass film, and the inferior science fiction film *Moon Zero Two* (1969). In between these two films, he took over direction of the troubled production of a Bette Davis film, *The Anniversary* (1967), based on William McIlwraith's play. Both *Moon Zero Two* and *The Anniversary* were made for Hammer and Baker's connection with the studio was consolidated with his first horror film, *The Vampire Lovers* (1970). This sensual reworking of Sheridan Le Fanu's *Carmilla* was followed by the lackluster *Scars of Dracula* (1970) with Christopher Lee* clearly going through the motions as Dracula. More interesting was Baker's next film, a gender reversal of the classic Dr. Jekyll and Mr. Hyde story as *Dr. Jekyll and Sister Hyde* (1971). Baker also directed two of the Amicus episodic films, the superior *Asylum** (1972), and *The Vault of Terror* (1972), together with an adaptation of the novel *Fengriffin,* which was titled *And Now the Screaming Starts!** (1972). He concluded his work on feature films with the kung fu vampire film *The Legend of the Seven Golden Vampires* (1973), shot in Hong Kong, and the horror spoof *The Monster Club* (1980). Baker, however, continued directing made-for-television films, including the excellent Sherlock Holmes adventure *The Masks of Death* (1984), with Peter Cushing* as Sherlock Holmes and John Mills,* a frequent star of Baker's films, as Dr. Watson. Baker worked extensively in television during this period, a practice that he began in the early 1960s with *Zero One* and *The Saint,* starring Roger Moore. His television work concluded with *The Good Guys* in 1992.

FILMS: The October Man (1947), The Weaker Sex (1948), Paper Orchid (1948), Morning Departure (1950), Highly Dangerous (1950), The House on the Square (1951), Don't Bother to Knock (1952), Night without Sleep (1952), Inferno (1953), Passage Home (1954), Jacqueline (1955), Tiger in the Smoke (1956), The One That Got Away (1957), A Night to Remember (1958), The Singer Not the Song (1960), Flame in the Streets (1961), The Valiant (1962), Two Left Feet (1962), Quatermass and the Pit (1967), The Anniversary (1967), Moon Zero Two (1969), The Vampire Lovers (1970), Scars of Dracula (1970), Dr. Jekyll and Sister Hyde (1971), Asylum (1972), And Now the Screaming Starts! (1972), The Vault of Horror (1972), The Legend of the Seven Golden Vampires (1973), and The Monster Club (1980).

BAKER, STANLEY (1927–1976). Stanley Baker occasionally played the role of a conventional hero, such as the airplane pilot, Captain Bardew, threatened by a unstable passenger (Richard Attenborough*) with a bomb in *Jet Storm* * (1959), or the stoic Lieutenant Chard who defied the might of the Zulu nation with his small band of Welsh soldiers at Rorke's Drift in 1879 in *Zulu* * (1964). But he was more distinctive as a villain or a morally problematic character, such as the broken down boxer who falls in with a group of misfits in *The Good Die Young* * (1954), his first major role. Prior to this, Baker alternated between the stage after his debut in 1944 and small film roles, beginning with *Undercover* in 1943.

Baker's ex-convict truck driver in Cy Endfield's* tough melodrama *Hell Drivers* * (1957), victimized by fellow drivers, epitomized Baker's distinctive contribution to the British cinema in the 1950s with his alienated persona and determination to survive life's obstacles—whatever the cost. Baker's raw, virile persona established him as a different kind of British film actor at this time, although by the end of the decade this trait was supplanted by a more socially conscious school of actors. Although he was not part of this cycle, Baker retained his place as a major figure in the late 1950s and 1960s, mainly in genre films such as the *Violent Playground* (1958), *Yesterday's Enemy* (1959), for which he was nominated as Best British Actor at the 1960 BAFTA Film Awards, and *Sands of the Kalahari* (1965), which reunited him with Endfield (*Hell Drivers* and *Zulu*).

Endfield's films emphasized Baker's virility. Joseph Losey,* on the other hand, emphasized his wounded vulnerability, a trait exploited in crime films such as *Blind Date* (1959) and *The Criminal* * (1960). Losey extended it further with Baker's masochistic Tyvian Jones drawn to evil Jeanne Moreau in *Eva* (1963), and the adulterous Oxford don in *Accident* * (1967).

Baker formed his own production company in the 1960s and produced a number of his own films, including *Zulu, Sands of the Kalahari, Robbery* (1967, based on the British Royal Mail robbery), and *Where's Jack?* (1969), with Tommy Steele playing opposite Baker. The 1970s were less kind to Baker, with only Peter Hall's *Perfect Friday* (1970), a caper film opposite Ursula Andress, *The Last Grenade* (1970), and Peter Collinson's espionage melodrama *Innocent*

Bystanders (1973) being of any interest. Baker was knighted just prior to his death from lung cancer in 1976.

FILMS: Undercover (1943), Obsession (1949), All Over the Town (1949), Your Witness (1950), The Rossiter Case (1950), Lilli Marlene (1950), Captain Horatio Hornblower (1951), Whispering Smith vs. Scotland Yard (1951), Home to Danger (1951), Cloudburst (1951), The Tell-Tale Heart (1953), The Red Beret (1953), Knights of the Round Table (1953), The Cruel Sea (1953), Hell below Zero (1954), Richard III (1954), The Good Die Young (1954), Beautiful Stranger (1954), Helen of Troy (1956), Alexander the Great (1956), A Hill in Korea (1956), Child in the House (1956), Checkpoint (1956), Hell Drivers (1957), Campbell's Kingdom (1957), Violent Playground (1958), Sea Fury (1958), The Angry Hills (1959), Yesterday's Enemy (1959), Jet Storm (1959), Blind Date (1959), Hell Is a City (1960), The Criminal (1960), The Guns of Navarone (1961), A Prize of Arms (1962), The Man Who Finally Died (1962), The Last Days of Sodom and Gomorrah (1962), In the French Style (1962), Eva (1963), Zulu (1964), Dingaka (1965), Sands of the Kalahari (1965), Robbery (1967), Accident (1967), Girl with a Pistol (1968), Where's Jack? (1969), Perfect Friday (1970), The Games (1970), The Last Grenade (1970), The Butterfly Affair (1970), Una Lucertola con la Pelle di Donna (1971), Innocent Bystanders (1972), Zorro (1974), and Bride to Be (1974).

BANKS, LESLIE (1890–1952). Although Leslie Banks's face was scarred during World War I, he resumed his acting career that had begun in the theater in 1911. He was forty-two years of age when he made his spectacular film debut as the sadistic Count Zaroff in an adaptation of Richard Connell's oft-filmed *The Most Dangerous Game* (1932). Bank's larger-than-life villain, who hunts down those unfortunate enough to find themselves stranded on his remote island, provided an indication of Banks's characteristic style, which, in some films, tended to the eccentric and the florid. In his fourth film, *The Fire Raisers* (1933), directed by Michael Powell,* Banks provides a stylized performance as an ambitious insurance assessor who, following a marriage to a woman with expensive tastes, breaks the law and joins Francis L. Sullivan's crooked scheme to deliberately torch buildings and claim the insurance money. Similarly, in *The Arsenal Stadium Mystery** (1939), Thorold Dickinson* emphasizes the eccentric behavior of Banks's Scotland Yard detective who selects a different form of headgear for each stage of the investigation. Banks was also ideally cast as the eccentric inventor of a revolutionary bomb site, desired by Nazi infiltrator John Mills,* in Anthony Asquith's* *Cottage to Let** (1941).

There were, of course, less flamboyant roles for Banks, particularly in Alfred Hitchcock's* 1934 version of *The Man Who Knew Too Much* and as the archetypal representative of the Imperial class, Commissioner R. G. "Lord Sandy" Saunders, in *Sanders of the River** (1935). In this film, his best screen role, Banks is superb as the iconic representative of the British Empire. His authoritarian, pipe-smoking, paternalistic district officer ends the film on the deck of his gunboat surveying his territory while his "children" celebrate his achievements in song. He represented the same class as Colonel Harry Blair in *Farewell Again* (1937) and Admiral Wetherby in *Ships with Wings* (1941), although Powell's intriguing film noir *The Small Back Room* (1949) treats Banks's Colonel Holland with less reverence. After the high points of *The Man Who Knew Too Much, The Arsenal Stadium Mystery,* and especially *Sanders of the River,* Banks appeared only in supporting roles, except for a celebrated performance in Laurence Olivier's* *Henry V* (1944). He also had a very good role as Oliver Wilsford, a fifth columnist and local squire, in Alberto Cavalcanti's *Went the Day Well?* (1943) and a key role as James Smith, the stern, puritanical father to the enigmatic *Madeleine** (1950). Banks died in 1952.

FILMS: The Most Dangerous Game (1932), I Am Suzanne (1933), Strange Evidence (1933), The Fire Raisers (1934), The Man Who Knew Too Much (1934), Sanders of the River (1935), Red Ensign (1935), The Night of the Party (1935), The Tunnel (1935), Three Maxims (1936), Debt of Honor (1936), Fire over England (1937), Wings of the Morning (1937), Farewell Again (1937), Jamaica Inn (1939), Sons of the Sea (1939), Guide Dogs for the Blind (1939), Dead Man's Shoes (1939), The Arsenal Stadium Mystery (1939), Twenty-One Days (1940), Busman's Holiday (1940), The Door with Seven Locks (1940), Neutral Port (1940), Ships with Wings (1941), Give Us More Ships (1941), Cottage to Let (1941), Went the Day Well? (1943), The Big Blockade (1942), Henry V (1944), Mrs. Fitzherbert (1947), The Small Back Room (1949), Madeleine (1950), and Your Witness (1950).

BATES, ALAN (b. 1934). When Robert Altman was promoting *Gosford Park* (2001) just after its release, he singled out Alan Bates for praise, noting that Bates worked the longest of his all-star cast, about ten or eleven weeks, and that Bates spent the first seven weeks in the background to many scenes, like an extra, before they filmed his scenes over the final four weeks. Altman noted that most American actors or anyone not trained in the theater would not be so generous to his fellow actors. In the tradition of British actors such as Ralph Richardson,* Bates's career appears less motivated by a desire for stardom than a need to perform in a wide variety of roles. This flexibility, and his constant shifting between the stage, television, and film, diminished his commercial viability. Bates won a scholarship to London's Royal Academy of Dramatic Arts and, after a period in the Royal Air Force and his stage debut at Coventry with the Midland Theatre Company, he joined the newly formed English Stage Company based at the Royal Court Theatre. This proved to be a significant moment for Bates as the Royal Court Theatre (and the work of Tony Richardson*) was important in the development of the British New Wave. Bates was also an integral part of this cycle as he starred in Richardson's staging of John Osborne's *Look Back in Anger* in 1956.

Bates's association with the Royal Court Theatre and Richardson was significant in starting his film career as Richardson cast him in *The Entertainer* (1960). He followed with a starring role in *Whistle Down the Wind* (1961) as a fugitive murderer who is thought to be Jesus Christ by three children when they discover him hiding in a North Country barn. Then came *A Kind of Loving** (1962), a key film in the New Wave with Bates as Vic, a young working-class husband trying to understand the needs and desires of his wife. His ability to suggest the inner turmoil of this essentially simple man won him a BAFTA Best British Film Actor nomination. Bates, fearing typecasting, wanted to exchange the role of Gabriel in *Far from the Madding Crowd* (1967) for that of Sergeant Troy. He felt Gabriel was no longer a challenge as he had played similar roles.

In terms of the cinema, the 1960s was a high point for Bates with international success as the reserved Englishman in *Zorba the Greek* (1964) opposite Anthony Quinn, followed by the inadequate lover in *Georgy Girl** (1966). John Frankenheimer's *The Fixer* (1968), with Bates as the Jew falsely imprisoned in Russia at the turn of the last century, won him a Best Actor nomination at the U.S. Academy Awards, while Ken Russell's* *Women in Love* (1969) attracted notoriety (unfairly) because of his nude wrestling scene with Oliver Reed. The role also won him a BAFTA nomination for Best Actor.

Bates has divided his time since the 1970s between film, television, and the stage. Yet, at the height of his screen career, after the critical accolades of *The Fixer* and a starring role in Joseph Losey's* *The Go-Between* (1970) as Julie Christie's* secret lover, Bates refused to take the easy way and exploit his fame— instead, he performed in Peter Medak's black comedy/drama *A Day in the Life of Joe Egg* (1972), concerning a couple who contemplate the mercy killing of their daughter because of her cerebral palsy. This tendency to focus on interesting projects rather than follow a commercial trajectory has pushed him to the edge, rather than the middle, of the mainstream cinema, although Paul Mazursky chose Bates for the male role in the influential *An Unmarried Woman* in 1978, opposite Jill Clayburgh. Bates has worked steadily since then, including important supporting roles in two big-budget Hollywood films released in 2002 (*The Mothman Prophecies* and *The Sum of All Fears*), despite personal tragedies involving his wife and son. In 1990 he was nominated Best Actor in a Supporting Role as Claudius at the BAFTA Film Awards for Franco Zeffirelli's *Hamlet* (1990).

FILMS: Three on a Gas Ring (short, 1960), The Entertainer (1960), Whistle Down the Wind (1961), A Kind of Loving (1962), The Running Man (1963), The Caretaker (1963), Nothing But the Best (1963), Zorba the Greek (1964), Insh'Allah (voice, 1965), Georgy Girl (1966), King of Hearts (1966), The Fixer (1967), Far from the Madding Crowd (1967), Hands Up! (1967), Women in Love (1969), The Go-Between (1970), A Day in the Life of Joe Egg (1970), Three Sisters (1970), Second Best (short, 1972), Impossible Object (1973), Butley (1973), In Celebration (1974), Royal Flash (1975), An Unmarried Woman (1977), The Shout (1978), The Rose (1978), Nijinsky (1979), Quartet (1981), The Return of the Soldier (1982), The Wicked Lady (1982), Britannia Hospital (1982), Duet for One (1986), A Prayer for the Dying (1987), We Think the World of You (1987), Force Majeure (1989), Docteur M (1990), Hamlet (1990), Mister Frost (1990), Secret Friends (1992), Silent Tongue (1994), The Grotesque (1996), The Cherry Orchard (1999), Gosford Park (2001), The Mothman Propecies (2002), and The Sum of All Fears (2002).

THE BEAUTY JUNGLE (Rank, 1964)—Drama. *Director:* Val Guest; *Producers:* Val Guest and F. Sherwin Green (associate); *Script:* Val Guest and Robert Muller; *Photography:* Arthur Grant; *Music:* Laurie Johnson; *Cast:* Ian Hendry

(Don McKenzie), Janette Scott (Shirley Freeman), Ronald Fraser (Walter Carey), Edmund Purdom (Rex Carrick), Jean Claudio (Armand), Kay Walsh (Mrs. Freeman), Norman Bird (Mr. Freeman), Janina Faye (Elaine), Tommy Trinder (Charlie Dorton), and Sydney James ("Butlin" judge).

The Beauty Jungle is one of the superior genre films directed by Val Guest* in the late 1950s and early 1960s that, until recently, has received little attention. A relatively large budget for the film was provided by Rank and it was filmed in CinemaScope on seaside and other locations, including Monte Carlo. As the film was directed and coscripted by Val Guest,* the film was anything but sentimental or positive as Guest emphasized the exploitative basis of beauty contests where sexual favors and economic considerations were more important than beauty or talent.

When cynical reporter Don McKenzie searches a tatty beachside for a news angle, he finds not only Tommy Trinder but Bristol typist Shirley Freeman, who is vacationing at the beach. McKenzie exploits Freeman's boredom with her mundane life, conservative family, and dull fiancé and seduces her with the prospect of public exhibition, sexual power, fame, and wealth.

After a series of humiliating experiences, Freeman learns quickly after receiving tips from a couple of "professional" contestants. As Freeman's ambition grows, McKenzie's control over her recedes in the face of her win-at-all-costs behavior. Finally, he realizes that Freeman's decision to sleep with him is merely payment for his services, just as she would reward other people who assist her career. It is only in the final moments of the film, after she has failed to win the Miss Globe contest, that the significance of her actions are apparent. This self-revelation is compounded when, as the reigning Rose of England winner, she is confronted by a surprise entry, her younger sister. Thus, Freeman is forced to contemplate what her sister will have to go through to get to the top.

The Beauty Jungle benefits from Arthur Grant's location photography, Guest's unsentimental direction, Ian Hendry's constantly on-the-make manager/reporter, and above all else, Janette Scott's convincing performance that always allows the audience more than a glimpse of her rock hard nature, even as a provincial typist enjoying the notoriety of her cheese-cake photo in the local paper. Later, the sweetness and innocence is subsumed by a hardened exterior expertly manufactured for her profession as Freeman's single-mindedness and naked ambition overwhelms her more sympathetic traits. Finally, after winning the Rose of England contest, her decision to abandon McKenzie at the celebratory party and wait on the bed of an impotent film star (Edmund Purdom), because he may assist her in the forthcoming Miss Globe contest, is both chilling and representative of the film's unsentimental tone.

THE BELLES OF ST. TRINIAN'S (London Film Productions, 1953)—Comedy. *Director:* Frank Launder; *Producers:* Sidney Gilliat and Frank Launder; *Script:* Sidney Gilliat, Frank Launder, and Val Valentine, based on the cartoons of Ronald Searle; *Photography:* Stanley Pavey; *Music:* Malcolm Arnold; *Cast:*

Alastair Sim (Millicent Fritton/Clarence), Joyce Grenfell (P. W. Ruby Gaines), George Cole (Flash Harry), Hermione Baddeley (Miss Drownder), Betty Ann Davies (Miss Waters), Renee Houston (Miss Brimmer), Beryl Reid (Miss Watson), Irene Handl (Miss Gale), Mary Merrall (Miss Buckland), Joan Sims (Miss Dawn), Lloyd Lamble (Superintendent Kemp-Bird), Richard Wattis (Manton Bassett), Guy Middleton (Eric Rowbottom-Smith), Eric Pohlmann (Sultan), and Sid James (Benny).

The Belles of St. Trinian's, the first of five films based on the anarchic schoolgirls depicted in the cartoons of Ronald Searle, assembled a superb cast of actors skilled in the traditions of British farce. In this world, everyone is corrupt or about to be corrupted—from the conservative public servants sent to investigate irregularities at the school (and end up seduced by the life of indolence and irresponsibility), to the opportunistic headmistress Millicent Fritton, with Alastair Sim* in a dual role as Fritton and her shady bookmaker brother. Sim is excellent as Fritton as she tries to retain a vestige of respectability even in the midst of the most cynical and self-serving actions. Twenty years before the horror genre equated children with evil (see *The Omen* [1976]), the St. Trinian's series associated them with anarchy.

The loose plot revolves around the battle between various groups—the staff, the head mistress, crooks, and the schoolgirls who are determined to make money from an imported horse. The plot merely provides an excuse to showcase the sharpness of the script and the skill of the cast. This includes Sim, George Cole, as the ultimate spiv, Flash Harry, and Joyce Grenfell as the severely repressed police woman who, tempted by the promise of marriage, goes undercover as a teacher at the school and bravely tries to impose a modicum of civilized behavior on the girls. This, of course, was doomed as evidenced in the hilarious hockey match between St. Trinian's and a nearby school, which results in the pitch being littered with bodies from the other school.

BILLY ELLIOT (BBC/Arts Council of England/Tiger Aspect/WT2/Working Title Films, 2000)—Family drama. *Director:* Stephen Daldry; *Producers:* Greg Brenman, Jon Finn, Charles Brand (executive), Tessa Ross (executive), David M. Thompson (executive), and Natascha Wharton (executive); *Script:* Lee Hall; *Cinematography:* Brian Tufano; *Music:* Stephen Warbeck; *Cast:* Julie Walters (Mrs. Wilkinson), Jamie Bell (Billy Elliot), Jamie Draven (Tony Elliot), Gary Lewis (Jackie Elliot), Jean Heywood (Grandma), Stuart Wells (Michael Caffrey), Mike Elliot (George Watson), Janine Birkett (Billy's Mum), and Nicola Blackwell (Debbie Wilkinson).

As a basic premise, it can be assumed that all feature films are contrived, in the sense that they have a point of view and try to elicit basic emotions in the viewer. Some films, however, work that little bit harder to exploit every possibility as scenes and plot developments strive to maximize feelings, such as sentimentality, in the viewer. *Billy Elliot* is one of these films. This is not necessarily a bad thing—it depends on the reasons for generating such feelings. An instructive companion film in this regard is *Brassed Off** (1996) as it draws on a similar economic and political context as *Billy Elliot* with the same threat to the welfare of mining communities in northern England.

A difference between the two films is that while *Billy Elliot* is set a few years before *Brassed Off,* during the strike of 1984, *Brassed Off* (set in 1992) follows through and points to the closure of the mines. Consequently, the underlying tone of *Brassed Off,* which utilizes a similar "triumph over adversity" plot, is permeated by a stronger sense of melancholy and anger. *Billy Elliot* is less concerned with such issues and uses the miners' strike as another dramatic obstacle to Billy achieving his personal dream.

Eleven years old, Billy lives with his father and brother, who are on strike from the local mine, and his grandmother. The film makes much of the masculine bias in the family that inhibits Billy's desire to dance, a desire that would have been encouraged if Billy's mother was still alive. Instead, Billy's father pushes his son into boxing, a sport in which Billy has no special talent. When the local ballet class, under the cynical eye of Mrs. Wilkinson, is forced to share the gym on Saturday with the boxing class, Billy is fascinated by the possibilities of dance. Billy's father prohibits Billy from participating in the ballet class and the film's dominant narrative strand concerns the escalating tension between father and son over this issue.

Mrs. Wilkinson, aware of this tension, agrees to prepare Billy in private for an audition to the Royal Ballet School. When Billy misses the audition, he breaks out in a defiant dance as an expression of his frustration. A similar dance later in the film convinces his father (a) that he has talent and (b) that homosexuality is not necessarily a prerequisite for all ballet dancers. It is no surprise that Billy succeeds in joining the Royal Ballet. The fact that the film works so well on an emotional level is due largely to the intensity of the presentation and the performance of Gary Lewis as the tormented father, straining to break through traditional stereotypes and understand a world that is alien to him.

The relationship between the two boys, Billy and his gay childhood friend, is touching—particularly at the end when Billy kisses him good-bye. A much more subtle presentation of the film's central theme, concerning opportunity and talent, comes near the end of the film after Billy achieves his dream and leaves his neighborhood for the last time. Nearby, a young girl watches him depart, a possibility that may never be available to her and other children from working-class backgrounds.

BILLY LIAR (Anglo-Amalgamated, 1963)—Comedy. *Director:* John Schlesinger; *Producer:* Joseph Janni; *Script:* Keith Waterhouse and Willis Hall, adapted from their play; *Cinematography:* Denys Coop; *Music:* Richard Rodney Bennett; *Cast:* Tom Courtenay (Billy Fisher), Wilfred Pickles (Geoffrey Fisher), Mona Washbourne (Alice Fisher), Ethel Griffies (Florence), Finlay Currie (Duxbury), Gwendolyn Watts (Rita), Helen Fraser (Barbara), Julie Christie (Liz), Leonard Rossiter (Shadrack), Rodney Bewes (Arthur Crabtree), George Innes (Stamp), and Leslie Randall (Danny Boon).

The release of *Tom Jones** and *Billy Liar* in 1963 marked, it has been argued, the end of the "kitchen sink" films and the start of the "Swinging London" cycle. The demarcation between the two cycles was not that simple as *Billy Liar* continued some of the patterns found in the earlier films—notably a critical presentation of British institutions. Both *Billy Liar* and *Room at the Top** (1958), for example, eschew any kind of nostalgia for the past as Joe Lampton and Billy Fisher live comprised lives. While Lampton is compromised by his ambition and chooses a loveless union, Fisher has to create a fantasy world just to survive the real world (of Bradford).

Fisher, known to his workmates as "Billy Liar" because he is a compulsive liar, escapes his dour existence by creating a fantasy life as the military leader of the fictional, semi-fascist state of Ambrosia. This fantasy supplies the power and control lacking in his daily life where he feels trapped in his job at the Shadrack and Duxbury funeral parlor. His sense of entrapment is compounded when he is confronted by his two fiancées, Rita and Barbara, who both want the one engagement ring he has purchased. Salvation comes in the form of Liz, an uninhibited woman who flits in and out of his life. Finally, Fisher decides to act on his dream and seek a job as a scriptwriter in London. He agrees to meet Liz at the local station at midnight. Once aboard the train, he loses his nerve and fabricates a story of requiring a milk drink that provides him with a convenient excuse to miss the train. Liz, knowing Billy only too well, leaves his suitcase on the platform and as Fisher walks home he imagines that he is leading the soldiers of Ambrosia up his local street, accompanied by the national anthem of Ambrosia. The last shot, however, devoid of his fantasy army, shows a sad figure entering "Hillcrest," his parent's semidetached house.

Billy Liar reveals the changes in northern Britain in the early 1960s. The film begins with a radio request program "Housewives Choice" over images of suburban houses and high-rise flats, as John Schlesinger* reworks Humphrey Jenning's *Listen to Britain*. Now the traditional smoke-belching factories and working-class terraces are replaced by a world of supermarkets, glib television presenters, and officious funeral parlor directors who extol the virtues of plastic coffins. Only Liz, the "dream girl," offers an alternative.

Overall, the mood in the film is disquieting—Fisher's dreams include killing people, such as his parents, who place obstacles in his way. The film shows that the only real obstacle confronting Fisher is a lack of courage combined with no obvious talent. His only achievement is the dubious pleasure offered by "Twisterella," a song cowritten by Fisher and his workmate Arthur Crabtree. *Billy Liar* was transformed into a stage musical and a television series.

BLACK NARCISSUS (The Archers/General Film Distributors, 1947)—Melodrama. *Director:* Michael Powell; *Producers:* Emeric Pressburger and Michael Powell; *Script:* Emeric Pressburger and Michael Powell, based on the novel by Rumer Godden; *Cinematography:* Jack Cardiff; *Music:* Brian Easdale; *Cast:* Deborah Kerr (Sister Clodagh), Sabu (Young Prince), David Farrar (Mr. Dean),

Flora Robson (Sister Phillipa), Esmond Knight (The Old General), Jean Simmonds (Kanchi), Kathleen Byron (Sister Ruth), Jenny Laird (Sister "Honey" Blanche), Judith Furse (Sister Briony), and May Hallatt (Angu Ayah).

Although *Black Narcissus* is set in the Himalayas, and Michael Powell* was offered the opportunity to shoot the film on location, almost all of the footage was filmed at Pinewood Studios, with a few exteriors in a tropical garden in Sussex. While this decision seemed perverse at the time, Powell's decision was correct and he created a masterpiece of repression and sensuality that could only have been created in the controlled conditions of a studio where Alfred Junge's sets, Jack Cardiff's cinematography, and Brian Easdale's score coalesce to create a magnificent film.

The story centers on the reaction of five nuns to an alien setting in the remote Himalayas when their religious order is offered the "House of Women," an abandoned "palace," which was once the home of the concubines of the kingdom's rulers. The nuns are lead by the relatively inexperienced Sister Clodagh, who demonstrates that intensity, dedication, and ambition are sometimes not sufficient to overcome all temptations. Clodagh is accompanied by Sister "Honey" Blanche, who is keen to help the local children, Sister Briony, who brings her medical skills to the mission, and Sister Phillipa, who is responsible for cultivating sufficient food for the women. The remaining nun, the troubled Sister Ruth, seeks an opportunity to make a fresh start. Each nun, however, succumbs to different temptations and the mission is abandoned after less than a year.

The film emphasizes the effect of the setting on the women—the combination of crystal air, incessant wind, and the sensual history of the "House of Women"— that nourishes feelings that Clodagh and Ruth have, up to their arrival, repressed. The camera foreshadows this theme as it tracks across the erotic murals in the wind-driven halls, a recurring motif that permeates the film. Without laboring the tensions and motivations of each woman, through dialogue, Powell slowly details the affect of the setting—Sister Phillipa, for example, ignores the needs of the group by growing flowers, such as honeysuckle and forget-me-nots, instead of food; Sister "Honey" ignores Sister Briony's advice and helps a terminally ill child, leading to a rupture between the mission and the locals who blame Honey for the child's death. Clodagh, on the other hand, finds that she is constantly distracted by thoughts of a failed romance in Ireland before she entered the religious order. Ruth's fragile emotional unity is shattered by the arrival of Mr. Dean, the British agent, who also unsettles Clodagh with his masculinity and refusal to respect her authority.

Dean's decision to introduce the sensual Kanchi into the mission, to stop her pestering him with her sexual advances, exacerbates tensions as Kanchi's response to the erotic murals is to break into an erotic dance before seducing the Young Prince. Sister Ruth's mind disintegrates due to sexual desire for Dean and jealousy of Clodagh. Finally, she rejects her habit for a scarlet dress. In one of the most provocative close-ups in the history of the cinema, Ruth slowly applies lipstick to her mouth as a taunting gesture to the shocked Mother Superior. Ruth then leaves the mission to offer herself to Dean in the valley. When Dean rejects her, she turns on Clodagh, stalking her through the dark corridors of the palace in a superbly choreographed combination of imagery and sounds—Easdale's haunting score was prerecorded before the shoot so that Powell could plan his shots. Finally, Ruth falls to her death as she attempts to murder Clodagh, forcing Clodagh to admit failure and return to Delhi, just as the rain begins to fall. A symbolic closure, relief comes as the nuns depart the "House of Women."

Black Narcissus benefits greatly from Junge's art direction and Cardiff's photography, supported by Easdale's impressive score. Cardiff won the Best Cinematography Award (Color) and Junge the Best Art Direction (Color) at the 1948 Academy Awards. Cardiff also won the 1948 Golden Globe for Best Cinematography and Deborah Kerr* the 1947 New York Film critics Award for Best Actress. Arguably, *Black Narcissus* is, if not the finest, at least one of the finest films produced in Great Britain.

BLACKMAIL (British International, 1929)—Thriller. *Director:* Alfred Hitchcock; *Producer:* John Maxwell; *Script:* Charles Bennett, Benn Wolf Levy, and Michael Powell; *Cinematography:* Jack Cox; *Music:* John Hubert Bath; *Cast:* Anny Ondra (Alice White), John Longden (Frank Webber), Cyril Ritchard (the Artist), Donald Calthrop (Tracy), Sara Allgood (Mrs. White), and Charles Paton (Mr. White).

Alfred Hitchcock's* first sound film, although it was initially designed as a silent, was jeopardized by lead actress Anny Ondra's heavy Czechoslovakian accent, so the British actress Joan Barry was used to supply the dialogue off camera while Ondra mimed the words. Although *Blackmail* has been described as "boldly experimental" with Hitchcock pushing his characteristic optical and aural subjectivity further than any other British director at that time, the basic themes are characteristic Hitchcock. Particularly important was the manner in which Hitchcock generated a strong sense of moral ambivalence in the audience as the central character, Alice White, betrays her dull policeman boyfriend Frank Webber in favor of a more exciting evening with an artist (Cyril Ritchard). Of course, this betrayal must be punished and the artist turns out to be a more relentless seducer than White initially anticipated, although her complicity, and the audience's complicity, in this arrangement is highlighted by Hitchcock in a number of scenes showing White in various stages of undress. After his ardor becomes too much for the heroine, she tries to fight him off and kills him with a bread knife before sneaking out of his apartment.

Hitchcock's moral ambiguity of this situation is intensified by Ondra's innate sensuality and her willingness to dress for the artist in the costume of one of his models—while he provides her with the sketch of a naked woman. On the other hand, the artist is shown to be less than desirable and, consistent with Hitchcock's darkly melodramatic world, deserves his fate.

After the killing, Hitchcock exploits the audience's sympathy for the hunted as White wanders through the city in a daze before rejoining her family. White's guilt intensifies when Webber joins the murder investigation and finds White's glove at the scene of the crime. He becomes legally and morally implicated when he covers up this evidence. The introduction of the blackmailer Tracy temporarily pushes the drama toward a more traditional moral schema of virtue (White) threatened by evil (Tracy). However, Tracy's death at the British museum triggers a morally problematic ending as White secretly confesses her guilt to Webber before the two lovers leave the police building—free, but emotionally scarred.

Hitchcock extends the formal possibilities of the classical feature film with *Blackmail*. For example, a recurring emphasis on the word "knife," at the expense of the other words at the family dinner table, highlights White's disturbed mental state. Similarly, Hitchcock utilizes the dead artist's painting of a jester in the final image as an ironic comment on "justice" as the two guilty lovers depart the police station. *Blackmail* is more than just a simple morality play. It is more a treatise on guilt presented within the tenets of melodrama.

BLANCHE FURY (Cineguild, 1947)—Costume melodrama. *Director:* Marc Allegret; *Producer:* Anthony Havelock-Allan; *Script:* Audrey Erskine-Lindop, Hugh Mills, and Cecil McGivern, based on the novel by Joseph Shearing (also known as Gabrielle Margaret Vere Long); *Cinematography:* Guy Green and Geoffrey Unsworth (exteriors); *Music:* Clifton Parker; *Cast:* Stewart Granger (Philip Thorn), Valerie Hobson (Blanche Fury), Walter Fitzgerald (Simon Fury), Michael Gough (Lawrence Fury), Maurice Denham (Major Fraser), Sybilla Binder (Louisa), Allen Jeayes (Mr. Weatherby), Susanna Gibbs (Lavinia), and Amy Veness (Mrs. Winterbourne).

In 1947–1948, four novels by Joseph Shearing (one of several pseudonyms used by Gabrielle Margaret Vere Long) were transformed into films. One of these films, *Blanche Fury,* was grouped as part of the cycle of popular 1940s costume melodramas. The commercial failure of *Blanche Fury,* relative to its large budget, effectively signaled the end of this cycle. Nevertheless, it remains one of the best examples of this genre with its confrontational story, intense characterizations, and striking use of color. This film also offered Valerie Hobson,* as the governess who marries into the Fury family, and Stewart Granger,* as the illegitimate heir to family estate, their best roles during this period.

Blanche is rescued from unsatisfactory domestic employment to the selfish Mrs. Winterbourne when invited by her uncle, Simon Fury, to join his household and care for her niece Lavinia. Blanche welcomes this change as her strong sense of independence makes her unsuitable for the subservient role of a "lady's companion." This resistance to control by others also causes problems in her subsequent marriage to Simon's weak son Lawrence, as Blanche tells him that she "has no intention . . . contrary to the fashion of our time, of being ordered about by my husband." Instead, Blanche is sexually attracted to Philip Thorn, the obsessive illegitimate heir to the estate who also works on the property. Thorn, who wants the Fury estate more than he wants Blanche, murders Simon and Lawrence after he learns that all legal avenues are closed with regard to his claim. However,

Lavinia remains in his way and Blanche, suspicious of Thorn's intentions toward the young girl, goes to the police and exposes Thorn's murder of her husband and uncle. The film concludes with a return to the opening moments as a doctor tends the dying Blanche after giving birth to Thorn's son. Thorn, on the other hand, faces his execution satisfied that his heir will finally regain the Fury estate.

The major weakness in *Blanche Fury* emanates from the poorly motivated presentation of Blanche's decision to go to the police to expose Thorn's murder of her husband and uncle. While Thorn's obsession with regaining the Fury estate is developed throughout the film, Blanche's decision, taken after watching Thorn prepare Lavinia for a dangerous horse jump, is perfunctory and abrupt. The love-hate motif familiar in film noir (e.g., as developed in *Double Indemnity* [1943]), involving the deterioration of love-lust following a crime, was common motif in the 1940s but in *Blanche Fury* it lacks the necessary development to render this crucial plot turn credible. Nevertheless, *Blanche Fury,* which remains faithful to its fatalistic premise, is one of the best examples of this genre.

BLOOD FROM THE MUMMY'S TOMB (Hammer, 1971)—Horror. *Director:* Seth Holt; *Producer:* Howard Brandy; *Script:* Christopher Wicking; *Cinematography:* Arthur Grant; *Music:* Tristram Cary; *Cast:* Andrew Keir (Professor Julien Fuchs), Valerie Leon (Margaret Fuchs/Queen Tera), James Villiers (Corbeck), George Coulouris (Professor Berrigan), Hugh Burden (Geoffrey Dandridge), Rosalie Crutchley (Helen Dickerson), Mark Edwards (Tod Browning), Aubrey Morris (Dr. Putnam), and James Cossins (Older Male Nurse).

Seth Holt, who joined Ealing in 1944 as an assistant editor and worked as a producer on *The Ladykillers** (1955) and other films before establishing himself as one of Britain's more talented directors, died while shooting *Blood from the Mummy's Tomb.* Hammer executive Michael Carreras completed the film and this may account for the incoherence in the latter part of the film. However, the film remains one of the less formulaic and more stylistically impressive horror films from Hammer.

When an archaeological expedition, consisting of Professor Julien Fuchs, Professor Berrigan, Geoffrey Dandridge, and Helen Dickerson, breaks into the sarcophagus of the evil Egyptian Queen Tera, the expedition discovers Tera's perfectly preserved severed right hand near her body. As Fuchs enters the tomb, his wife, back in England, dies giving birth to a daughter (Margaret). The baby also dies before suddenly coming back to life when Fuchs discovers Tera. This association becomes the film's dominant motif, the transference of (evil) power from Tera to Margaret Fuchs, rendering it less a traditional "Mummy" film and more a supernatural story in keeping with its source, *Jewel of the Seven Stars,* one of Bram Stoker's lesser known stories.

Fuchs takes Tera's body back to his house in London and, many years later, gives Tera's ruby ring to Margaret. After this action, members of the expedition begin to die in the same violent manner—a slashed throat. The film's final sequence is particularly dramatic—as Fuchs mutilates Tera's body, his house collapses on him, the villain Corbeck, and Margaret. The epilogue shows that only Margaret has survived—a babbling, hysterical wreck swathed in hospital bandages.

Blood from the Mummy's Tomb continues the cinematic fascination of the British horror film in the late 1960s and early 1970s with the destructive effects of the British family—a theme also found in *The Corpse** (1969), *Countess Dracula** (1970), *Demons of the Mind* (1971), which was also scripted by Christopher Wicking, *Hands of the Ripper* (1971), and *The Creeping Flesh* (1972). In *Blood from the Mummy's Tomb,* this theme surfaces as Tera attempts to control Fuchs through the body of his daughter, generating a perversely erotic situation enhanced by the sensual playing and revealing costumes worn by actress Valerie Leon.

An inferior large-budget remake followed eight years later by Warner Brothers entitled *The Awakening,* as it tried to cash in on the commercial success of *The Omen* (1976). However, the sparse fatalism and bleak ending of *Blood from the Mummy's Tomb* is a more honest presentation of the moral implications of Stoker's story than Warner's remake.

THE BLUE LAMP (Ealing, 1950)—Police/social problem film. *Director:* Basil Dearden; *Producers:* Michael Balcon and Michael Relph (associate); *Script:* T. E. B. Clarke, with additional dialogue by Alexander Mackendrick, based on a story by Ted Willis; *Cinematography:* Gordon Dines; *Music:* Ernest Irving; *Cast:* Jack Warner (P. C. George Dixon), Jimmy Hanley (P. C. Andy Mitchell), Dirk Bogarde (Tom Riley), Bernard Lee (Inspector Cherry), Robert Fleming (Sergeant Roberts), Peggy Evans (Diana Lewis), Gladys Evans (Mrs. Dixon), Meredith Edwards (P. C. Hughes), Patric Doonan (Spud), Clive Morton (Sergeant Brooks), Frederick Piper (Alf Lewis), and Betty Ann Davies (Mrs. Lewis).

The most popular British film released in 1950 was *The Blue Lamp* and although the central character, Jack Warner's* P. C. Dixon, was killed by Tom Riley midway in the film, the character was resurrected in 1955 in the long running BBC television program that concluded in 1976 when Warner was eighty-two-years old. The film, however, served a more specific social function: the dramatization of a fear of a new breed of criminal. To this end, *The Blue Lamp* utilizes an anonymous narrator who, over a montage of newspaper headlines at the start of the film, points to the escalation of crime and, over images of teenagers in grouped in suspicious circumstances, suggests that this trend was caused by the deterioration of communal and family values. This new breed of criminal, the narrator argues, lacks the "code, experience, and self-discipline of the professional thief," rendering them an inferior "class apart." The film dramatizes this problem by following the "typical" case of runaway teenager Diana Lewis, who, like many young people, came from a "home broken and demoralized by war." The answer, the narrator suggests, is to increase police numbers within the local community.

The youngest member of the Paddington Green police station, P. C. Andy Mitchell, is depicted as the surrogate son of P. C. George Dixon, a twenty-five-year veteran of the force. Mitchell's honesty is contrasted with the path followed by Tom Riley, a young petty criminal who graduates from theft to murder. The film's editing pattern emphasizes the differences between these two "worlds" as it crosscuts between the communal activities at the Paddington Green station (which includes choir practice and dart matches) to the sordid activities within Riley's apartment—notably Riley plans to rob the Coliseum Cinema with Spud and Alf Lewis. Following Dixon's murder outside the cinema, this pattern becomes more marked as the net closes in on Riley, culminating in his torment as the police, led by Mitchell, combine with the underworld to trap him at a greyhound meeting at the White City Stadium.

The Blue Lamp is one of Basil Dearden's* more interesting films in terms of its assimilation of different cinematic styles—ranging from the techniques associated with the police procedural film, including location shooting and a car chase, to its overly romanticized presentation of the daily life of a police constable. On the other hand, Dearden also invokes the highly stylized world of film noir in the scenes between Riley and Lewis within his apartment as he employs low-key lighting, unsettling camera angles, and suggestions of aberrant sexual desires— notably as Riley strokes the barrel of his gun while threatening Diana. Or in a later scene when the young girl wakes up to find the shadow of Riley menacingly cast over her.

Dirk Bogarde* has a strong sexual presence within the film and provides a disturbing contrast to the asexual Mitchell. Mitchell, in this respect, is the same as his mentor, the begonia-loving P. C. Dixon. Despite the film's overt social intentions, and despite the popularity of Warner's P. C. Dixon, it is this unsettling mixture of a disturbed sexuality and repressed violence in Riley that disrupts and overwhelms the film's celebration of communal cooperation between the police and the established underworld.

BLUE MURDER AT ST. TRINIAN'S (British Lion, 1957)—Comedy. *Director:* Frank Launder; *Producers:* Frank Launder and Sidney Gilliat; *Script:* Sidney Gilliat, Frank Launder, and Val Valentine, based on the cartoons by Ronald Searle; *Photography:* Gerald Gibbs; *Music:* Malcolm Arnold; *Cast:* Terry-Thomas (Romney), George Cole (Flash Harry), Joyce Grenfell (Sergeant Ruby Gates), Alastair Sim (Miss Millicent Fritton), Lionel Jeffries (Joe Mangan), Lloyd Lamble (Superintendent Kemp-Bird), Thorley Walters (Major), Judith Furse (Dame Maude Hackshaw), Richard Wattis (Bassett), Peter Jones (Prestwick), Lisa Gastoni (Myrna), Sabrina (Virginia), and Guido Lorraine (Prince Bruno).

The sequel to the popular *The Belles of St. Trinian's** (1954), *Blue Murder at St. Trinian's* retains and extends the basic premise of the first film. The anarchic schoolgirls of St. Trinian's, sing over the film's credits "the battle's to the strongest, might is always right, trample on the weakest" before they cheat their way into winning a UNESCO school competition with a trip to Europe so that they can offer themselves to a wealthy Italian, Prince Bruno. Their journey from England to Italy is complicated when the father of one of the girls, Joe Mangan, seeks refuge after stealing diamonds and uses the school trip as a means to avoid the police. He is disguised as the new headmistress, Dame Maude Hackshaw—the real Maude Hackshaw having been kidnapped and imprisoned by the girls soon after her arrival.

Alastair Sim,* as the former headmistress Millicent Fritton, is restricted to a couple of scenes at the beginning and end of the film, leaving George Cole, as the spiv Flash Harry, in the central role. Other familiar faces returning to their original roles include Joyce Grenfell as the love-smitten policewoman forced to go undercover again in the school in the hope that her fiancé of fourteen years, Superintendent Kemp-Bird, will marry her if she gains the reward money for capturing Mangan. Similarly, Richard Wattis reprises his role as the nerve-shattered bureaucrat who advises his successor Peter Jones that the "only thing to do, old man, is open a vein." Inveterate scene-stealer Terry-Thomas* is an addition to the original cast as the bus driver Romney, who romances Grenfell after he learns that the policewoman has a wealthy aunt. Sabrina also makes a brief appearance lying in bed in a negligee, reading a book as a fellow pupil describes her as the "school swot."

Arguably, the first two-thirds of *Blue Murder at St. Trinian's* contain the funniest scenes in all of the five St. Trinian's films, particularly when the army is called in to control the girls after Miss Fritton has been imprisoned. The ranks of the army are quickly decimated by the girls and after Superintendent Kemp-Bird enters the school and tells the commanding officer that "we're looking for a wanted criminal" (Mangan), the distraught army commander replies "there are at least two hundred of them here, my dear fellow." With the arrival of Dame Maude Hackshaw, who was selected by the British Education Ministry to administer St. Trinian's because of her experiences in running a borstal in Australia ("Kill or Cure Hackshaw"), the army is finally relieved of the responsibility of controlling the girls. As a parting gesture, the major foolishly decides to enter the school to tell the girls what he thinks of their behavior only to finally escape from the school building dressed in a girl's uniform.

BOGARDE, DIRK (1921–1999). Born Derek Van den Bogaerde in Hampstead, he was the son of the art editor of *The Times*. After a disastrous sojourn studying engineering drawing in Glasgow, where he was physically bullied, Bogarde returned to London and the Chelsea School of Art, but his real vocation was acting. In 1939, he joined the Q Theatre, at Kew, as a stagehand, and he became part of the cast for J. B. Priestley's *When We Are Married*. Bogarde also appeared in a bit part in the film *Come on George* (1939) before he was called up for military duty. Bogarde rose to the rank of captain during the war. After the experience of driving through the Belsen concentration camp in 1945, Bogarde said that after that nothing would frighten or disturb him as much again. After the war, Rank Studios took interest in Bogarde when he was spotted as the neurotic killer in the play *Power with Glory*. Although Bogarde did not think much of his early screen roles, such as Jean Simmons' savior in the thriller *So Long at the Fair* (1950),

both *Esther Waters** (1948), his first starring role, and *Once a Jolly Swagman**
(1948) provided Bogarde with something more than just the usual "matinee idol"
roles that characterized many of his films in the 1950s (especially after the success of *Doctor in the House** in 1954).

Bogarde's major break was as the small-time gangster Tom Riley, who shoots
Jack Warner,* in *The Blue Lamp** (1950) and his characterization as the sadistic
hood, with a problematic sexual bent, foreshadowed the more perverse characterizations that were found in his roles after *Victim** in 1961. Except for Joseph
Losey's* *The Sleeping Tiger* (1954), there were few indications in the 1950s of
what was to follow. In the 1960s, Bogarde reached his peak as he was able, with
minimum movement, to suggest much more than was in the dialogue. A prime
example is his manipulative Hugo Barrett in Losey's *The Servant* (1963) that, in
many ways, represents the pinnacle of his acting career. An ability to suggest a
kind of subterranean psychological disturbance is also evident in his sadistic
naval officer in *H.M.S. Defiant** (1962), in *Accident** (1967), and in *The Night
Porter* (1973).

These roles were made possible because of changes in the screen representation of male sexuality and masculinity in the late 1950s and 1960s. At the height
of his fame in the 1950s, Rank cast him in a succession of pleasant, somewhat
sexless, roles during a seven-year contract that, because of extensions for leave to
undertake other projects, lasted for seventeen years. His most popular roles during this period were in the "doctor" series, beginning with *Doctor in the House**
(1954), followed by *Doctor at Sea** (1955), with Brigitte Bardot, *Doctor at Large*
(1957), and *Doctor in Distress* (1963). This last film was an aberration and
belonged more to the mid-1950s. Following his role as the non-practicing homosexual barrister Melville Farr, and married to Sylvia Syms in *Victim,* Bogarde left
behind the "matinee idol" roles for greater challenges, culminating in his magnificent portrayal of the homosexual artist searching for beauty in Luchino Visconti's *Death in Venice* (1970), a performance that was matched only by his
decadent valet in *The Servant*.

As Bogarde sought more problematic roles, he left England for Europe, first to
Italy, to work with Visconti, and then to France where he lived on a farm in
Provence for nearly twenty years. Bogarde spent relatively little time working in
Hollywood after the disastrous experience of *Song without End* (1960), and
instead sought highly individualistic directors. After appearing in Rainer Werner
Fassbinder's adaptation of Vladimir Nabokov's *Despair* (1978), Bogarde semi-
retired from the screen to concentrate on his writing, producing seven successful
novels and a series of veiled autobiographical novels. Bogarde left Provence in
1986 and returned to live in London after Tony Forwood, his companion, fell ill.
Bogarde was knighted in 1992 and died of a heart attack in 1999 after suffering a
severe stroke in 1996 that left him partially paralyzed. His last film was Bernard
Tavernier's *Daddy Nostalgia* (1990).

Bogarde was the preeminent British film actor for more than twenty years and
he could have settled into a comfortable career exploiting the roles that made him

popular in the 1950s. Instead, he strove for excellence and variation, a not unexpected desire from an actor with an edgy personality (Terence Rattigan once remarked he's "got the courage to be a shit, has our Dirk"). This sometimes produced tension on the set, as director Roy Ward Baker* discovered when Bogarde opposed the casting of John Mills* in *The Singer Not the Song* (1960). Yet this very quality was the source of Bogarde's strong screen presence, reinforced by his decision to work in "difficult" films such as Liliana Cavani's *The Night Porter,* where he played an ex-Nazi in a sadomasochistic relationship with a woman he formerly abused in a concentration camp. Although this film provoked some discontent from his admirers, this was of little concern for Bogarde, who felt that audience adulation was rather silly.

Bogarde won the BAFTA Best British Actor Award for *The Servant* and as the television director in love with Julie Christie* in *Darling** (1965). He also received a BAFTA Lifetime Achievement Award in 1988.

FILMS: Come on George (1939), Dancing with Crime (1947), Esther Waters (1948), Quartet (1948), Once a Jolly Swagman (1948), Dear Mr. Prohack (1949), Boys in Brown (1949), The Blue Lamp (1950), So Long at the Fair (1950), The Woman in Question (1950), Blackmailed (1951), Penny Princess (1952), Hunted (1952), The Gentle Gunman (1952), Appointment in London (1953), Desperate Moment (1953), They Who Dare (1954), Doctor in the House (1954), The Sleeping Tiger (1954), For Better, for Worse (1954), The Sea Shall Not Have Them (1954), Simba (1955), Doctor at Sea (1955), Cast a Dark Shadow (1956), The Spanish Gardener (1956), Ill Met by Moonlight (1957), Doctor at Large (1957), Campbell's Kingdom (1957), A Tale of Two Cities (1957), The Wind Cannot Read (1958), The Doctor's Dilemma (1959), Song without End (1960), The Angel Wore Red (1960), The Singer Not the Song (1960), Victim (1961), We Joined the Navy (guest role, 1962), H.M.S. Defiant (1962), The Password Is Courage (1962), The Mind Benders (1962), I Could Go on Singing (1963), Doctor in Distress (1963), Hot Enough for June (1963), The Servant (1963), King and Country (1964), The High Bright Sun (1964), Darling (1965), Modesty Blaise (1966), Accident (1967), Our Mother's House (1967), Sebastian (1968), The Fixer (1968), The Damned (1969), Justine (1969), Oh! What A Lovely War (1969), Death in Venice (1970), The Serpent (1972), The Night Porter (1973), Permission to Kill (1975), A Bridge Too Far (1977), Providence (1977), Despair (1978), and Daddy Nostalgia (1990).

BONHAM CARTER, HELENA (b. 1966). It is now inadequate, and has been for some years, to stereotype Helena Bonham Carter as the personification of the costume film, the bodice-laden, genteel virgin associated with period or "heritage" melodramas. Even this association with the "costume film" is misleading as there is not just one costume role she plays but a range of characters with divergent personality traits, from the innocence of her sixteen-year-old monarch who would rule for only nine days in *Lady Jane* (1986), to the morally complex, driven, ruthless, ultimately vulnerable Kate Croy in *The Wings of the Dove** (1997), a role for which she received an Academy Award nomination and a BAFTA Best Actress Award nomination. As for "innocence," Croy's sexual manipulation of Linus Roache in *The Wings of the Dove* and her failed attempt to consummate her relationship with Richard Grant on the ground in the English countryside in *A Merry War/Keep the Aspidistra Flying* (1997) contradicts any attempt to categorize her as innocent—particularly as the scene begins with Bonham Carter, clad only in her stockings and underwear, inviting Grant to make love to her. This invitation is only withdrawn when she discovers that he has failed to bring any "protection." Such sequences are hardly in accord with Barbara Cartland's compliment of Bonham Carter for her "virginal aura" after she starred in the television adaptation of *A Hazard of Hearts* (1987).

The prevailing aristocratic image of Bonham Carter is reinforced by her family background as she is the great-granddaughter of Lord Herbert Henry Asquith, a Liberal prime minister of Britain, and granddaughter of Lady Violet Bonham Carter, politician and orator, as well as grandniece of director Anthony Asquith.* When her banker father suffered paralysis and blindness following an operation to remove a benign brain tumor, Bonham Carter placed a photo of herself with a casting agency resulting, eventually, in a commercial and, some time later, director Trevor Nunn selecting her to play the title role in *Lady Jane*. This was soon followed by the role that would generate widespread interest in her career and begin the "Bonham Carter" stereotype as Lucy Honeychurch in *A Room with a View* (1986). Since then, Bonham Carter has accepted a range of different roles: a drug addict in *Miami Vice* (1987); an independent woman in *Getting It Right* (1989); Woody Allen's adulterous wife in *Mighty Aphrodite* (1995); and a wheelchair-bound woman suffering from motor neurone disease with a desire for sex in *The Theory of Flight* (1998). These films were interspersed with "period" characterizations in *Hamlet* (1990), *Where Angels Fear to Tread* (1991), and *Howards End** (1992). Hopefully, the remnants of the Bonham Carter stereotype have been destroyed by the intensity of her nihilistic character in *Fight Club* (1999) and as Ari, an ape, in *Planet of the Apes* (2001).

FILMS: Lady Jane (1986), A Room with a View (1986), The Vision (1987), The Mask (1988), Getting It Right (1989), Francesco (1989), Hamlet (1990), Where Angels Fear to Tread (1991), Howards End (1992), Frankenstein (1994), Mighty Aphrodite (1995), Margaret's Museum (1995), Twelfth Night (1996), Shadow Play (1996), The Wings of the Dove (1997), A Merry War/Keep the Aspidistra Flying (1997), The Revengers' Comedies (1998), The Theory of Flight (1998), Fight Club (1999), Women Talking Dirty (1999), Carnivale (1999), and Planet of the Apes (2001).

BOULTING, ROY (1913–2001)/**BOULTING, JOHN** (1913–1985). Twin brothers, Roy Boulting and John Boulting alternated as director or producer on most of their films although Roy directed more films than John. After 1965, John worked only as a producer while Roy continued directing films and television programs into the mid-1980s. When John came back from the Spanish Civil War, he set up Charter Films with Roy. After their disastrous first film, *The Landlady* (1937), where Roy admitted they made numerous mistakes, they enjoyed considerable critical and commercial success with *Consider Your Verdict* (1938), based on a BBC playlet that ran as a support feature to the French film *Qai des Brumes* at the

Academy (London's first art house cinema) for more than six months. Later, it also enjoyed success across Britain. Both Boultings were active producing and directing propaganda documentaries during the war years—Roy assembled footage from front-line cameramen of the critical battle at El Alamein, which raged over ten nights at the end of October 1942, for *Desert Victory* (1942). The film also included new footage, shot by Roy. The film was a major success in Britain and the United States, where it was awarded an Oscar.

The Boulting brothers were forced on occasions to supplement their earnings by making one-off films for other production companies. Roy directed and John produced the expensive *Fame Is the Spur* (1946) for Two Cities but it failed at the box office. At other times, Roy directed films created by other people, such as the Cold War melodrama *High Treason* (1951) and *Run for the Sun* (1956), an adaptation of the popular 1932 thriller *The Most Dangerous Game,* for RKO starring Richard Widmark and Trevor Howard.* Roy's fee for these films was used to develop projects by the brothers for Charter Films, where they enjoyed considerable creative freedom.

Their most successful film of the 1940s, *Brighton Rock** (1947), directed by John, was acquired after Terence Rattigan, Anthony Asquith,* and Anatole de Grunwald were unable to come up with a working screenplay. Graham Greene discarded Rattigan's material and wrote his own screenplay. Roy then went to Brighton to search for appropriate locations and returned two weeks later with a shooting script, based on Greene's screenplay, which he gave to John who directed one of the edgiest gangster films ever made in Britain.

The injection of "realism" and social commentary into genre films characterized most of the Boulting brothers productions and, as Roy later argued, they tried to move beyond the "trite escapism to which British cinema had been wedded."[1] This included their cycle of satirical comedies in the 1950s, which represents the high water mark of the Boulting brothers' output. Films such as *I'm All Right Jack** (directed by John in 1959) that cast a jaundiced eye over the union movement and their collusion with employers, the army in *Private's Progress* (directed by John in 1956), lawyers (*Brothers-in-Law,* directed by Roy in 1957), the Civil Service (*Carlton-Browne of the F.O.,* directed by Roy in 1959), and the church (*Heavens Above!,* directed by John in 1963). During this period, the brothers adopted a policy of letting the writer direct while the other brother produced the film. They also developed a kind of "stock company" of familiar British actors, including Dennis Price, Ian Carmichael,* Richard Attenborough,* Terry-Thomas,* Irene Handl, and Kenneth Griffiths.

In 1958, the Boulting brothers joined the board of British Lion and played a prominent role in reestablishing the fortunes of this famous British film company. Over the next six years, British Lion was transformed into a flourishing enterprise. John died in 1985 and Roy, who was married six times, died in 2001. One of Roy's wives was Hayley Mills, whom he directed in *The Family Way** (1966) as the young bride who has trouble consummating her marriage to Hywel Bennett. Roy and Hayley married in 1971 and divorced in 1977.

John won the Best British Screenplay Award at the 1960 BAFTA Awards for *I'm All Right Jack* (shared with Frank Harvey and Alan Hackney) and both John and Roy were nominated for the same award for *Private's Progress* in 1957. Roy and John were nominated for the Golden Lion Award at the Venice Film Festival in 1950 for the thriller *Seven Days to Noon* (1950). Roy also won the 1944 New York Film Critics Award for Best Film for *Thunder Rock* (1942) and the 1949 New York Film Critics Award for Best Direction and Best Film for *Fame Is the Spur,* while John won the Best British Film Award at the 1951 BAFTA for *The Magic Box* (1951).

FILMS: Roy Boulting (as director): The Landlady (1938), Consider Your Verdict (1938), Trunk Crime (1939), Inquest (1939), Pastor Hall (1940), Dawn Guard (short, 1942), Thunder Rock (1942), Desert Victory (doc., 1943), Tunisian Victory (doc., codir., 1944), Burma Victory (doc., 1945), Fame Is the Spur (1947), The Guinea Pig (1948), Singlehanded (1951), High Treason (1951), Sailor of the King (1953), Seagulls over Sorrento (codir., 1954), Josephine and Men (1955), Run for the Sun (1956), Brothers-in-Law (1957), Happy Is the Bride (1958), Carlton-Browne of the F.O. (1959), Suspect (codir., 1960), A French Mistress (1960), The Family Way (1966), Twisted Nerve (1968), There's a Girl in My Soup (1970), Soft Beds, Hard Battles (1973), and The Last Word (1979).

John Boulting (as director): Journey Together (1946), Brighton Rock (1947), Seven Days to Noon (1950), The Magic Box (1951), Seagulls over Sorrento (codir., 1954), A Private's Progress (1956), Lucky Jim (1957), I'm All Right Jack (1959), Suspect (codir., 1960), Heaven's Above! (1963), and Rotten to the Core (1965).

BOX, MURIEL (1905–1991). Muriel Box began her film career working on scripts for British Instructional Films in the mid-1920s and, after her marriage to Sydney Box, they began writing one-act plays together in the 1930s. They formed their own company in 1939 to produce training and propaganda films. When Sydney suggested to Muriel that she should write and direct *Road Safety for Children* for the British government, the minister of information refused to allow Muriel to direct the film, replacing her with Ken Annakin, who did not have a fraction of Muriel's experience in the film industry. Muriel was to revisit this situation over the next thirty years. Even with her last film, *The Rattle of a Simple Man* (1964), Sidney had to intervene to convince executives at ABPC who objected to a female director, to allow her to proceed as director.

Muriel's greatest success, however, was not as a director but as a screenwriter with Sidney. They coauthored twenty-two screenplays, including their Oscar-winning script for *The Seventh Veil** (1945), which had its genesis in the use of narcosis on shell-shocked soldiers during World War II. After Muriel learned that the men were questioned while under the drug to reveal their inner thoughts, she reworked this concept into a script based on an artist who was traumatized by an event in her life. She followed the commercial and critical success of *The Seventh Veil* with *Daybreak* (1948), a strong, fatalistic drama of failed love between an executioner (Eric Portman*) and a lonely woman (Ann Todd*) who lives with him on a barge. *Daybreak* was less successful at the box office and attracted censorship problems that held up its release for more than two years.

In 1946, Sydney was placed in charge of Gainsborough Studios, with Muriel appointed head of the script department and Sydney's sister Betty elevated to the top position at Islington Studios. This trio produced nearly forty films in the next four years, including the clever film noir *Dear Murderer** (1947), with Portman and Greta Gynt* (co-produced by Muriel), and *Holiday Camp* (1947), with Jack Warner* and Kathleen Harrison. The success of this latter film led to a series of films based on the activities of the Huggett family.

Muriel's first film as director was *The Happy Family* (1952), coscripted by Muriel and Sydney. Sydney had to pretend it would be co-directed to conceal the fact that a woman was directing the film. Even then, financier John Woolf withdrew funding when he found out that Muriel was the director. Muriel's next film, *Street Corner* (1953), was devised as a reply to the absence of policewomen in *The Blue Lamp** (1950). Muriel's problems continued with *To Dorothy a Son* (1955) when U.S. star Shelley Winters resented the fact that the director was a woman, a situation that was replicated by Hildegarde Neff's attitude to Muriel in the Berlin thriller *Subway in the Sky* (1959).

Too Young to Love (1960), based on the play by Elsa Shelley, addressed questions of female promiscuity and the depiction of the medical and social ramifications, which resulted in an X certificate for the film. Although it was not a commercial success, Muriel was proud that the cast and crew were predominantly female. A more successful film was *Simon and Laura* (1955), with Muriel fighting Rank Studios to include Ian Carmichael* in the film version after seeing him develop the role in Alan Melville's successful West End play. This film, satirizing various aspect of television, exposed the "double life" of television stars (Peter Finch* and Kay Kendall) who battled each other off camera while pretending to be the perfect couple on-screen. Again, both Kendall and Finch opposed the appointment of a female director and asked to have Muriel removed from the film. Producer Earl St. John refused.

Muriel and Sydney were divorced in 1969, although they had ceased working together in 1959 when Sydney left the film industry for television. Muriel married Lord Gardiner, chancellor of the Exchequer, in 1971 and died in 1991.

FILMS (as director) The Happy Family (1952), Street Corner (1953), To Dorothy a Son (1955), The Beachcomber (1955), Simon and Laura (1955), Eyewitness (1956), The Passionate Stranger (1957), The Truth about Women (1959), Subway in the Sky (1959), This Other Eden (1959), Too Young to Love (1960), The Piper's Tune (1962), and Rattle of a Simple Man (1964).

BOYS WILL BE BOYS (Gainsborough, 1935)—Comedy. *Director:* William Beaudine; *Producer:* Michael Balcon; *Script:* Will Hay and Robert Edmunds; *Photography:* Charles Van Enger; *Music:* Louis Levy; *Cast:* Will Hay (Dr. Alec Smart), Gordon Harker (Faker Brown), Jimmy Hanley (Cyril Brown), Davy Burnaby (Colonel Crableigh), Norma Varden (Lady Dorking), Claude Dampier

(Theo P. Finch), Charles Farrell (Louis Brown), and Percy Walsh (Prison Governor).

Although *Boys Will Be Boys* was veteran music hall performer Will Hay's* third film, it was the first screen appearance of his amoral, proletarian school master who longs for middle-class acceptance. Hay's schoolmaster in this film is called Dr. Alec Smart, which, of course, provides the recurring opportunity for him to be called "Smart Alec." After allowing Brown, a convict, to forge an acceptable reference for him, Smart is appointed headmaster at Narkover Academy, a disreputable school filled with aspiring male criminals similar to St. Trinian's (for girls) two decades later.

The real appeal of the film resides in Hay's ability to transform logic into illogic, together with his problematic morality, which includes replacing the normal curriculum with cards and gambling. Brown's threat to expose Smart's fraudulent credentials forces Smart to employ him at the school. Brown, in turn, plans with his son, a student at the school, to steal an expensive necklace belonging to Lady Dorking, a member of the school board. This culminates in a prolonged rugby game as the necklace is hidden in the football. Smart inadvertently recovers the necklace and consolidates his position as head master.

Prior to the film's action climax, it gently satirizes many of the traditions of public school education including the initiation ceremonies imposed on new teachers and superficial traditions such as the bogus Founders' Day ritual. *Boys Will Be Boys* is hardly a subtle comedy and belongs within the traditions of the British music hall, especially with Hay's ability to make up "business" within its simplistic story line.

BRASSED OFF (Channel Four/Miramax/Prominent Features, 1996)—Social drama. *Director:* Mark Herman; *Producer:* Steve Abbott; *Script:* Mark Herman; *Cinematography:* Andy Collins; *Music:* Trevor Jones; *Cast:* Peter Postlethwaite (Danny), Tara Fitzgerald (Gloria), Ewan McGregor (Andy), Stephen Tompkinson (Phil), Jim Carter (Harry), Ken Colley (Greasley), Peter Gunn (Simmo), Mary Healey (Ida), Melanie Hill (Sandra), Philip Jackson (Jim), and Stephen Moore (McKenzie).

Of the British films released in the last part of the 1990s (including *The Full Monty** [1997] and *Billy Elliot** [2000]) utilizing a "triumph over economic adversity" plot, *Brassed Off* is the most fully realized. *Brassed Off* depicts the trials and tribulations of the Grimley Colliery brass band and was loosely based on the experiences of miners at Grimethorpe whose famous band supplied the sound track and musical extras.

The film is set in 1992 as the Conservative government launches another program of mining pit closures. The Grimley Colliery band is on the verge of folding due to the threatened closure of the mine. A young woman, Gloria, joins the band after entrancing band members with her dazzling performance of "Rodrigo's Concerto" on the flugelhorn. Although Gloria's father was a miner and band member, she works for the mining company, unbeknown to the other band members. This secret provides one of the film's many narrative strands within the overarching desire of bandleader Danny to take his band to the national finals in London. Danny is seemingly oblivious to the broader question of the closure and problems facing his son Phil—Phil's marriage is collapsing under debts accumulated during the last strike in 1984. There is also tension among the miners over the offer of a redundancy payment from the company if they will vote to close the mine. While all of the families need the money, it is the wives who maintain the struggle longest.

Against this turbulent background, *Brassed Off* juggles the more melodramatic aspects, including one-dimensional stereotypes such as the manipulative mining manager McKenzie, with many effective scenes—the touching romance between band members Andy and Gloria; sentimental scenes such as the band's rendition of *Danny Boy* outside Danny's hospital bed; rousing concert performances; and a bittersweet ending that reminds the viewer of the social cost of the government's policies.

Phil, the most troubled miner, is representative of the many problems faced by all miners—culminating in his near suicide after trying to make extra money as a part-time clown. Director/screenwriter Mark Herman cleverly uses this subplot to show Phil launching into a bitter tirade against Margaret Thatcher's policies at a children's party at the local church. The tone of the scene is sad and melancholic as the diatribe is delivered to a group of puzzled young children by a man dressed in a clown outfit—complete with red nose and oversized shoes.

Finally, Gloria realizes the extent of the suffering if the mine closes and offers three thousand pounds so that the band can participate in the national finals. After they win the contest, Danny, who has sneaked away from his hospital bed to watch his band, joins them on stage to tell the audience of the plight of the miners. Danny's speech is heightened by his previous indifference to the social consequences—all he cared about was the band. This moment disturbs the film's "feel good" ending and brings the audience back to reality and the fact that a way of life has been destroyed—the pit has closed and they are all out of work—"you can't have a colliery band without a bloody colliery," one band member observes. *The Full Monty* and *Billy Elliot,* on the other hand, just leave the audience with their happy endings and the social consequences recede into the background. *Brassed Off*, on the other hand, concludes with a written epilogue that reminds the viewer of the number of mine closures since 1984.

BRIEF ENCOUNTER (Cineguild, 1945)—Romance. *Director:* David Lean; *Producers:* Noël Coward, Anthony Havelock-Allan, and Ronald Neame; *Script:* David Lean, Ronald Neame, and Noël Coward, based on Coward's play *Still Life;* *Photographer:* Robert Krasker; *Music:* Sergey Rachmaninoff (from his Second Piano Concerto); *Cast:* Celia Johnson (Laura Jesson), Trevor Howard (Dr. Alec Harvey), Stanley Holloway (Albert Godby), Joyce Carey (Myrtle Baggot), Cyril Raymond (Fred Jesson), Everley Gregg (Dolly Messiter), and Marjorie Mars (Mary Norton).

David Lean* and Ronald Neame* adapted their screenplay for this film from Noël Coward's 1936 one-act play *Still Life* and it has been perceived over the years as almost the quintessential English film. Although the film's premise, two married people falling in love with each other, is a universal story line, the values and reactions of the two characters belong to a specific class (middle) and specific time period (1930s and 1940s). A comparison with the values and reactions of two similar groups in *Accident* * (1967) reveals the shift in moral assumptions, at least on the screen, over a twenty-year period.

The film is narrated via the consciousness of Laura Jesson, a middle-aged housewife who makes a trip each Thursday to the (fictional) provincial town of Milford by train to shop, exchange her library books, have lunch at the Kardomah (cafe), and finish the day with a matinee session of the local picture theater. The rest of the week is devoted to domestic chores and life with her less than passionate husband and two children. Each Thursday Laura travels back on the 5:43 train to Ketchworth. One day a cinder lodges in her eye and when she returns to the railway buffet, Dr. Alec Harvey removes the obstacle from her eye. He visits Milford each Thursday to relieve one of the surgeons at the local hospital before catching the 5:40 train in the opposite direction. Their love affair gradually blossoms as they continue to meet each Thursday.

At the time of its release, *Brief Encounter* was celebrated for its "realist" attributes. This is now difficult to understand as the film's expressive qualities are clearly evident in the stylized use of the railway station and the ever-present shadows that constantly remind us that the affair is ultimately doomed. The selection of a railway station and its drab buffet is inspired as it allows Lean to emphasize the "naturalism" of the film's surface while visually heightening those aspects relating to sex that remain unspoken—hence the recurring image of an express train shown rushing through the station and tunnel releasing steam, which functions as an appropriate sexual metaphor for the film's central dilemma: "We are neither of us free to love each other. There is too much in the way," cries Jesson.

Perhaps the most stylized device in the film is its use of Rachmaninoff's Second Piano Concerto, which is closely associated with Laura's fragile romantic aspirations. Her realization that she is falling in love with the idealistic doctor is beautifully signaled by a brief camera movement from a two-shot of Laura and Harvey to a close-up of Laura's face (and Rachmaninoff's music on the sound track), while Harvey is explaining his ideas on the power of preventive medicine. Aware of the change taking place, Harvey asks Laura to meet him next Thursday and the affair begins. In the end, however, family responsibility and commitment triumph over romance and sexual release.

Brief Encounter begins in the final moments of the love affair and the film is presented via a flashback that emphasizes the effect the affair has on Laura. The audience never sees other aspects of Harvey's life except as it relates to his meeting with Laura each Thursday. The film's climax occurs when Laura reluctantly agrees to go with Harvey to an apartment owned by one of his friends. The meaning of the scene is quite clear. Up to this point, the lovers are only shown together in public—at the movies, driving in the country, or lunching at the Kardomah and, on one special occasion, at the Grand Hotel. Just as Laura's sexual restraint ("I must control myself" and "I must be sensible") appears to collapse, the owner of the apartment returns home, forcing Laura to flee through the back entrance and the dark streets of Milford in shame. This effectively ends the relationship as the near hysterical heroine contemplates throwing herself under a passing train.

Brief Encounter was Lean's fourth film and he was the first British director nominated for an Academy Award. New York critics awarded Best Actress to Celia Johnson,* while the film won Best Picture at Cannes. It is uniformly well acted with a special mention to Joyce Carey as the guardian of the stale sandwiches at the station buffet who encourages Stanley Holloway's romantic/sexual attentions. Their relationship, together with her young assistant who only wants to be with her boyfriend, serves to emphasize the repression and restraint of the middle-class couple, Laura Jesson and Alec Harvey. The working class appear less inhibited.

BRIGHTON ROCK (Associated British, 1947)—Gangster. *Director:* John Boulting; *Producer:* Roy Boulting; *Script:* Graham Greene and Terence Rattigan; *Photography:* Harry Waxman; *Music:* Hans May; *Cast:* Richard Attenborough (Pinkie Brown), Hermione Baddeley (Ida Arnold), William Hartnell (Dallow), Harcourt Williams (Prewitt), Wylie Watson (Spicer), Nigel Stock (Cubitt), Alan Wheatley (Fred Hale), and Carol Marsh (Rose Brown).

From the first low-key image in the film introducing a young, brooding Richard Attenborough* as the mentally disturbed Pinkie Brown, the dark, psychological emphasis in this bleak gangster film is evident, representing a consolidation of both the formal and thematic attributes of what we now recognize as film noir. Seventeen-year-old Pinkie Brown assumes control of a group of small-time gangsters in pre–World War II Brighton when its leader is killed by a rival gang. Brown blames the killing on activities of a newspaper journalist, Fred Hale, who is visiting Brighton as part of a promotional stunt to increase circulation of his newspaper. After Brown kills Hale on the ghost train in the local amusement park, the film becomes more interested in the psychology of the young gangster. Brown has to reluctantly court and marry seventeen-year-old waitress Rose because her evidence could destroy his alibi. However, his plan to force his young bride to suicide is disrupted by blowsy entertainer Ida Arnold. Arnold becomes involved after the police declare that the journalist committed suicide when she believed he was murdered.

The U.S. release title for the film was *Young Scarface,* and Pinkie Brown shares the twisted sexuality of Howard Hawks's 1931 gangster classic. Baby-face Brown displays a deep hatred of people, especially those who are vulnerable, and his only pleasure comes from inflicting pain. After killing an elderly gang member, Spicer, Brown shows his true feeling for Rose—on their wedding night he records his contempt for her on a gramophone record as a wedding present. Instead of the expected declaration of love, Brown records: "You asked me to make a record of my voice. Well here it is. What you want me to say is I love you. Here is the truth. I hate you, you little slut. You make me sick. Why don't you get back to Nelson Place and leave me alone." The perverseness of this scene is emphasized by the composition with Brown in the foreground making his record-ing, while Rose, unable to hear him, looks adoringly at her husband as the camera slowly shifts toward her face. Rose does not hear this recording until the final scene in the film, after Pinkie's death. However, the record has become warped and all she hears is the first part: "You asked me to make a record of my voice. Well here it is. What you want me to say is I love you." At this point the record sticks on the repetition of "I love you, I love you." This ending was criticized as a sentimental mistake compared to the tragic ending in Graham Greene's novel. However, this is a misinterpretation as it is anything but sentimental. It is deeply ironic, bleak, and totally consistent with the overall tone of the film.

A superb film, *Brighton Rock* was popular with British audiences but enjoyed less success in the United States. Young, cherubic faced Attenborough, who had played the part of Pinkie Brown at the Garrick Theatre in 1943, brilliantly con-veyed the appropriate mixture of repression and violence and the film represented a profound change in the British gangster film. Three years later, the character of Tom Riley in *The Blue Lamp** (1950) displayed some of Brown's antisocial qual-ities, but *Brighton Rock* was a more confrontational film.

THE BROTHERS (Gainsborough, 1947)—Melodrama. *Director:* David Mac-donald; *Producer:* Sidney Box; *Script:* Muriel Box and Sidney Box, adaptation by David Macdonald, L. A. G. Strong, and Paul Vincent Carroll, based on the novella by L. A. G. Strong; *Cinematography:* Stephen Dade; *Music:* Cedric Thorpe Davie; *Cast:* Patricia Roc (Mary Lawson), Will Fyffe (Aeneas McGrath), Maxwell Reed (Fergus Macrae), Finlay Currie (Hector Macrae), Duncan Macrae (John Macrae), John Laurie (Dugald), Andrew MacDonald (Willie McFarish), James Woodburn (priest), and Megs Jenkin (Angustina).

Set on the Isle of Skye in 1900, *The Brothers* assumes some of the key attrib-utes of film noir with its sexual tension, repression, sadism, and bleak fatalism. Mary Lawson is sent to the island to live with and serve the all-male household of the Macraes, who are her distant relatives. The arrival of this young, pretty woman, however, triggers sexual hostility and tension, particularly from the eld-est son, John. This situation is aggravated by the feud between the Macraes and the McFarishes. When Willie McFarish attempts to rape Mary, the two clans con-front each other in a rowing race, leading to the demise of Hector, the head of the Macraes. On his death bed, Hector tells John to let Fergus marry Mary, but John ignores this as he covets her himself.

Mary loves Fergus and his neglect prompts her to accept a sexual invitation from Willie McFarish while rejecting similar advances from John. Although John marries another woman, Angustina, he cannot get Mary out of his mind so, after another rejection, he convinces Fergus to kill Mary. Fergus commits suicide and the film ends with Willie demanding that John be tied up and lashed to a cork in the ocean with a fish attached to his head as live bait for the skull-crushing sea eagles.

The Brothers is a challenging, impressive film that never allows any hint of sentimentality or romance to intrude on its unrelenting bleak depiction of Hebridean life at the turn of the century. Despite the location shooting and strong, naturalistic performances from Scottish character actors Will Fyffe, Duncan Macrae, Andrew Crawford, Finlay Currie, and John Laurie, the film was roundly criticized for its sadism and "morbidity." True, the film does include scenes of violence, such as Fergus cutting off his own thumb when it is trapped by a conger eel after putting his hand in the water to reach for a lobster, and also the death of an informer with a fish attached to this head. But it is also conveys a strong sense of authenticity and dramatic intensity.

BULLDOG JACK (Gaumont British, 1935)—Comedy/thriller. *Director:* Walter Forde; *Producer:* Michael Balcon; *Script:* Jack Hulbert, Gerard Fairlie, Sidney Gilliat, H. C. McNeile (as Sapper), and J. O. C. Orton; *Photography:* Mutz Greenbaum; *Music:* Louis Levy; *Cast:* Jack Hulbert (Jack Penington), Fay Wray (Ann Manders), Ralph Richardson (Morelle), Claude Hulbert (Algy Longworth), Gibb McLaughlin (Denny), Atholl Fleming (Bulldog Drummond), and Paul Gretz (Salvini).

Bulldog Drummond was an amateur detective celebrated in the popular novels written by "Sapper" after World War I. This popularity extended to a series of films, made in Hollywood and Britain in the 1920s and 1930s, with Ronald Coleman and Ralph Richardson* playing the detective at different times. *Bulldog Jack* is, however, not part of this series as it is primarily a parody of the formula with comedian Jack Hulbert, as cricketer Jack Penington, highlighting the ridiculous qualities of the Drummond mystique, primarily his unreasonable lack of fear and his simplistic view of the world. When Penington, accompanied by his foolish offsider Algy (played by Hulbert's brother Claude), impersonates Drummond after the detective is injured in a car crash, he agrees to help Ann Manders rescue her grandfather from the evil clutches of Morelle. Richardson, as Morelle, provides a dazzling parody of an archetypal master criminal.

After an amusing confrontation between the villains, Penington and Algy in the Bloomsbury Underground, Penington battles Morelle in the British Museum in a climax reminiscent of Alfred Hitchcock's* *Blackmail** (1929) and made more effective by the skill of art director Alfred Junge. With its clever mix of humor and thrills, the film succeeds due to its ability to combine parody with the excitement of the thriller—especially when Morelle attempts to crash a train in the London underground near the end of the film. *Bulldog Jack* remains a fascinating document that highlights the insular xenophobia of the Drummond formula while entertaining with slapstick and thrills.

BYRON, KATHLEEN (b. 1922). Sister Ruth, Kathleen Byron's sexually repressed nun in Michael Powell's* magical *Black Narcissus** (1947), is, within the context of the British cinema in the 1940s and 1950s, an amazing characterization. Sister Ruth's confrontation with Sister Clodagh, which is communicated largely via costume, makeup, and body language, has Ruth abandoning her nun's habit for a low-cut dress and lipstick. Powell, in a tight close-up, shows her applying the lipstick lasciviously to her mouth in a moment of great cinematic power, a moment made all the more powerful by Byron's careful underplaying in earlier scenes. Byron, however, had to fight Powell over the interpretation of the character, for, as Byron argued, Sister Ruth "didn't know she was mad." Unfortunately, Byron never again received the same opportunity to make such an impact on the screen.

Byron was still studying at the Old Vic Drama School when Deborah Kerr's* agent sent her to the people developing *The Young Mr. Pitt* (1941), and she won a small part in the film. Except for a supporting role in the propaganda drama *The Silver Fleet* (1943), Byron's career did not flourish until her series of films for Powell after World War II as a recording angel in *A Matter of Life and Death** (1946), Sister Ruth in *Black Narcissus,* and as David Farrar's* supportive girl-friend Susan in *The Small Back Room* (1949). This film faced censorship obstacles with its suggestion that Farrar and Byron were sexually active and cohabitating, although not married.

After another dangerously neurotic character in *Madness of the Heart* (1949), and a more conventional character in the costume melodrama *The Reluctant Widow* (1950), directed by Bernard Knowles, Byron was invited to Hollywood to play Ann Seymour in *Young Bess* (1953). When the studio wanted to add extra scenes between her and Charles Laughton (as Henry VIII), Byron declined as she was pregnant and returned home to Britain. Byron worked steadily throughout the 1950s, 1960s, and up to the mid-1970s, with supporting parts in films and television programs. She extended her career into the 1990s with the role of Mrs. Goddard in the 1996 adaptation of *Emma** and small role in Steven Spielberg's *Saving Private Ryan* (1998).

FILMS: The Young Mr. Pitt (1941), The Silver Fleet (1943), A Matter of Life and Death (1946), Black Narcissus (1947), The Small Back Room (1948), Madness of the Heart (1949), The Reluctant Widow (1950), Prelude to Fame (1950), Tom Brown's Schooldays (1951), The Scarlet Thread (1951), Life in Her Hands (1951), Hell Is Sold Out (1951), Four Days (1951), The House in the Square (1951), My Death Is a Mockery (1952), The Gambler and the Lady (1952), Young Bess (1953), Star of the Night (1953), The Night of the Full Moon (1954), Profile (1954), Secret Venture (1954), Handcuffs, London (1955), Hand in Hand (1960), Night of the Eagle (1962), Hammerhead (1968), Wolfshead: The Legend of Robin Hood (1969), Private Road (1971), Twins of Evil (1971), Nothing but the Night (1972), Craze (1973), The Abdication (1974), One of Our Dinosaurs Is Missing (1975), The Elephant Man (1980), Emma (1995), Les Misérables (1998), Saving Private Ryan (1998), and Diary (1998).

NOTE

1. McFarlane, *An Autobiography of British Cinema,* p. 79.

C

CAINE, MICHAEL (b. 1933). Born Maurice Joseph Micklewhite in the charity wing of St. Olave's hospital in south London, Michael Caine changed his acting name from Micklewhite to Caine after noticing a poster for the film *The Caine Mutiny* while talking to his agent in a phone box. He was born into a working-class family, left school at sixteen, and worked in a number of jobs until he was called up for national service, where he served with the Royal Fusiliers in Korea. Caine gained employment as assistant stage manager at the Horsham Repertory Company in Sussex before moving to the Lowestoft Repertory company in Suffolk, where he married Patricia Raines. From 1956 to 1962, Caine appeared in minor, often unbilled, film roles, small parts on television, and repertory theater before his theatrical break as the understudy to Peter O'Toole* in the hit play *The Long and the Short and the Tall* for its London season. He eventually replaced O'Toole and remained with the production when it moved to the provincial theaters.

His film break came when director Cy Endfield,* believing that Caine's "horsy" face was typical of the English aristocrat, disregarded his cockney background and speech and cast him as Lieutenant Gonville Bromhead in the story of British heroism at Rorke's Drift in South Africa in *Zulu** (1964). He followed this with the equally successful secret agent Harry Palmer in *The Ipcress File* (1965), a character he reprised in *Funeral in Berlin* (1966), followed by less successful films based on the same character in *The Billion Dollar Brain* (1967), *Bullet to Beijing* (1995), and *Midnight in St. Petersburg* (1997). After *The Ipcress File,* Caine became an international star with *Alfie** (1966), the cheeky, self-absorbed womanizer for which he was nominated for an Oscar and a Golden Globe Award.

Alfie defined Caine's screen person for many years although there were sporadic attempts to break away from this image, most notably as the ruthless southern landowner in the melodrama *Hurry Sundown* (1967). Audiences, however, preferred Caine in comedy and throughout the late 1960s and into the 1970s he appeared in a number of successful films—such as *The Italian Job* (1969), *Sleuth* (1972), *California Suite* (1978), and the rollicking Kipling yarn *The Man Who Would Be King* (1976). There was developing, however, another side to his screen persona that was not only morally problematic, but also dark and intense. He demonstrated this to great effect in war films such as *Play Dirty* (1968), Robert Aldrich's superb anti-war film *Too Late the Hero* (1970), and as the amoral hit man Jack Carter who redeems himself in Mike Hodges's tough film noir *Get Carter** (1971). Caine has maintained this dark, threatening persona throughout his career, usually in his best films, although some, such as *Blood and Wine* (1996) and *Quills* (2000), have not been always been commercially successful. This includes one of his best performances in the black comedy *A Shock to the System* (1990) as he kills his way to the top of the corporate ladder. In *Mona Lisa* (1986), on the other hand, Caine was celebrated by the critics for the intensity of his evil protagonist.

The other characteristic that emerged in Caine's career in the 1970s was a conscious decision to follow the money and appear in many nondescript films, often large budget and shot in pleasant locations, two factors assisting his decision to appear in films such as *Beyond the Poseidon Adventure* (1977), *The Swarm* (1978), *The Hand* (1981), *Blame It on Rio* (1984), and *Jaws: The Revenge/Jaws 4* (1987). Caine interspersed undemanding roles in mediocre films with quality performances in excellent films, such as *Educating Rita* (1983), for which he was nominated for Best Actor at the 1983 Academy Awards, and winning Best Actor at the BAFTA Film Awards. Woody Allan's *Hannah and Her Sisters* (1986) was another quality film and Caine won the 1986 Oscar for Best Supporting Actor.

In the 1990s, Caine's career started to slip even further after a succession of dire roles, such as the risible action film *On Deadly Ground* (1994), starring Steven Seagal, followed by the equally poor thriller *Bullet to Beijing* (1995). Always the quintessential screen actor, he revived his reputation with a standout performance in *Little Voice** (1998) and an Oscar for Best Supporting Actor as an abortionist in *The Cider House Rules* (1999) and as Helen Mirren's husband, and Ray Winstone's* stepfather, in *Last Orders* (2002). Caine was knighted Sir Maurice Micklewhite at Buckingham Palace on November 16, 2000. He owns a number of restaurants in England and Miami. Caine published a series of anecdotes in *Michael Caine's Moving Picture Show* (1988) and published his autobiography, *What's It All About,* in 1993.

FILMS: A Hill in Korea (1956), How to Murder a Rich Uncle (1957), The Steel Bayonet (1957), Blind Spot (1958), The Two-Headed Spy (1958), Carve Her Name with Pride (1958), The Key (1958), Passport to Shame (1958), The Danger Within (1959), Foxhole in Cairo (1960), The Bulldog Breed (1960), The Day the Earth Caught Fire (1961), Solo for Sparrow (1962), The Wrong Arm of the Law (1962), Zulu (1963), The Ipcress File (1965), Alfie (1966), The Wrong Box (1966), Gambit (1966), Funeral in Berlin (1966), Hurry Sundown (1966), Billion Dollar Brain (1967), Woman Times Seven (1967), Deadfall (1967), Play Dirty (1968), The Magus (1968), The Italian Job (1969), The Battle of Britain (1969), Too Late the Hero (1969), The Last Valley (1970), Get Carter (1971), Kidnapped

(1971), Zee and Co. (1971), Pulp (1972), Sleuth (1972), The Black Windmill (1974), The Marseilles Contract (1974), The Wilby Conspiracy (1975), The Romantic Englishwoman (1975), Peeper (1975), The Man Who Would Be King (1975), The Silver Bears (1976), The Eagle Has Landed (1976), A Bridge Too Far (1976), Harry and Walter Go to New York (1976), Beyond the Poseidon Adventure (1977), California Suite (1978), Ashanti (1978), The Swarm (1979), The Island (1979), Dressed to Kill (1980), The Hand (1981), Escape to Victory (1981), Deathtrap (1982), Educating Rita (1983), The Honorary Consul (1983), The Jigsaw Man (1983), Blame It on Rio (1984), Water (1984), The Holcroft Convenant (1984), Hannah and Her Sisters (1986), Sweet Liberty (1986), Half Moon Street (1986), Mona Lisa (1986), The Fourth Protocol (1986), The Whistle Blowers (1987), Jaws: The Revenge (1987), Surrender (1987), Dirty Rotten Scoundrels (1988), Without a Clue (1988), Mr. Destiny (1990), A Shock to the System (1990), Bullseye! (1991), Noises Off (1992), Blue Ice (1992), A Muppet Christmas (voice, 1993), On Deadly Ground (1994), Bullet to Beijing (1995), Blood and Wine (1996), Midnight in St. Petersburg (1997), Curtain Call (1997), Shadow Run (1998), Little Voice (1998), The Cider House Rules (1999), Get Carter (2000), Shiner (2000), Miss Congeniality (2001), Quills (2001), Last Orders (2002), Quicksand (2003), and The Quiet American (2003).

CALVERT, PHYLLIS (b. 1915–2002). *The Man in Grey** (1943) was a significant film in elevating all of its stars, James Mason,* Margaret Lockwood,* Stewart Granger,* and Phyllis Calvert, to film stardom. However, each actor was, to some extent, locked into a distinctive screen persona for some years. Hence Calvert, who began her film career in comedy, such as George Formby's* *Let George Do It* (1940), became the virtuous heroine in subsequent melodramas. Although *Fanny by Gaslight* (1944) offered Calvert a similar role, albeit with more substance and a better director (Anthony Asquith*), while *Madonna of the Seven Moons* (1944) provided her with (half) an opportunity to play a less virtuous character. In this film she played the mistress of a Florentine criminal as part of the schizoid personality of the same woman, the wife of an Italian merchant. In *They Were Sisters* (1945), Mason is, again, beastly but at least Calvert extracts revenge after he drives her sister to suicide. By *The Magic Bow* (1946), Calvert had had enough and tried desperately to get out of the film ("It was the *last* thing I wanted to do"),[1] but Rank forced her to co-star with Stewart Granger,* who played the violinist Paganini.

In the Frank Launder* and Sidney Gilliat* propaganda film *2000 Women* (1944), Calvert co-starred as a British woman interned by the Nazis in occupied France. However, Calvert's refusal to play a nun who falls in love with a British airman, played by Patricia Roc* in the film, damaged her friendship with Launder and Gilliat. Later in the decade, she was offered a better role as the feisty businesswoman Jackie Farnish in the melodrama *The Root of All Evil* (1947), where she battles fire, a deceitful lover, and bankruptcy on her way to monetary happiness. However, when her oil well is destroyed by fire she abandons her more "masculine" behavior and reverts to a more traditional feminine role and the arms of John McCallum.

While the 1940s represented the peak years of Calvert's popularity, one of her best roles came in the early 1950s as the mother of a young deaf girl in Alexander

Mackendrick's* *Mandy* (1952). This was an important film that marked a change in Calvert's career as she gradually switched to strong character parts, culminating with the role of Ingrid Bergman's sister in *Indiscreet* (1958). Prior to *Indiscreet,* Calvert had one of her last starring roles in the melodrama *It's Never Too Late* (1956), where she was riven by the demands of motherhood and the pleasures associated with being a celebrity writer. Calvert was nominated for the Best British Actress Award for *Mandy* at the 1953 BAFTA Film Awards.

FILMS: Discord (1933), Anne One Hundred (1933), School for Stars (1935), Two Days to Live (1939), They Came by Night (1940), Let George Do It (1940), Charley's Big-Hearted Aunt (1940), Neutral Port (1940), Inspector Hornleigh Goes to It (1941), Kipps (1941), The Young Mr. Pitt (1942), Uncensored (1942), The Man in Grey (1943), Fanny by Gaslight (1944), 2000 Women (1944), Madonna of the Seven Moons (1944), They Were Sisters (1944), Men of Two Worlds (1946), The Magic Bow (1946), The Root of All Evil (1947), Time out of Mind (1947), My Own True Love (1948), Broken Journey (1948), The Golden Madonna (1949), The Woman with No Name (1950), Appointment with Danger (1951), Mr. Denning Drives North (1951), Mandy (1952), The Net (1953), It's Never Too Late (1956), Child in the House (1956), Indiscreet (1958), A Lady Mislaid (1958), The Young and the Guilty (1958), Oscar Wilde (1960), Battle of Villa Fiorita (1965), Twisted Nerve (1968), Oh! What a Lovely War (1969), The Walking Stick (1970), and Mrs. Dalloway (1997).

A CANTERBURY TALE (The Archers, 1944)—World War II drama/parable. *Director:* Michael Powell; *Producers:* Michael Powell and Emeric Pressburger; *Script:* Michael Powell and Emeric Pressburger; *Cinematography:* Erwin Hillier; *Music:* Allan Gray; *Cast:* Eric Portman (Thomas Colpepper), Dennis Price (Sergeant Peter Gibbs), Sheila Sim (Alison Smith), Sgt. John Sweet (Sergeant Bob Johnston), Esmond Knight (Narrator, Seven-Sisters Soldier, Village Idiot), Charles Hawtrey (Thomas Duckett), Hay Petrie (Woodcock), George Merritt (Ned Horton), Edward Rigby (Jim Horton), and Freda Jackson (Prudence Honeywood).

One of the most oblique and disturbing wartime films, *A Canterbury Tale* was poorly received by critics (Caroline Lejeune described its theme as "unpleasant") and the general public. It was trimmed for the U.S. market with Kim Hunter added to the film, but it also failed there. Essentially, the film is a homage to Geoffrey Chaucer, and a certain kind of "Englishness." It involves three people who come together in the small village of Chillingbourne, ten miles from Canterbury. Each has suffered a loss or disappointment—the Land Girl Alison Smith believes that her fiancé has died in the war and that his parents disapprove of her, U.S. sergeant Bob Johnston believes that his girlfriend back in Oregon has lost interest in him, while the British sergeant Peter Gibbs devalues his peacetime occupation as an organist in a cinema.

The narrative pretext for keeping the trio together is provided by an attack on Smith soon after they arrive in Chillingbourne by the "Glue Man," a local man who places glue in the hair of women who are traveling within the village after dark. Despite the fact that ten other women have suffered similar attacks, the villagers appear relatively unconcerned so the trio set about trying to discover the identity of the "Glue Man." The fact that Michael Powell* and Emeric Pressburger* reveal quite early the identity of the "Glue Man" demonstrates that the "whodunit" aspect of the story is unimportant. Instead, they are much more interested in clarifying what constitutes the true "English" identity, an identity emanating from the England of Chaucer and William Shakespeare. Powell subsequently described this paean to a pastoral world as his version of "Why We Fight" that also assimilated his recurring "crusade against materialism."

A Canterbury Tale is a vision of England aligned with the views of Thomas Colpepper, gentleman farmer, magistrate, historian, and archaeologist. It is Colpepper's mission to emphasize the traditional virtues of pastoral England through his slide show and lecture. This, within the logic of the film, "legitimizes" his attacks on the young women of Chillingbourne as it deprives the soldiers of their companionship at night so they are left with nothing to do but attend his lectures. Colpepper is also central in restoring the faith of the troubled characters.

The film's reflexive narrative structure and oblique allegorical form renders *A Canterbury Tale* one of the curiosities of the British cinema. While other films during this period provided a clear, often simplistic, explanation of why people must get involved in the war, Powell and Pressburger embarked on a complex fable showing that the nation's roots lay in its pastoral history, a history celebrated by a man who has to resort to throwing glue into the hair of young women to attract listeners to this vision.

THE CAPTIVE HEART (Ealing, 1946)—War. *Director:* Basil Dearden; *Producers:* Michael Balcon and Michael Relph (associate); *Script:* Angus Macphail and Guy Morgan, based on a story by Patrick Kirwan; *Photography:* Douglas Slocombe; *Music:* Alan Rawsthorne; *Cast:* Michael Redgrave (Captain Karl Hasek), Mervyn Johns (Private Don Evans), Basil Radford (Major Ossy Dalrymple), Jack Warner (Corporal Ted Horsfall), Jimmy Hanley (Private Matthews), Jane Barrett (Caroline), Gordon Jackson (Lieutenant David Lennox), Ralph Michael (Captain Thurston), Derek Bond (Lieutenant Stephen Hartley), Guy Middleton (Captain Jim Grayson), Karel Stepanek (Herr Forster), Rachel Kempson (Celia Mitchell), Meriel Forbes (Beryl Curtess), Gladys Hanson (Mrs. Flo Horsfall), Rachel Thomas (Mrs. Evans), Robert Wyndham (Lieutenant Commander Robert Narsden), and Jack Lambert (Padre).

A significant portion of *The Captive Heart* was shot in Germany in a prisoner of war camp. The film intercuts life at home in Britain with British soldiers who were captured in France in 1940 and sent to a German prisoner of war camp. The film presents the stories of four men through an omnibus format. Captain Hasek, fleeing from the Gestapo, is forced to assume the identity of a dead British soldier, Geoffrey Mitchell. To prevent the Germans from becoming suspicious, he regularly writes to Mitchell's wife pretending to be her husband. The wife, not knowing her estranged husband is dead, tenderly replies to each letter. The content of Hasek's letters, narrated on the sound track by Michael Redgrave,* provides the emotional heart of the film with its mixture of vague optimism for a new society in Britain after the war combined with a profound sense of loneliness and anxiety ("deep down in the hearts of all of us there dwells a lonely ache, a desperate yearning for those we loved, and a fear of becoming forgotten men"). At other times, Hasek's letters are supported by images of the prisoners tending small gardens in the camp, playing games, or participating in various craft activities as they try to recreate "a little piece of England."

Other stories detail the hardship of war and the pain of separation. Scotsman Lennox loses his eyesight and writes to his girlfriend to break off their engagement. Pianist Lieutenant Hartley receives a letter from a spurned woman claiming that Hartley's wife has resumed an affair with a former lover while Private Evans learns that his wife has died after giving birth to a daughter. Inside the prison camp, Captain's Hasek's integration into the British community is paralleled by the reformation of young criminal, Private Matthews. Matthews forms a bond with the cheerful working-class Corporal Horsfall, played by Jack Warner.* This pairing of Jimmy Hanley and Warner was repeated in other films, most notably in *The Blue Lamp* * four years later.

While there are narrative similarities between *The Captive Heart,* which was produced shortly after World War II, and 1950s prisoner of war films, such as *The Colditz Story* * (1955), there are also basic differences, particularly in the depiction of the enemy. In the 1950s films, the enemy is generally forced into the background as these films are less interested in contrasting the virtues of British life with that of the enemy. *The Captive Heart,* on the other hand, retains a strong interest in celebrating those aspects of traditional England, summarized through references to the virtues of rural life, such as cricket on the village green on Saturday, home-made toffee, and gardens, as a means of contrasting life in England with the brutality and regimentation of the Germans. Unlike the relatively humane Kommandant in *The Colditz Story,* the Gestapo Forster, who periodically intervenes in the life of the prisoners in *The Captive Heart,* is another German screen sadist.

The Captive Heart is one of Ealing Studios' best films and the romantic intensity between Celia Mitchell and Captain Hasek is striking and rare for Ealing. The intensity is reinforced by the fact that it is based on deception as Hasek, initially, maintains communication with Celia only as a means of protecting himself by not arousing the suspicions of the Germans that he is not Geoffrey Mitchell. This deception is resolved by a series of shots as the film crosscuts between a spectacular eruption of sky rockets and Celia as she rushes to the phone to hear her lover's voice. Their words are not heard but through a clever combination of music and imagery, and an association between the exploding skyrockets and desire (used also by Alfred Hitchcock* in *To Catch a Thief* [1955]), Celia's passion is finally released. Love, communicated only through an interchange of letters, has triumphed, and Celia's acceptance of a new start with a man she has basically never seen, symbolizes the possibilities of a new start, a "new Britain," in 1946.

CARAVAN (Gainsborough, 1946)—Costume melodrama. *Director:* Arthur Crabtree; *Producers:* Harold Huth and Maurice Ostrer (executive): *Script:* Roland Pertwee, based on a novel by Lady Eleanor Smith; *Cinematography:* Stephen Dade with location photography by Cyril Knowles; *Music:* Walford Hyden. *Cast:* Stewart Granger (Richard Darrell), Jean Kent (Rosal), Anne Crawford (Oriana Camperdene), Dennis Price (Sir Francis Castleton), Robert Helpmann (Wycroft), John Salew (Diego), Gerard Heinz (Don Carlos), and Patricia Laffan (Betty).

Caravan, together with *Uncle Silas* (1947), best convey the conventions of nineteenth-century theatrical melodrama within the relatively brief flowering of costume melodrama. *Caravan,* with its formulaic characters, schematic story, and expressive settings drawn from the melodramatic conventions popularized by Guilbert de Pixerécourt in France in the early nineteenth century, provides a clear moral dichotomy between the evil aristocrat Sir Francis Castleton, with an appropriately excessive performance by Dennis Price, and the virtuous Oriana Camperdene and her lover, the heroic but impoverished Richard Darrell. A moral and physical counterpoint to fair-headed Oriana's pristine innocence is provided by Jean Kent, who virtually steals the film, as the dark, sultry gypsy dancer Rosal.

The film quickly sketches in the dominant character traits of Oriana, Francis, and Richard at the beginning, showing each as children. This prologue shows that cowardly Francis is no match for Richard and although both men love Oriana, she prefers Richard. Richard, however, will not marry Oriana until he establishes himself financially as a writer. To earn extra money he delivers an expensive piece of jewellery to Granada where he is ambushed and badly wounded by gypsy thieves hired by Wycroft, Francis's assistant. Although Richard is nursed back to health by gypsy dancer Rosal, he loses his memory and remains with her in their mountain hideout until she inadvertently mentions Oriana's name and his memory returns. Back in England, Oriana, believing Richard is dead, marries Francis and when Richard learns this he writes a bitter letter to Oriana. After their marriage, Francis's cruel and perverse nature is finally revealed to Oriana, particularly when he tries to humiliate her by inviting a group of prostitutes to dinner. Oriana flees to Spain, followed by Francis, where he dies. She is reunited with Richard after Rosal dies saving Richard.

The dialogue is suitably stylized ("serve the wine downwind or, so help me, I'll lay my cane across your shoulders") to match the schematic characterizations and moral polarities characteristic of melodrama. It is difficult to gauge whether the filmmakers intended to parody such conventions or merely push the story as far as it could go. The acting, particularly by Price and Australian ballet dancer-actor Robert Helpmann, is wildly excessive. Their dominant-submissive relationship provides some of the most bizarre moments in the film and Helpmann's Wycroft is one of the more openly gay figures in the British cinema before the relaxation of censorship strictures in the early 1960s, For example, Wycroft slyly feeling Richard's biceps during the voyage from England to Spain is hardly subtle.

CARLYLE, ROBERT (b. 1961). After a lead role in his second film, Ken Loach's* *Riff Raff* (1991), a social comedy about the bitter experiences of a newly arrived construction worker in London—gained partly because of Robert Carlyle's experience helping his father in the decorating business—Carlyle was cast in 1993 as "Albie" in a three-part episode of the *Cracker* television series, starring Robbie Coltrane. While Jimmy McGovern's script does not shrink from emphasizing Albie's murderous behavior, he also places him within a well-known social context, as a survivor of the Hillsborough disaster in Sheffield that killed many Liverpool soccer fans. This context provides an explanation for Albie's psychopathic reaction to a tabloid newspaper labeling the victims and survivors as "scum." Carlyle sought this part as "real" and "socially relevant" and from the moment that he was cast as Albie he spoke only with a Scouse accent for three months—even when a friend called him at 3 A.M. to test him out. Carlyle responded with a powerful performance—"I looked back at the tabloid reports of Hillsborough and it didn't take long to get angry. I sunk quite deep into that one. . . . The line between fiction and reality can get blurred. . . . I felt depressed and found it hard to function for two months afterwards."[2] As a result of the intensity Carlyle displayed in this role he won the 1995 BAFTA Scotland Best Actor Award.

Carlyle, who left school when he was sixteen, did not consider acting until a friend gave him a copy of Arthur Miller's *The Crucible* for his twenty-first birthday. This led to an amateur company at the Glasgow Arts Centre and, eventually, a place at the Royal Scottish Academy of Music and Drama. He left the academy midway through first term and it took the intervention of two tutors to persuade him to return. At the same time that Carlyle was attracting attention as the crazed Begbie in *Trainspotting* (1996), he was consolidating his career with television audiences as the star of *Hamish Macbeth,* the troubled but essentially humanist Glasgow policeman posted to the small Highlands town of Lochdubh. This duality, the psychopath Begbie and the gentle Hamish Macbeth, has typified his roles since 1996 and his determination not to be typecast, although there is a certain alienated quality that permeates most of his performances.

Carlyle's international breakthrough came with the spectacular success of *The Full Monty** (1997), with Carlyle as Gaz, the unemployed laborer who encourages a small group of unemployed workers to pay the bills as male strippers. In this film, he was able to assimilate a number of strands from his previous films—his strong affinity for working-class characters (such as *Riff Raff*) with the intensity of Albie and Begbie from *Trainspotting* and the romantic vulnerability of *Hamish Macbeth. The Full Monty* propelled Carlyle into the list of bankable international stars, a status marked by his casting as the chief villain opposite James Bond in *The World Is Not Enough* (1999). Carlyle, however, has not been content merely to exploit this newly acquired status with a succession of "easy" roles. He has mixed his more commercially accessible roles, such as the highwayman in *Plunkett and Macleane* (1999), the irresponsible Irish father in *Angela's Ashes* (1999), and the soccer coach in *There's Only One Jimmy Grimble* (2001), with some decidedly offbeat films, such as the commercially unpalatable *Ravenous* (1998), Antonia Bird's ambitious mixture of comedy, horror, and melodrama involving cannibalism in California in 1847, the petty criminal Ray trying to recover his stolen money in *Face* (1997), and a demented cameo as Daffy who points Leonardo DiCaprio toward a troubled paradise in *The Beach* (2000). Carlyle was awarded an OBE for services to drama in the 1999 and his favorite directors, so far, have been Loach (*Riff Raff* and *Carla's Song* [1996]) and Bird (*Priest* [1994], *Safe* [1993], *Face,* and *Ravenous*). Carlyle won the Best Actor Award at the 1998 BAFTA Film Awards for *The Full Monty.*

FILMS: Silent Scream (1989), Riff Raff (1990), Safe (1993), Being Human (1993), Priest (1994), Go Now (1995), The Lucky Suit (short, 1995), Trainspotting (1996), Carla's Song (1996), The Full Monty (1997), Face (1997), Ravenous (1998), Plunkett and Macleane (1999), Angela's Ashes (1999), The World Is Not Enough (1999), The Beach (2000), There's Only One Jimmy Grimble (2001), The 51st State (2002), To End All Wars (2002), Once Upon a Time in the Midlands (2002), and Black and White (2002).

CARMICHAEL, IAN (b. 1920). Born in Hull in 1920, Ian Carmichael was a major figure in the British cinema for less than a decade, primarily from 1955 to 1960, but during this period he appeared in a number of distinctive British films produced and directed by Roy Boulting* and John Boulting.* Educated at Scarborough Collage and trained at the Royal Academy of Dramatic Art, Carmichael developed his comedic skills in musical revues during the 1940s. He appeared in minor film parts in the late 1940s and he alternated between the stage and film in the early 1950s, including a supporting role in the Clark Gable and Lana Turner vehicle *Betrayed* (1954), which was Carmichael's only U.S. film.

When a film version of *Simon and Laura* was proposed, director Muriel Box* fought for Carmichael to repeat his stage character and, ultimately, he was the only member of the stage production retained for the film. Later, he played the central role of Simon in a British television production. Carmichael's breakthrough in the cinema took place when the Boulting brothers, who had seen him in a revue, wanted the same actor to play a similar character in both *Private's Progress* (1956) and *Brothers-in-Law* (1957). Carmichael's Stanley Windrush defined his screen persona. In *I'm All Right Jack* * (1959), Carmichael again essayed Stanley Windrush in an even better film and Carmichael's ability to generate humor from his mixture of innocence and ineptness provided the pretext for the Boulting brothers to apply their sharp satirical skills to key British institutions, such as the army, the unions, and employers organizations. Carmichael was a vital ingredient in these films as his innocence effectively counterpointed the deep-seated cynicism and made the social message more palatable to the general public. Carmichael, as a favor to the Boulting brothers, appeared briefly in *Heaven's Above!* (1963), the last of the quality satires from the Boultings.

Carmichael was never able to duplicate this successful period as he searched for a vehicle similar to the Cary Grant film *North by North West* (1959). There are certain parallels between the two actors as Carmichael's screen persona was that of a light leading man who could be placed in both comedic and dramatic situations where the humor came from his bemused reaction to various situations.

Carmichael also enjoyed popularity on television with his Bertie Wooster series in the 1960s, from the P. G. Wodehouse novels. Later, he starred in a television miniseries based on the Lord Peter Wimsey character created by Dorothy L. Sayers. In 1979, he published his autobiography, *Will the Real Ian Carmichael?*

FILMS: Bond Street (1948), Trottie True (1949), Dear Mr. Prohack (1949), Ghost Ship (1952), Time Gentleman Please (1952), Meet Mr. Lucifer (1953), Betrayed (1954), The Colditz Story (1955), Storm over the Nile (1955), Simon and Laura (1955), Private's Progress (1956), The Big Money (1956), Brothers-in-Law (1957), Lucky Jim (1957), Happy Is the Bride (1958), Left, Right and Centre (1959), I'm All Right Jack (1959), School for Scoundrels (1960), Light up the Sky (1960), Double Bunk (1961), The Amorous Prawn (1962), Heavens Above! (1963), Hide and Seek (1963), The Case of the '44s (1964), Smashing Time (1967), The Magnificent Seven Deadly Sins (1971), From beyond the Grave (1973), The Lady Vanishes (1979), Diamond Skulls (1989), and The Great Kandinsky (1996).

CARNIVAL (Twin Cities, 1946)—Romantic melodrama/film noir. *Director:* Stanley Haynes; *Producers:* John Sutro and William Sassoon; *Script:* Stanley Haynes, Guy Green, and Eric Maschwitz, with additional dialogue by Peter Ustinov, based on a novel by Compton McKenzie; *Cinematography:* Guy Green; *Music:* Nicholas Brodszky; *Cast:* Sally Grey (Jenny Pearl), Michael Wilding (Maurice Avery), Stanley Holloway (Charlie Raeburn), Bernard Miles (Trewhella), Jean Kent (Irene Dale), Catherine Lacey (Florrie Raeburn), Nancy Price (Mrs. Trewhella), Hazel Court (May Raeburn), and Michael Clarke (Fuzz).

Carnival is another example of the assimilation of film noir attributes into the 1940s British romantic melodrama (see also *Bedelia* [1946] and *So Evil My Love** [1948]). Although *Carnival* had been filmed before in 1931 (as *Dance Pretty Lady*), the 1946 version is dominated by an overwhelming sense of fatalism, which is conveyed by the film's opening images showing the dark, wet streets of London as a carriage brings three elderly woman to take away a newborn child from its mother. When Florrie Raeburn rejects an offer from three aunts to raise her child in a more respectable environment, the elderly women stand at the end of the nursing mother's bed and predict dire consequences for the child, Jenny, if it is not removed from her "immoral" surroundings (Florrie's husband is an alcoholic involved with the theater).

This prediction permeates the film, which is presented as a constant battle between temptation and repression. Jenny becomes a ballet dancer and, because of her immense beauty, attracts numerous men to her stage door. Jenny falls in love with Maurice Avery, a young artist who is determined to maintain his artistic independence by not marrying. Florrie's death occurs soon after Avery leaves for Spain and Jenny's younger sister, the crippled May, is left in Jenny's care. This double blow leaves Jenny financially and emotional vulnerable and she reluctantly accepts a marriage proposal from the religious Trewhella who offers to care for her and May on his farm in Cornwall.

After Jenny marries Trewhella and goes to Cornwall with May, she discovers the true extent of Trewhella bigotry and deep hatred for the immorality of "city folk." Encouraged by his mother, who urges her son to berate and punish his wife, Trewhella creates a religious hell for both Jenny and May. When Maurice finally comes to Cornwall and offers to take Jenny back to London, Trewhella kills Jenny. The doom that is anticipated in the opening minutes is thus realized at the close of the film.

Within this morality play, Jenny is not presented as a complex character. Sally Gray's* striking looks reinforce Jenny's function as a symbol of persecuted innocence, the victim of her father's irresponsibility, Trewhella's bigotry, her mother's sense of frustration, and Avery's selfishness. In other words, she is punished because of her class and her beauty and the effect this has on the people around her. The first renders Jenny socially powerless while the second provokes male desire, in Trewhella, which leads directly to her death.

Carnival emphasizes the unequal balance of power in Victorian society with regard to male and female desire. Ironically, this is remarked on by Trewhella to Jenny in his condemnation of the male lust directed toward the female dancers in the theater. Trewhella, his mother, and Jenny's aunts, personify sexual repression. Jenny, on the other hand, attempts to live by her own moral standards. She refuses Avery's offer to travel with him to Spain unless he marries her. On the other hand, she disputes Trewhella's moral authority over her. This results in her death. She is trapped by the prevailing codes with regard to female behavior. As a bleak representation of a cruel, male-dominated environment, *Carnival* certainly delivers.

CARRY ON CLEO (Anglo-Amalgamated, 1964)—Comedy. *Director:* Gerald Thomas; *Producer:* Peter Rogers; *Script:* Talbot Rothwell; *Cinematography:* Alan Hume; *Music:* Eric Rogers; *Cast:* Kenneth Williams (Julius Caesar), Sid James (Mark Anthony), Kenneth Connor (Hengist Pod), Charles Hawtrey (Seneca), Joan Sims (Calpurnia), Jim Dale (Horsa), Amanda Barrie (Cleopatra), Sheila Hancock (Senna Pod), Victor Madden (Sergeant Major), and Warren Mitchell (Spencius).

Although *Carry On* stalwarts Barbara Windsor and Hattie Jacques are missing, *Carry on Cleo* is the best entry in this long-running series. Utilizing the exterior sets from Twentieth Century Fox's multimillion dollar four-hour historical financial and creative failure *Cleopatra* (1963), which was shot at Pinewood Studios, *Carry on Cleo,* with a budget of less than two hundred thousand pounds, cleverly satirizes Fox's wooden saga with Kenneth William's excessively camp Julius Caesar delivering lines such as: "Infamy, infamy, oh they're all got in-for-me" as he is chased by Sid James's murderous henchmen. Instead of the knowing sexuality of Elizabeth Taylor as the Queen of the Nile, Amanda Barrie transforms Cleopatra into a seemingly innocent maiden who seduces Sid James (as Mark Anthony). Kenneth Connor returns as the weakling Hengist Pods, the Briton who, as usual, transforms into a ferocious fighter. Similarly, Charles Hawtrey as the lecherous Seneca and Kenneth Williams as the cowardly Caesar, repeat the characterizations developed in earlier *Carry On* films. Jim Dale confirms his status as the series' "leading man."

Two legal cases troubled the series—the use of the green and gold colors in relation to the slave market run by "Marcius and Spencius" caused problems as did the design of the initial poster, which worried Fox regarding its large investment in *Cleopatra.* Otherwise, the series continued to hone the James-Williams relationship to make this, the tenth entry, the sharpest one in the series.

CARRY ON SERGEANT (Anglo-Amalgamated Productions, 1958)—Comedy. *Director:* Gerald Thomas; *Producer:* Peter Rogers; *Script:* Norman Hudis and John Antrobus, based on the novel *The Bull Boys* by R. F. Delderfield; *Cinematography:* Peter Hennessy; *Music:* Bruce Montgomery; *Cast:* William Hartnell (Sergeant Grimshawe), Bob Monkhouse (Charlie Sage), Shirley Eaton (Mary Sage), Eric Barker (Captain Potts), Dora Bryan (Norah), Bill Owen (Corporal Bill Copping), Charles Hawtrey (Peter Golightly), Kenneth Connor (Horace Strong), Kenneth Williams (James Bailey), Hattie Jacques (Captain Clark), Terry Scott (Sergeant O'Brien), Gerald Campion (Andy Callaway), and Norman Rossington (Herbert Brown).

Carry on Sergeant was the first of the long-running series that flourished until the early 1970s, and then sporadically into the 1990s (*Carry on Columbus* [1992]). However, this film was not typical of the series. The bawdy, excessive humor of the later films was not evident in this entry, which consisted mainly of a series of standard army jokes. The fact that national service was still part of British life may have been a significant reason for the enormous popularity of the film. *Carry on Sergeant* did, however, provide a showcase for *Carry On* stalwarts such as Kenneth Connor as the hypochondriac Horace Strong, who, with the assistance of Hattie Jacques as the medical officer, makes the first of his last-minute transformations from weakling to hero. Similarly, Charles Hawtrey, as Peter Golightly, lives up to the camp implications of his name, and Kenneth Williams provides a toned down version of the excessive character that was to form such an integral part of the series.

There is even a sentimental narrative strand, inserted by scriptwriter Norman Hudis, in *Carry on Sergeant.* Training Sergeant Grimshawe, on the verge of retirement, expresses a wish that his last platoon will pass out as the star squad. This appears unlikely as his unit includes Hawtrey, Williams, Norman Rossington, as the camp failure, and Gerald Campion, a rotund misfit. After a series of embarrassing failures, the men rally together to make Grimshawe proud of them. The plot also includes a routine love affair between Bob Monkhouse and Shirley Eaton, who are separated when Monkhouse receives news of his call up during their wedding ceremony.

CASH ON DEMAND (Hammer, 1961)—Crime drama. *Director:* Quentin Lawrence; *Producer:* Michael Carreras; *Script:* David T. Chantler and Lewis

Greiffer, based on the play by Jacques Gillies; *Cinematography:* Arthur Grant; *Music:* Wilfred Josephs; *Cast:* Peter Cushing (Fordyce), André Morell (Hepburn), Richard Vernon (Pearson), Norman Bird (Sanderson), Barry Lowe (Harvill), Edith Sharpe (Miss Pringle), Lois Daine (Sally), Kevin Stoney (Detective Inspector Mason), and Vera Cook (Mrs. Fordyce).

Except for four exterior scenes, showing the (studio) street outside a bank in Haversham on Christmas Eve, *Cash on Demand* confines its action to the rooms of the bank. The dramatic pretext of the film is a robbery attempt, but the film is more concerned with the regeneration of Mr. Fordyce, a miserly bank manager. Fordyce, who treats his employees with cruelty and derision, is subjected to the scrutiny of "Colonel" Hepburn, a "gentleman" robber. Circumstances finally force Fordyce to turn to his employees for their help in this clever reworking of Charles Dickens's *A Christmas Carol.* Peter Cushing* and André Morell give, arguably, their best screen performances, especially Morell as the persuasive robber who is not content just to steal the bank's money but is determined to subject Fordyce to the kind of persecution that he inflicts on his employees.

The film begins with Sanderson, Harvill, Sally, Pearson, and Miss Pringle arriving for work on the day before Christmas. Their mood is jovial as they look forward to the Christmas party, but Fordyce's arrival signals the end of their happiness, beginning with his humiliation of Pearson over a faulty pen. The inquisition continues with Harvill over a minor irregularity in the bank's accounts, although it is soon obvious that Pearson, the chief clerk, is the real target of Fordyce's investigation. The arrival of a bank robber, "Colonel" Hepburn, disguised as security expert, transfers power from Fordyce to Hepburn after he convinces the bank manager that his [Fordyce] wife and child are being held prisoner. The bulk of the film's narrative expertly weaves together Hepburn's robbery attempt with a scrutiny of Fordyce's class-based attitudes and behavior. At the film's climax, Hepburn convinces Fordyce that if the police are notified in the hour after his escape, the manager's wife and child will die. When Pearson warns the police about Hepburn, Fordyce is forced to rely on his employees to convince the police that there has not been a robbery at the bank.

Cash on Demand, a low-budget genre film released during the height of the British New Wave, was ignored and today it is virtually unknown. The film deserves better than this—expertly photographed by veteran Arthur Grant, effectively directed by Quentin Lawrence, known mainly for his television work, with Cushing and Morell leading a great ensemble cast, *Cash on Demand* is an intelligent melodrama and, with minimal resources, maintains tension within its tale of regeneration. Hammer Films, which had revived itself as a production company after 1949 with low-budget crime melodramas, was, in 1961, enjoying a period of unprecedented fame and wealth with its cycle of popular horror films. With *Cash on Demand,* the studio returned to its origins.

THE CHALLENGE (London Films, 1938)—Alpine melodrama. *Directors:* Milton Rosmer and Luis Trenker (alpine sequences); *Producer:* Gunther Stapenhorst; *Script:* Emeric Pressburger, Patrick Kirwan, and Milton Rosmer; *Cinematography:* Albert Bentz and Georges Perinal; *Music:* Allan Gray; *Cast:* Luis Trenker (Jean-Antoine Carrel), Robert Douglas (Edward Whymper), Joan Gardner (Felicitas Favre), Mary Clare (Carrel's mother), Frank Birch (Reverend Charles Hudson), Geoffrey Wardwell (Lord Francis Douglas), Ralph Truman (Signor Giordano), and Bernard Miles (Villager).

Although *The Challenge* is based (loosely) on fact, the rivalry between England and Italy to reach the summit of the Matterhorn in the 1860s, the film retains many of the dramatic contrivances of melodrama in a plot involving loyalty, deception, and a last-minute rescue. In 1864, British climber Edward Whymper and his Italian guide Jean-Antoine Carrel climb further toward the summit of the Matterhorn than previous attempts. When Whymper insists on reaching the summit, Carrel tries to dissuade him because the conditions are not favorable. Whymper, however, continues until a landslide injures him, forcing Carrel to carry him back to a village at the base of the mountain. The two men pledge their friendship and commit themselves to climbing the mountain together the following year.

When a patriotic and well-resourced Italian expedition tries to solicit Carrel's help, he tells them that he is going with the Englishman Whymper. But, due to local machinations, both men are deceived and Whymper joins a British party while Carrel leads the Italian effort. Whymper, due to his radical plan of attacking the mountain from the Swiss side instead of the usual Italian entry point, reaches the summit before Carrel and the Italians. On the way down, four men from the victorious English group perish when a rope breaks. Whymper is charged with their death but when a magistrate dismisses the charge, the locals threaten to hang him. Meantime, Carrel saves his former friend by recovering the suspect rope from the mountain.

The Challenge was an Anglo-German production and the star of the film, Luis Trenker, directed the spectacular alpine sequences as well as the German version. British director Milton Rosmer directed the interiors for the English-language version. This division in directorial responsibility is significant. When the film is on the mountain, either on location or expertly shot studio exteriors, it is a spectacular drama. On the other hand, the interior scenes, set in Swiss and Italian villages, are static and tedious.

Actor and director Trenker, who was born to German parents in Italy, began his acting career in Germany in the 1920s opposite Leni Riefenstahl. He later directed and starred in a series of popular mountain films during the 1930s. In 1940, he was blacklisted by the Nazis following his production of *Der Feuerteufel* and after World War II the Allies banned his 1930s films. Nevertheless, Trenker continued directing in Germany throughout the 1950s and 1960s. *The Challenge* was also notable for being Emeric Pressburger's* first British screenplay. Producer Gunther Stapenhorst, who had worked with him in Germany in the 1930s, employed him. Pressburger's next film, *The Spy in Black* (1939), began his long partnership with Michael Powell.*

CHANCE OF A LIFETIME (Pilgrim Films, 1950)—Social drama. *Directors:* Bernard Miles and Alan Osbiston; *Producers:* Bernard Miles and John Palmer; *Script:* Walter Greenwood and Bernard Miles; *Cinematography:* Eric Cross; *Cast:* Basil Radford (Dickinson), Niall MacGinnis (Baxter), Bernard Miles (Stevens), Julien Mitchell (Morris), Kenneth More (Adam), Geoffrey Keen (Bolger), Josephine Wilson (Miss Cooper), John Harvey (Bland), Patrick Troughton (Kettle), and Hattie Jacques (Alice).

When *Chance of a Lifetime* was ready for release in 1950, the three major British circuits refused to distribute the film and only when a Board of Trade committee intervened that it finally received a release in Rank's Odeon cinemas. Little money or energy was spent on its promotion and the film was a commercial failure. The reluctance of the major distributors to release the film was primarily due to the film's "controversial" content.

When Dickinson, the owner of a plough factory, tired of fighting with his obstinate workers in a difficult economic climate, offers to let them run the business if they will pay him £120 per week. The workers select two men from their ranks, Stevens and Morris, to replace Dickinson but they soon discover that management is not as simple as they first thought. A large order from an East European government for the company's radical new plough offers economic salvation. However, after the factory has restructured its entire production line to accommodate this order the East Europeans cancel it due to a currency crisis All seems lost until Dickinson reappears to help the new management find other markets to sell the plough.

It is difficult today to understand the controversy over *Chance of a Lifetime* as the film is careful to avoid negative stereotyping of either capital or labor, with most of the workers presented as loyal and industrious and Dickinson, as the management figure, as humane and ultimately caring for his workers. The film reserves its hostility for those representatives of institutional capitalism, bankers and suppliers of materials, who feel threatened by this cooperative experiment in "democratic capitalism."

The film's solution is the cooperation between humane capitalism (Dickinson) and the new breed of worker (suitably named "Adam") not shackled by the industrial practices of the past. It marks a return to the optimistic, cooperative populism that characterized British cinema during World War II, a world that Bernard Miles, the codirector, coproducer, cowriter, and star of *Chance of a Lifetime,* obviously favored. In 1944, he coproduced, wrote, directed, and starred in *Tawny Pipit,* a populist film with a similar point of view. What rescues *Chance of a Lifetime* from its simplistic philosophy is the overall depth of acting performances throughout the film. Basil Radford stands out as the frustrated, but caring, factory owner, Geoffrey Keen and Niall MacGinnis as malcontents who undergo regeneration, a brash Kenneth More* as the prototype of the "new worker," and Josephine Wilson as the secretary who is able to broaden her loyalties to include the new management regime. Hattie Jacques, as one of the factory workers, has the best scene in the film with her mock seductive dance in front of an angry

MacGinnis. This is a key scene as she convinces him to share in the financial sacrifices needed to save the company.

CHARIOTS OF FIRE (Enigma Productions, 1981)—Sporting drama. *Director:* Hugh Hudson; *Producer:* David Puttnam; *Script:* Colin Welland; *Cinematography:* David Watkin; *Music:* Vangelis; *Cast:* Ben Cross (Harold Abrahams), Ian Charleson (Eric Liddell), Nigel Havers (Lord Andrew Lindsay), Ian Holm (Sam Mussabini), John Gielgud (Master of Trinity), Lindsay Anderson (Master of Caius), Nigel Davenport (Lord Birkenhead), Alice Krige (Sybil Gordon), Cheryl Campbell (Jennie Liddell), Dennis Christopher (Charles Paddock), Brad Davis (Jackson Scholz), Patrick Magee (Lord Cadogan), and Struan Rodger (Sandy McGrath).

The film begins with the words from Ecclesiastes, "Let us now praise famous men," and that is what it does. In a cunningly constructed screenplay, Colin Welland and David Putnam celebrate an all-embracing form of "Britishness" while including sufficient material and dramatic problems to prevent an overwhelming sense of simplistic national sentiment. Nowhere is this more evident than in the film's conclusion as the two men, the Scottish Presbyterian Eric Liddell and the Jewish Englishman Harold Abrahams, return to England after winning gold medals at the 1924 Olympics. While Liddell's return is joyously celebrated by his teammates and a large crowd, Abrahams's arrival is marked only by a sole supporter, his loyal girlfriend Sybil—despite a newspaper headline that boasts that Abrahams is now the "toast of England."

While criticizing the archaic values of the two Cambridge masters, played by John Gielgud* and Lindsay Anderson,* *Chariots of Fire* lovingly exploits the traditions, icons, and rituals associated with this past. Similarly, the film mixes the positive power of tradition with a vision of the future through the tactics and "entrepreneurial" values employed by Abrahams that looks to the future preparation of athletes with his adoption of a "professional" coach—or what the masters describe as a tradesman ethos that violates their dated vision of the elite amateur. This vision even includes the aristocracy with Lord Andrew Lindsay's decision to stand aside at the Olympics and allow Liddell to replace him in the 400 meters—after Lindsay has collected a medal in an earlier race. While Liddell runs for the "glory of God," and Abrahams is motivated by a desire to show that a Jew is as good as anybody, Lindsay represents the (master's) assumption that sport is both "fun" and an integral aspect of national character building.

Although the film carefully includes religious, class, and ethnic diversity, through the Italian and Arabic background of Abrahams's trainer (Sam Mussabini) and the early emphasis on Liddell's Scottishness, these differences are ultimately subsumed into a shared national identity. Yet, even here Welland and Puttnam insert a discordant note—when Abrahams and Mussabini drunkenly toast their success after Abrahams's win, Mussabini pointedly reminds him that his win was a personal one for both of them, the outsiders, and should not be perceived as a national triumph.

Chariots of Fire won Best Picture at the 1982 Academy Awards, Welland won Best Writing, Vangelis won Best Music, and Milena Canonero Best Costume Design, while Hugh Hudson was nominated for Best Director, Terry Rawlings Best Film Editing, and Ian Holm Best Supporting Actor. Canonero, Puttnam, and Holm won BAFTA Awards while Holm and Hudson won at Cannes. *Chariots of Fire* also won the Golden Globe for Best Foreign Film and cinematographer David Watkin won the New York Critics Circle Award, making this one of the most internationally celebrated and commercially successful British films of all time—despite that fact that it was financed largely from non-British money.

CHASE A CROOKED SHADOW (Associated British, 1958)—Thriller. *Director:* Michael Anderson; *Producers:* Douglas Fairbanks Jr. and Thomas Clyde; *Script:* David D. Osborn and Charles Sinclair; *Photography:* Erwin Hillier; *Music:* Matyas Seiber; *Cast:* Richard Todd (Ward Prescott), Anne Baxter (Kimberley Prescott), Herbert Lom (Police Commissioner Vargas), Alexander Knox (Chandler Brisson), and Faith Brook (Elaine Whitman).

In Barcelona, a man and a woman study a 16mm film detailing the layout of a villa. The owner of the villa, Kimberly Prescott, is first seen on the cover of a glossy magazine. Beneath her photo is a man's gun. Cut to Kimberly's villa eighty miles away on the coast of Spain as she farewells her uncle Chandler Brisson. As Brisson drives away, Kimberly's friendly smile becomes a more calculating facial gesture. Later that night, as Kimberly prepares for bed, the man from the first scene walks into her estate claiming to be her brother Ward Prescott.

This expert opening contains the elements for a clever suspense thriller. And it delivers. Although Kimberly, and the audience, know that the man is an impostor, he has all the correct credentials plus an intimate knowledge of Ward's movements. This includes his relationship with his sister up until his supposed death a year ago. The key questions are: Is Ward pretending to be Kimberly's brother as a means to claim part of her inheritance (the Prescotts are wealthy due to their South African diamond mine)? Are there sinister implications behind his sudden arrival with Mrs. Whitman?

For much of the film, Kimberly is presented as a traditional heroine trapped by the machinations of Ward, Mrs. Whitman, and Chandler Brisson. Even the local police officer, Vargas, is unable to help as Ward's documentation appears to be valid. Repeated attempts to escape are thwarted until Kimberly breaks down and reveals that she murdered her brother and stole jewellery from the family collection.

Chase a Crooked Shadow depends primarily on twists in the plot and the interplay between the three central characters, Ward, Kimberly, and Vargas, to maintain tension. The film's director Michael Anderson went on to more ambitious genre productions such as *Shake Hands with the Devil* (1959) and *The Quiller Memorandum* (1966). Nevertheless, *Chase a Crooked Shadow,* shot mostly at Elstree Studios with some location footage from Spain, efficiently inverts the conventions of the woman-in-distress thriller.

THE CHILTERN HUNDREDS (Two Cities, 1949)—Comedy. *Director:* John
Paddy Carstairs; *Producer:* George H. Brown; *Script:* William Douglas Home
and Patrick Kirwan; *Cinematography:* Jack Hildyard; *Music:* Benjamin Frankel;
Cast: Cecil Parker (Benjamin Beecham), A. E. Matthews (Lord Lister), David
Tomlinson (Lord Tony Pym), Lana Morris (Bessie Sykes), Majorie Fielding
(Lady Lister), Tom Macaulay (Cleghorn), Joyce Carey (Lady Caroline), Helen
Backlin (June Farrell), Laurence Naismith (reporter), Anthony Steel (Adjutant),
and Richard Wattis (Vicar).

The Chiltern Hundreds, one of the top-grossing British films of 1949, is dependent, to some degree, on awareness of the British postwar political context to
explain its commercial success. Set in the immediate postwar, Tony Pym invokes
an army regulation regarding compulsory leave for officers standing for parliament as a ruse to visit June, his U.S.-born fiancée. Because of the regulation,
Tony is compelled to stand for parliament as the Conservative candidate in the
general election. In the strong postwar swing to Labour, Tony loses the seat held
by the Pym family for many generations to his Labour opponent Cleghorn. When
Cleghorn is promoted to the House of Lords, Tony, despite opposition from his
conservative fiancée, stands in the by-election as a Labour candidate. This is all
too much for the family butler, Beecham, who opposes Tony as the Tory candidate and wins the seat after numerous recounts. Beecham then invokes the ancient
convention of "the Chiltern Hundreds" to withdraw from parliament and resumes
duties in the Pym household.

The major comedic attraction in the film is eighty-year-old A. E. Matthews as
Lord Lister, the head of the Pym household. A reflection of the then-prevailing
(postwar) attitude toward the aristocracy, as merely a legacy of the past,
Matthews enlivens proceedings with his out-of-kilter routines such as his obsession with killing all of the rabbits on the estate. Matthews dominates the first half
of the film, particularly in his interaction with his long-suffering wife who is
forced to flee when her husband spies a rabbit from the family living room. When
the rather banal romantic complications between Tony and the two women in his
life, fiancée June and maid Bessie, assume greater prominence in the second half,
the film loses steam.

The original play on which the film was based was by William Douglas Home,
a relative of the future Conservative British prime minister. The highlight of this
gentle comedy is the reaction of Lord Lister to a newspaper report describing him
as a "bloated capitalist" as he sits in a run-down kitchen peeling potatoes for the
family dinner.

CHRISTIE, JULIE (b. 1941). In the 1960s, Julie Christie made two films in
succession for director John Schlesinger,* *Billy Liar** (1963) and *Darling**
(1965). These films created a free-spirited image for Christie that captured the
public imagination. Born in India in 1941 and the daughter of British tea-planter,
Christie enrolled in the Central School of Speech and Training in London, determined to become an actress in the theater rather than the commercial cinema,

which she despised. Her poor opinion of the mainstream cinema was reinforced by her first two films, the comedies *Crooks Anonymous* (1962), where she played Babette LaVern, and *The Fast Lady* (1962), where she was courted by Stanley Baxter in his antique car.

Christie objected to the artificiality imposed on actresses of the time and, specifically, the need to look "like a china doll" all the time despite what was happening on screen. If she was to be in films, Christie wanted to act in films that emulated the French New Wave and she welcomed *Billy Liar* as the British equivalent. Christie especially enjoyed the fact that her character, Liz, displayed independence that, Christie maintained, emanated from the character's working-class background. *Darling* also offered Christie a role far removed from the ingenue roles she objected to. As the selfish Diana Scott, her display of sexual freedom and moral ambivalence had a strong impact on audiences and she won all of the major awards for that year, including the U.S. Academy Award for Best Actress, the BAFTA Film Award for Best Actress, and the New York Critics Circle Award for Best Actress.

Darling elevated Christie's status in the industry and she appeared in many big-budget British and U.S. films, with major directors, in the 1960s and early 1970s. These include the commercially successful *Doctor Zhivago* (1965), directed by David Lean,* François Truffaut's *Fahrenheit 451* (1967), where Christie appeared in the dual roles of Linda and Clarisse, Schlesinger's adaptation of Thomas Hardy's *Far from the Madding Crowd* (1967), and Richard Lester's *Petulia* (1968), which was filmed in the United States with an outstanding cast, including George C. Scott and Shirley Knight.

The selection of the director was, for Christie, the most important single factor in her decision to accept a film: "I've not been interested in roles, I'm interested in the director and I don't think that will change now. I am absolutely a believer in the auteur and I am convinced that the director is the only thing that really matters."[3] After Joseph Losey's* *The Go-Between* (1971), where Christie, in a period film, played a variation on her willful, selfish protagonist from *Darling*, she moved to the United States for *McCabe and Mrs. Miller* (1971), Robert Altman's anti-Western, which Christie considers one of her favorite films. It earned her an Oscar nomination for Best Actress. Her costar in *McCabe and Mrs. Miller* was Warren Beatty and the pair enjoyed a romance that lasted a number of years as well as producing two more films—the comedy *Shampoo* (1975) and the fantasy *Heaven Can Wait* (1978), a remake of *Here Comes Mr. Jordan* (1941). Between *McCabe and Mrs. Miller* and *Shampoo,* Christie costarred with Donald Sutherland, as the troubled couple visiting Venice, in Nicholas Roeg's* superb occult thriller *Don't Look Now** (1973), and Christie was nominated for the 1974 BAFTA Film Award for Best Actress.

Except for *Heat and Dust* (1983), where Christie returned to the country of her birth, she has avoided the large-budget film that characterized her first decade as a star. Instead, ideological considerations have been paramount in her choice of films "I think I could call myself a political person, so I had no option when it came to choosing roles."[4] This led to voice-overs in television documentaries dealing with social issues and specific film projects, such as the anti-war *The Return of the Soldier* (1982), Sally Potter's low-budget *The Gold Diggers* (1984), with an all-women crew, and the made-for-British television film *The Railway Station Man* (1992), which reunited Christie with Sutherland in a story based on the war in Ireland. Christie's most recent success was as Nick Nolte's troubled wife in Alan Rudolph's marital drama *Afterglow* (1997) for which she won the New York Critics Circle Award for Best Actress and an Oscar nomination.

FILMS: Crooks Anonymous (1962), The Fast Lady (1963), Billy Liar (1963), Young Cassidy (1964), Darling (1965), Doctor Zhivago (1965), Fahrenheit 451 (1966), Far from the Madding Crowd (1967), Tonight Let's Make Love (doc., 1967), Petulia (1968), In Search of Gregory (1970), The Go-Between (1971), McCabe and Mrs. Miller (1971), Don't Look Now (1973), Shampoo (1974), Nashville (1975), The Demon Seed (1977), Heaven Can Wait (1978), Memoirs of a Survivor (1981), The Animals Film (doc., 1981), The Return of the Soldier (1982), Les Quarantiemes Rugissants (1982), Heat and Dust (1983), The Gold Diggers (1984), Miss Mary (1986), Power (1986), Champagne amer (1986), Agent Orange: Policy of Poison (doc., 1987), Fools of Fortune (1990), Short Step (1991), Dragonheart (1996), Hamlet (1996), Afterglow (1997), Belphégor—Le fantôme du Louvre (2001), No Such Thing (2001), The Hermit of Amsterdam (2001), and I'm With Lucy (2002).

CIRCUS OF HORRORS (Lynx Films/Anglo-Amalgamated, 1960)—Horror. *Director:* Sidney Hayers; *Producers:* Julian Wintle and Leslie Parkyn; *Script:* George Baxt; *Cinematography:* Douglas Slocombe; *Music:* Muir Matheson and Franz Reizenstein; *Cast:* Anton Diffring (Dr. Rossiter/Dr. Schueler), Yvonne Monlaur (Nicole Vanet), Erika Remberg (Elissa Caro), Donald Pleasance (Vanet), Jane Hylton (Angela), Kenneth Griffith (Martin), Colette Wilde (Evelyn Morley Finsbury), Yvonne Romain (Melina), Jack Gwyllim (Superintendent Andrews), John Merivale (Edward Finsbury), and Chris Christian (Ringmaster).

Produced and distributed by the same company (Anglo-Amalgamated) that handled Michael Powell's* *Peeping Tom** (1960), *Circus of Horrors,* which was released straight after Powell's film, escaped the intense criticism that marked *Peeping Tom.* Both films signaled changes within the horror genre, especially with regard to the representation of violence. Both also shared certain thematic similarities. German-born actor Anton Diffring plays the sadistic plastic surgeon, Dr. Rossiter, who, after a botched operation on Evelyn Morley, flees England with his two assistants, Jane and Martin. After befriending Vanet, the owner of an impoverished circus, Rossiter, who changes his name to Schueler, successfully operates on the scarred face of Vanet's daughter. When a circus bear kills Vanet, Schueler assumes control of his circus.

Schueler only employs disfigured women and after operating on their faces transforms them into celebrated circus performers. However, the women are trapped by Schueler and when they try to leave the circus they die due to "accidents" arranged by him. One victim is murdered during her knife throwing act, another falls to her death during a high-wire performance, and the only woman that Schueler loves, Elissa, is torn to shreds during her lion-taming act.

After the circus returns to England from Europe, Evelyn Morley, a victim of Schueler's surgery, attends a performance just as the police close in on Schueler. The climax includes an effective moment of visual symmetry—as the victim (Evelyn) and the surgeon meet, the scars on her disfigured face match the scars, hidden by a bandage, on Schueler's face. Schueler is then killed by Evelyn in front of the Temple of Beauty when, running from the police, she drives her car over him.

The *Circus of Horrors* is a crude, albeit fascinating testament to the changes taking place within the British horror genre in the late 1950s. Also, just two years after his striking performance as the doomed family man on the Titanic in Roy Ward Baker's* *A Night to Remember* (1958), it is curious to see John Merivale in the minor, and nondescript, role of Evelyn Finsbury's husband.

THE CLAIRVOYANT (Gainsborough, 1935)—Supernatural thriller. *Director:* Maurice Elvey; *Producer:* Michael Balcon; *Script:* Charles Bennett and Bryan Edgar Wallace, based on a novel by Ernest Lothar; *Photography:* Glen MacWilliams; *Music:* Arthur Benjamin; *Cast:* Claude Rains (Maximus), Fay Wray (Renee), Mary Clare (Mother), Ben Field (Simon), Athol Stewart (Lord Southwood), Jane Baxter (Christine Shawn), and Felix Aylmer (Prosecutor).

The Clairvoyant is one of the best-looking Gainsborough films of the 1930s, courtesy of Glen MacWilliams's cinematography and Alfred Junge's art direction. The film also benefits from the performance by Claude Rains and an intriguing screenplay by Charles Bennett. The story concerns Maximus, a professional mind reader who discovers one night during a mind reading performance that when he is near a particular member of the audience, Christine Shawn, he really has the ability to perceive future events. The predictive power emanating from this strange alliance is confirmed during a train trip when Maximus, who is on the train with Christine, predicts that the train will crash.

Rapid fame and notoriety flow to Maximus following this event. This is reinforced with the general public when he is able to predict a hundred to one winner at the Grand National horse race. The remainder of the film is primarily concerned with the source of his power and whether it is a positive or negative attribute. Maximus's mother explains that his grandfather also had this power and it killed him. She urges her son to never utilize it again. He fails to take this advice and when a mine disaster occurs, Maximus is arrested. In the grand tradition of melodrama, Maximus is saved when, during his trial, he predicts that the miners will escape due to an air pocket.

The Clairvoyant also deals with a marital rift between Maximus and Renee over his spiritual rapport with Christine. The strength of the film resides in its strong dramatic premise and the efficiency of the overall production, especially Claude Rains's high standard performance as the troubled clairvoyant.

CLAYTON, JACK (1921–1995). With the financial failure of the big-budget *The Great Gatsby* (1974), and the disappointment of the Disney-produced *Something*

Wicked This Way Comes (1983), Jack Clayton's reputation suffered despite the fact that he directed two of the best films ever produced in Britain: *Room at the Top** (1959) and *The Innocents** (1961). In terms of films he directed, Clayton was anything but prolific although he worked in the British film industry for more than fifty years, despite suffering a stroke in 1977.

Born in 1921 in Brighton, Clayton entered the film industry in 1936 at London Films as a "gofer" who went straight into the editing department. After the war, Clayton was working as a first assistant when, during the production of *An Ideal Husband* (1947), he was promoted to production manager. This was followed in 1951 by his elevation to the status of associate producer for Romulus Films and Clayton stayed with the Woolf brothers for the rest of the decade. Beginning with *Moulin Rouge* in 1952, directed by John Huston, and soon followed by another Huston film, the offbeat quasi-thriller *Beat the Devil* (1953), Clayton worked as a producer throughout the 1950s. Impressed by Clayton's work, Huston offered him the chance to produce his next four films but Clayton, wanting to direct, refused the offer and remained with Romulus.[5] Clayton's breakthrough came after he persuaded the Woolf brothers to let him direct a thirty-two minute adaptation of Gogol's *The Overcoat*. The resultant short *The Bespoke Overcoat* (1955) won an Oscar. However, Clayton had promised to remain with the Woolf brothers for two years if they financed the film.

Finally, in 1959 Clayton realized his ambition when the Woolf brothers agreed to let him direct *Room at the Top* after they had acquired the rights to John Braine's prestigious novel. Clayton's film was an important breakthrough as it started the move to the north by British filmmakers to exploit the bleak industrial landscape. The film also provided a more mature representation of sexual desire and a morally complex protagonist (Joe Lampton).

Clayton selected Laurence Harvey* for the lead role after working with him in the 1950s in films such as *The Good Die Young** (1954) and *Three Men in a Boat* (1956). *Room at the Top* won Best Film at the 1958 BAFTA Film Awards. He was also nominated for Best Director at the Academy Awards that year. The film, which was a commercial success in the United States, was a major breakthrough for both the director and the stars.

After the success of *Room at the Top,* Clayton was offered a number of similar film projects but, in keeping with the pattern of the rest of his career, he refused to repeat himself. *The Innocents*, his next film, was an adaptation of Henry James's *Turn of the Screw* with Deborah Kerr* as the sexually repressed governess. Both *Room at the Top* and *The Innocents* share ambiguous, downbeat endings, a feature of Clayton's films with his penchant for disturbed protagonists. This also described Clayton's next film, *The Pumpkin Eater* (1964), with Anne Bancroft, the mother of eight children, who discovers that husband Peter Finch* has been unfaithful. It was followed by *Our Mother's House* (1967), a Gothic story concerning a group of children determined to survive together after their mother's death, and *The Great Gatsby* (1974), Clayton's faithful adaptation of F. Scott Fitzgerald's seminal novel of desire, class, and murder.

The commercial failure of *The Great Gatsby,* combined with his illness, slowed Clayton down, although, as a director, he was never prolific. Only one film, *The Lonely Passion of Judith Hearne* (1987), and a made-for-television film *Memento Mori* (1992), both starring Maggie Smith, followed the failed *Something Wicked This Way Comes* before his death in 1995. Aside from his awards for *Room at the Top, The Innocents* was nominated for Best British Film at the 1962 BAFTA Film Awards and *The Pumpkin Eater* was nominated for the Best British Film at the 1965 BAFTA Film Awards.

FILMS (as director): The Bespoke Overcoat (short, 1955), Room at the Top (1959), The Innocents (1961), The Pumpkin Eater (1964), Our Mother's House (1967), The Great Gatsby (1974), Something Wicked This Way Comes (1983), and The Lonely Passion of Judith Hearne (1987).

THE COLDITZ STORY (British Lion, 1955)—War. *Director:* Guy Hamilton; *Producer:* Ivan Foxwell; *Script:* Ivan Foxwell and Guy Hamilton, based on the novels *The Colditz Story* and *The Latter Days* by P. R. Reid; *Photography:* Gordon Dines; *Music:* Frances Chagrin; *Cast:* John Mills (Pat Reid), Eric Portman (Colonel Richmond), Christopher Rhodes ("Mac" McGill), Lionel Jeffries (Harry Tyler), Bryan Forbes (Jimmy Winslow), Ian Carmichael (Robin Cartwright), Richard Wattis (Richard Gordon), Frederick Valk (Kommandant), Eugene Deckers (La Tour), Guido Lorraine (Polish Officer), Theodore Bikel (Vandy), Anton Diffring (Fischer), and Denis Shaw (Priem).

In 1940, troublesome British, French, Polish, and Dutch prisoners of war were transferred to Colditz Castle in Germany and the film begins with the arrival of two British prisoners, Pat Reid and "Mac" McGill, at Colditz. This film, like many other 1950s British war films, is less concerned with polarizing the drama into "us" and "them" ("good" British and "evil" Germans) and more with the effects of the war on a small group of British soldiers. Consequently, the narrative pattern in the film is less didactic and more episodic.

After a number of unsuccessful escape attempts, Reid and McGill devise a clever plan to escape by climbing down from the auditorium to the German quarters and then walk out of the camp dressed as German officers. The film is less concerned with the actual mechanics involved in executing this plan than in the human dimension involving McGill's participation. As Colonel Richmond points out to him, McGill would be easily recognized by the Germans due to his unusual height and extroverted behavior in the camp. McGill, who desperately wants to escape from Colditz, initially refuses to accept Richmond's advice that his participation would jeopardize the whole escape plan. However, prior to the actual attempt, McGill virtually commits suicide by scaling a fence around the camp and his death removes the only weakness in the plan as McGill's spot goes to the more nondescript British prisoner Jimmy Winslow.

The Colditz Story focuses on a succession of failed attempts, mainly by the British prisoners, although there is some recognition of the French and Polish efforts. Personal heroics remain largely understated as the film emphasizes the need for group discipline. Similarly, the film is careful to avoid stereotyping the Germans as inherently sadistic. Although the Kommandant (Frederick [Fritz] Valk) has the necessary physical attributes associated with the "brutal German," he is shown to be an essentially humane man determined to avoid needless bloodshed in his camp.

The strength of *The Colditz Story* emanates from the quality of the esensemble, with Eric Portman superb as the reluctant leader of the British contingent. Ian Carmichael* and Richard Wattis, as two "theatrical" British prisoners, also stand out, particularly during their flamboyant drill parade that is used to distract the Germans during an unsuccessful escape attempt. This relatively low-key war film contributed to the popularity of the British war film in the 1950s and it was nominated for a BAFTA Award for Best Film in 1956.

COMFORT, LANCE (1908–1966). After *The Edge of the World* in 1937, Michael Powell* vowed to never again work on the formulaic, low-budget films that he had been directing since 1931. Similarly, Thorold Dickinson* found it "terribly difficult" to make films that he was not interested in. Lance Comfort, however, was the antithesis of such artists. Comfort, similar to other British directors such as Arthur Crabtree, Bernard Knowles, and Lawrence Huntington, was a "journeyman director" who accepted most projects offered to him and he could be relied on to produce (within budgetary, script, and casting limitations) superior genre films that would surpass all reasonable expectations.

Comfort entered the industry in the latter half of the 1920s, first as an animator and cameraman on a series of medical research films. Over the next fifteen years, he acquired experience as a sound recordist, assistant director, and director on several short films made for children. Comfort's first feature film as a director, the ponderous *Penn of Pennsylvania* (1941), was largely shaped by the demands of World War II and the need to consolidate U.S.–British relations. It was not until his next film, *Hatter's Castle** (1941), that Comfort found his dramatic niche within the realm of the Gothic and melodrama. Comfort's skillful use of the Gothic and melodrama in *Hatter's Castle* transformed A. J. Cronin's turgid 1931 novel into a gripping study of hubris and failed ambitions, dramatizing the failed dreams and excesses of James Brodie (Robert Newton*). Because of the film's association with the Cronin novel, *Hatter's Castle* was one of Comfort's few "prestige" productions, although he did direct other A films in the 1940s.

Comfort's best film, and one of the best films produced in Britain in the 1940s, was *Great Day** (1945). Unlike *Penn of Pennsylvania, Great Day* was not just another propaganda film designed to reinforce the hands-across-the-sea military alliance between Britain and the United States. The film's primary subject matter, the visit of Eleanor Roosevelt to the Women's Institute of Denley, a small village in England, would suggest that this was a factor in the initial decision to make this film during the war years. Yet Roosevelt's visit provides little more than a pretext to dramatize the complexities of postwar adjustment—largely through the personal problems of World War I veteran Captain Ellis (Eric Portman*), problems that are intensified by the end of the war. Ellis's mental state, which is shown to be fragile throughout the film, collapses after an incident in the local pub and near the end of the film he contemplates suicide. It is Comfort's assured handling of Ellis's deterioration, largely through the stylistic elements of composition, lighting, and music, that elevates *Great Day* to a superior level. Instead of focusing on the integration of the community, as would be expected in such a film, Comfort has the courage to detail the disintegration of a respected military leader who longs for the simplicities of war but cannot face the complexities of peace.

After *Great Day,* Comfort's next film starred Britain's most popular female actress of the mid- to late 1940s, Margaret Lockwood,* in the film noir *Bedelia* (1946) where Lockwood plays a murderess who dislikes men, especially Ian Hunter, her second husband. He followed this with two superb psychological melodramas, *Temptation Harbour* (1947) and *Daughter of Darkness** (1948). The latter, a bizarre film, does not have a counterpart in the British cinema of the 1940s. It effectively utilized elements of the Gothic in its story of an Irish woman, Emmy Beaudine (Siobhan McKenna), who cannot understand or control her repressed sexual feelings. These feelings periodically erupt in moments of extreme violence, and even murder. Comfort refused to polarize the drama by caricaturing Emmy as a simple melodramatic villain; instead, he creates a sympathetic context for the audience to understand her behavior. This sympathy, in turn, provides a critique of the false security, stability, and "pleasures" of life in pastoral England (the Tallent Farm in Yorkshire) to expose a society riddled by repression, both sexual and social. At a time when most British film critics were celebrating literary adaptations and "realist" fare, such as *Oliver Twist* (1948), *Hamlet* (1948), *The Winslow Boy** (1948) *The Fallen Idol* (1948), and *Scott of the Antarctic* (1948), there was little chance that they would celebrate the cinematic pleasures of *Daughter of Darkness.*[6]

After the *Portrait of Clare* in 1950, starring Margaret Johnston and Richard Todd,* Comfort's status within the film industry declined to a point where, by the mid-1950s, he was directing and producing half-hour episodes of *Douglas Fairbanks Presents* for U.S. television. *Assignment Foreign Legion* and *Ivanhoe,* also for television, soon followed. This fall from grace was not due to any decline in Comfort's talent as a director but was largely due to changes in patterns of production and exhibition within the British film industry in the late 1940s and early 1950s. The revival of the empire and war films, the decline of the psychological melodrama, and the reduced status of the crime film, where Comfort was to find much of his employment in the 1950s and 1960s, resulted in his relegation to the less prestigious levels of the co-feature (the middle-budget film that shared the billing) and the B film (that appeared on the bottom half of the bill).

Comfort continued to work at this lower level of the British film industry until his death in 1966, aged fifty-eight. In the 1950s and 1960s, he directed twenty features that, despite limited budgets, represented some of his best work, including the unusual *Bang! You're Dead* (1954), which Alfred Hitchcock* adapted for his U.S. television series, *Touch of Death* (1962), *Tomorrow at Ten* (1962), *The*

Break (1963), and *Blind Corner* (1963). Comfort's last two films were *Devils of Darkness* (1964), his only color film, and the musical *Be My Guest* (1965). Both, fittingly, were resolutely generic.

FILMS: Sandy Steps Out (short, 1938), Laddie's Day Out (short, 1939), Judy Buys a Horse (1939), Thoroughbreds (short, 1939), Penn of Pennsylvania (1941), Hatter's Castle (1941), Those Kids from Town (1942), Squadron Leader X (1942), Escape to Danger (1943), Old Mother Riley Detective (1943), When We Are Married (1943), Hotel Reserve (1944), Great Day (1945), Bedelia (1946), Temptation Harbour (1947), Daughter of Darkness (1948), The Silent Dust (1949), Portrait of Clare (1950), Home to Danger (1951), The Girl on the Pier (1953), The Genie (1953), The Triangle (1953), Bang! You're Dead (1954), Eight O'Clock Walk (1954), The Last Moment (1954), Port of Escape (1956), The Man in the Road (1956), Face in the Night (1957), At the Stroke of Nine (1957), The Man from Tangier (1957), The Ugly Duckling (1959), Make Mine Million (1959), The Breaking Point (1961), Rag Doll (1961), Pit of Darkness (1961), The Break (1962), The Painted Smile (1962), Tomorrow at Ten (1962), Touch of Death (1962), The Switch (1963), Live It Up (1963), Blind Corner (1963), Devils of Darkness (1964), and Be My Guest (1965).

CONNERY, SEAN (b. 1930). Born Thomas Sean Connery in Edinburgh on August 25, 1930. Since his Academy Award for Best Supporting Actor in *The Untouchables* in 1987, Connery's status has continued to rise and he is now a major star. There were long periods in the 1970s, after he decided to abdicate the role of James Bond in 1971 (after *Diamonds Are Forever*), when there was doubt as to whether his films would attract the large audiences of his Bond films. To his credit, Connery chose a number of offbeat roles in the later Bond period and throughout the 1970s. Some of these films, including two from Sidney Lumet (*The Hill** [1965] and *The Offence* [1973]), were confrontational films that presented the actor with more morally complex characters than earlier roles, especially 007.

Connery joined the British navy when he was fifteen and after three years he left and subsequently worked in a number of jobs, ranging from coffin polisher to milkman. It was his interest in bodybuilding that led to modeling, culminating in him representing Scotland at the Mr. Universe contest. Connery also expressed an interest in acting, joining the sailor chorus in the London production of *South Pacific* in 1951. Thereafter, repertory and minor roles in films paralleled his more substantial work in British television, including Vronsky in *Anna Karenina,* Hotspur in *The Age of Kings,* and the lead role in a live performance of *Requiem for a Heavyweight* in 1957.

The hot-headed truck driver in *Hell Drivers** (1957) was followed by the Lana Turner melodrama *Another Time, Another Place* (1958), the vicious O'Bannion in *Tarzan's Greatest Adventure** (1959), the lead in the Disney film *Darby O'Gill and the Little People* (1959), and an Irish crook in *The Frightened City* (1961)—before James Bond and *Dr. No** in 1962. While Ian Fleming opposed casting Connery as the hero of his novels, Terence Young, the director of *Dr. No,* added a veneer of sophistication to Connery's "masculinity" and Connery became a star after *Goldfinger* in 1964. He was not, however, content to just exploit the Bond image as he parlayed his status into less formulaic roles, beginning with his enigmatic protagonist in Alfred Hitchcock's* *Marnie* (1964), a stubborn army prisoner who refuses to cower before a sadistic prison officer in *The Hill,* and a nonconformist poet in *Fine Madness* (1966). Thus, Connery began the pattern of alternating James Bond with more challenging roles, including his Irish mine worker fighting exploitation in Pennsylvania in the 1870s in *The Molly Maguires* (1970).

Connery was thus able to combine the popular appeal of 007 with a reputation as a "quality," versatile actor. In his most recent phase when he often assumed the function of both star and executive producer, which began in 1992 with *Medicine Man* (1992), he has been able to retain his appeal as a leading man (although well into his sixties) through vehicles such as *The Rock* (executive produced by Connery in 1996) and *Entrapment* (produced by Connery in 1999).

Connery won the 1988 BAFTA for Best Actor for *The Name of the Rose* (1986), the 1988 Golden Globe for Best Supporting Actor in *The Untouchables,* and the Best Actor Award at the 1965 New York Film Critics Circle Awards for *The Hill.* A major contributor to the Scottish Nationalist Party, he received a knighthood in 1999.

FILMS: Lilacs in the Spring (1955), Geordie (1955), No Road Back (1957), Time Lock (1957), Action of the Tiger (1957), Hell Drivers (1957), Another Time, Another Place (1958), Darby O'Gill and the Little People (1959), Tarzan's Greatest Adventure (1959), The Frightened City (1961), On the Fiddle (1961), The Longest Day (1962), Dr. No (1962), From Russia with Love (1963), Goldfinger (1964), Marnie (1964), Woman of Straw (1964), Thunderball (1965), The Hill (1965), Un Monde Noveau (1966), A Fine Madness (1966), You Only Live Twice (1967), Shalako (1968), The Molly Maguires (1970), The Red Tent (1970), The Anderson Tapes (1971), Diamonds Are Forever (1971), The Offence (1973), Zardoz (1974), Murder on the Orient Express (1974), Ransom (1975), The Wind and the Lion (1975), The Man Who Would Be King (1975), Robin and Marian (1976), The Next Man (1976), A Bridge Too Far (1977), Meteor (1979), The First Great Train Robbery (1979), Cuba (1979), Outland (1981), Time Bandits (1981), The Man with the Deadly Lens (1982), Five Days One Summer (1982), Sword of the Valiant (1983), Never Say Never Again (1983), The Highlander (1986), The Name of the Rose (1986), The Untouchables (1987), The Presidio (1989), Indiana Jones and the Last Crusade (1989), Family Business (1989), The Hunt for Red October (1990), The Russia House (1990), Robin Hood: Prince of Thieves (1991), Highlander II—The Quickening (1991), Medicine Man (1992), Rising Sun (1993), Wrestling Ernest Hemingway (1993), A Good Man in Africa (1994), Just Cause (1995), First Knight (1995), The Rock (1996), Dragonheart (1996), A Life Less Ordinary (1997), The Avengers (1998), Playing by Heart (1998), Entrapment (1999), and Finding Forrester (2000).

THE CORPSE (Cannon/Abacus, 1969)—Horror. *Director:* Viktors Ritelis; *Producer:* Gabrielle Beaumont; *Script:* Olaf Pooley; *Cinematographer:* John Mackey; *Music:* John Hotchkis; *Cast:* Michael Gough (Walter Eastwood),

Yvonne Mitchell (Edith Eastwood), Sharon Gurney (Jane Eastwood), Simon Gough (Rupert Eastwood), Olaf Pooley (Reid), and David Butler (Gregson).

This independent, very low-budget production, scripted by actor Olaf Pooley, provides a chilling dramatization of the resilience and evil effects of British patriarchy. The film also reworks the familiar horror theme involving the "return of the repressed." After the murder of a sadistic insurance executive (Walter Eastwood) by his much-abused wife (Edith) and daughter (Jane), his corpse keeps returning from the dead. What is even more threatening is that Walter harbors strong incestuous desires (signaled early in the film when Walter rubs his hand over a bicycle seat recently vacated by Jane) toward his sixteen-year-old daughter and he takes every opportunity to humiliate and beat her.

After years of abuse, Edith and Jane poison Walter but his corpse keeps reappearing even after the women push it over a cliff in a wooden box. At the film's climax, it returns to terrorize the two women into total submission. The film's epilogue shows Walter resuming his customary position at the head of the table at breakfast time as he converses with his son Rupert, a replica of his father, leaving wife and daughter in a terrified, and fatally weakened, position within the household. There is nothing to stop Walter's perversions at the close of *The Corpse*.

Although *The Corpse* borrows some of the narrative aspects of *Les Diaboliques* (1955), its execution is uniquely British and differs considerably from the French film. Michael Gough is excellent as the sadistic patriarch. Although the production suffers from obvious budgetary restrictions and a muted climax, as well as director Viktors Ritelis's overreliance on close-ups and images of inconsequential objects, the film's critique of patriarchy is strong. The film's low budget obviously gave it the commercial freedom to avoid making compromises that would have softened its point of view, particularly with regard to its confrontational ending.

CORRIDOR OF MIRRORS (Appollo Films, 1948)—Gothic. *Director:* Terence Young; *Producer:* Rudolph Cartier; *Script:* Rudolph Cartier and Edana Romney, based on the novel by Christopher Massie; *Cinematography:* Andre Thomas; *Music:* Georges Auric; *Cast:* Eric Portman (Paul Mangin), Edana Romney (Mifanwy Conway), Barbara Mullen (Veronica), Hugh Sinclair (Owen Rhys), Alan Wheatley (Edgar Orsen), Joan Maude (Caroline Hart), Bruce Belfrage (Sir David Conway), Leslie Weston (Mortimer), Thora Hird (Old Woman), and Christopher Lee (Charles).

Corridor of Mirrors is a relatively little-known Gothic story of a woman, Mifanwy Conway, who is intrigued by the mysterious Paul Mangin. Mangin takes Conway away from her comfortable existence into a dark, perverse fantasy, a world inspired by a four-hundred-year-old Italian painting of a young woman. Initially, Conway is eager to assist Mangin, but as the extent of his obsession becomes apparent, she becomes frightened by his possessive tendencies and retreats back to the less threatening world of her conventional boyfriend Owen Rhys. Mangin refuses to let go of his dream and invites Conway to a lavish Venetian ball and, intrigued, Conway leaves Rhys to participate in the festivities. Afterwards, she refuses to take part in his fantasy. When a woman, Caroline Hart, is murdered in one of Mangin's bedrooms, he takes the blame rather than have his fantasy subjected to public scrutiny. Some years later, Conway returns to view Mangin at Madame Tussaud's wax museum where she learns the identity of the real killer, a demented woman living with Mangin. Mifanwy then returns home to husband Rhys and their three children.

Corridor of Mirrors was supposedly influenced by the dramatic premise and formal style of Jean Cocteau's *Beauty and the Beast* (1946). It is, however, a traditional Gothic story as director Terence Young, in his debut feature film, emphasizes Mangin's house and the objects inside of it. The film, with its constant low-key photography and perverse sexual implications, including Mangin's desire to transform Conway into another woman (this predates *Vertigo* [1958] by more than a decade), shares the same troubling qualities as Lance Comfort's* *Daughter of Darkness,* * which was released in the same year. The film also benefits from Andre Thomas's lighting as it takes years off Portman's face and assists the leading lady (Edana Romney), who coscripted the film, by adding dramatic tension into what is largely a stilted performance.

COSH BOY (Romulus, 1953)—Crime. *Director:* Lewis Gilbert; *Producer:* Daniel M. Angel; *Script:* Lewis Gilbert and Vernon Gilbert Harris, based on the play *Master Crook* by Bruce Walker; *Photography:* Jack Asher; *Music:* Lambert Williamson; *Cast:* James Kenney (Roy Walsh), Joan Collins (Rene Collins), Robert Ayres (Bob Stevens), Hermione Baddeley (Mrs. Collins), Hermione Gingold (Queenie), Betsy Ann Davies (Elsie Walsh), Laurence Naismith (Inspector Donaldson), Frederick Piper (Mr. Easter), Walter Hudd (Magistrate), Sid James (Sergeant), and Ian Whittaker (Alfie Collins).

Cosh Boy, the first British film to receive an X certificate, dramatized a growing fear of juvenile delinquency as an emerging social problem in Britain. The film's release coincided with the murder trial of teenager Christopher Craig and his older companion Derek Bentley. The solution provided in the film to this "problem" was restoration of strict family discipline. In *Cosh Boy* the film suggests that "soft parents," such as Elsie Walsh and the absence of a strong father figure (Roy's father died in World War II), were responsible for the emergence of young criminals such as Roy Walsh.

Walsh rules over a gang of teenage criminals who rob women at night by hitting them with a cosh while stealing their handbags. After Walsh and Alfie Collins, one of his companions, are arrested and ordered to undertake community service, he develops the local youth center into a base for his criminal activities. At the youth center, Walsh meets, terrorizes, and seduces Rene Collins. After impregnating her, Walsh callously rejects her marriage plea, forcing Collins into an unsuccessful suicide attempt and, consequently, the loss of her baby. At the same time, Walsh organizes and participates in a robbery of the local sports stadium where he shoots one of the workers. Cornered by Bob Stevens, the manager of the stadium, who also happens to be his mother's new husband, Walsh eagerly anticipates the arrival of the police who, he believes, will save him from a thrashing from his stepfather. The police agree to go away for ten minutes so that Stevens can lash Walsh with his trouser belt and the film ends with the sound of the young man's screams as the police walk from the house.

Although *Cosh Boy* was severely criticized by most of the daily papers, it remains a valuable insight into this period. James Kenney, who repeated his stage role, gives a strong performance as the sadistic, cowardly Roy Walsh.

COTTAGE TO LET (Gainsborough, 1941)—Espionage thriller. *Director:* Anthony Asquith; *Producer:* Edward Black; *Script:* Anatole de Grunwald, J. O. C. Orton, and Geoffrey Kerr, based on his play; *Cinematography:* Jack E. Cox; *Music:* Louis Levy; *Cast:* Leslie Banks (John Barrington), Alastair Sim (Charles Dimble), John Mills (Flight Lieut. George Perry), Jeanne De Casalis (Mrs. Barrington), Carla Lehmann (Helen Barrington), George Cole (Ronald Mittsby), Michael Wilding (Alan Trently), Frank Cellier (John Forest), Muriel Aked (Miss Fernery), and Catherine Lacey (Mrs. Strokes).

Both Hollywood and Britain responded, initially, to World War II with semi-comic espionage films. In Hollywood, films such as *All Through the Night* (1942) were similar in their mixture of comedy and propaganda to British films such as *Cottage to Let.* Paradoxically, as the fortunes of World War II brightened for both Britain and the United States in 1945, the films grew darker and more problematic.

Cottage to Let is set in a Scottish village where John Barrington, a slightly eccentric scientist, develops a revolutionary bombing device for British planes. The Barringtons also rent cottages on their estate, and their tenants include wounded Royal Air Force pilot George Perry and the mysterious Charles Dimble. The British government, fearing German capture of Barrington and his invention, plant a government agent on the estate as they suspect Barrington's assistant, Alan Trently, of Nazi sympathies. With British agents and German spies on the estate, the narrative is primarily a series of "red herrings" and revelations as to the true identity of the spies and government agents.

The film's simplistic presentation of espionage and politics is highlighted by its use of a teenage evacuee Ronald Mittsby, particularly when he hides in the trunk of the German spy's car after he kidnaps Barrington. A last-minute rescue by the army and the "surprise" unmasking of the Nazi spy George Perry by the seemingly inept Charles Dimble brings the film to a close in a shoot-out in a bazaar tent full of distorting mirrors, a device exploited much more expressively, and excessively, by Orson Welles seven years later in *The Lady from Shanghai.*

COUNTESS DRACULA (Hammer, 1970)—Horror. *Director:* Peter Sasdy; *Producer:* Alexander Paal; *Script:* Jeremy Paul; *Cinematography:* Kenneth Talbot; *Music:* Harry Robinson; *Cast:* Ingrid Pitt (Countess Elizabeth Bathory), Nigel Green (Captain Dobi), Sandor Eles (Imre Toth), Maurice Denham (Master

Fabio), Lesley-Ann Down (Illona), Patience Collier (Julie), and Nike Arrighi (Gypsy Girl).

The murderous behavior of Countess Elizabeth Bathory, the daughter of an ally of Ferdinand I of Hapsburg, who was born in 1560, and married to Ferenz Nadasdy, has fed the vampire myth for many years. Bathory, who did not live with her husband for most of their marriage, moved from castle to castle slaughtering young women (some estimates reach six hundred) for their blood. Bathory believed their blood would rejuvenate her skin. In 1610, she was condemned to death and walled up (alive) in her bedroom.

Based on *The Bloody Countess,* Valentine Penrose's book on Bathory, Hammer produced *Countess Dracula* and, following her success in *The Vampire Lovers* (1970), cast Polish-born actress Ingrid Pitt in the title role. This role provided more of a challenge to Pitt as she, in effect, had to play two parts, the bitter, aging Countess Elizabeth Bathory who desires the dashing young soldier Imre Toth and a "young" woman who, in actuality, is Elizabeth after partaking of her blood baths that transform her into a much younger woman. This provides a pretext for Elizabeth to kill a series of young women.

Elizabeth's scheme is complicated by the fact that Toth believes that the "young" Elizabeth is her daughter Illona, when Illona has been kidnapped to prevent her from interfering with her mother's plan. Elizabeth's deception is exposed when she is caught bathing in the blood of her latest victim. In *Countess Dracula,* director Peter Sasdy emphasizes the destructive relationship between parents and their children, the theme of his first film *Taste the Blood of Dracula* (1969). *Countess Dracula,* with its strong anti-maternal theme, points to society's fixation with youthfulness. There is an inherent sadness in Elizabeth's obsession with beauty and sexual gratification to the point where she is prepared to sacrifice her daughter Illona for the opportunity to be young again. The film also reinforces a traditional Hammer theme—the decadence of the aristocracy and their exploitation of the working class. The young peasant women of the village literally rejuvenate the aristocracy with their blood.

CRICHTON, CHARLES (1910–1999). Because of the huge success of the comedy *A Fish Called Wanda** (1988), Charles Crichton, after a thirty-three-year absence from feature films, was celebrated as one of the preeminent directors associated with the "Ealing comedy." The comedies produced at Ealing Studios in the late 1940s and the 1950s, however, varied considerably, as one would expect from directors as diverse as Robert Hamer,* Alexander Mackendrick,* and Crichton. Paradoxically, the streak of affectionate cruelty that pervades Crichton's *A Fish Called Wanda* is closer to the tone of Hamer's and Mackendrick's films.

Educated at Oxford University, Crichton befriended Zoltan Korda and established himself within the film industry as an editor where he worked on a number of important London Film productions. From 1935 to 1940, he edited key films such as *Sanders of the River** (1935), *Things to Come* (1936), *Elephant Boy*

(1937), and *The Thief of Baghdad* (1940). Believing he was about to be called up for military duty, Crichton marked time by editing propaganda documentaries (*The Young Veterans* [1941] and *Yellow Caesar* [1941]) for Alberto Cavalcanti. When he was not called up (because he was working on propaganda films), Crichton joined Ealing Studios as an editor and began directing propaganda films, such as *For Those in Peril* (1944), with David Farrar.* This film, celebrating the work of the Air-Sea Rescue Service, was shot in the English Channel.

Crichton's first major feature was *The Golfing Story,* an episode in the portmanteau supernatural film *Dead of Night** (1945). Basil Radford, the star of *The Golfing Story* with Naunton Wayne, assisted Crichton in the delivery and pacing of this episode. Crichton's next film for Ealing, *Hue and Cry** (1947), firmly established his reputation as a director of film comedy and after helping Mackendrick sort out the disastrous first cut of *Whisky Galore!* (1994), Crichton worked as a film and television director for the rest of his career.

*The Lavender Hill Mob** (1951) was Crichton's biggest hit in the 1950s, although this film was originally conceived as a thriller following the passage of gold-laden miniature Eiffel Tower souvenirs from person to person. However, producer Michael Truman, working with scriptwriter "Tibby" Clarke and Crichton, reworked the script by focusing on two men who conceived and executed the robbery of gold ingots, and, with the casting of Stanley Holloway and Alec Guinness,* the film was transformed into a comedy.

Crichton worked successfully in genres other than comedy for Ealing, particularly the war film *Against the Wind** (1948), where Jack Warner* played one of his rare screen villains as the collaborator working against British agents in occupied France, and the sentimental drama *The Divided Heart* (1954), based on a true story of a custody battle involving a young boy. Crichton also directed the melodrama *Hunted* (1952), with Dirk Bogarde* as a murderer who forms an attachment with a young boy. After leaving Ealing, Crichton directed another melodrama about a man hunted by the police, *Floods of Fear* (1958), starring Howard Keel. Crichton also continued with comedies that resembled, less successfully, his earlier films such as *Law and Disorder* (1958) and *The Battle of the Sexes* (1959).

Crichton's career as a top film director faded in the 1960s, especially after a failed sojourn to Hollywood for the *Birdman of Alcatraz* (1962), which he left after falling out with the film's star Burt Lancaster. Crichton worked mainly on television programs for most of the decade (*The Avengers*) and throughout the 1970s (*Space 1999, The Professionals,* and *The Return of the Saint*) until John Cleese approached him in 1983 with an idea to make a comedy with Cleese as a barrister. Cleese and Crichton worked on this concept for the next four years and in 1987 their script for *A Fish Called Wanda* went before the camera with Crichton, aged seventy-seven, directing what was to become one of Britain's most successful screen comedies.

Crichton was nominated as Best Director and for the Best Writing and Original Screenplay Award at the 1989 Academy Awards. He won the Michael Balcon

Award at the 1989 BAFTA Awards. He was also nominated for Best Director and Best Film. In 1951, Crichton was nominated for the Golden Lion Award for *The Lavender Hill Mob* at the Venice Film Festival. Crichton died in London in 1999.

FILMS (as director): For Those in Peril (1944), Painted Boats (1945), Dead of Night (1945), Hue and Cry (1947), Against the Wind (1948), Another Shore (1948), Train of Events (1949), Dance Hall (1950), The Lavender Hill Mob (1951), Hunted (1952), The Titfield Thunderbolt (1953), The Love Lottery (1954), The Divided Heart (1954), The Man in the Sky (1957), Floods of Fear (1958), Law and Disorder (1958), The Battle of Sexes (1959), The Boy Who Stole a Million (1960), The Third Secret (1964), He Who Rides a Tiger (1965), and A Fish Called Wanda (1988).

THE CRIMINAL (Anglo-Amalgamated, 1960)—Gangster. *Director:* Joseph Losey; *Producer:* Jack Greenwood; *Script:* Alun Owen and Jimmy Sangster; *Cinematography:* Robert Krasker; *Music:* John Dankworth; *Cast:* Stanley Baker (Johnny Bannion), Sam Wanamaker (Mike Carter), Margit Saad (Suzanne), Gregoire Aslan (Frank Saffron), Patrick Magee (Chief Warden Barrows), Jill Bennett (Maggie), Rupert Davies (Mr. Edwards), Laurence Naismith (Mr. Town), Noel Willman (Prison Governor), and Tom Bell (Flynn).

The transformation in the screen persona of Stanley Baker* in the second half of the 1950s, from his villains in *Checkpoint* (1956) and *Campbell's Kingdom* (1957), and working-class victim in *The Good Die Young** (1954), to the heroic truck driver in *Hell Drivers** (1957), was symptomatic of changes taking place in the British crime film. The rise of Baker, from supporting villains to lead roles, emerged mostly in the films of U.S. expatriate directors Cy Endfield* and Joseph Losey.* In the late 1950s, Losey made two important films with Baker: *Blind Date* (1959), an intriguing detective mystery, and *The Criminal.*

In *The Criminal,* Alun Owen rewrote Jimmy Sangster's script and Owen, together with Losey, transformed and subverted many of the film's generic conventions. Losey and Owen were more concerned with the activities of one prisoner, Johnny Bannion (Baker), and his physical and existential entrapment in a greedy, materialistic society. The film begins with Bannion as the kingpin of his cell block, although another convict, Frank Saffron, rules the prison with Chief Warden Barrows. After Bannion is released, he resumes his criminal activities by robbing a racetrack but Maggie, a jealous ex-girlfriend, informs on him and he is sent back to prison for fifteen years after burying the money in a field. Former colleague Mike Carter kidnaps Suzanne, Bannion's new girlfriend, thereby forcing Bannion to make a deal with Saffron to escape in exchange for the money. After his escape, Bannion is betrayed and dies on his knees as he attempts to recover the money from a snow-covered field.

Losey transforms this seemingly conventional gangster story into a parable that warns of the dangers of the growing corporatization of daily life. Bannion represents individualism in the highly organized world of crime. Carter, on the other hand, represents the "new breed" of businessmen-criminals. In the film's final scene, Carter cradles the dying Bannion in an attempt to find out where he has buried the money. When he fails to gain this information, he brutally throws Bannion's body aside.

Bannion, loosely based on information provided by Soho gangster Albert Dimes, is not only an anachronistic figure, but also a contradictory one—sadistic, tough, vulnerable, romantic, and individualistic. In the confined world of the prison, Bannion is able to survive. Outside prison, he is trapped by his inability to adapt to the changed circumstances.

The Criminal, seemingly rooted within the generic conventions of the prison film, provoked derision from critics in 1960. While many of these critics were celebrating the "adult" pleasures and "realism" of *Saturday Night and Sunday Morning,* which was released at the same time as *The Criminal,* there are thematic associations between both films. For example, Bannion's individualistic ethos provokes confrontation with the "organization," producing an alienated protagonist similar to the antiheroes of the New Wave films. *The Criminal,* however, eschews the "realism" of the New Wave for an expressionistic style, particularly in the stylized prison scenes captured by Robert Krasker's photography.

THE CROOKED ROAD (Argo Film Productions, 1965)—Adventure. *Director:* Don Chaffey; *Producers:* David Henley and Jack O. Lamont (executive); *Script:* J. Garrison, based on the novel *The Big Story* by Morris West; *Cinematography:* Stephen Dade; *Music:* Bojan Adamic; *Cast:* Robert Ryan (Richard Ashley), Stewart Granger (Duke of Orgagna), Nadia Grey (Cosima), Marius Goring (Harlequin), and George Coulouris (Carlo).

Although *The Crooked Road* is not a very good film, it provides Robert Ryan, one of the great actors of the U.S. cinema, with his only lead role in a British film. Ryan, whose film career had started to decline in the early 1960s, believed, mistakenly, that *The Crooked Road* would restore his status as the basic story, based on Australian author Morris West's novel, provided him with an opportunity to break away from the Western villains and military officers that had characterized much of his career in the 1950s and 1960s. Ryan's liberal political beliefs attracted him to the role of a crusading U.S. newspaperman investigating the embezzlement of state funds by a government leader, the duke of Orgagna. Ryan also welcomed the romantic scenes with Nadia Grey (Cosima) in the script. Such scenes were a rarity for Ryan. Thus, Ryan was cast against type as the hero, as was Stewart Granger* (normally a hero) as the corrupt leader of a fictitious European country.

The film was shot in black and white on location in Yugoslavia, and, due to its small budget, the number of exterior scenes were restricted and most of the film was shot in a villa on a small island. The film's small budget also shows in the bland lighting, excessive dialogue, and almost total absence of action scenes. The inability of the filmmakers to utilize the local scenery and atmosphere, except for a relatively small number of awkward outdoor scenes, meant that the film could have been shot much more expertly back in London. The basic plot, involving Ashley's investigation into the De's fraudulent activities and his involvement with an old girlfriend, the duke's current wife, was a reasonable dramatic premise. Although Ryan and Granger are good, script and budgetary problems ultimately defeat them.

CROUPIER (Channel Four Films, 1998)—Film noir. *Director:* Mike Hodges; *Producers:* Jonathan Cavendish, Christine Ruppert, and James Mitchell (executive producer); *Script:* Paul Mayersberg; *Cinematography:* Michael Garfath; *Music:* Simon Fisher-Turner; *Cast:* Clive Owen (Jack Manfred), Kate Hardie (Bella), Alex Kingston (Jani de Villiers), Gina McKee (Marion), Nicholas Ball (Jack Manfred Sr.), Nick Reding (Giles Cremorne), Alexander Morton (David Reynolds), and Paul Reynolds (Matt).

Mike Hodges directed the best British crime film of the early 1970s in *Get Carter** (1971) and the best British crime film of the late 1990s in *Croupier.* After the success of *Get Carter,* Hodges worked in Hollywood on *Pulp* (1972) and *The Terminal Man* (1974), and, following the comic book excesses of *Flash Gordon* (1980), drifted into relative obscurity, punctuated by an occasional film, such as his adaptation of the Jack Higgins's novel *A Prayer for the Dying* (1987). *Croupier* is the work of a mature filmmaker working with a limited budget to deliver a personal, multi-layered film.

Paul Mayersberg is also a significant influence on this film. Mayersberg's script develops a world of paradoxes and metaphors based around gambling as a metaphor for life. Mayersberg's main character is the cold, detached Jack Manfred. There is, however, an inherent dichotomy within Manfred. Although he refuses to gamble, as the odds are too great, he takes great risks, risks that are rationalized through his fictional surrogate, Jake. Thus, Jack the croupier, who takes perverse pleasure watching his customers lose their money, readily sleeps with Bella, a fellow croupier, and takes Jani, a South African gambler, away for the weekend, despite a prohibition from his gambling establishment that forbids croupiers from fraternizing with colleagues or customers.

The film begins with Jack, who was born in South Africa, suffering from writer's block. Although he is desperate for money, he cannot fulfil the demands of his philistine publisher, Giles Cremorne, for a soccer book with plenty of action and sex. Jack, with the assistance of his father, secures a job as a croupier where he finds that he is fascinated (again) by the prospect of watching people lose their money. His live-in girlfriend Marion is less enthusiastic about the prospect of living with a croupier rather than a struggling writer. Jack, who is half in love with Marion, meets two women, Bella, a fellow croupier who also despises the punters, and Jani, a gambler who invites Jack to participate in a plan to rob the casino. Jack, rationalizing away his objections through his voice-over, agrees, leading to an unexpected, somewhat oblique, ending.

Croupier, consistent with the world of film noir, is a deeply cynical film, as Jack's publisher, Giles Cremorne, is almost a caricature of the crass publisher with little interest in quality writing, only in sales. The film's dominant motif, gambling, is a perfect expression of disaffection. Jack only succeeds through chance. Even after Marion's death and his success as an anonymous novelist, there is no sign of redemption or regeneration as Jack replaces the romantic, caring Marion with the cynical Bella. Bella is the perfect match for Jack's alienated point of view as she is a woman who spent a year as a sadomasochistic prostitute as it provided no emotional or sexual interaction with her customers—a social condition that also approximates the rules of the casino for its employees. Similarly's, Jack's detachment and alienation from the gamblers is not moral but sadistic—he enjoys watching people lose their money. Yet, as the narrative shows, when the price is right he also succumbs to the temptations of illicit sex and criminal behavior.

While Hodges and Mayersberg infuse *Croupier* with a quasi-realistic atmosphere, it is a very stylized film, opening on the metal center of a spinning wheel as the carriage spins around its center, replaced by the image of Jack Manfred as the camera dollies around him in the casino. These contrasting images of stasis and movement provide an effective summary of the film's basic premise, the alienated croupier seemingly detached from the world of risk takers. As the film progresses this duality, contrasting Jack's control with the addiction of the gamblers, it is cleverly subverted by Jack's alter ego, Jake, the risk taker. Clive Owen, as Jack, is perfect as the croupier who has one good novel in him. Jack's realization of this fact begins with the pleasure he takes in his physical transformation from the bohemian would-be writer, with dyed blonde hair, to the repressed, controlled croupier with his slicked-down black hair and accompanying uniform, his impersonal evening dress.

Even the history of the distribution and exhibition of *Croupier* reinforces the film's central thesis, that life is a gamble. When the film was completed in 1998, the BBC was no longer interested in promoting the film as there had been a change in management. Mayersberg complained that they did not even produce one poster for promotion as the film was destined not to have a cinema release but go straight to television. After thirteen copies were sent to the U.S. festival circuit and a subsequent theatrical release, *Croupier* received glowing reviews, which led to openings in Britain, Europe, and Australia, and a nomination for Mayersberg at the 2001 Edgar Allan Poe Awards. Yet, consistent with the inherent irony of the film, because it had been shown briefly on television, *Croupier* was ruled ineligible for U.S. awards. An unjust fate for Owen, Hodges, and Mayersberg.

THE CRUEL SEA (Ealing, 1953)—War. *Director:* Charles Frend; *Producers:* Michael Balcon (executive) and Leslie Norman; *Script:* Eric Ambler, based on the novel by Nicholas Monsarrat; *Photography:* Gordon Dines; *Music:* Alan Rawsthorne; *Cast:* Jack Hawkins (Captain Ericson), Donald Sinden (Lieutenant Lockhart), John Stratton (Sub-lieutenant Ferraby), Denholm Elliott (Sub-lieutenant Morell), Stanley Baker (Lieutenant Bennett), John Warner (Sub-lieutenant Baker), Bruce Seton (Bob Tallow), Liam Redmond (Jim Watts), Virginia McKenna (Julie Hallam), Moira Lister (Elaine Morell), June Thorburn (Doris Ferraby), and Megs Jenkins (Glad Tallow).

During the early to mid-1950s, the war film reemerged as one of the most popular genres in the British cinema. This resurgence in popularity was partly due to the critical and commercial success of *The Cruel Sea,* the most popular film in Britain in 1953. There are significant differences between the war films produced in the 1950s and those produced during World War II. A significant difference, for example, was the treatment of the enemy who, in the 1950s films, receded into the background and functioned as only one of many obstacles facing the British serviceman. In *The Cruel Sea,* the Germans are largely absent, except for their periodic attacks on British shipping and they merely provide a context for the real drama that focuses on the relationships of the men of the HMS *Compass Rose* and, in particular, the relationship between Captain Ericson and Lieutenant Lockhart, his second-in-command.

The film begins in 1940 when Ericson is placed in command of a corvette with an inexperienced crew, such as Lockhart, Ferraby, Morell, and Baker, who have had no battle experience. Although there are sporadic visits back to the shore, as the men visit wives and family, the film is more concerned with their interrelationships and reactions to the various situations that affect the ship. There is a tentative romance between Lockhart and Julie Hallam, a young woman working at the naval central command and this allows the film to contrast two dominant cultural stereotypes of the war and postwar period: the loyal, caring girlfriend (Julie) with the selfish woman of the world, Morell's show business wife Elaine, who cares nothing for her husband's safety and is only interested in her own pleasures, sexual and otherwise. The shore visits also serve as a reminder that the danger from the German military machine during the early war years was felt not only at the front but also at home, as Bob Tallow discovers when he returns to his bombed house and his dead sister.

Many of the British war films produced during the 1950s, including *The Cruel Sea,* eliminated, or reduced, the "us" and "them" ideology of the 1940s films, replacing the communal theme of the war years with a celebration of the professional officer class—epitomized by Jack Hawkins,* the most popular actor in Britain in 1953–1954. This shift allowed a degree of vulnerability and self-doubt to enter the film. This occurs in *The Cruel Sea* when Captain Ericson decides to drop depth charges on what he believes to be an enemy submarine circling below a group of British sailors waiting to be rescued. Although the depth charges fail to destroy the German U-boat, they kill the sailors in the water. This action provokes an emotional breakdown in Ericson and he is nursed through this period by Lockhart. Later, Ericson is redeemed when his decision to pursue and destroy a U-boat is vindicated, despite a lack of confidence from other members of the crew.

There is a strong class subtext to *The Cruel Sea,* with the only working-class officer, the sadistic Lieutenant Bennett, quickly removed from the *Compass Rose* in favor of a more harmonious upper-middle-class group. The film emphasizes the hardships of war. The underlying bitterness in Ericson's realization that "war is just a matter of killing the enemy" is reaffirmed at the end of the film when he notices that, despite the loss of most of his men on the *Compass Rose,* he has sunk only two German U-boats in five years.

Eric Ambler's screenplay for *The Cruel Sea* was nominated for an Academy Award in 1954 while both Hawkins and the film were nominated for BAFTA Film Awards.

CUMMINS, PEGGY (b. 1925). If it had not been for two low-budget films, one filmed in Hollywood (*Gun Crazy* [1949]) and one filmed in England (*Night of the Demon* [1957]), Peggy Cummins would have been little more than a footnote in the history of the cinema. Born in Wales, Cummins's classic fresh-faced physical features, with her open face and blonde curly hair, proved, in some ways, to be more of a hindrance than a help to the overall development of her film career as she was relentlessly typecast as the bland heroine in many 1950s British films. After a number of minor films, such as *Old Mother Riley Detective* (1943), in the early 1940s, Cummins was brought to Hollywood by Twentieth Century Fox to star in its controversial production of *Forever Amber* (1947), Kathleen Winsor's novel of a woman who exploited her sexual prowess to enter the court of Charles II. Studio head Darryl F. Zanuck, however, was disappointed with the early rushes of the film and replaced Cummins with the dark, sensuous Fox contract player Linda Darnell. Cummins was compensated with lead roles in a number of Fox productions, such as the blackmailer in the period melodrama *Moss Rose* (1947), opposite Victor Mature, Eleanor Apley in Joseph L. Mankiewicz's *The Late George Apley* (1947), a gentle satire of Boston conservatism starring Ronald Coleman, and the Western adventure *Green Grass of Wyoming* (1948), before returning to England for another film directed by Mankiewicz, *Escape* (1948), opposite Rex Harrison.

The response to these U.S. films was not sufficient for Fox to keep Cummins on contract and before her permanent return to Britain in 1949, Hollywood independent low-budget producers Maurice King and Frank King cast Cummins opposite John Dall in the noir masterpiece *Deadly Is the Female/Gun Crazy* (1949). Such a role, combining sexual and emotional complexity, would never again be offered to Cummins. As Annie Laurie Starr, a carnival con woman, this fresh-faced actress brilliantly captured Starr's conflicting impulses, combining the sympathetic qualities of a doomed romantic with a gun fetish and an uncontrollable desire to kill.

There were some compensating roles for Cummins in British films in the 1950, such as Muriel Box's* *Street Corner* (1953), which was a kind of reply to *The Blue Lamp** (1950) as it focused on the daily work of policewomen, and Stanley Baker's* ally in Cy Endfield's* *Hell Drivers** (1957) who exposes a corrupt truck haulage racket. Unfortunately, more typical fare for Cummins was the bland comedy *Always a Bride* (1953), opposite Terence Morgan, and *The Captain's Table* (1959), with Cummins sadly underutilized as Mrs. Judd, one of a number of women pursuing the captain (John Gregson) of a luxury liner.

It was another independent production, *Night of the Demon,* directed by Jacques Tourneur, that provided Cummins with her second best role as Joanna Harrington, a young teacher who asks visiting U.S. psychologist (Dana Andrews) to investigate the death of her scientist father. While Harrington quickly grasps the role of the supernatural in causing his demise, the American steadfastly refuses to acknowledge the power of the occult, provoking intense danger for both Cummins and Andrews. After the inane comedy *In the Doghouse* (1961), Cummins retired from films leaving behind two great films (*Gun Crazy* and *Night of the Demon*) and a handful of interesting roles (*Moss Rose, Escape,* and *Hell Drivers*).

FILMS: Dr. O'Dowd (1939), Salute John Citizen (1942), Old Mother Riley Detective (1943), English without Tears (1944), Welcome, Mr. Washington (1944), Moss Rose (1947), The Late George Apley (1947), Green Grass of Wyoming (1948), Escape (1948), That Dangerous Age (1949), Deadly Is the Female/Gun Crazy (1949), My Daughter Joy (1950), Who Goes There? (1952), Street Corner (1953), Meet Mr. Lucifer (1953), Always a Bride (1953), To Dorothy a Son (1954), Love Lottery (1954), March Hare (1955), Hell Drivers (1957), Night of the Demon (1957), Carry on Admiral (1957), The Captain's Table (1959), Your Money or Your Wife (1960), Dentist in the Chair (1960), and In the Doghouse (1961).

THE CURSE OF FRANKENSTEIN (Hammer, 1957)—Horror. *Director:* Terence Fisher; *Producers:* Anthony Hinds and Michael Carreras (executive); *Script:* Jimmy Sangster, based on the story by Mary Shelley; *Cinematography:* Jack Asher; *Music:* James Bernard; *Cast:* Peter Cushing (Baron Victor Frankenstein), Hazel Court (Elizabeth), Robert Urquhart (Paul Krempe), Christopher Lee (The Creature), Melvyn Hayes (Young Victor), Valerie Gaunt (Justine), Paul Hardtmuth (Professor Bernstein), and Alex Gallier (Priest).

The Curse of Frankenstein is a significant film in the history of the British cinema and in the development of the horror genre. Its commercial success came at a time when the British film industry was going through one of its periodic low points (*The Curse of Frankenstein* was the most commercially successful British film produced in 1957), and this film, almost single-handedly raised the status of its production company, Hammer Studios, from the depths of the industry to the most commercially viable production house in Britain.

The success of *The Curse of Frankenstein* in the United States inspired interest from the Hollywood studios in this small British studio, which had specialized in different genres for the B picture market since its production of *The Mystery of Marie Celeste,* starring Bela Lugosi, in 1935. With *The Curse of Frankenstein,* Hammer found its niche, the historical horror film. The studio gave new life to the genre by adding violence, sex, color, and style. *The Curse of Frankenstein* also provided a breakthrough for Terence Fisher,* who entered the British industry in 1933. With this film, Fisher found an appropriate genre for his talents and he directed seventeen more horror films for Hammer, including the enormously successful remake of *Dracula* in 1958.

The Curse of Frankenstein differs considerably from Universal's groundbreaking 1931 version, directed by British filmmaker James Whale. Hammer's 1957 version, which upset British critics with its violence, was enriched by

Fisher's creative use of color and captures the novel's underlying sadism. This is most apparent in Fisher's characterization of Baron Victor Frankenstein as a sadist, driven by self-interest and ego to create human life. The difference is also apparent in the presentations of the creature and the scientist. While Frankenstein and the creature in the 1931 version are opposites, in the 1957 version the murderous urges of the creature mirror the actions of his creator who kills the elderly Professor Bernstein to acquire his brain while also orchestrating the murder of his pregnant mistress Justine. Fisher emphasizes this aspect with a close-up of Frankenstein's calm reaction while standing outside a locked door listening to Justine's cries as his creature kills her.

The film is told in flashback one hour before Frankenstein's execution for the murder of Justine as he tries to convince a priest that the creature killed Justine. Even as a boy, Frankenstein is most unattractive with his aloof manner and ultra-precise social skills. After the death of his parents, he employs a tutor, Paul Krempe, to develop his intellect and scientific skills. Later, as an adult Frankenstein revives a dead puppy and this motivates his desire to create a human being. Krempe, however, strongly opposes Frankenstein and he functions as the ethical face of science for the remainder of the film.

Frankenstein is presented as amoral with little concern for obstacles that might obstruct his main goal. For example, sex, romance, and social areas of life are of little interest to him—his sexual needs are met by Justine and his niece Elizabeth is brought into the household to provide him with a wife. The scenes in the laboratory demonstrate Fisher's skillful use of composition, color, and sounds as the scientist works toward the creation of human life. The film also benefits from Fisher's determination to present the story straight, without any sense of parody that had entered the genre in the 1940s and 1950s, including Universal's decision to assimilate the creature into a 1948 Bud Abbott and Lou Costello comedy (*Abbott and Costello Meet Frankenstein*). On the other hand, Fisher's 1957 production demonstrated there still was considerable life in Mary Shelley's creature with another six sequels over the next sixteen years, concluding with *Frankenstein and the Monster from Hell* in 1973, Fisher's fifth, and Hammer's seventh, Frankenstein film. Fisher died soon after finishing this film.

CUSHING, PETER (1913–1994). In 1957, at the age of forty-four, Peter Cushing's career was radically transformed by the success of *The Curse of Frankenstein.** This film not only changed Cushing's life, but also the career of Christopher Lee* and the status of Hammer Studios. Cushing had been active on the stage, in supporting parts in films, and on television (notably his performance in the BBC production of George Orwell's *1984*) in the previous twenty years, but *The Curse of Frankenstein,* followed by his performance as Van Helsing in *Dracula** (1958), and a starring role in the Hammer remake of *The Mummy** (1959), elevated him to stardom.

After studying at London's Guildhall School of Music and Drama, Cushing made his stage debut in 1935 with the Connaught Repertory Company of Worthing. After adopting the billing of "Peter Ling," which Cushing dropped when agents believed he was Chinese, he crossed over to the United States where he worked on Broadway and in supporting roles in the cinema. His first film, ten days after his arrival in the United States, was as the stand-in for Louis Hayward in James Whale's *The Man in the Iron Mask* (1939). As Hayward had to portray twins in the film, Cushing's "role" was optically eliminated in the final print. Whale, however, impressed by Cushing's skill in delivering dialogue, gave him a small speaking part. After another bit part in a Laurel and Hardy film, *A Chump at Oxford* (1940), George Stevens expanded Cushing's status to second male lead to Carole Lombard in *Vigil in the Night* (1940). After portraying Clive of India in *Hidden Master* (1940), part of MGM's *John Nesbitt's Passing Parade* series of shorts, Cushing began to attract attention within Hollywood. With World War II raging, he returned home to the stage. On his way east across the United States, Cushing worked in the art department in Michael Powell* and Emeric Pressburger's* *The 49th Parallel* (1941).

After the war, Cushing's first major film role in Britain came about when Laurence Olivier* cast him as Osric in his film version of *Hamlet* (1948). This was followed by a prolonged overseas sojourn through Australia and New Zealand with the Olivier Company. On his return to Britain, Cushing alternated theater and television work with supporting parts in British-based films with U.S. directors, such as *Moulin Rouge* (1952), *The Black Knight* (1954), *The End of the Affair* (1955), *Magic Fire* (1956), and *Alexander the Great* (1956). After a supporting role in Joseph Losey's* *Time without Pity* (1957), Cushing's break came with *The Curse of Frankenstein.* Compared with Colin Clive's slightly unhinged scientist in the 1931 version, Cushing brought a degree of studied intelligence and dignity to the character. Cushing argued that the scientist was not intrinsically evil and defends his actions on the grounds that the ends justify the means. He was, Cushing maintains, obsessed by his desire to create life..

After *The Curse of Frankenstein,* Hammer's follow-up horror (or what Cushing preferred to describe as "fantasy") film was *Dracula,* with Cushing as Van Helsing. *Dracula* contrasted Cushing with the tall, elegant Christopher Lee, who transformed the vampire into a more sensuous figure. Both actors were now "fixed" in the public imagination as a kind of "horror double" act (a trio if you add in director Terence Fisher* who was instrumental in the success of these film). The type-casting of Cushing and Lee extended to non-horror films such as *The Hound of the Baskervilles* (1959), where Cushing built on his Van Helsing persona with his rational, imperious Sherlock Holmes opposed to Lee's Sir Henry Baskerville. This film was also directed by Fisher for Hammer. One notable break in horror roles for Cushing came with the low-budget Hammer crime film *Cash on Demand** (1961), where he played a bank manager forced to reconsider his cruel behavior toward his employees by a "gentleman bank robber." In this film, Cushing gave, arguably, his best screen performance.

Cushing appeared as Baron Frankenstein seven times over a fifteen-year period for Hammer and there were shifts in the characterization over the years as audience tastes changed. For example, Cushing's sadistic baron in *Frankenstein Must Be Destroyed,* directed by Fisher in 1969, extends the baron's evil side to a point where he virtually replaces the monster as the source of terror by brutally victimizing all who come into contact with him. Similarly, throughout the late 1960s and 1970s Cushing reworked familiar roles in films such as the vampire hunter in Roy Ward Baker's* *The Vampire Lovers* (1970), the doctor who exposes the curse of the Fengriffen family in Baker's *And Now the Screaming Starts!** (1973), the puritanical witch-hunter Weil in *Twins of Evil* (1971), and the deranged headmaster in *Fear in the Night* (1972).

Cushing had to withdraw from some projected roles in 1970–1971, such as *Blood from the Mummy's Tomb** (1972), after completing one day of shooting, and *Lust for a Vampire* (1970), because of his wife's illness. After she died, he threw himself into a large number of projects, many of them low-budget films dependent on Cushing's name and professionalism to attract fans to the genre. In the French-made *Tendre Dracula* (1976), Cushing played a vampire for the first time, and in *Shock Waves* (1977) he was a Nazi officer who had assembled a battalion of zombies during the war and was forced to try and eliminate them after the war. During this period, Cushing's most famous role was the evil commander of the Deathstar in *Star Wars* (1977). After a long absence, Cushing returned to the stage in 1975 in Henry James's *Washington Square,* but his most prominent medium remained the cinema with occasional television work.

Cushing, described by Olivier as "one of the best screen actors," published *Peter Cushing: An Autobiography* in 1986, which he began in the 1970s as a way of dealing with the pain of his wife's death. He followed this in 1988 with *Past Forgetting—Memoirs of the Hammer Years,* which focused more on his film career. Cushing died of cancer on August 11, 1994.

FILMS: The Man in the Iron Mask (1939), A Chump at Oxford (1940), Vigil in the Night (1940), Laddie (1940), The Howards of Virginia (1940), Women in War (1940), The Hidden Master (short, 1940), Dreams (short, 1940), The New Teacher (short, 1941), They Dare Not Love (1941), The 49th Parallel (1941), It Might Be You (short, 1947), Hamlet (1948), Moulin Rouge (1952), The Black Knight (1954), The End of the Affair (1955), Magic Fire (1956), Alexander the Great (1956), Time without Pity (1956), Violent Playground (1957), The Curse of Frankenstein (1957), The Abominable Snowman (1957), The Revenge of Frankenstein (1958), Dracula (1958), John Paul Jones (1959), The Flesh and the Fiends (1959), The Mummy (1959), The Hound of the Baskervilles (1959), Cone of Silence (1960), The Brides of Dracula (1960), Mania (1960), Sword of Sherwood Forest (1960), Suspect (1960), The Hellfire Club (1961), The Naked Edge (1961), Cash on Demand (1961), Night Creatures (1962), Captain Clegg (1962), The Devil's Agent (1962), The Man Who Finally Died (1967), Fury at Smuggler's Bay (1963), Day of the Triffids (1963), The Gorgon (1964), The Evil of Frankenstein (1964), Dr. Terror's House of Horrors (1965), She (1965), The Skull (1965), Doctor Who and The Daleks (1965), Island of Terror (1966), Daleks' Invasion Earth AD 2150 (1966), Frankenstein Created Woman (1967), The Mummy's Shroud (1967), Torture Garden (1967), The Blood Beast Terror (1967), Island of the Burning Doomed (1967), Some May Live (1967), Night of the Big Heat (1967), Corruption (1968), Frankenstein Must Be Destroyed (1969), Doctors Wear

Scarlet (1969), Scream and Scream Again (1970), One More Time (1970), The Vampire Lovers (1970), I, Monster (1971), The House That Dripped Blood (1971), Twins of Evil (1971), Panico en el Transsiberiano (1972), Dracula A.D. 1972, Asylum (1972), The Creeping Flesh (1972), Tales from the Crypt (1972), Fear in the Night (1972), Nothing but the Night (1972), Dr. Phibes Rises Again (1972), From beyond the Grave (1973), And Now the Screaming Starts! (1973), The Legend of the 7 Golden Vampires (1974), Shatter (1974), The Satanic Rites of Dracula (1974), Madhouse (1974), Frankenstein and the Monster from Hell (1974), The Beast Must Die (1974), Tendre Dracula (1975), Legend of the Werewolf (1975), The Ghoul (1975), Trial by Combat (1976), Land of the Minotaur (1976), At the Earth's Core (1976), Star Wars (1977), The Uncanny (1977), Die Standarte (1977), Shock Waves (1977), Hitler's Son (1978), Touch of the Sun (1979), Arabian Adventure (1979), Black Jack (1980), Monster Island (1981), Sword of the Valiant (1982), House of the Long Shadows (1983), Top Secret! (1984), and Biggles: Adventures in Time (1986).

NOTES

1. McFarlane, *An Autobiography of British Cinema,* p. 111.
2. Quoted in an interview with Andrew Smith, Method Man, *The Weekend Australian,* May 15/16, 1999, p. 4.
3. McFarlane, *An Autobiography of British Cinema,* p. 125.
4. McFarlane, *An Autobiography of British Cinema,* p. 126.
5. See N. Sinyard, *Jack Clayton,* Manchester, Manchester University Press, 2000, p. 24.
6. See B. McFarlane, *Lance Comfort,* Manchester, Manchester University Press, 1999, p, 88.

D

THE DAM BUSTERS (Associated British, 1955)—War. *Director:* Michael Anderson; *Producers:* Robert Clarke and W. A. Whittaker; *Script:* R. C. Sheriff, based on the novel *Enemy Coast Ahead* by Paul Brickhill; *Cinematography:* Erwin Hillier; *Music:* Leighton Lucas and Eric Coates; *Cast:* Richard Todd (Wing Commander Guy Gibson), Michael Redgrave (Barnes Wallis), Ursula Jeans (Mrs. Wallis), Derek Farr (Group Captain J. N. H. Whitworth), Patrick Barr (Captain Joseph Summers), John Fraser (Flight Lieutenant Hopgood), Denys Graham (Flying Officer L. G. Knight), Bill Kerr (Flight Lieutenant Martin), Raymond Huntley (Ministry Official), Nigel Stock (Flight Lieutenant Spafford), Laurence Naismith (Farmer), and Patrick McGoohan (Guard).

Richard Todd,* who plays Commander Guy Gibson, claimed that *The Dam Busters* was the "best military war picture ever made."[1] Although the box office receipts in 1955 provided support for Todd's assertion, there are better British war films (e.g., see *The Captive Heart** [1946]), and even more compelling and morally problematic home front films (see Michael Powell* and Emeric Pressburger's* *The Small Back Room* [1949]), but *The Dam Busters* is a sturdy example of the popular cycle of mid-1950s films that looked back to World War II as a means to celebrate British military achievements and sacrifices during that period.

The film consists of two interconnected sections. The first part details the obstacles faced by English design engineer Barnes Wallis in 1942 to produce a "bouncing bomb" that would destroy German dams on the Moehne, Eder, and Sorbe Rivers in the Ruhr heartland. Conservative bureaucrats in Whitehall oppose Wallis until he receives military support, leading to Commander Guy Gibson's involvement and the formation of a special squadron to carry out the intricate requirements of the mission—particularly the need for extreme low-level flying so that the bombs can be dropped in such a way that they will skip along the surface of the water, slide down the dam face, and then explode alongside the dam wall. Although much of the first part of the film is conventional, there are small, touching moments, such as the reaction of Wallis to another failed demonstration on Reculver Beach. Pulling up his trousers, he wades into the water to recover fragments of his bomb after the Whitehall men have abandoned the inventor in disgust. Similarly, there is something peculiarly British in the film's opening scene as Wallis, surrounded by his children in the back yard, experiments with marbles and a bath tub full of water.

The second half of the film necessarily shifts the emphasis away from Wallis to Gibson and his men as they practice low-level flying, followed by the prolonged climax as the planes cross enemy territory to reach the Ruhr. The film crosscuts between the war room back in England, a tense Wallis, and the planes making their dangerous trek across the water toward the dam wall. Although the mission succeeds, fifty-six men are killed and Wallis confides to a tired Gibson the morning after the mission that if he had known the losses were going to be so heavy he would not have proceeded with his experiment. Wallis's confession is reinforced by Michael Anderson's selection of images that emphasize the enormity of the losses and the film closes in a downbeat manner as Gibson walks back to his room to write letters to the relatives of the dead and missing.

Because the specific details of Wallis's invention were still top secret in 1954, the actual bombs depicted in the film were the wrong shape, which in actuality resembled a stubby cylinder. Also, when the film was released in the United States, Gibson's dog Nigger, who is killed in the film, is dubbed Trigger to avoid any racial problems. John Coates's recurring musical motif in the film, *The Dam Busters March,* was popular on radio in the 1950s and the film was nominated for Best British Film and Best Film from Any Source at the 1956 BAFTA Awards. R. C. Sheriff's literate script, from Paul Brickhill's novel *Enemy Coast Ahead,* was also nominated for Best British Screenplay.

DANCE WITH A STRANGER (Goldcrest Films, 1985)—Biographical drama/film noir. *Director:* Mike Newell; *Producers:* Roger Randall-Cutler and Paul Cowan (associate); *Script:* Shelagh Delaney; *Cinematography:* Peter Hannan; *Music:* Richard Hartley; *Cast:* Miranda Richardson (Ruth Ellis), Rupert Everett (David Blakely), Ian Holm (Desmond Cussen), Matthew Carroll (Andy), Tom Chadborn (Anthony Findlater), Jane Bertish (Carole Findlater), Stratford Johns (Morrie Conley), Joanne Whalley (Christine), and David Troughton (Cliff Davis).

After Ruth Ellis has fired six bullets into racing car driver and lover David Blakely, *Dance with a Stranger* concludes with a sad, confused letter written by Ellis to Blakely's mother trying to explain her action. In the letter, Ellis blames Blakely's friends, Anthony and Carol Findlater, for causing his death because of their class-based prejudice to Blakely's relationship with Ellis. The letter thus foregrounds one of the film's dual narrative strands—the obvious class difference between Ellis and Blakely. The other is sexual obsession, which, in the end destroys Ellis and Blakely. Director Mike Newell* forces the audience to focus on these aspects—not only is the Ellis-Blakely relationship permeated by obsessive, irrational behavior, but also in the way the film obsessively comes back time and time again to the same pattern—Ellis and Blakely fight followed by sex followed by betrayal followed by sex followed by violence. The only other characters that are allowed to intrude on this pattern are Desmond Cussen, Ellis's long-suffering admirer, and Andy her son. The only information we learn about Cussen and Andy is restricted to the effect that Ellis and Blakely have on their lives.

Ellis, a bar manager with a shady past, divorced and an ex-prostitute with a Marilyn Monroe hairstyle, becomes the lover of Blakely, a spoiled, immature racing car driver. Ellis murders Blakely in 1955 and becomes the last woman in England to go to the gallows. *Dance with a Stranger* does not moralize and the film is not a just a melodrama of victims and villains, at least as far as Ellis and Blakely are concerned. Even the immature, self-centered Blakely is allowed moments of sympathy while Ellis struggles, unsuccessfully, to establish a stable environment for Andy, who committed suicide later in life.

Ellis declares "I've never had any kind of peace" and her inability to retain the necessary distance in her relationship with Blakely, as required by a professional working woman with male customers, gives the film a real sense of noirish fatalism. This sense of inevitability and doom is expressed through the dark visuals, the costumes, and the settings. *Dance with a Stranger* is one of the finest British films of the 1980s, with near perfect performances from Miranda Richardson and Ian Holm. Holm has the more difficult role in that he is able to project a sliver of dignity while ritually humiliating himself before Ellis. Also, Newell and Shelagh Delaney never deviate from their relentless focus on the destructive effects of class restrictions and sexual obsession.

Holm won the Best Supporting Actor Award at the 1986 Boston Society of Critics Awards and Newell won the Young Cinema Award at Cannes in 1985.

DANGER ROUTE (Amicus, 1968)—Espionage. *Director:* Seth Holt; *Producers:* Max Rosenberg and Milton Subotsky; *Script:* Meade Roberts, based on the novel *The Eliminator* by Andrew York; *Cinematography:* Harry Waxman; *Music:* John Mayer; *Cast:* Richard Johnson (Jonas Wilde), Carol Lynley (Jocelyn Kirby), Barbara Bouchet (Mari), Sylvia Syms (Barbara Canning), Gordon Jackson (Stem), Diana Dors (Rhoda Gooderich), Harry Andrews (Canning), Maurice Denham (Peter Rovenspur), Sam Wanamaker (Lucinda), David Bauer (Bennett), Robin Bailey (Parsons), and Reg Lye (Balin).

Richard Johnson was one of the actors in consideration for the part of James Bond in the first Bond film *Dr. No* (1962) and the actor's urbane, suave screen persona would have suited the role of 007. In *Danger Route,* this persona is utilized as a plot device as Jonas Wilde charms and exploits a number of women, particularly the sad Rhoda Gooderich. But the film demonstrates that this persona is basically misleading or incomplete as it is used by Wilde to carry out his espionage activities. Otherwise, he is shown as a dour character wanting desperately to escape from his position as a professional killer for the British espionage service.

Danger Route is also different from the Bond series in other ways—it is devoid of gadgets, chases, prolonged action sequences, and the gratuitous sex and violence that increasingly characterized the Bond series after 1964. *Danger Route* is not devoid of sex and violence, but its usage is integral to the plot and, in most cases, neither titillating nor humorous. The use of violence, particularly at the end of *Danger Route* when Wilde deliberately breaks the neck of his girlfriend and enemy agent, Jocelyn Kirby, comes as a shock and few producers today would allow a scene where the central (and most sympathetic) character inflicts such a callous, if justified, action on an unarmed female. The pessimistic tone and complex plotting of *Danger Route* makes it much closer to films such as *The Quiller Memorandum* (1966) and *The Naked Runner* (1967).

The basic plot of *Danger Route* illustrates the film's bleak mood as Wilde, who is periodically employed by the British to kill enemy agents and defectors, learns that Stem, his close friend and business partner, is an international mercenary selling Wilde's services to the highest bidder. Stem's duplicitous instructions to Wilde have caused the deaths of a number of loyal agents. Wilde learns this after he has carried out his latest mission to kill Balin, a defector protected by the Central Intelligence Agency. To execute Balin, Wilde exploits the loneliness of Rhonda Gooderich, a deserted wife working as a housekeeper, so that he can infiltrate an enemy stronghold. Wilde's relationship with other women, including his girlfriend Jocelyn Kirby (Carol Lynley), Mari (Barbara Bouchet) as the agent planted in Wilde's operation by the Americans, and Barbara Canning (Sylvia Syms), the elitist wife of his superior. However these romantic interludes appear perfunctory and do not develop in any satisfactory way—except to emphasize Wilde's sour, ruthless disposition.

After Wilde kills Balin, he is captured by Lucinda, a U.S. operative, who tells Wilde that he is being used by both sides—"some jobs for them, some jobs for us"—Lucinda points to the need to flush out the double agent in the British system who is betraying Wilde. Unlike the polarized thrillers of the 1940s and 1950s, where moral qualities were largely distributed according to political allegiances so that the West was shown as good and the East bad, *Danger Route* dramatizes a more morally and politically complex world where good and evil are the not the product of political systems and different ideologies. Instead, the film presumes a world devoid of moral absolutes where institutions, whatever their ideological bias, are inherently corrupt. "Trust," as Lucinda tells Wilde, "went out in the forties—only someone forgot to tell the British."

DANGER WITHIN (British Lion, 1959)—War. *Director:* Don Chaffey; *Producer:* Colin Lesslie; *Script:* Bryan Forbes, Michael Gilbert, and Frank Harvey Jr., based on the novel *Death in Captivity* by Michael Gilbert; *Cinematography:* Arthur Grant; *Music:* Francis Chagrin; *Cast:* Richard Todd (Lieutenant-Colonel David Baird), Bernard Lee (Lieutenant-Colonel Huxley), Richard Attenborough

(Captain Bunter Phillips), Michael Wilding (Major Charles Marquand), William Franklyn (Captain Tony Long), Donald Houston (Captain Roger Byford), Dennis Price (Captain Rupert Callender), Peter Arne (Captain Benucci), and Terence Alexander (Lieutenant Gibbs).

One of the last of the popular cycle of British prisoner of war films in the 1950s, *Danger Within* reworks many of the narrative conventions of the genre, popularized by films such as *The Colditz Story** (1955). This includes the use of a theatrical performance in both films to distract the enemy while the prisoners escape. This sense of familiarity is reinforced by the casting of such stalwarts as Richard Todd,* Michael Wilding, Donald Houston, and Richard Attenborough* and the use of such character stereotypes as the effeminate theatrical prisoner (Callender), the angry escape organizer (Baird), the sadistic enemy officer (Benucci), and the wily senior officer (Huxley) who, initially, is thought to be too conservative. *Danger Within* knowingly plays with such characters and situations.

Danger Within is set in northern Italy during the summer of 1943. The plot revolves around the repeated failure of escape attempts, much to the frustration of the escape committee comprising David Baird, Bunter Phillips, Roger Byford, and Tony Long. Captain Benucci, who taunts the escapees before shooting them in cold blood, foils each attempt. The ease with which the Italians catch the prisoners convinces Baird, and other members of the escape committee, that there is a traitor. While the audience is given his identity, Captain Tony Long, early in the film, the British prisoners of war only discover the truth just prior to executing their plan to tunnel out of the camp in broad daylight during a performance of *Hamlet.*

One of the distinguishing features of *Danger Within,* compared to the earlier films, is the degree of distrust and hostility within the British community. While there is some initial hostility between John Mills* and his senior officer, Eric Portman,* in *The Colditz Story,* this aspect is intensified between Huxley and Baird. Similarly, while the earlier films assume that all British prisoners wish to escape, this assumption is humorously subverted by Captain Rupert Callender's annoyance when Huxley tells him that the escape attempt must take precedence over his production of *Hamlet.* Similarly, the "knowingness" of the film, coming after so many other prisoner of war films in the 1940s and 1950s, is indicated prior to the film's credits, with documentary footage depicting military destruction and death. As the credits begin, the film cuts to the image of a British solder lying face down in the dirt, presumed dead. At the end of the credits, however, the seemingly dead man's hand comes up from the ground as he casually scratches his bottom before he turns around and moves away.

DARLING (Anglo-Amalgamated, 1965)—Social parable. *Director:* John Schlesinger; *Producers:* Joseph Janni and Victor Lyndon (associate); *Script:* Fredric Raphael; *Cinematography:* Kenneth Higgins; *Music:* John Dankworth; *Cast:* Dirk Bogarde (Robert Gold), Laurence Harvey (Miles Brand), Julie

Christie (Diana Scott), Jose Luis de Villalonga (Cesare), Roland Curram (Malcolm), Basil Henson (Alec Prosser-Jones), and Helen Lindsay (Felicity Prosser-Jones).

Darling was one of the most influential British films of the 1960s. Building on her carefree characterization in *Billy Liar** (1963), Julie Christie,* who headed south to London at the end of *Billy Liar,* emerged from *Darling* with an Academy Award and as a star of considerable power and influence. In *Darling,* Frederic Raphael's script and John Schlesinger's* direction combine to present a morality tale exposing the superficiality of society and the "empty" values of its inhabitants.

This is dramatized through the experiences of Diana Scott, a fashion model, who experiences life through fashion photography, art galleries, charity functions, decadent sex parties, and conspicuous consumption. Along the way, Diana has a less-than-satisfactory relationship with three men—Robert Gold, a liberal television reporter, Miles Brand, a totally self-absorbed advertising executive, and Malcolm, a gay fashion photographer. The film ends with Scott trapped in a loveless marriage as the "trophy" wife of an Italian aristocrat.

Darling signals its intentions with its first scene over the credits, as a billboard showing starving children is replaced by a large-sized close-up of the carefully cultivated image of Diana Scott promoting her life story in a magazine interview. Thus, narcissism replaces social commitment and conscience. This theme is reiterated throughout the film, particularly in the way Scott's voice-over is usually subverted by contrasting visual images that expose her as facile and self-serving. Despite the clear intention of the film, not all members of the audience were repelled by Scott's choice of lifestyle, as Christie explains: "Here was a woman who didn't want to get married, didn't want to have children. . . . Darling wanted to have everything . . . of course she had to be punished for it. But there was an element of possibility for women, of a new way of living, which is why the film was a success."[2]

Scott thus offered women a characterization that combined sexual freedom with power, although she is ultimately punished by Gold's rejection, which consigns her to a life of duty and ritual in a loveless marriage. The journey and her experiences were, for some people, worth the price. Scott's appeal is also enhanced by the fact that just about everybody else in the film is presented in a negative way—from her ritual-bound ultra-conservative parents and sister, to the perversely decadent advertising executive Miles Brand who introduces Scott to a world of orgies and political power. Brand, who is unable to demonstrate any feelings of love and compassion, provides the pretext for Scott to escape from a more "normal" existence with Gold. Yet, as the film suggests, it is more Scott's decision rather than Brand's influence that closes off this possibility as her interest in personal advancement, power, publicity, and wealth is evident long before Brand comes into her life.

Darling was nominated for Best Picture at the 1966 Academy Awards and Christie won Best Actress, Julie Harris won Best Costume Design (black and white), and Frederic Raphael won Best Writing, Story, and Screenplay. Dirk Bogarde* won the 1966 BAFTA Film Award for Best British Actor, Christie for Best British Actress, Raphael for Best British Screenplay, and the film won the 1966 Golden Globe Award for Best English Language Foreign Film. Christie also won the Best Actress Award from the 1966 National Board of Review. At the New York Film Critics Circle Awards, Schlesinger won Best Director, Christie Best Actress, and *Darling* Best Film.

DAUGHTER OF DARKNESS (Paramount British, 1948)—Gothic drama. *Director:* Lance Comfort; *Producers:* Victor Hanbury and James A. Carter (executive); *Script:* Max Catto, based on his play *They Walk Alone; Cinematography:* Stanley Pavey; *Music:* Clifton Parker; *Cast:* Anne Crawford (Bess Stanforth), Maxwell Reed (Dan), Siobhan McKenna (Emmy Beaudine), George Thorpe (Mr. Tallent), Barry Morse (Robert Stanforth), Liam Redmond (Father Corcoran), Honor Blackman (Julie Tallent), David Greene (David Price), Denis Gordon (Saul Trevethick), and Grant Tyler (Larry Tallent).

Daughter of Darkness was released in the same year as a number of critically acclaimed British films, such as *The Winslow Boy,* * *The Fallen Idol,* and *Hamlet,* and it, not surprisingly, disappeared quickly after largely tepid newspaper reviews. Yet, *Daughter of Darkness* is a challenging film that deserves recognition after years of critical neglect, as does its underrated director Lance Comfort.*

It is not difficult to understand the reaction to *Daughter of Darkness* as the film violated many of the canons of critical respectability prized in 1948. For a start, the film is thematically confronting and emotionally challenging and eschews the realist aesthetic that was celebrated by most British critics of the time. The film also denies the customary film presentation whereby the viewer is allowed to relate to a virtuous hero or heroine who is threatened or violated by a person with evil intent. This, with little change, could have been the basis of *Daughter of Darkness* where the evil, Emmy Beaudine, infiltrates and corrupts a conventional British family (the Tallent family). To his credit, Comfort never allows such as simplistic premise to develop.

Daughter of Darkness details the strange story of Emmy Beaudine, a young Irish girl ejected from her village following the demands of the local women. She is sent to work on the Tallent Farm in Yorkshire. Before she leaves Ireland, however, Beaudine meets a boxer, Dan, who works in a traveling carnival. Dan, excited by Beaudine's presence at the ringside, batters his opponent before pursuing Beaudine into the darkness where he is seriously maimed by Beaudine's nails after rejecting his sexual advances. This incident is part of a recurring pattern in the film as Beaudine expresses both love and hate toward her male suitors. Sexual desire repeatedly transforms into sexual violence.

The presentation of Beaudine differs from the traditional conception of the femme fatale, which was popular in both British and Hollywood films in the 1940s. She is as much a victim of her own repressions, as those inflicted on her by a patronizing class system. Unlike protagonists in films such as *Blanche Fury* *

(1947), she does not exploit her sexual powers in attempt to better her social position. Instead, the Tallent Farm seems to offer Beaudine an opportunity to make a new start although the local men on the farm soon fall under her spell. The first murder occurs when Dan's carnival sets up camp near the farm and the Tallents force a reluctant Beaudine to come with them to the carnival. This results in Dan's death. When a local boy also dies, Bess Stanforth, who lives on the farm with her husband Robert, becomes suspicious of Beaudine and her strange ways (such as the mysterious organ playing that takes place in the local church each night) and attempts to evict her from the farm. Beaudine, as retribution for what she feels is a form of victimization, seduces and kills Bess's young brother Larry. Bess retaliates by forcing Beaudine onto the moors at night where Dan's mongrel dog kills her.

The dramatic subtext in *Daughter of Darkness* is overt, involving the sexual repression inflicted on women by repressive social and religious systems. Beaudine, to combat this pernicious code, constructs an alternative world in her head that has little connection to her everyday reality. Her desire for romance and sex is perverted into overwhelming feelings of guilt and self-disgust resulting in sexual violence, a product of her rage and frustration.

Daughter of Darkness, with a budget of two hundred thousand pounds and three weeks of location shooting in Cornwall, was not a financial success and represented a setback to Comfort's career, which saw him relegated to low-budget films in the 1950s and 1960s. Yet the film's mixture of Gothic and horror establishes it as one of the most startling British films of the 1940s. Although it was produced too late in the decade to cash in on the brief vogue for Gothic melodrama in the early and mid-1940s (such as *The Man in Grey** [1943]), it is problematic that such a thematically confronting film would have attracted a large audience at any time.

DAVIES, TERENCE (b. 1945). The union of novelist Edith Wharton and director Terence Davies for *The House of Mirth** (2000) seems, in some ways, quite natural. Davies's cinema is highly disciplined, stark, elegiac, poetic, and deeply critical of aspects of society. He began with a trilogy of black and white shorts: *Children* (1974), *Madonna and Child* (1980), and *Death and Transfiguration* (1983), followed by two (color) feature films, *Distant Voices, Still Lives* (1988) and *The Long Day Closes* (1992). Davies's films are imbued with his formative experiences growing up in a Catholic, working-class family in Liverpool. His memories of his brutal father and protective mother are, in some ways, not totally unlike Gary Oldman's destructive youthful experiences in South London. Whereas Oldman dramatized his early years in the stylized, confrontational realism of *Nil by Mouth** (1997), Davies's experiences have been mediated through a different style, marked by its schematic formalism and languid pacing, a style where memory is presented in a stylized form that emphasizes meaning through a combination of image and, in his early films, radio voices, songs, and other evocative sounds.

In *The House of Mirth,* Davies, after the less than successful attempt to transform these qualities to the U.S. South in *The Neon Bible* (1995), directed one of the great art films. The rich, mediated language of *The House of Mirth* provides a dramatic structure to assimilate the concerns of his earlier films. Wharton's novel of persecution and hypocrisy allows him the opportunity to rework, develop, and dramatize his core concerns. Thus, over four feature films and three shorts he has consolidated his status as an auteur of high quality. *The House of Mirth* was nominated for a BAFTA Award for Best British Film and Davies for Best Director in 2001 by the London Film Critics Circle Award. *The Long Day Closes* and *The Neon Bible* were both nominated at Cannes for the Golden Palm Award, while *Distant Voices, Still Lives* was successful at Cannes in 1988.

FILMS: Children (short, 1974), Madonna and Child (short, 1980), Death and Transfiguration (short, 1983), Distant Voice, Still Lives (1988), The Long Day Closes (1992), The Neon Bible (1995), and The House of Mirth (2000).

THE DAY THE EARTH CAUGHT FIRE (British Lion, 1961)—Science fiction. *Director:* Val Guest; *Producers:* Val Guest and Frank Sherwin Green (associate); *Script:* Wolf Mankowitz and Val Guest; *Cinematography:* Harry Waxman; *Music:* Stanley Black; *Cast:* Janet Munro (Jeannie), Leo McKern (Bill Maguire), Edward Judd (Peter Stenning), Michael Goodliffe (Night Editor), Bernard Braden (News Editor), Reginald Beckwith (Harry), Gene Anderson (May), and Arthur Christiansen (Editor).

Directed by one of the best British genre directors, Val Guest,* *The Day the Earth Caught Fire* hints at, without really exploiting, the East-West tensions of the Cold War. The film adopts a more universal outlook by blaming mankind in general, and scientists in particular, while taking a swipe at the secrecy of the British bureaucracy for hiding news of the catastrophe.

Two simultaneous nuclear explosions at the North and South Poles disturb the earth's orbit, forcing the planet toward the Sun. This news is kept from the public until Peter Stenning, a demoted *Daily Express* reporter, learns the truth from a British Public Service telephone operator (Jeannie). The film's dual narrative strands, Stenning's regeneration after falling from marital and professional grace due to his excessive drinking, and the threat to the world as scientists attempt to restore the earth to its correct orbit by detonating four nuclear explosions, are linked. While Stenning redeems himself, the outcome of the threat to the world is less clear with the *Daily Express* preparing two front page headlines—one proclaiming the success of the explosions ("World Saved"), the other signaling disaster for the earth ("World Doomed"). Ultimately, the sound of birds on the sound track and the final image of a church steeple, combined with Edward Judd's lyrical, semireligious voice-over, is sufficient to suggest a positive outcome.

The Day the Earth Caught Fire is hampered by a small budget resulting in cheap special effects that are combined with newsreel footage. The film also suffers from the use of black and white, rather than color (the opening and closing reels were tinted yellow in the release print). Nevertheless, real-life newspaper editor Arthur Christiansen blends in with the professional actors and *The Day the Earth Caught Fire* is one of the more intelligent science fiction films of this period.

DEAD OF NIGHT (Ealing, 1945)—Supernatural/horror. *Directors:* Alberto Cavalcanti, Charles Crichton, Basil Dearden, and Robert Hamer; *Producers:* Michael Balcon, Sidney Cole (associate), and John Croyden (associate); *Script:* John V. Baines, E. F. Benson, T. E. B. Clarke ("Golfing Story" based on a story by H. G. Wells), and Angus MacPhail; *Cinematographers:* Stan Pavey, Douglas Slocombe, and Jack Parker; *Music:* Georges Auric; *Cast:* Mervyn Johns (Walter Craig), Michael Redgrave (Maxwell Frere), Naunton Wayne (Larry Potter), Basil Radford (George Parratt), Roland Culver (Eliot Foley), Mary Merrall (Mrs. Foley), Googie Withers (Joan Cortland), Ralph Michael (Peter Cortland), Frederick Valk (Dr. van Straaten), Anthony Baird (Hugh Grainger), Sally Ann Howes (Sally O'Hara), Esme Percy (Mr. Rutherford), Peggy Bryan (Mary), Robert Wyndham (Dr. Albury), Miles Matheson (Hearse Driver), and Michael Allen (Jimmy).

This portmanteau film was influential in the development of the horror genre. Later, in the early 1970s specialist horror companies such as Amicus utilized this form. None matched the power of *Dead of Night,* especially the eerie quality of its linking story, directed by Basil Dearden* and written by E. F. Benson. Architect Walter Craig accepts an invitation to visit a house in rural Kent. As soon as he enters the house, Craig experiences an uneasy feeling that he has been there before, a feeling confirmed when he meets other people gathered at the house. Each guest then recounts a supernatural experience.

Racing car driver Hugh Grainger begins by telling his story of waking up in hospital after an accident only to see a horse-driven hearse in the street below. Grainger declines an offer from the driver of the hearse to join him ("room for one more"). The next day, as Grainger goes to board a London bus, he notices that the bus driver was the driver of the hearse and Grainger is invited to board the bus with the same words—"room for one more." Shocked, Grainger declines this offer and the bus subsequently crashes over a bridge, killing all of the passengers.

The story of the hearse driver, directed by Dearden and written by Benson, is followed by "The Haunted Mirror," directed by Robert Hamer* and scripted by John Baines. A young woman, Joan, buys an early Victorian mirror as a present for her fiancé Peter Cortland. When Cortland looks into the mirror, he sees only a room from an earlier period. Joan does not share Peter's vision. After their marriage, Peter's vision disappears. However, it eventually returns accompanied by a change in his attitude, so Joan visits the antique dealer who sold her the mirror. The dealer tells Joan that the mirror's first owner was an active man who, after falling from his horse, was confined to his bedroom. His inactivity caused a rapid deterioration in his mental condition and he starts to suspect that his wife is unfaithful. He kills his wife and then cuts his own throat in front of the mirror. When Joan returns home with this story Peter accuses her of infidelity and attacks her. During her struggle with Peter, Joan looks into the mirror and sees a Victorian room in the mirror. She breaks the spell by shattering the mirror. Peter and Joan now resume a staid, comfortable lifestyle, free of conflict and excitement.

Another guest, young Sally O'Hara, tells of a Christmas party when, during a game of hide-and-seek, she consoles a young boy who is crying. The boy, she subsequently discovers, was murdered some years ago. This ghost story, directed by Alberto Cavalcanti and scripted by Angus MacPhail, is followed by the weakest episode, a long comedy turn by Basil Radford and Naunton Wayne, reprising their sport-obsessed gentlemen from *The Lady Vanishes* (1938) and *Night Train to Munich* (1940). They play a pair of golfing fanatics who both fall in love with Mary, a young woman. After their golfing skills deteriorate, owing to their infatuation with Mary, they decide to settle the issue with a round of golf. George Parratt (Radford) wins, after cheating, so Larry Potter (Wayne) commits suicide in a lake near the golf course. Potter, however, returns to haunt Parratt and he eventually replaces Parratt in Mary's bed.

This labored sketch, directed by Charles Crichton* and scripted by T. E. Clarke, and based on a story by H. G. Wells, precedes the film's most famous segment, the story of the dummy who takes over the consciousness of ventriloquist Maxwell Frere. This results in Frere being involved in a series of violent acts, culminating with the "dummy's" domination of the ventriloquist's mind. This story, directed by Cavalcanti and scripted by Baines, formed the basic premise of Richard Attenborough's* feature film *Magic* (1978), starring Anthony Hopkins.

The film concludes in a symmetrical fashion by reprising the opening minutes. Walter Craig, having strangled the psychiatrist Dr. van Straaten in his nightmare, is woken by a phone call inviting him to visit a house in Kent. As Craig approaches the same house, "The End" titles appear. Music is used to indicate his sense of dread as he enters the house (again).

DEAR MURDERER (Gainsborough, 1947)—Film noir. *Director:* Arthur Crabtree; *Producer:* Betty E. Box; *Script:* Sidney Box and Muriel Box, based on the play by St. John Clowes; *Cinematography:* Stephen Dade; *Music:* Ben Frankel; *Cast:* Eric Portman (Lee Warren), Greta Gynt (Vivien Warren), Dennis Price (Richard Fenton), Maxwell Reed (Jimmy Martin), Jack Warner (Inspector Pembury), Hazel Court (Avis Fenton), Andrew Crawford (Sergeant Fox), and Jane Hylton (Rita).

Although Greta Gynt* complained that Arthur Crabtree was not a "strong director," *Dear Murderer* demonstrates that when the material was good, as in this film, Crabtree could produce an above average melodrama. *Dear Murderer,* based on St. John Clowes's play, is a superior example of the British film noir cycle that was evident in the mid- to late 1940s. The story involves a jealous husband Lee Warren, his unfaithful wife Vivien, Vivien's former lover Richard Fenton, and her current lover Jimmy Martin. Lee, unhinged by his wife's serial infidelity, murders Fenton and then incriminates Martin. Seemingly trapped, Vivien concocts her own scheme to murder her husband, retain his money, and resume her affair with Jimmy.

Although Lee's ingenious murder scheme, and the subsequent game of cat-and-mouse with Inspector Pembury, occupies most of the screen time, Vivien dominates the film. Gynt, one of the few perennial "wicked women" of the British cinema, has one of her best roles as a selfish, sensual woman who subjugates everything, and every one, to her carnal desires.

Unlike most of the femme fatales in U.S. film noir, Vivien wants more than material comforts, she wants sexual satisfaction, a desire that is not met by Lee. This is indicated by a clever sequence of images early in the film—stranded on business in New York, Lee phones his wife in London and seeks reassurance that she still loves him. Vivien, framed by a painting of herself in the background, reassures her husband. However, as she declares her love for him the camera pulls back to show a man's hand (belonging to Jimmy Martin) sliding into the frame to gently touch her shoulder. The narcissistic implications of her painting indicates the self-centered, pleasure-seeking basis of all of her actions.

Later, after Fenton's death and Martin's arrest, Lee presumes that he has the upper hand in his relationship with Vivien. While her initial reaction is to leave her husband with a note addressed to "Dear Murderer," she soon returns. However, another strong image—contrasting areas of light and shadow crisscrossing Vivien's face and body as she sits in front of her triple dressing room mirror—indicates that her return will not be on her husband's terms. Vivien seduces her husband into believing that she is still in love with him while plotting his death so that she may resume her sexual relationship with Martin. As Lee dies from a fatal overdoes of sleeping tablets, Vivien explains: "You've got to die so that I may go on living as I want to." Unfortunately, Inspector Pembury ultimately traps Vivien after she leaves behind an incriminating ring.

The British film noir cycle differed from the Hollywood films in terms of their overall tone. While the U.S. films were intense and melodramatic, the British films often contained their stories of betrayal and murder within a more "civilized" surface. For example, when Lee returns to London from New York to murder Fenton, the two men carry on a polite discourse, despite the fact that Fenton is aware that Lee knows of his affair with Vivien. Even after Lee indicates that he is going to kill Fenton, this sense of civility remains with Lee telling Fenton that he will let him go if he can point out flaws in his plan to murder him. After Fenton fails, Lee chides him by pointing out that "you were a bit of a failure as a lawyer. I'm glad that my life didn't depend on your arguments."

DEARDEN, BASIL (1911–1971)/**RELPH, MICHAEL** (b. 1915). The films of Basil Dearden and Michael Relph, as a director/producer/writer team, from 1943, or officially from 1949, until Dearden's death in a car accident in 1971, included a series of high-quality "socially conscious" genre films. Relph described them as more than just "entertainment" films. This approach is evident in one of their first films, *Frieda* (1947), a melodrama that exposed less desirable aspects of postwar British society. It dramatizes the reaction of a British country town to a young German woman (Mai Zetterling) who accompanies her British prisoner of war husband (David Farrar*) to his hometown during World War II. In *The Blue Lamp** (1950), a commercially successful film for Ealing, Dearden and Relph, working from a script from T. E. B. Clarke and a story by Ted Willis, used the British police film to point to the dangers of a "new breed" of postwar criminal. A high point in this blend of entertainment and overt social discourse occurred at the end of the decade with *Sapphire* (1959), a murder mystery that used racial prejudice as the motivation for the death of a young music student.

Two years later, Dearden directed and Relph produced *Victim** (1961), a crime film that included an attack on homophobia within its more generic elements. Although the film is careful to obscure the exact nature of the relationship between Dirk Bogarde* and a young gay man who kills himself, it does include a scene where Bogarde explains the intensity of his sexual attraction for the man in a painful confession to his wife (Sylvia Syms). *Victim* also offers a critique of the prevailing British law that made homosexuality an offense, punishable by a prison sentence. Other films that blended generic conventions with strong social themes included *The Ship that Died of Shame* (1955), a thinly veiled critique of postwar disillusionment in Britain, and *Life for Ruth* (1962), which dramatized the negative effects of religious fundamentalism.

Dearden and Relph had separate careers prior to forming their partnership in 1943 at Ealing. Dearden, born Basil Dear, changed his name to avoid confusion with director Basil Dean when he worked as stage manager to Dean. Dearden followed Dean to Ealing, where Dearden had the opportunity to work as a screenwriter, production manager, associate producer, and co-director of three Will Hay* comedies (beginning with *The Black Sheep of Whitehall* [1941]). With *The Bells Go Down* (1943), a sentimental drama focusing on the activities of a volunteer fire unit, and the allegorical drama *Halfway House* (1943), Dearden assumed sole directorial responsibilities.

Relph was the art director on *The Bells Go Down,* and on subsequent films directed by Dearden (such as *They Came to a City* [1944], *Dead of Night** [1945], *The Captive Heart** [1946], and *Saraband for Dead Lovers* [1948]). He started as an apprentice art director with Michael Balcon at Gaumont-British in 1932, before moving to Warner Brothers (British) and then to Ealing as a set designer and art director. In 1943, Alberto Cavalcanti, Ealing director (and producer of *Halfway House*), suggested to Balcon that Relph team with Dearden on future projects. Relph, however, did not receive a producer's credit until *The Captive Heart* because Balcon appropriated the "producer's" credit on all Ealing productions for many years. In 1948, Relph also produced *Kind Hearts and Coronets.**

Relph directed two films, *Davy* (1958) and *Rockets Galore* (1958), with Dearden acting as producer. Although Relph was credited as co-director on *The Gentle Gunman* (1952), *The Square Ring* (1953), and *Out of the Clouds* (1955), this was more an attempt by Dearden to acknowledge Relph's creative input by giving him a co-director credit. Otherwise, Relph was primarily a designer and producer of their films. There was little of substance from Relph after Dearden's death, but during their peak years of creativity from the late 1940s to the early 1960s, Dearden and Relph were a formidable team. Relph was nominated for Best Art Direction for *Saraband for Dead Lovers* at the 1950 Academy Awards, and *Sapphire* won Best British Film at the 1960 BAFTA Film Awards.

FILMS: Basil Dearden (as director): The Black Sheep of Whitehall (codir., 1941), The Goose Steps Out (codir., 1942), My Learned Friend (codir., 1943), The Bells Go Down (1943), The Halfway House (1943), They Came to a City (1944), and Dead of Night (1945).

Basil Dearden (as director) and Michael Relph (as producer or associate producer): The Captive Heart (1946), Frieda (1947), Saraband for Dead Lovers (1948), Train of Events (1949), The Blue Lamp (1949), Pool of London (1950), Cage of Gold (1950), I Believe in You (1951), The Gentle Gunman (1952), The Square Ring (1953), The Rainbow Jacket (1954), The Ship that Died of Shame (1955), Out of the Clouds (1955), Who Done It? (1956), The Green Man (uncredited, 1956), The Violent Playground (1957), The Smallest Show on Earth (1957), Sapphire (1959), The League of Gentlemen (1959), Desert Mice (1959), Man in the Moon (1960), Victim (1961), The Secret Partner (1961), All Night Long (1961), Life for Ruth (1962), A Place to Go (1963), The Mind Benders (1963), Woman of Straw (1964), Masquerade (1965), Khartoum (1966), Only When I Larf (1968), The Assassination Bureau (1968), and The Man Who Haunted Himself (1970).

Michael Relph (as director) and Basil Dearden (as producer): Davy (1957), and Rockets Galore (1958).

DEFENCE OF THE REALM (Hemdale, 1985)—Thriller. *Director:* David Dury; *Producers:* Robin Douet, Lynda Myles, and David Puttnam (executive); *Script:* Martin Stellman; *Cinematography:* Roger Deakins; *Music:* Richard Harvey; *Cast:* Gabriel Byrne (Nick Mullen), Greta Scacchi (Nina Beckman), Denholm Elliott (Vernon Bayliss), Ian Bannen (Dennis Markham), Fulton Mackay (Victor Kinsbrook), Bill Paterson (Jack Macleod), David Calder (Harry Champion), Frederick Treves (Arnold Reece), and Robbie Coltrane (Leo McAskey).

The paranoid thriller has long been associated with the post-Watergate Hollywood cinema, with films such as *The Parallax View* (1974) and *All the President's Men* (1976). *Defence of the Realm* shares many of the attributes of these films, particularly *All The President's Men,* with its complex story line involving the investigation of deep-seated political corruption. The film utilizes the distinctive imagery of dark, threatening compositions that hint at danger or evil lurking just beyond the edge of each frame.

When reporter Nick Mullen uncovers a story linking prominent left-wing British politician Dennis Markham with a prostitute and East German spy, his newspaper employers reward him with a front page story and a by-line. Later, when pressure is mounting to force the politician to resign his parliamentary seat, Mullen learns from veteran journalist Vernon Bayliss that Markham may have been set up and that there is a more significant story beyond the politician's fall from grace. Mullen, basking in the glory of his scoop, is not convinced. However, after Bayliss dies Mullen, with the assistance of Nina Beckman, Markham's secretary, and an anonymous informer, realizes that there has been an attempt to silence the disgraced left-wing politician. Slowly, they uncover a widespread conspiracy involving a cover-up of the near crash of a U.S. nuclear bomber in England.

Director David Dury, with his background in television documentary films, efficiently utilizes the devices and conventions of this genre. The film, with its use of television excerpts and eavesdropping devices is reminiscent of *The Conversation* (1974). The ending, however, is too perfunctory, even for a paranoid thriller. The building, with Mullen and Beckman inside, explodes after we learn that Mullen has successfully exposed the cover-up by ignoring the British press in favor of European newspapers. *Defence of the Realm* is a fine contribution to the genre and deserved a much wider audience.

DENCH, JUDI (b. 1934). Judi Dench's stated preference for the stage over film and television is well known although she has been relatively prolific since *Mrs. Brown* in 1997. Initially, she was wary because film and television, she felt, restricted the potential for an actor to hone and develop a character over successive performances, and because the best take, from an actor's point of view, may not necessarily be the one used in the film. Dench cites her experience on *Room with a View* (1985), where she was required to go mad and attack a man selling postcards. When director James Ivory viewed the rushes, he praised Dench's performance—but the scene never appeared in the film. This was due, allegedly, to the fact that the central character, played by Helena Bonham Carter,* was having an "off day."[3]

Dench, born in York, studied at London's Central School of Speech and Drama before making her stage debut in 1957. Her film debut was in 1964 in the Charles Crichton* thriller *The Third Secret,* starring Stephen Boyd and Jack Hawkins.* She followed with *A Study in Terror* (1965), an exploitative mixture of horror and mystery with Sherlock Holmes investigating murders committed by Jack the Ripper. Dench was more prominent in her second film for Crichton, *He Who Rides the Tiger* (1965), as the romantic interest in this tale of a cat burglar. Her most notable film role in the 1960s was in the ultra low-budget *Four in the Morning* (1965) as a housewife trapped by the ever-constant demands of her baby. The film's episodic structure and documentary and improvised style appealed to Dench as it approximated the nature of the theatrical experience. Her performance won the 1966 BAFTA Award for Most Promising Newcomer.

As Dench has not been dependent on film or television for establishing and maintaining an acting career, she has been selective in her choice of film roles, although the location and timing of the production are also important considerations. As she explains, "I don't mind doing a film in summer but I don't want to do one in winter—not when I have to get up at half past four in the morning."[4] However, after the death of her husband Dench plunged herself into work and even agreed to participate in *The Shipping News* (2002), co-starring Kevin Spacey and Julianne Moore, even though it was filmed in freezing conditions in Newfoundland.

Dench has a rich body of film and television work—including her performance as the wife of Anthony Hopkins in *84 Charing Cross Road* (1987), a role that was added for the film, Mistress Quickly in *Henry V* (1989), as Arabella in *Tea with Mussolini* (1999), one of a group of expatriate British women who raise a young boy in Florence in the 1930s, and, in one of her best screen roles to date, as Queen Victoria in *Mrs. Brown* (1997) who is comforted by Highland horseman John Brown (Billy Connolly) after the death of her husband. Recently, her performance as (the older) Iris Murdoch in *Iris* (2002) was well received. A more unusual role for Dench was an ongoing cameo as M in the long-running James Bond series, beginning with *GoldenEye* in 1995, followed by *Tomorrow Never Dies* (1997) and *The World Is Not Enough* (1999). Dench also won an Academy Award for a (brief) supporting role as Queen Elizabeth in *Shakespeare in Love* (1998).

Since the early 1980s, Dench has appeared regularly on television. This included prestige productions such as *Mr. and Mrs. Edgehill* (1985), opposite husband Michael Williams in *A Fine Romance,* and the long-running award-winning situation comedy, *As Time Goes By,* co-starring Dench with Geoffrey Palmer as the middle-aged couple who reignite their teenage romance following a chance meeting. Another notable made-for-television film for Dench was *The Last of the Blonde Bombshells* (2000), a bittersweet romantic story of a recently widowed middle-aged woman who decides to reform her 1940s (mostly) female swing band. This film reunited Dench with Ian Holm, who was a colleague at Stratford. He also co-starred with her in *Wetherby* (1985) and *Mr. and Mrs. Edgehill.*

In 1996, Dench was the first performer to win two Olivier Awards for two different roles. She was awarded the Order of the British Empire in 1970 and made a dame of the British Empire in 1988. She was nominated for an Academy Award for *Mrs. Brown* and for *Chocolat* (2000). She won a BAFTA Television Award for the *A Fine Romance* (1981), the Best Actress BAFTA Award for *Mrs. Brown,* the 2001 Best Actress Television Award for *The Last of the Blonde Bombshells,* and Best Performance by an Actress for *Iris* at the 2002 BAFTA Awards, as well as receiving BAFTA nominations for Best Supporting Actress for *Wetherby,* for *84 Charing Cross Road,* for *A Handful of Dust*, and for *Chocolat.*

FILMS: The Third Secret (1964), A Study in Terror (1965), He Who Rides the Tiger (1965), Four in the Morning (1966), A Midsummer Night's Dream (1968), Luther (1973), Dead Cert (1974), Wetherby (1985), A Room with a View (1985), The Angelic Conversation (narr., 1985), 84 Charing Cross Road (1986), A Handful of Dust (1987), Henry V (1989), Jack and Sarah (1994), GoldenEye (1995), Hamlet (1996), Mrs. Brown (1997), Tomorrow Never Dies (1997), Shakespeare in Love (1998), Tea with Mussolini (1999), The World Is Not Enough (1999), Chocolat (2000), Iris (2001), The Shipping News (2002), and The Importance of Being Earnest (2002).

THE DEVIL RIDES OUT (Hammer, 1968)—Horror. *Director:* Terence Fisher; *Producer:* Anthony Nelson Keys; *Script:* Richard Matheson, based on the novel by Dennis Wheatley; *Cinematography:* Arthur Grant; *Music:* James Bernard; *Cast:* Christopher Lee (Duc de Richleau), Charles Gray (Mocata), Nike Arrighi (Tanith), Leon Greene (Rex Van Ryn), Patrick Mower (Simon Aaron), Paul

Eddington (Richard), Sarah Lawson (Marie), Rosalyn Landor (Peggy), and Gwen Ffrangcon Davies (Countess).

Director Terence Fisher* was disappointed with his inability to develop the love interest between Rex Van Ryn and Tanith in *The Devil Rides Out*. Fisher felt that this weakened the ability of the audience to relate to these characters. However, he underestimated the many positive aspects of the film—particularly Christopher Lee's* commanding performance as Duc de Richleau, the French aristocrat who battles an equally powerful figure, Mocata, for the soul of two vulnerable people, de Richleau's friend Simon Aaron and a young woman Tanith.

Lee, after many years as Dracula, or Dracula surrogates, was finally allowed to bring his characteristic qualities of strength, authority, power, and determination to a heroic character. Fortunately, Charles Gray, in his best screen role, was cast opposite Lee as the film required both a strong hero and a strong villain. *The Devil Rides Out* dramatizes Fisher's fascination for the elemental conflict between Good and Evil. Nowhere is this better illustrated than the long suspenseful sequence when de Richleau, Richard, Peggy, and Simon spend a terrifying night within a pentagram while the Devil tries to lure one of them into breaking the circle. The Devil's use of sentiment, an apparition of Richard and Marie's daughter Peggy calling to her parents, and terror, a gigantic tarantula threatening both the group and "Peggy," precedes his appearance on horseback in the room in an effort to fragment the people within the pentagram.

Based on Dennis Wheatley's novel, the narrative structure of *The Devil Rides Out* resembles the episodic pattern of the Saturday afternoon serials, with its three-part pattern of threat/climax/renewed threat. The film's strong visual appeal was made possible because Hammer provided a larger than usual budget so that the film could have a period (1925) setting—Fisher always preferred period settings for his "fantasy" films as he maintained that this assisted audience acceptance of the "grim fairy tale" aspects. Unfortunately, *The Devil Rides Out* was not a commercial success in the United States, an important market for Hammer's films, and, after one more Wheatley adaptation (*The Lost Continent* [1968]), a planned series based on his novels was dropped.

THE DEVILS (Warner Brothers, 1971)—Religious drama. *Director:* Ken Russell; *Producers:* Ken Russell, Robert H. Solo, and Roy Baird (associate); *Script:* Ken Russell, based on the play by John Whiting and the novel *The Devils of Loudun* by Aldous Huxley; *Cinematography:* David Watkin; *Music:* Peter Maxwell Davies; *Cast:* Vanessa Redgrave (Sister Jeanne), Oliver Reed (Urbain Grandier), Dudley Sutton (Baron De Laudardemont), Max Adrian (Ibert), Gemma Jones (Madelaine), Murray Melvin (Mignon), Michael Gothard (Father Barre), Christopher Logue (Cardinal Richelieu), Georgina Hale (Philippe), Brian Murphy (Adam), and Graham Armitage (Louis XIII).

An opening title to *The Devils* reminds the audience that the film was based on actual people and historical events. Ken Russell,* however, spends the rest of the film eradicating any sense of historical veracity. Although the film is based on

Aldous Huxley's novel and John Whiting's play, the film is clearly a Russell production and audiences and reviewers reacted accordingly. The critical response was polarized between repulsion and adoration. Russell, in close collaboration with Derek Jarman's sets, provided a very stylized interpretation.

When a Catholic priest, Urbain Grandier, is made governor of the fortified city of Loudun, with its mixed Protestant and Catholic population, he incurs the wrath of Baron De Laudardemont, who represents Cardinal Richelieu. Grandier, a notorious womanizer, is then confronted with false charges that he molested Mother Superior, Sister Jeanne, and infected her with demons. He is burned at the stake, thus allowing De Laudardemont to raze Loudun.

While Oliver Reed attempts a realistic presentation of the victimized priest, his performance is swamped by Russell's excessive presentation. This excess extends to stylized performances from the supporting cast and historically absurd costumes—the witch-hunter, Father Barre, with his long blonde hair and John Lennon glasses, for example, is both historically and dramatically inappropriate. Unfortunately, an opportunity to show the association between religious hysteria and political machinations is lost.

The Devils, released by Warner Brothers, was symptomatic of a number of films released in the early 1970s during a period of rapid liberalization of the censorship process. This encouraged filmmakers to explore "adult" films such as *Straw Dogs* (1971), *A Clockwork Orange* (1971), *Deliverance* (1972), and *Last Tango in Paris* (1973). However, *The Devils* was an excessive reaction to this liberalization and did not have the compensating thematic complexity to warrant its confronting presentation.

DICKINSON, THOROLD (1903–1984). Thorold Dickinson, educated at Oxford University, had a busy career although he made relatively few feature films. Dickinson's temperament was not suited to that of the journeyman director who was prepared to work on virtually any project given to him. Instead, his films often emanated from his political interests, a quality that did not always serve him well. For example, *Men of Two Worlds* (1946) suffers from an earnestness in its tale of superstition and education in an African village. On the other hand, *Gaslight** (1940) and *The Queen of Spades* (1949), two costume films, provided the necessary generic structure for Dickinson to produce his best work.

Gaslight, Dickinson's version of Patrick Hamilton's play, preceded the more famous MGM version by five years and yet Dickinson's film is superior to the Hollywood version, capturing the pervasive sadism in this Gothic story more expertly than George Cukor's version. Even MGM realized the superiority of Dickinson's film by trying to destroy the negative of the British version before the release of its 1944 film.

Dickinson began his career with Paris-based George Pearson in the mid-1920s and over the next few years he worked as an editor, production manager, and assistant director before directing his first film, *High Command,* in 1937. This starred Lionel Atwill in a story of adultery and murder in a West African fortress.

Dickinson went to Spain during its civil war for two documentaries in 1938, followed by the enjoyable murder-mystery *The Arsenal Stadium Mystery** (1939). Here, Dickinson undermined the formulaic elements of the story by focusing more on the eccentric behavior of Leslie Banks,* a Scotland Yard detective. During World War II, he supervised and directed military training films and one of these films, *Next of Kin* (1942), received a theatrical release. After the war, Dickinson directed *Secret People* (1952), an espionage drama concerning the assassination of a fascist dictator by left-wing migrants in prewar London. In 1952, Lindsay Anderson* published a book on the *Making a Film: The Story of Secret People.* Dickinson then left Britain for Israel to become an adviser on film and he directed his final feature film, *Hill 24 Doesn't Answer* (1955), in Israel.

Although Dickinson's output was sparse, he contributed to the film community in many other ways—including a long period as vice president of the Association of Cine-Technicians from 1936 to 1953, as director of the United Nations Office of Public Information from 1956 to 1960, where he supervised a number of UN documentaries, and as a film academic from 1960, becoming Britain's first professor of film in 1967. Dickinson published *A Discovery of Cinema* in 1971 and died in 1984.

FILMS: The High Command (1937), Spanish ABC (codir., doc.,1938), Behind Spanish Lines (codir., doc., 1938), The Arsenal Stadium Mystery (1939), Gaslight (1940), Westward Ho (doc., 1940), Yesterday Is over Your Shoulder (doc., 1940), The Prime Minister (1941), Next of Kin (1942), Men of Two Worlds (1946), The Queen of Spades (1949), Secret People (1952), The Red Ground (doc., 1953), and Hill 24 Doesn't Answer (1955).

DIVORCING JACK (BBC Films/Winchester Films/Scala Productions/Arts Council of England/Arts Council of Northern Ireland, 1998)—Black comedy/thriller. *Director:* David Caffrey; *Producers:* Robert Cooper, Georges Benayoun (coproducer), Frank Manion (coproducer), Chris Craib (coexecutive), Marina Gefter (coexecutive), Gary Smith (coexecutive), David M. Thompson (executive), Stephen Woolley (executive), and Nik Powell (executive); *Script:* Colin Bateman, based on his novel; *Cinematography:* James Welland; *Music:* Adrian Johnston; *Cast:* David Thewlis (Dan Starkey), Rachel Griffiths (Lee Cooper), Jason Isaacs (Cow Pat Keegan), Laura Fraser (Margaret), Richard Gant (Charles Parker), Laine Megaw (Patricia), Bronagh Gallagher (Taxi Driver), Robert Lindsay (Michael Brinn), and Kitty Aldridge (Agnes Brinn).

Set in the near future, Belfast 1999 as it prepares for independent elections, Dan Starkey, satirical journalist, serious drinker, and irresponsible husband, meets Margaret, an arts student, in a park and takes her to a party at his house. When Dan's wife Patricia kicks him out, Dan spends the night with Margaret. The following night Dan returns from the fish and chip shop to find Margaret has been shot a number of times. Before she dies, she whispers what sounds like "divorcing Jack" to Dan. Distressed, Dan then attacks and kills a figure coming up the stairs, who turns out to be Margaret's mother. Chased by the police and various Irish paramilitary groups, Dan sets out to find Margaret's killer, which leads him into a political conspiracy involving an incriminating audio tape and the man likely to be Northern Ireland's first prime minister. David Caffrey skillfully blends the conventions of the chase film and "paranoid" conspiracy, overlaid with a strong strand of black humor.

Nothing is sacred in the film, including the more serious aspects of the situation in Northern Ireland, a factor that alienated some critics who complained such material should not form the basis for a comedy. Colin Bateman's literate script, based on the novel he wrote while working as a satirical journalist for a newspaper, favors no side of the conflict. The only speech occurs at the film's climax when Dan believes he is about to be killed. His reaction is to expose the opportunism of politicians, such as the film's "savior" figure, Michael Brinn, and the senseless violence of the paramilitary groups.

Divorcing Jack is never sentimental, the pace never falters, and David Thewlis is superb as the cynical journalist forced to confront the harsh realities of a desperate situation. While Dan's self-image is found in a film poster on his wall—*Destry Rides Again*—the film repudiates such romantic perceptions. Instead, Bronagh Gallager, the foul-mouthed taxi driver who appears at the start and end of the film, provides a more reliable indication of the film's overall tone. Thewlis was nominated for the Best Performance by a British Actor in an Independent Film at the 1998 British Independent Film Awards and both Caffrey and Bateman won their categories at the 1999 Fantasporto Awards.

DOCTOR AT SEA (Rank, 1955)—Comedy. *Director:* Ralph Thomas; *Producer:* Betty E. Box; *Script:* Jack Davies and Nicholas Phipps, adaptation by Richard Gordon; *Cinematography:* Ernest Steward; *Music:* Bruce Montgomery; *Cast:* Dirk Bogarde (Dr. Simon Sparrow), Brigitte Bardot (Helene Colbert), James Robertson Justice (Captain Hogg), Brenda de Banzie (Muriel Mallet), Maurice Denham (Easter), Michael Medwin (Trail), Hubert Gregg (Archer), James Kenney (Fellowes), Raymond Huntley (Captain Beamish), Geoffrey Keen (Hornbeam), George Coulouris (Carpenter), Jill Adams (Jill), Joan Sims (Wendy), and Noel Purcell (Corbie).

Although *Doctor at Sea* was released uncut by Republic Pictures in the United States in 1956, the U.S. censor, the Production Code Administration, regretted that a "bad breast exposure" of Brigitte Bardot in *Doctor at Sea* proved impossible to eliminate.[5] This incident provided one of the few exciting moments in this mild sequel to *Doctor in the House* (1954). The *Doctor* series were significant in establishing Dirk Bogarde as a major British film star and producer Betty E. Box fought for him in the role of Simon Sparrow at a time when, Bogarde claimed, Rank Studios believed he could only play "spivs and Cockneys."[6]

Simon Sparrow is forced to take a job as a doctor aboard the SS *Lotus*, bound for South America, to avoid the amorous advances of the daughter of his employer. A cargo ship, Sparrow reasons, offers the advantage of no passengers, hence no women. Sparrow's subsequent romance with Brigitte Bardot (who is wasted in her first English language film) is remarkably tame. Despite the female interest in him, Sparrow's most exciting adventure is getting drunk with a fellow officer in an all-night binge and finishing up in jail.

James Robertson Justice performs the same function in *Doctor at Sea* as he did in *Doctor in the House* (as Lancelot Spratt, the tyrannical head of St. Swithin's hospital). The only difference is a change of name. In *Doctor at Sea,* he plays Captain Hogg, who, faced with the prospect of marrying Muriel Mallet, the "man-hungry" daughter of the owner of the shipping line, gets drunk and goes berserk at the end of the film. The film's script, by Jack Davies and Nicholas Phipps, was nominated for a BAFTA Film Award in 1956.

DOCTOR IN THE HOUSE (Rank, 1954)—Comedy. *Director:* Ralph Thomas; *Producer:* Betty E. Box; *Script:* Richard Gordon and Nicholas Phipps, based on Richard Gordon's novel; *Cinematography:* Ernest W. Steward; *Music:* Bruce Montgomery. *Cast:* Dirk Bogarde (Simon Sparrow), Muriel Pavlow (Joy), Kenneth More (Richard Grimsdyke), Donald Sinden (Benskin), Kay Kendall (Isobel), James Robertson Justice (Lancelot Spratt), Donald Houston (Taffy), Suzanne Cloutier (Stella), Geoffrey Keen (Dean), and Nicholas Phipps (Magistrate).

*Genevieve,** costarring John Gregson, Dinah Sheridan, Kenneth More,* and Kay Kendall, was the top grossing British film in 1953. *Doctor in the House,* costarring Dirk Bogarde,* More, Muriel Pavlow, and Donald Sinden, was the top grossing film of 1954. Both films were cosy and professional, with a nonconfrontational sense of humor—even though the hierarchy at Rank (namely Sir John Davis and Earl St. John) were wary of financing them. Both films also marked important stages in the careers of Bogarde and More. Bogarde, as the nervous, sensitive medical student Simon Sparrow, gently romances Pavlow, delivers a baby, and finally graduates, unlike More's Richard Grimsdyke and Sinden's Benskin.

Bogarde also emerged from this film a genuine film star, the passive, stolid leading man Rank wanted him to be, eliminating the more dangerous, morally problematic traits of his earlier roles. The success of this film was also important in consolidating More's career after a strong showing in *Genevieve*—More won the 1955 BAFTA Best Actor Award for *Doctor in the House* as Grimsdyke, a perennial student living off his grandmother's £1,000 a year allowance. The self-confident, caring aura he exudes throughout the film, a more positive characterization than his mildly lecherous Ambrose Claverhouse in *Genevieve,* would serve him well in the next few years as Douglas Bader in *Reach for the Sky* (1956) and the resourceful butler in *The Admirable Crichton* (1957).

The film's simple plot places Sparrow, the new student at St. Swithin's teaching hospital, with repeat students—Grimsdyke, and his Austrian fiancée Stella, the (mildly) womanizing Benskin, and the rugby fanatic Taffy. With an authoritarian, cold-hearted dean, authoritarian, warm-hearted Chief Surgeon Lancelot Spratt, a predictable story, gentle humor, and middle-class values, the film was enormously successful, topping the box office for 1954 and winning the Best British Film Award at the 1954 BAFTA Film Awards. There were six follow-up films and a television series. Why? Director Ralph Thomas explained that the film was about something that people, up to that time, held in awe—doctors and hospitals. *Doctor in the House,* Thomas maintains, broke through that awe by finding humor in familiar medical situations. Also, Thomas points out, the *Doctor* films provided a more "realistic" form of comedy than the Ealing films of the late 1940s and early 1950s and the bawdy, "seaside postcard" humor of the *Carry On* series.[7]

DONAT, ROBERT (1905–1958). Despite a lifelong fight against chronic asthma and self-doubt, Robert Donat was one of the best British screen actors. After taking elocution lessons to overcome a stutter when he was eleven, Donat developed a classically trained speaking voice that was used to advantage in his films. At a young age he performed in repertory theater before making his London stage debut in 1930. After two minor films, Donat's breakthrough came with a supporting role as Thomas Culpepper in *The Private Life of Henry VIII** (1933). The film was a major commercial success, particularly in the United States, where Donat was cast in the lead role in the Hollywood production of *The Count of Monte Cristo* (1934). Although Donat was selected by Warner Brothers to star in its large-scale swashbuckler *Captain Blood* (1935), he withdrew just before shooting began, leaving the way open to Errol Flynn to star in his first major role.

Donat alternated between the stage and the British cinema for the rest of the 1930s, appearing in a number of outstanding films, particularly as Richard Hannay in Alfred Hitchcock's* masterly thriller *The Thirty-Nine Steps* (1935). He was the archetypal Hitchcockian hero, able to expertly deliver a mixture of comedy and sex appeal. After *Knight without Armour* (1937), costarring Marlene Dietrich, Donat appeared in MGM films produced in London that established him as a major international film star: *The Citadel* (1938), the A. J. Cronin story of a doctor forced to examine his ideals after material desires distort his outlook, and *Goodbye, Mr. Chips* (1939), a sentimental tale of dedication and sacrifice by a British school master. His performance in this latter film, where he was required to age from his mid-twenties to his eighties, won him the 1940 Oscar for Best Actor. This followed his Oscar nomination for Best Actor for *The Citadel* in 1939.

The 1940s and 1950s were not as rewarding as poor health restricted his career. Nevertheless, he was very effective as Sir Robert Morton, the conservative barrister and politician who defends a boy unjustly charged with stealing a five-shilling postal order in *The Winslow Boy** (1948). The script by Terence Rattigan and Anatole de Grunwald, based on Rattigan's play, provided Donat with another opportunity to demonstrate his expert delivery of well-written lines. Donat directed himself in a screen version of *The Cure for Love* (1950). He died soon after telling Ingrid Bergman in *The Inn of the Sixth Happiness* (1958) that "We shall not see each other again, I think. Farewell."

FILMS: Men of Tomorrow (1932), That Night in London (1932), The Private Life of Henry VIII (1933), Cash (1933), The Count of Monte Cristo (1934), The Thirty-Nine Steps (1935), The Ghost Goes West (1935), Knight without Armour (1937), The Citadel (1938), Goodbye, Mr. Chips (1939), The Young Mr. Pitt (1942), The New Lot (1943), The

Adventures of Tartu (1943), Perfect Strangers (1945), Captain Boycott (1947), The British—Are They Artistic? (short, 1947), The Winslow Boy (1948), The Cure for Love (1950), The Magic Box (1951), Royal Heritage (narr., 1952), Lease of Life (1954), The Stained Glass at Fairford (voice, 1956), and The Inn of the Sixth Happiness (1958).

DON'T LOOK NOW (British Lion, 1973)—Psychological thriller. *Director:* Nicholas Roeg; *Producers:* Peter Katz, Frederick Muller, Steve Previn, and Anthony B. Unger (executive); *Script:* Chris Byrant and Allan Scott, based on the story by Daphne DuMaurier; *Cinematography:* Anthony Richmond; *Music:* Pino Donaggio; *Cast:* Julie Christie (Laura Baxter), Donald Sutherland (John Baxter), Hilary Mason (Heather), Clelia Matania (Wendy), and Massimo Serato (Bishop Barbarrigo).

One of the most profoundly disturbing films in the British cinema, *Don't Look Now* still evokes a mixture of terror and fascination nearly thirty years after its release. The film was also Nicholas Roeg's* most coherent, thematically power-ful film that, like many of his films, benefited from its complex juxtaposition of images and sounds, time and space.

John Baxter and his wife Laura move to Venice after the death of their daugh-ter Christine, who drowned in a pond near the family home in England. John is hired to restore a sixteenth-century church in Venice and during a visit to a local restaurant Laura meets two English women, Wendy and her blind sister Heather, who is a psychic. Heather tells Laura that she has seen Christine in a vision and that she also fears for the safety of John in Venice. When their son (Baxter) is injured in an accident at his English school, Laura flies home. During her absence, John sees Laura on a funeral boat with Heather and Wendy, although she is in England, not Venice.

John begins following a small person in a red raincoat—similar to the one worn by his daughter when she died—along the long dark passages throughout Venice. When John finally catches up with the red raincoat it turns out to be a murderous dwarf who kills John with his knife. The film closes with a reprise of the earlier image of Laura, in black, on the funeral boat with Wendy and Heather and the realization that John's earlier "vision" was, in fact, a flash-forward to his own funeral. This summary does not do justice to the film as Roeg constantly intrigues with his complex association of images—some of which counterpoint the dramatic logic of the story while providing resonances of other scenes. Ironi-cally, John, who is shown to possess a visionary gift like Heather, denies this attribute, which leads to his death. Laura, on the other hand, who accepts Heather's visions, has no such ability.

Roeg, with his first two images, signals his determination not to be constrained by classical conventions regarding the presentation of time and space. The first shot zooms in on the pond where Christine will die followed by small points of light through a screened window. The first image is accompanied by the sound of rain while a man is heard humming and the sound of a church bell. This second image refers to a future scene of John working in his hotel room in Venice. The film then returns to a more sequential pattern, ending with Christine's death in the pond. Later, Roeg alternates images of John and Laura having sexual intercourse with shots of their dressing afterwards to suggest the ease and normality of their relationship.

More complex associations emanate from the Roeg's use of two white and red toy balls during the film—the white ball refers to Christine and her death in the pond as she tries to retrieve the ball, followed by the use of a second white ball signalling her son's recovery in hospital when a young boy is shown playing with his ball. The red ball, on the other hand, invokes more sinister feelings—created not only in the red coat worn by the dwarf, but also the red wine that spreads across John's slide photograph as his daughter dies in the pond.

The high quality of the film was recognized at the 1974 BAFTA Film Awards with a Best Director Award for Roeg, a Best Actor Award for Donald Sutherland, Best Actress for Julie Christie,* and Best Cinematography for Anthony Richmond. The film was also nominated for Best Film and Graeme Clifford for Best Film Editing.

DORS, DIANA (1931–1984). Born Diana Fluck in Swindon in 1931, her stunning figure and facial beauty facilitated her entry into the British film industry at the age of fifteen playing characters much older than her real age. Yet, the industry did not know what to do with this talented youngster and her early roles, such as her brief appearance as a nightclub "hostess" in *Dancing with Crime* (1947), reinforced the "miniature Mae West" tag that curtailed her opportunities as an actress for most of her career.

Even after 1950, and her early Rank period, Diana Dors was restricted by the kinds of roles offered by the studio. She had to leave Rank for Associated British Picture Corporation to win her most coveted role, the convicted murderess in *Yield to the Night* (1956). Otherwise, there was little variety from the playful, teasing sexuality evident in films such as *Value for Money* (1955), where Dors appears as a mercenary showgirl, to the more seriously sexual Vicki in *Passport to Shame* (1958). Dors contributed to this persona in the 1950s by participating in numerous stunts and "photo opportunities," the most notable being the so-called mink bikini (which was rabbit), which Dors used to attract photographers during the Venice Film Festival. Also, Dors told reporters that she was the "only sex symbol England produced since Lady Godiva." Consequently, she was often linked, in the mind of the general population, with less talented British performers such as Sabrina. This was reinforced by her publicity tag as the "English Marilyn Monroe," an image compounded by appearances in film such as *An Alligator Named Daisy* (1955) opposite Donald Sinden.

There were, however, a few roles of substance, especially *A Kid for Two Farthings* (1954), directed by Carol Reed,* where Dors appeared opposite the consummate British actress Celia Johnson.* This was followed by her best role, the convicted murderess sentenced to hang for killing her boyfriend in *Yield to the Night,* J. Lee Thompson's* film noir which gave Dors an opportunity to perform in a more complex role. Earlier, in 1953 Lee Thompson cast Dors in another strong prison drama, *The Weak and the Wicked*. Despite good reviews for these films, Dors was unable to secure the Hollywood contract she desired. A starring role opposite comedian George Gobel in the contrived comedy *I Married a Woman* (1956) was a rare U.S. appearance for the actress.

After the 1950s, Dors was relegated to supporting parts and superficial sex comedies that mostly relied on her name for box office appeal. By the 1970s, her career had slumped to the tawdry depths of *Adventures of a Taxi Driver* (1976) and *Keep It up Downstairs* (1976), although there were some brief appearances in more acceptable films, such as Jerzy Skolimowski's *Deep End* (1970) and the gender-reversal revenge Western *Hannie Caulder* (1971), starring Raquel Welch. After one of her better roles, as Violet in Joseph Losey's* screen adaptation of the play *Steaming* in 1984, Dors died of cancer in May of that year.

FILMS: The Shop at Sly Corner (1946), Holiday Camp (1947), Dancing with Crime (1947), Oliver Twist (1948), Good Time Girl (1948), My Sister and I (1948), Penny and the Pownall Case (1948), Here Comes the Huggetts (1948), Diamond City (1948), The Calender (1948), Vote for Huggett (1948), It's Not Cricket (1949), A Boy, a Girl and a Bike (1949), Dance Hall (1950), Lady Godiva Rides Again (1951), Worm's Eye View (1951), The Last Page (1951), My Wife's Lodger (1951), The Weak and the Wicked (1952), Is Your Honeymoon Really Necessary? (1952), It's a Grand Life (1953), The Great Game (1953), The Saint's Return (1954), The Saint's Girl Friday (1954), A Kid for Two Farthings (1954), Value for Money (1954), An Alligator Named Daisy (1955), Miss Tulip Stays the Night (1955), As Long As They're Happy (1955), Yield to the Night (1956), The Unholy Wife (1956), I Married a Woman (1956), The Long Haul (1956), The Love Specialist (1957), Tread Softly Stranger (1958), Passport to Shame (1959), Scent of Mystery (1960), On the Double (1961), The Big Bankroll (1961), King of the Roaring Twenties (1961), Mrs. Gibbons' Boys (1962), West Eleven (1963), Allez France (1964), The Sandwich Man (1966), That Swinging City (1966), Beserk! (1967), Danger Route (1967), Hammerhead (1968), Baby Love (1969), There's a Girl in My Soup (1970), Deep End (1971), Hannie Caulder (1971), The Pied Piper of Hamelin (1971), Every Afternoon (1972), The Amazing Mr. Blunden (1972), Steptoe and Son Rides Again (1973), Theatre of Blood (1973), Nothing but the Night (1973), Craze (1974), Bedtime with Rosie (1974), The Amorous Milkman (1974), Swedish Wildcats (1974), Three for All (1974), From beyond the Grave (1975), Adventures of a Taxi Driver (1976), Confessions of a Driving Instructor (1976), Keep It up Downstairs (1976), The Groove Room (1977), Adventures of a Private Eye (1977), The Galaxy Affair (1979), The Plank (1979), Dr. Jekyll and Mr. Hyde (1980), and Steaming (1984).

DR. NO (Eon Productions/United Artists, 1962)—Action/espionage. *Director:* Terence Young; *Producers:* Albert R. Broccoli and Harry Saltzman; *Script:* Richard Maibaum, Johanna Harwood, Terence Young (uncredited), and Wolf Mankowitz (uncredited), based on the novel by Ian Fleming; *Cinematography:* Ted Moore; *Music:* Monty Norman and John Barry; *Cast:* Sean Connery (James Bond), Ursula Andress (Honey Ryder), Joseph Wiseman (Dr. No), Jack Lord (Felix Leiter), Bernard Lee (M), Anthony Dawson (Professor Dent), Zena Marshall (Miss Taro), John Kitzmiller (Quarrel), Eunice Grayson (Sylvia Trench), and Lois Maxwell (Miss Moneypenny).

In 1953, the first James Bond novel (*Casino Royale*) was published, followed by a television adaptation by CBS in the United States. Despite public enthusiasm for Ian Fleming's novels, it was not until Albert ("Cubby") Broccoli broke away from his partnership with Irving Allan in Warwick Films and joined with Harry Saltzman, who had just left Woodfall Films, that *Dr. No,* the first James Bond film, was produced. When Saltzman paid $50,000 for the rights to Fleming's novels for six months in 1961, he needed a Bond film in production very quickly. Thus, Saltzman and Broccoli approached United Artists, who agreed to finance a film based on one of Fleming's novels. David Pickard, the executive at United Artists who fostered this deal, encouraged the selection of *Dr. No* as the first film primarily for budgetary reasons (as costs could be restricted) and because, Pickard argued, it established the basic style of film they were seeking as part of a series. For an initial investment of just less than $1 million, *Dr. No* provided a more than satisfactory financial return on its first run and even greater profits over the long term with an estimated gross of approximately $60 million. Thus, Broccoli, Saltzman, and United Artists had initiated one of the most successful movie franchises in the history of the cinema.

The decision to use Terence Young as the director for the first Bond film was also crucial as Young imbued the film with a lot of his own attributes, especially the way in which he heightened Fleming's sense of style, dry humor, and casual flamboyance. Young's contribution cannot be underestimated as he worked closely with Sean Connery.* There was nothing in Connery's previous roles to suggest he would be appropriate. Connery was not the first choice; Cary Grant was considered but rejected as the studio realized that he would not participate in a long-running series if *Dr. No* was successful. When Roger Moore was unavailable owing to television commitments, Connery was selected.

What Connery's Bond did have, that subsequent Bond actors lacked, was an inner toughness, a thinly veiled suggestion of sadism and cruelty. This surfaced not only in his callous remarks (when a carload of SPECTRE agents burn to death in a car accident, Bond flippantly tells a workman that "I think they must have been going to a funeral"), but also in his readiness to kill both men and women in cold blood. After Professor Dent, a SPECTRE agent, makes an attempt on his life, Bond casually shoots him a couple of times despite the fact that Dent's gun is empty. Bond's last shot hits Dent in the back. Connery was also the most overtly sexual of the Bond characters—while others would use the sexual interludes as a form of light relief, Connery's Bond was a sexual predator who easily separated love from sex, as demonstrated in his first film. As a means of filling in time while waiting for an assassination attempt, he has sexual intercourse with Miss Taro, a SPECTRE agent.

Bond's lack of self-doubt and physical invincibility characterizes the Bond series right from the start. *Dr. No* combines elements from the superhero world of the comic strip and movie serials with a thin layer of topicality involving the Cold War, rapid technological changes, and specific incidents, such as the Cuban missile crisis of the early 1960s. The determination of Dr. No to threaten U.S. rockets launched from Cape Canaveral from his nuclear laboratory on Crab Key in the West Indies refers, obliquely, to these aspects. This is reinforced by the Chinese and/or Asian background of most of the villains and the source of Bond's assistance in the film, an agent from the Central Intelligence Agency (Felix Leiter).

Dr. No was not the most financially successful Bond film. However, it established many of the basic elements, including the "Bond Girl," in this case Ursula Andress as Honey Ryder (Andress's voice was considered to have too much of an accent and was dubbed by Monica van der Zyl). Her spectacular entrance into the film, as she emerges from the sea in a white bikini, is as notable in its own way as Connery's first scene at the gambling table where his voice, hands, and other body parts precede his first close-up and, what was to become a familiar trademark, his slightly Scottish accented "Bond, James Bond." Also, the supervillain Dr. No began a long line of powerful, increasingly bizarre, adversaries for Bond. The tone of the series was also established by Ken Adam's opulent sets—notably Dr. No's oval room where he questions the luckless Professor Dent.

Dr. No, compared with the Bond films after *Goldfinger* in 1964, contained relatively little of the self-parody (despite the film's inclusion of Goya's portrait of the Duke of Wellington in Dr. No's lair on Crab Island) that characterized the series after 1964. Also, the gadgets did not overwhelm the film as they tended to do after 1964. Instead, *Dr. No* is, almost, a "quasi-realistic film," particularly the first half, which draws on the conventions of the thriller and the espionage genres. This is evident in the opening sequence as three "blind men" change into hired killers to remove a British agent in Jamaica.

DRACULA (Hammer, 1958)—Horror. *Director:* Terence Fisher; *Producers:* Anthony Hinds and Michael Carreras (executive); *Script:* Jimmy Sangster; *Cinematography:* Jack Asher; *Music:* James Bernard; *Cast:* Peter Cushing (Dr. Van Helsing), Christopher Lee (Count Dracula), Michael Gough (Arthur Holmwood), Melissa Stribling (Mina Holmwood), Carol Marsh (Lucy), John Van Eyssen (Jonathan Harker), Olga Dickie (Gerda), Valerie Gaunt (Vampire Woman), Janina Faye (Tania), Barbara Archer (Inga), and Charles Lloyd Pack (Dr. Seward).

After the surprising commercial success of *The Curse of Frankenstein** (1957) in the United States, the Hollywood studios courted the small Hammer Film Company. In 1958, Universal announced that it was providing Hammer access to its entire library of horror films. Earlier, when Hammer began shooting its version of *Dracula* in late 1957, Universal acted as co-financier and distributor. This new version of Bram Stoker's novel also utilized most of the creative team that produced *The Curse of Frankenstein,* director Terence Fisher,* producer Anthony Hinds, music by James Bernard, cinematography by Jack Asher, art director Bernard Robinson, and, significantly, Jimmy Sangster for the script.

Sangster's script for *Dracula* includes many of the elements in Stoker's novel, even though it is set in 1885, twelve years before the novel was published. While Jonathan Harker is no longer a shipping clerk but a vampire hunter, the film retains the novel's sense of vulnerability and dread as Harker infiltrates Count Dracula's castle to discover an urbane, seemingly civilized aristocrat. The tone is established by Harker's narration, from his diary, as he arrives in sunshine at Dracula's castle: "The castle appeared innocuous enough in the warm afternoon sun and all seemed normal ... but for one thing. ... There were no birds singing."

Count Dracula's entry into the film provides a highlight through the combination of Fisher's composition and cutting and Christopher Lee's* height and voice. As a woman in a nightgown pleads with Harker to help her escape from the castle, Dracula appears in shadow at the top of the stairs and as he moves down the stairs toward Harker the aristocratic resonance of the Count is emphasized by Lee's welcome to his guest. This entry was crucial to both Lee's career and Hammer's interpretation of Stoker's character as the aristocratic Count alternated between displays of charm with red-eyed fury as he kills his victims.

This mixture of arousal and terror proved enormously successful as Hammer updated Universal's 1931 version. After Harker's death in Dracula's castle, his scientific friend, Dr. Van Helsing, follows him but arrives just as Dracula leaves his castle. Returning home, he informs Mina and Arthur Holmwood of Harker's death but is prevented from seeing Lucy Holmwood, Harker's fiancée, due to her anaemia. Lucy, however, allows Dracula into her bedroom each night until he transforms her into a vampire. When Lucy attempts to lure young Tania, the housekeeper's daughter, away from the house at night, Van Helsing pushes a stake through her heart. Dracula next seduces Holmwood's wife, Mina, and only Van Helsing's intervention, allowing sunlight into Dracula's crypt, prevents her total conversion into a vampire.

The significance of Hammer's *Dracula* is quite profound with its attack on Victorian morality and social customs. This aspect is effectively encapsulated when Van Helsing and Holmwood hide outside in the garden as a way of both protecting Mina and capturing Dracula. Mina has allowed Dracula to reside within the house, in the basement and as the two pillars of Victorian respectability, the rational scientist and the patriarchal head of the household, wait in the dark and the cold, Dracula is in the compliant Mina's bedroom transforming her into his image. Similarly, Lucy actively encourages Dracula's nocturnal visits by ordering the housekeeper to remove the garlic plants, placed there by Van Helsing to protect her. She opens her bedroom window and makes herself ready on the bed for his visit.

Van Helsing, the cold, rational scientist, is aware of Dracula's appeal as he dictates his thoughts into a primitive recording machine: "[The] victims consciously detest being dominated by vampirism, but are unable to relinquish the practice, similar to addiction to drugs." The count easily infiltrates and subverts the British middle class, which is revealed, through the characterization of Holmwood and Harker, to be ineffectual in combating his erotic mixture of sensuality and dread. No wonder many British critics expressed moral outrage when it was first released.

THE DRUM (London Films, 1938)—Frontier melodrama/empire film. *Director:* Zoltan Korda; *Producer:* Alexander Korda; *Script:* Lajos Biros, Hugh Gray, Patrick Kirwan, and Arthur Wimperis, based on the novel by A. E. W. Mason; *Cinematography:* Georges Perinal and Osmond Borradaile (location shooting); *Music:* John Greenwood (Miklos Rozsa—uncredited); *Cast:* Sabu (Prince Azim), Raymond Massey (Prince Ghul), Roger Livesey (Tony Carruthers), Valerie Hobson (Mrs. Carruthers), David Tree (Lieutenant Escott), Francis L. Sullivan (Governor), and Desmond Tester (Bill Holder).

Producer Alexander Korda,* with brothers Vincent (art director) and Zoltan (director), reworked the dramatic and thematic basis of *Sanders of the River** (1935) for *The Drum. The Drum* was the second of their successful celebrations of the British Empire (*The Four Feathers* [1939] was the third). Each film assumes that British rule is a good thing and has lasting benefits for the local population.

As in other films in the cycle, there is a pro-British local leader (Prince Azim), presented in a positive manner, and an anti-British fanatic (Prince Ghul). There is also a British officer, Captain Carruthers, and it is his function to protect the Indian people from Ghul. To carry out his duty, he is almost eager to die for them. For example, prior to his attendance at a banquet organized by Ghul, and knowing that he is going to be ambushed, Carruthers refers to earlier British imperial leaders who have died on behalf of the empire. This includes Sir Lewis Cavagnari at Kabul and General Gordon at Khartoum. Carruthers speculates that "a not unusual preliminary to our establishing law and order is the murder of one of our representatives." Carruthers then, happily, goes off to the banquet (and possibly death).

Ghul wants to restore the old Moghul empire in India, beginning with the elimination of the British in the border state of Toket. He murders his brother, a pro-British ruler, and threatens young Prince Azim. Azim seeks help from Carruthers and his wife. Azim also forms a close friendship with cockney drummer boy Bill Holder. Their friendship demonstrates that age (they are both young boys) can break down barriers based on class, caste, and religion. Adults, the film suggests, are locked into their prejudices.

When Carruthers returns to Toket, Prince Ghul invites him, and a number of British soldiers, to a banquet where, at the sound of the third beating of a large drum, Ghul plans to murder his guests. This, Ghul argues, will demonstrate the fallibility of the British to his fellow Indians. Prince Azim upsets Ghul's plan by sending a warning to Carruthers on a drum, a message that was taught to him by Holder. Ghul dies in the subsequent battle and British rule is restored in Toket.

Zoltan Korda excels in the action sequences. Filmed in Technicolor, most of the film was shot either at Denham or in the hills of Wales. Through the judicious use of matte shots, the Himalayas were imposed on exterior shots of the Welsh hills from material filmed by a second unit in Chitral. The interior scenes are less impressive. The film was nominated for the "Mussolini Cup" for Best Film at the 1938 Venice Film Festival.

NOTES

1. See McFarlane, *An Autobiography of British Cinema,* p. 565.
2. Quoted in Robert Murphy, *Sixties British Cinema*, London, BFI Publishing, 1992, p. 124.
3. McFarlane, *An Autobiography of British Cinema,* p. 164.
4. McFarlane, *An Autobiography of British Cinema,* p. 165.
5. A. Slide, *"Banned In The USA"*. *British Films in the United States and Their Censorship. 1933–1960.* London, I. B. Tauris, 1998, p. 157.
6. McFarlane, *An Autobiography of British Cinema,* p. 69.
7. See McFarlane, *An Autobiography of British Cinema,* pp. 557–558.

E

THE EMBEZZLER (Kenilworth, 1954)—Drama. *Director:* John Gilling; *Producers:* Robert Baker and Monty Berman; *Script:* John Gilling; *Cinematography:* Jonah Jones; *Music:* John Lanchberry; *Cast:* Charles Victor (Henry Paulson), Zena Marshall (Mrs. Forrest), Cyril Chamberlain (Johnson), Leslie Weston (Piggott), Avice Landone (Miss Ackroyd), Peggy Mount (Mrs. Larkin), and Michael Craig (Dr. Forrest).

The Last Holiday, * which was released four years before *The Embezzler,* is concerned with a middle-aged man, believing that he has little time to live, changes his life completely by resigning from his job and taking off to a seaside resort, determined to make full use of his remaining time. *The Embezzler* tells a similar story, only this time the victim is fifty-four-year-old Henry Paulson, a bank clerk in a loveless marriage with a nagging wife. When his doctor tells him that he has less than two years to live, he buys a ticket to France. However, Paulson's bank manager catches him stealing money from the bank to finance his adventure and Paulson is forced to hide out in a boarding house in the seaside resort of Eastbourne. At the boarding house, Paulson assists a young wife, Mrs. Forrest, who is being blackmailed by Johnson, her former lover. When Paulson steps in to protect her, he succumbs to a fatal heart attack.

This is another low-budget, unpretentious drama from Robert S. Baker and Monty Berman's Kenilworth Productions. *The Embezzler* stands out from other Kenilworth Productions due to John Gilling's sharp script and direction and the strong performance from character actor Charles Victor as the hapless man who dies a hero. Michael Craig, in an early role, plays the husband of the blackmail victim.

EMMA (Miramax, 1996)—Romance. *Director:* Douglas McGrath; *Producers:* Patrick Cassavetti, Steven Haft, Donna Grey (associate), Bob Weinstein (executive), Harvey Weinstein (executive), and Donna Gigliotti (executive); *Script:*

Douglas McGrath, based on the novel by Jane Austen; *Cinematography:* Ian Wilson; *Music:* Rachel Portman; *Cast:* Gwyneth Paltrow (Emma Woodhouse), Jeremy Northam (Mr. Knightly), Toni Collette (Harriet Smith), Greta Scacchi (Mrs. Weston), Alan Cumming (Reverend Elton), Ewan McGregor (Frank Churchill), Sophie Thompson (Miss Bates), Phyllida Law (Mrs. Bates), James Cosmos (Mr. Weston), and Kathleen Byron (Mrs. Goddard).

The English village of Highbury in 1814 was, in a period when most people did not travel very far, a closed community dominated by social rituals and agreed practices. Emma Woodhouse, a wealthy twenty-one-year-old, has little to do with her time except play matchmaker for those deemed worthy of her attention. After orchestrating the union of Mr. and Mrs. Weston, Emma sets her sights on her less privileged friend Harriet Smith and steers her toward Reverend Elton, even though Harriet is interested in a local farmer.

Elton prefers Emma so she transfers Harriet's attention to the dashing Frank Churchill. To bring Frank and Harriet together, Emma invites members of the local community to a picnic where the domineering Mrs. Elton irritates her. When Frank suggests a game whereby everybody will be invited to amuse Emma by telling stories—the only limitation is that dull stories will be limited to three— Emma, frustrated by Elton's wife, sharply reminds Miss Bates, who always repeats everything three times for her deaf mother, that the limit is three. Within the insular context of Highbury, Emma's retort is a major social gaffe and Bates, and everybody else, is stunned and Mr. Knightly, a family friend, reprimands Emma.

The fact that this is presented as a seminal moment in the film highlights the insular basis of Highbury's highly developed system of codes and rituals. A parallel between the rigidity of this social system and the world of U.S. teenagers also forms the basis of the Hollywood teen comedy *Clueless* (1995). *Emma* is a subtle directorial debut film for U.S. scriptwriter Douglas McGrath (*Bullets over Broadway* [1994]) and, surprisingly, the performance of Hollywood actress Gwyneth Paltrow blends easily with the high-quality cast, including Jeremy Northam as Mr. Knightly, Emma's eventual partner, Juliet Stevenson as Mrs. Elton, Ewan McGregor as Frank Churchill, mother and daughter Phyllida Law and Sophie Thompson (sister of Emma Thompson) as Mrs. and Miss Bates, Greta Scacchi as Emma's mentor, and Australian Toni Collette, who reprieves aspects of her performance in *Muriel's Wedding* (1994) as Harriet Smith.

The score for *Emma,* one of the finest romantic scores in recent years, by Rachel Portman won the 1997 Oscar for Best Musical Score while Ruth Myers was nominated for Best Costume Design. McGrath was nominated at the 1997 Writers Guild of America Awards for his script.

ENDFIELD, CY RAKER (1914–1995). After an education at Yale and New York City's Theater School, Endfield worked in Hollywood as a writer and, later, director on MGM's *Our Gang* series of shorts. After World War II, Endfield began directing feature films for "poverty row" studios, such as Monogram with

Gentleman Joe Palooka (1946), before leaving Hollywood for England following his blacklisting during the anti-communist purge that swept Hollywood with the resumption of the House Committee on Un-American Activities hearings in 1947.

Working under different names in England, such as Hugh Raker and C. Raker, Endfield directed British television series and low-budget films (such as *Impulse* [1954] for Tempean Films, and *The Master Plan* [1955]). However, in 1956 he formed a working partnership with actor Stanley Baker* and their first film, the robust *Hell Drivers** (1957), stood out at the time for its sheer visual excitement and rapid narrative pacing as it told its story of ex-convict truck driver Baker who is threatened by Patrick McGoohan and the other drivers when he exposes corruption in their trucking company. Endfield's presentation of the competition between the drivers as they race against each other, and the clock, in delivering their cargo is a highlight. Another melodrama followed with *Sea Fury* (1958), which involved sexual passion on a tugboat as first mate Stanley Baker battles captain Victor McLaglen over the favors of Luciana Paluzzi.

The culmination of the Endfield-Baker partnership, and the high point in Endfield's film career, was the exciting epic *Zulu** (1964), the celebration of the defense of a small British garrison at Rorke's Drift in 1879 during the Zulu Wars. Most of the second half of the film was one battle sequence after another, as the Welsh soldiers fight off successive attacks, with Endfield responding with a series of superbly choreographed battle sequences. Later, in 1979, after Enfield had basically left the film industry, his script depicting the events prior to the battle at Rorke's Drift, was adapted in *Zulu Dawn* (1979). Before his film career collapsed following the disastrous *De Sade* (1969), Endfield made one more tough melodrama with Stanley Baker, Stuart Whitman, Susannah York, Harry Andrews, and Nigel Davenport battling each other and simian attackers after their plane crashes in the Kalahari Desert in *Sands of the Kalahari* (1965).

FILMS (as director): Radio Bugs (short, 1943), Dancing Romeo (short, 1944), Tale of a Dog (short, 1944), Gentleman Joe Palooka (1946), Stork Bites Man (1947), The Argyle Secrets (1948), Joe Palooka in the Big Fight (1949), The Underworld Story (1950), The Sound of Fury (1950), Tarzan's Savage Fury (1952), Colonel March Investigates (1952), The Limping Man (1953), The Secret (1954), Impulse (1954), The Master Plan (1955), Child in the House (1956), Hell Drivers (1957), Sea Fury (1958), Jet Storm (1959), Mysterious Island (1961), Hide and Seek (1963), Zulu (1964), Sands of the Kalahari (1965), De Sade (1969), and Universal Soldier (1971).

ESTHER WATERS (Wessex/Rank, 1948)—Melodrama. *Directors:* Ian Dalrymple and Peter Proud; *Producers:* Ian Dalrymple and Peter Proud; *Script:* Michael Gordon and William Rose, based on the novel by George Moore; *Cinematography:* H. E. Fowle and C. M. Pennington; *Music:* Dr. Gordon Jacob; *Cast:* Kathleen Ryan (Esther Waters), Dirk Bogarde (William Latch), Cyril Cusack (Fred), Ivor Barnard (Randal), Fay Compton (Mrs. Barfield), Margaret Diamond (Sarah), and Mary Clare (Mrs. Latch).

Esther Waters provided Dirk Bogarde* with his first starring role as William Latch, the irresponsible groom, who seduces the new maid, Esther Waters, and then runs off with another woman. The story covers twenty years in the life of Esther in the late nineteenth century. Esther leaves her position at a large horse-training property after she becomes pregnant. Returning to London, Esther suffers seven years of hardship trying to raise her son while trying to earn sufficient money to keep them together. When she achieves a modicum of financial stability, and the promise of marriage from a kindly minister (Cyril Cusack), Latch reenters Esther's life and they marry.

This time the relationship flourishes and Esther puts aside her religious objections to gambling and drinking by helping Latch run his public house and book-making operation. After three years of marriage, Latch falls ill and Esther again faces money problems, particularly after her husband places all of their money on the 1885 Derby. After Latch dies in hospital, just as his horse loses the Derby, Esther returns to her first employer in the in the country.

Esther Waters is traditional melodrama. Esther personifies virtue in an ungodly world of gambling, drinking, and extramarital sex. Although Esther is exposed to these sins, she finally finds peace and security at the Barfield property and a mistress who shares her religious views. The film utilizes the traditional narrative rhythm associated with melodrama involving a rapid, alternating pattern of emotional "highs" and "lows." Thus, whenever Esther appears lost a savior figure or fortuitous event "rescues" her—in the form of a kindly policeman or cleric or even Mrs. Barfield. However, the obstacles faced by Esther are a lot tougher than most films and include a baby sitter who, for five pounds, kills sickly children.

Esther Waters, a large-scale production, contains excellent performances from Kathleen Ryan, Bogarde, Margaret Diamond, and Cyril Cusack as the minister who loves her. The film was not a commercial success—Bogarde subsequently described it as a "gloomy movie"—and Ian Dalrymple was forced to take over direction of the film from Peter Proud. Proud, who was an art director, never directed again, nor did Dalrymple, who worked for the next twenty years in the British film industry as a producer and screenwriter.

In Hollywood, Joseph Breen, representing the Hollywood Production Code Administration, objected to a number of aspects of the script including Latch's seduction of Esther and the birth of an illegitimate child. Breen also decreed that Latch had to be free of Peggy, the woman he ran away with, when he returns to Esther after a seven-year absence. Above all else, Breen maintained that the "compensating moral values" found in George Moore's novel, which offset the "sin" of Esther's relationship with Latch, must be emphasized in the film.[1] Hence, the seven years of suffering that Esther undergos after the birth of her illegitimate baby. The film finally received a certificate for release in the United States in 1949 and Eagle-Lion Films released it as *The Sin of Esther Waters* in 1951.

EVERGREEN (British-Gaumont, 1934)—Musical. *Director:* Victor Saville; *Producer:* Michael Balcon; *Script:* Marjorie Gaffney and Emlyn Williams, based on the play by Benn W. Levy; *Cinematography:* Glen McWilliams; *Music:* Lorenz Hart, Richard Rodgers, and Harry Woods; *Cast:* Jessie Matthews (Harriet Green), Sonny Hale (Leslie Benn), Betty Balfour (Maudie), Ivor McLaren (Marquis of Staines), Barry Mackay (Tommy Thompson), and Hartley Power (George Treadwell).

At the end of *Evergreen,* after Harriet Green has discarded most of her clothes in front of a first-night theater audience to reveal that she is a young woman, and not the sixty-year-old former star she had been impersonating, the audience expresses their disgust. At this point, Harriet's costar, Tommy Thompson, jumps in and tells them: "You've been had? What about me? I've been in love with her for weeks and had to go about London calling her Mummy."

The Freudian implications of this scenario are obvious. This musical, based on a sharp script by (primarily) Marjorie Gaffney, exploits the comedic and sexual possibilities inherent in a young woman's rise to fame by pretending to be her dead mother, and then falling in love with a man with whom she shares a house and is forced to assume, in public, the role of his mother as well. This bizarre plot provides an entertaining context for the talented Jessie Matthews, working at the peak of her powers, to fully exploit. Matthews is ably supported by U.S. dancer and choreographer Buddy Bradley, director Victor Saville,* and a impressive number of musical sequences, including an art deco interpretation of Fritz Lang's *Metropolis* (1927).

Evergreen opens with the farewell performance of Edwardian music star Harriet Green, who is leaving the stage to marry the Marquis of Staines. However, just prior to the marriage, a former lover, and father of Harriet's daughter, appears to blackmail her. Harriet decides that she must flee London for anonymity in South Africa and leaves behind her daughter to be raised by another woman in London. Harriet dies in South Africa and twenty-five years later her daughter, Harriet junior, tries unsuccessfully to start a theatrical career. A brash publicity man, Tommy Thompson, engineers a plan, with the help of her mother's former theater friends, Leslie Benn and Maudie, to jump start Harriet's career by claiming that the former musical star was making a comeback. While this deception is successful in Harriet's professional life, it causes romantic problems for Harriet and Tommy, who have fallen in love.

They are forced, through circumstances, to live together as mother and son. In a prolonged sequence detailing their sexual frustration, visually reiterated by a strategically placed nude statue in the foreground of one scene, Saville cleverly exploits the natural inclinations of Harriet and Tommy, in their bedclothes, alone in a sumptuous house. The humor of this situation emanates from the agony and frustration of their inability to act on their desires.

Saville used a similar premise in *The Faithful Heart* (1933) with Edna Best playing both mother and daughter. In *Evergreen,* however, he successfully combines the emotional appeal of melodrama, particularly a sentimental court scene where mother and daughter are brought together in song, with the sexual freedom and visual pleasures offered by the genre, to produce one of the Britain's finest musicals.

EXPRESSO BONGO (Conquest Productions/British Lion, 1959)— Drama/musical. *Director:* Val Guest; *Producers:* Val Guest and Jon Penington (associate); *Script:* Wolf Mankowitz, based on the play by Wolf Mankowitz and Julian Moore; *Cinematography:* John Wilcox; *Music:* Robert Farnon, David Heneker, Julian Moore, Monty Norman, Val Guest, Bunny Lewis, Norrie Paramour, and Paddy Roberts; *Cast:* Laurence Harvey (Johnny Jackson), Sylvia Syms (Maisie King), Yolande Donlan (Dixie Collins), Cliff Richard (Bongo Herbert), Meier Tzelniker (Gus Mayer), Ambrosine Phillpotts (Lady Rosemary), Eric Pohlmann (Leon), Gilbert Harding (Gilbert Harding), Hermione Baddeley (Penelope), Reginald Beckwith (Reverend Tobias Craven), Avis Bunnage (Mrs. Rudge), Kenneth Griffith (Charlie), Susan Hampshire (Cynthia), and Wilfred Lawson (Mr. Rudge).

When young pop star Bongo Herbert appears on stage to promote his new record *The Shrine on the Second Floor,* a contrived celebration of his mother when, in fact, he despises her, he tells the audience that "it is not generally known, I'm a deeply religious boy." Herbert then acquiesces to the predatory desires of aging U.S. entertainer Dixie Collins. In one telling scene, Herbert, who has deliberately inveigled himself into Collins's apartment late at night, slumps drunkenly onto her bed as Collins eyes her prey while removing her earrings. This scene fits perfectly within the film's cynical tone, effectively encapsulated by hustler Johnny Jackson when he tells long-suffering girlfriend Maisie King that "it's a bastards world and I'm a fully paid up member."

At the beginning of the film, Jackson, who lives on the edge of the entertainment business, sees a chance to make some money with a young singer who he renames "Bongo Herbert." Aspects of the seedy Soho entertainment business dominate the first half of the film as Jackson pushes his protégé into a recording contract and television appearances. The second half, however, is less interesting as the film reverts to a more familiar pattern tracing the after-effects of Bongo's sudden fame and the battle between Jackson and Collins for the body and soul of the young singer. Both eventually lose out to wily record owner Gus Mayer.

Val Guest's* films, particularly in the late 1950s and 1960s, are characterized by their energy and melodramatic intensity and *Expresso Bongo* is no exception. Although it is a flawed film, particularly in its reliance on broad cultural and class stereotypes, Laurence Harvey* as the shallow hustler-agent Johnny Jackson, and Sylvia Syms, as the sympathetic stripper Maisie King, provide striking performances while Cliff Richard, in his second film role, is suitably pliable as the young singer.

At the 1960 BAFTA Film Awards, Harvey was nominated for the Best British Actor Award and Wolf Mankowitz for Best British Screenplay.

NOTE

1. See Slide, *"Banned in the USA,"* pp. 61–62.

F

THE FAMILY WAY (British Lion, 1966)—Family comedy/social drama. *Director:* Roy Boulting; *Producer:* John Boulting; *Script:* Bill Naughton, based on his play *All in a Good Time; Cinematography:* Harry Waxman; *Music:* Paul McCartney; *Cast:* Hayley Mills (Jenny Fitton), Hywel Bennett (Arthur Fitton), John Mills (Ezra Fitton), Marjorie Rhodes (Lucy Fitton), Avril Angers (Liz Piper), John Comer (Leslie Piper), Wilfred Pickles (Uncle Fred), Barry Foster (Joe Thompson), Murray Head (Geoffrey Fitton), Liz Fraser (Molly Thompson), Thorley Walters (The Vicar), and Margaret Lacey (Mrs. Harris).

Surprising as it may seem today, the release of *The Family Way* generated controversy in the mid-1960s. This was due to a number of factors—the film's basic subject matter, the inability of newly married Jenny and Arthur Fitton to consummate their marriage; the fact that former child star Hayley Mills was cast as Jenny and her father, John Mills,* as her father-in-law; followed by the news that Hayley Mills had fallen in love with the film's director, Roy Boulting,* thirty-three years her senior.

The theatrical basis of *The Family Way* is evident, particularly in the film's closing shot, which reproduces the emotional effect of the use of tableau in nineteenth-century theatrical melodrama to maximise the emotional effect. Here, the film's dark secret is openly acknowledged by Ezra and Lucy Fitton. This secret, that Ezra's close boyhood pal Billy Stringfellows was really Arthur's father, and that Arthur was conceived during a brief affair between Ezra's wife, Lucy, and Billy, is hinted at throughout the film. The "revelation" during the epilogue reminds the audience that the film was not only concerned with Arthur's (temporary) impotence, the aspect that preoccupied most critics, but the deteriorating relationship between Ezra and Lucy.

The source of Arthur's impotence is his relationship with Ezra. Their contrasting personalities and inability to understand each other emanate from this "dark" secret. When Ezra challenges Arthur to an arm wrestling contest during the wedding celebration, Arthur is about to best Ezra when he looks into the old man's face and loses his motivation to continue the contest. Similarly, the realization that Ezra is sleeping in the next room, separated only by thin walls, inhibits Arthur's libido. Both narrative strands come together when Jenny's parents confront Ezra and Lucy with the news that Arthur and Jenny have not, after a period of some weeks, had sexual intercourse. At this point, the film shifts the source of the "problem" from Arthur and Jenny to Ezra and Lucy and, specifically, Ezra's decision to take Billy on his honeymoon with Lucy many years ago. Thus, just as the "blockage" to Arthur's pleasure is removed at the end of the film when he resumes a delayed honeymoon with his wife, so the psychological "blockage" between Ezra and Lucy is similarly removed, or at least, openly acknowledged.

Marjorie Rhodes, in a role that showcased her great talent, deservedly won the Best Supporting Actress Award from the National Board of Review in 1967 and the Best Supporting Actress Award from the (U.S.) National Society of Film Critics in 1968. John Mills was awarded Best Actor at the 1967 San Sebastian International Film Festival.

FARRAR, DAVID (1908–1995). After five years stage experience, David Farrar was approached by Victor Hanbury, the head of RKO Radio Pictures in Britain, and offered a small role in a film to be shot at Shepparton Studios. Over the next ten years, from 1937 to 1946, he appeared in supporting roles in major films (such as a Nazi posing as a British officer in Alberto Cavalcanti's *Went the Day Well?* [1942]) and lead roles in minor films (*Sheepdog of the Hills* [1941] and *Meet Sexton Blake* [1944]). During this period, he honed his screen acting skills. With his matinee idol good looks, powerful voice, and masculine presence, Farrar's breakthrough role came as Mr. Dean in Michael Powell* and Emeric Pressburger's* magical *Black Narcissus** (1947).

The period from 1947 to 1951 represents the high point in Farrar's career. He displayed the requisite degree of earthy sensuality in *Black Narcissus.* In a similar role, in *Mr. Perrin and Mr. Traill** (1948), he upsets the masters at an elite boy's boarding school. This preceded his best performance as the disturbed bomb disposal expert in the Powell-Pressburger film *The Small Back Room* (1948). Farrar had not completed *Mr. Perrin and Mr. Traill* when he began the tense climax to *The Small Back Room,* a beach scene in Dorset where Farrar has to defuse a bomb that has already killed another expert. Farrar's irresponsible squire in *Gone to Earth* (1950) completed his films for Powell and Pressburger after he withdrew from their production of *The Red Shoes** (1948).

The second part of Farrar's screen career began in 1951 when he was cast as Sir Guy of Devon, opposite Ann Blyth, in the U.S. production of *The Golden Horde* for Universal Studios, his first appearance in a number of costume films over the next nine years. During this period, Farrar worked mostly in Hollywood, including two films directed by Hollywood veteran Allan Dwan (*Escape to Burma* [1955] and *Pearls of the South Pacific* [1955]) for RKO Radio. He occasionally returned to Britain for films such as *Lilacs in the Spring* (1954), *Lost**

(1955), Guy Green's crime melodrama with Farrar as Inspector Craig investigating the kidnapping of a baby, in *I Accuse!* (1958), with Farrar as the brother of Alfred Dreyfus in José Ferrer's production, and the *Son of Robin Hood* (1958).

Farrar retired from the screen after completing his role of Xerxes in *The 300 Spartans* (1962) for Twentieth Century Fox. Faced with the prospect of character parts, Farrar left screen acting for a life in South Africa although he was only fifty-four years of age. Farrar died in South Africa in 1995.

FILMS: Return of the Stranger (1937), Head over Heals (1937), Silver Top (1937), Sexton Blake and the Hooded Terror (1938), A Royal Divorce (1938), Danny Boy (1941), Penn of Pennsylvania (1941), Sheepdog of the Hills (1941), Suspected Person (1942), Went the Day Well? (1942), The Dark Tower (1943), The Night Invader (1943), They Met in the Dark (1943), Headline (1943), The Hundred Pound Widow (1943), For Those in Peril (1943), Meet Sexton Blake (1944), The World Owes Me a Living (1945), The Echo Murders (1945), The Trojan Brothers (1946), Lisbon Story (1946), Black Narcissus (1947), Frieda (1947), The Small Back Room (1948), Mr. Perrin and Mr. Traill (1948), Diamond City (1949), Gone to Earth (1950), Cage of Gold (1950), The Late Edwina Black (1951), Night without Stars (1951), The Golden Horde (1951), Duel in the Jungle (1954), Lilacs in the Spring (1954), The Black Shield of Falworth (1954), The Sea Chase (1955), Pearl of the South Pacific (1955), Escape to Burma (1955), Lost (1956), Battle of the River Plate (narr., 1956), Woman and the Hunter (1957), I Accuse! (1958), Son of Robin Hood (1958), Solomon and Sheba (1959), John Paul Jones (1959), Watusi (1959), Middle of Nowhere (1960), Beat Girl (1960), The Webster Boy (1960), and The 300 Spartans (1962).

FATHER BROWN (Facet Productions/Columbia, 1954)—Detective/comedy. *Director:* Robert Hamer; *Producers:* Paul Finder Moss and Vivian A. Cox (associate); *Script:* Thelma Schnee and Robert Hamer, based on the stories by G. K. Chesterton; *Cinematography:* Harry Waxman; *Music:* Georges Auric; *Cast:* Alec Guinness (Father Brown), Joan Greenwood (Lady Warren), Peter Finch (Gustave Flambeau), Cecil Parker (The Bishop), Bernard Lee (Inspector Valentine), Sidney James (Parkinson), Gerard Oury (Inspector Dubois), Ernest Clark (Bishop's Secretary), John Salew (Station Sergeant) Eugene Deckers (French Cavalry Officer), Ernest Thesiger (Vicomte), and John Horseley (Inspector Wilkins).

This is a gentle detective story of redemption. When Father Brown fails to dissuade the police and the Catholic Church from sending a valuable religious artifact from London to Rome under police guard, due to the threat from the notorious art thief Gustave Flambeau, Father Brown takes the artifact and travels from London to Paris where Flambeau, disguised as a priest, steals it. Brown, motivated not by revenge, although his career is under some jeopardy from the Catholic hierarchy, but by a determination to redeem Flambeau, tracks the master thief down to his estate in provincial France, retrieves the artifact, and celebrates in the redemption of Flambeau.

Father Brown is, deliberately, devoid of suspense and the usual conventions associated with the detective film, although Inspector Valentine merely functions as an obstacle to Brown's investigation. The film is a low-key religious parable optimistically celebrating the pleasures and virtues of the non-material world. This was director Robert Hamer's* third last film before his premature death in 1963. He was nominated for the Golden Lion Award at the 1954 Venice Film Festival.

FIELDS, GRACIE (1898–1979). In 1936, music hall performer Gracie Fields was the most popular film star in Britain and she retained her popularity until the end of the decade. It dipped during World War II when she left England for Hollywood when her Italian-born director husband Monty Banks was threatened with internment. Never entirely comfortable with films, Fields was primarily a music hall performer with the ability to align herself closely with the values and interests of her working-class audiences, the class into which she was born in Lancashire in 1898. As the decade progressed, her appeal developed beyond these limitations into an artist with broad, populist appeal enhanced by the growing patriotism of the late 1930s. Unashamedly optimistic and sentimental, these qualities transferred to the cinema, with Fields generally cast as a non-glamorous, asexual character who often mediated on behalf of others.

When Fields entered the cinema with *Sally in Our Alley* in 1931, the experience was not a happy one due to the film's chaotic production conditions. It was not until Banks took over her career that she felt more comfortable with the filmmaking experience. Fields, because of her music hall popularity, was well paid, beginning with a £40,000 per picture deal at the start of her film career. J. B. Priestley was hired to work on the script of Field's best film, *Sing As We Go* (1934), which assimilated elements of the 1930s depression into the story. Fields was cast as Gracie Platt, a mill girl who bargains with management on behalf of her fellow workers. Her British film career ended with her move to Hollywood, where she made three films. Fields regained her popularity as a performer after the war. She was awarded Dame Commander of the Order of the British Empire in 1979, the year of her death.

FILMS: Sally in Our Alley (1931), Looking on the Brighter Side (1932), This Week of Grace (1933), Love, Life and Laughter (1934), Sing As We Go (1934), Look up and Laugh (1935), Queen of Hearts (1936), The Show Goes On (1937), We're Going to Be Rich (1938), Keep Smiling (1938), Shipyard Sally (1939), Holy Matrimony (1943), Stage Door Canteen (1944), Molly and Me (1945), and Paris Underground (1945).

FINCH, PETER (1916–1977). Peter Finch, born in England, and raised in France and India before spending most of his formative years in Australia, was one of the finest screen actors of his generation. Finch's early roles in Australian films, after his stage debut in 1935, included the young farmer in the popular *Dad and Dave Come to Town* (1938), a German spy impersonating an Australian in *The Power and the Glory* (1941), and an English soldier in the war film *The Rats of Tobruk* (1944). Finch also supplied voice-over to propaganda documentaries during World War II as well as acting as assistant director on a documentary on

Arnhem Land Aborigines (*Primitive Peoples* [1947]). Thirteen years later, Finch made another documentary, the award-winning film set in Ibiza (*The Day* [1960]), which he wrote and directed.

Throughout the 1940s, Finch worked extensively in Australian radio dramas although it was his stage work that attracted the attention of Laurence Olivier* and Vivien Leigh during Olivier's well-publicized theatrical tour of Australia and New Zealand in 1948. Finch returned with Olivier to the London stage and, with the support of Michael Balcon and Harry Watt, he made his British film debut as a murderer in *Train of Events* (1949). There was, however, little indication in his early screen performances of the consummate screen actor he was to become in the 1960s and 1970s, although his gentleman art thief in Robert Hamer's* detective film *Father Brown* (1954) provides some indication of his talent. Finch also appeared in a number of Hollywood films during this period, including the troubled production of *Elephant Walk* (1954), where Vivien Leigh's mental problems overwhelmed her and she had to be replaced by Elizabeth Taylor.

Finch developed his screen acting technique, a medium he preferred to the stage, throughout the 1950s. He brought an edge to most performances, even in lesser films such as Michael Powell's* *Battle of the River Plate* (1956), which was notable only for Finch's tragic naval officer Captain Langsdorff. During the 1950s, he won the 1957 BAFTA Film Award for Best British Actor as Joe Harmon in the British production of *A Town Like Alice* (1956). Finch returned to Australia for location work on two more British films—the rough and ready swagman who takes his daughter away from his estranged wife in *The Shiralee* (1957), based on the novel by D'Arcy Niland, and the bold bushranger Captain Starlight in *Robbery under Arms* (1957).

By the early 1960s, Finch was the consummate screen actor, particularly as the jaded Labour politician in *No Love for Johnnie** (1961), and the unfaithful husband in *The Pumpkin Eater* (1964). During this period, from 1960 to 1964, Finch produced his most sustained sequence of fine performances. This included his middle-aged novelist romantically involved with a young farm girl, played by Rita Tushingham in *Girl with Green Eyes* (1964). It was the period from 1971 to his death in 1976 that strengthened his international reputation, particularly with *Sunday Bloody Sunday* (1971), where he played a Jewish homosexual doctor involved in a romantic triangle, with Glenda Jackson* and Murray Head. Both Finch and Jackson love Head in this controversial film, which was followed five years later with *Network,* his most famous performance as the "mad prophet of the airwaves."

Finch died of a heart attack in California while promoting this film and he was (posthumously) awarded the 1977 Academy Award for Best Actor. This followed an earlier nomination for *Sunday Bloody Sunday.* Finch also won the 1978 BAFTA Award for Best Actor for *Network,* the 1972 Award for *Sunday Bloody Sunday,* the 1962 Award for *No Love for Johnnie,* the 1961 BAFTA Award for Best British Actor for *The Trials of Oscar Wilde* (1960), and the 1957 Award for *A Town Like Alice.*

FILMS: Dad and Dave Come to Town (1938), Mr. Chedworth Steps Out (1939), The Power and the Glory (1941), Another Threshold (doc., 1942), While There's Still Time (doc., 1942), South West Pacific (doc., 1943), Jungle Patrol (doc., 1944), The Rats of Tobruk (1944), Red Sky at Morning (1945), A Son Is Born (1946), Primitive Peoples (doc., 1947), Train of Events (1949), The Miniver Story (1950), The Wooden Horse (1950), The Story of Robin Hood (1952), The Heart of the Matter (1953), The Story of Gilbert and Sullivan (1953), Elephant Walk (1954), Make Me an Offer! (1954), Father Brown (1954), Josephine and Men (1955), Passage Home (1955), Simon and Laura (1955), The Dark Avenger (1955), A Town Like Alice (1956), The Battle of the River Plate (1956), Robbery under Arms (1957), Windom's Way (1957), The Shiralee (1957), Operation Amsterdam (1958), The Nun's Story (1959), Kidnapped (1959), The Sins of Rachel Cade (1960), The Trials of Oscar Wilde (1960), The Day (doc., 1960), No Love for Johnnie (1961), I Thank a Fool (1962), In the Cool of the Day (1962), Girl with Green Eyes (1963), The Pumpkin Eater (1964), First Men in the Moon (1964), Judith (1965), The Flight of the Phoenix (1965), 10:30 P.M. Summer (1966), Far from the Madding Crowd (1967), The Legend of Lylah Clare (1968), The Red Tent (1969), The Greatest Mother of Them All (1969), Sunday Bloody Sunday (1971), Something to Hide (1971), England Made Me (1971), Lost Horizon (1972), Bequest to the Nation (1973), The Abdication (1974), Network (1976), and Raid on Entebbe (1976).

FINNEY, ALBERT (b. 1936). An actor with enormous power and charisma, Albert Finney has spent the greater part of his career avoiding type casting and the coveted status of the "film star." He once said he was not the "romantic type" and he was only "happy in character roles." This attitude is reflected in his choice of roles as there have been a number of times in his career, particularly in the period following *Tom Jones** (1963), when Finney was courted by the Hollywood studios with the prospect of major roles in big-budget U.S. films. Instead, Finney returned to the stage and a more marginal career in the film industry.

A bookie's son from Salford Lancashire, Finney was prominent among the "northern" actors who dominated the British theater in the middle and late 1950s. After graduating from the Royal Academy of Dramatic Arts in 1955, Finney worked as Laurence Olivier's* understudy in Shakespearian productions, occasionally replacing Olivier in *Coriolanus* and other plays produced at Stratford-on-Avon. He made his film debut with a small part in *The Entertainer* (1960), starring Olivier. His next film, Karel Reisz's *Saturday Night and Sunday Morning* (1960), was not only a landmark New Wave film, but established a distinctive screen persona for Finney, a persona he challenged many times over the next four decades. Finney's performance as Arthur Seaton also reinforced many of the characteristic traits of male characters in the New Wave films. This included a mixture of defiance and selfishness overlaid by a raw sexuality, traits that were not common in most male protagonists in the British cinema up to this time.

Despite the strong critical support for *Saturday Night and Sunday Morning,* it was, Finney claimed, his performance in *Tom Jones* that established his international reputation. In *Tom Jones,* Finney played a more "audience friendly" character compared with his anti-social lathe factory worker in *Saturday Night and*

Sunday Morning. However, he did not capitalize on the popularity of this film with similar roles, as Michael Caine* did after *Alfie* (1966).* Instead, he followed with a relatively minor role as a Russian soldier in Carl Foreman's sprawling war drama *The Victors* (1963), and the lead role as a psychotic killer in Reisz's remake of the Emlyn Williams's play *Night Must Fall* (1964). Finney, at this point in his career, preferred the stage and his film appearances were sporadic throughout the 1960s. His best role in this period was opposite Audrey Hepburn in *Two for the Road* (1967), Stanley Donen's comedy-drama of two people trying to retrieve their marriage. Finney followed this in 1968 with his commercially unsuccessful directorial debut *Charlie Bubbles* (1967), opposite Liza Minnelli in her screen debut.

Finney's penchant for character roles was evident in the 1970s, as he appeared as Ebenezer Scrooge in a musical version of *Scrooge* (1970), the heavily disguised, and irritating, detective Hercule Poirot in *Murder on the Orient Express* (1974), and the very theatrical touring actor, allegedly based on Donald Wolfit, in *The Dresser* (1983). Finney occasionally demonstrated his prowess in a demanding role, such as *Shoot the Moon* (1981), Alan Parker's searing drama detailing the breakdown in a marriage. Finney won an Academy Award nomination as George Dunlap, the middle-aged man experiencing a mid-life crisis.

After *Shoot the Moon,* Finney's best role was as the heroic, aging gunman Leo O'Bannion in the Dashiell Hammett–inspired gangster film *Miller's Crossing* (1990), from the highly creative Joel Coen and Ethan Coen. He was also impressive as the sad school teacher in the underrated screen remake of Terence Rattigan's play *The Browning Version* (1994). Increasingly, Finney's best work was found on British television, such as *A Rather English Marriage* (1998), for which he won the BAFTA Television Award for Best Actor. He also appeared in a supporting role, opposite Julia Roberts, as the jaded lawyer Ed Masry in Steven Soderbergh's *Erin Brockovich* (2000), which generated more award nominations for Finney for Best Supporting Actor from the U.S. Academy Awards, the British Academy, and the Golden Globe Awards. This followed earlier awards for *Saturday Night and Sunday Morning* at the 1961 BAFTA for Most Promising Newcomer, the 1963 New York Critics Circle Award for Best Actor (*Tom Jones*), and the 1971 Golden Globe for Best Motion Picture Actor (*Scrooge*).

FILMS: The Entertainer (1960), Saturday Night and Sunday Morning (1960), Tom Jones (1963), The Victors (1963), Night Must Fall (1964), Two for the Road (1966), The Picasso Summer (1967), Charlie Bubbles (1967), Scrooge (1970), Gumshoe (1971), Alpha Beta (1972), Murder on the Orient Express (1974), The Duellists (1977), Loophole (1980), Shoot the Moon (1981), Looker (1981), Wolfen (1981), Annie (1981), The Dresser (1983), Under the Volcano (1984), Orphans (1987), Miller's Crossing (1990), Playboys (1992), Rich in Love (1992), The Browning Version (1994), A Man of No Importance (1995), The Run of the Country (1996), Washington Square (1997), Breakfast of Champions (1999), Simpatico (1999), Erin Brockovich (2000), Traffic (2001), and Delivering Milo (2001).

FIRE OVER ENGLAND (London Films, 1937)—Historical drama. *Director:* William K. Howard; *Producer:* Erich Pommer; *Script:* Clarence Dane and Sergei

Nolbandov, based on the novel by A. E. W. Mason; *Cinematography:* James Wong Howe; *Music:* Richard Addinsell; *Cast:* Flora Robson (Queen Elizabeth), Raymond Massey (Phillip II of Spain), Leslie Banks (Earl of Leicester), Laurence Olivier (Michael Ingolby), Vivien Leigh (Cynthia), Morton Selten (Lord Burleigh), Tamara Desni (Elena), Lyn Harding (Sir Richard Ingolby), George Thirlwell (Gregory), Henry Oscar (Spanish Ambassador), Robert Rendel (Don Miguel), Robert Newton (Don Pedro), Donald Calthrop (Don Escobal), Charles Carson (Admiral Valdez), and James Mason (Hilary Vane).

Alexander Korda's* patriotic celebration of Great Britain, and thinly disguised attack on Nazi Germany, was performed largely by a British cast, led by Flora Robson* as the strong, romantically frustrated Queen Elizabeth and Laurence Olivier* as her courtier. The production talent, however, was primarily European: producer Erich Pommer, scriptwriter Sergei Nolbandov, U.S. director William Howard, and the talented Hollywood cinematographer James Wong Howe. This is one of the most impressive looking British films of the late 1930s, with massive halls and other sets to complement Howe's lighting. It is also a static, dull film that relies largely on Robson's theatrical speeches and Olivier's dash and romantic interludes with Vivien Leigh to retain audience interest.

In the late sixteenth century, Britain is facing invasion from Philip II of Spain and the cash-strapped court of Queen Elizabeth is covertly endorsing profitable raids on Spanish ships. After Michael Ingolby's father is executed by the Spanish Inquisition, he volunteers to replace the English traitor, Hilary Vane (James Mason*) and visit Philip's court, posing as Vane, to discover the names of the English traitors plotting against Elizabeth. Ingolby's infiltration of Philip's court, jeopardized by the presence of a former lover Elana, now married to Don Pedro, provides one of the rare moments of tension in the film. Ingolby escapes with the names, and Queen Elizabeth confronts her traitors and orders them, led by Ingolby, to set fire to the Spanish ships sailing toward Britain. In this propaganda film, thinly disguised as an historical epic, it is little surprise that the British foil the Spanish invasion at the end of the film, in preparation for the real German air attack three years later.

A FISH CALLED WANDA (MGM, 1988)—Comedy. *Director:* Charles Crichton; *Producer:* Michael Shamberg, Steve Abbott (executive), John Cleese (executive), and John Comfort (executive); *Script:* John Cleese and Charles Crichton; *Cinematography:* Alan Hume; *Music:* John Du Prez; *Cast:* John Cleese (Archie Leech), Jamie Lee Curtis (Wanda Gerschwitz), Kevin Kline (Otto West), Michael Palin (Ken), Maria Aitken (Wendy Leech), Tom Georgeson (George), Patricia Hayes (Mrs. Coady), Geoffrey Palmer (Judge), and Cynthia Caylor (Portia Leech).

A Fish Called Wanda is a very funny comedy. Its conventional narrative form (farce) provides an opportunity to include a series of mildly "offensive" jokes, mainly concerned with the killing of dogs, the eating of live fish, and a display of male nudity in front of (unimpressed) young children and (embarrassed) adults.

The film was a major commercial success in Britain, the United States, Australia, and many other countries. Some critics were disappointed that it was not more surreal and adventurous. However, veteran Ealing director Charles Crichton* (who was seventy-seven when he made the film) and John Cleese produced a consistently funny film, expertly performed by a team of professionals, especially Kevin Kline as the psychopath Otto and Jamie Lee Curtis in the best role of her career.

The basic plot concerns four jewel thieves—Americans Otto and Wanda joining British crooks George and Ken to commit a jewellery heist. After they successfully complete the robbery, Otto and Wanda betray George to the police. George hides the jewels before he is taken into custody so Otto and Wanda are forced to find out where the jewels have been secreted. While Wanda works on George's defense lawyer Archie Leech, Ken tries to kill Mrs. Coady, the only witness to the crime. Wanda succeeds in seducing Archie, and also falling in love with him, and Ken, inadvertently, causes Mrs. Coady's death after killing her dogs in successive mishaps. Unlike Crichton's famous 1951 heist film *The Lavender Hill Mob,** where the police finally catch the inoffensive Alec Guinness* and Stanley Holloway, Wanda and Leech successfully evade the authorities.

Kline won an Oscar at the 1989 Academy Awards for Best Supporting Actor, Crichton was nominated for Best Director and Best Original Writing, while Cleese was nominated for Best Writing, Best Original Screenplay. Cleese won the Best Actor Award at the 1989 BAFTA Film Awards, as did Michael Palin for Best Actor in a Supporting Role. Kline (Best Actor), Curtis (Best Actress), Maria Aitken (Best Actress in a Supporting Role), Crichton (Best Direction), John Jympson (Best Editing), and Cleese (Best Original Screenplay) were nominated at these Awards as was Crichton and producer Michael Shamberg for best film. Cleese and Curtis were also nominated at the 1989 Golden Globe Awards.

FISHER, TERENCE (1904–1980). There have been many phases in Terence Fisher's career in the British film industry. After a lengthy period as clapper boy and editor in the 1930s, Fisher was promoted to director and worked on minor melodramas in the late 1940s within the Rank organization. His best film during this first phase, which Fisher co-directed with Anthony Darnborough, was *So Long at the Fair* (1950), a Gothic mystery that utilizes the 1889 Paris Exposition as an integral part of the plot as Jean Simmons, assisted by Dirk Bogarde,* searches for her missing brother (David Tomlinson). Fisher and Darnborough also co-directed a dull version of Noël Coward's drawing room melodrama *The Astonished Heart* (1949), but a more instructive film, in terms of the future direction of Fisher's career, was *To the Public Danger* (1948), a B film produced at Rank's Highbury Studios, which was designed to "showcase" its "Company of Youth" personalities. *To the Public Danger,* based on a radio play by Patrick Hamilton, was the best film to come out of this series of low-budget films.

After his period at Rank ended, Fisher worked on a succession of low-budget films at Hammer Studios, and elsewhere, and he also supplemented his income with television programs (including the immensely popular *Robin Hood* series starring Richard Greene) in the early and mid-1950s. Fisher's breakthrough, however, came with *The Curse of Frankenstein** (1957). Prior to this, there was little real indication in his films prior to 1957 of what was to come in the next two years and the impact he was to have in resurrecting the horror genre.

The Curse of Frankenstein, and many of his other horror films at Hammer, provided Fisher with an appropriate dramatic form to explore his recurring theme—the Manichaean struggle between the good and evil. While this struggle is evident in other genres, it is an integral aspect of Fisher's horror film. His films from 1957 to 1959 included the best screen version of *Dracula** (1958), the best screen version of *The Hound of the Baskervilles* (1959), and the best screen version of *The Mummy** (1959). All of these, and other films directed by Fisher, were characterized by his ability to generate a strong dramatic atmosphere from limited resources. This included startling editing rhythms, poetic ellipses, and a masterly use of color and composition.

His formal skill was matched by the rich thematic basis of his films where issues of class, scientific rationalism, and religious values were scrutinized within an entertaining generic context. Fisher's *Dracula,* for example, heightens the erotic aspects of the tale and contrasts the sensual relationship of the vampire and (mostly) female victims with the sadistic behavior of the representatives of Christianity who drive their stakes into the bodies of the "infected" women. Dracula emerges in this film as a more problematic manifestation of society's repressed fears than other versions of this tale.

The inherent sensuality and depictions of sadism in Fisher's horror films invoked complaints from the critics although the films were embraced by the public in both Britain and the United States. The success of *The Curse of Frankenstein* and *Dracula* elevated Hammer to the position of the most successful British production company at the time. It also transformed the careers of Fisher, Peter Cushing,* and Christopher Lee,* who had been working in minor parts for many years. After *The Curse of Frankenstein, Dracula,* and *The Mummy,* Lee rejected any horror role that required heavy makeup, which was coupled with his desire to avoid typecasting. His absence from Fisher's follow-up vampire film *The Brides of Dracula* (1960) weakened the film. Lee did not return to the role of the count until Fisher's excellent *Dracula, Prince of Darkness* in 1965, except for an Italian parody (*Tempi Duri per I Vampiri* [1959]). After *The Brides of Dracula,* Cushing did not return to the part of Van Helsing for another twelve years with *Dracula A.D. 1972* (1972).

In 1962, Fisher made his most romantic film, and one of his worst commercial failures, in *The Phantom of the Opera.* Almost devoid of violence, suspense, and terror, the film did not employ the traditional unmasking of the phantom at the climax and concentrated instead on the doomed love of the phantom (Herbert Lom) for opera singer Christine (Heather Sears). After the commercial failure of *The Phantom of the Opera,* Hammer's most expensive film up until that time, Fisher left the studio and was reduced to working on dismal parodies. This included films such as *The Horror of It All* (1963), starring crooner Pat Boone, and a trio of science fiction films for low-budget U.S. distributors such as Lippert and Planet: *The Earth Dies Screaming* (1964), *Island of Terror* (1966), and *The Night of the Big Heat* (1967), the last one with Lee and Cushing.

With his return to Hammer later in the decade, Fisher concluded his career with three excellent films that reworked many of the themes and motifs established in his "golden" period of the late 1950s. *The Devil Rides Out** (1967) foregrounds the elemental Manichaeistic polarities that dominate his best films. For his final two films, Cushing returned to the character that rejuvenated his film career in 1957. *Frankenstein Must Be Destroyed* (1969) was a bleak film with the Baron replacing the monster as the real villain. He followed with *Frankenstein and the Monster from Hell* (1973), which was Fisher's fifth Frankenstein film and Hammer's seventh. An even bleaker film, it confines the story within the walls of an asylum. Fisher died in 1980.

FILMS (as director): Colonel Bogey (1948), Song of Tomorrow (1948), To the Public Danger (1948), Portrait from Life (1948), Marry Me (1949), The Astonished Heart (1948), So Long at the Fair (1950), Home to Danger (1951), Wings of Danger (1952), A Stolen Face (1952), The Last Page (1952), Distant Trumpet (1952), Mantrap (1953), Four Sided Triangle (1953), Spaceways (1953), Blood Orange (1953), Face the Music (1954), Three's Company (1954), Stranger Came Home (1954), Murder by Proxy (1954), Mask of Dust (1954), Final Appointment (1954), Children Galore (1954), Stolen Assignment (1955), The Flaw (1955), The Last Man to Hang (1956), The Gelignite Gang (1956), The Curse of Frankenstein (1957), Kill Me Tomorrow (1957), Dracula (1958), The Revenge of Frankenstein (1958), The Hound of the Baskervilles (1959), The Mummy (1959), The Man Who Could Cheat Death (1959), The Stranglers of Bombay (1960), The Brides of Dracula (1960), The Two Faces of Dr. Jekyll (1960), Sword of Sherwood Forest (1960), The Curse of the Werewolf (1961), The Phantom of the Opera (1962), Valley of Fear (1962), The Horror of It All (1963), The Gorgon (1964), The Earth Dies Screaming (1964), Dracula, Prince of Darkness (1966), Island of Terror (1966), Frankenstein Created Woman (1966), The Night of the Big Heat (1967), The Devil Rides Out (1968), Frankenstein Must Be Destroyed (1969), and Frankenstein and the Monster from Hell (1973).

FORBES, BRYAN (b. 1926). A talented actor, writer, producer, and director, Bryan Forbes has not been fully appreciated for his contribution to the British film industry. Forbes entered the film industry in the late 1940s with small parts in Michael Powell's* *The Small Back Room* (1949), *All over the Town* (1949), and *Dear Mr. Prohack* (1949). His best role during this period was as the cad in Guy Hamilton's adaptation of the long-running J. B. Priestley play *An Inspector Calls* (1954). Forbes was often cast as a working-class "lad" or a prisoner of war (*The Wooden Horse* [1950] and *The Colditz Story** [1955]), but not an officer— when he auditioned for *The Cruel Sea** (1953), Forbes received a rejection letter informing him that he was "not officer material."[1]

During the 1950s, Forbes often worked in U.S.–British co-productions with U.S. "stars" whose careers were waning, such as Alan Ladd. Forbes also contributed to the scripts of three genre films with Ladd, the Arthurian adventure *The Black Knight* (1954), with Forbes supplying additional dialogue, the war film *The Red Beret* (1953), and the whaling adventure *Hell below Zero* (1954). However, it was not until another U.S.–British co-production, the war drama *The Cockleshell Heroes* (1955), directed by and starring José Ferrer, that Forbes received his first screenplay credit.

In 1960, two of Forbes's best scripts were produced. First, the controversial story of the persecution of a union man who refuses to join an unofficial strike in *The Angry Silence* (1960). Although Forbes received a good deal of criticism from the union movement, especially the miners' union, he was nominated for the 1961 Oscar for Best Writing. Forbes followed with an even better script for *The League of Gentlemen** (1960), a deeply ironic caper film that transforms 1950s military icons, such as Jack Hawkins,* Richard Attenborough,* and Roger Livesey, into antisocial bank robbers.

Forbes made his directorial debut with the allegorical tale of young Hayley Mills mistaking murderer Alan Bates* for Jesus Christ in *Whistle Down the Wind* (1961). He followed with *Séance on a Wet Afternoon* (1964), and although the film failed to reach a wide public it contained superb performances from Kim Stanley, as a disturbed medium, and Attenborough as her husband. This film is representative of the low-key style so characteristic of his best films. He also directed the downbeat, realist drama *The L-Shaped Room* (1963), starring Leslie Caron as a young Frenchwoman who comes to England to give birth to her child. Unfortunately, the failure of *Séance on a Wet Afternoon* (and *Life for Ruth* [1962]) caused the collapse of Allied Filmmakers, the production company set up by Forbes with Attenborough, Michael Relph,* Basil Dearden,* and Hawkins in 1960 to make films for distribution by Rank.

Forbes continued to write and direct throughout the 1960s, including the caustic anti-war film *King Rat* (1965), starring George Segal as a self-serving prisoner of war, and the black comedy *The Wrong Box* (1966). In 1969, Forbes was appointed head of production at EMI's Elstree Studios, but this only lasted to 1971, when Elstree was eventually demolished. He was prolific, but less successful, throughout the 1970s and early 1980s with *International Velvet* (1978), a sequel to MGM's *National Velvet* (1944), and the commercially successful "gender" thriller *The Stepford Wives* (1975), which inspired a series of inferior sequels. He co-scripted *Chaplin* (1992) for Attenborough and married actress Nanette Newman, who worked in a number of his films. Forbes is also a prolific author of fiction and nonfiction.

FILMS (as actor): The Tired Men (short, 1943), The Small Back Room (1949), All over the Town (1949), Dear Mr. Prohack (1949), The Wooden Horse (1950), Green Grows the Rushes (1951), Flesh and Fury (1952), The World in His Arms (1952), Appointment in London (1953), Sea Devils (1953), Wheels of Fate (1953), The Million Pound Note (1954), An Inspector Calls (1954), Up to His Neck (1954), The Colditz Story (1955), Passage Home (1955), Last Man to Hang (1955), The Quatermass Xperiment (1955), Now and Forever (1956), Satellite in the Sky (1956), The Extra Day (1956), It's Great to Be Young (1956), The Baby and the Battleship (1956), Quatermass II (1957), The Key (1958), I Was Monty's Double (1958), Yesterday's Enemy (1959), The League of Gentlemen (1960), The Guns of Naverone (1961), A Shot in the Dark (1964), Of Human Bondage (1964), The Slipper and the Rose (1976), International Velvet (1978), and The Restless Natives (1985).

FILMS (as director): Whistle Down the Wind (1961), The L-Shaped Room (1962), Séance on a Wet Afternoon (1964), King Rat (1965), The Wrong Box (1966), The Whisperers (1966), Deadfall (1966), The Madwoman of Chaillot (1969), The Raging Moon (1970), The Stepford Wives (1975), The Slipper and the Rose (1976), International Velvet (1978), Sunday Lovers (1980), Better Late Than Never (1982), and The Naked Face (1984).

FORMBY, GEORGE (1904–1961). Initially a regional comedian popular in the north and the Midlands, Lancashire-born George Formby enjoyed wide appeal throughout Britain in the 1930s and early 1940s. Formby's films established a repetitive formula with him as an inept, sexually innocent lad desiring a girl who should have been out of his league—generally played by an attractive actress on her way up, such as Kay Walsh, Phyllis Calvert,* and Googie Withers.* Despite his physical and intellectual deficiencies, Formby's character would emerge triumphant, marked by his catch phrase, "It turned out nice again, hasn't it?"

Radio played a significant role in establishing Formby's popularity and by the late 1930s he was the most popular male film star in Britain. His films also inserted musical interludes into their simple plots with Formby singing his simple ditties, laced with their thinly veiled sexual meanings, often phallic, on his small ukulele. However, just as the *Carry On* series from the late 1950s to the 1970s was able to inject overt sexual material in a period when film censorship was relatively strict, Formby was also able to avoid censure because his character was never sexually threatening or even "realistic." Typically, as in *Turned out Nice Again* (1941), Formby worked for a women's underwear manufacturer who specialize in "reinforced" woolly combinations. This, of course, provided a context for his distinctive humor. Formby's films lost favor after World War II and following the failure of *George in Civvy Street* in 1946 he returned to the music hall and radio.

FILMS: By the Shortest of Heads (1915), Boots, Boots (1934), Off the Dole (1935), No Limit (1935), Keep Your Seats, Please (1936), Keep Fit (1937), Feather Your Nest (1937), It's in the Air (1938), I See Ice! (1938), Trouble Brewing (1939), Come on, George! (1939), Spare a Copper (1940), Let George Do It (1940), Turned out Nice Again (1941), South American George (1941), Much Too Shy (1942), Get Cracking (1943), Bell-Bottom George (1943), Her Snoops to Conquer (1944), I Didn't Do It (1945), and George in Civvy Streets (1946).

THE 49TH PARALLEL (Ortus, 1941)—War/propaganda. *Director:* Michael Powell; *Producers:* Michael Powell, John Sutro, George H. Brown (associate), and Roland Gillett (associate); *Script:* Emeric Pressburger; *Cinematography:* Freddie Young; *Music:* Ralph Vaughan Williams; *Cast:* Leslie Howard (Phillip Armstrong Scott), Raymond Massey (Andy Brock), Laurence Olivier (Johnnie), Eric Portman (Lieutenant Hirth), Anton Walbrook (Peter), Niall MacGinnis (Vogel), John Chandos (Lohrmann), Glynis Johns (Anna), Finlay Currie (Albert, the Factor), Basil Appleby (Jahner), Peter Moore (Kranz), Raymond Lovell (Lieutenant Kuhnecke), and Charles Victor (Andreas).

The 49th Parallel is a significant film in the history of the British film industry for many reasons. It was the most popular film in Britain in 1941 and it elevated Eric Portman* into the top rank of British actors. It was the only full-length feature film to be financed by the Ministry of Information and is one of the best propaganda films produced by any country during World War II. Emeric Pressburger's* script was both intelligent and courageous as there were considerable institutional obstacles to the film before ever going into production.

There is also a characteristic Michael Powell* and Pressburger off-centered quality to the film, particularly when it is compared with the typical propaganda film in this period. For a start, it was rare to place the enemy, the Germans, at the center of the film—particularly as there is always a danger that the audience will develop sympathy for the hunted—in this case six Nazi seaman forced to flee Canadian authorities after their U-boat is destroyed by the Canadian Air Force while trying to hide in the Gulf of St. Lawrence. Any possibility of audience empathy with the Germans is addressed by Powell and Pressburger at the start of the film as German ruthlessness and an unquestioning adherence to a central figure (Adolf Hitler) is evident.

Pressburger's script offers a unifying discourse on the importance of diversity within a democracy, a diversity that finally unifies all those opposed to the totalitarianism of the Nazi ideology. This theme is developed in each encounter in the film. The first "debate," or ideological confrontation, is between a French Canadian fur trapper Johnnie and the leader of the Germans, Lieutenant Hirth. Hirth attempts to solicit Johnnie's sympathies by promising that the Nazis will address French Canadian separatism after their victory. Johnnie, however, is not impressed and tells Hirth that the French Canadians have their own institutions and he points to the pattern of monolithic subjugation of different cultures by Germany in the past.

After the Germans shoot Johnnie, they come across a Hutterite community of German immigrants, a place where Hirth expects support for their cause. However, when Hirth extols the virtues of Hitler's philosophy in an address to the Hutterite community, they respond, through their leader Peter, that Hitler's "New Order" is anathema to the Hutterites. Again, the Nazis are forced to move on and they lose another member of their group when they execute Vogel after he tries to remain with the Hutterites.

The next encounter is between the two remaining Germans, Hirth and Lohrmann, and an effete English anthropologist Phillip Armstrong Scott. Scott lives in remote Canada in a tepee with his collection of paintings by Pablo

Picasso and Henri Matisse. His interest in the writings of Ernest Hemingway and, especially, Thomas Mann's *Magic Mountain* confirms Hirth's belief that the British are soft and decadent. This belief is shown to be false as Scott beats Lohrmann in a fistfight (with each punch he tells Lohrmann: "That's for Matisse, that's for Picasso, that's for me") after the Nazis slash his paintings.

The last episode takes place on a train headed for the United States between Hirth, the last German, and a Canadian soldier, Andy Brock, a deserter. When Hirth extols the virtues of Hitler's New Order, Brock's anger and patriotism surfaces and he prevents Hirth from crossing into the United States, a neutral country in 1941. The Powell-Pressburger film presents its drama as a confrontation between the forces of civilization (the Allies) and the forces of ruthlessness and evil (the six Germans).

Pressburger's script, deservedly, won an Oscar for Best Writing, Original Story at the 1943 Academy Awards and the film was nominated for Best Picture.

FOUR WEDDINGS AND A FUNERAL (Polygram, 1994)—Comedy. *Director:* Mike Newell; *Producers:* Duncan Kenworthy, Richard Curtis (coexecutive), Eric Fellner (executive), and Tim Bevan (executive); *Script:* Richard Curtis; *Cinematography:* Michael Coulter; *Music:* Richard Rodney Bennett; *Cast:* Hugh Grant (Charles), Andie MacDowell (Carrie), James Fleet (Tom), Simon Callow (Gareth), John Hannah (Matthew), Kristin Scott-Thomas (Fiona), David Bower (David), Charlotte Coleman (Scarlett), Rowan Atkinson (Father Gerald), Corin Redgrave (Hamish Banks), Sophie Thompson (Lydia Hibbott), David Haig (Bernard Delaney), Anna Chancellor (Henrietta), Timothy Walker (Angus), and Sara Crowe (Laura).

The slight narrative premise that links the four weddings and the funeral is Charles's inability to commit to a long-term relationship. Henrietta, whom he abandons at the altar, describes him as "serial monogamist," a fact that Charles even acknowledges during his witty best man speech after the first wedding. Yet, the film is determined not to leave any character unhappy and the film's epilogue provides a satisfying closure even for Henrietta, as well as the rest of Charles's unmarried friends. This includes Fiona (Kristin Scott Thomas), who is last seen ogling Prince Charles.

Mike Newell* has directed more complex, morally problematic films, such as *Donnie Brasco* (1997), but the clever structure of *Four Weddings and a Funeral,* with its emphasis on communal celebrations—the four weddings and Gareth's funeral—with no boring extraneous material, such as vocational or domestic problems, resulted in an outstanding success. The credit must be shared with Richard Curtis's script and the self-deprecating mannerisms of Hugh Grant, who had been playing variations of the humble, bumbling, absent-minded, witty Charles for more than a decade. Grant is also surrounded by inveterate scene-stealers such as Simon Callow as Gareth (the gay Scotsman who dies while energetically dancing at the third wedding), Scott-Thomas's Fiona, James Fleet as Tom (an even more bumbling English caricature than Charles), and Rowan Atkinson (a nervous priest who finds it almost impossible to complete the second marriage ceremony between Bernard and Lydia). Add John Hannah with his reading of the W. H. Auden poem *Funeral Blues* at Gareth's funeral, and the film provides a lively celebration of friends who resumed their friendship at every function.

Curtis's script also varies the tone, with the second wedding a standout as it exploits Charles's pain when he discovers that Carrie is engaged to a wealthy Scotsman. His misery escalates when he is surrounded by a number of bitter ex-girlfriends after the wedding, including the tearful Henrietta. Finally, Charles is trapped in a closet while Bernard and Lydia consummate their marriage (again and again).

Four Weddings and a Funeral won the BAFTA Best Film Award in 1995, Grant won Best Actor, Scott Thomas Best Supporting Actress, and Newell the David Lean Award for Direction. The film also won Best Foreign Film in France and Australia, the Golden Screen Award in Germany, while Grant won a Golden Globe Award in the United States and Curtis the Writers Guild of America Award for Best Screenplay.

FROM RUSSIA WITH LOVE (Eon Productions/United Artists, 1963)—Espionage/adventure. *Director:* Terence Young; *Producers:* Harry Saltzman and Albert R. Broccoli; *Script:* Richard Maibaum and Johanna Harwood (adaptation) from Ian Fleming's novel; *Cinematography:* Ted Moore; *Music:* John Barry; *Cast:* Sean Connery (James Bond), Daniela Bianchi (Tatiana Romanova), Pedro Armendariz (Kerim Bey), Lotte Lenya (Rosa Klebb), Robert Shaw (Donald "Red" Grant), Bernard Lee (M), Eunice Grayson (Sylvia Trench), Martine Beswick (Zora), Lois Maxwell (Miss Moneypenny), Desmond Llewelyn (Major Boothroyd—Q), Vladek Sheybal (Kronsteen), and Eric Pohlmann (voice of Ernst Stavros Blofeld).

The second James Bond film, *From Russia with Love,* brought back most of the personnel from *Dr. No*,* including director Terence Young, scriptwriters Richard Maibaum and Johanna Harwood, and series regulars Sean Connery* as Bond, Bernard Lee as M, and Lois Maxwell as Miss Moneypenny. Even co-star Daniela Bianchi's voice was dubbed, as was Ursula Andress's in *Dr. No.* Desmond Llewelyn made his first appearance as Major Boothroyd (subsequently known as "Q"), John Barry's distinctive score became much more prominent, as did the emphasis on Bond's sexual prowess and flippant asides. This film also increased the number of the spectacular action pieces, particularly in the last part of the film with an extended fight between Bond and SPECTRE agent Donald "Red" Grant within the confined spaces of the Orient Express. This is followed by a helicopter attack and a boat chase before Bond's final confrontation with SPECTRE's Rosa Klebb. Like *Dr. No,* the plotting in *From Russia with Love* was not overwhelmed with the gadgets (with a specially designed suitcase that exudes smoke that saves Bond on the Orient Express the only notable invention) and the excessive amount of self-parody that characterized future Bond films—beginning with the pre-title scene in *Goldfinger* (1964).

From Russia with Love is one of Ian Fleming's best novels and the film is faithful to its emphasis on Cold War intrigue in Istanbul. Bond, attracted by the lure of a Russian agent (Tatiana Romanova) and a special decoding machine (the Lektor), travels to Istanbul, where he forms an alliance with Kerim Bey (Pedro Armendariz in his final screen appearance). However, chess champion Kronsteen, a SPECTRE agent, sets in motion a complicated plot that upsets the delicate political balance in Istanbul. The scheme involves Tatiana's allegiance to her Russian superior, Rosa Klebb, who unknown to Tatiana, has defected to SPECTRE. Tatiana is used as the bait to kill Bond—because Bond killed Dr. No in the first film. After Bond steals the decoding machine from the Russians, Grant sets after Bond to kill him and steal the machine. Grant fails.

The film retains much of the novel's tension and political intrigue. Its relatively "serious" tone, interspersed by romance and sex, differentiates *From Russia with Love* from subsequent entries in this series.

THE FULL MONTY (Fox Searchlight Pictures/Channel Four Films/Redwave Film, 1997)—Comedy/social drama. *Director:* Peter Cattaneo; *Producer:* Uberto Pasolini; *Script:* Simon Beaufoy; *Cinematography:* John de Borman; *Music:* Anne Dudley; *Cast:* Robert Carlye (Alex "Gaz" Garfield), Tom Wilkinson (Gerald Arthur Cooper), Mark Addy (Dave Althorpe), Paul Barber (Barrington "Horse" Mitchell), Steve Huison (Lomper), Hugo Speer (Guy), Emily Woof (Mandy Garfield), Lesley Sharp (Jean), William Snape (Nathan Garfield), Deidre Cooper (Linda Cooper), Bruce Jones (Reg), and Paul Butterworth (Barry).

Six unemployed workers learn two things from watching their wives and girlfriends at a Chippendale strip show. First that women respond enthusiastically to male strippers and second, having watched the women use a male urinal, that women can urinate standing up. Both discoveries frighten the men and compound their insecurities—sexual and otherwise—and while the film initially focuses on male insecurities, it also shows them regaining a sense of self-worth. A male strip show provides the pretext for this to take place.

Set in Sheffield at a time when the city is suffering from the economic effects of the Thatcher period, the film is based on a series of troubled relationships. Each character has a specific problem: Gaz's marriage has collapsed and he is in trouble with his young son Nathan; Dave is suffering from recurring bouts of impotence due to his weight and inability to find a decent job; Lomper has no male friends, but a dependent mother; and Gerald, the only middle-class member of the group, is terrified that his wife will find out that he has lost his job as foreman at the mill. The remaining members of the troupe are Guy, who has an added physical advantage over other men, an advantage that can only be fully realized when his G-string comes off, and Horse, a middle-aged man with a bad hip who admits that while his "break-dancing days are over . . . there's always the funky chicken."

Simon Beaufoy's script could easily have degenerated into a series of low-level comedy turns, but the film, by focusing firmly on the lives of these desperate men, never resorts to cheap laughs and retains a sense of dignity for them. They succeed, despite many obstacles, and the final image clearly shows that they have regained their confidence. However, unlike *Brassed Off* (1996), where triumph is mitigated by a final reminder of the devastating impact of the government's economic policies, *The Full Monty* avoids this with its "feel-good" ending. Each man achieves his personal goal: Dave and his wife are reunited, Gaz and his son are reunited, and Lomper now has Guy as a sexual partner. Gaz's ex-wife is even in the audience cheering him on at the end.

NOTE

1. McFarlane, *An Autobiography of British Cinema,* p. 191.

G

GASBAGS (Gainsborough, 1940)—Comedy. *Director:* Marcel Varnel; *Producer:* Edward Black; *Script:* Marriott Edgar and Val Guest; *Cinematography:* Arthur Crabtree; *Cast:* Chesney Allen (Ches), Bud Flangagan (Bud), Jimmy Gold (Goldy), Teddy Knox (Knoxy), Charlie Naughton (Charlie), Jimmy Nervo (Cecil), Moore Marriott (Jerry Jenkins), Wally Patch (Sergeant Major), Frederick Valk (Sturmfuehrer), Eric Clauvering (Scharffuehrer), Anthony Eustrel (Gestapo Officer), Carl Jaffe (Gestapo Chief), and Irene Handl (Wife).

In 1933, the first Crazy Gang show was produced at the London Palladium. The concept grew out of the appearance of three double acts on the same bill—Bud Flanagan and Chesney Allen, Jimmy Nervo and Teddy Knox, and Charlie Naughton and Jimmy Gold. The first show was such a success that there were six more Crazy Gang shows and three films—*Okay for Sound* (1937), *The Frozen Limits* (1939, which Graham Greene thought was "the funniest English picture yet produced"),[1] and *Gasbags*.

Gasbags was released at an anxious time for the British people as the country was facing invasion from Germany following the fall of Norway. Yet, *Gasbags* is quite surreal and it provides evidence of neither fear or the overt jingoism evident in Hollywood films produced in the period following the Japanese attack on Pearl Harbor.

The Crazy Gang, as members of the British army, operate an illegal fish and chip stall from their barrage balloon in Hyde Park. When a strong gale lifts the balloon and the six comics to the western front, they meet up with a platoon of (captured) French soldiers and are placed in a German concentration camp. Other inmates include a squadron of Adolf Hitler look-alikes who have been imprisoned because of their refusal to impersonate the Führer at times when he is likely to be assassinated. The Gang escapes, after Knoxy replaces Hitler at a banquet where the Gestapo plans to kill the impersonator, thereby engendering public sympathy for Hitler. However, Knoxy, because of his total ineptitude, survives the assassination attempt and the Gang escape to the Siegfried line, where they commandeer a secret tunneling weapon to burrow under the sea back to London.

This is a funny, stupid film. It is significant as it provides an opportunity for audiences to appreciate this mad talented group of comedians, although their natural medium was the London Palladium, not the cinema.

GASLIGHT (British National, 1940)—Gothic melodrama. *Director:* Thorold Dickinson; *Producers:* John Corfield and Richard Vernon (associate); *Script:* A. R. Rawlinson and Bridget Boland, based on the play *Angel Street* by Patrick Hamilton; *Cinematography:* Bertrand Knowles; *Music:* Richard Addinsell; *Cast:* Anton Walbrook (Paul Mallen/Louis Barre), Diana Wynyard (Bella Mallen), Frank Pettingell (B. G. Rough), Cathleen Cordell (Nancy), Robert Newton (Vincent Ullswater), Jimmy Hanley (Cobb), and Mary Hinton (Lady Winterbourne).

The 1940 British production of Patrick Hamilton's Gothic melodrama *Gaslight* was released in the United States as *Angel Street* and when MGM decided to produce a Hollywood version with Charles Boyer and Ingrid Bergman, the U.S. studio not only bought the rights to the film, but also allegedly tried to destroy existing prints to remove competition for their version. Despite the high production values of the Hollywood version, which was rewarded at the 1945 Academy Awards, Thorold Dickinson's* version is far better as it conveys a stronger sense of perversity and sadism than the sanitized MGM version. Aside from Dickinson's intelligently restrained direction, the film benefits from Anton Walbrook's performance as the continental villain, Paul Mallen/Louis Barre. Walbrook's ability to blend charm with a sense of violence is particularly effective as it is constrained by his icy exterior and sadistic behavior. Similarly, Diana Wynyard is suitably fragile, both physically and emotionally, as the wife tormented after she comes across a letter that reveals her husband's true identity.

The film begins with a murder at 12 Pimlico Square as an elderly woman is killed by a man searching for the woman's rubies. Twelve years later, Paul Mallen and his wife Bella take up residence in an adjoining apartment and Bella begins to doubt her sanity as personal items disappear and then suddenly reappear. Bella's plight is intensified by her husband's sexual flirtations with the family maid, Nancy, who despises Bella's weakness. Fortunately, a retired policeman, Rough, takes an interest in Paul and assists Bella in exposing Paul's machinations.

Gaslight is a fine example of Victorian Gothic melodrama, with its dark, sadistic male tormenting a vulnerable woman. The family residence, consistent with the conventions of the Gothic form, plays a crucial part in the woman's distress. When Paul enters the empty apartment at number 12, he turns up the gas, causing the gaslight in his own home to dim and flicker, which, together with the disappearance and reappearance of personal items, threatens Bella's fragile mental state. Bella's vulnerability is heightened by Nancy's disdainful manner toward her mistress and the humiliating revelation that Paul and Nancy are conducting an affair within the apartment.

The power and pleasure of melodrama, particularly the Gothic variation, often emanates from the ending and that moment when the virtuous victim turns the tables on her tormenting protagonist. *Gaslight* fully delivers in this regard as the film climaxes with Paul tied to a chair while pleading with Bella to cut the ropes restraining him. Bella is thus able to enact her revenge on her cruel husband by feigning the distressed, uncertain psychological condition that Paul tried to induce throughout the film.

GENEVIEVE (Rank/Sirius, 1953)—Comedy. *Director:* Henry Cornelius; *Producer:* Henry Cornelius; *Script:* William Rose; *Cinematography:* Christopher Challis; *Music:* Larry Adler; *Cast:* Dinah Sheridan (Wendy McKim), John Gregson (Alan McKim), Kenneth More (Ambrose Claverhouse), Kay Kendall (Rosalind Peters), Geoffrey Keen (Policeman), Joyce Grenfell (Hotel Proprietress), Reginald Beckwith (Motorist), Arthur Wontner (Old Gentleman), and Michael Medwin (Husband).

Near the start of *Genevieve,* one of the most popular films produced in Britain in the 1950s, married couple Wendy and Alan McKim squabble over the annual Vintage Car Rally from London to Brighton. While Wendy would prefer to go to a party, Alan is determined to participate in the rally in his 1904 Darracq automobile ("Genevieve"). Wendy, dressed in her pyjamas, softens her attitude after she discovers a new hat that Alan has bought for her for the rally. So she returns to their bedroom, leans down and begins kissing Alan, also dressed in pyjamas. As the camera pans past Alan and Wendy kissing on the bed to a vintage photo of Genevieve, lying near the foot of the bed, an anonymous voice is heard over this image explaining: "What is taking place here is by now an old story but surprising as it may now seem, it was quite illegal as late as 1896"—at this point the next scene appears showing the source of the voice, a radio commentator, at the start of the car rally. However, this clever blending of sound (from the next scene) with the image of the current scene provides a humorous moment that manages, through clever composition and editing, to be both funny and subtle (and also avoid the censor's wrath).

Much of the credit for this fine film most go to director Henry Cornelius and scriptwriter William Rose (*The Ladykillers** [1955])—both of whom worked for Ealing. Cornelius even offered the script to Ealing but the head of production, Michael Balcon, suggested they take it to Pinewood. The Pinewood executives, however, were less than impressed by the film after they viewed a preview print and, thus, one of the classic British films was nearly shelved.

The story involves Alan and Wendy McKim, their friend Ambrose Claverhouse and his date Rosalind Peters (Kay Kendall in a role that was important to her career). While the film is best remembered for the car race from Brighton to London, and the succession of auto mishaps, the story also contains a degree of sexual openness not readily associated with the British cinema in the early 1950s. The film makes clear that Ambrose brings a different woman to the rally each year for one purpose only, and this fact exacerbates the sexual tension between the two men as Wendy was Ambrose's date for the 1949 rally. She, like his other dates, also stayed overnight at Brighton with Ambrose, the year before she married Alan. This aspect is made transparent when Rosalind tells Wendy that Ambrose is only interested in two things—old cars and that "other thing"—a line that the Production Code Administration demanded be deleted when the film was released in the United States.[2]

The sexual jealousy between the two men and the tension between Alan and Wendy over her participation in the 1949 rally with Ambrose provides an undercurrent for most of the film and supplies the motivation for the idiotic determination of both men to best each other in the race. This tension, however, dissipates in the last section as the film is content to milk the humor as both vehicles struggle to reach the finish line at Westminster Bridge.

One of the most identifiable aspects of *Genevieve* was the distinctive harmonica score supplied by Larry Adler, who was nominated for an Oscar at the 1955 Academy Awards, as was William Rose's script. Kenneth More* won the Best Actor Award at the 1954 BAFTA Film Awards and the film won both Best British Film and Best Film from Any Source at the same awards. *Genevieve* also shared the 1955 Golden Globe Award for Best Foreign film.

GEORGY GIRL (Columbia, 1966)—Comedy/romance. *Director:* Silvio Narizzano; *Producers:* Robert A. Goldston and Otto Plaschkes; *Script:* Peter Nicholls and Margaret Forster, based on Margaret Forster's novel; *Cinematography:* Kenneth Higgins; *Music:* Alexander Faris; *Cast:* James Mason (James Leamington), Alan Bates (Jos), Lynn Redgrave (Georgy), Charlotte Rampling (Meredith), Bill Owen (Ted), Clare Kelly (Doris), Denise Coffey (Peg), and Rachel Kempson (Ellen).

The so-called Swinging London cycle of British film followed the New Wave in the 1960s, peaking in the mid-1960s with films such as *Darling** (1965), *The Knack* (1965), *Georgy Girl, Alfie** (1966), and *To Sir with Love* (1967). There were many factors that encouraged this cycle, including the physical reconstruction of London, beginning after World War II, plus concomitant shifts within the composition of the city's population (age, race, and social background) and a concentrated program of self-promotion by newspapers and magazines. These films also assimilated changes in values with regard to sex, marriage, employment, ambition, and the family.

The "swinging" element in these films was not necessarily sexual but often just odd moments when the story would seemingly stop while characters would run, jump, or merely wander amidst familiar London settings, such as Edgware Road. For example, there is a typical moment in *Georgy Girl* when Jos (Alan Bates,* complete with "mod" cap and suit) wanders in a children's playground prior to his wedding. Similarly, near the end of the film he prances at the end of a pier to mark the end of his relationship with Georgy. Such scenes today appear forced, but *Georgy Girl* was a huge success for Columbia, the U.S. studio that financed the film. This popularity was reinforced by the The Seekers' hit song that is used over the credits in the film.

The film's plot is simple. Georgy, a virgin in her early twenties, moves between her Maida Vale apartment, which she shares with self-centered party girl Meredith, and the affluent Leamington mansion where her parents are servants to James Leamington, and where Georgy runs a small kindergarten. Georgy, living in the shadow of Meredith, lacks self-esteem and her only expression of control, which she periodically exploits, is her sexual power over the wealthy James Leamington. Leamington, who has known Georgy since she was a very young child, and describes himself as a kind of surrogate parent, offers her a contract to be his mistress, an offer that Georgy refuses. Meredith, on a whim, decides that the party life has become boring and decides to keep the baby she has conceived with boyfriend Jos. Georgy, however, becomes a surrogate parent to the unborn baby, a role she continues after its birth when Meredith, who marries Jos, disowns the baby (Sarah).

Georgy and Jos, with Sarah, live together until Jos decides that he cannot continue this personally restrictive lifestyle. The film rejects a conventional happy ending (Georgy, Jos, and Sarah) in favor of the more unconventional ending of Georgy marrying Leamington, a man who is more than twice her age. This is made even more morally problematic by the fact that Georgy does not love Leamington and he has been a kind of surrogate parent to her for many years. Georgy's father clearly condones this relationship. Rachel Kempson, who plays Leamington's neurotic wife, was Lynn Redgrave's mother in real life.

"Swinging London" is not an accurate description of the film's dominant mood. Instead, there is a prevailing a sense of sadness, failed relationships, and poor marriages. This mood is accentuated by Redgrave's (who accepted the part after her sister Vanessa declined) performance as a young woman who wants more than just a life of service. The only alternative lifestyle offered in the film is Meredith's promiscuous party life. Ultimately, the film suggests, servitude and sacrifice is Georgy's destiny. This is confirmed by the final image of Georgy, in her wedding dress, driving away on her honeymoon with Leamington clutching Sarah. The pleasures of "Swinging London" seem even more unobtainable to Georgy.

GET CARTER (MGM British, 1971)—Crime/gangster. *Director:* Mike Hodges; *Producer:* Michael Klinger; *Script:* Mike Hodges, based on the novel *Jack's Return Home* by Ted Lewis; *Cinematography:* Wolfgang Suschitzky; *Music:* Roy Budd; *Cast:* Michael Caine (Jack Carter), Ian Hendry (Eric Paice), Britt Ekland (Anna Fletcher), John Osborne (Cyril Kinnear), Tony Beckley (Peter), George Sewell (Con McCarty), Geraldine Moffat (Glenda), Dorothy White (Margaret), Rosemarie Dunham (Edna), Petra Markham (Doreen), Alun Armstrong (Keith), Bryan Mosley (Cliff Brumby), Glynn Edwards (Albert Swift), Bernard Hepton (Thorpe), and Terence Rigby (Gerald Fletcher).

There are examples of tough British gangster films in the late 1940s, such as *They Made Me a Fugitive** (1947) and *Brighton Rock** (1947). There are fewer examples in the 1950s and 1960s. *Get Carter* was released with little publicity in

1971 and has over the past thirty years deservedly acquired a reputation of one of the finest British gangster films.

Jack Carter is working in London for Gerald Fletcher when he learns of the death of his estranged brother in Newcastle. He is warned by Fletcher not to go north and interfere with the local criminals as Fletcher has an arrangement with local gangster Cyril Kinnear. Carter ignores Fletcher's advice and returns home to Newcastle, where he becomes suspicious about the circumstances concerning his brother's death in car accident. As he moves closer to the truth, the locals turn nasty and Carter is caught between the corrupt Kinnear and members of his own gang who have been sent by Fletcher to bring him back to London. This request becomes even more ominous when Fletcher learns that Carter has been sleeping with his wife Anna.

The turning point in the film occurs when Carter views a pornographic film showing the seduction of his brother's young daughter Doreen. This provides the moral context justifying Carter's subsequent behavior. This aspect is also intensified by the film's suggestion that Doreen may even be Carter's daughter. Henceforth, Carter sets out to kill everybody concerned with the exploitation of Doreen in the pornographic film.

Get Carter transfers the setting of Ted Lewis's novel from somewhere around Doncaster, probably the steel town of Scunthorpe, to Newcastle. This proves to be an inspired choice as the city, and its potent atmosphere of the old and the superficially modern, is effectively exploited by Mike Hodges. The setting for the final scene, by the sea at Seaham, County Durham, is an evocative mixture of nature and industry. Carter places Eric Paice's body in one of the coal carts heading out to sea as he walks jauntily alongside the cart swinging the gun that has just battered Paice to death. Carter, pleased that he has avenged his brother and the exploitation of Doreen, is executed by an unseen hit man. The last image shows Carter's body lying on the beach.

Get Carter, with a reasonable budget of $750,000, was released by MGM when it was in financial trouble and the film was virtually thrown away to the U.S. drive-in circuit. MGM remade it as *Hit Man,* with a U.S. black cast, the following year. The only film nomination *Get Carter* received was a 1972 BAFTA nomination for Best Supporting Actor for Ian Hendry's performance as the chief villain Eric Paice. Mainstream critics at the time were dismayed by the film's complex plotting and Carter's lack of remorse. During the film, he kills Cliff Brumby by throwing him off the roof of a car park, Albert Swift is knifed by Carter, and Paice is bashed to death. Similarly, Carter shows little emotion as he watches the villains push his car, with a woman (Glenda) in the trunk, off a pier into the water. Later, in an attempt to incriminate Kinnear, he injects another woman (Margaret) with drugs before drowning her in Kinnear's lagoon. While the commentators were appalled by Carter's actions, particularly as it involved the murder of women, each action is justified by the moral context established in the film. Carter is the only moral agent—as Hodges points out through the book Carter reads while traveling from London to Newcastle: Raymond Chandler's *Farewell,*

My Lovely—another "knight" forced to dispense his own justice in a corrupt world. A third-rate Hollywood version of *Get Carter,* starring Sylvester Stallone, was released in 2000.

GIELGUD, JOHN (1904–2000). Sir John Gielgud belonged to a generation of British stage actors in the 1920s, 1930s, and the 1940s—including Laurence Olivier* and Ralph Richardson*—who only contributed sporadically to the British cinema. This generation preferred the theater. Gielgud, whose Hamlet was considered the "high-water mark of English Shakespearian acting" in 1930, showed little interest in film acting until he went to Hollywood in the early 1950s to play Cassius in *Julius Caesar* (1953), directed by Joseph Mankiewicz. During the production of this film, Gielgud carefully studied James Mason's* film technique, especially the way Mason used his close-ups to suggest meaning without grimacing. Thereafter, he approached screen acting more seriously. However, it was not until the late 1970s that Gielgud performed extensively in the cinema with fine performances in *Providence* (1977) and *A Portrait of the Artist as a Young Man* (1977). He was, however, restricted by the type of film roles offered to him.

Gielgud came from a theatrical family. He was the grandnephew of stage actress Ellen Terry and, after training at the Royal Academy of Dramatic Arts, was playing Hamlet by the age of twenty-six. He made his debut at the Old Vic when he was eighteen. Considerable success on the British and U.S. stage in the late 1920 and throughout the 1930s persuaded Gielgud that he did not need the cinema and he turned down Alexander Korda* in the mid-1930s for a proposed version of *Hamlet.* He also rejected MGM's offer to appear opposite Norma Shearer in its version of *Romeo and Juliet* (1936), with Leslie Howard eventually accepting the lead role. Gielgud did accept a lead role in Alfred Hitchcock's* *Secret Agent* (1936), opposite Madelaine Carroll, after Hitchcock told Gielgud that his film would be a "modern-dress Hamlet." But the film reinforced Gielgud's suspicions about the cinema and he was disappointed with Hitchcock for favoring, in his opinion, Carroll in most set-ups. He also noted that Peter Lorre stole most of the remaining scenes. Similarly, in an earlier film, *The Good Companions* (1933), Gielgud complained that Jessie Matthews* dominated both screen space and screen billing, although the film provided him with an opportunity to sing.

Gielgud won a Tony Award for directing the play *Big Fish, Little Fish* on Broadway and was nominated for Best Supporting Actor for *Becket* (1964) at the 1965 Academy Awards. Throughout the late 1970s, 1980s, and 1990s, he enlivened many films with his flamboyant, theatrical cameos that, on occasion, developed into something more substantial. In many ways, Gielgud's definitive screen persona was encapsulated by his portrayal of Dudley Moore's butler in *Arthur* (1981), a role that gave impetus to his film career with a Best Supporting Actor at the 1982 Academy Awards. Thereafter, with a few notable exceptions, Gielgud was used in numerous films to add "class" with his well-judged cameo performances, such as his BAFTA–nominated performance as David Helfgott's mentor in the Australian film *Shine* (1996). A more serious opportunity came when Peter Greenaway* accepted Gielgud's suggestion that he would be ideal as Prospero in Greenaway's cinematic reworking of William Shakespeare's *The Tempest* in *Prospero's Books* (1991).

Age did not slow Gielgud down although film and television became more significant than the theater. He worked in his nineties, playing the pope in *Elizabeth* (1998) when he was ninety-four. Gielgud, knighted in 1953, died in 2000. He published a number of books, including an early autobiography, *Early Stages,* in 1939.

FILMS: Who Is the Man? (1924), The Clue of the New Pin (1929), Insult (1932), The Good Companions (1933), Full Fathom Five (voice only, doc., 1934), The Secret Agent (1936), Hamlet (1939), The Prime Minister (1941), An Airman's Letter to His Mother (short, 1941), Unfinished Journey (short, 1943), Shakespeare's Country (short, 1944), A Diary for Timothy (short, 1946), Julius Caesar (1953), Romeo and Juliet (voice only, 1954), Richard III (1955), Around the World in Eighty Days (1956), The Barretts of Wimpole Street (1956), Saint Joan (1957), The Immortal Land (voice only, short, 1958), Becket (1964), Hamlet (voice only, 1964), The Loved One (1965), Chimes at Midnight (1966), Sebastian (1967), Assignment to Kill (1967), To Die in Madrid (1967), October Revolution (narr., 1967), The Charge of the Light Brigade (1968), The Shoes of the Fisherman (1968), Oh! What a Lovely War (1969), Eagle in a Cage (1970), Lost Horizon (1972), Eleven Harrowhouse (1974), Gold (1974), Murder on the Orient Express (1974), Galileo (1974), Aces High (1974), Joseph Andrews (1976), A Portrait of the Artist As a Young Man (1977), Providence (1977), Murder by Decree (1978), Caligula (1978), The Conductor (1979), The Human Factor (1979), The Elephant Man (1980), The Formula (1980), Priest of Love (1980), Arthur (1981), Sphinx (1981), The Lion of the Desert (1981), Chariots of Fire (1981), Gandhi (1982), The Vatican Pimpernel (1982), Invitation to the Wedding (1983), The Wicked Lady (1983), Scandalous (1984), The Shooting Party (1984), Time after Time (1985), Plenty (1985), Leave All Fair (1985), Ingrid (voice, doc., 1985), The Whistle Blower (1986), Bluebeard, Bluebeard (1987), Appointment with Death (1988), Arthur 2: On the Rocks (1988), Getting It Right (1989), Strike It Rich (1990), Prospero's Books (1991), Shining Through (1992), The Power of One (1992), First Knight (1994), Haunted (1995), Hamlet (1996), The Portrait of a Lady (1996), Shine (1996), Looking for Richard (1996), Dragonheart (voice, 1996), The Leopard Son (voice, 1996), The Quest for Camelot (voice, 1998), Elizabeth (1998), and The Tichborne Claimant (1998).

GILBERT, LEWIS (b. 1920). After working as a child actor in British silent films, and into the 1930s, Lewis Gilbert worked as an assistant director before directing documentaries for the Royal Air Force during World War II. He moved on to low-budget feature films after the war, such as *The Little Ballerina* (1947) and *Cosh Boy** (1952), starring James Kenney as the teenage thug Roy Walsh in Britain's first X-certificate film. Gilbert followed this tough genre film two years later with another bleak crime film, *The Good Die Young** (1954), which included a number of U.S. actors associated with film noir, such as Gloria Grahame, John Ireland, and Richard Basehart.

It was, however, Gilbert's war films, often co-produced and co-written by Gilbert, that consolidated his reputation in the industry in the mid- to late 1950s, especially the sentimental *Reach for the Sky* (1956). This film told the heroic story of Douglas Bader's against-all-odds effort to remain a pilot despite the loss of both legs. *Reach for the Sky,* a major commercial success in most English-speaking countries, except the United States, was the first in a series of films Gilbert directed starring Kenneth More.* This included *The Admirable Crichton* (1956), another film version of the J. M. Barrie comedy of class reversal, *Sink the Bismark!* (1960), an exciting World War II drama involving the British attempts to destroy the legendary German battleship, and *The Greengage Summer* (1961), a bittersweet story of female infatuation with More miscast as the object of a teenager's (Susannah York) desire. Gilbert followed this with the period naval drama *H.M.S. Defiant* (1962), a tense film characterized by strong contrasting performances by Dirk Bogarde* and Alec Guinness.*

As the fortunes of the British film industry changed, so did Gilbert, who was able to adjust and change his style and genres to suit the times. In the mid-1960s, he directed and produced the successful social comedy *Alfie** (1966). Gilbert's versatility was further demonstrated with *You Only Live Twice* (1967), with Sean Connery* as James Bond, and two films with the bland Roger Moore as Ian Fleming's spy, *The Spy Who Loved Me* (1977), one of Moore's better outings as 007, and *Moonraker* (1979). More interesting were Gilbert's gentle social comedies: *Educating Rita* (1983), with Julie Walters as the mature student and Michael Caine* as her reluctant professor, and *Shirley Valentine* (1989), with Pauline Collins repeating her Broadway and London stage role as the middle-aged woman trying to recapture her passion in Greece.

Reach for the Sky won Best British Film at the 1957 BAFTA Film Awards, *Alfie* was nominated for Best British Film at the 1967 British Awards, winning a Special Jury Prize at Cannes and a Oscar nomination at the 1967 Academy Awards. *Educating Rita* won Best Film at the 1984 BAFTA Film Awards and *Shirley Valentine* was nominated for Best Film at the 1990 BAFTA Film Awards.

FILMS: Sailors Do Care (doc., 1944), The Ten-Year Plan (doc., 1945), Arctic Harvest (doc., 1946), Under One Roof (doc., 1946), Fishing Grounds of the World (doc., 1947) The Little Ballerina (1947), Marry Me (1949), Once a Sinner (1950), There Is Another Sun (1951), It's a Small World (1951), Scarlet Thread (1951), Emergency Call (1952), Cosh Boy (1952), Time Gentlemen Please (1952), Johnny on the Run (1953), Albert RN (1953), The Good Die Young (1954), The Sea Shall Not Have Them (1954), Cast a Giant Shadow (1955), Reach for the Sky (1956), The Admirable Crichton (1956), A Cry from the Streets (1958), Carve Her Name with Pride (1958), Ferry to Hong Kong (1959), Sink the Bismark! (1960), Light up the Sky (1960), The Greengage Summer (1961), H.M.S. Defiant (1962), The Seventh Dawn (1964), Alfie (1966), You Only Live Twice (1967), The Adventurers (1970), Friends (1971), Paul and Michelle (1974), Operation Daybreak (1975), Seven Nights in Japan (1976), The Spy Who Loved Me (1977), Moonraker (1979), Educating Rita (1983), Not Quite Jerusalem (1984), Shirley Valentine (1989), Stepping Out (1991), and Haunted (1995).

THE GOOD DIE YOUNG (Romulus Productions, 1954)—Crime/film noir. *Director:* Lewis Gilbert; *Producer:* Jack Clayton (associate); *Script:* Lewis

Gilbert and Vernon Harris, based on a novel by Richard Macaulay; *Cinematography:* Jack Asher; *Music:* Georges Auric; *Cast:* Laurence Harvey (Miles "Rave" Ravenscourt), Gloria Grahame (Denise), Richard Basehart (Joe), Joan Collins (Mary), John Ireland (Eddie), Rene Ray (Angela), Stanley Baker (Mike), Margaret Leighton (Eve Ravenscourt), Robert Morley (Sir Francis Ravenscourt), Freda Jackson (Mrs. Freeman), James Kenney (David), Susan Shaw (Doris), and Lee Patterson (Tod Maslin).

The Good Die Young is quintessential film noir and it benefits from an outstanding cast, including such iconic noir actors as Gloria Grahame (*Crossfire* [1947], *In a Lonely Place* [1950], and *The Big Heat* [1953]), Richard Basehart (*He Walked by Night* [1948]), and John Ireland (*Railroaded* [1947], *The Gangster* [1947], and *Raw Deal* [1948]). To this list add British actors such as Stanley Baker,* Freda Jackson, James Kenney (*Cosh Boy*), and Susan Shaw (*To the Public Danger* [1948]). The mood of the film was captured by Jack Asher's high-contrast black and white photography in such characteristic scenes such as Baker's death in the gutter late at night or the image of Ireland's body laying on the railway tracks. The script by director Lewis Gilbert* and Vernon Harris was based on prolific Hollywood scriptwriter Richard Macaulay's novel—Macaulay scripted numerous films for Warner Brothers in the 1930s, including *Brother Rat* (1938) and *The Roaring Twenties* (1939), plus the bizarre RKO film noir *Born to Kill* (1947).

The film's fatalistic narrative structure focuses on the reasons why four ex-servicemen (Eddie is a deserter while the others were discharged) decide to rob a postal van. Ex-soldier Joe returns to England from the United States to persuade his British wife Mary to return with him to the United States. Mary, on the other hand, is pressured by her selfish mother to stay in England. Joe, who was forced to leave his job in the United States, runs out of money and reluctantly participates in the robbery. Eddie deserts the U.S. military to stay with his duplicitous actress-wife Denise when he discovers that she is having an affair with her leading man. Mike, a battered and aging boxer, loses his funds for a tobacconist shop when his wife lends the money to her criminal brother. Finally, the psychotic "Rave," in need of money when his father Sir Francis Ravenscourt refuses to lend him any more to finance his gambling debts, convinces Joe, Eddie, and Mike to join him in the robbery of a postal van.

The robbery goes wrong and the men are forced to hide the money in a churchyard grave. "Rave" kills Eddie and Mike before confronting Joe at the airport. Both men are killed in a shoot-out, leaving Mary alone on the airport tarmac near the plane that would have taken them back to the United States. The film ends with a narrator's warning that the money would not have helped the men. Nothing, the narrator insists, would allow them to escape their fate. A suitably bleak film noir sentiment.

GORING, MARIUS (1912–1998). In 1958, Marius Goring had a co-starring role as a murderous doctor opposite Rick Jason and Lisa Gastoni in *Family Doctor.*

This was one of five films Goring made that year and although none of them were especially significant, he was a strong presence in each film. Although *Family Doctor* was little more than a routine murder mystery based on a series of deaths in a British village, it was typical of the type of films in which Goring labored for so many years.

Born on the Isle of Wight, Goring attended universities at Cambridge, Frankfurt, Munich, Vienna, and Paris before his first stage appearance in 1925 at Cambridge. This was followed by his London debut in 1927 and his West End debut in 1934. During the war, he made many BBC service broadcasts. Goring also made his first major screen appearance as a German naval officer, the first of many such roles, in Michael Powell's* World War I espionage thriller *The Spy in Black* (1939).

This association with Powell and Emeric Pressburger* proved to be rewarding for Goring as after World War II they provided him with his most prestigious screen roles—notably as Operator 71 in the fantasy *A Matter of Life and Death** (1946), and, two years later, as the composer Julian Craster who falls in love with the tragic heroine in *The Red Shoes** (1948). Other noteworthy roles included the wealthy yachtsman who lusts after Ava Gardner in *The Barefoot Contessa* (1954), the Nazi officer who falls in love with Maria Schell in *So Little Time* (1952), and another German in Powell's war film *Ill Met by Moonlight* (1957).

The recurring image of Goring in British films is that of the sophisticated, decadent villain—for example, see his evil Communist Commandant Anton Razinski in Roy Ward Baker's* espionage drama *Highly Dangerous* (1950), his murderous schoolmaster in Ronald Neame's* film noir *Take My Life** (1947), and the relatively large number of Germans he played throughout his career. However, aside from the films for Powell, one role that demonstrates Goring's range was as the tragic, vulnerable schoolmaster Vincent Perrin in Lawrence Huntington's melodrama *Mr. Perrin and Mr. Traill** (1948). In this film, Perrin is forced to confront his own weaknesses as he reacts adversely to the arrival of David Farrar,* a new teacher, and Perrin is, alternatively, vindictive, caring, jealous, and ultimately heroic.

Goring starred in two British television series, as Sir Percy Blakeney in *The Adventures of the Scarlet Pimpernel* in the mid-1950s and *The Expert* in the late 1960s. He died of cancer in 1998.

FILMS: Rembrandt (1936), The Amateur Detective (1936), Dead Men Tell No Tales (1938), Consider Your Verdict (1938), The Spy in Black (1939), Flying Fifty Five (1939), Pastor Hall (1940), The Case of the Frightened Lady (1940), The Big Blockade (1941), The Night Invader (1943), The Story of Lilli Marlene (1944), Night Boat to Dublin (1946), A Matter of Life and Death (1946), Take My Life (1947), The Red Shoes (1948), Mr. Perrin and Mr. Traill (1948), Odette (1948), Highly Dangerous (1950), Circle of Danger (1951), Pandora and the Flying Dutchman (1951), The Magic Box (1951), So Little Time (1952), Nachts auf den Strassen (1952), The Man Who Watched Trains Go By (1952), Rough Shoot (1952), The Mirror and Markheim (voice, 1953), Break in the Circle (1955), The Adventures of Quentin Durward (1955), The Barefoot Contessa (1955),

Ill Met by Moonlight (1957), The Truth about Women (1958), The Moonraker (1958), Family Doctor (1958), Son of Robin Hood (1958), I Was Monty's Double (1958), Whirlpool (1959), The Angry Hills (1959), The Treasure of San Teresa (1959), Desert Mice (1959), Beyond the Curtain (1960), The Unstoppable Man (1960), Exodus (1960), The Inspector (1960), The Devil's Daffodil (1962), The Devil's Agent (1962), The Crooked Road (1964), Up from the Beach (1965), The 25th Hour (1967), Girl on a Motorcycle (1968), Subterfuge (1968), First Love (1970), Zeppelin (1971), The Girl in Blue Velvet (1978), and Strike It Rich (1990).

THE GOVERNESS (Arts Council of England/BBC/Pandora Cinema/Parallax Pictures, 1998)—Historical drama. *Director:* Sandra Goldbacher; *Producers:* Sarah Curtis and Sally Hibbin (executive); *Script:* Sandra Goldbacher; *Cinematography:* Ashley Rowe; *Music:* Ed Shearmur; *Cast:* Minnie Driver (Rosina da Silva/Mary Blackchurch), Tom Wilkinson (Charles Cavendish), Harriet Walter (Mrs. Cavendish), Florence Hoath (Clementina Cavendish), Jonathan Rhys-Meyers (Henry Cavendish), Bruce Meyers (Rosina's Father), and Diana Brooks (Rosina's Mother).

Set in 1840s England, Rosina da Silva, the daughter of a Jewish merchant, enters domestic service after her father is murdered. Rosina, faced with very few options, such as marriage or domestic service, favors employment rather than an arranged marriage to a middle-aged fish merchant. However, to get a suitable position Rosina must disguise her Jewish background, pose as a gentile, Mary Blackchurch, and travel to the Scottish Isle of Skye and the Cavendish family.

Rosina's duties within the Cavendish family are primarily to educate young Clementina. This offers this energetic woman little challenge and so Rosina becomes intrigued by the experiments of Charles Cavendish to capture and retain images on light-sensitive paper. Charles, who has a problematic relationship with his elitist wife, is delighted by the young woman's interest in his work. Rosina, however, wants more and initiates an affair with Charles, boldly pulling his hand up her leg as he tries to arrange a suitable pose for a photograph. The affair blossoms until Rosina disrobes Charles while he is sleeping so that she can take a nude photograph of him—this action causes Charles to terminate the affair. After his son Henry declares his infatuation with Rosina, Charles vindictively disregards Rosina's contribution to his scientific achievements when an influential scientist visits him from London. Rosina, hurt not only by Charles ending their relationship, but also by ignoring her scientific assistance, leaves the Cavendish household after depositing the naked photo of Charles with his wife. The film's epilogue shows Rosina as a successful photographer, documenting her Sephardic Jewish community, while disregarding Charles's attempt to renew their relationship.

Written and directed by Sandra Goldbacher, *The Governess* is inflected by a modern sensibility and Minnie Driver's Rosina is not a woman of the 1840s but displays the values and manners of an independent woman of the late twentieth century. This is evident in her sexual assertiveness with Charles and also her domination of young Henry Cavendish, who is forced to strip by the governess so that she can examine his body. Similarly, the ending is motivated more by feminist polemics rather than historical verisimilitude as Rosina seeks, and achieves, retribution on the gentile family while dedicating herself to her own community. Nevertheless, *The Governess* is an intriguing reworking of a popular British formula, the dependent woman forced into domestic service. Differences in attitudes and values since the 1940s can be discerned in a comparison between the characterization and ending in *The Governess* with such 1940s films as *Blanche Fury** (1947) and *Esther Waters** (1948).

GRANGER, STEWART (1913–1993). Stewart Granger and James Mason* were the two most popular male British film stars in the 1940s. Both men, however, had different screen images. Mason's brooding intensity (*The Night Has Eyes** [1942] and *The Man in Grey** [1943]) was more morally ambivalent than the Granger persona, which rarely deviated from the dashing, heroic image he grew to resent. However, Granger did regret missing out on the lead roles in *Quo Vadis?* (1951) and *Ben-Hur* (1959), two parts that would have only reinforced his stereotypical image as a strong hero figure.

After putting aside his plans for a career in medicine, due, as Granger readily admits, to the fact that such a career required dedication and prolonged study, he found work as an extra in 1933. This followed eighteen months at Webber-Douglas School of Dramatic Art. Appearances in repertory theater prepared Granger for an acting career began in the early 1940s with films such as *Convoy* (1940) and *Secret Mission* (1942). The role of Swinton Rokeby, the romantic hero who tries to save Phyllis Calvert* from a loveless marriage and a cruel husband (James Mason*) in *The Man in Grey*, created sufficient public interest to elevate Granger to stardom. He followed *The Man in Grey* with the lead roles in a series of Gainsborough melodramas, including *Fanny by Gaslight* (1944) and *Madonna of the Seven Moons* (1944). Granger disliked both films ("they both had drippy characters").[3] The only compensation was that *Fanny by Gaslight* was directed by Anthony Asquith,* who he thought was a more competent director than Arthur Crabtree (*Madonna of the Seven Moons* and *Caravan** [1946]) and Bernard Knowles (*The Magic Bow* [1946]) who were, in Granger's view, primarily cameramen. Similarly, Granger considered Leslie Arliss, the director of one of his most popular films, *Love Story* (1944), a better writer than director.

In between these florid melodramas, Granger had one of his best roles as the villainous Ted Purvis who tries to seduce John Mill's* wife in *Waterloo Road* (1945). Although Granger wanted to continue playing villains, his strong matinee idol features led to more conventional roles—with one notable exception, the bitter Phillip Thorn, who seduces Valerie Hobson* and kills her husband in Marc Allegret's grim tale of twisted emotions in *Blanche Fury** (1948).

Granger left England in 1949 for Hollywood, hoping to keep more of his salary from the high British tax rates, and he was signed by MGM for *King Solomon's Mines* (1950), directed by British director Compton Bennett. This successful remake was followed by a succession of historical melodramas—*Soldiers Three*

(1951), *Scaramouche* (1952), *The Prisoner of Zenda* (1952), *Young Bess* (1953), and *Beau Brummell* (1954). Only the seafaring melodrama *All the Brothers Were Valiant* (1953), the Western *The Last Hunt* (1956), both opposite Robert Taylor, and the British-filmed Victorian melodrama *Footsteps in the Fog* (1955) offered Granger the chance to play villains. *Footsteps in the Fog,* an intriguing tale of deceit and blackmail, also provided Granger with the opportunity to appear on-screen with his then-wife Jean Simmons, although both characters demonstrate little affection toward each other. Granger plays an employer who has murdered his wife and Simmons the mercenary maid who blackmails him. Standard adventure films (such as *North to Alaska* [1960], with John Wayne), Westerns (such as *Gun Glory* [1957]), and lackluster comedies (such as *The Little Hut* [1957]) were characteristic of his roles in the 1950s.

The 1960s were less kind to Granger as, devoid of a studio contract, he spent the decade in independent productions. This period included a series of German-made Westerns, based on the stories of Karl May, that were filmed in Europe. In 1964, Granger first appeared as Old Surehand (also known as Old Shatterhand), the white blood brother of the Apache Chief Winnetou. This series, which began in 1963 with Lex Barker in *The Treasure of Silver Lake/Der Schatz im Silbersee,* continued when Granger replaced the former Hollywood Tarzan in *Among Vultures/Unter Geiern* 1964), and he continued for two more films: *Flaming Frontier/Old Surehand* (1965) and *Rampage at Apache Wells/Der Olprinz* (1965). These three films were popular in Europe and paved the way for the Italian Westerns later in the decade. An unsuccessful safari melodrama *The Last Safari* (1967), directed by veteran Hollywood director Henry Hathaway, was Granger's last starring role. He turned to television and the stage throughout the 1970s and 1980s.

Granger, born James LaBlanche Stewart, died in 1993. Granger believed that very few, if any, of his films were worthwhile. His autobiography, *Sparks Fly Upwards,* was published in 1981.

FILMS: A Southern Maid (1933), Over the Garden Wall (1934), Give Her a Ring (1934), Mademoiselle Docteur (1937), So This Is London (1937), Convoy (1940), Secret Mission (1942), Thursday's Child (1943), The Lamp Still Burns (1943), The Man in Grey (1943), Fanny by Gaslight (1944), Love Story (1944), Madonna of the Seven Moons (1944), Waterloo Road (1945), Caravan (1946), Caesar and Cleopatra (1946), The Magic Bow (1946), Captain Boycott (1947), Blanche Fury (1948), Saraband for Dead Lovers (1948), Woman Hater (1948), Adam and Evalyne (1948), King Solomon's Mines (1950), The Light Touch (1951), Soldiers Three (1951), The Wild North (1952), Scaramouche (1952), The Prisoner of Zenda (1952), Young Bess (1953), Salome (1953), All the Brothers Were Valiant (1954), Beau Brummell (1954), Green Fire (1955), Moonfleet (1955), Footsteps in the Fog (1955), Bhowani Junction (1956), The Last Hunt (1956), Gun Glory (1957), The Little Hut (1957), The Whole Truth (1958), Harry Black and the Tiger (1958), North to Alaska (1960), The Secret Partner (1961), The Swordsman of Sienna (1961), Commando (1962), La Congiura Der Dieci (1962), Sodom and Gomorrah (1962), The Shortest Day (1963), The Legion's Lost Patrol (1963), The Crooked Road (1964), Among Vultures (1964), The Secret Invasion (1964), Flaming Frontier (1965), Rampage at Apache Wells

(1965), Killer's Carnival (1965), Red Dragon (1966), Target for Killing (1966), Requiem for a Secret Agent (1966), The Trygon Factor (1967), The Last Safari (1967), The Wild Geese (1978), and Hell Hunters (1978).

GRAY, SALLY (b. 1916). If Sally Gray made films for one of the major Hollywood studios during the 1940s, it would be reasonable to assume that she would have been a major film star as she was blessed with a stunning face, blonde hair, a distinctively sensual voice, acting talent, and a strong cinematic presence. However, like Greta Gynt* and other notable British female actors in the 1940s who exuded a strong sense of sex appeal, Gray worked steadily without the worldwide fame that would have accompanied a Hollywood career. Evidence of this was the increased status enjoyed by James Mason,* Stewart Granger,* Deborah Kerr,* and others who left England for Hollywood (and fame and fortune).

Born Constance Vera Steadman, Sally Gray studied at the Fay Compton School of Acting, making her first appearance, as Constance Stevens, in School for Scandal in 1930. However, it was not until the mid-1930s that her film career gathered strength with a succession of musicals, light comedies, and two appearances in RKO's popular detective series based on the adventures of the Saint. Although the series began in Hollywood in 1938, it switched to London for two films in the late 1930s and early 1940s: The Saint in London (1939), starring George Sanders as Simon Templar ("The Saint") and Gray as Penny Parker, a socialite, followed by The Saint's Vacation (1941), with British actor Hugh Sinclair replacing Sanders as Templar and Gray as Mary Langdon, a newspaper reporter assisting the Saint to resolve an Axis plot against the Allies in Switzerland.

After The Saint's Vacation, Gray had a starring role opposite Anton Walbrook in Brian Desmond Hurst's Dangerous Moonlight (1942) as a U.S. journalist who assists her husband, a Polish concert pianist shot down during the Battle of Britain, recover his musical talent. After this popular film, Gray did not appear in another film for four years as, allegedly, she suffered a nervous breakdown. In 1946, Gray returned to the screen as nurse "Freddie" Linley in one of the best British films of the 1940s, the clever detective/comedy/mystery Green for Danger.* Gray is a crucial element in the complicated plot as her beauty and sex appeal fulfills a necessary plot function by explaining why doctors Leo Genn and Trevor Howard* are behaving so strangely in a country hospital during World War II.

Gray followed Green for Danger with the role of Jenny Pearl, the music hall ballerina in Stanley Haynes's engrossing melodrama Carnival* (1946), who makes the fatal mistake of marrying Bible-quoting farmer Bernard Miles after a rift with her true love Michael Wilding. An even superior film followed, Alberto Cavalcanti's masterly film noir They Made Me a Fugitive* (1947), with Gray caught up in the criminal activities of Griffith Jones and his attempt to destroy former Royal Air Force officer Trevor Howard. Gray, after a vicious beating from Jones, passes judgment on her tormentor: "He's not even a respectable crook, just cheap, rotten, after-the-war trash."

The Mark of Cain* (1947), Gray's next film, was not as commercially success-ful as her previous two films, but provided another strong role as Sarah Bonheur, who, inadvertently, motivates Eric Portman's* poisoning of his brother. In *Obses-sion** (1949), Gray is less innocent as Storm Riordan, Robert Newton's* unfaith-ful wife, whose adulterous behavior provokes Newton into imprisoning her lover. In between *The Mark of Cain* and *Obsession,* Gray starred in Lance Comfort's* intriguing domestic melodrama *Silent Dust* (1948) as Angela Rowley, who mar-ries Derek Farr, believing that her husband, Nigel Patrick, died in the war. Although Gray made two more films, she lost interest in the film industry in the early 1950s, preferring to concentrate on her marriage to Lord Oranmore, the Baron Mereworth.

FILMS: School for Scoundrel (1930), Lucky Days (1935), Cross Currents (1935), Check-mate (1935), Cheer Up (1936), Calling the Tune (1936), Saturday Night Revue (1937), Cafe Collette (1937), Sword of Honour (1938), Over She Goes (1938), Mystery of Room 13 (1938), Lightning Conductor (1938), Hold My Hand (1938), The Saint in London (1939), A Window in London (1939), Honeymoon Merry-Go-Round (1939), Lambeth Walk (1940), The Saint's Vacation (1941), Dangerous Moonlight (1941), Green for Dan-ger (1946), Carnival (1946), They Made Me a Fugitive (1947), The Mark of Cain (1947), Silent Dust (1948), Obsession (1949), Escape Route (1952), and The Keeper (1976).

GREAT DAY (RKO–British, 1945)—Melodrama. *Director:* Lance Comfort; *Producer:* Victor Hanbury; *Script:* John Davenport and Wolfgang Wilhelm, from Lesley Storm's play; *Cinematography:* Erwin Hiller; *Music:* William Alwyn; *Cast:* Eric Portman (Captain Ellis), Flora Robson (Mrs. Ellis), Sheila Sim (Mar-garet Ellis), Philip Friend (Geoffrey Winthrop), Isabel Jeans (Lady Mott), Mar-jorie Rhodes (Mrs. Mumford), Margaret Withers (Miss Tyndale), Walter Fitzgerald (Bob Tyndale), and Maire O'Neill (Mrs. Walsh).

One of the best British films of the 1940s, *Great Day* points both to the need for communal solidarity due to the war while highlighting difficulties associated with the transition to peace. The film begins and ends in a conventional manner, celebrating the strong community support for the hands-across-the sea military alliance between Britain and the United States during World War II. The context for this expression is the proposed visit by Eleanor Roosevelt to the Women's Institute of Denley village. The patriotism and communal solidarity expressed in the film was expected during World War II. What is unusual for a wartime film, however, is that the film does not focus on unity within the community but on ten-sion and division.

Within the overarching context of the Denley women preparing for the visit of the U.S. First Lady, the film explores two main narrative strands. The first, and most important, focuses on the anxieties and disintegration of Captain Ellis, a World War I veteran who, despite his superficial bluff and bravado, suffers from a sense of estrangement from his community. This is due to his inability to find a sufficient reason for living in a seemingly idyllic place like Denley after the glory and responsibilities he enjoyed during World War I. Ellis is particularly embittered because, as some remind him, he is nothing more than a relic of a past war. The "old days," his wife tells him, "are dead and done with," while the village barmaid complains that "he [Ellis] never lets you forget the captain."

The second strand concerns his daughter Margaret, who, despite loving a young army captain, is tempted to accept the security offered by a middle-aged farmer, Bob Tyndale. The plight of Margaret's mother, who her daughter feels is trapped by "Dad's swaggering and drinking and clinging to the past," provides the motivation for Margaret to accept Tyndale's offer of marriage. This follows her mother's advice that "security may sound dull but it does give you your freedom." Captain Ellis, on the other hand, warns his daughter not to get trapped, a clear reference to his own situation that despite all of the superficial attractions of the village, it provides no outlet or satisfaction for a person like him.

The self-destructive aspects of Ellis's personality, provoked by drink and a need to impress U.S. and British soldiers, erupts when he is denied credit in the local pub. This causes Ellis to try and steal a ten-shilling note from a woman's purse. After the police charge him with theft, Ellis contemplates suicide in the local river. However, unlike Lesley Storm's play, Ellis decides not to kill himself and his daughter arrives to tell him that "it's sometimes braver to live than to die." Margaret also decides to follow her heart and marry the young soldier rather than the middle-aged farmer and both, tentatively, rejoin the communal celebrations at the end of the film.

Great Day is a complex film that exposes the plight of those, such as a former military leader, who feel alienated from their communities. At this point, Lance Comfort* utilizes expressive lighting to highlight Ellis's torment. For example, when Ellis tries to explain his behavior to his wife prior to his attempted suicide, Eric Portman's* face is partly covered in shadow while his wife receives full lighting. Here, Ellis explains that "I was never frightened during the war. But I was frightened in peace—of a wife being dependent on me." Ellis breaks down and admits that while he was a leader of men in World War I, he is "conscious of the enormity of the responsibilities of a man's role in peacetime: 'He's the lover, the protector, the strong man. Or he wants to be. In my case no fresh supplies came in.'" *Great Day* anticipates the end of the simplicities of war and the complexities of peace.

GREAT EXPECTATIONS (Cineguild, 1946)—Melodrama. *Director:* David Lean; *Producer:* Ronald Neame; *Script:* Anthony Havelock-Allan, David Lean, Ronald Neame, Kay Walsh, and Cecil McGivern, based on the novel by Charles Dickens; *Cinematography:* Guy Green; *Music:* Walter Goehr; *Cast:* John Mills (Pip), Valerie Hobson (Estella/Molly), Bernard Miles (Joe Gargery), Martita Hunt (Miss Havisham), Alec Guinness (Herbert Pocket), Francis L. Sullivan (Mr. Jaggers), Jean Simmons (Young Estella), Finlay Currie (Magwitch), Anthony Wager (Young Pip), Freda Jackson (Mrs. Gargery), Ivor Barnard (Mr. Wemmick), Eileen Erskine (Biddy), and Torin Thatcher (Bentley Drummle).

The dramatic function of Pip in this, the best cinema version of *Great Expectations,* was, according to the instructions given to John Mills* by director David

Lean,* to be seen as a "coat-hanger" for the other great characters that dominate the story. The "grotesque" characters as Mills described them—such as the formidable lawyer Jaggers, played by Francis L. Sullivan, and eccentric Miss Havisham, played by Martita Hunt—matched the tone of Guy Green's low-key lighting and the carefully selected settings, particularly the memorable confrontation between young Pip and the convict Magwitch in the graveyard scene that opens the film. This sense of horror is reinforced during Pip's visits to Havisham's mansion with the aging woman eerily dressed in wedding clothes surrounded by the decaying preparations of her abortive wedding, including a mice-ridden cake and a clock that remains fixed at the time of the wedding. These scenes, together with the Havisham's perverse plan to punish all males, points to the centrality of a Gothic sensibility to this film.

After Pip assists Magwitch in the graveyard, he is summoned by Miss Havisham to amuse her and Pip is subjected to the taunts of Estella, which only intensifies his infatuation with the young girl. When a mysterious benefactor, through the lawyer Jaggers, informs Pip that he will be provided with the means to live the life of a gentleman, Pip assumes that his patron is Havisham as Jaggers is her lawyer. Later, he learns that Magwitch is his benefactor and that the convict's finances came from his successful farming activities in New South Wales. Magwitch dies soon after attempting to escape from England and Jaggers tells Pip that, consistent with the tenets of melodrama, Magwitch's long lost daughter is Estella. Estella, as part of Havisham's plan, accepts an offer of marriage from the elitist Bentley Drummle. He rejects her when he discovers her background. Pip returns to his childhood home and finds Estella living in Havisham's decrepit mansion. Pip convinces Estella to leave the gloomy mansion and join him in the sunlight.

The film makes other changes from Dickens's novel but Lean, with wife Kay Walsh, and producer Ronald Neame,* retains the essential melodramatic structure of Dickens's novel, complete with his characteristic use of coincidence and bursts of sentimentality. The film was rewarded with Best Picture, Best Director, and Best Writing nominations at the 1948 Academy Awards with John Bryan and Wilfred Shingleton winning Oscars for Best Art Direction–Set Direction, Black and White, and Guy Green for Best Cinematography, Black and White. *Great Expectations* was also notable in providing Alec Guinness* his first major film role as Herbert Pocket, after appearing as an extra in *Evensong* in 1936. It also assisted the career of seventeen-old Jean Simmons as the young Estella. In 1988, Simmons played Miss Havisham in a television mini-series adaptation of Dickens's novel.

GREEN FOR DANGER (Individual Pictures/Rank, 1946)—Detective. *Director:* Sidney Gilliat; *Producers:* Sidney Gilliat and Frank Launder; *Script:* Sidney Gilliat and Claude Guerney; *Cinematography:* Wilkie Cooper; *Music:* William Alwyn; *Cast:* Sally Gray (Nurse Frederica "Freddie" Linley), Trevor Howard (Dr. Barney Barnes), Leo Genn (Mr. Eden), Rosamund John (Nurse Esther Sanson), Alastair Sim (Inspector Cockrill), Judy Campbell (Sister Marion Bates), Megs Jenkins (Nurse Woods), Henry Edwards (Mr. Purdy), Ronald Adam (Dr. White), George Woodbridge (Detective Sergeant Hendricks), and Moore Marriott (Joseph Higgins).

When Robert Morley was unavailable for the role of Inspector Cockrill in *Green for Danger* due to a stage commitment, Alastair Sim* was cast as the eccentric policeman Cockrill, derived from Christianna Brand's novels, was an amiable English police detective wandering through Kent looking for criminals. The film improves on its source with a multi-layered script from Sidney Gilliat* and Claude Gurney, deftly blending comedy and romance with the conventions of the traditional English detective story.

Cockrill's narration begins the film by telling the audience that the village postman, Joseph Higgins, will be the first to die in a country hospital and that among the six members of the hospital staff who care for Higgins, one will die. Higgins is taken to the hospital when he is injured by debris from a "doodlebug" (a German V-2 rocket). Although the story is confined to the hospital grounds and buildings, as Cockrill ferrets out information leading to the traditional denouement with all of the suspects gathered together as the detective points to the guilty party, it never weakens the film. This is because Gilliat's script and direction make each of the suspects interesting. While anaesthetist Doctor Barnes and surgeon Mr. Eden clash over nurse Linley, other suspects have their own reasons for committing murder.

A hospital dance brings the suspects together and nurse Bates, inflamed by Eden's attraction to Nurse Linley, hysterically breaks into the festivities to announce that she knows how Higgins was killed. When she returns to the operating room at night to retrieve the evidence, she is stabbed to death in one of the film's more visually chilling moments. The killer appears from the shadows dressed in a white operating uniform. When Cockrill convinces Nurse Linley to duplicate the circumstances surrounding Higgins's death in the operating room, the policeman discovers, just in time, that the bottles supplying oxygen have been switched and the fatal cylinder painted green. When Cockrill exposes Nurse Sanson as the killer, Eden fails to prevent her suicide.

Green for Danger walks a fine line between droll comedy (when Barnes explains to Cockrill that it is the impurities in "laughing gas" (nitrous oxide) that cause people to laugh, Cockrill replies: "Rather like our music halls."), a traditional British detective story, and a whimsical parody of the form. It is also marked by excellent performances from the six suspects, Sally Gray,* Leo Genn, Trevor Howard,* Rosamund John, Megs Jenkins, and especially Judy Campbell as the lovesick nurse. Sim is also perfect as the deceptively complex Inspector Cockrill in this satisfying film.

THE GREEN MAN (British Lion Film Corporation, 1956)—Farce. *Director:* Robert Day; *Producers:* Sidney Gilliat, Frank Launder, and Leslie Gilliat (associate); *Script:* Sidney Gilliat and Frank Launder, based on their play; *Cinematogra-*

phy: Gerald Gibbs; *Music:* Cedric Thorpe Davie; *Cast:* Alastair Sim (Hawkins), George Cole (William Blake), Terry-Thomas (Charles Boughtflower), Jill Adams (Ann Vincent), Raymond Huntley (Sir Gregory Upshott), Colin Gordon (Reginald Willoughby-Cruft), Avril Angers (Marigold), Eileen Moore (Joan Wood), Dora Bryan (Lily), John Chandos (McKechnie), Cyril Chamberlain (Sergeant Bassett), Richard Wattis (Doctor), Arthur Lowe (Radio Salesman), and Michael Ripper (Waiter).

Robert Day directed this farce, based on a script by Frank Launder* and Sidney Gilliat* from their play. The film, like all good farces, gradually escalates into absolute chaos. The film builds from the desire of clock maker and assassin Hawkins to kill Sir Gregory Upshott. When vacuum salesman William Blake stumbles onto the plot, he travels to the rural hotel The Green Man with Ann Vincent to foil the assassination. This is preceded by a series of comic episodes involving a body in a piano. A bomb is planted by Hawkins at the hotel just as Sir Gregory is trying to get a young woman, Joan Wood, into bed without anybody knowing that he is at the hotel. However, Blake and Vincent, initially, mistake Charles Boughtflower for Sir Gregory, as Boughtflower has also escaped from his wife to spend a weekend with a hotel receptionist. Eventually, Blake and Vincent discover the bomb and save Upshott's life as the police arrest Hawkins.

The basic premise of the film, based on a series of mistaken identities and confused reactions, benefits from skillful performances. This includes familiar faces such as Terry-Thomas* as the cad who is worried that his wife has sent somebody to spy on him, Raymond Huntley as the vain, lecherous politician, Alastair Sim* as the scheming assassin, George Cole as the harassed vacuum salesman, and, particularly, Colin Gordon as the BBC announcer Reginald Willoughby-Cruft. Willoughby-Cruft keeps returning to his house to find his fiancée Ann Vincent in compromising positions with vacuum salesman Blake. Willoughby-Cruft finally warns Blake that "I'd thrash the life out of you—if I didn't have to read the nine o'clock news."

GREENAWAY, PETER (b. 1942). Peter Greenaway is a painter who makes films that display little regard for the formal conventions and cinematic devices of the mainstream or classical cinema. Greenaway dismisses the techniques of the classical cinema as merely devices for recording drama, devices that belong to the theater and the novel. The cinema, he argues, took a wrong turn when it became, primarily, a narrative medium. Visual expression for him is not to tell stories but to make a singular visual statement about the world and all that is in it. Thus, he dislikes stories built around cause and effect and the psychologically motivated characters that populate much of the cinema.

As a result, Greenaway is aware that his films will not appeal to mainstream audiences. Hence, budgets must be kept tight, on the average below £2 million. His first film *The Draughtsman's Contract* (1982) was a limited commercial success and it combined aspects of Restoration tragedy and comedy with conventions from the traditional English detective genre. However, the deliberate artificiality of the costuming and dialogue ensured that audiences did not mistake it for a popular genre film.

Greenaway, born in Wales, studied at the Walthamstow College of Art and began making experimental films while working as a film editor for the Central Office of Information. After spending several years producing short films, Greenaway directed *Goole by Numbers* (1976), which provided a link to his feature film *Drowning by Numbers* (1988) with its interest in numerology. Greenaway's breakthrough film in the United States, and arguably his best, was *The Cook, the Thief, His Wife and Her Lover* (1989). Here, he uses the conventions of theatrical melodrama, while retaining his customary artificiality through his intricate pattern of color coding. The film also expressed his anger at the political situation in Britain in the 1980s where, he maintained, the excesses of the consumer society coalesced in the greedy figure of the thief in this reworking of a Chaucerian medieval parable.

Prospero's Books (1991), a visually challenging reworking of William Shakespeare's play *The Tempest,* also abandons any semblance of a cause and effect narrative structure in favor of a celebrating John Gielgud,* the actor (who appeared as Prospero four times on stage), as a correspondence between Prospero as fiction and Shakespeare the person. Greenaway showed that although the cinema is normally loathe to present simultaneous action in anything more complex than crosscutting between two lines of action, he would make three films in one utilizing the background, foreground, and middle perspective simultaneously. The prodigious amount of nudity in the film may explain why it was Greenaway's greatest commercial success in the United States. *The Belly of an Architect* (1987) was nominated for the Golden Palm Award at the 1987 Cannes Film Festival, as was *Drowning by Numbers* at the 1988 Festival where it won Best Artistic Contribution. *8 1/2 Women* (1999) was nominated for the Golden Palm Award at the 1999 Festival.

FILMS: Train (short, 1966), Revolution (short, 1967), Love, Love, Love (short, 1968), Windows (short, 1975), Water (short, 1975), Goole by Numbers (short, 1976), A Walk through H (short, 1978), Vertical Features Remake (short, 1978), The Falls (short, 1980), The Draughtsman Contract (1982), A Zed and Two Noughts (1986), The Belly of an Architect (1987), Drowning by the Numbers (1988), The Cook, the Thief, His Wife and Her Lover (1989), Prospero's Books (1991), Rosa (1992), The Baby of Macon (1993), Stairs I Geneva (doc., 1995), The Pillow Book (1996), Lumiere and Company (1997), and 8 1/2 Women (1999).

GREENWOOD, JOAN (1921–1987). "Sexy" is not a description that characterizes most British actresses of the 1940s, especially at Ealing Studios where Joan Greenwood made her best films. However, this exquisite actress always exuded sensuality on the screen, largely through her distinctively "throaty" voice. Trained at the Royal Academy of Dramatic Art, Greenwood was on stage at eighteen and her breakthrough in the cinema came in 1943 when Leslie Howard cast her in his propaganda film *The Gentle Sex.* Although she appeared in films produced during World War II, it was in the period after the war that provided Greenwood with her best roles, especially Sibella in *Kind Hearts and Coronets** (1949). In this role, Greenwood combined a frank delight in sexual activity with a mercenary, amoral view of the world. These characteristics are also evident in the Ealing comedy *The Man in the White Suit** (1951). Greenwood, as Daphne Birnley, the daughter of the owner of the Birnley textile mill, is encouraged to seduce the hapless Sidney Stratton who has developed an indestructible, dirt-resistant material. After humiliating the men into paying for her services, Daphne betrays them by showing Stratton how to escape from their clutches.

Greenwood's distinctive husky voice and measured delivery of her lines hinted at layers of erotic depth, such as Lady Warren in *Father Brown** (1954). When the script allowed these traits to emerge more fully, as in Greenwood's Lady Bellaston in *Tom Jones** (1963), no one was more effective. She was rewarded with an Oscar nomination for her brief appearance in Tony Richardson's* film. Greenwood's Peggy Macroon in Ealing's *Whisky Galore!* (1949) allowed a more comic dimension of this persona while the melodrama *The White Unicorn* (1947), with Greenwood as a young mother who attempts suicide and infanticide, portrays her more as a victim of male irresponsibility. In Roy Ward Baker's* *The October Man** (1947), Greenwood gave emotional and physical support for the psychologically troubled John Mills.* Their reunion on an overhead railway bridge after Mills contemplates suicide provides an intense climax in the film. Greenwood, however, rarely found film roles that allowed the full development of her unique talent even though she worked in cinema, television, and the theater up until her death in 1987. Greenwood was married to the British stage and screen actor André Morell, who died in 1978.

FILMS: John Smith Wakes Up (1940), My Wife's Family (1941), He Found a Star (1941), The Gentle Sex (1943), They Knew Mr. Knight (1945), A Girl in a Million (1946), The Man Within (1947), The October Man (1947), The White Unicorn (1947), Saraband for Dead Lovers (1948), The Bad Lord Byron (1949), Whisky Galore! (1949), Kind Hearts and Coronets (1949), Mr. Peek-a-Boo (1950), Flesh and Blood (1951), Young Wive's Tale (1951), The Man in the White Suit (1951), The Importance of Being Earnest (1951), Knave of Hearts (1954), Father Brown (1954), Moonfleet (1955), Lucky Jim (1957), Stage Struck (1958), Horse on Holiday (voice, 1959), Mysterious Island (1961), The Amorous Prawn (1962), Tom Jones (1963), The Moon-Spinners (1964), Girl Stroke Boy (1971), The Uncanny (1977), The Hound of the Baskervilles (1977), The Water Babies (1978), and Little Dorrit (1987).

GUEST, VAL (b. 1911). Energy, determination, and a lack of pretension marks Val Guest's long, prolific career in the British film industry. A former film journalist for the *Hollywood Reporter,* Guest broke into the film industry with his scripts for Will Hay's* comedies and, later, for the Crazy Gang. Guest continued to write even after he became an established director and he claimed to have directed only two films where he did not also work on the script. After learning his craft with second-unit work on films directed by Marcel Varnel, Guest, who was contracted to Gainsborough Studios, was asked to script a Ministry of Information short warning of the danger of spreading disease through careless sneezing (*The Nose Has It,* 1942).[4] He agreed, providing he could also direct the film. *The Nose Has It,* Guest claimed, attracted attention after two newspaper critics claimed that this short, starring Arthur Askey, was better than the U.S. feature film (*My Gal Sal* [1942)]) on the same program.

Gainsborough invited him to write and direct *Miss London Ltd* (1943) for Askey and for the rest of the 1940s and the early 1950s Guest's output consisted mainly of comedies, such as *Miss Pilgrim's Progress* (1950), *Penny Princess* (1951), and *Mr. Drake's Duck* (1951), starring his wife, the U.S. actress Yolande Donlan, *Men of Sherwood Forest* (1954), starring Hollywood actor Don Taylor as Robin Hood, and the tense Cold War thriller *They Can't Hang Me** (1955) demonstrated that Guest could easily shift across genres and tap into shifts within both the film industry and society. After his move to Hammer Films, to make *The Lyons in Paris* (1954) with Bebe Lyon and Ben Lyon, Anthony Hinds asked Guest to look at a science fiction script based on the successful *Quartermass* television series and, although reluctant at the start, Guest became an enthusiastic fan of the genre. He directed *The Quatermass Xperiment* that helped stabilized Hammer's financial status that, in turn, lead to it purchasing the rights to the Frankenstein character and *The Curse of Frankenstein** (1957).

Guest followed with *Quatermass II** (1957), a chilling political allegory based on alien infiltration of the top echelons of the British government. *The Day the Earth Caught Fire** (1961) was another major science fiction success for him he shared the 1962 BAFTA Award for Best British Screenplay with Wolf Mankowitz for this film. This period, from the middle of the 1950s through to the early 1960s, included most of Guest's best films, such as *Yesterday's Enemy* (1959, nominated for Best British Film at the 1960 BAFTA Film Awards), *Hell Is a City* (1960, nominated for Best British Screenplay at the 1961 BAFTA Film Awards), *Jigsaw* (1962), a film version of his own novel, *80,000 Suspects* (1963), plus *Expresso Bongo** (1959), with Laurence Harvey* as the shady agent who discovers, and then loses, rock and roll singer Cliff Richard.

Toward the end of this fertile period, Guest co-wrote, produced, and directed one of his best films: *The Beauty Jungle** (1964), a similar film to *Expresso Bongo* with regard to its cynical attitude to the entertainment industry, in this case corruption within beauty contests. After 1964, Guest never matched the sustained quality of this period. He continued to work steadily throughout the rest of the 1960s, 1970s, and early 1980s, although some of the films produced during this period, such as the weak sex comedies *Au Pair Girls* (1972) and *Confessions of a Window Cleaner* (1974), are noteworthy only in that they demonstrate his opportunistic ability to adapt to changes within the industry.

FILMS (as director): The Nose Has It (short, 1942), Miss London (1943), Give Us the Moon (1944), Bees in Paradise (1944), I'll Be Your Sweetheart (1945), Just William's Luck (1947), William Comes to Town (1948), Murder at the Windmill (1949), Miss Pilgrim's Progress (1950), The Body Said No! (1950), Mr. Drake's Duck (1951), Penny

Princess (1952), Life with the Lyons (1954), The Runaway Bus (1954), Men of Sherwood Forest (1954), Dance Little Lady (1954), They Can't Hang Me (1955), Break in the Circle (1955), The Lyons in Paris (1955), The Quatermass Xperiment (1955), The Weapon (1955), It's a Wonderful World (1956), Carry on Admiral (1957), Quatermass II (1957), The Abominable Snowman (1957), Camp on Blood Island (1958), Up the Creek (1958), Further up the Creek (1958), Life Is a Circus (1959), Yesterday's Enemy (1959), Expresso Bongo (1959), Hell Is a City (1960), The Full Treatment (1961), The Day the Earth Caught Fire (1961), Jigsaw (1962), 80,000 Suspects (1963), The Beauty Jungle (1964), Where the Spies Are (1965), Casino Royale (codir., 1967), Assignment K (1967), When Dinosaurs Ruled the Earth (1970), Tomorrow (1970), Au Pair Girls (1972), Confessions of a Window Cleaner (1974), The Diamond Mercenaries (1975), The Shillingbury Blowers (1980), Dangerous Davies—The Last Detective (1980), and The Boys in Blue (1983).

GUILLERMIN, JOHN (b. 1925). A British director who made the best Tarzan film, *Tarzan's Greatest Adventure** (1958), John Guillermin was comfortable with genre films, having studied the Hollywood studio system in the 1940s. Because of his preference for melodrama and popular stories, Guillermin's films have received little scholarly attention. Yet, when the material was right, he was one of the most efficient and innovative British directors of his generation—as Hollywood recognized in the 1970s when he was entrusted with a number of big-budget productions, especially the commercially successful, but ultimately routine, all-star extravaganza *The Towering Inferno* (1974).

Guillermin's Hollywood films, which also included a dull remake of *King Kong* (1976) and the even more abysmal *King Kong Lives* (1986), overshadow the consistently fine films he made in England from the mid-1950s (*Town on Trial* [1957]) to the mid-1960s (*Guns at Batasi* [1964]). After an education at the City of London, military service during World War II with the Royal Air Force, and a brief period working on documentaries in France, Guillermin entered the British film industry in the late 1940s with his script for *Melody in the Dark* (1948). A series of low-budget films followed where Guillermin served as producer, writer, and director (*High Jinks in Society* [1949] and *Torment* [1950]), leading to (slightly) higher budgets and Margaret Rutherford* in *Miss Robin Hood* (1952), with Rutherford trying to retrieve the family whisky formula.

In 1957, Guillermin made his mark with the well-paced police film *Town on Trial,* which benefited from a strong cast that included John Mills,* Charles Coburn, Derek Farr, and Alec McCowen, involving murder in a small British town. He followed with *I Was Monty's Double* (1958), based on the true story of the successful attempt by British intelligence to divert the Germans in North Africa by having an actor pose as General Bernard Montgomery. The British-based production of *Tarzan's Greatest Adventure,* with location filming in Kikuyu country in Kenya, marked a new phase in this long-running series as Guillermin and producer Sy Weintraub rejected the juvenile tone of the previous Tarzan films. They replaced it with a more mature, complex representation of Tarzan (Gordon Scott) who seeks retribution from Anthony Quayle, Sean Connery,* and Niall MacGinnis after they murder everybody at a remote outpost. Guillermin continued in this vein with Jock Mahoney as Tarzan in *Tarzan Goes to India* (1962), which proved to be the highest grossing Tarzan film to this point in time.

In between the two Tarzan films, Guillermin directed two fine crime dramas: *Never Let Go* (1960) and *The Day They Robbed the Bank of England* (1960). *Never Let Go* was a story of desperation and alienation involving an inoffensive cosmetics salesman (Richard Todd*) who tries to recover his new Ford Anglia from car thief Peter Sellers.* Criticized by critics for its "realistic" use of violence, *Never Let Go* provided Todd with one of his least characteristic film roles as an unsuccessful salesman who undertakes an existential journey to recover his property at all costs. *The Day They Robbed the Bank of England* was a carefully constructed caper film detailing the efforts of the Irish Republican Army to rob the Bank of England and Guillermin followed this with a Peter Sellers film *Waltz of the Toreadors* (1962), based on Jean Anouilh's story of a lusty retired military officer with a desire for young women.

A full-blooded war drama involving British soldiers in Africa, *Guns at Batasi,* with Richard Attenborough,* preceded Guillermin's French-based drama *Rapture* (1965) and the beginning of his Hollywood career with the commercially successful *The Blue Max* (1966), with George Peppard as the World War I German ace. *The Blue Max* was the first of three films directed by Guillermin starring Peppard, with Peppard as a private detective in *P. J.* (1968), followed by the melodrama *House of Cards* (1968), with Peppard as an adventurer dragged into a fascist conspiracy, led by Orson Welles.

Guillermin's versatility in working efficiently in virtually all genres was in evidence in his next film, the war drama *The Bridge at Remagen* (1969), based on the defense of a bridge in Europe by a group of Allies in the final years of World War II. Yet another genre film followed. Inspired by the liberalization of the sex and violence in the Italian Western, Guillermin shot *El Condor* (1970) in Spain although the film was set in nineteenth-century Mexico. Jim Brown and Lee Van Cleef co-star as a pair of adventurers after gold lodged in a Mexican fortress.

Throughout the 1970s and 1980s, Guillermin worked in films with larger budgets but less distinction. The low point was *Sheena* (1984), with Tanya Roberts as queen of the jungle in this camp attempt to recreate the spirit of the serial queens of the 1940s. However, he redeemed himself in his last film, *The Tracker* (1988), an HBO Western starring Kris Kristofferson as Noble Adams, who tracks down a killer who has kidnapped a young girl. Ultimately, it was the unpretentious generic material such as *The Tracker* that brought the best out of Guillermin, as opposed to his overblown Hollywood films of the 1970s.

FILMS: Melody in the Dark (script, 1948), High Jinks in Society (1949), Torment (1950), The Smart Aleck (1951), Four Days (1951), Two on the Tiles (1952), Song of Paris (1952), Miss Robin Hood (1952), Operation Diplomat (1953), The Crowded Day (1954), Adventure in the Hopfields, (1954), Thunderstorm (1956), Town on Trial (1957), The Whole Truth (1958), I Was Monty's Double (1958), Tarzan's Greatest Adventure (1959), Never Let Go (1960), The Day They Robbed the Bank of England (1960), Waltz of the Toreadors (1962), Tarzan Goes to India (1962), Guns at Batasi (1964), Rapture (1965), The Blue Max (1966),

P. J. (1969), House of Cards (1968), The Bridge at Remagen (1969), El Condor (1970), Skyjacked (1972), Shaft in Africa (1973), The Towering Inferno (1974), King Kong (1976), Death on the Nile (1978), Mr. Patman (1980), Sheena (1984), and King Kong Lives (1986).

GUINNESS, ALEC (1914–2000). Alec Guinness established himself on the British and U.S. stage in the 1930s and 1940s before making his film debut with *Great Expectations** (1946) (he appeared as an extra in *Evensong* in 1936). Guinness considered the cinema as a legitimate medium for actors, unlike the disdainful attitude expressed by his mentor John Gielgud* (at least until relatively late in Gielgud's career). Guinness, initially, considered the cinema as "a mystery,"[5] an adventure, and his choice of roles reflected his determination not to be typecast. This attitude led to his suggestion that he should play all eight members of the d'Ascoyne family in *Kind Hearts and Coronets** (1949). This approach was also evident when he was offered the part of the stiff military martinet in *Tunes of Glory* (1960). This was a logical casting decision following his Oscar-winning performance as an uncompromising military officer in *The Bridge on the River Kwai* (1957). However, Guinness wanted a different kind of role and insisted that he play the robust, hard-drinking Jock Sinclair. This spirit of adventure and risk lasted throughout his career, as evidenced by his support for Anthony Waller's British–German–Russian low-budget thriller *Mute Witness* (1994), when he appeared unbilled as a master criminal in his last feature film.

Guinness was born Alec Guinness de Cuffe in Marylebone on April 2, 1914. His mother's name was Agnes Cuffe and his father's name was left blank on the birth certificate. When Guinness was five years old, his mother married a Scottish army captain David Stiven and for the next nine years Guinness believed his name was Alec Stiven. It was not until he was fourteen that he was told that his real name was Guinness. He never met his biological father. After working as an advertising copywriter, Guinness was attracted to the theater and studied at the Fay Compton School of Acting, where Gielgud awarded him an acting prize and, more importantly, two minor roles in the 1934 production of *Hamlet*. Four years later Guinness played Hamlet himself.

After the success in *Kind Hearts and Coronets,* Guinness appeared in a rare failure as the meek reporter Whimple in *A Run for Your Money** (1949). He learned from this experience that he was not comfortable playing parts that were too close to his own personality. For the next five decades, he ranged across a wide variety of character roles. Ealing Studios was important to his career, particularly in casting him as the obsessive inventor Sidney Stratton who creates an indestructible, dirt-resistant material in *The Man in the White Suit** (1951). Guinness starred in another major Ealing comedy the same year, *The Lavender Hill Mob,** opposite Stanley Holloway. He followed it four years later with an even better film, *The Ladykillers,** thanks to the skill of director Alexander Mackendrick* and an assortment of bizarre characters. Here, Guinness gives one of his most notable performances as the psychotic Professor Marcus, who is outwitted by Katie Johnson.

David Lean's* commercially successful epics of the 1960s showcased Guinness's ability to work his characters from the outside in, where makeup, costume, and "bits of business" combined to create a distinctive persona. This process worked also with Fagin in *Oliver Twist* (1948), where Guinness defied the studio's order to play the character straight. Instead, he developed, with the aid of makeup, a larger than life figure that aroused charges of anti-Semitism in the United States and elsewhere.

This approach is also apparent in the Lean epics, as Prince Faisal in *Lawrence of Arabia* (1962) and Zhivago's half-brother in *Doctor Zhivago* (1965), and the Indian professor Godbole in *A Passage to India* (1984). His distinctive character parts culminated in his role as Luke Skywalker's mentor Obi-Wan Kenobi in *Star Wars* (1977), a role he repeated in the sequels *The Empire Strikes Back* (1980) and *Return of the Jedi* (1983). It was also a character he hated so much that he wanted George Lucas to kill him off so as to eliminate him from any more sequels. Instead, Guinness favored roles such as George Smiley in the BBC television productions of John Le Carré's cynical espionage stories *Tinker, Tailor, Soldier, Spy* (1979) and *Smiley's People* (1982).

Guinness, knighted in 1959, was awarded a Special Academy Award in 1979 for "advancing the art of screen acting through a host of memorable and distinguished performances." Guinness was nominated for the Academy Award for Best Actor for *The Lavender Hill Mob,* he won for *The Bridge on the River Kwai,* he was nominated for Best Supporting Actor for *Star Wars,* and nominated again for *Little Dorrit* (1987). Guinness died of liver cancer on August 5, 2000.

FILMS: Evensong (1936), Great Expectations (1946), Oliver Twist (1948), Kind Hearts and Coronets (1949), A Run for Your Money (1949), Last Holiday (1950), The Mudlark (1950), The Lavender Hill Mob (1951), The Man in the White Suit (1951), The Card (1952), The Square Mile (narr., 1953), The Captain's Paradise (1953), The Malta Story (1953), Father Brown (1954), To Paris with Love (1954), The Prisoner (1955), Rowlandson's England (narr., 1955), The Ladykillers (1955), The Swan (1956), Barnacle Bill (1957), The Bridge on the River Kwai (1957), The Scapegoat (1958), The Horse's Mouth (1959), Our Man in Havana (1959), Tunes of Glory (1960), A Majority of One (1961), H.M.S. Defiant (1962), Lawrence of Arabia (1962), The Fall of the Roman Empire (1964), Situation Hopeless . . . But Not Serious (1964), Doctor Zhivago (1966), Hotel Paradiso (1966), The Quiller Memorandum (1966), The Comedians (1967), Cromwell (1970), Scrooge (1970), Brother Sun, Sister Moon (1972), Hitler: The Last Ten Days (1973), Murder by Death (1976), Star Wars (1977), The Empire Strikes Back (1980), Raise the Titanic! (1980), Little Lord Fauntleroy (1980), Return of the Jedi (1983), Lovesick (1983), A Passage to India (1984), Little Dorrit (1987), A Handful of Dust (1988), Kafka (1992), A Foreign Field (1993), and Mute Witness (1994).

GYNT, GRETA (1916–2000). Greta Gynt, born Margrethe Woxholt in Oslo, Norway, in 1916, was one of the few British actresses in the 1940s and 1950s who consistently exuded sex appeal and glamor. She worked, however, in an industry that, on most occasions, did not know how to exploit these attributes and Gynt made many undistinguished films. Nevertheless, she did appear in a handful of films that allowed her peculiar talent to flourish. Gynt, who selected her name because of the *Peer Gynt Suite* by Edvard Grieg, was naturally dark haired but changed her hair color to blonde after arriving in England from Norway when she was nineteen. This was done at the suggestion of her agent, Christopher Mann, whom she married. Mann also had success with Madeleine Carroll's career when she changed her dark hair to blonde.

Gynt's major break, after a couple of years of low-budget thrillers (such as *Sexton Blake and the Hooded Terror* [1938]) and comedies (*Boys Will Be Girls* [1937]), was in the Thorold Dickinson's* murder-mystery *The Arsenal Stadium Mystery* (1939) as the sexually permissive Gwen Lee, a persona that characterized her subsequent film roles. In the mid- to late 1940s, this persona matured in films such as *Take My Life* (1947) and *Dear Murderer* (1947). In *Take My Life,* Gynt has the best role of her career as Phillipa Shelley, an opera singer forced to investigate the circumstances leading to the death of her husband's (Hugh Williams) former girlfriend. When her husband is convicted of the murder, Shelley's enquiries lead to a remote public school in Scotland and Marius Goring.* Gynt's next film was as Vivien Warren, an adulterous woman who betrays her husband (Eric Portman*) in the film noir *Dear Murderer. Mr. Perrin and Mr. Traill* (1948) provided Gynt with yet another variation of this persona as the vivacious school nurse Isobel Lester who attracts both Goring and David Farrar,* leading to the death of the former.

Gynt, who would have been more comfortable in Hollywood films, finally got her chance when MGM invited her to appear in *Soldiers Three* (1951), but this film, relatively late in Gynt's career, offered little and she soon returned to Britain and a succession of mediocre films in the 1950s. She did, however, outshine the imported Hollywood star Arlene Dahl in the melodrama *Fortune Is a Woman* (1957). Gynt died in London on April 2, 2000.

FILMS: Sangen Till Henne (1934), Boys Will Be Girls (1937), The Last Curtain (1937), Sexton Blake and the Hooded Terror (1938), The Last Barricade (1938), Too Dangerous to Live (1939), Dark Eyes of London (1939), She Couldn't Say No (1939), The Arsenal Stadium Mystery (1939), The Middle Watch (1939), Two for Danger (1940), Bulldog Sees It Through (1940), Room for Two (1940), Crooks Tour (1940), The Common Touch (1941), It's That Man Again (1942), Tomorrow We Live (1942), Mr. Emmanuel (1944), London Town (1946), Take My Life (1947), Dear Murderer (1947), Easy Money (1947), Mr. Perrin and Mr. Traill (1948), The Calender (1948), Shadow of the Eagle (1950), I'll Get You for This (1951), Soldiers Three (1951), Whispering Smith Hits London (1952), I'm a Stranger (1952), The Ringer (1952), Three Steps in the Dark (1953), The Last Moment (1953), Forbidden Cargo (1954), Devil's Point (1954), See How They Run (1955), The Blue Peter (1955), Dead on Time (1955), Born for Trouble (1955), Keep It Clean (1956), My Wife's Family (1956), Fortune Is a Woman (1957), Morning Call (1958), The Witness (1959), The Crowning Touch (1959), Bluebeard's Ten Honeymoons (1960), and The Runaway (1964).

NOTES

1. Graham Greene, *The Pleasure Dome,* London, Secker and Warburg, 1972, p. 252.
2. Slide, *"Banned In The USA,"* p. 69.
3. McFarlane, *An Autobiography of British Cinema,* p. 230.
4. See McFarlane, *An Autobiography of British Cinema,* p. 257.
5. See McFarlane, *An Autobiography of British Cinema,* p. 260.

H

HAMER, ROBERT (1911–1963). Every national cinema has examples of a director who demonstrates talent well above the ordinary who, after a few excellent films, suddenly falters. One such director was Robert Hamer. It is hard to think of a sequence of British films by one director (except perhaps Alfred Hitchcock's* films between 1934 and 1937) better than *Pink String and Sealing Wax** (1945), *It Always Rains on Sunday** (1947), *Kind Hearts and Coronets** (1949), and *The Spider and the Fly** (1949). Yet, by 1954 and *To Paris with Love,* Hamer's talent, as shown in his early films, was not so evident. By 1963, he was dead from symptoms associated with his alcoholism.

Hamer was the son of British character actor Gerald Hamer. After an education at Cambridge University, he worked for London Films as a clapper boy and by 1938, at Denham, he was a cutting room assistant for Erich Pommer. At Denham, Hamer edited *St. Martin's Lane* (1938), Hitchcock's *Jamaica Inn* (1939), and other films before joining Ealing Studios in 1941 as an editor and, from 1943, an associate producer.

Hamer made his directorial debut with the "Haunted Mirror" sequence in the portmanteau fantasy thriller *Dead of Night** (1946). This segment, depicting the mirror worlds of respectability and evil, a recurring theme in Hamer's best films, which focused more on the dark side of human nature. Thus, in *Pink String and Sealing Wax,* the dangerous world of Googie Wither's* public house disturbs and overwhelms the sterile domesticity of Mervyn Johns' Victorian family. Similarly, in Hamer's masterpiece *Kind Hearts and Coronets,* audience pleasure is derived from watching Denis Price wreak havoc on the D'Ascoyne family. Hamer's preceding film, *It Always Rains on Sunday,* shows a family, and a community, breaking down under the pressures of sexual desire and marital betrayal. In Hamer's next film, *The Spider and the Fly,* expedience and male friendship overpower the constraints of the law and heterosexual romance.

After these five films, Hamer's decline is evident although there is considerable pleasure in the gentle detective comedy film *Father Brown** (1954), with Alec Guinness* and Peter Finch* reprising aspects of the Eric Portman*–Guy Rolfe relationship from *The Spider and the Fly*. In *The Long Memory** (1952), Hamer's last really good film, he dramatized the perverse pleasure of alienating oneself from society. Hamer died at the age of fifty-two.

FILMS (as director): Dead of Night (1945), Pink String and Sealing Wax (1945), It Always Rains on Sunday (1947), Kind Hearts and Coronets (1949), The Spider and the Fly (1949), His Excellency (1951), The Long Memory (1952), To Paris with Love (1954), Father Brown (1954), The Scapegoats (1958), and School for Scoundrels (1959).

HARVEY, LAURENCE (1928–1973). Laurence Harvey was, for most of his career, roundly criticized by critics and fellow actors for his difficult behavior and perceived lack of acting talent. Even his most celebrated role, as Joe Lampton in *Room at the Top** (1959), provoked dissent from those who dismissed his performance as "an impersonation of a Northerner" and a "sop to the old star system."[1] Yet, every film and performance must, on one level at least, be considered within the social and filmic context of the period in which it was released and *Room at the Top,* released in the same year as *Look Back in Anger,* was a seminal film in the development of the British New Wave. His performance as the ambitious Lampton was an important element in this film finding a large audience.

Harvey had been around for many years prior to *Room at the Top*. Born Laruschka Mischa Skikne in Lithuania, and raised in South Africa, where he began his theatrical career, his first British film (*House of Darkness*) was released in 1948 and he alternated between low-budget films and the stage for the next few years. After *Women of Twilight* (1952), Romulus, a small studio owned by the Woolf brothers, assisted Harvey's film career for many years, in films such as *The Good Die Young** (1954), produced by John Woolf. In this film noir, directed by Lewis Gilbert,* he starred as the psychotic "mastermind" Miles "Rave" Ravenscourt, a charismatic man in need of money after his wealthy wife (Margaret Leighton, who later married Harvey) refuses to finance his indulgences. He followed with the lead role in another Romulus film, *I Am a Camera** (1955), a bowdlerized adaptation of Christopher Isherwood's platonic relationship with entertainer Sally Bowles during the rise of fascism in Berlin in the 1930s. However, this film, which was based on the John van Druten play, and was converted into the stage musical and film *Cabaret* (1972), suffered because of the censorship strictures of the 1950s that prohibited direct acknowledgment of Isherwood's homosexuality.

Harvey also appeared in a number of costume films in the 1950s, including *King Richard and the Crusaders* (1954) and *Storm Over the Nile* (1955), a remake of *The Four Feathers* (1939). His career received some impetus from the comedy *Three Men in a Boat* (1956), although his performance as Lieutenant Lionel "Buster" Crabbe in *The Silent Enemy** (1958) was more interesting as it detailed Crabbe's successful attempt to foil a plan by the Italians to destroy British shipping near Gibraltar with midget submarines during World War II.

Harvey's relationship with fellow actors and directors throughout his career was not always cordial, although Michael Craig, who costarred with Harvey in *The Silent Enemy,* said that off-camera Harvey was relaxed and wonderful to be with but in front of the camera he "became all stiff and started to 'act.' "[2] Daniel Angel, who produced one of Harvey' early films, *Women of Twilight,* thought he was a "bloody good actor," while Muriel Box,* who directed him in *The Truth about Women* (1959), claimed he was the most difficult actor she ever worked with, a feeling also shared by actress Kathleen Byron,* who worked with him on *The Scarlet Thread* (1951). On the other hand, Jack Clayton,* who directed Harvey in *Room at the Top,* was pleased with him.

After the success of *Room at the Top,* Harvey was in great demand, even from Hollywood, and he co-starred with John Wayne in the overlong epic *The Alamo* (1960). Then came his best role, as the brainwashed assassin Raymond Shaw in John Frankenheimer's paranoid thriller *The Manchurian Candidate* (1962), a role some critics unkindly noted that he was born to play. The quality of Harvey's films deteriorated in the 1960s, except for a supporting role in *Darling* * (1965). He directed *The Ceremony* in 1963 and, following the death of director Anthony Mann, Harvey completed the filming of the espionage drama *A Dandy in Aspic* (1968). He also starred in and directed his last film *Welcome to Arrow Beach* (1974), a strange movie about a Vietnam veteran who kills people to meet his taste for human flesh. Harvey assisted in the editing of the film from his sickbed and died of stomach cancer in November 1973.

Harvey was nominated for the 1960 Oscar for Best Actor and the 1959 BAFTA Best British Actor Award for *Room at the Top.* He also received a nomination at the 1960 BAFTA Awards for *Expresso Bongo* * (1960) for his role as Johnny Jackson, the hustler who tries to elevate young rocker Cliff Richard to musical stardom.

FILMS: House of Darkness (1948), Man on the Run (1948), The Dancing Years (1948), The Man from Yesterday (1949), Landfall (1949), the Black Rose (1950), Cairo Road (1950), There Is Another Sun (1951), Scarlet Thread (1951), A Killer Walks (1952), Innocents in Paris (1952), I Believe in You (1952), Women of Twilight (1952), Knights of the Round Table (1953), The Good Die Young (1954), King Richard and the Crusaders (1954), Romeo and Juliet (1954), Storm over the Nile (1955), I Am a Camera (1955), Three Men in a Boat (1956), After the Ball (1957), The Truth about Women (1958), The Silent Enemy (1958), Power among Men (1958), Room at the Top (1959), Expresso Bongo (1960), The Alamo (1960), Butterfield 8 (1960), The Long and the Short and Tall (1960), Summer and Smoke (1961), Two Loves (1961), Walk on the Wild Side (1962), The Wonderful World of the Brothers Grimm 1962), The Manchurian Candidate (1962), A Girl Named Tamiko (1962), The Running Man (1963), The Ceremony (1963), The Outrage (1964), Of Human Bondage (1964), The Love Goddess (1965), Darling (1965), Life at the Top (1965), The Spy with a Cold Nose (1966), A Dandy in Aspic (1968), Fight for Rome (1968), The Winter's Tale (1968), Rebus (1968), The Magic Christian (1969), She and He (1969), WUSA (1970), Escape to the Sun (1972), Night Watch (1973), and Welcome to Arrow Beach (1974).

HATTER'S CASTLE (Paramount British, 1941)—Melodrama. *Director:* Lance Comfort; *Producer:* Isadore Goldsmith; *Script:* Paul Merzbach and Rudolph

Bernaur, with scenario and dialogue by Rodney Ackland, from the novel by A. J. Cronin; *Cinematography:* Max Greene; *Music:* Horace Shepherd; *Cast:* Robert Newton (James Brodie), Deborah Kerr (Mary Brodie), James Mason (Dr. Renwick), Beatrice Varley (Mrs. Brodie), Emlyn Williams (Dennis), Enid Stamp-Taylor (Nancy), Henry Oscar (Grierson), Anthony Bateman (Angus Brodie), and Stuart Lindsell (Lord Winton).

After his debut feature film, the dull *Penn of Pennsylvania* (1941), Lance Comfort* established his credentials with this striking version of A. J. Cronin's popular novel, which was first published in 1931. Comfort heightens the melodramatic potential of the novel and provides a filmic adaptation, as opposed to a literal translation, of Cronin's story of a patriarchal bully whose overwhelming desire to perpetuate and elevate his name through his "castle." Ultimately, he brings pain and death to his family.

In 1879 in the Scottish town of Levensford, James Brodie bullies his family, employees, and the local townspeople and carries on a brazen affair with the local barmaid Nancy while suppressing Mary, his daughter, who wants to get out into the world and meet other people, particularly young Dr. Renwick. Brodie, however, prevents Renwick from treating his wife and seeing his daughter. This dictatorial behavior prevents Mary from attending the county ball. Instead, Nancy's lover, Dennis, sneaks away from the festivities and seduces Mary. After learning of Mary's pregnant condition, Dennis rejects her and she is forced to leave Levensford after her father throws her out of his house.

The establishment of a rival hat shop threatens Brodie's vulnerable financial position and his reluctance to adjust his lifestyle to his declining income leads to financial ruin. At the same time, Brodie exerts pressure on his son Angus to be the best student at the local school by winning a scholarship. This pressure causes the boy to break into the headmaster's office so that he can read the exam questions. Brodie's reaction to his son's disgrace causes Angus to commit suicide and, with his wife and son dead, his wealth gone, and Mary believed dead, Brodie attacks the symbol of his ambitions—his castle. He dies in the ensuing blaze. Mary, who lost Dennis's child, is reunited with Renwick at her father's funeral.

Hatter's Castle was a perfect vehicle for Robert Newton's* florid acting style and he excels in this biting study of ambition and patriarchy. Comfort emphasizes the melodramatic basis of Cronin's story—even including a snowstorm as Brodie heartlessly ejects his pregnant daughter from the family castle. *Hatter's Castle* is a strong, unflinching example of British melodrama.

HAWKINS, JACK (1910–1973). A 1950s British cinematic icon, Jack Hawkins worked primarily in theater in the 1930s and 1940s. With only intermittent film roles, such as a small part in the first sound version of *The Lodger* in 1932, he did not emerge as a full-fledged film star until the 1950s. After World War II, with the support of Alexander Korda,* Hawkins developed a popular screen image that combined strength, decency, and a benevolent authoritarianism.

His career benefited from a strong supporting role, opposite Tyrone Power, in the epic adventure *The Black Rose* (1950). This was followed by *Mandy* (1952), with Hawkins as a caring teacher, and his most famous role as Captain Ericson in the World War II military drama *The Cruel Sea** (1953). Other prominent military figures followed (such as Major Warden in David Lean's* *The Bridge on the River Kwai* [1957] and General Allenby in *Lawrence of Arabia* [1962]). When he was not playing military officers, he could be seen as a police officer in films such as *Home at Seven* (1952), *The Long Arm* (1956), and John Ford's day in the life of a British inspector (*Gideon's Day* [1958]). This persona, which exuded authority and reliability, also transferred to historical epics such as Howard Hawks's *Land of the Pharaohs* (1955), with Hawkins as Pharaoh Cheops, and *Ben-Hur* (1959), with Hawkins as Quintus Arrius. A rare deviation from this heroic image was his communist "Interrogator" in the Cold War drama *The Prisoner* (1955), with Alec Guinness* as the cardinal who is the subjected to Hawkins's inquisition. Hawkins was nominated for the 1956 BAFTA Best British Award for this role.

The League of Gentlemen* (1959), arguably Hawkins's best film, depends, to a certain extent, on the image developed by Hawkins in the 1950s as the film extended, and critiqued, the largely middle-class virtues encapsulated by his 1950s' military films. In *The League of Gentlemen,* the object of the "military operation" is not the usual pro-social objective, but a bank robbery with Hawkins as the embittered Lieutenant Colonel Hyde, soured by enforced retirement after twenty-five years of service.

League of Gentlemen was produced by Allied Film Makers, a company established by Hawkins with Richard Attenborough,* Basil Relph,* Basil Dearden,* and Bryan Forbes,* who wrote the screenplay for the film. A strong supporting role as the crazed Reverend Witt in *Zulu** (1964), plus other roles in the 1960s that projected a less heroic image, preceded an operation on Hawkins's larynx for throat cancer in 1966 that resulted in the loss of his voice. However, with the support of other filmmakers, Hawkins continued to act until his death in 1973 with his voice dubbed in post-production (often by actor Charles Gray). In his penultimate film *Theatre of Blood* (1973), Hawkins was not required to speak during his brief role as a husband forced into killing his wife by a demented Shakespearian actor (Vincent Price). Hawkins was nominated for BAFTA Film Best British Actor Awards for *Mandy, The Cruel Sea, The Prisoner,* and *The Long Arm,* and he was producer on Peter Medak's irreverent black comedy *The Ruling Class* (1972).

FILMS: Bird of Prey (1930), The Lodger (1932), A Shot in the Dark (1933), The Jewel (1933), I Lived with You (1933), The Good Companions (1933), The Lost Chord (1934), Death at Broadcasting House (1934), Autumn Crocus (1934), Peg of Old Dury (1935), The Frog (1936), Beauty and the Barge (1937), Who Goes Next? (1938), A Royal Divorce (1938), Murder Will Out (1939), The Flying Squad (1940), Next of Kin (1942), The Fallen Idol (1948), Bonnie Prince Charlie (1948), The Small Back Room (1949), The Elusive Pimpernel (1950), State Secret (1950), The Black Rose (1950), No Highway in the Sky

(1951), The Adventurers (1951), Home at Seven (1952), The Planter's Wife (1952), Mandy (1952), Angels One Five (1953), Twice upon a Time (1953), The Malta Story (1953), The Cruel Sea (1953), Front Page Story (1954), The Intruder (1954), The Seekers (1954), Touch and Go (1955), The Prisoner (1955), Land of the Pharaohs (1955), The Long Arm (1956), Fortune Is a Woman (1957), The Bridge on the River Kwai (1957), The Man in the Sky (1957), Two-Headed Spy (1958), Gideon's Day (1958), Ben-Hur (1959), The League of Gentlemen (1959), Two Loves (1961), Lafayette (1961), Five Finger Exercise (1962), Lawrence of Arabia (1962), Rampage (1963), Zulu (1964), The Third Secret (1964), Guns at Batasi (1964), Lord Jim (1965), Masquerade (1965), Judith (1966), Poppies Are Also Flowers (1966), Shalako (1968), Great Catherine (1968), Monte Carlo or Bust (1969), Oh! What a Lovely War (1969), Twinky (1969), The Adventures of Gerard (1970), Waterloo (1970), The Beloved (1970), When Eight Bells Toll (1970), Nicholas and Alexander (1971), Kidnapped (1971), Young Winston (1972), Escape to the Sun (1972), Theatre of Blood (1973), and Tales That Witness Madness (1973).

HAY, WILL (1888–1949). The popular image of Will Hay, saddled with his pince-nez and a general air of shabbiness, was that of a flustered schoolmaster desperately trying to cover up his own inadequacies—a character he developed on radio in 1922 with his "St. Michael's School" sketches and, beginning in 1934, in the cinema. Hay's catch phrase was "good morning boys." The characteristic traits of Hay's incompetent headmaster, who was largely devoid of romantic feelings or attachments, extended to his other authority figures such as the inadequate station master in *Oh, Mr. Porter!* (1937), and his Sergeant Dudfoot in *Ask a Policeman* (1939). In reality, Hay was the antithesis of his screen and radio image as he was a talented astronomer.

Hay, like other northern performers, such as George Formby and Gracie Fields, developed his comic expertise and masterly timing over a long period in the hard world of the music halls, beginning in 1909. His first major film, *Boys Will Be Boys** (1935), reprised his school teacher persona, and this was the first of three Hay comedies directed by American William Beaudine. In the second film, *Windbag the Sailor* (1936), the toothless Moore Marriott and the overweight Graham Moffat joined Hay and they were perfect foils over a number of films, many of which were scripted by Val Guest,* Marriott Edgar, and Hay himself. Marcel Varnel replaced Beaudine for *Oh, Mr. Porter,* with Hay as a less than capable station master who captures a group of smugglers.

Hay jettisoned Marriott and Moffat, who were replaced by Claude Hulbert, when he left Gainsborough for Ealing during World War II. Varnel directed his first film at his new studio, *The Ghost of St. Michael's* (1941), which reprised Hay's earlier characterization of a seedy schoolmaster who befuddles a group of Nazi spies with his devastating incompetence. Hay, however, co-directed his final three films, including *The Black Sheep of Whitehall* (1941), with Hay as a shabby teacher running a correspondence school, and *The Goose Steps Out* (1942), with Hay instructing Germans in British customs. Hay's films at Ealing failed to match the popularity of his earlier films at Gainsborough. After *My Learned Friend* (1943), a bizarre comedy involving a murderous psychopath (Mervyn Johns) threatening lawyers Hay and Hulbert, he retired from the screen. Hay died in 1949.

FILMS: Those Were the Days (1933), Radio Parade of 1935 (1934), Dandy Dick (1935), Boys Will Be Boys (1935), Where There's a Will (1936), Windbag the Sailor (1936), Oh, Mr. Porter! (1937), Good Morning Boys (1937), Old Bones of the River (1938), Hey! Hey! USA (1938), Where's That Fire? (1939), Convict 99 (1939), Ask a Policeman (1939), The Ghost of St. Michael's (1941), The Black Sheep of Whitehall (1942), The Goose Steps Out (1942), Go to Blazes (1942), The Big Blockade (1942), and My Learned Friend (1943).

HELL DRIVERS (Rank/Aqua, 1957)—Trucking melodrama. *Director:* Cy Raker Endfield; *Producer:* Benjamin Fisz; *Script:* Cy Raker Endfield and John Kruse, based on a story by John Kruse; *Cinematography:* Geoffrey Unsworth; *Music:* Hubert Clifford; *Cast:* Stanley Baker (Tom Yately), Herbert Lom (Gino), Peggy Cummins (Lucy), Patrick McGoohan (Red), William Hartnell (Cartley), Wilfred Lawson (Ed), Sid James (Dusty), Jill Ireland (Jill), Alfie Bass (Tinker), Gordon Jackson (Scottie), David McCallum (Jimmy), Sean Connery (Tom), George Murcell (Tub), Wensley Pithey (Pop), Marjorie Rhodes (Ma West), Beatrice Varley (Mrs. Yately), Robin Bailey (Assistant Manager), and John Horseley (Doctor).

Hell Drivers was not only one of the best British films of the 1950s, it was also the kind of film that gives genre a good name. It was notable for consolidating Stanley Baker's* status within the British film industry as well as providing Sean Connery* with a supporting role as a reckless truck driver before his major film break as James Bond in *Dr. No** (1962).

Tom Yately, who has just been released from prison, gains a job as a truck driver with a shady company who only hire men prepared to break the speed limit while delivering gravel by driving dangerously on narrow rural roads. Yately joins the other drivers at the local boarding house run by Ma West. When a fight breaks out at the village dance and he refuses to support the other drivers by joining in, because of his prison record, the men, lead by Red, try to force Yately out of the company. When Gino, the only truck driver who supports Yately, is killed by Red, Yately intervenes and exposes the collusion between Red and Cartley, the company manager.

The appeal of the film does not reside in its generic elements but in Baker's performance and Endfield's* robust direction. There are many distinctive aspects—such as Marjorie Rhodes, as the tough Ma West, introducing Yately to the rules of her boarding house. Also, the sexual tension between Peggy Cummins's Lucy and Yately, a tension exacerbated by Yately's sense of loyalty to Gino, who also loves Lucy. Lucy is drawn to Yately's rough sexuality while also feeling guilty about her relationship with Gino. Above all else, Endfield makes sure that the film moves at a breakneck pace, not only on the roads with some superb action scenes, but also in the boarding house and cafe scenes that crackle with violence and sharp dialogue. The only time sentimentality threatens to stall the film occurs when Yately visits his crippled brother Jimmy in London. The arrival of Beatrice Varley, as Tom's mother, who vents her bitterness toward her ex-convict son, soon ends such feelings. Similarly, the truck drivers, who are presented as a group of social misfits working only for the bonus money, remain (with the exception of Gino) a vicious pack driven only by self-interest. There is no sense of community. *Hell Drivers* is a tough, uncompromising film.

HILARY AND JACKIE (Arts Council of England/British Screen/Channel Four Films/Intermedia Films/Oxford Film Company, 1998)—Domestic drama. *Director:* Anand Tucker; *Producers:* Nicolas Kent, Andrew Paterson, Guy East (executive), Ruth Jackson (executive), and Nigel Sinclair (executive); *Script:* Frank Cottrell Boyce, based on the novel *A Genius in the Family* by Hilary du Pre and Piers du Pre; *Cinematography:* David Johnson; *Music:* Barrington Pheloung; *Cast:* Emily Watson (Jackie duPré), Rachel Griffiths (Hilary du Pré), James Frain (Daniel Barenboim), David Morrissey (Kiffer), Charles Dance (Derek du Pre), Celia Imrie (Iris du Pre), Bill Paterson (Cello Teacher), and Nyree Dawn Porter (Dame Margot Fonteyn).

This biography of the relationship between sisters Hilary and Jackie du Pré, from their childhood in the early 1950s to Jackie's death from multiple sclerosis in 1987, could have been sensationalized and utterly depressing. The fact that it is not is largely due to the film's intelligent treatment of the more bizarre episodes in Jackie's life, such as her request to sleep with Kiffer, Hilary's husband, and Jackie's erratic behavior in the latter stages of her life. The film also benefits from strongly contrasting performances between the two lead actresses, with Emily Watson as the vibrant, intense Jacqueline du Pré and the more subdued, but equally effective, Rachel Griffiths as Hilary.

The film, above all, captures the intensity of the relationship between the two girls/women, and it this intensity that remains the central aspect of the film. For example, the initial motivation for Jackie's dedication to the cello, the film suggests, was just to be with her sister who showed promise as a flautist at an early age. Similarly, Hilary's painful decision that Kiffer, for the sake of Jackie's deteriorating mental state, should have sexual intercourse with her sister is rendered plausible by its presentation in the film. As Hilary tells Kiffer: "She [Jackie] just needs proof that someone loves her" and the intensity of the relationship between the two women supersedes all other relationships and concerns.

After presenting the early years, the film utilizes a non-linear, "parallel" narrative structure by first showing Hilary's "story," including her marriage to Kiffer and their move to a rural farmhouse, followed by Jackie's "story" that, periodically, overlaps earlier details of Hilary's story. Although this device offers some useful information, and occasionally provides an insight into the differences between the two women, it does slow the narrative down. The major weakness, however, concerns the lack of information concerning Jackie's marriage to the talented pianist and conductor Daniel Barenboim (possibly because he is still a very public figure). The breakdown in their relationship, the film suggests, seems to result from the effects of Jackie's illness, but there are also suggestions that this is only part of the story.

The film suggests that despite her fame and public acclaim, Jackie really wanted Hilary's life of family and stability. This theme is reinforced early in the film when Jackie, alone overseas on a concert tour, sends her soiled clothes home to be laundered by her mother. While the family, when they receive the clothes, view this action with some disdain, the audience is allowed to understand Jackie's motivation when she is shown wallowing in the laundered clothes on her hotel bed as their smell takes away, for a moment, her extreme longing to be home with Hilary and the rest of her family.

The film begins and ends with a slightly surreal sequence at the beach when Jackie and Hilary, as young girls, play only to be interrupted by the shadow of a mysterious woman near the water's edge. The fatalism of this sequence pervades the rest of the film. Jackie is diagnosed with multiple sclerosis when she is twenty-seven. The film devotes relatively little of its two hours running time to Jackie's final years—she did not die for another fourteen years after the initial diagnosis. Instead, her full-blown illness is introduced late in the story with the film choosing, correctly, to emphasize, the life-affirming aspects of Jackie's relationship with Hilary and her unique musical ability—accentuated by Watson's uncanny ability to duplicate Jackie's physical reactions to her music, plus a brief, exciting, impromptu performance of "You Really Got Me" between Jackie and Barenboim.

THE HILL (MGM, 1965)—Prison. *Director:* Sidney Lumet; *Producer:* Kenneth Hyman; *Script:* Ray Rigby and R. S. Allen, based on Ray Rigby's play; *Cinematography:* Oswald Morris; *Music:* Art Noel and Don Pelosi; *Cast:* Sean Connery (Joe Roberts), Harry Andrews (Regimental Sergeant Major Bert Wilson), Ian Bannen (Sergeant Charlie Harris), Alfred Lynch (George Stevens), Ossie Davis (Jacko King), Roy Kinnear (Monty Bartlett), Jack Watson (Jock McGrath), Ian Hendry (Staff Sergeant Williams), Michael Redgrave (Medical Officer), and Norman Bird (Commandant).

Ray Rigby served as a private during World War II. He was placed in field detention on two occasions. His experiences in the punishment center served as the inspiration for his script, based on his play *The Hill,* one of the most confronting British films of the 1960s. The film is characterized by uniformly excellent performances from an all-male cast, especially Sean Connery,* escaping from his James Bond persona as the tough, stubborn Joe Roberts, imprisoned in a British military center in the Libyan desert after striking an officer. Robert's action was provoked by an order to lead his men into a futile battle. Soon after his arrival, Regimental Sergeant Major Wilson indicates that he "wants" Roberts, he wants to break his spirit of independence. Wilson runs the camp as his personal prison, supported by the sadistic Staff Sergeant Williams, who wants to break everybody.

Roberts is placed with four other prisoners—Jacko King, who suffers racial taunts until he finally breaks; Jock McGrath, who initially despises Roberts for his failure to follow orders; George Stevens, who dies following a concentrated session of walking up and down the man-made hill; and Monty Bartlett, the spiv who cares only for himself. Eventually, McGrath joins Roberts and King and their desire to bring Williams to justice for Stevens's death. The film closes on an indeterminate note. Just as the men seemed to have convinced the weak medical officer (Michael Redgrave) to investigate Williams, the men jeopardize this decision by unleashing their frustrations on the sadistic officer.

Harry Andrews, in a role he seemed destined to play, stands out as the cunning disciplinarian, innately aware that Roberts represents a threat to his autocratic behavior. Andrews was rewarded with a Best Supporting Actor Award from the 1965 American National Board of Review and he was also nominated for Best British Actor at the 1966 BAFTA Film Awards, as was Sidney Lumet for Best British Film, Ray Rigby for Best British Screenplay, and Herbert Smith for Best British Art Direction, while Oswald Morris won Best British Cinematography (black and white). Rigby also won the Best Screenplay Award at the 1965 Cannes Film Festival. However, the award ceremonies neglected the strong performance of Ian Hendry as the sadist Williams. Similarly, Ian Bannen contributed another nervy, guilt-ridden performance as Sergeant Harris, the only British officer with a conscience, while Roy Kinnear was effective as the self-interested coward Monty Bartlett.

HINDLE WAKES (Gainsborough, 1931)—Melodrama. *Director:* Victor Saville; *Producer:* Michael Balcon; *Script:* Victor Saville and Angus MacPhail, based on the play by Stanley Houghton; *Cinematography:* Mutz Greenbaum; *Cast:* Belle Chrystal (Jenny Hawthorne), Sybil Thorndike (Mrs. Hawthorne), Edmund Gwenn (Chris Hawthorne), Norman McKinnel (Nat Jeffcote), Mary Clare (Mrs. Jeffcote), John Stuart (Alan Jeffcote), Muriel Angelus (Beatrice Farrar), A. G. Poulton (Sir Timothy Farrar), Ruth Peterson (Mary Hollins), and Lionel Roberts (Bob Parker).

Hindle Wakes, Stanley Houghton's spirited reworking of the tenets of the "fallen woman" melodrama, had been adapted by Maurice Elvey for the British screen in 1927, but Victor Saville's* 1931 film was the first sound version. It was remade as *Holiday Week* in 1952. The different value systems of each generation, especially the clash between traditional and "modern" representations of female sexual desire, dominate the film although questions of class and the power of wealth are never far below the surface.

When young Lancashire mill worker Jenny Hawthorne and girlfriend Mary Hollins go to Blackpool for their annual vacation, Jenny meets Alan Jeffcote, the son of the owner of the mill in which she works. Unlike Mary, Jenny is not content to spend the vacation just going to dances but wants "some fun" and so she and Alan leave Blackpool and spend a few days together in an expensive hotel where they register as husband and wife. Jenny tries to cover her tracks by leaving behind a post-dated postcard for Mary to mail to Jenny's parents from Blackpool. However, this scheme backfires when Mary dies in an accident and Jenny's parents discover the postcard.

The issue of female virtue and male responsibility occupies the second half of the film as Alan does not want to marry Jenny because he is engaged to Beatrice Farrar, the daughter of another mill owner. On the other hand, Jenny's mother (played with melodramatic relish by Sybil Thorndike) and father are anxious to protect their daughter's name by her marrying Alan. Alan's father, unlike his wife, also insists that Alan "do the right thing" by marrying Jenny. Hence, the social pressure on Jenny to conform to the wishes of her parents, and society, is immense but, in a revealing explanation to Alan, she shocks everybody by telling Alan that, like him, she merely wanted "some fun" and would never consider marrying him.

To the film's credit, it reworks this basic tenet of the "fallen woman" tale by refusing to punish Jenny for her "modern" views, although there is the conventional image near the end of Jenny, the "fallen woman," leaving her home and her mother's threats, and walking off into the dark night. The final scenes are more optimistic and provide a more traditional closure, based on class—Alan returns to Beatrice and his legacy as the (future) owner of two major mills, while Jenny is last seen flirting with Bob Parker, another mill worker.

The early films of Saville, such as *Hindle Wakes,* require closer analysis, as this is an impressive film. At times the dated regional dialect and the "creaky" theatrical structure of Houghton's story threaten the film, but Saville's innovative composition and editing, aided by Mutz Greenbaum's dramatic lighting, rejuvenates the entire production. Belle Chrystal as Jenny and Norman McKinnel, repeating his role from the 1927 film as Alan's father, articulate the different worldviews that underpin the film.

HITCHCOCK, ALFRED (1899–1980). Of Alfred Hitchcock's fifty-three films, twenty-eight were British (including the four U.S.–produced films) and, following François Truffaut's interview with Hitchcock in the 1960s, it has been common to divide his output into the (lesser) British films and the (superior) U.S. films. This is an oversimplification as many of the recognizable themes and formal elements of his U.S. films were developed in England in the 1920s and 1930s. This crude dichotomy was perpetuated by Hitchcock himself in the Truffaut interviews where he speaks of the English version of *The Man Who Knew Too Much** (1934) as the work of a "talented amateur" compared with the professionalism of his 1956 U.S. version. Yet, this ignores the historical context as there was twenty years between each film and it would have been interesting to know what he would have produced if he had remained in Britain after 1940. Indeed, working with David O. Selznick in the 1940s, and within the Hollywood studios in the 1950s and 1960s, together with the effect that the Production Code had on all U.S. films, meant that Hitchcock's films were always subject to some form of constraint. It could be argued that it was such constraints, and Hitchcock's ability to circumvent them, that gave his films their multi-layered intensity.

Critics, eager to unravel the recurring themes in Hitchcock's cinema, often resort to correlating stories and known facts from his childhood with scenes in his films. Thus, recycled stories emphasize that he was raised in a strict Catholic family where he was required by his mother to stand at the end of her bed and recount his experiences for the day. Similarly, there is the much quoted story of his father sending young Alfred to the local police station where he was placed in jail for ten minutes because "that's what we do with boys who are naughty." Thus, his films are sometimes reduced to crude themes—such as Hitchcock's supposed "mother fixation" in films such as *Psycho* (1960) and *Notorious* (1946), which also includes a scene showing Claude Rains confessing to his mother as she lies in bed. More interesting, however, is the way Hitchcock developed formal elements of classical narration, such as optical subjectivity, and extended their function within his films.

Hitchcock was born in London on August 13, 1899, into a lower-middle-class Catholic family. After working as a clerk in a cable manufacturing company, Hitchcock moved into the advertising department, where he worked with print advertisements. This provided him with his entry into the film industry in 1920 as a title designer for Famous Players-Lasky, which was opening a studio in London. He directed sequences for the ill-fated *Number 13* (1922), which was shut down when the money ran out, before taking a job as a scenario writer for Gainsborough Pictures at Islington in 1923. After working as co-director on *Always Tell Your Wife* (1923), he performed the functions of scriptwriter, assistant director, and art director on *The White Shadow* (1924), *The Passionate Adventurer* (1924), and *The Prude's Fall* (1924). Hitchcock's first film as sole director was *The Pleasure Garden* (1925), which was filmed in Munich, and this was followed by another German co-production, *The Mountain Eagle* (1926). Hitchcock's period in Germany has often been cited as exposing him to the specific stylistic features of German expressionism and Soviet montage, which can be seen in his subsequent films, although these elements were tempered by the demands of his chosen genre, the thriller.

It was, however, Hitchcock's next film, *The Lodger** (1926), a suspense story of a man mistaken for Jack the Ripper, which provided a critical breakthrough for the director. He also began the practice of making a brief cameo appearance with this film. Hitchcock married Alma Reville in the same year (1926), although he had known her since his period at Famous Players-Lasky, where she was a writer. In 1927, Hitchcock left Gainsborough for the Elstree Studios at British International Pictures where he wrote his own screenplay for a boxing film *The Ring* (1927). *Blackmail** (1929), his last silent film, was also released as Britain's first synchronous sound feature. It brought him more critical acclaim due to the subjective use of sound to heighten the heroine's confusion at a critical moment in the film.

The Man Who Knew Too Much prefigured a rich period for Hitchcock, followed by *The Thirty-Nine Steps* (1935), *Secret Agent* (1936), *Sabotage* (1936), *Young and Innocent* (1937), and *The Lady Vanishes** (1938). This completed his contract with Gaumont-British. Hitchcock, keen to try his hand in the Hollywood studio system, accepted an offer from Selznick. As he had some time before he was required in the United States, Hitchcock completed one more British film, *Jamaica Inn* (1939), before leaving for the United States, where he planned to film a version of the sinking of the Titanic. However, Selznick scrapped this and Hitchcock directed *Rebecca* (1940), which won the Oscar for Best Picture in 1940, although Hitchcock did not win Best Director. In fact, Hitchcock never won an Oscar for Best Director, although he was nominated for *Rebecca, Lifeboat* (1944), *Spellbound* (1945), *Rear Window* (1954), and *Psycho*. Earlier, Hitchcock won the New York Critics Film Circle Award for Best Director for *The Lady Vanishes*.

A series of superb films followed (including his personal favorite, *Shadow of a Doubt* [1943]), interspersed by the adventurous, but commercially unsuccessful *Rope* (1948) and *Under Capricorn* (1949), before the masterpieces of the 1950s and early 1960s. This included Hitchcock's brilliant reworking of the Cornell Woolrich short story (*Rear Window*) and the audacious *Vertigo* (1958), which pushed the formal and thematic boundaries of the classical Hollywood cinema further than anybody had dared to go up to that point. The quality of his films deteriorated after *The Birds* (1963), although his penultimate film *Frenzy* (1972) brought him back to England. Hitchcock was knighted in 1980, a few months before his death. In 1968, he was awarded the Irving G. Thalberg Memorial Award.

FILMS: Number 13 (1922), Always Tell Your Wife (1923), The Prude's Fall (1924), The Pleasure Garden (1925), The Mountain Eagle (1926), The Lodger (1926), The Ring (1927), Easy Virtue (1927), Downhill (1927), The Farmer's Wife (1928), Champagne (1928), The Manxman (1929), Blackmail (1929), Murder (1930), Juno and the Paycock (1930), Elstree Calling (1930), The Skin Game (1931), Rich and Strange (1931), Number Seventeen (1932), Waltzes from Vienna (1933), The Man Who Knew Too Much (1934), The Thirty-Nine Steps (1935), Secret Agent (1936), Sabotage (1936), Young and Innocent (1937), The Lady Vanishes (1938), Jamaica Inn (1939), Rebecca (1940), Foreign Correspondent (1940), Suspicion (1941), Mr. and Mrs. Smith (1941), Saboteur (1942), Shadow of Doubt (1943), Lifeboat (1944), Adventure Malgache (short, 1944), Bon Voyage (short, 1944), Spellbound (1945), Notorious (1946), The Paradine Case (1947), Rope (1948), Under Capricorn (1949), Stage Fright (1950), Strangers on a Train (1951), I Confess (1953), Rear Window (1954), Dial M for Murder (1954), To Catch a Thief (1955), The Man Who Knew Too Much (1955), The Wrong Man (1956), The Trouble with Harry (1956), Vertigo (1958), North by Northwest (1959), Psycho (1960), The Birds (1963), Marnie (1964), Torn Curtain (1966), Topaz (1969), Frenzy (1972), and Family Plot (1976).

H.M.S. DEFIANT (Columbia, 1962)—Naval melodrama. *Director:* Lewis Gilbert; *Producer:* John Brabourne; *Script:* Nigel Kneale and Edmund North, based on the novel by Frank Tilsley; *Cinematography:* Christopher Challis; *Music:* Clifton Parker; *Cast:* Alec Guinness (Captain Crawford), Dirk Bogarde (Lieutenant Scott-Padget), Anthony Quayle (Vizard), Tom Bell (Evans), Victor Madden (Dawlish), Walter Fitzgerald (Admiral Jackson), Maurice Denham (Mr. Goss), Nigel Stock (Senior Midshipman Kilpatrick), Richard Carpenter (Lieutenant Ponsonby), Peter Gill (Lieutenant D'Arblay), David Robinson (Harvey Crawford), Russell Napier (Flag Captain), and Murray Melvin (Wagstaffe).

Although *H.M.S. Defiant* is set in 1797, with the possibility of a French invasion of England, the sea battles between the two countries provide little more than an historical backdrop to the confrontation between Captain Crawford and his second in charge, Lieutenant Scott-Padget. Scott-Padgett, who has successfully destroyed the careers of two previous captains, displays suggestions of sexual perversity; he is a sadist who wants to indulge himself in frequent floggings of the crew.

Captain Crawford is hampered in this battle by the presence of his young son on the ship and Scott-Padget, aware that Captain Crawford cannot be seen to display any form of favoritism toward his son, exploits Crawford's vulnerability. When Crawford is badly injured by losing an arm during another skirmish with the French, Scott-Padget assumes command and the floggings resume, heightening tensions on the ship. A subplot concerns the efforts of the men on the ship to obtain better conditions on admiralty ships through a charter of grievances and when the actions of Scott-Padget provoke a mutiny, the sailors redeem themselves during a sea battle.

The historical context for the film has a strong contemporary relevance (early 1960s) in the battle for better conditions. The real significance of the film resides in the performances of Alec Guinness* and Dirk Bogarde,* who enliven a familiar plot. The film was not as successful at the box office as expected and producer John Brabourne argued that the film's tough presentation of the issues weakened its appeal for women.[3] The miniatures and other special effects used in sea battles were supervised by Howard Lydecker, the Hollywood veteran who produced, with his brother, high-quality special effects with minimal resources at Republic Studios from the 1930s to the 1950s.

HOBSON, VALERIE (1917–1998). Early in her career, after her return from Hollywood in 1936, Valerie Hobson was constricted by the parts available to her. Later, in the 1940s she was cast in roles that emphasized her imperious facial features, strong characters tinged by repression and calculation. Hobson was notable in Michael Powell's* *The Spy in Black* (1939), as the double agent Frau Till/Jill Blacklock, the woman torn between desire and security in the costume melodrama *Blanche Fury* * (1947), and the dominant liquor-hating Edith d'Ascoyne in Robert Hamer's* masterpiece *Kind Hearts and Coronets* * (1949). This film also benefits from the contrast between the glacial Hobson and the sensual, scheming Joan Greenwood.*

Hobson, however, had a brief career in Hollywood prior to this and, while still a teenager, she was signed to a contract to Universal Studios in 1934 and worked steadily for a year or so in Hollywood films, including the *Bride of Frankenstein* (1935), as Henry Hull's wife in *Werewolf of London* (1935), and *Chinatown Squad* (1935). Hobson returned to Britain in 1936 and appeared in the successful comedy-thriller *This Man Is News* (1938) and the even more successful paean to the British Empire *The Drum* * (1938). However, in the 1940s Hobson went from one from good film to another—notably as both Estella and her mother Molly in

David Lean's* masterly adaptation of *Great Expectations** (1946), where Hobson provided a suitable contrast with the actress (Jean Simmons) who played the young Estella.

*Interrupted Journey** (1949), which followed *Kind Hearts and Coronets,* allowed Hobson to essay one of her few conventional roles in the 1940s as the concerned wife of husband (Richard Todd*) who is planning to run away with another woman. This was followed by one of Hobson's strangest roles as the willful mother of young John Howard Davies in *The Rocking Horse Winner** (1949), a bizarre drama of a small boy with the ability to pick horse race winners while on his rocking horse. Eventually, Davies rocks himself to death to satisfy his materialistic mother.

Hobson, who died in 1998, was married at one time to producer Anthony Havelock-Allan, who produced a number of her films in the 1940s, including the costume melodrama *Blanche Fury.* This color film was a favorite of the actress as she enjoyed working with cinematographers Guy Green and Geoffrey Unsworth. Hobson and Havelock-Allan divorced in 1952 and she virtually retired from the screen after marrying John Profumo, a junior minister in the Conservative British government. Although Profumo was a key figure in the political and sex scandal that rocked the British establishment in 1963, they remained married and dedicated themselves to social work.

FILMS: Eyes of Fate (1933), Two Hearts in Waltz Time (1934), The Path of Glory (1934), Badger's Green (1934), Strange Wives (1934), Great Expectations (1934), Oh, What a Night (1935), Rendezvous at Midnight (1935), Werewolf of London (1935), Bride of Frankenstein (1935), The Mystery of Edwin Drood (1935), Chinatown Squad (1935), The Great Impersonation (1935), Life Returns (1935), August Weekend (1936), Tugboat Princess (1936), The Secret of Stamboul (1936), No Escape (1936), Jump for Glory (1937), The Drum (1938), Q Planes (1938), This Man Is News (1938), This Man in Paris (1939), The Spy in Black (1939), The Silent Battle (1939), Contraband (1940), Atlantic Ferry (1941), Unpublished Story (1942), The Adventures of Tartu (1943), The Years Between (1946), Great Expectations (1946), Blanche Fury (1947), The Small Voice (1948), Train of Events (1949), Kind Hearts and Coronets (1949), The Interrupted Journey (1949), The Rocking Horse Winner (1949), The Card (1951), Who Goes There? (1952), Meet Me Tonight (1952), The Voice of Merrill (1952), Background (1954), and Knave of Hearts (1954).

HOPKINS, ANTHONY (b. 1937) The most celebrated British film actor working today, Anthony Hopkins, in some ways, represents a continuation of the classically trained British actors who emerged in the 1920s and 1930s, such as Laurence Olivier, Ralph Richardson and John Gielgud. There is, however, a difference between Anthony Hopkins and his predecessors—basically Olivier, Richardson, Gielgud et al. had little respect for the cinema in their formative years and, until late in their lives, always favored the stage over the cinema. On the other hand Hopkins performed in television and film relatively early in his career and has favored the latter during his most creative period. Hopkins made his stage debut in *The Quare Fellow* in 1960 and this was followed by four years of repertory work before *Julius Caesar* in London. His first film appearance was in *The White Bus* (1966) but he was much more active on television during the 1970s and early 1980s and he appeared in a number of critically acclaimed, award-winning productions such as the mini-series QBV11 (1971), *The Lindbergh Kidnapping Case* (1976) and as Hitler in *The Bunker* (1981). Hopkins won Best Actor Emmy Awards for these last two productions.

Hopkins has been compared with another famous Welsh actor, Richard Burton, although a significant difference between the two men is that Hopkins has retained control of his acting career and, unlike Burton, his most prestigious work has come in the latter half of his career. Hopkins now enjoys the rare status of a critically celebrated actor who is also a film star. This took some time as he appeared in a succession of lackluster films in the 1970s and 1980s such as Richard Attenborough's *Magic* (1978), which developed the basic premise of an episode from the 1947 classic *Dead of Night* with Hopkins as Corky, the emotionally fragile ventriloquist tormented by his murderous dummy; *The Bounty* (1984), a revisionist interpretation of the famous mutiny with Hopkins's Captain Bligh confronting Mel Gibson's Fletcher Christian; *The Desperate Hours* (1990), Michael Cimino's disappointing remake of the 1955 film with Hopkins as the head of a household terrorized by Mickey Rourke and other escaped convicts.

These films, which failed to establish Hopkins as a major film star, were interspersed by superior made for television films, such as his hugely enjoyable eccentric Yorkshire vet Siegfried in *All Creatures Great and Small* (1974) and the unhinged father who loses custody of his child in Mike Newell's *The Good Father* (1987). These television productions also received a limited cinema release in some countries whilst Hopkins also starred in a number of medium or low budget films which were (mostly) overlooked by the public or distributors—such as *84 Charing Cross Road* (1986) with Hopkins as the London bookseller who forms a trans-Atlantic friendship with a New York woman (Anne Bancroft) over a twenty-year period. Hopkins also traveled to Australia to star in the gentle social comedy *Spotswood* (1991), also known as *The Efficiency Expert* in the U.S., involving a management consultant who comes to value the working class culture and comradeship of the workers in a small factory that makes moccasins.

Spotswood, in fact, marked the end of Hopkins's period as a character actor or lead actor in small budget films. Whilst filming *Spotswood* in Melbourne in 1991 *The Silence of the Lambs* (1991) was released in the U.S. and his performance as Hannibal Lecter radically changed his status within the (Hollywood) film industry. Hopkins was now a film star *and* a critically celebrated actor. He won the Best Actor award at the 1992 Academy Awards and the 1992 BAFTA Awards. But it was not only the awards he won, as he had been winning awards for some years, but also the effect that his performance as Hannibal Lector had on audiences throughout the world.

He now became a much sought after lead actor in large budget films, especially after the Merchant Ivory production of *Howards End* (1992) with Hopkins as the calculating businessman Henry J. Wilcox. In Francis Ford Coppola's ambitious production of *Bram Stoker's Dracula* (1992) Hopkins followed in the footsteps of Laurence Olivier and Peter Cushing, and many others, as the vampire hunter Van Helsing; *Remains of the Day* (1993) was a return to the prestige British film with Hopkins as the repressed, self-sacrificing butler who works closely with the head housekeeper (Emma Thompson) to keep a large manor functioning in the 1930s whilst its lord (James Fox) promotes his pro-Nazi sympathies. As C. S. Lewis in *Shadowlands* (1993) Hopkins is the Oxford don attracted to independent American poet Joy Grisham (Debra Winger), and, to courageously demonstrate his range, Hopkins accepted the controversial role of *Nixon* (1995) in Oliver Stone's idiosyncratic interpretation of the disgraced American president.

During the last half of the 1990s Hopkins continued to alternate between demanding roles, such as Hopkins as a self-centered artist (Pablo Picasso) in James Ivory's *Surviving Picasso* (1996), and large budget projects such as *Amistad* (1997), Steven Spielberg's recreation of the plight of the slaves on the Spanish slave ship *La Amistad* with Hopkins, as John Quincy Adams, supplying the courtroom speech which climaxes the film. Whilst he appeared in a number of lackluster films during this period, including *The Mask of Zorro* (1998) and *Meet Joe Black* (1998). Hopkins also starred in the under-appreciated David Mamet scripted outdoor drama *The Edge* (1997). This film, a mixture of typical Mamet elements combining betrayal and confrontation with his usual multi-layered dialogue, was set in the wilderness and physical action formed an integral part of the story. After *Titus,* 1999), Julie Taymor's long, violent interpretation of Shakespeare's *Titus Andronicus,* which was filmed in Italy with Hopkins in the title role, he took a long sabbatical from acting except for supplying a voice-over in *Mission: Impossible II* (2000) and narrating *How the Grinch Stole Christmas* (2000). However, the chance to reprise his role as Hannibal Lecter in the disappointing sequel *Hannibal* (2001) appears to have regenerated his enthusiasm for the cinema with strong roles in subsequent films such as the sentimental fantasy *Hearts in Atlantis (2001), The Devil and Daniel Webster* (2002) and a return to Hannibal Lecter in *Red Dragon* (2002), a remake of Michael Mann's *Manhunter* (1986).

Hopkins was nominated for the Best Actor Award for *Remains of the Day* at the 1994 Academy Awards, for *Nixon* at the 1995 Awards, and Best Supporting Actor for *Amistad* at the 1997 Awards. Hopkins won the BAFTA Award for Best Actor for *Shadowlands* in 1994 and a BAFTA television award for Best Actor for his role in the *War and Peace* miniseries (1973). In 1969, in his second film, Hopkins was nominated for Best Supporting Actor for *The Lion in Winter.* When Stanley Kubrick's 1960 production of *Spartacus* was restored in 1991, Hopkins imitated the voice of Laurence Olivier (who died in 1989) for a restored scene where Marcus Crassus (Olivier) tries to have sex with the slave Antoninus (Tony Curtis). Hopkins was knighted in 1993.

FILMS: The White Bus (1966), The Lion in Winter (1968), Hamlet (1969), The Looking Glass War (1970), When Eight Bells Toll (1971), Young Winston (1972), A Doll's House

(1973), Juggernaut (1974), The Girl From Petrovka (1974), Audrey Rose (1977), A Bridge Too Far (1977), Magic (1978), International Velvet (1978), A Change of Seasons (1980), The Elephant Man (1980), The Bounty (1984), 84 Charing Cross Road (1986), The Dawning (1988), A Chorus of Disapproval (1988), Desperate Hours (1990), The Silence of the Lambs (1991), Spotswood (1991), Freejack (1992), Howards End (1992), Bram Stoker's Dracula (1992), Chaplin (1992), The Trial (1993), The Innocent (1993), The Remains of the Day (1993), Shadowlands (1993), The Road to Wellville (1994), Legends of the Fall (1994), Nixon (1995), August (1996), Surviving Picasso (1996), The Edge (1997), Amistad (1997), The Mask of Zorro (1998), Meet Joe Black (1998), Instinct (1999), Titus (1999), Mission Impossible 11 (2000), How the Grinch Stole Christmas (2000, voice only), Hannibal (2001), Hearts in Atlantis (2001), Bad Company (2002), The Devil and Daniel Webster (2002), Red Dragon (2002).

HOSKINS, BOB (b. 1942). Balding and stocky with a strong working-class image, Bob Hoskins is Britain's best-known character actor. He regularly works on both sides of the Atlantic following his U.S. success with *Who Framed Roger Rabbit* (1988). A film that is closer to the roots of Hoskins is *Twenty Four Seven** (1997), with Hoskins as Alan Darcy, a middle-aged man with a dream to establish a boxing club for economically depressed youths in his home town. Ultimately, Darcy fails due to a combination of bad luck and personal flaws, a recurring feature of many of the characters played by Hoskins throughout his career.

Director Neil Jordan, with coscreenwriter David Leland, provided Hoskins with the opportunity to extend his image by adding a romantic dimension to this persona in his award-winning performance as a petty criminal turned chauffeur for a high-class prostitute (Cathy Tyson) in the bittersweet drama *Mona Lisa* (1986). While Hoskins attracted widespread critical recognition for this British film, two years later he captured the attention of U.S. audiences with his performance as a U.S. fictional icon, the hard-boiled detective in Roger Zemeckis's mixture of live action and animation in *Who Framed Roger Rabbit.*

After virtually falling into acting at the age of twenty-five, following a series of short-term jobs, including a stint in the Norwegian merchant marines, Hoskins developed his acting skills in the theater, including performances with the prestigious Royal Shakespeare Company. His early film roles were less successful, beginning with a brief part in *Up the Front* (1972), and it was not until a key role as a gangster who finds his empire is under threat in John Mackenzie's gangster film *The Long Good Friday* (1981) that Hoskins attracted any substantial interest as a film actor. This role, which combined a mixture of ruthlessness and vulnerability, defined his screen persona for some time, although he has tried to vary this image over the years—as the shoe salesman romancing Cher in *Mermaids* (1990), as J. Edgar Hoover in Oliver Stone's interpretation of *Nixon* (1995), as Maggie Smith's vulnerable suitor in Jack Clayton's* *The Lonely Passion of Judith Hearne* (1987), as a sinister caterer in Atom Egoyan's *Felicia's Journey* (1999), and as Nikita Krushchev in the war film *Enemy at the Gates* (2001). Fred

Schepisi's touching drama of friendship and human flaws, *Last Orders* (2002), gave Hoskins his best role in recent years as Ray, the funny-sad punter who cares for Michael Caine's wife (Helen Mirren).

Hoskins starred in, and was also executive producer, for the failed version of Joseph Conrad's *Secret Agent* (1996), and he directed and wrote the screenplay for *The Raggedy Rawney* in 1987. Hoskins was nominated for an Academy Award for *Mona Lisa* and he won the BAFTA Award, the Cannes Film Festival Award, and a Golden Globe for Best Actor for this film. Earlier, Hoskins was nominated for the Best Actor Award at the 1982 BAFTA Film Awards for *The Long Good Friday.*

FILMS: Up the Front (1972), The National Health (1973), Inserts (1975), Royal Flash (1975), Zulu Dawn (1979), The Long Good Friday (1980), Pink Floyd—The Wall (1982), The Honorary Consul (1983), Lassiter (1984), The Cotton Club (1984), Brazil (1985), Mona Lisa (1986), Sweet Liberty (1986), A Prayer for Dying (1987), The Secret Policeman's Third Ball (voice, 1987), The Lonely Passion of Judith Hearne (1987), Who Framed Roger Rabbit (1988), The Raggedy Rawney (1988), Mermaids (1990), Heart Condition (1990), The Favour, the Watch and the Very Big Fish (1991), Shattered (1991), Hook (1991), Blue Ice (1992), The Inner Circle (1991), Passed Away (1992), The Super Mario Bros. (1993), The Big Freeze (1993), Nixon (1995), Balto (voice, 1995), Rainbow (1995), Ding Dong (1995), The Secret Agent (1996), Michael (1996), Twenty Four Seven (1997), Spice World (1997), Cousin Bette (1998), Parting Shots (1998), Captain Jack (1998), A Room for Romeo Brass (1999), Felicia's Journey (1999), The White River Kid (1999), Let the Good Times Roll (1999), American Virgin (2000), Enemy at the Gates (2001), Last Orders (2002), Where Eskimos Live (2002), and The Sleeping Dictionary (2002).

THE HOUSE ACROSS THE LAKE (Hammer, 1954)—Film noir. *Director:* Ken Hughes; *Producer:* Anthony Hinds; *Script:* Ken Hughes, based on his novel *High Wray; Cinematography:* Walter Harvey; *Music:* Ivor Slaney; *Cast:* Alex Nicol (Mark Kendrick), Hilary Brooke (Carol Forest), Paul Carpenter (Vincent Gordon), Hugh Dempster (Frank), Peter Illing (Harry Stevens), Sid James (Beverly Forest), Alan Wheatley (Inspector MacLennan), and Susan Stephen (Andrea Forest).

Before Hammer Studios became strongly associated with historical horror films, such as *The Curse of Frankenstein** (1957) and *Dracula** (1957), it specialized in low-budget crime films with second-string or fading Hollywood stars, such as Robert Preston in *Cloudburst* (1951), *The Last Page* (1952) with George Brent, and *Stolen Face* (1952) with Paul Henreid and Lizabeth Scott. One of the best examples of this cycle, *The House across the Lake,* was based on the novel *High Wray* by the film's director, Ken Hughes.

Hughes incorporates many of the archetypal elements found in *Double Indemnity* (1943) in his film, notably the sexual entrapment of a male character by a femme fatale desirous of killing her husband. In *The House Across the Lake,* duplicitous Carol Forest schemes to kill her wealthy husband after she learns that he is dying and plans to cut off her financial benefits after his death. Consequently, Carol exploits the sexual hunger of jaded, failed novelist Mark Kendrick, who lives across the lake from the Forest mansion. Kendrick, for his part, struggles with his conscience as he forms a friendship with Carol's husband, Beverly, and his daughter.

The film's short running time requires that little time is wasted on subplots and the film strips the familiar conventions back to their generic essence. Consequently, the viewer is made aware that Kendrick's attempts to break away from Carol are futile and that, eventually, he will participate in Beverly's death. Familiarity with the genre's inherent fatalism means that once the murder is executed, the love affair between Carol and Kendrick will turn sour resulting in Kendrick's confession. This is an assured film providing minor Hollywood actor Alex Nicol with a rare opportunity to excel in a role different from the western villains he often played.

THE HOUSE OF MIRTH (Granada Film Production/Arts Council of England/Glasgow Film Fund, 2000)—Tragedy. *Director:* Terence Davies; *Producers:* Olivia Stewart, Bob Last (executive), Pippa Cross (executive), and Alan J. Wands (coproducer); *Script:* Terence Davies, based on the novel by Edith Wharton; *Cinematography:* Remi Adefarasin; *Music:* Adrian Johnston; *Cast:* Gillian Anderson (Lily Bart), Eric Stoltz (Lawrence Selden), Dan Aykroyd (Gus Trenor), Eleanor Bron (Mrs. Peniston), Anthony LaPaglia (Sim Rosedale), Laura Linney (Bertha Dorset), Terry Kinney (George Dorset), Jodhi May (Grace Stepney), Elizabeth McGovern (Carry Fisher), and Penny Downie (Judy Trenor).

With the movie set in New York, 1905, Lily Bart emerges out of the shadows and steam from a nearby train to meet the only man she will ever love, Lawrence Selden. This opening signals a sentimental, romantic period drama. Nothing could be further from the truth as *The House of Mirth* is not a period film but an uncompromising dramatization that the "heart of fools is in the house of mirth." After meeting Selden, Lily gently coaxes an invitation out of him to visit his apartment, thereby breaking a social code for an unmarried woman of her class. Lily's action, by today's standards, may appear slight, but within the rigid code of her society it is a mistake. Her rebelliousness and independence of spirit, combined with her integrity and an inability to accept advice from those more aware of the ramifications of violating the rigid codes of New York society, lead to her downfall. This path begins as she leaves Selden's apartment and meets the rich Jewish businessman Sim Rosedale. As a consequence of her actions, Lily is forced to concoct a clumsy lie, the first in a series of bad decisions leading to her estrangement from society and death by suicide.

The House of Mirth, based on Edith Wharton's caustic satire of Belle Époque New York, is similar to Martin Scorsese's adaptation of Wharton's *The Age of Innocence* (1993), and also Iain Softley's brilliant adaptation of Henry James's *The Wings of the Dove** (1997). James was a close friend of Wharton and their novels share a similar desire to expose old patrician New York as duplicitous and hypocritical, condemning those who cannot live within its codes to isolation and disgrace. Terence Davies,* working with a more limited budget, eschews the lavishness of the earlier films to focus on the small moments, those moments that gradually trap Lily and provide, within the limitations of her moral code, no alternative except death. Although the pacing may seem languid, the film's delicate tension seamlessly assimilates Wharton's rich dialogue into Davies's evocative imagery and sounds, producing a fully realized film, not just a "tasteful" literary adaptation.

Occasionally, the film foregrounds its own expertise, such as the long transition from the dust sheets covering the great town house where Lily lives, across the rainy streets of New York and their vacated estates, to the sun drenched shores of the Mediterranean, finishing in Monte Carlo and devastation for her as she allows Bertha Dorset to falsely incriminate her in a scandal that will lead to her expulsion from New York society. Here, Davies amplifies Lily's realization of what it means to be "useless" in the world. Trained in only one vocation, to find a rich husband, she cannot come to terms with the men who are attracted to her—they are dull (Percy Gryce), married (George Dorset and the lecherous Gus Trenor), physically unattractive and social unacceptable (Sim Rosedale), or insufficiently wealthy (Lawrence Selden).

The House of Mirth is a compelling, painful film. Bart's downward trajectory is steady and the film is unyielding in its denial of the usual pleasures of retribution and catharsis where victimization, such as that inflicted on Lily, is involved. There are many opportunities for such pleasures in the narrative, but the film steadfastly allows none of them to eventuate. For example, early in the film Lily acquires letters that incriminate her nemesis, Bertha Dorset. But she refuses to use them even though it would restore her position in society and address her financial plight. When she is finally tempted to exploit them, fate conspires against her and the opportunity lapses. Lily is a victim of a cruel, uncaring society that believes, as she ruefully admits, "where a woman is concerned the truth is a story that's easiest to believe."

Lily contributes to her own downfall, making her a rare tragic figure in the cinema as she cannot reconcile her vocation, to marry a wealthy man, with a contradictory impulse that draws her toward Selden and away from dull, respectable men such as Gryce. Consequently, she is unable to exist either within or without society. Unable to meet the puritanical standards of either Gryce or her wealthy Aunt Julia, Lily forgoes a lucrative opportunity to marry Gryce and is bypassed in her aunt's will in favor of the scheming Grace Stepney. On the other hand, she refuses to meet the sexual demands of Trenor or match the viciousness of Bertha Dorset. Trapped between different social expectations, Lily commits suicide, and the final scene, showing Selden weeping by her bed as the scarlet liquid from the fatal bottle stains her white sheets, remains one of the most desolate images in the history of the cinema.

HOWARD, TREVOR (1916–1988). Although Trevor Howard, like many British actors, spent nearly ten years on the British stage before film stardom in the

1940s, he was, for the rest of his career, primarily a film actor, and one of Britain's best. There were many reasons for his preference for film but paramount was his dislike for playing the same part night after night. Howard trained at the Royal Academy of Dramatic Art before his London debut in 1934 and, after his discharge from the Royal Artillery, he appeared in *The Way Ahead** (1944) and *The Way to the Stars* (1945).

His big chance came with his next film as the decent, middle-class, but repressed, Dr. Alec Harvey in *Brief Encounter** (1946), who conducts a romance with a married woman (Celia Johnson*) at a railway junction. The drab, ordinary railway setting for much of the film, and the basic premise of the film involving desire that could not be consummated, struck a chord with audiences. The success of the film launched Howard's career and it made him, for a brief period, a romantic leading man in films such as *I See a Dark Stranger** (1946), opposite Deborah Kerr,* as Ann Todd's* on again off again lover in *The Passionate Friends** (1949), and as an innocent man who romances Anouk Aimée while caught up in Tunisian gun smuggling racket in *The Golden Salamander* (1950).

During this period, however, there were clear indications that Howard was capable of vastly different roles, especially as Clem Morgan, a recently discharged Royal Air Force man seeking excitement in the postwar period in *They Made Me a Fugitive** (1947). When Morgan is framed for murder, he finds that he is a fugitive caught between the police and a vicious criminal and this downbeat film represents an inverse of the gentle world of *Brief Encounter*—the most romantic scene in *They Made Me a Fugitive* occurs when Sally Gray* removes buckshot from Morgan's infected back. Similarly, Howard's no-nonsense Major Calloway provides an effective counterpoint to the naïve Holly Martins (Joseph Cotton) in *The Third Man** (1949) and Howard's Dr. Barney Barnes is sufficiently unstable to make him a murder suspect in *Green for Danger** (1946).

Throughout the 1950s, he moved more into villainous roles and character parts, such as the ex-Nazi who pursues Richard Widmark and Jane Greer through the South American jungle in Roy Boulting's* *Run for the Sun* (1956), and the love-starved broken-down sea captain who lusts for a young stowaway (Elsa Martinelli) in Guy Hamilton's *Manuela** (1957), for which Howard was nominated as Best British Actor at the 1958 BAFTA Awards. Howard won this award the next year in the lackluster romance *The Key* (1958). However, Howard's move to strong character parts culminated with his performance as Dean Stockwell's drunken father in *Sons and Lovers* (1960), which earned him an Oscar nomination. By the time of *The Charge of the Light Brigade* in 1968, and another nomination at the BAFTA Awards, he had settled into a profitable career in British, U.S., and international films as one of the most recognizable British character actors. Although many of these films were mediocre, including dreary pot-boilers such as *Catch Me a Spy* (1971) and dull all-star vehicles such as *Meteor* (1979), the prolific Howard also appeared in the odd gem, such as Sidney Lumet's tough police drama *The Offence* (1972), opposite Sean Connery.* Howard, married to British actress Helen Cherry, died in 1988.

FILMS: The Way Ahead (1944), The Way to the Stars (1944), Brief Encounter (1945), Green for Danger (1946), I See a Dark Stranger (1946), They Made Me a Fugitive (1947), So Well Remembered (1947), The Passionate Friends (1949), The Third Man (1949), The Golden Salamander (1950), Odette (1950), The Clouded Yellow (1950), Outcast of the Islands (1951), Lady Godiva Rides Again (1951), The Gift Horse (1952), The Heart of the Matter (1953), The Lovers of Lisbon (1954), The Stranger's Hand (1954), April in Portugal (short, 1955), The Cockleshell Heroes (1955), Around the World in Eighty Days (1956), Run for the Sun (1956), Interpol (1957), Manuela (1957), The Key (1958), The Roots of Heaven (1958), Moment of Danger (1959), Sons and Lovers (1960), Mutiny on the Bounty (1962), The Lion (1962), Man in the Middle (1963), Father Goose (1964), Operation Crossbow (1965), Von Ryan's Express (1965), The Saboteur: Code Named Morituri (1965), The Liquidator (1965), The Poppy Is Also a Flower (1966), Triple Cross (1966), The Long Duel (1967), Pretty Polly (1967), The Charge of the Light Brigade (1968), The Battle of Britain (1969), Twinky (1969), Ryan's Daughter (1970), Catch Me a Spy (1971), Mary, Queen of Scots (1971), The Night Visitor (1971), Kidnapped (1971), Ludwig (1972), Pope Joan (1972), The Offence (1972), Who? (1973), Craze (1973), A Doll's House (1973), Persecution (1974), 11 Harrowhouse (1974), Hennessy (1975), Death in the Sun (1975), Conduct Unbecoming (1975), The Bawdy Adventures of Tom Jones (1975), Eliza Fraser (1976), Aces High (1976), Slavers (1977), The Last Remake of Beau Geste (1977), Stevie (1978), Superman (1978), Meteor (1979), The Missionary (1979), Hurricane (1979), The Sea Wolves (1980), Sir Henry at Rawlinson End (1980), Windwalker (1980), The Shillingbury Blowers (1980), Light Years Away (1981), Gandhi (1982), Sword of the Valiant (1983), The Missionary (1982), Dust (1984), Foreign Body (1985), Time after Time (1985), White Mischief (1987), The Unholy (1988), and The Dawning (1988).

HOWARDS END (Merchant-Ivory Productions, 1992)—Period drama. *Director:* James Ivory; *Producer:* Ismail Merchant; *Script:* Ruth Prawer Jhabvala, based on the novel by E. M. Forster; *Cinematography:* Tony Pierce-Roberts; *Music:* Richard Robbins; *Cast:* Anthony Hopkins (Henry Wilcox), Emma Thompson (Margaret Schlegel), Vanessa Redgrave (Ruth Wilcox), Helena Bonham Carter (Helen Schlegel), Samuel West (Leonard Bast), James Wilby (Charles Wilcox), Jemma Redgrave (Evie Wilcox), Nicola Duffett (Jacky Bast), Prunella Scales (Aunt Juley), Adrian Ross-Magenty (Tibby Schlegel), and Joseph Bennett (Paul Wilcox).

The best and most celebrated of the Merchant-Ivory productions, *Howards End* benefits greatly from its strong source material: E. M. Forster's story of class conflict and Edwardian hypocrisy. The film also benefits, compared to other Merchant-Ivory Productions, from the stronger than usual ending that brings together the film's major protagonists, thus providing a more cathartic closure. Rooted within the tenets of good melodrama, the film's closure functions to restore both a social and a dramatic equilibrium as Margaret Schlegel renounces her intention to leave her husband Henry Wilcox while Wilcox, in return, announces his decision to leave Howards End to Margaret and, more importantly, through Margaret to her nephew, Helen's illegitimate child.

The films of Merchant-Ivory often provoke a polarized response from the critics and the public. Ranging from the cries of "boring" for their elegant settings and conservative style of filmmaking, to, at the other extreme, celebrations of their "civilized" stories that are sometimes seen as an antidote to the "low-brow" melodramas and "sex comedies" that seemingly dominate the contemporary popular cinema. However, whatever the faults of earlier Merchant-Ivory films, *Howards End* is a very good film. The virtues of the film are established in the opening sequence as Ruth Wilcox strolls in the grounds of her country house (Howards End) in the late evening while representatives of two middle-class families, Wilcox and Schlegel, inhabit the interior of the house. Ruth's separation from the protagonists is not merely geographical but also ideological as she mediates the more extreme views of each family. The values of the Wilcox family are encapsulated within its patriarch, Henry Wilcox, who favors the virtues of commerce, while expressing a strong distrust of people and little interest in breaking down class barriers ("The poor are poor, and one's sorry for them—but there it is"). The Schlegel family, on the other hand, believes in the benefits of the arts, which it combines with an interest in social welfare and class justice.

When Ruth Wilcox dies, leaving Howards End to Margaret Schlegel (in a note that Henry Wilcox destroys), Margaret becomes the go-between for the two families, and the values they represent, after accepting Henry Wilcox's offer of marriage. The dull, unthinking Charles Wilcox and feisty, progressive Helen Schlegel represent more extreme positions within the film's social spectrum ranging from arch conservatism to a freethinking liberalism. The catalyst for bringing these different elements into conflict is Leonard Bast, a lower-middle-class young man married to Jacky, a working-class girl. When circumstances bring Bast into Helen's orbit, he suffers, inadvertently, through the good intentions of the Schlegel family and Henry's indifference. Eventually, each element comes together at Howards End, the film's symbol of the virtues (and faults) of Edwardian England.

The acting, as in most Merchant-Ivory Productions, is uniformly good, particularly Emma Thompson,* Vanessa Redgrave, and Anthony Hopkins*, who has the most difficult task of creating sympathy for the reactionary Henry Wilcox. *Howards End* was nominated for nine Academy Awards, with Thompson winning Best Actress, Luciana Arrighi and Ian Whittaker Best Art Direction, and Ruth Prawer Jhabvala Best Screenplay. Thompson also won Best Actress at the BAFTA Film Awards and *Howards End* won Best Film.

HUE AND CRY (Ealing, 1947)—Comedy. *Director:* Charles Crichton; *Producers:* Henry Cornelius (associate) and Michael Balcon; *Script:* T. E. B. Clarke; *Cinematography:* Douglas Slocombe; *Music:* Georges Auric; *Cast:* Alastair Sim (Felix H. Wilkinson), Jack Warner (Jim Nightingale), Harry Fowler (Joe Kirby), Valerie White (Rhona), Jack Lambert (Inspector Ford), Frederick Piper (Mr. Kirby), Vida Hope (Mrs. Kirby), Heather Delaine (Dorrie Kirby), Stanley Escane (Roy), Gerald Fox (Dicky), Douglas Barr (Alec), Joan Dowling (Clarry), and Arthur Denton (Vicar).

Although *Hue and Cry* was promoted in 1947 as "the Ealing film that begs to differ," it did not immediately inspire the comedic cycle known as the "Ealing comedies." The next, more influential comedy, *Passport to Pimlico,* was released more than two years after *Hue and Cry. Hue and Cry* was a commercial and critical success and there are obvious similarities between the two films—which is not surprising as regular Ealing writer, T. E. B. Clarke, scripted both films, characterized by a strong sense of community and a common purpose.

Part of the appeal of *Hue and Cry* is the film's extensive use of London's bomb sites, particularly during the film's rousing climax when the boys, led by Joe Kirby, trap the fur-thieves who have been committing a series of robberies. Although some fanciful critics tried to establish a link between this film and the distinctive style ("neorealist") of the Italian filmmakers at that time, *Hue and Cry* is a fantasy with predominantly studio interiors, masterfully photographed by Douglas Slocombe, with some location sequences documenting the markets, docklands, and other war-affected locations around London.

When young Joe Kirby realizes that his favorite comic strip, *The Trump,* is being used by a criminal mastermind (Jack Warner's* hearty crook, Jim Nightingale) to let his gang know where and when to commit their robberies, he begins his investigation. The police fail to believe Kirby, so he enlists his gang of young boys, and one girl (Clarry), to solve the crime. The famous climax to the film shows hundreds of English schoolboys rallying to Kirby's call to trap the thieves near the docks.

Although *Hue and Cry* appears to be little more than just a well-photographed, slightly violent, children's film, its appeal in 1947 to British audiences was strong. Perhaps this emanated from the optimistic, light-hearted tone of the film, epitomized by the "torture" of Rhona, one of the villains, as Joe and the boys attempt to discover the identity of the master criminal. The form of the "torture" is not very threatening and Rhona easily dismisses their attempts to tickle her feet. The boys, however, have more success when they confront her with a white mouse and they, eventually, unmask the criminal mastermind and destroy his gang—without the help of adults or the police. British audiences warmly supported such fanciful, populist sentiments in the depressingly cold winter of 1947.

HURT, JOHN (b. 1940). After training as a painter at St. Martin's School of the Arts, John Hurt made his London stage debut in 1962 and, for some years, the stage was his primary medium. His first screen role was in *The Wild and the Willing* (1962), a domestic melodrama involving a university student's affair with the wife of a professor. With age, Hurt's physical appearance matched his ability to convey mental and physical pain, traits that were evident early in his career when he played the innocent Timothy Evans in *10 Rillington Place* (1970), a man who was hanged in 1944 for crimes he did not commit. In 1976, he gave a BAFTA award-winning performance as the extroverted Quentin Crisp in the television drama *The Naked Civil Servant.*

The definitive victim essayed by Hurt during this period was as John Merrick in *The Elephant Man* (1980), and Hurt, layered beneath dense makeup and costume, captured the inner pain of the protagonist through his phrasing and voice.

He deservedly was nominated for Best Actor at the 1981 Academy Awards and won the BAFTA Film Award for Best Actor for *The Elephant Man.*

Hurt alternated this ability to elicit audience sympathy, which included a Best Supporting Actor Award at the 1979 BAFTA Film Awards for *Midnight Express* (1978) and a 1980 Best Supporting Actor nomination for his alien-riddled crewman in *Alien* (1979), with portrayals of villainy. His villains often seemed elite and convincingly expressed contempt in roles such as Caligula, in the BBC miniseries *I, Claudius* (1976), and the hit man Braddock who is sent to Spain to bring back informer Terence Stamp in Stephen Frears's black comedy/gangster film *The Hit* (1984).

Hurt's other prevailing persona projected moral dissipation and sexual depravity in films such as *White Mischief* (1987), which dramatized the foibles and sexual games of an indulgent British colony at Happy Valley in Kenya in the early 1940s. A potentially more challenging role for Hurt, which allowed him to combine both victimization and moral ambiguity, was as Stephen Ward, who gained entry to the highest levels of British society in *Scandal** (1989). However, a more adventurous interpretation of this period by director Michael Caton-Jones would have provided Hurt with the ability to demonstrate more facets of his acting talent.

Throughout the 1990s, Hurt has been prolific with lead performances in small- and medium-budget productions that are not really mainstream films—films such as *Love and Death on Long Island* (1997), with Hurt as a British writer infatuated with an actor (Jason Priestley), the cynical espionage drama *The Commissioner* (1998), the Irish drama *Night Train* (1998), and Gus Van Sant's uneven *Even Cowgirls Get the Blues* (1994). Hurt also appeared in supporting roles in big-budget films that exploited his ability to bring dramatic color to otherwise mediocre productions, such as *Rob Roy* (1995) and *Wild Bill* (1995).

FILMS: The Wild and the Willing (1962), A Man for All Seasons (1966), The Sailor from Gibraltar (1967), Sinful Davey (1969), Before Winter Comes (1969), In Search of Gregory (1969), 10 Rillington Place (1970), Mr. Forbush and the Penguins (1971), The Pied Piper (1972), Little Malcolm (1974), La Linea Del Fiume (1975), The Ghoul (1975), The Disappearance (1977), East of Elephant Rock (1977), Midnight Express (1978), Watership Down (1978), The Shout (1978), Alien (1979), Heaven's Gate (1980), The Elephant Man (1980), History of the World, Part 1 (1981), Night Crossing (1981), Partners (1982), The Plague Dogs (voice, 1982), The Osterman Weekend (1983), Champions (1983), Success Is the Best Revenge (1984), Nineteen Eight-Four (1984), The Hit (1984), The Black Cauldron (voice, 1985), After Darkness (1985), Jake Speed (1986), Spaceballs (1987), White Mischief (1987), Rocinante (1987), Vincent: The Life and Death of Vincent Van Gogh (doc., 1987), The Hunting of the Snark (1987), From the Hip (1987), Aria (1987), The Storyteller (1987), Poison Candy (1988), Bengali Night (1988), Deadline (1988), Scandal (1989), Windprints (1990), The Field (1990), Romeo-Juliet (1990), Little Sweetheart (1990), Frankenstein Unbound (1990), King Ralph (1991), I Dreamt I Woke Up (doc., 1991), Lapse of Memory (1992), Six Characters in Search of an Author (1992), L' Oeil Qui Ment (1992), Even Cowgirls Get the Blues (1993), Monolith (1993), Betrayal (voice, 1994), Second Best (1994), Thumbelina (voice, 1994), Rob Roy (1995), Wild Bill (1995), Two Nudes Bathing (1995), Saigon Baby (1995), Dead Man (1976), Love and Death on

Long Island (1997), Contact (1997), Tender Loving Care (1997), Brute (1998), The Commissioner (1998), The Climb (1998), All the Little Animals (1998), You're Dead (1998), New Blood (1999), If . . . Dog . . . Rabbit (1999), The Tigger Movie (voice, 2000), and Lost Souls (2000).

NOTES

1. See G. Brown, "Paradise Found and Lost: The Course of British Realism," in R. Murphy (ed.), *The British Cinema Book,* London, BFI Publishing, 1997, p. 193.
2. McFarlane, *An Autobiography of British Cinema,* p. 146.
3. McFarlane, *An Autobiography of British Cinema,* p. 93.

I

I AM A CAMERA (Romulus, 1955)—Sex comedy/drama. *Director:* Henry Cornelius; *Producer:* Jack Clayton; *Script:* John Collier, based on the John Van Druten play that was based on the novel *Berlin Stories* by Christopher Isherwood; *Cinematography:* Guy Green; *Music:* Malcolm Arnold; *Cast:* Julie Harris (Sally Bowles), Laurence Harvey (Christopher Isherwood), Shelley Winters (Natalie Landauer), Ron Randell (Clive), Anton Diffring (Fritz Wendel), Lea Seidl (Frau Schneider), Patrick McGoohan (Swede), and Frederick Valk (Doctor).

Director Henry Cornelius wanted to shoot *I Am a Camera* in Berlin, the location for Christopher Isherwood's stories that formed the basis of both the film and John Van Druten's play. However currency problems denied the production company, Romulus, the opportunity to film in Berlin. This proved a major limitation as the sterility of the film is due, partly, to the endless studio interiors for a story demanding a sense of history and a strong atmosphere. The film's second major obstacle was the subject matter of the play, particularly Isherwood's homosexuality, Sally Bowles's casual, nonmoralistic attitude to sex, and her abortion in the third act. This immediately created problems, especially in the United States.

When a copy of Van Druten's play was submitted to Joseph Breen in May 1953, Breen pointed to code violations. *I Am a Camera* was released in the United Kingdom with an X certificate and without the Production Code Seal in Los Angeles on July 21, 1955, and later in Cleveland, Cincinnati, New York, Chicago, and Detroit. However, the film was condemned in August 1955 by the Catholic lobby group, the National Legion of Decency (*I Am a Camera* was one of four British film condemned by the league—the others were *The Girl from Maxim's* [1933], *Living Dangerously* [1936], and *The Private Life of Henry VIII** [1933]). Bowles's characterization in the film was a problem for Geoffrey Shurlock, Breen's successor, and he objected that her character lacked the "proper compensating moral values." The issue of abortion was also a major obstacle—even after changes to the code in December 1956, it remained explicit in this regard: "The subject of abortion shall be discouraged, shall never be more than suggested, and when referred to shall be condemned." Consequently, Shurlock reiterated in December 1956 that *I Am a Camera* would not receive code approval as abortion in the film was treated "lightly" and not condemned.[1] This severely limited distribution of the film within the United States and weakened its financial potential.

It is a pity that the film was not entirely worthy of the controversy surrounding its release, although the play's subject matter was always going to create a challenge to the filmmakers. The film also suffers from its own self-imposed weaknesses, particularly the decision to downplay the historical context, the rise of Nazism, and the growth of anti-Semitism. This latter aspect is treated in a stolid, heavy-handed manner through the romance between Fritz Wendel, Isherwood's friend, and Natalie Landauer, a wealthy Jewish woman.

Considering the volatility of this period, the film lacks the requisite sense of excitement and terror and replaces it with a dull treatment of the platonic relationship between Bowles and Isherwood. Julie Harris, who repeated her stage portrayal as Sally Bowles, was nominated for the Best Foreign Actress Award at the 1956 BAFTA Film Awards.

The story is told in flashback. When Isherwood, who describes himself in the film as "not the marrying kind," attends a book launch in London, he discovers that the author is Bowles. The film then moves back to Berlin in 1931 when they first meet, a time of limited money for the pair, except for a period of affluence supplied by a U.S. playboy (Clive), who is attracted to Bowles. After Clive moves on, leaving Bowles pregnant, Isherwood, reluctantly, offers to marry her but the issue of abortion, mysteriously and conveniently, disappears after Bowles tells Isherwood one morning that she is not pregnant. While Bowles tries to explain this away by pointing to her mistake in counting the days, the film is most unconvincing. Similarly, the film fails to provide a correlation between the rise of Nazism and the suppression of religious, social, and sexual freedom.

I KNOW WHERE I'M GOING! (The Archers, 1945)—Romance. *Director:* Michael Powell; *Producers:* Michael Powell, Emeric Pressburger, and George R. Busby (associate); *Script:* Michael Powell and Emeric Pressburger; *Cinematography:* Erwin Hillier; *Music:* Allan Gray; *Cast:* Wendy Hiller (Joan Webster), Roger Livesey (Torquil MacNeil), George Carney (Mr. Webster), Pamela Brown (Catriona Potts), Finlay Currie (Ruairidh Mor), Murdo Morrison (Kenny), Margot Fitzsimmons (Bridie), Captain C. W. R. Knight (Colonel Barnstaple), Jean Cadell (Postmistress), Petula Clarke (Cheril), Catherine Lacey (Mrs. Robinson), Valentine Dyall (Mr. Robinson), John Laurie (John Campbell), Graham Moffat (Royal Air Force Sergeant), Nancy Price (Mrs. Rebecca Crozier), Walter Hudd (Hunter), and Norman Shelley (Sir Robert Ballinger).

Michael Powell* and Emeric Pressburger* continue their anti-materialism, "money isn't everything" theme in *I Know Where I'm Going!* a recurring motif in their previous film, *A Canterbury Tale** (1944). Powell's ability to move audiences with his grasp of cinematic language is evident early in the film as banker's daughter Joan Webster farewells her father in Manchester to travel to a remote island (Kiloran) off the west coast of Scotland. Joan's decision to marry an older, wealthier man, Sir Robert Ballinger, the corporate head of Consolidated Chemical Industries, provides the audience with an insight into her character. Powell, however, reveals her anxiety about the forthcoming marriage through a succession of surreal images where top hats dissolve into train chimneys and Joan's dream of marriage to Sir Robert transforms into a marriage to his corporation. These surreal images are replaced by a more lyrical presentation during the final stages of Joan's journey to Kiloran.

While waiting to cross to Kiloran, Joan forms a friendship with Torquil Mac-Neil, a British naval officer, who also wants to travel across the strait to Kiloran to spend his leave on his island—Torquil is the Laird of Kiloran. Gradually, Joan falls in love with the impoverished laird, a process that is enhanced by the fact that Sir Robert is never seen in the film (his voice is heard at one point), although Powell and Pressburger studiously avoid the usual clichés in developing their love story.

I Know Where I'm Going! is another spiritual film from Powell and Pressburger, who assimilate aspects from Hebridean myth, Scandinavian legend, and a local curse concerning Torqil's inability to enter a local castle, into their story. The exteriors were filmed with most of the cast, except Roger Livesey, on location. Livesey was appearing in a West End play, necessitating the use of a double for shots with Wendy Hiller. This is an elegiac, relaxed film, with little contrived drama, and even Joan Webster, superbly played by Wendy Hiller, who is shown to be willfully materialistic early in film, is never a negative stereotype.

Hiller, who expressed a distaste for other films directed by Powell, argued that *I Know Where I'm Going!* was the "warmest, most compassionate and likeable"[2] of all his films. The film's basic story line provides potential for conflict between the characters based on sexual desire and jealousy concerning Torquil, Sir Robert, and Joan, or Joan, Torquil, and his childhood friend Catriona Potts. Such generic contrivances are never allowed to intrude on the film's gentle celebration of the timeless "reality" of this distinctive landscape, which was first celebrated by Powell in *The Edge of the World* (1937).

I SEE A DARK STRANGER (Individual/Rank, 1946)—Espionage thriller. *Director:* Frank Launder; *Producers:* Frank Launder and Sidney Gilliat; *Script:* Frank Launder, Sidney Gilliat, and Wolfgang Wilhelm; *Cinematography:* Wilkie Cooper; *Music:* William Alwyn; *Cast:* Deborah Kerr (Bridie Quilty), Trevor Howard (Lieutenant David Bayne), Raymond Huntley (Miller), Garry Marsh (Captain Goodhusband), Tom Macauley (Lieutenant Spanswick), Olga Lindo (Mrs. Edwards), Norman Shelley (Man in Straw Hat), David Tomlinson (Intelligence Officer), Katie Johnson (Old Lady), Gerald Case (Colonel Dennington), and Torin Thatcher (Policeman).

In *I See A Dark Stranger,* Frank Launder* and Sidney Gilliat* maintain the light tone and high quality of such earlier thrillers as *The Lady Vanishes** (1938) and *Night Train to Munich* (1940), both scripted by Launder and Gilliat. *I See a Dark Stranger* was scripted by Launder toward the end of World War II. Perversely, the film manipulates the audience's sympathy by depicting the plight of a British-hating Irish woman (Bridie Quilty) who, for much of the film, evades British authorities in her role as a German spy. Ultimately, of course, Bridie finally redeems herself, motivated by love and a gradual awareness that the desires of the individual must, in times of a national crisis, be subjugated to the concerns of the larger community (those identified with the Allies).

The film begins with a deliberately confusing prologue showing a man skulking around the Isle of Man at night before reverting to a flashback to the Irish village of Ballygarry in 1937 as young Bridie listens to heroic tales told by her father, of Irish resistance to English persecution. The film quickly shifts to 1944 and twenty-one-year-old Bridie's determination to carry on the fight against the English after the death of her father. When a former member of the Irish Republican Army tries to dissuade Bridie from confronting the English at this time, Bridie is recruited by Miller, a German spy sent to help Oscar Pryce escape from British custody in the west of England. Pryce has vital information for the German military authorities and after he and Miller die (with Bridie forced to dump Miller's body over a cliff), Bridie goes to the Isle of Man to retrieve a notebook hidden by Pryce before his capture. When Bridie discovers that the notebook contains the destination of the D day landing, she decides that her personal animosity toward the British is less significant than the lives of the men who will die if she passes this information on to the Germans—so she burns the notebook. An important motivation for this change of heart is her feelings for David Bayne, a love-smitten British officer who follows her to the Isle of Man.

The comic stereotypes used throughout *I See a Dark Stranger,* particularly the depiction of the Irish, are balanced by two not very intelligent British intelligence officers, with Garry Marsh and Tom Macaulay reprising the comedic function of Basil Radford and Naunton Wayne in *The Lady Vanishes* and *Night Train to Munich.* The star of the film, however, is Deborah Kerr* and this film, together with Michael Powell's* *Black Narcissus** (1947), provided the basis for Kerr's move to Hollywood in the late 1940s. Kerr won the New York Critics Circle Award for Best Actress in 1947 (which included her performances for both *I See a Dark Stranger* and *Black Narcissus*).

ICE COLD IN ALEX (Associated British, 1958)—War. *Director:* J. Lee Thompson; *Producer:* W. A. Whittaker; *Script:* Christopher Landon and T. J. Morrison; *Cinematography:* Gilbert Taylor; *Music:* Leighton Lucas; *Cast:* John Mills (Captain Anson), Sylvia Syms (Sister Diana Murdoch), Anthony Quayle (Captain van der Poel), Harry Andrews (Sergeant Tom Pugh), Diane Clare (Sister Denise Norton), Liam Redmond (Brigadier), Richard Leech (Captain Crosbie), Peter Arne (British Officer), Allan Cuthbertson (Staff Officer), and David Lodge (CMP Captain).

Representing the high point of the 1950s British war film, *Ice Cold in Alex* is, in many ways, the most subversive. At the end of the film, Captain van der Poel, a German spy posing as South African officer, tells his British colleagues that "it has been quite an experience, all against the desert, the greater enemy. I have learned a lot about the English, so different from all I have been taught." Gradually throughout the 1950s, the depiction of the enemy, the Germans, was "softened" or the genre ignored them to concentrate on divisions within a group of British soldiers. By the late 1950s, it was possible to show that not all Germans were bad—this pattern began with *The One That Got Away* in 1957 and *Ice Cold in Alex* followed the next year. In this film, the German (van der Poel) is a "hero" figure who rescues the British at key points in their six-hundred-mile journey from Tobruk to Alexandria. The film concludes not with the three British survivors, Captain Anson, Sergeant Pugh, or Sister Murdoch, but with the German as he is taken away in a British jeep as a prisoner of war—but not as a spy—thanks to the protection offered to van der Poel by Anson, Pugh, and Murdoch.

Ice Cold in Alex is also notable for the presentation of the central British officer, Captain Anson, played by one of the major icons of this genre, John Mills.* In this film, Anson is a flawed figure, a burnt out survivor of the desert campaign who requires regular doses of alcohol to keep him functioning—the only reason he allows van der Poel to join their ambulance unit in the first place is that he has three bottles of gin. When confronted by the Germans in the desert, Anson panics, causing the death of Sister Denise Norton as the Germans fire at the ambulance as it attempts to escape. Again, at various times during their journey, it is van der Poel who retrieves the situation, not Anson. Anson's major contribution lies in his ability to keep his promise to stay away from alcohol after Norton's death—a promise he keeps until they arrive in Alexandria, where he shares a cold beer with his colleagues.

When *Ice Cold in Alex* was released by Twentieth Century Fox in 1960 in Los Angeles, it had been cut to 79 minutes. The British version ran 125 minutes and the British censor demanded ninety cuts in the script, provoking an angry response from director J. Lee Thompson.* More recently, Mills complained that most of his love scene with Sylvia Syms had been removed, as in the version available today, while Syms talks of loves scenes. That is, more than one, and that one of these scenes "caused a lot of trouble at the time! I think they had to cut one close-up of what looked like an exposed bosom. In fact, all John did was to undo some buttons and I know I still had a bra on."[3]

Anthony Quayle was nominated for Best British Actor and the film was nominated as Best British Film at the 1959 BAFTA Film Awards. Lee Thompson won the FIPRESCI Award at the 1958 Berlin International Film Festival.

AN IDEAL HUSBAND (Icon Entertainment/Pathe, 1999)—Comedy of manners/ romantic melodrama. *Director:* Oliver Parker; *Producers:* Bruce Davey, Uri Fruchtman, and Barnaby Thompson; *Script:* Oliver Parker, based on the play by Oscar Wilde; *Cinematography:* David Johnson; *Music:* Charlie Mole; *Cast:* Rupert Everett (Lord Arthur Goring), Cate Blanchett (Lady Gertrude Chiltern), Jeremy Northam (Sir Robert Chiltern), Julianne Moore (Mrs. Laura Cheveley), Minnie Driver (Mabel Chiltern), John Wood (Earl of Caversham), Lindsay Duncan (Lady Markby), Peter Vaughan (Phipps), Jeroen Krabbe (Baron Arnheim), and Ben Pullen (Tommy Trafford).

An intrinsic difficulty in adapting Oscar Wilde's 1895 play for movie audiences today arises from the changes in shared social values over the past one hundred years. For example, the balance of power between men and women was considerably different in late Victorian England than it is today—women were assumed to be, as the Earl of Caversham points out, stupid and devoid of common sense—and Caversham is presented in the film as basically a sympathetic character! Such attitudes are intrinsic, although questioned, in Wilde's play, and they provide an added layer of pleasure as the film quietly subverts such perceptions. For some people, the motivation of the characters may be difficult to accept as their behavior is predicated on values that have long been repudiated or ameliorated.

The perfect husband, and virtuous politician, Sir Robert Chiltern is threatened with blackmail by Mrs. Cheveley. Cheveley is in possession of a letter that establishes that Sir Robert acted improperly some years ago when he leaked a vital document pertaining to the Suez Canal to the German financier Baron Arnheim in exchange for £110,000 and the opportunity for a career in politics. Robert worries that if this fact is exposed his virtuous wife Gertrude will lose all respect for him. Thus, he asks Lord Goring, an indolent womanizer, to mediate. Cheveley, who has invested in a dubious venture in Argentina, wants Robert to alter a negative government report on the project. Cheveley, however, has a weakness for Goring and, unknown to Robert, makes a wager that if Robert does not weaken and delivers a negative verdict to Parliament, she will give Goring the incriminating letter. On the other hand, if Robert abandons his principles Goring must marry her.

The contrivances of the plot do not really matter. What really matters is the writing and the delivery and here the film excels. The performances of the five central characters, including Minnie Driver as Robert's sister and Goring's ultimate romantic partner, are excellent and the film retains the spirit of Wilde's play. Especially good is Rupert Everett as Lord Goring with his dry bon mots ("To love oneself is the beginning of a lifelong romance"). Goring has a love-hate relationship with his father, Lord Caversham, who is forever trying to convince his son about the need to get married. Cate Blanchett captures the right balance of indignation and affection for Robert, while Julianne Moore embellishes the malicious Cheveley with a suggestion of a romantic obsession (for Goring) and a cynical awareness of the ways of the (male) world.

Thankfully, director and screenwriter Oliver Parker resists the temptation to "modernize" the film by providing a direct association to the "Clinton affair"—both involve a popular politician who tries desperately to keep a past indiscretion from his wife, the media, and the public. Instead, the film perpetuates Wilde's dictum that everybody is a little corrupt, encapsulated in Goring's assertion that "morality is simply the attitude we adopt toward people we dislike."

I'M ALL RIGHT JACK (British Lion, 1959)—Social comedy. *Director:* John Boulting; *Producer:* Roy Boulting; *Script:* John Boulting, Frank Harvey, and

Alan Hackney, based on the novel *Private Life* by Alan Hackney; *Cinematography:* Mutz Greenbaum; *Music:* Ron Goodwin; *Cast:* Ian Carmichael (Stanley Windrush), Terry-Thomas (Major Hitchcock), Peter Sellers (Fred Kite/Sir John Kennaway), Richard Attenborough (Sidney de Vere Cox), Dennis Price (Bertram Tracepurcel), Margaret Rutherford (Aunt Dolly), Irene Handl (Mrs. Kite), Liz Fraser (Cynthia Kite), Miles Malleson (Mr. Windrush), Marne Maitland (Mr. Mohammed), John Le Mesurier (Waters), Raymond Huntley (Magistrate), Victor Madden (Knowles), Kenneth Griffiths (Dai), Sam Kydd (Shop Steward), Ronnie Stevens (Hooper), Esme Cannon (Spencer), David Lodge (Card Player), and Fred Griffiths (Charlie).

Richard Attenborough,* who played one of the capitalist crooks (Sidney de Vere Cox) in *I'm All Right Jack,* described the film as an "expression of the Boultings' disillusioned radical views,"[4] which manifested itself in a series of films that focused on various British institutions—beginning with the right-wing paranoia of *High Treason* (1951), to their satirical depictions of the army (*Private's Progress* [1956]), the legal system (*Brothers-in-Law* [1957]), university life (*Lucky Jim* [1957]), the Foreign Office (*Carleton-Browne of the F.O.* [1959]) and the church (*Heaven's Above* [1963]).

In 1959, the Roy Boulting* and John Boulting* turned their attention to Capital and Labor in *I'm All Right Jack* and they brought back most of the central characters from *Private's Progress.* They also added Peter Seller's* dictatorial union leader Fred Kite, complete with a Hitler-type moustache. This film boosted Seller's career and he won the Best British Actor Award. John Boulting, Frank Harvey,* and Alan Hackney also received the Best British Screenplay Award at the 1960 BAFTA Film Awards. Liz Fraser was nominated for the Most Promising Newcomer Award for her performance as Cynthia, Fred Kite's sexually aggressive daughter who, while listening to Bertram Tracepurcel's dull speech to the workers in his factory, suddenly shows interest when Stanley Windrush tells her that Bertram is extolling the benefits of "commercial intercourse."

When Windrush graduates from Oxford, he seeks a job in industry. Windrush fails a series of interviews, with one ending when he vomits into a confectionery vat. Windrush, unwittingly, becomes part of scam devised by his Uncle Bertram Tracepurcel and former army colleague Sidney de Vere Cox to bring the production of missiles to a halt in Bertram's factory. This will cause a lucrative Middle Eastern arms contract to go to a subsidiary company owned by Cox. Bertram and Cox select Windrush as the person most likely to alienate the unions and provoke a strike. The scheme goes according to plan until Windrush causes a strike not just in Tracepurcel's plant but throughout the entire British industry, including Cox's factory.

Finally, as in *The Man in The White Suit** (1951), union and management conspire to get rid of Windrush and he retreats to a nudist colony with his father. Even Raymond Huntley, who appears late in the film as a magistrate to chastise Windrush, was surprised at the unflattering depictions of the workers in the film: "It is amazing," Huntley said later, "that the union tolerated the film at the time. They might just as easily have walked out and pulled the plugs!"[5]

The film attacks both Capital and Labor. The most telling caricature, however, is Kite. The film presents him as self-important, dictatorial, and ignorant—he imagines the life of a worker in the Soviet Union as "cornfields, and ballet in the evening."

IN WHICH WE SERVE (Two Cities, 1942)—War. *Directors:* Noël Coward and David Lean; *Producers:* Noël Coward and Anthony Havelock-Allan (associate); *Script:* Noël Coward; *Cinematography:* Ronald Neame; *Music:* Noël Coward; *Cast:* Noël Coward (Captain Edward V. Kinross), John Mills (Ordinary Seaman "Shorty" Blake), Bernard Miles (Chief Petty Officer Walter Hardy), Celia Johnson (Alix Kinross), Kay Walsh (Freda Lewis), Michael Wilding ("Flags," Second Lieutenant), Richard Attenborough (Young Sailor), Ann Stephens (Lavinia Kinross), Daniel Massey (Bobby Kinross), Joyce Carey (Katherine Lemmon Hardy), Kathleen Harrison (Mrs. Blake), Dora Gregory (Mrs. Lemmon), Philip Friend ("Torps"), Frederick Piper (Edgecomb), Walter Fitzgerald (Colonel Lumsden), James Donald (Ship's Doctor), Jill Stephens (May Blake), Juliet Mills (Freda's Baby), and Leslie Howard (Voice).

In Which We Serve was one of the most significant films of World War II, released at a time when the war was not going all that well for the Allies. Viewed today, sixty years after its release, the didactic or propaganda intentions of the film are transparent, especially the series of addresses by Captain Edward V. Kinross to the men of HMS *Torrin* (in reality, the audience at the time). "This is the story of a ship," the audience is informed at the start of the film as the plight of the men of the *Torrin,* and their response, serve as a simple metaphor of the problems facing Britain in 1941–1942.

Three survivors, Captain Kinross, Chief Petty Officer Walter Hardy, and Ordinary Seaman "Shorty" Blake, representative of a specific social class (Kinross: upper-middle class; Hardy: lower-middle class; Blake: working class)—these men represent a British class system based on mutual respect and sympathy. This is made clear during one of the flashbacks when Blake, enjoying his honeymoon on train with Freda, meets Kinross, who introduces Blake to his wife Alix as "one of my shipmates." In the film's final scene, Kinross shakes the hand of every survivor as they file past him.

Although the film touches on major military landmarks, such as evacuation from Dunkirk, the German blitz, and the Battle of Britain, it utilizes these events primarily to reinforce a sense of communal solidarity and the need for personal sacrifice. This is reiterated through Kinross's response to the news that a number of his men died during a ferocious battle with the enemy: "If they had to die, what a way to go." The film is also careful to point to the fact that Hardy's wife and mother perish on the home front. The interests of the individual, the film emphasizes, must be relegated to the wider concerns of British society and the need to defeat the enemy. When Hardy receives the news of his loss from Blake, he congratulates Blake on the birth of his child before moving off to mourn his loss.

Like most successful propaganda films produced during World War II, *In Which We Serve* draws on shared images and perceptions of unity and national coherence. As Kinross's clings to the raft, his thoughts go back to his Georgian house in Devon, his dutiful wife Alix, and their two children. These scenes emphasize a sense of order and tradition as they share tea on their lawn. This contrasts with the ebullience displayed by working-class Freda Blake when she greets Shorty on leave and Kath Hardy's warm response to her husband's raucous singing of "Roll Out the Barrel" in a music hall. Each response is class based and forms part of a social apex with Kinross at the peak. He is always photographed above his men in his speeches reminding them of their duties and responsibilities as the film assumes that each class is aware of its appropriate position in society.

In Which We Serve was developed by Noël Coward after Filippo Del Guidice, who had been sent off to an internment camp at the start of the war because he was Italian, asked him to devise a film about the British war effort. Although Coward was initially reluctant, the inspiration of Lord Louis Mountbatten, a friend of Coward, and the sinking of Mountbatten's destroyer the HMS *Kelly* off Crete, provided the basis for the story and producer Anthony Havelock-Allen invited David Lean,* an editor, to assist Coward. Coward also selected Ronald Neame* as his cameraman.

Coward's initial script was far too long and included sections set in the Caribbean and the Cafe de Paris involving socialites before the war. Havelock-Allan, Lean, and Neame persuaded Coward to leave the script with them, and Lean decided, with Coward's approval, to tell the story of one ship. Coward's influence, through Mountbatten, was also significant in obtaining support from the British navy despite strong opposition from the Ministry of Information, who objected to a story that focused on the sinking of a British ship. There were also objections to the casting of Coward as a captain in the Royal Navy. Guidice went ahead and shot the film, initially on credit, and after ten days of shooting Lean put together a reel of footage for British Lion, who provided a financial guarantee.

In Which We Serve went on to become the most commercially successfully British film in 1942 and it was also popular in the United States despite a well publicized controversy where the Production Code Administration demanded that expressions of profanity, such as "hell," "God," "bastard," and "lousy," be deleted. The U.S. distributor, United Artists, appealed to the board of directors of the Motion Picture Producers and Distributors of America, which provided some support for United Artists' claim, but demanded the deletion of ten expressions of profanity, including four new deletions that were not previously noted. United Artists agreed to the original deletions, but not the new changes, and Joseph Breen issued a certificate in December 1942.[6]

Coward won an Honorary Award for his "outstanding production achievement" at the 1943 Academy Awards and the film was nominated for Best Picture and Coward for Best Writing, Original Screenplay at the 1944 Academy Awards. *In Which We Serve* won Best Picture at the 1942 National Board of Review and the 1942 New York Film Critics Circle Awards.

THE INNOCENTS (Twentieth Century Fox, 1961)—Psychological drama/horror. *Director:* Jack Clayton; *Producer:* Jack Clayton; *Script:* William

Archibald, Truman Capote, and John Mortimer, based on the novel *The Turn of the Screw* by Henry James; *Cinematography:* Freddie Francis; *Music:* Georges Auric; *Cast:* Deborah Kerr (Miss Giddens), Martin Stephens (Miles), Pamela Franklin (Flora), Megs Jenkins (Mrs. Grose), Michael Redgrave (The Uncle), Peter Wyngarde (Peter Quint), and Clytie Jessop (Miss Jessel).

Jack Clayton* was asked many times after the release of *The Innocents* as to whether the ghostly influence of Pete Quint and Miss Jessel actually existed or was a figment of the disturbed imagination of the governess (Miss Giddens). Clayton always avoided giving a direct answer to this question and the film provides sufficient evidence to support both points of view. The same is true of the film's source, *The Turn of the Screw,* written in 1898 by Henry James.

While *The Innocents* was widely praised at the time of its release, some critics have subsequently criticized Clayton's restrained, measured interpretation. Such criticism was not justified as the film slowly develops an association between the disintegration of Giddens's mental state and the aberrant sexual relationship between the dead governess (Miss Jessel), Quint, and the children, Miles and Flora.

Miles and Flora are left in Giddens's care by their London-based uncle who has no desire to visit or have any knowledge of them. Giddens, initially, feels well disposed to both children although she gradually becomes distressed by her inability to "save" them from the sexual influence and control of Jessel and her brutal lover, the late Peter Quint.This is a masterly film that builds to a terrifying, enigmatic climax.

The Innocents is also visually splendid with its black and white cinematography and CinemaScope. Although Clayton initially objected to the use of CinemaScope, the film's use of close-ups serves to heighten the sense of ambiguity and anxiety and emphasizes Giddens's growing trauma and sense of dread. This is evident, for example, in the devastating effect Miles's lingering kiss has on the governess. The casting of Deborah Kerr* is a masterstroke as her sympathetic screen persona, a mixture of humanity and repressed sexuality, effectively counterpoints her moral disintegration. Her performance is enhanced by the cinematography of Freddie Francis, which he acknowledged as his favorite film, and Georges Auric's score.

Although there have been a number of remakes, and a banal prequel (*The Nightcomers* [1971]), none come close to Clayton's version.

THE INTERRUPTED JOURNEY (Valiant, 1949)—Film noir/melodrama. *Director:* Daniel Birt; *Producer:* Anthony Havelock-Allen; *Script:* Michael Pertwee; *Cinematography:* Erwin Hillier; *Music:* Stanley Allach; *Cast:* Valerie Hobson (Carol North), Richard Todd (John North), Christine Norden (Susan Wilding), Tom Walls (Mr. Clayton), Ralph Truman (Inspector Waterson), Vida Hope (Miss Marchment), Alexander Gauge (Jerves Wilding), Dora Bryan (Waitress), and Vincent Ball (Workman).

Richard Todd,* who burst into prominence with his second film *The Hasty Heart* (1949), changed direction with his third film *The Interrupted Journey.*

Todd, as John North, plays a weak, unfaithful husband caught up in a desperate situation triggered by his sexual desire for another woman. The moral context for the film is established early when John, a relatively unsuccessful writer, decides to leave his wife, Carol, and run away with Susan Wilding, the wife of his publisher. John panics when he sees Susan's husband on the same train as the one that is taking them to an illicit hotel rendezvous. He pulls the emergency cord and then runs across a field to his wife, who lives close by. Just as John returns home, however, he hears the train crash and many of the passengers, including Susan, are killed. Although he denies being on the train, a railway officer (Mr. Clayton) suspects that John pulled the emergency cord.

Gradually, John's "nightmare" intensifies as evidence is produced that he was on the train with Susan and he eventually breaks down and confesses to Carol and Clayton. When new evidence is discovered that the accident was not caused by John's actions, he appears to be free. When more evidence reveals that Susan was not killed in the train accident but died with a bullet in her back, John becomes the prime suspect. With Carol's support, he evades the police and confronts the real killer, Susan's husband (Jerves), in a hotel room. However, just as Jerves fires his gun into the hapless husband, John wakes up from his nightmare, tells Susan that he is not going away with her, and returns to his wife.

Although the dream ending appears contrived, the film carefully simulates the qualities of a "nightmare" via the coincidental plot twists, accentuated by the sparse production values and Erwin Hillier's low-key lighting. Todd and Valerie Hobson* convey the appropriate degree of angst as the troubled husband and wife. The ending is similar to, but not as morally complex as Fritz Lang's *The Woman in the Window* (1944).

IT ALWAYS RAINS ON SUNDAY (Ealing, 1947)—Family melodrama/crime. *Director:* Robert Hamer; *Producers:* Michael Balcon and Henry Cornelius (associate); *Script:* Henry Cornelius, Robert Hamer, and Angus MacPhail, based on the novel by Arthur La Bern; *Cinematography:* Douglas Slocombe; *Music:* Georges Auric; *Cast:* Googie Withers (Rose Sandigate), Jack Warner (Detective Sergeant Fothergill), Edward Chapman (George Sandigate), Susan Shaw (Vi Sandigate), Patricia Plunkett (Doris Sandigate), John McCallum (Tommy Swann), Sidney Taffler (Morry Hyams), John Slater (Lou Hyams), Jimmy Hanley (Whitey), Alfie Bass (Dicey), John Carol (Freddie), David Lines (Alfie Sandigate), Michael Howard (Slopey Collins), Nigel Stock (Ted Edwards), John Salew (Caleb Neesley), Frederick Piper (Detective Sergeant Leech), and Jane Hylton (Bessie Hyams).

From 1945 to 1949, Robert Hamer* directed four of the best films ever produced by the British film industry—*Pink Sting and Sealing Wax** (1945), *It Always Rains on Sunday, Kind Hearts and Coronets** (1949), and *The Spider and the Fly** (1949). These films, with the exception of the last, were produced at Ealing Studios, although they were not typical of Ealing's output at this time.

Aspects of *It Always Rains on Sunday* troubled Joseph Breen and the Production Code Administration in the United States. For example, the casual manner in which Rose Sandigate invites her former lover, the escaped convict Tommy Swann, to strip off his prison clothes in front of her clearly suggests that they had a sexual relationship before he went to jail, and the local censorship board in Massachusetts demanded the deletion of this scene.[7]

Set in London's East End, *It Always Rains on Sunday* focuses on the activities of the Sandigate family, and members of the local community, in the period that stretches from dawn to midnight on a rainy Sunday. Rose Sandigate is married to George, a dull man, fifteen years her senior, whom she does not love and she takes her frustrations out on his daughters, particularly the sexually active Vi, who is having an affair with a married man (Morry Hyams). The other daughter, the dutiful Doris, is embroiled in a minor row with her boyfriend Ted over an offer from Lou Hyams to work in one of his establishments. Doris eventually declines his offer.

When Tommy Swann enters her life, Rose sees a chance for sexual fulfillment and romance. Frustrated by her family responsibilities, Rose tears the dress off Vi, leaving her exposed in her underwear. Vi is presented in the film as a younger "mirror" image of Rose—only Vi has the freedom that Rose covets. A flashback shows Swann with Rose and he is arrested just as they attempt to leave Bethnal Green. Now, at least in Rose's imagination, Swann represents a chance to escape. After finding him hiding in the Anderson shelter in the backyard, she moves him into the house and, when George goes out for his weekly darts match at the pub, into their bedroom, and, more suggestively, their bed. Thus, Hamer is able to bypass restrictions imposed by censorship at that time while making quite explicit the carnal attraction between Rose and the gangster Swann.

Finally, Slopey Collins, a local newspaperman, suspects that Rose may be hiding Swann. When he enters the Sandigate house, Swann erupts and attacks both the newspaperman and Rose. After an exciting, noirish chase through the dark streets of London, culminating in a railroad marshalling yard, Swann is captured by Detective Sergeant Fothergill (Jack Warner*). The film ends with George forgiving Rose, condemning her to a life lacking in passion or excitement in the East End, a place she has been trying to escape since puberty.

IT STARTED IN PARADISE (Rank, 1952)—Drama. *Director:* Compton Bennett; *Producers:* Sergei Nolbandov and Leslie Parkyn; *Script:* Marghanita Laski, with additional dialogue by Hugh Hastings; *Cinematography:* Jack Cardiff; *Music:* Malcom Arnold; *Cast:* Jane Hylton (Martha Watkins), Muriel Pavlow (Alison), Terence Morgan (Edouard), Ian Hunter (Arthur Turner), Brian Worth (Michael), Martita Hunt (Mme. Alice), Kay Kendall (Lady Caroline), Ronald Squire ("Mary Jane"), and Joyce Barbour (Lady Burridge).

Produced the year after the release of the Joseph L. Mankiewicz's classic *All about Eve* (1950), *It Started in Paradise,* which shares aspects of Mankiewicz's film, focuses on the world of haute couture and the fortunes of a London fashion house from 1938 to 1950. The first section in *It Started in Paradise* is dramatically strong and director Compton Bennett and cinematographer Jack Cardiff give the film a distinctive sense of style as the ambitious Martha Watkins plots to get rid of her aging mentor Mme. Alice. Her scheme comes to fruition after a disappointing show as Watkins convinces Alice to take an overseas vacation while she (Watkins) looks after the fashion house—Martita Hunt as the aging designer is effectively vulnerable at this point, supported by low-key lighting and dramatic use of dark blue to highlight her sense of betrayal.

The support of Alice's financial backer, Arthur Turner, is crucial to Watkins's plans and she cold-bloodedly seduces the middle-aged man. Bennett captures the different motivations and feelings of both parties through a simple action—the way they place their glass down so that they may kiss. This action is shown a number of times throughout the film. For example, a close-up of Watkins's hand as she carefully places her glass on the floor captures the calculated nature of her actions in exchanging sex for Turner's financial backing. On the other hand, Turner, who is in love with Watkins, lets his glass crash to the floor in his eagerness to kiss her. Later, after Edouard, a British con man posing as a French aristocrat, seduces Watkins in the hope of exploiting the fashion house, he places his glass gently on a table beside her upended glass as he prepares to kiss her. She loves him and he, eventually, deserts her. Finally, when Alison, Watkins's former assistant, kisses her colleague Michael at the end of the film, both glasses crash to the floor as a sign of their true love.

When Watkins falls from grace in the fashion industry, Alison replaces her as chief designer, although her motives are pure (unlike the scheming successor to Anne Baxter in *All about Eve*). The final section in *It Started in Paradise* is a disappointment, as it contains neither the requisite ruthlessness nor the biting humor of the Mankiewicz film. Although Ronald Squire as the fashion critic Mary Jane is sporadically allowed to inject a degree of cynicism into the film, its conventional climax, a prolonged fashion show with the mandatory happy ending for all concerned, is a disappointing end to an intriguing premise. Rank twelve years later, with its production of *The Beauty Jungle** (1964), developed more fully some of the ideas introduced in *It Started in Paradise*.

It Started in Paradise provided Jane Hylton, a long-serving supporting player in many British films in the late 1940s and 1950s, a rare starring role, and she does not disappoint as the manipulative designer Martha Watkins.

NOTES

1. See Slide, "*Banned In The USA*," pp. 80–82.
2. McFarlane, *An Autobiography of British Cinema*, p. 296.
3. McFarlane, *An Autobiography of British Cinema*, p. 550.
4. McFarlane, *An Autobiography of British Cinema*, p. 35.
5. McFarlane, *An Autobiography of British Cinema*, p. 311.
6. See Slide, "*Banned In The USA*," pp. 82–84.
7. See Slide, "*Banned In The USA*," p. 85.

J

JACKSON, GLENDA (b. 1936). A distinctive, strong actress, Glenda Jackson entered the British film industry in the late 1960s at a time when the industry began to falter following the cessation of U.S. funding. Jackson, primarily through her initial association with the flamboyant director Ken Russell,* made a powerful impact in her early films and she was never afraid to tackle difficult roles. Jackson, the daughter of a Liverpool bricklayer, supported herself after leaving school at sixteen while nurturing a desire to act. Theater director Peter Brook provided her initial break when he cast her as the assassin Charlotte Corday in *The Persecution and Assassination of Jean-Paul Marat as Performed by the Inmates of the Asylum of Charenton under the Direction of the Marquis De Sade* in his 1964 award winning theatrical production. Two years later, Jackson reprised the role in the film adaptation before entering into a creative association with Russell, beginning with one of her best roles as Gudrun Brangwen in *Women in Love* (1969). This resulted in the first of her two Oscars for Best Actress—the second coming four years later in a totally different film, the Hollywood romantic comedy *A Touch of Class* (1973), co-starring George Segal.

The Jackson-Russell collaboration in the late 1960s and early 1970s was productive for both participants with films such as *Music Lovers* (1971), Russell's controversial interpretation of Peter Tchaikovsky's life, with Jackson cast as the unstable, sexually provocative Nina. This was followed by a cameo in Russell's homage to the Hollywood musical *The Boy Friend* (1971). In between these two films, Jackson was Alex Greville, caught in a romantic triangle with her lover Murray Head and his lover Peter Finch* in *Sunday Bloody Sunday* (1971). In this groundbreaking film, directed by John Schlesinger,* Jackson garnered another Oscar nomination and a BAFTA Award for Best Actress. Jackson was cast opposite a number of strong actors, such as Finch, Tony Britton, and Peggy Ashcroft and during this film she realized that in film acting you were playing to the camera, not to the other performers,[1] an insight that may help explain the fact that, at times, the camera seems mesmerized by her performance.

Subsequent films with Russell in the 1980s, *Salome's Last Dance* (1988) and *The Rainbow* (1989), were less successful, both artistically and commercially. Jackson also won an Emmy Award for the British miniseries *Elizabeth R* (1971) and later received universal critical accolades for her portrayal of actress Patricia Neal's recovery from a stroke in *The Patricia Neal Story* (1981). Jackson's long-held interest in politics finally took precedence over her acting career and, after winning a seat in the British Parliament as the Labour member for Hampstead in 1992, she retired from acting.

FILMS: This Sporting Life (1963), The Persecution and Assassination of Jean-Paul Marat as Performed by the Inmates of the Asylum of Charenton under the Direction of the Marquis De Sade (1966), The Benefit of the Doubt (1967), Tell Me Lies (1968), Negatives (1968), Women in Love (1969), The Music Lovers (1971), Sunday Bloody Sunday (1971), The Boy Friend (1971), Mary, Queen of Scots (1972), Triple Echo (1972), A Touch of Class (1973), Bequest to the Nation (1973), The Maids (1974), Hedda (1975), Il Sorriso del Grande Tentore (1975), The Romantic Englishwoman (1975), The Incredible Sarah (1976), Nasty Habits (1976), H.E.A.L.T.H. (1979), The Class of Miss MacMichael (1979), House Calls (1979), Stevie (1979), Lost and Found (1979), Hopscotch (1980), And Nothing But the Truth (1982), The Return of the Soldier (1982), Turtle Diary (1985), Beyond Therapy (1987), Business as Usual (1987), Salome's Dance (1988), The Rainbow (1989), King of the Wind (1990), and Doombeach (1990).

JASSY (Gainsborough, 1947)—Historical melodrama. *Director:* Bernard Knowles; *Producer:* Sidney Box; *Script:* Campbell Christie, Dorothy Christie, and Geoffrey Kerr, based on the novel by Norah Lofts; *Cinematography:* Jack Asher and Geoffrey Unsworth; *Music:* Henry Geehl; *Cast:* Margaret Lockwood (Jassy Woodroffe), Patricia Roc (Dilys Helmar), Dennis Price (Christopher Hatton), Basil Sydney (Nick Helmar), Dermot Walsh (Barney Helmar), Esma Cannon (Lindy), Cathleen Nesbitt (Elizabeth Twisdale), Linden Travers (Mrs. Helmar), Nora Swinburne (Mrs. Hatton), Ernest Thesiger (Sir Edmund Follesmark), Jean Cadell (Meggie), John Laurie (Woodroffe), Torin Thatcher (Bob Vicks), Maurice Denham (Jim Stoner), and Alan Wheatley (Sir Edward Walker).

Jassy, produced near the end of the cycle of Gainsborough melodramas, was more sentimental than most other films in this cycle. The casting of Margaret Lockwood* as the gypsy girl Jassy Woodroffe invokes memories of her role as Hesther, the ambitious working-class girl in *The Man in Grey** (1943). Both characters use their friendship with another woman to assist their ambitions. However, Jassy's motivations are, unlike Hester's, ultimately honorable.

When Jassy's father is killed by the local squire Nick Helmar, she is forced into service and while working at an exclusive girls school she meets Dilys who takes Jassy back to her home. Jassy is in love with Barney Hatton, whose father lost the family mansion to Nick Helmar and when Nick proposes marriage, the gypsy girl agrees to his proposal providing that he deeds Barney's former mansion to her.

After the marriage, he falls from the horse. Jassy, and her faithful mute servant Lindy, tend to Nick's wounds, but when Jassy leaves the house to visit Dilys, Lindy poisons Nick with rat-bane. Jassy, who possesses psychic powers, intuits Nick's demise even though she is miles away and her reaction at the time of his death incriminates her at the subsequent murder trial. In true nineteenth-century melodramatic fashion, after Jassy has been declared guilty, the mute girl Lindy regains her voice and confesses to killing Nick. Jassy gives the house to Barney who, fortuitously, declares his love for her after, seemingly, loving Dilys for most of the film.

Jassy, because of its literal dependence on seemingly dated melodramatic conventions (such as the mute who regains her voice to establish the appropriate states of innocence and guilt and Jassy's extraordinary psychic powers) renders the film a prime example of the Gainsborough melodrama.

JET STORM (British Lion Film, 1959)—Aviation melodrama. *Director:* Cy Raker Endfield; *Producer:* Steven Pallos; *Script:* Cy Raker Endfield and Sigmund Miller; *Cinematography:* Jack Hildyard; *Music:* Thomas Rajna; *Cast:* Richard Attenborough (Ernest Tilley), Stanley Baker (Captain Bardow), Hermione Baddeley (Mrs. Satterly), Diane Cilento (Angelica Como), Virginia Maskell (Pam Leyton), Harry Secombe (Binky Meadows), Sybil Thorndike (Emma Morgan), Mai Zetterling (Carol Tilley), Elizabeth Sellars (Inez Barrington), David Kossoff (Dr. Bergstein), Patrick Allen (Mulliner), Marty Wilde (Billy Forrester), Paul Carpenter (George Towers), Megs Jenkins (Rose Brock), George Rose (James Brock), Paul Eddington (Victor Tracer), Lana Morris (Jane Tracer), Bernard Braden (Otis Randolph), Barbara Kelly (Edwina Randolph), Jackie Lane (Clara Forrester), Neil McCallum (Gil Gilbert), Cec Linder (Colonel Coe), and Jeremy Judge (Jeremy Tracer).

In 1960, an independent company in Hollywood produced a film about a bomb aboard a plane, *Jet over the Atlantic,* with Guy Madison as the pilot. This followed *The High and the Mighty* with John Wayne in 1954. These early "disaster" films culminated with *Airport* in 1970, which spawned a number of sequels. The basic narrative premise was similar in each film—domestic and/or romantic problems affecting an all-star cast aboard a plane under threat. The year before *Jet over the Atlantic, Jet Storm* was released.

Ernest Tilley plants a bomb under the wing of a domestic plane flying from London to New York so that he can kill James Brock, who was responsible for the death of his daughter in a car accident. Tilley also wishes to punish the rest of the passengers as they, to his way of thinking, form part of an uncaring world where a little girl's death can go unpunished. The news of this threat provokes different reactions from the passengers—Victor Tracer confesses his infidelity to his wife, who forgives him; the recently widowed Mrs. Satterly declares that she never loved her wealthy husband and now fears that having done the hard labor (twenty-eight years of marriage) she will not live to enjoy the spoils; Otis and Edwina Randolph, traveling to New York for a divorce, decide they still love each other; and co-pilot Gil Gilbert falls in love with flight attendant Pam Leyton.

Aside from the soap-opera characterizations, the dramatic focus is on Captain Bardow's attempt to dissuade Tilley from detonating the bomb. Dissatisfied with the captain's progress, the villainous Mulliner organizes some of the passengers into a vigilante group who, at first, beat up Tilley, and when this fails, decide to kill James Brock so that Tilley will not have a reason to detonate his bomb. Inadvertently, Brock dies when he smashes a window and is sucked out of the plane. This does not deter Tilley and it takes an eight-year-old boy, Jeremy Tracer, to stop the deranged man from activating his bomb. The dramatic tension is interspersed with the good-natured banter between Sybil Thorndike and Harry Secombe. *Jet Storm,* with its less than a 90-minute running time, is preferable to the 130 minutes of *Airport,* or any of its all-star sequels.

JOE MACBETH (Columbia, 1955)—Gangster. *Director:* Ken Hughes; *Producer:* Mike Frankovich; *Script:* Philip Yordan; *Cinematography:* Basil Emmott; *Music:* Richard Taylor; *Cast:* Paul Douglas (Joe Macbeth), Ruth Roman (Lily Macbeth), Bonar Colleano (Lennie), Gregoire Aslan (Duca), Sidney James (Banky), Nicholas Stuart (Duffy), Minerva Pious (Rosie), and Walter Crisham (Angus).

This film project should have been a total disaster—a U.S.–style gangster film (the British crime film rarely used the rise-and-fall prototype favored by Hollywood) by prolific Hollywood scriptwriter Philip Yordan, filmed entirely in England (with the inclusion of a couple of stock shots to try to establish a Chicago setting), with British-supporting actors playing U.S. gangsters. On top of this, the script is based on William Shakespeare's play with less-than-subtle names changes ("Duffy" for McDuff and so on). However, the film succeeds largely due to Ruth Roman's intense performance as the scheming, ambitious Lily Macbeth. Another asset is the mise-en-scène and Ken Hughes's sharp compositions capturing the tortured presence of Paul Douglas wilting before his willful wife.

The familiar story charts the rise of Joe Macbeth to the position of right-hand man in the Chicago gang controlled by Duca. Lily reminds Joe that he is the third number one and each of his predecessors had been killed by Duca. Thus, Lily urges, Joe should get in first. Initially, Joe resists his wife: "For crying out loud, what do you want? We got the house, we got money, we're sitting pretty. Isn't that enough?" Lily, however, replies, "No, Joe, it isn't."

Lily forces Joe to invite Duca to their country house where, in the major set piece in the film, Macbeth murders his boss in their lake. When he cannot retrieve the knife from the body, his wife completes the task. After Joe assumes leadership of the gang, everything starts to fall apart as Joe begins to suspect everybody of plotting against him. He kills his closest friend Banky, and then murders Banky's son and Lennie's wife and daughter. Macbeth's power within the gang deteriorates further when he reacts adversely to the vision of Banky's ghost at a gang banquet. Lennie avenges the death of his family by killing Joe (after Joe accidentally shoots Lily) and then Lennie is killed (offscreen) by the police.

Joe Macbeth is, ultimately, a triumph of style over content. It demonstrates the skill of Hughes and his affinity with this dark, noirish material—the year before the release of *Joe Macbeth* Hughes wrote and directed *The House across the Lake** (1954), a cut-price version of *Double Indemnity* (1944). Both films are representative of the last vestiges of the low-budget crime thrillers that were distributed as co-features (equal billing with similar films). With significant structural changes in the film industry (with CinemaScope and the widespread use of color) and society (leading to the fragmentation of the film audience), such films began to disappear. *Joe Macbeth* was a Columbia Studios production, one of the last Hollywood studios to abandon such films.

JOHNSON, CELIA (1908–1982). In some ways, Celia Johnson is the female equivalent of those (male) British stage actors who, sporadically, appeared in the cinema only when their stage commitments allowed. In Johnson's case, family responsibilities also restricted her film output, but there was little doubt that her artistic soul was in the theater, not the cinema. A pity as her quiet style of underplaying was suited to the medium of film. Nevertheless, for one role, Laura Jesson in *Brief Encounter** (1946), Johnson earned a place in the history of the British cinema. Johnson seemed so perfect for this role that it is difficult to imagine anybody else in it—certainly not Sophia Loren, who appeared opposite Richard Burton in the 1974 made-for-television remake. Johnson's other notable film role was as Ethel Gibbons in *This Happy Breed* (1944), a celebration of the endurance of the British lower-middle class between the two world wars. Johnson's Gibbons was the epitome of British stoicism.

Johnson made her stage debut in 1928 and her film debut in a wartime short in 1941, followed by Alix Kinross, the commander's wife in *In Which We Serve** (1942). After *Brief Encounter,* Johnson performed mostly on the stage, with limited opportunities in films such as *The Holly and the Ivy* (1952), as Jenny Gregory, one of Ralph Richardson's* daughters, and *The Captain's Paradise* (1953), as one of Alec Guinness's* wives. At least a strong supporting role in *The Prime of Miss Jean Brodie* (1968), which earned Johnson a Best Supporting Actress Award at the 1970 BAFTA Film Awards, ended her film career on a good note.

FILMS: A Letter from Home (short, 1941), In Which We Serve (1942), Dear Octopus (1943), This Happy Breed (1944), Brief Encounter (1946), The Astonished Heart (1949), I Believe in You (1952), The Holly and the Ivy (1952), The Captain's Paradise (1953), A Kid for Two Farthings (1955), The Good Companions (1957), and The Prime of Miss Jean Brodie (1968).

NOTE

1. See McFarlane, *An Autobiography of British Cinema,* p. 317.

K

KERR, DEBORAH (b. 1921). Prior to 1953, the screen image of Deborah Kerr was one of elegance, dignity, and a repressed sensuality, traits brilliantly exploited by Michael Powell* in *Black Narcissus** (1948). However, in 1953 Kerr fought hard for the role of the adulteress Karen Holmes in *From Here to Eternity* and, with the success of this film (Kerr was nominated for the Best Actress Award at the 1954 Academy Awards) she was able to expand her acting opportunities.

Kerr's early films at MGM (such as the heroine Elizabeth Curtis in *King Solomon's Mines* [1950] and Princess Flavia in *The Prisoner of Zenda* [1952]) perpetuated the persona developed in the British cinema in the 1940s. However, her success in *From Here to Eternity* encouraged producers to cast Kerr in films with more "adult" themes, such as *Tea and Sympathy* (1956), where Kerr reprised her 1953 Broadway role as a woman who cares for a troubled (seemingly homosexual) young man, *The Proud and the Profane* (1956), which was similar to her role in *From Here to Eternity,* the feisty English governess in *The King and I* (1956), the tragic Anne Larsen in *Bonjour Tristesse* (1958), and Ida Carmody, Robert Mitchum's long-suffering wife forced to confront the obstacles of the Australian outback in *The Sundowners* (1960).

Deborah Jane Kerr-Trimmer was born in Scotland in 1921, the daughter of Captain Arthur Kerr-Trimmer, and trained as a dancer in Bristol, winning a scholarship to the Sadler's Wells Ballet School. Kerr gradually shifted her interest from ballet to acting and she performed with the Oxford Repertory Company in 1939–1940. Over the next seven years, Kerr shared her time between the British cinema and the stage, beginning with *Major Barbara* (1940), followed by starring roles in two Lance Comfort* films in 1941, the dull *Penn of Pennsylvania* and the intense domestic melodrama *Hatter's Castle,** where the twenty-year-old Kerr matched the performance of the idiosyncratic Robert Newton.* Perhaps Kerr's best British role, prior to *Black Narcissus,* was as the pro–Irish Republican Army heroine battling the British secret service and Nazi sympathizers in Frank Launder* and Sidney Gilliat's* superb espionage-romance-adventure *I See a Dark Stranger** (1946).

Kerr's best British film, and her ticket to Hollywood, was as Sister Clodagh, the earnest, dedicated, sexually repressed young nun struggling to hold her mission together in the "House of Women" in the Himalayas in *Black Narcissus*. Fifteen years later, Kerr reprised aspects of this performance, within a more mature persona, as the governess Miss Giddens in *The Innocents** (1961). After this film, Kerr's opportunities in the 1960s failed to match her outstanding roles of the 1940s and 1950s. Kerr semi-retired from feature films after the disappointing domestic melodrama *The Arrangement* (1969), directed by Elia Kazan. Kerr returned, sporadically, to television projects in the 1970s and 1980s and to one film as the repressed, recently widowed former memsahib who develops a tentative relationship with her Indian neighbor in *The Assam Garden* (1985).

Kerr received an Honorary Award at the 1994 Academy Awards following a record number of nominations for Best Actress without ever winning the award for *Edward, My Son* (1949), *From Here to Eternity, The King and I, Heaven Knows Mr. Allison* (1957), *Separate Tables* (1958), and *The Sundowners*. Similarly, Kerr was nominated for the BAFTA Film Award for Best Actress for *The End of the Affair* (1955), *Tea and Sympathy, The Sundowners,* and *The Chalk Garden* (1963). The New York Critics Circle Awards were kinder to Kerr as she won the Best Actress Award on three occasions, for *Black Narcissus, Heaven Knows Mr. Allison,* and *The Sundowners*. Kerr has lived in Switzerland for many years with her husband, novelist Peter Viertel.

FILMS: Major Barbara (1940), Love on the Dole (1941), Penn of Pennsylvania (1941), Hatter's Castle (1941), The Day Will Dawn (1942), The Life and Death of Colonel Blimp (1943), Perfect Strangers (1945), I See a Dark Stranger (1946), Black Narcissus (1947), The Hucksters (1947), If Winter Comes (1948), Edward, My Son (1949), Please Believe Me (1949), King Solomon's Mines (1950), Quo Vadis? (1951), Thunder in the East (1951), The Prisoner of Zenda (1952), Julius Caesar (1953), Young Bess (1953), Dream Wife (1953), From Here to Eternity (1953), The End of the Affair (1955), The King and I (1956), The Proud and the Profane (1956), Tea and Sympathy (1956), Heaven Knows Mr. Allison (1957), An Affair to Remember (1957), Kiss Them for Me (voice, 1957), Separate Tables (1958), Bonjour Tristesse (1958), The Journey (1958), Count Your Blessings (1959), Beloved Infidel (1959), The Sundowners (1960), The Grass Is Greener (1960), The Naked Edge (1961), The Innocents (1961), The Chalk Garden (1963), The Night of the Iguana (1964), Marriage on the Rocks (1965), Eye of the Devil (1966), Casino Royale (1967), Prudence and the Pill (1968), The Gypsy Moths (1969), The Arrangement (1969), and The Assam Garden (1985).

KIND HEARTS AND CORONETS (Ealing, 1949)—Comedy. *Director:* Robert Hamer; *Producers:* Michael Balcon and Michael Relph (associate); *Script:* Robert Hamer and John Dighton, based on the novel *Israel Rank* by Roy Horniman; *Cinematography:* Douglas Slocombe; *Music:* Ernest Irving; *Cast:* Dennis Price (Louis Mazzini/his Father), Valerie Hobson (Edith), Joan Greenwood

(Sibella), Alec Guinness (Ascoyne d'Ascoyne/Henry d'Ascoyne/Canon d'Ascoyne/Admiral d'Ascoyne/General d'Ascoyne/Lady Agatha d'Ascoyne/ Lord d'Ascoyne/Ethelred, Duke of Chalfont), Audrey Fildes (Mrs. Mazzini), John Penrose (Lionel), John Salew (Mr. Perkins), Hugh Griffiths (Lord High Steward), Cecil Ramage (Lord High Steward), Miles Malleson (Hangman), Clive Morton (Prison Governor), and Arthur Lowe (Reporter).

One of the great British films, *Kind Hearts and Coronets* derived its title from a Tennyson couplet, quoted by Edith d'Ascoyne to the film's protagonist, Louis Mazzini, to reassure him that he is worthy to eat at the table of Henry d'Ascoyne:

Kind hearts are more than coronets
And simple faith than Norman blood.

Just like the rest of the film, the title is deeply ironic as Mazzini only pretends to be humble so as to ingratiate himself with Edith and Henry d'Ascoyne. In fact, Louis views himself as the equal of all the d'Ascoynes and he is as prone to issue judgments based on class ("Yes, Sibella was pretty enough in her suburban way . . . but her face would have looked out of place under a coronet"). Only the obstinacy of the Duke of Chalfont, Louis believes, denies him his rightful place in the d'Ascoyne family. His sense of injustice provides the motivation for the film as he proceeds to murder most members of the d'Ascoyne family. He is also driven by the need to avenge his mother who was alienated from the d'Ascoynes after she married an Italian singer, Mazzini's father. His bitterness is intensified after his mother's death when the Duke of Chalfont refuses to bury her in the family crypt.

Kind Hearts and Coronets has a cool, ironic surface. It is also a funny, passionate film that subtly manipulates the audience into a morally comprised position by almost willing the deaths of the d'Ascoynes so that Louis may achieve his dream. This complicity is accentuated by Robert Hamer's* presentation of the killings—mostly rendered offscreen or in long shot—as in the famous image of Louis talking to Edith while smoke appears over Edith's shoulder indicating her husband's death. Similarly, a long shot shows the punt carrying the lecherous Ascoyne d'Ascoyne and his girlfriend over a weir as they make love. Yet, as the U.S. censors noted, the tone of the film changed in the presentation of the final death, that of Ethelred, the Duke of Chalfont. Ethelred is filmed in alternating close-ups as Mazzini coldly explains to the Duke why he is going to die before shooting him with his hunting gun. This killing is both brutal and ironic—earlier Louis had refused to participate in hunting as he was opposed to "blood sports."

The first killing takes place after Ascoyne d'Ascoyne insults Mazzini, who is working as a humble draper. Mazzini follows Ascoyne, and his female companion, to Maidenhead, where he forces their punt over a weir. At their demise, Mazzini remarks: "I was sorry about the girl, but found some relief in the reflection that she had presumably, during the weekend, already undergone a fate worse than death." This remark is accentuated by Dennis Price's ironic, detached delivery of his lines. The death of Henry d'Ascoyne follows when Mazzini substitutes explosive material in Henry's darkroom, followed by the poisoning of Canon d'Ascoyne. When suffragette Lady Agatha d'Ascoyne attempts to balloon over London so that she can drop feminist leaflets, she is brought down by Mazzini's arrow. General d'Ascoyne is murdered when a pot of caviar explodes, and Admiral d'Ascoyne dies through his own stubbornness and incompetence when he goes down with his ship. Lord d'Ascoyne, the banker, dies of a stroke leaving only Ethelred, the Duke of Chalfont. Mazzini is arrested just after he becomes the tenth Duke of Chalfont—not for the murder of the six members of the d'Ascoyne family but for a death that he did not cause, the suicide of Lionel, the husband of his mistress Sibella.

The major characters in *Kind Hearts and Coronets* are all morally flawed. The two women attracted to Mazzini, the ambitious, sensual Sibella, marries the dull Lionel as he offers material security. Nevertheless, Sibella refuses to let marriage impede her sexual pleasure and she regularly visits Mazzini at his St. James's apartment. When Mazzini warns her that if she continues to visit him she is "playing with fire," Sibella replies, "At least it warms me." Similarly, after Mazzini asks Sibella whether she enjoyed her honeymoon with Lionel she replies, "Not at all, not all, not at all"—her intonation suggests that her husband is a poor lover compared to Mazzini. Mazzini is also attracted to Henry d'Ascoyne's glacial widow Edith and he uses Sibella until an appropriate time has lapsed after Henry's death and he can marry Edith.

The story is told via Mazzini's narration of his memoirs, which he writes in his prison cell while awaiting his execution for Lionel's death. Sibella visits him in jail with a veiled offer—she will produce a "miracle," Lionel's suicide note, if Mazzini will "eliminate" Edith. Mazzini agrees although his voice-over indicates that he may not go through with the deal after he has been released from prison. The audience is denied the answer and as he walks out through the prison gates both Sibella and Edith are waiting for him. Then, a reporter from *Titbits* asks Mazzini if he will sell his memoirs to the magazine, the memoirs that Mazzini left in the prison cell.

This wonderfully subversive ending, which invites the audience to speculate as to what might happen to Mazzini—will the prison governor retrieve the memoirs and execute Mazzini for killing the d'Ascoyne family—or will Mazzini be able to talk his way back into his cell and retrieve the papers? The Breen Office (Production Code Administration) in the United States was clearly aware of the implications of this ending and refused to provide a seal of approval. Producer Michael Balcon agreed, for the U.S. release print, to insert an additional scene at the end showing Mazzini's memoirs in the hands of the prison governor. This removed most of the U.S. objections, although Breen objected to the final killing and the line "and sent the fool of the family into the church." *Kind Hearts and Coronets* was finally released by Eagle-Lion Films in 1950, six minutes shorter than the British version.[1]

The final irony concerning *Kind Hearts and Coronets,* despite its excellence, was that producer Michael Balcon was right when he warned Robert Hamer* that he, Hamer, was attempting one of the hardest feats possible—trying to sell irony to the British public. The decidedly inferior comedy *The Chiltern Hundreds** out-grossed *Kind Hearts and Coronets* in 1949, although Hamer's film was nominated for Best British Film at the 1949 BAFTA Film Awards. Alec Guinness,* who played all eight members of the d'Ascoyne family, won the 1950 American National Board of Review Award for Best Actor, and Hamer was nominated for Golden Lion Award at the 1949 Venice Film Festival. Price, who gave the performance of his career as Louis Mazzini, and Joan Greenwood,* as the calculating, passionate Sibella, were overlooked.

A KIND OF LOVING (Anglo-Amalgamated, 1962)—Domestic drama. *Director:* John Schlesinger; *Producer:* Joseph Janni; *Script:* Willis Hall and Keith Waterhouse, based on the novel by Stan Barstow; *Cinematography:* Denys Coop; *Music:* Ron Grainger; *Cast:* Alan Bates (Vic Brown), June Ritchie (Ingrid Rothwell), Thora Hird (Mrs. Rothwell), Bert Palmer (Mr. Brown), Malcom Patton (Jim Brown), Gwen Nelson (Mrs. Brown), Pat Keen (Christine), David Mahlowe (David), Jack Smethurst (Conroy), James Bolan (Jeff), and Patsy Rowlands (Dorothy).

A Kind of Loving, John Schlesinger's* first feature film as director and possibly his best British film, is a deceptive film in some ways as it does not seem to share the intensity and class hostility of other films categorized as part of the British New Wave (such as *Look Back in Anger* [1959] and *This Sporting Life** [1963]). While the film details various aspects of working-class rituals, it is more concerned with issues emanating from gender expectations, the difficulties of marital compromise, and problems associated with living with the in-laws (a central theme also in *The Family Way** [1966]).

The two central protagonists are Vic Brown, a draughtsmen in a Lancashire factory, and Ingrid Rothwell, who works in the same factory as a typist. Vic, whose ideas of sex and women are shaped by the sexist perceptions of his mates, ranging from the larrikin Jeff to the more sexist Conroy, and the "girlie" magazine that he carries around with him, is attracted to blonde Ingrid. After a tentative courtship, the relationship develops. Vic, however, is frustrated by Ingrid's reluctance to totally consummate their relationship (Schlesinger uses couples kissing and indulging themselves in the background and foreground to heighten Vic's frustration) and he begins to drift away from her. Ingrid, aware of Vic's loss of interest, invites him to her mother's house where, hesitantly, she participates in sexual intercourse even though Vic failed to bring a condom with him.

Vic terminates the relationship and tells Jeff that some days he "fancies" Ingrid but at other times he is feels only repulsion. However, Ingrid is pregnant and Vic, reluctantly, agrees to marry her. After a brief, and happy, honeymoon, the marriage is threatened by the animosity between Vic and Ingrid's mother, Mrs. Rothwell. Forced to live in Rothwell's house, Vic resents his mother-in-law's control over his wife. Rothwell, on the other hand, has little respect for Vic because of the circumstances surrounding her daughter's "forced" marriage. This hostility escalates after Rothwell fails to contact Vic when Ingrid loses the baby. It comes to a head after Vic's pub-crawl with Conroy and Rothwell repeatedly calling him a "filthy pig" after he vomits on her carpet. Vic leaves Ingrid but he is forced to reevaluate his ideas when his family provide little sympathy. Vic persuades his wife to accompany him while they look for alternative accommodation and Ingrid agrees to give their marriage a second chance by moving out of her mother's house despite the fact that he can only provide meager living conditions due to his small salary.

Virtually all of the characters in *A Kind of Loving* are flawed. Schlesinger allows a degree of sympathy for Vic and Ingrid and confines his criticism mainly to Ingrid's mother and, to a lesser extent, the factory bully Conroy. While the film studiously avoids melodramatic excess, Ingrid's mother, and what she stands for, veers dangerously close to an ideological caricature and her persecution of Vic shifts the last section of the film into a more polarized drama of victims and villains. Mrs. Rothwell, superbly played by veteran Thora Hird, is the kind of character that was often targeted for critical treatment during the New Wave—she is sexually repressed, gullible with regard to the media, obsessed with material aspects, particularly her overly neat semi-detached house, and, despite her working-class background, despises working-class institutions, such as the pub and the union movement. Rothwell, in her final confrontation with Vic, wearing her outsized glasses with decorative frames, allows years of frustration to erupt in her excessive display of disgust with Vic.

Schlesinger won the Golden Berlin Bear Award at the 1962 Berlin International Film Festival and *A Kind of Loving* was nominated for Best British Film and Best Film from Any Source at the 1963 BAFTA Awards, while Alan Bates* was nominated for Best British Actor and Willis Hall and Keith Waterhouse for Best British Screenplay.

KORDA, ALEXANDER (1893–1956). Aside from J. Arthur Rank, Britain only had one real film mogul, Hungarian-born Alexander Korda, who established the basis for his empire with one film, *The Private Life of Henry VIII** (1933), a gigantic and surprising hit. The film broke the first-day box office records at Radio City Music Hall in New York. This success allowed Korda to build the lavish Denham Studios in 1935 and he became a partner to Charles Chaplin, Mary Pickford, and Douglas Fairbanks in United Artists in the same year. Korda received the first knighthood awarded to a British producer in 1942 and after World War II forged a deal with David O. Selznick that resulted in *The Third Man** (1949). There were also many failed projects but he believed that if the British cinema was to be an international cinema, it must first be an "intensely national" cinema.

Born Sandor Kellner, Korda began his career as a director in Hungary in 1914, after writing about the cinema since 1911. Korda established an independent film studio in Budapest in 1916, but left for Vienna after his arrest during the Miklós Horthy dictatorship. Korda continued to produce films in Vienna before moving to Germany and Hollywood, where he had little success at Fox and First National. He then moved to Paris, working in the French subsidiary of Paramount, and, finally, Britain in 1931, where he established London Films. After a couple of low-budget films, Korda produced and directed the film that was to change the British film industry, *The Private Life of Henry VIII*. With a budget of £60,000, the film grossed more than £500,000 on first release and this encouraged Korda, with financial assistance from the Prudential Assurance Company, to build studios at Denham in Buckinghamshire. When Korda became a partner in United Artists, and United Artists acquired a half share of the Odeon chain of theaters, Korda's films were assured of distribution throughout the United Kingdom. Korda, however, failed to establish a regular market in the United States with his expensive productions and although he lost control of Denham in 1938, he continued film production by leasing space at Denham until he left for Hollywood in 1940.

Korda's films of the late 1930s utilized many international filmmakers, including his brother and director Zoltan Korda, who was responsible for many of the best films of the empire cycle in the 1930s (*Sanders of the River** [1935], *The Drum** [1938], and *The Four Feathers* [1939]), his brother and art director Vincent Korda, Hungarian scriptwriters Lajos Biró and Arthur Wimperis, and French cameraman Georges Perinal. Korda tried to duplicate the success of *The Private Life of Henry VIII* with *The Private Life of Don Juan* (1934) and *Rembrandt* (1936) and then he did not return to directing until *Lady Hamilton* (1941), a favorite of his friend Winston Churchill, which was filmed in Hollywood with Laurence Olivier* and Vivien Leigh.

Korda returned from Hollywood to Britain in 1944 and reopened the studios at Elstree under the MGM logo, where he made *Perfect Strangers* (1945), costarring Robert Donat* and Deborah Kerr.* Korda left MGM after one film and rebuilt his empire at London Films by purchasing British Lion, a major distribution company, plus a share of Shepperton Studios and the Worton Hall Studios at Isleworth. He also arranged distribution of his films in the United States through Twentieth Century Fox. Korda also attracted many of the best filmmakers from Rank, including Michael Powell,* Emeric Pressburger,* Olivier, David Lean,* and Carol Reed.* While Korda only directed one more film, a lackluster adaptation of Oscar Wilde's *An Ideal Husband** (1947), his company was actively producing some of the more formally and thematically innovative films of this period, including *Mine Own Executioner** (1947), *Anna Karenina* (1948), Reed's *The Fallen Idol* (1948), *The Third Man*,* *The Tales of Hoffman* (1951), *Cry the Beloved Country* (1951), *Breaking the Sound Barrier* (1952), *Hobson's Choice* (1954), and *Richard III* (1955). Korda, who was the first major producer to sell the rights to his films to television in the 1950s, was active up until his death, and his final project was *Smiley* (1956), set in the Australian outback. Korda was married to actresses Maria Corda and Merle Oberon.

FILMS (English-language films as director): The Stolen Bride (1927), The Private Life of Helen of Troy (1927), Yellow Lily (1928), Night Watch (1928), Love and the Devil (1929),

The Squall (1929), Her Private Life (1929), Lilies of the Field (1930), Women Everywhere (1930), The Princess and the Plumber (1930), Service for Ladies (1932), Wedding Rehearsal (1933), The Private Life of Henry VIII (1933), The Girl from Maxim's (1933), The Private Life of Don Juan (1934), Rembrandt (1936), Lady Hamilton (1941), Perfect Strangers (1945), and An Ideal Husband (1947).

NOTE

1. See Slide, *"Banned In The USA,"* pp. 89–91.

L

THE LADY VANISHES (Gainsborough, 1938)—Espionage adventure. *Director:* Alfred Hitchcock; *Producer:* Edward Black; *Script:* Sidney Gilliat and Frank Launder, based on the novel *The Wheel Spins* by Ethel Lina White; *Cinematography:* Jack Cox; *Music:* Louis Levy; *Cast:* Margaret Lockwood (Iris Henderson), Michael Redgrave (Gilbert Redman), Paul Lukas (Dr. Hartz), Dame May Whitty (Miss Froy), Cecil Parker (Eric Todhunter), Linden Travers ("Mrs." Margaret Todhunter), Naunton Wayne (Caldicott), Basil Radford (Charters), Mary Clare (Baroness), Emile Boreo (Hotel Manager), Googie Withers (Blanche), and Catherine Lacey ("The Nun").

The Lady Vanishes, Alfred Hitchcock's* penultimate film before leaving England for Hollywood, is generally considered the quintessential British Hitchcock film, utilizing the familiar Hitchcock premise of the likeable character whom nobody will believe, within a light, comedic context. The film walks a fine line between comedy, adventure, and propaganda (the film was produced a year before Britain's declaration of war against Germany), although the film is set in the fictional country of Bandrika, supposedly somewhere in the Balkans, the uniforms and casting, notably Paul Lukas as the villain Dr. Hartz, indicate that they are really German.

Most of *The Lady Vanishes* takes place on a train traveling across central Europe bound for England. The basic plot is economically established early in the film as the passengers wait for their train at a Bandrikan hotel. The McGuffin Inn, the dramatic "excuse" employed by the film to bring its collection of eccentric characters together, is initiated by an elderly British woman (Miss Froy), posing as a governess, who possesses espionage information to take back to England. The early section at the inn also establishes the film's romantic premise. As Iris Henderson prepares to leave Bandrika and return, reluctantly, to England to marry a wealthy suitor, her peace is interrupted by the activities of Gilbert Redman, an ethnomusicologist gathering material for a book on folk songs. The love-hate between Henderson and Redman is interspersed by the musings of the cricket-obsessed Caldicott and Charters, who are rushing back to Manchester to see a test match between England and Australia.

When Froy disappears on the train, after befriending Henderson, no one will believe the young woman. Gilbert, impressed by her sincerity, comes to accept her story. Within the dramatically closed space of the train, Hitchcock, aided by scriptwriters Sidney Gilliat* and Frank Launder* (who reworked the characters and the events in this film in their 1940 thriller *Night Train to Munich*), is able to indulge his gently sadistic game of cat and mouse with the audience as Henderson and Redman are seemingly frustrated every time they appear to be on the brink of solving the mystery of Froy's disappearance. With the aid of a patriotic English-woman posing as a nun, Henderson and Redman solve the mystery, convince Caldicott and Charters that there is a conspiracy, and commandeer the train so that they can take it to a neutral country. However, before they find safety, the pacifist on the train, the lecherous Eric Todhunter, is exposed as a coward and killed by the enemy when he attempts to reason with them—a topical reference to the futility of diplomacy when it is not supported by force.

The Lady Vanishes was a key film in Hollywood's wanting to secure the services of Hitchcock. He won the New York Critics Circle Award for Best Director in 1938.

THE LADYKILLERS (Ealing, 1955)—Comedy. *Director:* Alexander Mackendrick; *Producers:* Michael Balcon and Seth Holt (associate); *Script:* William Rose; *Cinematography:* Otto Heller; *Music:* Tristram Cary; *Cast:* Alec Guinness (Professor Marcus), Cecil Parker (Major Courtney), Herbert Lom (Louis Harvey), Peter Sellers (Harry Robinson), Danny Green ("One Round" Lawson), Jack Warner (The Superintendent), Katie Johnson (Mrs. Louisa Alexandra Wilberforce), Philip Stainton (Sergeant), Stratford Johns (Security Guard), Edie Martin (Lettice), and Frankie Howard (The Barrow Boy).

Late into *The Ladykillers,* there is scene showing the motley group of gangsters who are forced to participate in a tea party organized by Mrs. Wilberforce for her elderly female friends. The gangsters, fearful that Wilberforce will expose the fact that they have just committed a robbery, stand around helplessly with cups of tea and cakes while their leader, Professor Marcus, reluctantly plays "Silver Threads among the Gold" on the piano. The men are, in effect, emasculated by the situation and the manifestations of Victorian values. While U.S. scriptwriter William Rose and director Alexander Mackendrick,* in his last film for Ealing before leaving for Hollywood, may have intended this scene, and the rest of the film, to satirize English stasis and complacency, it also perpetuates the film's dominant theme—the triumph of tradition over contemporary corruption and superficiality.

This is reiterated when Wilberforce tells the gangsters that her twenty-first birthday party in Pangbourne was ruined by the announcement of the death of Queen Victoria. This theme is effectively encapsulated in Wilberforce's old Victorian town house in St. Pancras (St. Pancras station, which can be seen from the house on occasions, is used as an icon of an earlier period). The house appears in the film's first image as a lopsided villa in a cul-de-sac with the railway in the background. The house is also stuffed with faded memories of the past—including Wilberforce's parrot (General Gordon) and the photographs of her husband, Captain Wilberforce, who died going down with his ship—and her only visitors are elderly women. Into this nineteenth-century world comes five representations of crime (and social change)—Cecil Parker's ex-officer con man, Danny Green's dimwitted muscleman, Herbert Lom's Soho gangster, Peter Sellers's* Teddy-boy crim, and, the most bizarre of all, Alec Guinness's* sinister criminal mastermind Professor Marcus, complete with oversized dentures. They are no match for Wilberforce, and her house, and what it stands for—significantly, the men perish not in the house, but in a symbol of change, the railway.

The gangsters, who use the upper rooms in Wilberforce's house to plan a robbery, try to hide their activities under an unlikely disguise as a practicing string quartet. They never escape Wilberforce or her house—as they prepare to leave, Green accidentally catches the handle of his cello case in the door of the house. When he tries to pull it free the cello breaks open revealing the stolen money to Wilberforce. This forces the men to return to the house. After failing to persuade her not to contact the police, their attempts to kill Wilberforce fail miserably. Instead, they kill each other, confirming Marcus's assessment—"It was a good plan but for the human element." In the final moments, when the police refuse to believe Wilberforce's claim that she has the money from the robbery, the old lady walks back to her house (and £60,000) after buying a new umbrella and making a small donation to a street artist working on a portrait of Winston Churchill, another icon of Victorian values.

The Ladykillers was nominated for Best Film, Katie Johnson deservedly won an award for the Best British Actress and Rose for the Best British Screenplay at the 1956 BAFTA Film Awards, while Rose also received an Oscar nomination for his ingenious script at the 1957 U.S. Academy Awards.

LAST HOLIDAY (Associated British Picture Corporation, 1950)—Comedy/ social parable. *Director:* Henry Cass; *Producers:* Stephen Mitchell, A.D. Peters, and J. B. Priestley; *Script:* J. B. Priestley; *Cinematography:* Ray Elton; *Music:* Frances Chagrin; *Cast:* Alec Guinness (George Bird), Beatrice Campbell (Sheila Rockingham), Kay Walsh (Mrs. Poole), Gregoire Aslan (Gambini), Jean Colin (Daisy Clarence), Muriel George (Lady Oswington), Brian Worth (Derek Rockingham), Esme Cannon (Miss Fox), Bernard Lee (Inspector Wilton), Sid James (Joe Clarence), Madam Kirkwood-Hackett (Miss Hatfield), Wilfred Hyde-White (Chalfont), Ernest Thesiger (Sir Trevor Leamington), and Eric Maturin (Wrexham).

In the late 1940s, J. B. Priestley formed his own film production company and then wrote an original script before inviting Henry Cass, a former stage director, to direct. The basic premise is intriguing—George Bird is told by his local doctor that he has Lampington's Disease, which will cause him to die within weeks. This news provokes a character reversal in the normally reticent Bird—he resigns from his job as an agricultural machinery salesman and withdraws all of his savings so he can live at an expensive seaside hotel. At the hotel, guided by Mrs. Poole, the hard-bitten housekeeper-with-a-heart-of gold, he adopts the role of a wealthy man of mystery and this persona naturally attracts the other guests— thereby allowing George to dispense advice and help to those in need.

Robert S. Baker, who produced *The Embezzler* (1954), a low-budget film based on a similar idea, described this narrative concept as "the man who played God."[1] George is attracted to Sheila Rockingham, the wife of a young man who has fallen on hard times. This relationship, between George and Sheila highlights the film's major weakness: a lack of focus and clarity. We never really know the exact basis, and the status, of the relationship between Rockingham and Bird. Initially, it appears that she is developing an interest in another (wealthy) guest, Wrexham, to assist her husband. However, when he appears in the hotel lounge for the first time, Cass provides a single shot of Sheila looking at George in a suggestive manner as she shifts her attention from Wrexham to Bird. Bird responds, she kisses him, and then confesses that she is still in love with Derek, her husband. Later, when Bird provides money to assist the couple, the sexual tension between Rockingham and Bird reappears only to dissipate when he learns that he does not have a terminal disease—he celebrates this news with Mrs. Poole. During the course of the film, he makes sexual overtures to both women and although, because of the censorship restrictions, sexual innuendoes had to be necessarily oblique—in this film they are merely confusing.

A contrived twist concludes the film—Bird, free of the threat of death from Lampington's Disease, is killed driving back to the hotel to rejoin the other guests at a dinner they have organized in his honor. Unaware of his death, most of the guests, peeved by his absence, regress to their selfish, class-bound attitudes. Thus, the film suggests, he has little lasting effect on their lives and his ability to create a sense of community and cooperative behavior is exposed as illusory. Surprisingly, for a film marketed as a light comedy, the film ends on a despairing note as Mrs. Poole, distressed by the news of Bird's death, walks into the darkness of the hotel garden. The final image is a shadow, accompanied by the sounds of the old violinist that opened the film. *Last Holiday,* with its low—key ending, was a commercial failure, although much of blame can be directed to Cass's lackluster direction and Priestley's script, despite strong performances from Alec Guinness,* Beatrice Campbell, Sid James, and especially Kay Walsh.

THE LATE EDWINA BLACK (Romulus, 1951)—Mystery/gothic. *Director:* Maurice Elvey; *Producer:* Ernest Gartside; *Script:* Charles Frank and David Evans, based on the play by William Dinner and William Moray; *Cinematographer:* Stephen Dade; *Music:* Allan Gray; *Cast:* David Farrar (Gregory Black), Geraldine Fitzgerald (Elizabeth Grahame), Roland Culver (Inspector Martin), Jean Cadell (Ellen), Mary Merrall (Lady Southdale), and Harcourt Williams (Dr. Septimus Prendergast).

When Edwina Black dies, suspicion is immediately cast on her husband, Gregory, and Edwina's maid, Elizabeth Grahame, as they had been carrying on an affair for some time. Ellen, the elderly housekeeper, loved Edwina and disapproved of Gregory's relationship with Elizabeth. Enter Inspector Martin from Scotland Yard, who demonstrates that Edwina was murdered by arsenic poisoning. After Martin leaves, the love between Gregory and Elizabeth turns sour as each suspects the other of the murder. Eventually, Martin rounds the suspects up in the kitchen and recreates the crime before exposing Ellen as the murderer. Knowing that she was about to die, Edwina convinced Ellen to administer poison to her so that Gregory will be blamed for the death—thereby destroying the love affair between Gregory and Elizabeth. Gregory and Elizabeth reconcile at the end, determined that Edwina's malice will not prevent their marriage and honeymoon in Venice.

The Late Edwina Black draws on a sturdy mixture of conventions from the classical detective genre and Gothic fiction. The legacy of the dead wife haunts the illicit lovers throughout the film, perpetuating guilt, dread, and death. Her memory permeates the house, particularly the wind chimes that ring out at key moments to remind the lovers of the dead wife's presence. Similarly, Edwina's housekeeper Ellen remains obsessively faithful to the memory of her dead mistress (as in the archetypal Gothic film *Rebecca* [1940]).

The film is basically restricted to four characters, although Mary Merrall has one effective scene as Lady Southdale. After Edwina's funeral, she reminds Elizabeth that the world is a cruel place for penniless young women and old women, as the events in the film demonstrate.

LAUGHTER IN PARADISE (Associated British Pictures, 1951)—Comedy. *Director:* Mario Zampi; *Producer:* Mario Zampi; *Script:* Michael Pertwee and Jack Davies; *Cinematography:* William McLeod; *Music:* Stanley Black; *Cast:* Alastair Sim (Deniston Russell), Fay Compton (Agnes Russell), Guy Middleton (Simon Russell), George Cole (Herbert Russell), Hugh Griffith (Henry Russell), Ernest Thesiger (Endicott), Beatrice Campbell (Lucille Grayson), Mackenzie Ward (Benson), E. A. Matthews (Sir Charles Robson), Joyce Grenfell (Elizabeth Robson), Eleanor Summerfield (Sheila Wilcott), John Laurie (Gordon Webb), Anthony Steel (Roger Godfrey), Veronica Hurst (Joan Webb), and Audrey Hepburn (Cigarette Girl).

An early scene in *Laughter in Paradise* shows Alastair Sim,* in a smoking jacket, standing next to a bronze bust of William Shakespeare while dictating the contents of his latest pulp thriller (*Blood Lust*) to his secretary Sheila Wilcott: "I walked into the room and there stood Petal, her silken hair languorously caressing one fair cheek, her lips red and inviting. I walked over to her and slugged her in the mouth. No, no, change that Miss Wilcott to slugged her in the kisser." It is Sim's performance as a reluctant pulp author (Captain Deniston Russell) that makes *Laughter in Paradise* such as comedic joy.

When inveterate prankster Henry Russell dies while trying to set fire to a newspaper, he provides £50,000 pounds to his four relatives—Deniston, the playboy

Simon, timid bank clerk Herbert, and the bitter spinster Agnes. Each relative is given a set task he or she must achieve before claiming the money. Deniston has to spend twenty-eight days in jail without telling his fiancée, army officer Elizabeth ("Fluffy") Robson or her father, the right-wing magistrate, Sir Charles Robson; Simon must marry the first eligible woman he talks to; Herbert must hold up his bank manager; and Agnes must work as a domestic for twenty-eight days.

While there is considerable humor in each escapade, Deniston's failed attempts to get himself arrested provides the most sustained source of humor. Especially his attempt to carry out a smash and grab on a jewellery store with a neatly wrapped brick. This, like the other failed attempt to steal from a department store, provides Sim with opportunities to demonstrate his impeccable comic timing and gift of mime. Veteran supporting actor Guy Middleton also appears as the playboy Simon, who is conned into a marriage with gold-digger Lucille Grayson. Even though the film's punch line denies each character the promised £50,000, each, with the possible exception of Simon, emerges from his or her task better off in some way—Herbert is appointed manager of a branch of the bank after inadvertently foiling a robbery, Agnes realizes that she was a bitter woman and acts as a matchmaker for a young couple, and Deniston sheds his fiancée "Fluffy" for Sheila, a woman who appreciates his literary "talent."

LAUNDER, FRANK (1906–1997)/**GILLIAT, SIDNEY** (1908–1994). There were a number of excellent producer-director teams in the British cinema, such as Basil Dearden* and Michael Relph,* Roy Boulting* and John Boulting,* Betty E. Box and Ralph Thomas, and Frank Launder and Sidney Gilliat. Launder and Gilliat came together in 1935 as screenwriters and continued working closely together until *The Great St. Trinian's Train Robbery* in 1966. Although both men worked sporadically after 1966, with Launder serving as executive producer on the Gilliat directed thriller *Endless Night* (1972), and Launder also functioning as executive producer on the Dick Emery comedy *Ooh, You Are Awful (1972),* they produced little of real substance after the early 1960s. From the beginning, their collaborations were often characterized by an ability to blend comedy with drama. *The Lady Vanishes,** directed by Alfred Hitchcock* in 1938, is a case in point. The film was based on Ethel Lina White's novel *The Wheel Spins.* After initial production problems, Hitchcock was hired and Gilliat, although he was now employed by MGM, worked with Launder in the evening revising the script. Gilliat devised the cricket-loving characters Charters and Caldicot although, after the film's release, Hitchcock claimed sole credit for their inclusion. Similarly, their adaptation of Christianna Brand's classic whodunit, *Green for Danger** (1946), directed by Gilliat, gave Alastair Sim* one of his best roles as Inspector Cockrill.

After failing to complete his university degree, Gilliat drifted into the film industry in the late 1920s with the assistance of the *Evening Standard* film critic Walter Mycroft. Initially, Gilliat checked unsolicited manuscripts and later provided titles for silent films, including *Under the Greenwood Tree* (1929). Gilliat co-wrote *Rome Express* (1932) and many other 1930s films, including the Jack

Hulbert comedy-thriller *Bulldog Jack** (1935). *Seven Sinners* (1936) brought Gilliat and Launder together and they based their script on Arnold Ridley's play, *The Wrecker,* which had also been filmed in 1928.

Launder joined the story department at British International Pictures in 1928 and he, like Gilliat, was a prolific screenwriter in the early 1930s. Later, they reworked elements from their script of *The Lady Vanishes,* including Basil Radford and Naunton Wayne as the cricket fanatics Charters and Caldicott in the World War II propaganda thriller *Night Train to Munich* (1940), directed by Carol Reed.* Their first directorial credit was another propaganda film, *Millions Like Us* (1943), codirected by Launder and Gilliat, although they rarely codirected films after this as they felt it did not work and preferred to alternate as either producer or director after working on the script. As a general principle, Launder favored broad farce, such as the bizarre St. Trinian's films, with Gilliat more at home with social comedies such as *Only Two Can Play* (1961), although it is difficult to be really specific in attributing individual responsibility for the special qualities of films such as *I See a Dark Stranger** (1946).

In 1945, Launder and Gilliat formed their own company, Individual Pictures, and Gilliat was nominated for Best British Screenplay at the 1956 BAFTA Film Awards for *Constant Husband* (1955), which he shared with Val Valentine. Gilliat and Launder's screenplay for *The Green Man** (1956) was nominated for Best British Screenplay at the 1957 BAFTA Film Awards. Gilliat died in 1994, and Launder died three years later.

FILMS: Sidney Gilliat (as director): Millions Like Us (codir., 1943), Waterloo Road (1944), The Rake's Progress (1945), London Belongs to Me (1948), State Secret (1950), The Story of Gilbert and Sullivan (1953), The Constant Husband (1954), Fortune Is a Woman (1957), Left, Right and Centre (1959), Only Two Can Play (1961), The Great St. Trinian's Train Robbery (codir., 1966), and Endless Night (1972).

Frank Launder (as director): Millions Like Us (codir., 1943), 2,000 Women (1944), I See a Dark Stranger (1946), Captain Boycott (1947), The Blue Lagoon (1949), The Happiest Days of Your Life (1950), Lady Godiva Rides Again (1951), Folly to Be Wise (1953), The Belles of St. Trinian's (1954), Geordie (1955), Blue Murder at St. Trinian's (1957), The Bridal Path (1959), The Pure Hell of St. Trinian's (1961), Joey Boy (1965), The Great St. Trinian's Train Robbery (codir., 1966), and The Wildcats of St. Trinian's (1980).

THE LAVENDER HILL MOB (Ealing, 1951)—Comedy. *Director:* Charles Crichton; *Producers:* Michael Balcon and Michael Truman (associate); *Script:* T. E. B. Clarke; *Cinematography:* Douglas Slocombe; *Music:* Georges Auric; *Cast:* Alec Guinness (Holland), Stanley Holloway (Pendlebury), Sid James (Lackery), Alfie Bass (Shorty), Marjorie Fielding (Mrs. Chalk), Edie Martin (Miss Evesham), John Salew (Parkin), Ronald Adam (Turner), John Gregson (Farrow), Clive Morton (Station Sergeant), Sidney Taffler (Clayton), Eugene Deckers (Customs Official), Audrey Hepburn (Chiquita), and Patrick Barr (Divisional Detective Inspector).

The Lavender Hill Mob won the Best Film Award at the 1952 BAFTA Awards, beating *The Man in the White Suit** (1951). *The Lavender Hill Mob* was also one of Ealing's most commercially successful films. The basic idea came to scriptwriter T. E. B. Clarke's while he was working on *Pool of London* (1951), an Ealing drama. Michael Balcon, the head of production at Ealing, suggested that Clarke transform the script into a comedy based on the theft of gold bullion from the Bank of London. Allegedly, representatives from the bank also provided specific advice to Clarke as to how the robbery might successfully take place.

The resultant film, unlike the complex use of irony and metaphor in the harder-edged Ealing films such as *Kind Hearts and Coronets** (1949) and *The Man in the White Suit,* is simple and gentle. Holland, a disillusioned bank clerk, devises a plan to rob gold bullion from the Bank of England as it is being transported. Holland recruits Pendlebury, another boarder in his south London boarding house, to assist. Pendlebury produces souvenir models of the Eiffel Tower in his small factory and Holland's plan is to melt the gold down into souvenir models and ship them to Paris. Holland also inveigles two working-class professional thieves, Shorty and Lackery, into his "gang."

The plan does not proceed smoothly, the men ship the bullion to Paris, where, inadvertently, six Eiffel Tower souvenirs are sold to English schoolgirls visiting the tower. Holland and Pendlebury retrieve five of the models but the sixth girl refuses to part with her souvenir and it ends up with her father at a London police exhibition. The film concludes with a parody of the car chase from *The Blue Lamp** (1950) as Holland and Pendlebury race through the streets of London in a stolen police car. Although Pendlebury is eventually captured, Holland escapes to South America. At this point, the film returns to the opening scene where Holland is telling his story to a man in a restaurant. To meet the requirements of both the British and U.S. censors, the last shot shows that the man listening to Holland's story is a policeman sent to bring Holland back to England.

The humor in *The Lavender Hill Mob* is based on gently reversing social stereotypes—the mild, loyal bank clerk secretly dreaming of robbing his employer, the elderly boarding house landlady (Mrs. Chalk) obsessed by crime fiction, and the professional crooks, Lackery and Shorty, who trust Pendlebury and Holland to return to Britain with their share of the loot. The humor is broadly played, particularly by Stanley Holloway (Pendlebury), as he and Alec Guinness* (Holland) suffer one obstacle after another while activating their "fool-proof" plan. In a different period, they probably would have succeeded in getting away with the bullion for, as Pendlebury excitedly exhorts when he realizes that Holland is proposing they rob the Bank of England, "By Jove Holland, it's a good job we're both honest men."

Clarke won an Oscar at the 1953 Academy Awards for Best Writing, Story and Screenplay, Guinness won the Silver Ribbon Award for Best Actor from the Italian National Syndicate of Film Journalists, and Charles Crichton* was nominated at the 1952 Venice Film Festival.

THE LEAGUE OF GENTLEMEN (Allied Filmmakers/Rank, 1960)—Heist film. *Director:* Basil Dearden; *Producer:* Michael Relph; *Script:* Bryan Forbes, based on the novel by John Boland; *Cinematography:* Arthur Ibbetson; *Music:* Philip Green; *Cast:* Jack Hawkins (Norman Hyde), Nigel Patrick (Peter Race), Roger Livesey ("Padre" Mycroft), Richard Attenborough (Edward Lexy), Bryan Forbes (Martin Porthill), Kieron Moore (Stevens), Terence Alexander (Rupert Rutland-Smith), Norman Bird (Frank Weaver), Robert Coote (Bunny Warren), Melissa Stribling (Peggy), and Nanette Newman (Elizabeth).

Peter Race, a disgraced former transport major in the British army, visits the home of retired army Lieutenant-Colonel Norman Hyde to discuss Hyde's plan to rob a London bank. Race notices an oil painting of a woman in Hyde's house and innocently asks Hyde if the woman is Hyde's wife. Hyde confirms that is. Noticing that there is no sign of a woman's influence in the house, Race then asks is she dead and Hyde replies: "No, I am sorry to say the bitch is still going strong." Thus, instead of exploiting the obvious sentimental possibilities, the film takes a tougher line and this is symptomatic of the entire film that assimilates the conventions of the heist film with a deeply humorous satire on the conventions of the British war film, the most popular British genre of the 1950s. The significance of this scene between Race and Hyde is even more profound if you consider the popular screen image, in the 1950s, of the two actors, especially Jack Hawkins,* who was regularly cast throughout the 1950s as a dependable, authority figure—such as Inspector George Gideon in *Gideon's Day* (1958) or Major Warden in *The Bridge on the River Kwai* (1958), or, in his most famous role, Captain Ericson in *The Cruel Sea** (1953). Similarly, Nigel Patrick, while less typecast, often appeared in similar roles, such as the Scotland Yard detective in *Sapphire* (1959) and the doomed Lieutenant Manson in *Morning Departure* (1950). The motivation for the robbery for Hyde is to exact some form of revenge on a society in which he was forced to retire from the army after twenty-five years of service.

The League of Gentlemen, however, is even more slyly subversive than just this. Except for Hyde, all of the other ex-army personnel recruited for the bank job are disgraced army officers who have fallen on hard times since World War II. This aspect is reinforced by the casting of familiar actors, such as Roger Livesey as the former quartermaster captain who committed an act of "gross indecency" in a public place and is now forced to make a living as a religious con man with a penchant for porn magazines. Similarly, Kieron Moore, a former supporter of the fascist Lord Haw Haw, was expelled from the army for a homosexual act. Norman Bird appears as a ex-explosives captain who caused the death of four men when he got drunk on his watch. Patrick is involved in the black market, Bryan Forbes* is forced to live off wealthy women, and Terence Alexander is humiliated by his wealthy, promiscuous wife who taunts him, while naked in the bath, by pointing out that "the war's been over a long time—nothing's rationed any more, there's plenty to go around." Richard Attenborough* completes the group as an ex-radio lieutenant who sold secrets to the enemy during the war.

Hyde, after reading an account of a military-style robbery on a U.S. bank in the novel *The Golden Fleece,* recruits seven ex-army specialists to execute a similar robbery in London. To obtain the necessary weapons, the men rob an army base, posing as a British army inspection team, and then, after careful planning, steal a large amount of money from a bank after releasing gas cylinders to cause maximum confusion. However, an inquisitive child writes down the license plate of a car used in the robbery, which, eventually, leads the police back to the group. While the conventions of the heist, or caper, film are skillfully executed by Basil Dearden,* working from Forbes's script, the film's extra layer is its cutting satire on class and military values. The film was the first commercial success for Allied Filmmakers, set up by Hawkins, Attenborough, Forbes, Dearden, and Michael Relph* with the assistance of Rank, and although the group had subsequent successes, such as *Whistle Down the Wind* (1961), which was Forbes's directorial debut, the company soon folded. Forbes was also nominated for a BAFTA Award in 1961 for Best British Screenplay for *The League of Gentlemen.*

LEAN, DAVID (1908–1991). In 1970, David Lean went to New York to promote his second last film, *Ryan's Daughter.* At a function chaired by Richard Schickel, prominent U.S. critics, lead by Pauline Kael, savaged the film for its indulgent, old-fashioned qualities (although he defended it by saying that the critics had missed the fact that the film was "intentionally over-romantic") and for being hopelessly out of step with the (brief) "New Wave" of low-budget, youth-oriented U.S. films such as *Easy Rider* (1969). Lean, who had enjoyed a long period of critical and commercial success, especially with *Doctor Zhivago* (1965), which alone earned more than the total revenue of all of Lean's films prior to 1965, was badly shaken by the reaction to *Ryan's Daughter* and vowed never to make another film. Later in the decade, however, he began preparing *A Passage to India* (1984), which was perceived as a triumphant return with Oscar and BAFTA nominations for Best Film. Lean's face also appeared on the cover of *Time* magazine accompanied by a celebratory article by Schickel, his old nemesis. At the time of Lean's death, he was preparing a film version of Joseph Conrad's *Nostromo.*

In a television interview with Melvyn Bragg following the release of *A Passage to India,* Lean extolled the importance of his training as an editor, especially the period he spent in the 1930s editing news reels for Gaumont-British News and British Movietone News. The essence of this craft, Lean pointed out, was based on this expertise and, especially, speed. Yet, Lean, the film director, made only five feature films in the last thirty-four years of this life, preferring inordinately detailed preparation followed by lengthy shooting schedules in exotic locations and painstaking post-production work, carefully supervised by him.

On the set, Lean was not considered sympathetic to the difficulties faced by his actors. Alec Guinness* worked with him on many films, beginning with *Great Expectations** in 1946, his Oscar-winning *The Bridge on the River Kwai* (1957), through to Lean's final film where Guinness appeared as the Indian intellectual

Professor Godbole in *A Passage to India.* Guinness criticized Lean's inability to impart his vision to the actors and he fell out so badly with Lean over their different interpretations of Guinness's character (Colonel Nicholson) during the production of *The Bridge on the River Kwai* that both men only communicated through producer Sam Spiegel for a period. This disagreement between the director and his leading actor was not helped by Lean's comment to Guinness when he met him at Colombo airport prior to shooting that he (Lean) really wanted Charles Laughton for Guinness's role as Colonel Nicholson. Similarly, James Fox, who worked with him on *A Passage to India,* claimed that Lean was not interested in the way actors internalized a role as he was only concerned with a mechanical form of acting that contributed to his overall vision for the "look" of the film.

Lean was raised in the London suburb of Croydon in a conservative household that prohibited attendance at the movies. He was a poor student at school although he displayed an aptitude for photography when he was given a camera. After a dreary year working as a clerk in an accountancy firm, his father helped him acquire a job at Gaumont-British, where he worked in numerous menial roles, including wardrobe assistant, before his promotion to the editing room. He excelled in this position and when Noël Coward wanted a technician to assist him direct *In Which We Serve** (1942), Lean was recommended by a number of filmmakers as the finest editor in Britain at that time. Coward directed the actors, leaving Lean to the camera set-ups and virtually everything else. Lean later claimed that Coward became so bored with the filmmaking process he left directing the film entirely to him after a while.

Three more films based on Coward's works followed. With *Brief Encounter** (1945), he was nominated for the 1947 Oscar for both Best Director and Best Writing, which he shared with Anthony Havelock-Allan and Ronald Neame.* Lean followed this film with the two finest screen adaptations of Charles Dickens's *Great Expectations* and *Oliver Twist* (1948). The next three films, where Lean worked with his then-wife Ann Todd* (*The Passionate Friends** [1949], *Madeleine** [1950], and *The Sound Barrier* [1952]), are sometimes cited, incorrectly, as lesser Lean films. *The Passionate Friends* was a complex reworking of the theme of the conflict between desire and marital duty (found also in *Brief Encounter*), and *Madeleine* was a morally problematic story of a woman who may have killed her lover. These two fine films differ greatly from the international epics that characterized the next phase in his career.

Following *Hobson's Choice* (1954) with Charles Laughton, Lean began his period of international filmmaking in foreign locations with *Summer Madness* (1955), starring Katharine Hepburn, and he devoted the rest of his career to five multi-star long epics. While these films retained Lean's fascination with oddball characters, such as T. E. Lawrence (in *Lawrence of Arabia* [1962]) and Colonel Nicholson (*The Bridge on the River Kwai*), who were eccentric to the point of madness, and themes involving thwarted love and social repression, these themes and characterizations were often pushed into the background and dwarfed by

Lean's lush production values and desire for pictorial perfection. Lean was knighted in 1984 and died in 1991.

FILMS: In Which We Serve (codir., 1942), This Happy Breed (1944), Blithe Spirit (1945), Brief Encounter (1945), Great Expectations (1946), Oliver Twist (1948), The Passionate Friends (1949), Madeleine (1950), The Sound Barrier (1952), Hobson's Choice (1954), Summer Madness (1955), The Bridge on the River Kwai (1957), Lawrence of Arabia (1962), Doctor Zhivago (1965), Ryan's Daughter (1970), Tomorrow Is Yours (short, 1977), and A Passage to India (1984).

LEE, CHRISTOPHER (b. 1922). In *The Wicker Man** (1973), Christopher Lee was Lord Summerisle, the intelligent, urbane Gaelic aristocrat dedicated to the worship of pagan gods responsible for bringing food and prosperity to his island. When a police officer (Edward Woodward) arrives from the mainland to investigate the apparent disappearance of a young girl, Lee, seemingly, assists the policeman but in the film's chilling climax he leads the islander's pagan chants while the young officer is sacrificed, by fire, in a giant wicker man. This role, in many ways, encapsulates the image of Lee as a representative of those forces that are not accessible to ordinary humans, as intelligent, powerful, dangerous, and mostly evil. To his credit, he also brought a certain sadness and self-knowingness to his most famous creation, Count Dracula, in a long series of films for Hammer.

There was, however, nothing in Lee's background to indicate that he would eventually become one of the most well-known actors in the history of the horror film (rivaled only by Boris Karloff). The son of Lieutenant Colonel Jeffrey Lee of the King's Royal Rifle Corps and an Italian contessa, he lived in Switzerland for a period during his childhood after the divorce of his parents. When his mother married a banker, the uncle of Ian Fleming, Lee moved back to London, where he had the opportunity to perform at the Summerfields Preparatory School in Oxford before attending Wellington College. During World War II, he served in liaison with the Rhodesian police and the Royal Air Force, before receiving a transfer to Special Operations. After the war, Lee's cousin, Count Niccolo Carandini, the Italian ambassador in London, suggested that Lee consider acting as a profession, but the head of Denham Studios told Lee that he was too tall to make a successful actor. Nevertheless, his cousin arranged a meeting with Del Guidice at Two Cities, a division of Rank, and he was given a standard seven-year Rank contract, beginning with a one-line of dialogue in Terence Young's elegant film noir *Corridor of Mirrors** (1948).

Lee appeared in eleven films in the next eighteen months, mostly small roles although he did have a featured role in the low-budget *Penny and the Pownall Case* (1948) as the leader of a continental underground organization assisting the escape of German war criminals. During this period, Lee realized that his height was a disadvantage together with his appearance, which was not considered "typically British" by casting agents. By 1950, even small roles began to dry up although he did appear in *Captain Horatio Hornblower* (1950) for Warner Brothers. His last picture under his Rank contract was *Valley of the Eagles* (1951).

After this, he was forced to seek work as a freelance actor, including working as the stand-in for Burt Lancaster in *The Crimson Pirate* (1952). Many television series, such as *Colonel March of Scotland Yard,* where he appeared with Karloff, followed. In terms of the cinema, it was not until *Beyond Mombasa* (1956), and the part of a big game hunter, that Lee received a substantial screen credit, followed by three war-related films. The first was Nicholas Ray's *Bitter Victory* (1957), where Lee clashed with Ray over how a sergeant of the Brigade of Guards would behave. This was followed by *Ill Met by Moonlight* (1957) and *The Traitor* (1957).

Lee's big break came when Hammer was searching for a tall actor to play the monster in *The Curse of Frankenstein** (1957). As Lee's career was not developing as strongly as he would have wished after ten years in the business, he went after the part in what would be his thirty-fifth film. After the film was completed, but before it was released, he returned to supporting roles, including the villainous Marquis St. Evremonde in *A Tale of Two Cities* (1958). The success of *The Curse of Frankenstein* enabled Lee to rejoin director Terence Fisher* and Peter Cushing* for his most famous role as *Dracula** (1958). The combination of Lee's powerful screen presence, plus the film's use of graphic violence, sadism, and sensuality, and Fisher's masterly direction, resulted in *Dracula* being a great financial success. This established a screen image that stereotyped Lee for many years. However, after appearing as Kharis in *The Mummy** (1959), directed by Fisher, Lee refused to make any more horror films requiring elaborate makeup.

Surprisingly, given the strong commercial success of *The Curse of Frankenstein* and *Dracula,* Lee's career did not flourish as much as it should have after *Dracula,* and while Hammer promoted Cushing in a series of British horror films, Lee languished in low-budget French, German, and Italian films, such as *The Hands of Orlac* (1960), *Ercole al centro della terra* (1961), *Das Ratsel der Roten Orchidee* (1962), and *Sherlock Holmes and the Deadly Necklace* (1962), as Sherlock Holmes. He also had supporting roles in British films, such as *Terror of the Tongs* (1961), *Taste of Fear* (1961), and *The Pirates of Blood River* (1961). Although Lee hoped that the German production of *Sherlock Holmes and the Deadly Necklace,* co-directed by Fisher and Frank Witherstein, would transform his career, the poor script and shoddy production values destroyed his hopes for a series of Sherlock Holmes films.

When Lee married Danish model Birgit Kroencke in 1961, he moved to Switzerland to live and, because of tax reasons, was unable to appear in British films for a year, so he starred in more low-budget European films, mostly with horror and Gothic story lines. Returning to Britain in 1964, he received top billing for the first time in a Hammer film in the non-horror *Devil-Ship Pirates* (1964), followed by *The Gorgon* (1964), where the traditional Hammer casting of Lee and Cushing was reversed so that Lee played the hero and top-billed Cushing the villain. In the popular Amicus omnibus *Dr. Terror's House of Horror* (1964), Lee was the acerbic art critic Franklyn Marsh, who learns that his future is bleak when Cushing reads from the tarot cards. Significantly, Lee received top billing in this film over Cushing for the first time, a position he retained for all future Hammer productions.

Lee's status as the pre-eminent British horror film star was consolidated by his role as the Oriental master villain in *The Face of Fu Manchu* (1965), produced by Hallam Films. Hammer, after the success of this film, must have regretted rejecting Lee's suggestion in the early 1960s that it purchase the rights to the Sax Rohmer's novels. He followed this with a series of low-budget sequels: *The Brides of Fu Manchu* (1966), *The Vengeance of Fu Manchu* (1967), *The Blood of Fu Manchu* (1968), and *The Castle of Fu Manchu* (1970). In between the Fu Manchu series, Lee enjoyed top billing in *Rasputin, the Mad Monk* (1965) and a welcome return to the role that created his reputation in *Dracula, Prince of Darkness* (1965), directed by Fisher. This was followed by one of Lee's best roles, and films, as the aristocratic Duc de Richleau in Fisher's *The Devil Rides Out** (1967), which transformed, to a certain degree, Lee's screen image as he represented a positive force combating the evil Charles Gray in the film. Unfortunately, the commercial failure of this film, and a subsequent Denis Wheatley adaptation (*The Lost Continent* [1968]), caused Hammer to lose interest in further films based on Wheatley's novels.

While Lee continued to make one Dracula film a year for Hammer, with mixed results, he was becoming anxious about the quality of the series although it continued to consolidate his reputation with the public as the most prominent horror actor of his generation, an image he was increasingly willing to parody, as in *The Magic Christian* (1969). A chance for him to break away from the restrictions of this image came when he was cast in a strong supporting role in Billy Wilder's *The Private Life of Sherlock Holmes* (1970), as Sherlock's brother Mycroft. This was one of Lee's most enjoyable film experiences as it showed the general public that he was capable of a wider range of roles than had previously been offered to him. He subsequently appeared in his first Western, *Hannie Caulder* (1971), as the blacksmith who assists Raquel Welch to obtain revenge on the men who raped her, and *The Three Musketeers* (1973), as Rochefort. Lee also began purchasing film properties in the hope of producing superior genre films but his first attempt, *Nothing But the Night* (1972), a supernatural thriller co-starring Cushing for his own production company Charlemagne Productions, failed at the box office.

Since the mid-1970s, Lee continued his move away from the horror genre, including a prominent role in *The Man with the Golden Gun* (1974) as Francisco Scaramanga, James Bond's (Roger Moore) principal adversary. Lee also starred in *Jinnah* as Mohammed Ali Jinnah, the founder of Pakistan, in a 1998 U.S., British, and Pakistani co-production. In recent years, he has, selectively, returned to the genre that made him famous, including his role as the Burgomeister in Tim Burton's retelling of Washington Irving's *Sleepy Hollow* (1999). Recently, Lee appeared in the film adaptation of one of his favorite books, as Saruman the White in Peter Jackson's adaptation of J. R. R. Tolkien's *Lord of the Rings: The Fellowship of the Ring* (2001). As these three films were shot back to back in

New Zealand throughout 1999 and 2000, Lee will appear in the sequels, *Lord of the Rings: The Two Towers,* scheduled for release in late 2002, and *Lord of the Rings: The Return of the King,* scheduled for release in late 2003.

FILMS: Corridor of Mirrors (1948), One Night with You (1948), Hamlet (1949), Saraband for Dead Lovers (1948), Song of Tomorrow (1948), Penny and the Pownall Case (1948), My Brother's Keeper (1948), Scott of the Antarctic (1948), Trottie True (1949), Prelude to Fame (1950), They Were Not Divided (1950), Valley of Eagles (1951), Captain Horatio Hornblower (1951), Paul Temple Returns (1952), Babes in Baghdad (1952), The Crimson Pirate (1952), Moulin Rouge (1952), Top Secret (1952), Innocents in Paris (1953), Thought to Kill (1953), The Triangle (1953), The Death of Michael Turbin (1954), Destination Milan (1954), The Final Column (1954), Police Dog (1955), That Lady (1955), The Warriors/The Dark Avengers (1955), Crossroads (1955), Man in Demand (1955), Stranglehold (1955), Cockleshell Heroes (1955), Storm over the Nile (1955), Beyond Mombasa (1955), Alias John Preston (1956), Port Afrique (1956), Private's Progress (1956), The Battle of the River Plate (1956), Fortune Is a Woman (1956), Ill Met by Moonlight (1957), Bitter Victory (1957), The Traitor (1957), The Curse of Frankenstein (1957), The Truth about Women (1957), A Tale of Two Cities (1958), Dracula (1958), Corridors of Blood (1958), The Battle of the V. I. (1958), Tempi duri per I vampiri/Hard Times for Dracula (1959), The Hound of the Baskervilles (1959), The Mummy (1959), The Treasure of San Teresa (1959), The Man Who Could Cheat Death (1959), Too Hot to Handle (1960), The City of the Dead (1960), Beat Girl (1960), The Two Faces of Dr. Jekyll (1960), The Hands of Orlac (1960), The Terror of the Tongs (1960), Ercole al centro della terra (1961), The Devil's Daffodil (1961), The Pirates of Blood River (1961), Taste of Fear (1961), Das Ratsel der Roten Orchidee (1962), The Doctor from Seven Dials (1962), The Devil's Agent (1962), The Longest Day (1962), Sherlock and the Deadly Necklace (1962), Castle of Terror (1963), Crypt of Horror (1963), Katarsis (1963), Faust (1963), Night Is the Phantom (1963), The Devil Ship Pirates (1964), Castle of the Living Dead (1964), Dr. Terror's House of Horrors (1964), The Gorgon (1964), The Skull (1965), She (1965), The Face of Fu Manchu (1965), Dracula, Prince of Darkness (1965), Five Golden Dragon (1965), Rasputin, the Mad Monk (1966), Psycho Circus (1966), The Brides of Fu Manchu (1966), Theatre of Death (1966), Night of the Big Heat (1967), Torture Chamber of Dr. Sadism (1967), Victims of Terror (1967), The Devil Rides Out (1968), The Vengeance of Fu Manchu (1968), Curse of the Crimson Alter (1968), The Face of Eve (1968), Dracula Has Risen from the Grave (1968), The Blood of Fu Manchu (1969), Scream and Scream Again (1969), The Oblong Box (1969), The Bloody Judge (1969), Philosophy in the Boudoir (1969), Taste the Blood of Dracula (1969), One More Time (1969), Julius Caesar (1969), The Magic Christian (1969), The Castle of Fu Manchu (1970), Vampir (1970), Vampir (1970), The Shady Place (1970), The House That Dripped Blood (1970), The Private Life of Sherlock Holmes (1970), The Scars of Dracula (1970), Bram Stoker's Count Dracula (1970), I, Monster (1971), Hannie Caulder (1971), Nothing But the Night (1972), Horror Express (1972), Death Line (1972), Dracula A.D. 1972 (1972), The Creeping Flesh (1972), The Wicker Man (1973), The Butcher, the Star and the Orphan (1973), The Three Musketeers (1973), The Satanic Rites of Dracula (1973), The Man with the Golden Gun (1974), Dark Places (1974), The Four Musketeers (1974), Diagnosis: Murder (1974), The Legend of Dracula (1975), To the Devil a Daughter (1975), Killer Force (1975), The Keeper (1976), Whispering Death (1976), Starship Invasions (1977), Revenge of the Dead (1976), End of the World (1977), Airport '77 (1977), Return from Witch Mountain (1978),

The Passage (1978), Caravans (1978), Nutcracker Fantasy (1979), Jaguar Lives! (1979), Dracula and Son (1979), Arabian Adventure (1979), Bear Island (1979), The Silent Flute (1979), 1941 (1979), Serial (1980), The Salamander (1981), Desperate Moves (1981), An Eye for an Eye (1981), A Desperate Case (1981), Safari 3000 (1982), The Last Unicorn (voice, 1982), The Return of Captain Invincible (1983), New Magic (1983), House of the Long Shadows (1983), The Rosebud Beach Hotel (1984), Mask of Murder (1985), Howling II: Your Sister Is a Werewolf (1985), The Girl (1986), Jocks (1988), The Land of Faraway (1987), Dark Mission (1988), The French Revolution (1989), The Return of the Musketeers (1989), Murder Story (1989), L'Avaro (1989), Honeymoon Academy (1990), Treasure Island (1990), The Care of Time (1990), Gremlins 2: The New Batch (1990), The Rainbow Thief (1990), Incident at Victoria Falls (1991), Curse III: Blood Sacrifice (1991), Shogun Warrior (1992), Jackpot (1992), Police Academy 7: Mission to Moscow (1994), Funny Man (1994), A Feast at Midnight (1995), The Stupids (1995), Tale of the Mummy (1998), Jinnah (1998), Sleepy Hollow (1999), Lord of the Rings: The Fellowship of the Ring (2001), and Star Wars: Episode II : Attack of the Clones (2002).

LEE THOMPSON, J. (b. 1914). In terms of directorial longevity in the U.S. cinema, John (Jack) Lee Thompson, after Alfred Hitchcock,* was the most successful British director to work in Hollywood after a substantial career in the British cinema. Lee Thompson's U.S. career followed a similar pattern to John Guillermin.* Both directors produced a number of very efficient British films in the late 1950s before the lure of larger budgets persuaded them to move to Hollywood in the 1960s and 1970s. In terms of quality, both directors failed to match their British films in Hollywood—with one exception, Lee Thompson's first U.S. film, the masterly *Cape Fear* (1962).

Born in Bristol, Lee Thompson joined the Nottingham Repertory where he made his stage debut as an actor in 1931. In 1934, at the age of twenty, he made a decisive shift by joining British International in their script writing department. The late 1930s was a great training period for Lee Thompson, including a stint as dialogue director on *Jamaica Inn* (1939), directed by Hitchcock. Hitchcock remained a formative influence on him.

While serving in the Royal Air Force during World War II, Lee Thompson continued to write for the theater, and, in 1951, one of his plays that had been successfully staged in 1942, *Murder without Crime,* was adapted to the cinema with Lee Thompson directing. However, it was his second film as a director, the low-budget thriller *The Yellow Balloon* (1953), based on the premise of a criminal pursuing a young boy after he has witnessed a killing, that attracted controversy as the British censors burdened the film with an X classification, which weakened its commercial potential.[2]

Lee Thompson demonstrated in his 1950s British films his interest and expertise with story lines based on melodrama, into which he often assimilated moral and social issues—this was most evident in *Yield to the Night* (1956), in this story of a woman sentenced to death for killing her boyfriend. He also directed four musicals, including *An Alligator Named Daisy* (1955) for Rank. After the critically successful *Woman in a Dressing Gown* (1957), which won him the International Critics Prize, and the Best Actress Award for Yvonne Mitchell, at the Berlin Film Festival, Lee Thompson completed four films that represented the peak of his film career in terms of creativity: *Ice Cold in Alex** (1957), a superior film that challenged many of the prevailing conventions of the 1950s British war film; *North West Frontier** (1959), a late example of the empire film that, while extolling some of the characteristic ideological virtues of the empire, also accommodated the changed political context; *The Guns of Navarone* (1961), an exciting adventure based on Alastair MacLean's story of the small group of Allied fighters determined to destroy a large German cannon on a Greek Island; and *Cape Fear,* Lee Thompson's masterpiece, which addresses, within the dramatic structure of the revenge thriller, a number of key ethical issues.

After the commercial and critical success of *The Guns of Navarone,* Lee Thompson moved to the United States, the fulfilment of a long-held desire to be a working Hollywood director. However, *Cape Fear* represented the apex of his film career even though he worked steadily in Hollywood for another twenty-eight years. With a few (minor) exceptions (*Return from the Ashes,* shot in England in 1965, *Conquest of the Planet of the Apes* [1972], and *The White Buffalo* [1977]), there is little of real interest after *Cape Fear* as most of his U.S. films are devoid of the thematic complexity and left-leaning social themes that characterized many of his British films. While Lee Thompson never lost his ability as a craftsman to expertly execute spectacle and action, many of his U.S. films appear simplistic, even reactionary—especially some of the films he directed for Charles Bronson in the 1970s and 1980s (e.g., see *Death Wish 4: The Crackdown* [1987]).

FILMS (as director): Murder without Crime (1951), The Yellow Balloon (1953), The Weak and the Wicked (1954), For Better or Worse (1954), As Long As They're Happy (1955), An Alligator Named Daisy (1955), Yield to the Night (1956), The Good Companions (1957), Woman in a Dressing Gown (1957), Ice Cold in Alex (1957), No Trees in the Street (1959), Tiger Bay (1959), North West Frontier (1959), I Aim at the Stars (1960), The Guns of Navarone (1961), Cape Fear (1962), Taras Bulba (1963), Kings of the Sun (1963), What a Way to Go (1964), John Goldfarb, Please Come Home (1964), Return from the Ashes (1966), Eye of the Devil (1968), Mackenna's Gold (1968), Before Winter Comes (1969), The Most Dangerous Man in the World (1969), Country Dance (1970), Conquest of the Planet of the Apes (1972), Battle of the Planet of the Apes (1973), Huckleberry Finn (1974), The Reincarnation of Peter Proud (1974), St. Ives (1976), The White Buffalo (1977), The Greek Tycoon (1978), The Passage (1979), Cabo Blanco: Where Legends Are Born (1980), Happy Birthday to Me (1980), 10 to Midnight (1983), The Evil That Men Do (1983), The Ambassador (1984), King Solomon's Mines (1985), Murphy's Law (1986), Firewalker (1986), Death Wish 4: The Crackdown (1987), Messenger of Death (1988), and Kinjite: Forbidden Subjects (1989).

LEIGH, MIKE (b. 1943). Mike Leigh developed an unusual method of preparing his film scripts through extensive periods of improvisation with his actors. This improvisation, however, occurs only in script development, not in the actual shooting of the film, which is carefully structured to heighten the "realism" of the script. This technique involves long periods of rehearsal before shooting that, in the case of *Secrets and Lies* (1996), can take up to five months before the cameras start rolling. In effect, Leigh's style is no less "fictional" than other film directors who mix comedy with melodrama within a quasi-realist aesthetic, although Leigh's prevailing tone is characteristically pessimistic, even in his seemingly optimistic films such as *Topsy-Turvy** (1999). Although Leigh has sometimes, mistakenly, been aligned with the overtly political films directed by Ken Loach,* his work is more in the comic tradition of the Boulting Brothers,* especially their 1950s films such as *Private's Progress* (1956) and *I'm All Right Jack** (1959). Surprisingly, a lesser influence on Leigh has been the British films of the New Wave realism of the late 1950s and early 1960s, although their grey industrial landscapes inspired Leigh to make films in the first place.

Leigh left school at seventeen to train as an actor at the Royal Academy of Dramatic Art. Unlike the older tradition of British actors such as Ralph Richardson* and John Gielgud,* his first love was not the stage, where he spent many years in the 1970s and 1980s, but the cinema. His period working in the theater, which he describes as a "period of exile," followed his first film, *Bleak Moments* (1971), which was based on his play. During this "period of exile,"[3] Leigh made a number of short films at the London Film School and 16mm films for television, such as *Meantime* (1983), which was not released theatrically anywhere in the world except Australia. The success of *High Hopes* in 1989 changed Leigh's fortunes, winning awards at Venice and other film festivals. Although this was Leigh's most overtly political film, he denied that even this anti-Thatcher film was specifically "English" but more concerned with more universal issues, such as "how and when and whether to have babies" and the problems of growing old—issues that emanate from his fascination with the "populist" cycle of living and dying.

In 1993, the release of Leigh's most controversial film, *Naked,* polarized critics with its "rambling" narrative structure following the "adventures" of David Thewlis and his confrontational philosophy of life. The film attracted criticism from feminist and other groups. However, the overall reaction proved to be a positive for Leigh with a BAFTA nomination for Best Film, plus success at Cannes with Leigh winning the Best Director Award and Thewlis Best Actor. *Secrets and Lies* consolidated Leigh's place in the industry with further awards (including a BAFTA Award for Best Film and Screenplay and more success at Cannes) and a wide commercial release. *Career Girls* (1997) was less successful, although Leigh's interpretation of the trials and tribulations of Gilbert and in *Topsy-Turvy* was, to some critics, an unlikely film for Leigh but the film is so imbued by his love for their music, combined with his characteristic scrutiny of their foibles and rituals, to disarm most viewers. The resultant film was irresistible, although a liking for their music, especially *The Mikado,* does help. *Topsy-Turvy* was nominated for the Best British Film and Best Screenplay at the 2000 BAFTA Film Awards and the Best Screenplay Award at the 2000 Academy Awards, following an earlier nomination Leigh received for Best Director and Best Screenplay for *Secrets and Lies* in 1997.

FILMS: Bleak Moments (1971), Meantime (mainly television, 1983), High Hopes (1989), Life Is Sweet (1990), A Sense of History (short, 1992), Naked (1993), Secrets and Lies (1996), Career Girls (1997), Topsy-Turvy (1999), and All or Nothing (2002).

LITTLE FRIEND (Gaumont-British, 1934)—Family drama. *Director:* Berthold Viertel; *Producer:* Robert Stevenson; *Script:* Christopher Isherwood, Margaret Kennedy, Heinrich Fraenkel, and Berthold Viertel, based on the novel *Kleiner Freundin* by Ernst Lothar; *Cinematography:* Gunther Krampf; *Music:* Louis Levy; *Cast:* Matheson Lang (John Hughes), Lydia Sherwood (Helen Hughes), Nova Pilbeam (Felicity Hughes), Arthur Margetson (Hilliard), Jean Cadell (Miss Drew), Jimmy Hanley (Leonard Parry), Cecil Parker (Mason), Finlay Currie (Grove), and Gibb McLaughlin (Thompson).

Between 1934 and 1936, German poet and theater and film director Berthold Viertel completed three films for Gaumont-British (*Little Friend, The Passing of The Third Floor Back,* and *Rhodes of Africa*). After establishing his career in Germany in the 1920s, Viertel moved to Hollywood for a prolific (eight films for Warner Brothers and Paramount), but unhappy period. When Viertel left the United States in 1932 for Europe, his wife Salka Steuermann remained behind as a scriptwriter at MGM. At Gaumont-British, Michael Balcon assigned Robert Stevenson as Viertel's producer for *Little Friend,* together with German exiles such as Heinrich Fraenkel to help with the script, which transposed the setting of the story from Vienna to London. Alfred Junge was the art director and Gunther Krampf the cinematographer.

The narrative basis of *Little Friend* could have been adapted for a Shirley Temple vehicle in Hollywood but in the hands of Christopher Isherwood, Margaret Kennedy, and the German exiles it has a much tougher edge than any comparable Hollywood film during this period. The film begins with Felicity Hughes (Nova Pilbeam in her first screen performance) in bed coming out of a nightmare involving distorted adult voices that transform into the sounds of her parents arguing outside her door. The argument is based on John Hughes's, Felicity's father, concern that his wife Helen is having an affair with Hilliard, an actor friend of Helen's who always refers to Felicity as his "little friend." As the marriage continues to deteriorate, Felicity becomes more and more upset, a condition that is exacerbated by her loneliness, as Helen spends most of her time with Hilliard and her father is preoccupied with business activities. This situation worsens after John leaves the family home.

When Leonard Parry, a working-class youth, rescues Felicity from a potential road accident, he becomes her friend. This allows the film to include class criticism as Felicity's elitist friends reject Leonard because of his working-class background. The situation between John and Helen worsens and Felicity, in an attempt to bring her parents together, visits Hilliard to persuade him to stop seeing Helen. Felicity discovers her mother in Hilliard's bedroom. At the subsequent divorce proceedings, Felicity tries to protect her mother's reputation and when it appears unlikely that her parents will ever reconcile their differences, Felicity attempts suicide by turning on the gas fire in her bedroom. After Leonard and Miss Drew, Felicity's governess, save the young girl, her parents decide to reunite for the sake of their daughter.

Aside from the direct references to Helen's affair with Hilliard, and the confronting climax of the young girl's attempted suicide, *Little Friend* could be classified as a sentimental melodrama. However, Viertel's direction continually pressures the slight narrative material to yield a more significant drama and Viertel, through his use of a very mobile camera, his unorthodox compositions, and the deployment of ingenious lighting patterns, with pinpoint shafts of light directed at specific objects and performers, produces a film that, stylistically, is well in advance of most British films in the early to mid-1930s.

These devices are not employed just for their own sake but form part of Viertel's aim to present the story from a young girl's point of view. Viertel also provides the opportunity for the audience to view the whole story as a nightmare, a figment of Felicity's imagination, with the beginning and end of the film forming the start and end of her dream. Aside from this reading, the final shot, which functions to provide a seemingly happy ending, with Felicity's parents gathered on the young girl's bed to mark their reunion, is, in itself, quite problematic as the scene is characterized by a noticeable lack of enthusiasm from Helen to the return of her husband. Her reluctance to embrace Hughes is obvious, for as she tells Felicity, her love for her husband has diminished due to a number of factors—that he is always at work, that they do not have shared interests (the film stresses that John is a businessman with a businessman's point of view compared to his wife's interest in the arts), and that he is much older than her. *Little Friend* is a superior melodrama and is evidence that Viertel had more to offer the cinema than just two more films for Gaumont-British, the last films he would ever complete.

LITTLE VOICE (A Scala Production, 1998)—Musical/drama. *Director:* Mark Herman; *Producers:* Laurie Borg (coproducer), Nik Powell (executive), Stephen Woolley (executive), Bob Weinstein (coexecutive), Harvey Weinstein (coexecutive), and Paul Webster (coexecutive); *Script:* Mark Herman, based on the play *The Rise and Fall of Little Voice* by Jim Cartwright; *Cinematography:* Andy Collins; *Music:* John Altman; *Cast:* Brenda Blethyn (Mari Hoff), Michael Caine (Ray Say), Jane Horrocks (Laura Hoff—"LV"), Ewan McGregor (Billy), Jim Broadbent (Mr. Boo), Philip Jackson (George), and Annette Badland (Sadie).

This mixture of Grand Guignol, domestic melodrama, and cabaret musical is one of the strangest films to emerge in recent years. Based on Jim Cartwright's stage play, the film opens Cartwright's play without ever dropping its theatrical basis. The characters, particularly Brenda Blethyn as Laura Hoff's ("LV") vicious, selfish, and sad mom, and Michael Caine* (who steals the film, particularly at the climax with his passionate, angry rendition of Roy Orbison's "It's Over"), play to the back stalls with their larger-than-life performances. Jane Horrocks is also outstanding as the pathologically shy LV.

The screen musical, in its traditional form, largely consists of two acts of obstacles and frustration, punctuated by songs and dance performances, leading to the joyous, cathartic, final act that recognizes the young, unknown talent who succeeds brilliantly. Not so in *Little Voice*. Although there is a brief, tentative attempt to establish LV's liberation from her domestic hell as she watches young Billy release his pigeons, the ending is resolutely downbeat. LV's refusal to perform deflates the sense of joy and satisfaction from her one triumphant performance.

LV lives with her mother, Mari, in rooms above a record store that was owned by her late father. LV escapes Mari's insults and sexual adventures by remaining mute much of the time and escaping to her bedroom to listen to recordings of the great standards of the 1940s and 1950s, sung by artists such as Judy Garland, Shirley Bassey, Billie Holiday, and Marilyn Monroe. When Mari brings down-on-his-luck agent Ray Say back to her house for a quick "roll," Say hears LV singing upstairs and quickly recognizes the young girl's talent. Say then recruits local nightclub owner Mr. Boo, and after some difficulty, they hear LV sing "Over the Rainbow." LV's first cabaret performance, however, is a disaster but Say persists and convinces her, via a parable about a bluebird, to perform again. This time LV, imagining she is only performing for her father, sheds her inhibitions and belts out one standard after another to a rapt audience.

Say and Mr. Boo, convinced they have somebody that will bring them a lot of money, invite a London agent to LV's next performance. LV, however, points out that she promised only one performance and retreats to her pathologically shy condition, leaving Say and Mr. Boo to entertain, miserably, the large audience. Say turns on Mari and dashes any hope of marriage and when a fire destroys LV's house, Billy saves the young woman.

LV's transformation in the nightclub, with Jane Horrocks singing many of the great standards, is clearly the film's high point. Unlike the narrative trajectory of the traditional musical, where such plot machinations normally provide a pretext for show-stopping musical numbers, *Little Voice* quickly brings its audience down to earth with its sad, bleak final act. *Little Voice* received the Alexander Korda Award for Best British Film in 1999, Blethyn was nominated for an Oscar at the 1999 Academy Awards for Best British Supporting Actress, and Caine and Horrocks were nominated at the 1999 BAFTA Awards. While Caine won the Golden Globe Award for Best Performance in a Motion Picture Comedy/Musical, Horrocks was nominated for the Best Actress Award for the same category. Caine also won the 1999 London Critics Award for Best Supporting Actor.

LOACH, KEN (b. 1936). Ken Loach is a unique British filmmaker. He has steadfastly rejected classical techniques of filmmaking while maintaining a steady output of film and television programs for forty years—rejecting traditional narrative structures, popular genres, and the use of "stars" to sell a film and develop empathy for his characters. His films also reject the use of simple emotions, such as sentimentality, and devices such as suspense. Instead, he favors developing patterns of meaning through the juxtaposition of sequences and the assimilation of non-professional people with professional actors. Loach normally denies his actors detailed rehearsal periods with a completed script, preferring instead a loose story outline to capture the "spontaneity" of the scene. Loach's main concerns are political and social. Despite the vagaries of the prevailing political climate, he has maintained a consistent a left-wing ethos, beginning with his earliest television productions such as *Up the Junction* (1965) and *Cathy Come Home* (1966).

Graduating from Oxford University, Loach joined the BBC in 1962 at the time when the New Wave British cinema was still in vogue, although he had had little affection for it and, initially, considered it in opposition to the formal and ideological projects he had in mind. Loach felt that this cycle merely exploited the North and the working class for dramatic effect. He was more interested in long-term commitment and social change and he formed a creative partnership with producer Tony Garnett to make political films and television programs. While *Cathy Come Home* exposed the suffering of the urban homeless, *Poor Cow,** his film debut in 1967, lacked the consistent tone of his television work.

This was rectified with his next film, *Kes* (1969), a searing critique on the class limitations of the British education system. Unhappy at home and at school, a young working-class boy (David Bradley) redirects his energies to nursing back to health and training an injured kestrel. Loach refused to sentimentalize the material and his ending offers little real hope for the future. Loach continued his critique of basic social institutions with *Family Life* (1971), transferring his focus from a young boy to the plight of a vulnerable woman exploited by her family and the medical system.

The 1970s and most of the 1980s were difficult for Loach in terms of the cinema so, initially, he worked with Garnett on feature-length films for (BBC) television. After leaving Garnett and the BBC in 1981, he made documentaries for Channel 4, although four of his programs were banned by the channel. The critical success of *Hidden Agenda* in 1990, winning a Special Jury Prize at the 1990 Cannes Film Festival, revived his film career. *Hidden Agenda,* while not diluting Loach's social criticisms concerning the role of security forces in Northern Ireland, was a more "mainstream" film utilizing the conventions of the political thriller.

Since *Hidden Agenda,* Loach's cinema films have included humor (*Riff-Raff* [1991] and *Raining Stones* [1993]) and romance (*My Name Is Joe* [1998]) as a sign of a confident, more financially secure filmmaker extending his social program into different forms. Loach's films have, over a long period, received critical recognition at film festivals—*Kes* was nominated for the 1971 BAFTA Film Award for Best Screenplay, *Raining Stones* was nominated for the Alexander Korda Award for Best British Film in 1994, as was *Land and Freedom* (1995) in 1996 and *My Name Is Joe* in 1999. *Looks and Smiles* (1981) was nominated for the Golden Palm Award at Cannes in 1981, followed by *Hidden Agenda* in 1990, winning a Jury Prize, *Raising Stones* in 1993, *Land and Freedom* in 1995, and *My Name Is Joe* in 1998.

At the time of the screening of *The Navigators* (2001) at the Melbourne Film Festival, Loach told an interviewer that he has not mellowed over the years. "I certainly haven't mellowed in terms of taking the soft option. . . . Out of respect, you have to be as rigorous as you can with yourself, the subject matter and the ideas you're arguing for."[4] As evidenced by *The Navigators* and its examination of the privatisation of Britain's rail network and the effect it has on a group of workers, there is no indication that Loach has repudiated his formal and ideological concerns. The film, based on a script by Rob Dawker, who died of asbestos-induced cancer, foregrounds the rivalry between workers when their job security is threatened by the use of short-term contracts.

FILMS: Poor Cow (1976), Kes (1970), Family Life (1971), Black Jack (1979), The Gamekeeper (1980), Looks and Smiles (1981), Fatherland (1986), Hidden Agenda (1990), Riff-Raff (1992), Raining Stones (1993), Ladybird, Ladybird (1994), Land and Freedom (1995), Carla's Song (1996), My Name Is Joe (1998), Bread and Roses (2000), The Navigators (2001), and Sweet Sixteen (2002).

LOCKWOOD, MARGARET (1916–1990). Margaret Lockwood was the most popular British actress in the mid-1940s following her performance in a series of costume melodramas. In the 1930s, as an ingenue and pallid leading lady in British and two Hollywood films, she made little impact. Similarly, when Lockwood attempted to broaden her range in the 1950s, her film career quickly dissipated. Her popularity was confined to 1940s and, in effect, one genre (costume melodrama).

Born in India, Lockwood made her stage debut at the age of twelve, trained at RADA, with her first film appearance in *Lorna Doone* in 1934. Two films in 1938 gave her career some impetus: *Bank Holiday,* an early film directed by Carol Reed* concerning the experiences of a group of British vacationers, and Alfred Hitchcock's* classic train mystery *The Lady Vanishes,* with Lockwood as Iris Henderson the plucky heroine who, with the assistance of Michael Redgrave and Dame May Whitty, foils a German espionage scheme. She also starred in Reed's *Night Train to Munich* (1940), where scriptwriters Frank Launder* and Sidney Gilliat* reworked many of the elements of their script for *The Lady Vanishes.*

The Stars Look Down (1940), another film directed by Reed (Lockwood subsequently appeared in seven of his films), gave Lockwood the opportunity to play a negative character as Michael Redgrave's* selfish wife. This proved to be a stepping stone for Lockwood as she radically escalated her evil qualities in her next few films, beginning with the willfully wicked Hester Snow in her breakthrough film *The Man in Grey* (1943). In this film, Snow betrays innocent Phyllis Calvert,* seduces Calvert's husband (James Mason*), and dies a violent death. The popularity of *The Man in Grey* was exceeded by her next costume melodrama, *The Wicked Lady* (1945), with Lockwood as Barbara Worth, the bold adventuress who removes every obstacle to her dual life as a highway robber ("I'd rather shoot a man than a horse") and a "respectable" lady of the manor (Lady Skelton).

The Wicked Lady provides a reliable indication of the kind of "evil" manifested by Lockwood in these films and their calculated mixture of sex and sadism. These potentially threatening elements are, however, mitigated by her less-than-threatening persona, and she pales in comparison to the genuine sense of evil generated by the actresses who populated the U.S. film noir during the 1940s (such as Jane Greer, Lizabeth Scott, and Barbara Stanwyck). A more threatening representation of evil came in Lockwood's next film, the film noir *Bedelia* (1946), directed by Lance Comfort* with Lockwood in the title role as the man-hating wife of Ian Hunter, whom she tries to poison after killing her first husband.

*Jassy** (1947) represented a return to costume melodrama with Lockwood as a gypsy girl accused of causing her husband's death in this visually splendid color film. The only notable films after this were *Madness of the Heart* (1949), an excessive melodrama with Lockwood as businesswoman Lydia Garth, and Roy Ward Baker's* anticommunist adventure *Highly Dangerous* (1950), with Lockwood as a British scientist who, with the assistance of newspaperman Dane Clark, gathers espionage information from behind the Iron Curtain. Otherwise, Lockwood's film career quickly disintegrated, especially after *Laughing Anne* (1953) and *Trouble in the Glen* (1953), where she co-starred opposite U.S. actors Orson Welles and Forrest Tucker. Following one of her best performances in *Cast a Dark Shadow* (1955), where she was nominated for the BAFTA Film Award for Best British Actress, Lockwood did not appear in another film for twenty-one years until her appearance as the cruel step-mother in Bryan Forbes's* musical adaptation of the Cinderella story, *The Slipper and the Rose* (1976). Lockwood died in 1990 and her autobiography, *Lucky Star,* was published in 1955.

FILMS: Lorna Doone (1934), The Case of Gabrielle Perry (1935), Some Day (1935), Honours Easy (1935), Man of the Moment (1935), Midshipman Easy (1935), Jury's Evidence (1936), The Amateur Gentleman (1936), Beloved Vagabond (1936), Irish for Luck (1936), The Street Singer (1937), Who's Your Lady Friend? (1937), Dr. Syn (1937), Melody and Romance (1937), Owd Bob (1938), Bank Holiday (1938), The Lady Vanishes (1938), A Girl Must Live (1939), Susannah and the Mounties (1939), Rulers of the Sea (1939), The Stars Look Down (1940), Night Train to Munich (1940), Girl in the News (1940), Quiet Wedding (1941), Alibi (1942), The Man in Grey (1943), Dear Octopus (1943), Give Us the Moon (1944), Love Story (1944), A Place of One's Own (1945), I'll Be Your Sweetheart (1945), The Wicked Lady (1945), Bedalia (1946), Hungry Hill (1946), Jassy (1947), The White Unicorn (1947), Look before You Love (1948), Cardboard Cavalier (1949), Madness of the Heart (1949), Highly Dangerous (1950), Trent's Last Case (1952), Laughing Anne (1953), Trouble in the Glen (1954), Cast a Dark Shadow (1955), and The Slipper and the Rose (1976).

THE LODGER (Gainsborough, 1926)—Drama. *Director:* Alfred Hitchcock; *Producers:* Michael Balcon and Carlyle Blackwell Sr.; *Script:* Alfred Hitchcock and Eliot Stannard, based on the novel by Marie Belloc Lowndes; *Cinematography:* Baron Ventimiglia; *Cast:* Ivor Novello (Jonathan Drew), Jane Tripp (Daisy Bunting), Malcom Keen (Joe Betts), Marie Ault (Mrs. Bunting), and Arthur Chesney (Mr. Bunting).

Alfred Hitchcock* maintained that the success of *The Lodger* was crucial to the continuation of his career in the British film industry after three previous films failed to make much impact at the box office. *The Lodger* contains many of the traits that characterized Hitchcock's later films, including his ability to generate and maintain a pervasive sense of unease in the audience. This, even in 1926, was the product of his visual mastery of the medium with a carefully planned shooting pattern that regularly inserted point-of-view shots into the overall system. *The Lodger* was characterized by critics as a more expressionistic example of Hitchcock's cinema, influenced by his experience in Germany, but many of the touches found in this film were repeated, in different ways, and in subsequent films—even the famous image of Jonathan Drew pacing his room as seen through a floor made of thick, transparent glass.

When a suspicious stranger, Jonathan Drew, suddenly arrives at the Bunting household, following a series of murders in surrounding neighborhoods, suspicion gradually falls on the newcomer. Drew's sense of alienation is heightened by the jealous behavior of a local police detective, Joe Betts, who resents Drew's interest in his girlfriend Daisy Bunting. The bulk of *The Lodger*'s narrative is concerned with a carefully orchestrated cat-and-mouse game as to Drew's guilt and it is not until the film's final moments, when Drew tells Daisy why he came to this neighborhood, to catch the serial killer and avenge the murder of his sister, that he is seen to be innocent.

Drew's habit of leaving the house each night arouses the suspicions of Betts and Mrs. Bunting. Subsequently, he is arrested leading to a spectacular climax. After Drew escapes from police custody, he is rendered immobile when he becomes imprisoned on an iron fence, with his handcuffs caught in the iron spokes, as a vengeful mob, believing that Drew is the killer, beat his body with their fists. Finally, Drew is rescued by Betts after the detective learns that the real killer has been arrested. This happy ending represents a change from the ending in the novel and the ending used in subsequent versions of this story in 1932, 1944, and 1953.

THE LONELINESS OF THE LONG DISTANCE RUNNER (Woodfall Films, 1962)—Social drama. *Director:* Tony Richardson; *Producer:* Tony Richardson; *Script:* Alan Sillitoe, based on his novella; *Cinematography:* Walter Lassally; *Music:* John Addison; *Cast:* Tom Courtenay (Colin Smith), Michael Redgrave (Governor), James Bolan (Mike), Avis Bunnage (Mrs. Smith), Alec McCowen (Brown), Topsy Jane (Audrey), Julia Foster (Gladys), Joe Robinson (Roach), Dervis Ward (Detective), Philip Martin (Stacy), John Thaw (Bosworth), and James Fox (Ranley School Runner).

Over the years, Tony Richardson* has had a difficult time with critics, but in *The Loneliness of the Long Distance Runner* one cannot question the commitment and intensity of the film's anger directed at those institutional forces designed to subjugate working-class youths like Colin Smith. Although Richardson can be criticized for his jumble of French New Wave influences, particularly the speeded-up action, the film never deviates from its social views that, at times, border on a form of nihilism. For example, Smith espouses views that for working-class youths like him there is little point in "slaving my guts out for the bosses to get all the profits." Few mainstream films, particularly today, have the commercial courage to present such a confronting film devoid of sentimentality and compromise.

Colin Smith, a stubborn eighteen year old, is sent to Ruxton Towers after robbing a baker's shop with close friend Mike. Ruxton Towers represents a microcosm of English life, designed to produce capitalist (low-wage) fodder by a governor interested in only using the institution to further his ambitions and ego. Elementary trade skills, manual labor, and sport prevail and when the governor recognizes Smith's athletic ability, he favors him within the institution in the hope that the youth can win a prestigious athletics long-distance race against a neighboring public school.

Smith, initially, goes along with the governor's hopes, only to deny him ultimate victory after seemingly defeating his competition. When Smith stops a few meters from the finishing line, a close-up of Smith's triumphant smile is crosscut with a close-up of the governor's face and his realization that Smith has not only sabotaged the race, but also rejected the values perpetuated at Ruxton Towers. The film's epilogue shows the price paid by Smith as the governor walks through the shed where Smith and the other boys dismantle gas masks. This time the governor refuses to recognize Smith as the camera finally rests on the barren, desolate image of a gas mask.

The Loneliness of the Long Distance Runner provides sufficient motivation for Smith's actions in its many flashbacks and jump cuts—all detailing the conditions and compromises expected of Smith and other working-class youths. A weekend with Mike and two girls at the beach at Skegness provides their only escape that, the film shows, is also illusory as both couples resent returning to their miserable prospects in urban Nottingham. Frequently, Smith's mind wanders back to the past during his long training session in the woods that, in turn, offer another (illusory) sense of freedom. Walter Lassally's camera effectively conveys a world without real hope. Tom Courtenay's debut won him the Most Promising Newcomer Award at the 1963 BAFTA Film Awards.

THE LONG MEMORY (Rank, 1952)—Film noir/melodrama. *Director:* Robert Hamer; *Producer:* Hugh Stewart; *Script:* Frank Harvey, based on the novel by Howard Clewes; *Cinematography:* Harry Waxman; *Music:* William Alwyn; *Cast:* John Mills (Phillip Davidson), John McCallum (Superintendent Bob Lowther), Elizabeth Sellars (Fay Lowther), Eva Bergh (Ilse), Geoffrey Keen (Craig), John Chandos (Boyd), John Slater (Pewsey), Thora Hird (Mrs. Pewsey), Vida Hope (Alice Gedge), John Horseley (Bletchley), Laurence Naismith (Hasbury), Michael Martin Harvey (Jackson), Mary Mackenzie (Gladys), and Harold Lang (Boyd's Chauffeur).

Phillip Davidson leaves prison after serving twelve years for a murder he did not commit. He was convicted primarily due to the testimony of brain-damaged boxer Pewsey and Fay, Davidson's ex-girlfriend, who lied to protect her father at the trial. Davidson, bent on revenge, moves into a cabin on an abandoned barge on the coast of Kent. The dramatic power of the film is conveyed through director Robert Hamer's* ability to draw a close association between the bleak imagery of this desolate area, with its sparse, windblown vegetation, poverty-ridden shacks, and abandoned boats and Davidson's strong sense of alienation from traditional society. "Home" has never been depicted in such a stark manner.

Davidson's desire for revenge takes him to London, where Fay now lives with her husband, Superintendent Bob Lowther. Davidson eventually learns that the man he supposedly killed, Boyd, is alive and prosperous, operating his black market activities on the Thames. Davidson's only real ally in this story of redemption and regeneration is a displaced woman, Ilse, who comes to live with him after he rescues her from a rape attack. Although Davidson, initially, wants nothing to do with Ilse, her belief in his innate goodness and her devotion to him gradually tempers his obsession for revenge.

Finally, he decides that it "is not worth it." Although there is a perfunctory climax, with Boyd attempting to kill Davidson, the focus of *The Long Memory* resides in Davidson's (and Ilse's) sense of alienation and estrangement—and the many ways the film conveys the breakdown of traditional and/or populist values and the prejudicial role of basic institutions, such as the media and the justice system. Superintendent Lowther, appointed to uphold the law, lives with Fay, a woman that he knows is guilty of perjury. Hamer, in a telling scene, intercuts the bedroom conversation between Lowther and Fay, shown isolated in their single beds, with an angled shot of Davidson and Ilse, with their heads nearly touching, in their cabin at night. While the representatives of society (Lowther and Fay) are presented as repressed and anxious, society's outcasts (Ilse and Davidson) are shown to be intimate and open.

Ilse and Davidson function as parallel characters within the film—both have been unjustly treated. Ilse, as a victim of war ("Our village was burned. What happened to my father and mother I never knew. Since then I've never had a place to be where I was happy."), shows Davidson how to recover ("Bad things have happened to me but I'm not bad."). After Boyd's death and Lowther's apology to Davidson for his years in prison, Ilse tells the policeman that Davidson "does not need anything that you can do. He just needs to be alone" as the two wounded lovers retreat back to their isolated cabin on the coast of Kent. Although *The Long Memory* is a story of regeneration, it is not a story of assimilation as the two lovers choose to remain estranged from society.

LOSEY, JOSEPH (1909–1984). In surveys of Joseph Losey's career, it is reasonably common for his films created during his Hollywood period, from *The Boy with Green Hair* in 1947 to *M* (1951), and his early films in England—directed under pseudonyms such as Victor Hanbury (for *The Sleeping Tiger* [1954]) and Joseph Walton (for *Intimate Stranger* [1956])—to be dismissed as "minor" works. Arguably, it is Losey's bloated films in the late 1960s, such as *Modesty Blaise* (1966), *Boom* (1968), and *Secret Ceremony* (1968), that should be relegated to the category of "minor works." Born in La Crosse, Wisconsin, Losey entered the entertainment industry via live presentations at the Radio City Music Hall before drifting into New Deal Theatre projects and film classes with Eisenstein in Moscow. His first films were industrial shorts before working as a staff director on MGM's "Crime Does Not Pay" series.

After war service, Losey directed stage productions in Hollywood, including a production of Bertold Brecht's *Galileo* (starring Charles Laughton) in 1947. That same year he directed his first feature film for RKO, the socially conscious *The Boy with Green Hair,* which was singled out by the House Committee on Un-American Activities (HUAC) for its pacifist sentiments. This film, with Dean Stockwell as the boy who is persecuted because of the color of his hair, assimilates a "progressive" ideology within a traditional Hollywood narrative structure. Similarly, *The Lawless* (1949), a melodrama, focuses on the prejudicial treatment of Mexican American fruit pickers in southern California. Another Hollywood film, *The Prowler,* starring Van Heflin as a man who cannot control his destructive desires, established a link between Losey in the early 1950s and the complex reworking of this theme in films such as *The Servant* (1963) and *Accident** (1967).

While Losey was directing *Stranger on the Prowl* in 1951 in Italy, he was named by scriptwriter Leo Townsend, who was testifying before HUAC, as a member of the Communist Party and Losey fled to England. With the support of Dirk Bogarde,* who was to become an integral part of Losey's career in the 1960s, Losey directed the domestic melodrama *The Sleeping Tiger,* involving the betrayal of Alexander Knox by his wife (Alexis Smith) and her young lover (Bogarde). This film was not only significant in reestablishing Losey's film career, but also in providing Bogarde with one of his best roles in the 1950s as a youth who betrays his mentor by insinuating himself in the affections of his wife.

Following the disappointment of *The Gypsy and the Gentleman* (1958), after which Rank terminated his contract, Losey directed a pair of innovative crime thrillers: *Blind Date* (1959) and *The Criminal** (1960), both starring Stanley Baker.* These two films are not only superior genre films; they also mark a stylistic transition between Losey's generic films of the 1950s and his shift to the conventions of the art-cinema and an overt concern with more confronting themes such as repression and guilt. This change is evident in *Eva* (1962) with Baker in a perverse relationship with his mistress (Jeanne Moreau) and his wife (Virna Lisi), followed by his greatest film, *The Servant,* with James Fox in an even more perverse relationship with his servant (Bogarde) and Bogarde's lover (Sarah Miles).

Losey worked with Bogarde again (effectively) in *King and Country* (1964) and the Harold Pinter scripted *Accident,* a complex rendering of a morally problematic academic milieu involving Bogarde and two of his students (Michael York and Delphine Seyrig). These films highlight Losey's fascination with the inequities of the British class system, a theme he returned to with a vengeance in *The Go-Between* (1971), the tragic story of a boy who mediates between a selfish aristocrat (Julie Christie*) and a love-stricken farmer (Alan Bates*). Losey left Britain in the 1970s for France, but he returned for his final film, a disappointing film adaptation of the stage play *Steaming* (1984).

Losey, who died in 1984, won the Golden Palm for *The Go-Between* at the 1971 Cannes Film Festival. He was nominated for Best Direction for this film at the 1972 BAFTA Film Awards. Earlier, in 1968, *Accident* was nominated for Best British Film at the BAFTA Awards and won the Grand Jury Prize at the 1967 Cannes Film Festival. *The Servant* was nominated at the 1963 BAFTA Film Awards and *Mr. Klein* (1976) won a Best Director Award for Losey at the 1977 Cesar Awards in France.

FILMS: Pete Roleum and His Cousins (short, 1939), A Child Went Forth (short, 1941), Youth Gets a Break (short, 1941), A Gun in His Hand (short, 1945), The Boy with Green Hair (1948), The Lawless (1949), The Prowler (1950), M (1951), The Big Night (1951), Stranger on the Prowl (1952), The Sleeping Tiger (1954), A Man on the Beach (1955), The Intimate Stranger (1956), Time without Pity (1957), The Gypsy and the Gentleman (1958), Blind Date (1959), The Criminal (1960), The Damned (1961), Eva (1962), The Servant (1963), King and Country (1964), Modesty Blaise (1966), Accident (1967), Boom (1968), Secret Ceremony (1968), Figures in a Landscape (1970), The Go-Between (1971), The Assassination of Trotsky (1972), A Doll's House (1973), Galileo (1974), The Romantic Englishwoman (1975), Mr. Klein (1976), Les Routes du Sud (1978), Don Giovanni (1979), La Truite (1982), and Steaming (1984).

LOST (Rank, 1955)—Thriller. *Director:* Guy Green; *Producer:* Vivian Cox; *Script:* Janet Green; *Cinematography:* Harry Waxman; *Music:* Benjamin Frankel; *Cast:* David Farrar (Inspector Craig), David Knight (Lee Cochrane), Julia Arnall (Sue Cochrane), Anthony Oliver (Sergeant Lyel), Meredith Edwards (Sergeant Davies), Eleanor Summerfield (Sergeant Cook), Everley Gregg (Viscountess), Marjorie Rhodes (Mrs. Jeffries), and Ann Turner (Mrs. Robey).

Guy Green, one of the top cinematographers in the British cinema during the second half of the 1940s, worked on many of David Lean's* films, including *Great Expectations** (1946), *The Passionate Friends** (1949), and *Madeleine** (1950). *Lost* was his third film as a director and it is an unpretentious thriller based on the kidnapping of a young child. The film focuses almost entirely on the reactions of the various parties, such as the distressed parents, the harassed police, and an intrusive media. The person responsible for kidnapping the child, a psychologically disturbed mother who recently lost her own baby, only enters the film near the end.

One of the virtues of *Lost* is Janet Green's clever script, which continually takes the parents and police into dead ends that, nevertheless, appear logical at the time. In fact, it is one of the seemingly innocuous clues introduced early in the film, the torn page of a paperback thriller found near the boy's baby carriage, that provides the link to the kidnapper's identity and whereabouts. The almost single-minded focus of the script on the kidnapping, and its ramifications, gradually produces an escalation of tension as the police and parents fear that the child may have been murdered. In a film that largely eschews physical thrills, the introduction of a bogus blackmail operation near the end provides a prelude to the film's climax involving the distressed kidnapper as she threatens to kill the baby and herself by jumping off a cliff.

Mostly, the narrative is not diverted by extraneous personal information concerning the police and their private lives, except as it details the effect the kidnapping has on the baby's parent's, Lee and Sue Cochrane. Other diversions emphasize that the police not only have to deal with this investigation, but also with more routine matters, such as a case of bigamy involving the redoubtable Marjorie Rhodes (Mrs. Jeffries).

NOTES

1. See McFarlane, *An Autobiography of British Cinema,* p. 47.
2. See S. Chibnall, *J. Lee Thompson,* Manchester, Manchester University Press, 2000, pp. 50–51.
3. McFarlane, *An Autobiography of British Cinema,* p. 359.
4. J. Schembri, "Man of the People," *The Age, July 26, 2002, p. 3.*

M

MACKENDRICK, ALEXANDER (1912–1992). One of the most talented British directors, Alexander Mackendrick's film output was limited, with a number of aborted projects. Virtually all of his films are worthy of repeat viewings. Born in the United States to Scottish parents, Mackendrick developed his filmmaking skills working on propaganda shorts for the Ministry of Information during World War II before joining Ealing as a screenwriter and, subsequently, as a director of five films for the studio, beginning with the comedy *Whisky Galore!* (1949). This film established Mackendrick's ability to subvert expectations and present a less comfortable view of communal life in Britain than most other films from Ealing. *The Man in the White Suit** (1951) encapsulates his non-sentimental worldview with its critique of both unions and employers while refusing to sentimentalize his protagonist.

The difference between the general perception of the "warm-hearted Ealing ethos" and Mackendrick's films is most apparent in his final film for the studio, *The Ladykillers** (1955), a masterpiece depicting the subjugation of Alec Guinness's* gang to the Victorian world of Mrs. Wilberforce and her lopsided house in St. Pancras. After this film, Mackendrick left England for Hollywood and his greatest film, the film noir masterpiece *Sweet Smell of Success* (1957), which demonstrated not only that Tony Curtis could act, but also provided Burt Lancaster with one of his greatest roles as J. J. Hunsecker, the sadistically powerful gossip columnist with the ability to destroy careers. Unfortunately, this film, with its clear resonance to the pernicious effects of the blacklist and the career-destroying activities of the House Committee on Un-American Activities in the 1950s, was not a commercial success and it was some years before it was recognized as a masterpiece.

As the *Sweet Smell of Success* did not provide the necessary fillip for Mackendrick's career in the tough Hollywood market, he returned to Britain only to discover that things were not any better. He only completed three more films before he died—*Sammy Going South* (1963), which was filmed in Africa, the bittersweet *A High Wind in Jamaica* (1965), with Anthony Quinn giving one of his best performances as a pirate, and *Don't Make Waves* (1967), one of the few Tony Curtis comedies of any significance. This last one was a sharp satire on Californian lifestyles. Mackendrick also worked, uncredited, on the black comedy *Oh Dad, Poor Dad, Mama's Hung You in the Closet and I'm Feeling So Sad* (1967), starring Rosalind Russell and Robert Morse.

After this film, Mackendrick left the industry for a position teaching film at the Californian Institute of the Arts, which he held nearly to his death in 1993. Mackendrick was nominated, with Roger MacDougall and John Dighton, for the Best Screenplay Award at the 1953 Academy Awards for *The Man in the White Suit*. He won the Special Jury Prize at the 1952 Venice Film Festival for *Mandy* (1952).

FILMS: Kitchen Waste (short, 1942), Contraries (short, 1943), Whisky Galore! (1949), The Man in the White Suit (1951), Mandy (1952), The "Maggie" (1953), The Ladykillers (1955), Sweet Smell of Success (1957), Sammy Going South (1963), A High Wind in Jamaica (1965), and Don't Make Waves (1967).

MADELEINE (Cineguild, 1950)—Crime/film noir. *Director:* David Lean; *Producer:* Stanley Haynes; *Script:* Stanley Haynes and Nicholas Phipps; *Cinematography:* Guy Green; *Music:* William Alwyn; *Cast:* Ann Todd (Madeleine Smith), Norman Wooland (William Minnoch), Ivan Desny (Emile L'Anglier), Leslie Banks (James Smith), Barbara Everest (Mrs. Smith), Elizabeth Sellars (Christina), Patricia Raine (Bessie Smith), Eugene Deckers (Thuau), Andre Morell (Defending Counsel), Barry Jones (Prosecuting Counsel), Ivor Barnard (Mr. Murdoch), and Jean Cadell (Mrs. Jenkins).

At the end of the 1940s, David Lean* made two films with his then-wife Ann Todd* (the other one was *The Passionate Friends** [1948]) and although these films failed to match the commercial success of Lean's earlier films, such as *Brief Encounter** (1945) and *Great Expectations** (1946), *Madeleine* is one of his finest films. Lean's precise, almost clinical, visual style is ideally suited to the film's emotionally complex subject matter and the director cleverly exploits the recessive screen persona of Todd as the enigmatic Madeleine Smith. Cinematographer Guy Green, at the request of Lean, transformed his normal desire to achieve a "realistic look" into a more expressionistic lighting style for Todd, emphasizing her cheek bones through a carefully positioned overhead lighting pattern, similar to the style devised by Josef von Sternberg for Marlene Dietrich in her Paramount films in the early 1930s (see, particularly, *The Devil Is a Woman* [1935]).

Todd, who began in the British cinema in 1932, enjoyed great success as the masochistic, emotionally fragile pianist Francesca in *The Seventh Veil** (1945) and her performance as Madeleine Smith cleverly exploits the submissive mannerisms of the earlier film, with a number of scenes visually emphasizing her vulnerability before the two, seemingly dominant, males in her life—her lover Emile L'Anglier and her father James Smith. However, Madeleine is much more than a submissive Scottish lady torn between the forbidden pleasures offered by Emile and the social demands of Victorian society. Madeleine subtly resists the intense pressure from her father to marry the wealthy, but dull, William Minnoch as she tries to both live within the repressions imposed by Victorian society while indulging her sexual desire for Emile. After Emile rejects Madeleine's offer to run away and get married, she realizes that her French lover is more interested in her family's social position and wealth than in marriage to her.

Emile's rejection follows the sexual consummation of their relationship and Lean leaves little doubt as to their sexual behavior through his judicious insertion of a passionate dance sequence at a highland festival as Madeleine and Emile engage in foreplay. When Madeleine falls over in a dark forest, and looks up with anticipation at Emile towering over her, Lean cuts to the frenzy of the dancers performing in the village below. Following the purchase of arsenic by Madeleine from a local chemist, Emile suffers two bouts of poisoning with the last one being fatal. Madeleine is tried for murder and the jury finds the charge "not proven." The film concludes with a voice-over pointing out that she is deemed neither innocent or guilty—Lean's final close-up of Madeleine's sly smile as she leaves the court leaves little doubt as to her guilt.

Lean, together with scriptwriters Stanley Haynes and Nicholas Phipps, transformed a real court case, which took place in Glasgow in 1857, into a study of the destructive power of Victorian patriarchy. The film makes is quite clear that the real motivation for Madeleine's actions emanate from James's authoritarian control over his family, in particular, the (lack of) rights accorded to women. The repression of female desire leads to betrayal that culminates in murder. The scenes between Todd and Leslie Banks* are both revealing and powerful as the patriarch tries to impose his will on Madeleine. She, in turn, subverts his authority.

THE MAN IN GREY (Gainsborough, 1943)—Melodrama. *Director:* Leslie Arliss; *Producer:* Edward Black; *Script:* Margaret Kennedy, Doreen Kennedy, and Leslie Arliss, based on the novel by Lady Eleanor Smith; *Cinematography:* Arthur Crabtree; *Music:* Cedric Mallabey; *Cast:* Margaret Lockwood (Hesther Snow), James Mason (Marquis of Rohan), Phyllis Calvert (Clarissa Richmond), Stewart Granger (Peter Rokeby/Swinton Rokeby), Helen Haye (Lady Rohan), Raymond Lovell (Prince Regent), Martita Hunt (Miss Patchett), and Beatrice Varley (Gypsy).

The Man in Grey elevated Stewart Granger,* James Mason,* and Phyllis Calvert* into the top rank of British stars while consolidating the reputation of Margaret Lockwood* in the mid-1940s. Although the story in *The Man in Grey* stretches back from the early 1940s to the Regency period, history provides only a cursory context for the film's dominant dramatic structure, the elemental basis of all melodrama involving the subjugation of virtue and its ultimate liberation. This was dependent on a clear moral dichotomy that is found in this film on many levels—from the fair-headed representation of innocence (Calvert's Clarissa Richmond), to Lockwood's dark-haired Hesther Snow, who, like most melodramatic villains, betrays the heroine's trust after insinuating herself into her world.

Mason's brooding, sadistic Marquis of Rohan is contrasted by the virtuous Swinton Rokeby. Once established, these stereotypes do not develop or change within the course of the story—Hesther and Rohan are as evil at the end as they are at the start when Hesther befriends Clarissa at Miss Patchett's school for girls. Later, Hesther, having fallen on hard times, accepts Clarissa's offer of assistance and becomes her companion. Clarissa, in a loveless marriage with Rohan, is desperate for a companion and Hesther repays Clarissa's trust by becoming Rohan's mistress. Rohan, who despises his wife's innocence, is attracted by Hesther's ruthless behavior.

This villainy is counterbalanced by the heroic Rokeby, the Jamaican-born dispossessed landowner, who accepts a position as the librarian on the Rohan estate and falls in love with Clarissa. The lovers are doomed as Rokeby, desperate to regain his inheritance in the West Indies, leaves England after promising to come back to Clarissa once he regains his land. Clarissa falls ill in the interim period and Hesther eventually kills her. Rohan, who lives by the family motto "Who dishonors us dies," then takes his cane and beats Hesther to death.

A key ingredient in classic melodrama is the intensity of the catharsis generated by the climax when virtue finally overcomes evil. This is evident with Rohan's graphic murder of Hesther. Yet, Rohan survives and only in the film's epilogue, set in the 1940s, does innocence achieve complete liberation as Clarissa is finally reunited with Rokeby—in the form of a symbolic unification between their descendants.

The Breen Office (Production Code Administration) in the United States objected to *The Man in Grey* because the requisite compensating moral values were not sufficiently dramatized in the film.[1] This moral ambivalence was due, in part, to the film's ending, with the lack of retribution for Rohan, but it also emanated from the strong (female) audience appeal for Mason's sensual, sadistic Rohan. Rohan, devoid of normal heroic qualities, struck a chord with audiences in the 1940s and Mason's screen persona, introduced prior to *The Man in Grey* with his authoritarian "hero" in *The Night Has Eyes** (1942), was fixed in the imagination of the British public until he left England for Hollywood after the *Odd Man Out* (1947).

THE MAN IN THE WHITE SUIT (Ealing, 1951)—Comedy. *Director:* Alexander Mackendrick; *Producers:* Michael Balcon and Sidney Cole (associate); *Script:* John Dighton, Alexander Mackendrick, and Roger MacDougall, based on MacDougall's play; *Cinematography:* Douglas Slocombe; *Music:* Benjamin Frankel; *Cast:* Alec Guinness (Sidney Stratton), Joan Greenwood (Daphne Birnley), Cecil Parker (Alan Birnley), Michael Gough (Michael Corland), Ernest Thesiger (Sir John Kierlaw), Howard Marion Crawford (Cranford), Henry Mollison (Hoskins), Vida Hope (Bertha), Patric Doonan (Frank), Duncan Lamont (Harry), Colin Gordon (Hill), Miles Matheson (the Tailor), Mandy Miller (Gladdie), and Judith Furse (Nurse Gamage).

While much of the credit for *The Man in the White Suit* must go to Alec Guinness,* as the hapless inventor Sidney Stratton, and director Alexander Mackendrick,* credit must also go to scriptwriter John Dighton. Two years earlier, Dighton coscripted with Robert Hamer* *Kind Hearts and Coronets.* * Both films share a common element—a tough, unsentimental edge that was not found in most other Ealing comedies. In *The Man in the White Suit,* this "edge" is a social critique.

The setting for Mackendrick and Dighton's parable is an unnamed northern industrial town with competing textile factories. When the unauthorized experiments of young Sidney Stratton are discovered, he is dismissed by the Corland mill, his seventh dismissal since his ejection from Cambridge University. Through sheer luck, Stratton is able to ingratiate himself into the research facilities at the Birnley mill, where he continues his (unauthorized) work. After being discovered working on his own project to develop a new type of cloth, Stratton is ejected from the mill and the research manager pours Sidney's discovery down the drain. Sidney is determined to tell the mill owner what he has discovered and in a series of farcical scenes he attempts to get into Birnley's mansion as the butler repeatedly ejects him. Within the house, Birnley is desperately trying to find the man responsible (Stratton) for the expenditure blowout in the research department.

Stratton befriends Birnley's daughter Daphne and she convinces her father that Sidney is well on the way to discovering a material that does not wear out and is totally stain resistant. Birnley, motivated only by greed, agrees to finance Stratton's experiments. After a series of explosions, Sidney produces his miracle fabric, which is made up into a luminous white suit. However, Corland and the other mill owners bring in the industry's aging patriarch, Sir John Kierlaw, to persuade Birnley and Stratton that the fabric must never be produced as it would destroy the economic foundation of the industry. The local union agrees with this stand and Stratton, with only Daphne's support, is chased throughout the town until it discovers that the material is not stable and Sidney is left standing in the street at night clothed only in his underwear as the mob tears his white suit to shreds.

The Man in the White Suit, which was Mackendrick's and Guinness's favorite film, is a rich parable critical of industry practices and the alienation of science from society. The film also repudiated the often-sentimental communal populism espoused by other Ealing films. While Capital and Labor form an uneasy alliance in *The Man in the White Suit,* it is not based on communal idealism, only self-interest. The film is more intelligent than just this and does not present an easy polarization of the drama into a simple victim (Stratton) and villain (unions and mill owners) dichotomy—despite Daphne's reference to Sidney's visual status as a "knight in shining armor" when he first appears before her in his luminous white suit.

Sidney is not beyond criticism as to his single-minded obsession with science. This is made transparent late in the film when, trying to evade the mob, he asks his former landlady, Mrs. Watson, for help. Sidney is astonished when she refuses: "Why can't you scientists leave things alone? What's to become of my bit of washing when there is no washing to do?" At this admonishment Sidney's will to continue with his fabric dissipates. He becomes aware, for the first time, that his discovery will only hurt vulnerable people in society, such as Mrs. Watson, who is dependent on washing other people's dirty clothes to make ends meet. As his willpower disintegrates, so does the fabric in his suit.

The film's final scene, narrated by Birnley, is optimistic that the mill owners have seen the last of Stratton as he walks away from the mill, seemingly defeated. However, in a clever, subversive touch, the film's sound track offers a more problematic ending as the familiar bubbling sounds of Stratton's fabric experiment is heard over the music—indicating that, perhaps, Sidney is not finished with them yet.

When the mill owners, led by the eagle-like Kierlaw, fail to bribe or physically intimidate Stratton, they seize on Daphne's friendship with Stratton as a way of repressing his invention. When Daphne's fiancé, Michael Corland, joins in with Kierlaw and the other owners eager to push Daphne into using her sexual power to change Sidney's mind ("you're a very attractive woman"), she humiliates the mill owners by forcing them to openly state what they have in mind (Daphne: "I'm not experienced in these matters, but I've always understood this work was very well paid"). When the others are reluctant to spell it out in monetary terms, the evil Kierlaw welcomes Daphne's openness and suggests £2,000. Daphne raises the offer to £5,000, making explicit the association between capitalism and prostitution where everything, ultimately, has a price.

The Man in the White Suit was nominated for the Best British Film at the 1952 BAFTA Awards. Dighton, Mackendrick, and Roger MacDougall were also nominated at the 1953 Academy Awards for their script.

THE MAN WHO COULD WORK MIRACLES (London Films, 1936)—Fantasy. *Director:* Lothar Mendes; *Producer:* Alexander Korda; *Script:* H. G. Wells, based on his short story *The Man Who Had to Sing; Cinematography:* Harold Rosin; *Music:* Mischa Spoliansky; *Cast:* Roland Young (George McWhirter Fotheringay), Ralph Richardson (Colonel Winstanley), Edward Chapman (Major Grigsby), Ernest Thesiger (Mr. Maydig), Joan Gardner (Ada Price), Sophie Stewart (Maggie Hooper), George Zucco (Moody), and George Sanders (Indifference).

In the mid-1930s, Alexander Korda's* London Films produced two science fiction/fantasy films: *Things to Come* (1936) and the more modest *The Man Who Could Work Miracles,* both scripted by H. G. Wells from his stories. In the latter, three Gods give superhuman powers to George McWhirter Fotheringay, an ordinary draper's assistant, as a test of the maturity and development of the human race. Fotheringay, initially, astounds the locals, and himself, with his ability to make a lamp turn upside down, heal a woman's arm, and clean up the draper's shop via his newly acquired magical powers. When he accidentally sets a rose tree on a constable, he is forced to send the policeman to hell, and then to San Francisco.

Fotheringay discovers that the only thing he cannot do is change human emotions. After he fails to make Ada Price fall in love with him, the film becomes more philosophical as Fotheringay is forced to consider larger issues, such as human greed and his greedy employer's desire to monopolize wealth. Major Grigsby offers him £3,000 a year for the exclusive rights to his powers. A more humane perspective is presented through Mr. Maydig's plea to have Fotheringay eradicate disease, war, and poverty. This brings Fotheringay into conflict with the establishment, represented by Colonel Winstanley. After Fotheringay explains that his (lower-middle and working) class wants change, Winstanley makes it clear that the establishment has a vested interest in retaining the status quo and the elderly colonel (played by thirty-five-year-old Ralph Richardson* in a rich cameo performance) attempts to kill Fotheringay. Finally, Fotheringay decides that he is going to act out of self-interest and he creates a palace, populated by the most the world's wisest and most powerful people. Ultimately, Fotheringay is disappointed in their resistance to his demand for a new world order and he throws the earth off its axis. It is left to the Gods to re-establish order.

The Man Who Could Work Miracles was produced at Korda's London Films with its European expertise and interests. The film was only a mediocre success at the British box office.

MANUELA (British Lion, 1957)—Romantic melodrama. *Director:* Guy Hamilton; *Producer:* Ivan Foxwell; *Script:* William Woods, Ivan Foxwell, and Guy Hamilton, based on the novel by William Woods; *Cinematography:* Otto Heller; *Music:* William Alwyn; *Cast:* Trevor Howard (James Prothero), Elsa Martinelli (Manuela Hunt), Pedro Armendariz (Mario Constanza), Donald Pleasance (Evans), Jack MacGowran (Tommy), Leslie Weston (Bleloch), Peter Illing (Agent), Max Butterfield (Bliss), and Harold Kasket (Pereira).

Manuela is an unlikely British film, particularly as it was produced during a period when the British cinema rarely focused on the power and significance of sex. Director Guy Hamilton, who later directed some of the most commercially successful James Bond films (*Goldfinger* [1964] and *Diamonds Are Forever* [1971]), suggested that *Manuela* was "a very French film in mood" and that it "was fairly strong meat and had the censors right on edge."[2] In some ways, it is similar to Roy Ward Baker's* *Passage Home* (1955), where the presence of Diane Cilento on a steamer crossing from South America to England provokes tension among the all-male crew. Cilento's effect is greatest on Peter Finch's* authoritarian captain, who finally snaps and tries to force himself on her. The most notable difference between *Passage Home* and *Manuela* is that in the latter film Elsa Martinelli's Manuela, who is only seventeen years old in the film, offers herself to the alcoholic forty-three-year-old Captain Prothero (Trevor Howard*), who readily succumbs to her beauty.

Hamilton also argues that *Manuela* is a morality play that was "unusually direct (for a British film) about the destructive power of sexuality."[3] The meaning of the film is not as clear as he suggests, as its warning can be interpreted in a number of ways. Manuela is brought aboard Prothero's ship when it is docked in South America by sailor Mario Constanza after she offers to have sexual intercourse with him if he smuggles her aboard. Manuela later refuses to fulfill her part of the bargain. When she is discovered by the captain, he initially is outraged and plans to dump both Constanza and Manuela on a nearby island. However, he changes his mind and spends the next few days with Manuela in his cabin.

Manuela has a strong effect on Prothero, and Hamilton dramatizes his central theme concerning the destructive effect of sex through a fire on the ship. As Prothero neglects his duties, the fire eventually forces him to abandon ship. The eruption of the fire parallels the eruption of Prothero's sexual appetite, leading to the loss of his ship. Conversely, the film also shows the positive effect Manuela has on the captain. Prothero was a burnt-out, bitter alcoholic before Manuela enters his world and her vitality and sensuality rejuvenates him.

The ending of the film is more optimistic than Hamilton implies. Constanza, on Prothero's orders, tells Manuela that the captain perished after the ship sank as Prothero is concerned that he is too old for Manuela and that the life of a captain is not suited to a long-term romance. However, he wavers in the final shot as he turns around and walks back to her. Thus, love (and sex) conquers all barriers including age and vocation. The only character aboard the ship who resents Prothero's relationship with Manuela, the Bible-reading First Mate Evans, is killed by Constanza when he threatens Prothero's reputation after the sinking of the ship—this murder seems, despite censorship strictures, to go unpunished.

Manuela provided Howard with one of his best screen roles in the 1950s and he was nominated for the Best British Actor Award at the 1958 BAFTA Awards.

THE MARK OF CAIN (Two Cities/Rank, 1947)—Melodrama. *Director:* Brian Desmond Hurst; *Producer:* W. P. Lipscomb; *Script:* W. P. Lipscomb (adaptation), Francis Crowdy, and Christianna Brand, based on the novel *Airing in a Closed Carriage* by Joseph Shearing; *Cinematography:* Erwin Hillier; *Music:* Bernard Stevens; *Cast:* Eric Portman (Richard Howard), Sally Gray (Sarah Bonheur), Patrick Holt (John Howard), Dermot Walsh (Jerome Thorn), Denis O'Dea (Sir William Godfrey), Edward Lexy (Lord Rochford), Therese Giehse (Sister Seraphine), Maureen Delaney (Daisy Cobb), Helen Cherry (Mary), Vida Hope (Jennie), and James Hayter (Dr. White).

Four novels written by Joseph Shearing, a pseudonym for Gabrielle Margaret Vere Long, were produced as films in 1947 and 1948. While *Moss Rose* was produced in Hollywood, *Blanche Fury** (1948), *So Evil My Love** (1948), and *The Mark of Cain* were all produced in England. All four films involve their female protagonists in betrayal, murder, and unhappy relationships. *The Mark of Cain* does not differ from this pattern in any significant way although its female protagonist is not nearly as complex, assertive, or as interesting as her counterparts in *So Evil My Love* and *Blanche Fury*. Instead, the virtues of *The Mark of Cain* reside more in Alex Vetchinsky's striking Victorian sets and Erwin Hillier's low-key photography.

Two brothers, Richard Howard and John Howard from the north of England, fall in love with British-born, French-raised Sarah Bonheur when they visit France to purchase cotton for their mill. Sarah, initially, is attracted to Richard's high culture leanings although she ultimately favors the more masculine advantages of John. Although the marriage produces a child, Sarah is unhappy with John's dictatorial, boorish behavior and, encouraged by Richard, investigates the possibilities of a divorce. When Sarah learns that Victorian law favors the husband, and that she will have to leave her daughter with John if she abandons the marriage, she decides to stay. Ironically, as John's health, and overt masculine power, deteriorates, Sarah is increasingly attracted to her husband. Richard, thwarted by Sarah's reconciliation with John, poisons his brother and frames Sarah for the crime, planning to save her at the trial. Richard's bizarre performance in the courtroom fails to save Sarah and she is found guilty. Only the intervention of Jerome Thorn, who is attracted to Sarah, saves her from the gallows when he plays on Richard's mental disintegration.

The Mark of Cain is less interesting than either *Blanche Fury* or *So Evil My Love* due to the fact that Sally Gray's* Sarah Bonheur is little more than a victim, or pawn, of the sibling rivalry involving Richard and John. Nevertheless, director Brian Desmond Hurst, supported by superb cinematography, provides a strong dramatic context for this elemental melodrama with its biblical subtext. Primarily, it is a story of virtue (Bonheur) struggling to survive and overcome the demands of the Howard family in particular, and the iniquities of Victorian patriarchy in general.

MASON, JAMES (1909–1984). Aside from the classical, theatrically trained British actors, such as Laurence Olivier,* Ralph Richardson,* and John Gielgud,* James Mason, along with Dirk Bogarde* and Sean Connery,* was one of the greatest screen actors to come out of Britain. There have been many phases in Mason's career and many strong performances. In the 1930s, after stage work with the Old Vic and Dublin's Gate Company, Mason appeared in the low-budget "quota quickies," such as *Late Extra* (1935), with supporting roles in better films such as *Fire over England** (1936), *The Return of the Scarlet Pimpernel* (1937), and *Hatter's Castle** (1941). An important early starring role for Mason, which helped define his screen persona for much of the 1940s, was as the brooding war-affected composer in *The Night Has Eyes** (1942) who arouses strong passion in a vulnerable heroine (Joyce Howard) trapped in his isolated mansion on the Yorkshire moors.

Mason's ability to convincingly project a feeling of repressed violence and sexual sadism, coupled with suggestions of emotional disturbance, was further developed in his breakthrough role as the sadistic Marquis of Rohan in *The Man in Grey** (1943). Although Rohan was an unmitigated villain, some of these qualities were also evident as Nicholas, Ann Todd's* mentor in *The Seventh Veil** (1946). Todd, like Howard in *The Night Has Eyes,* welcomes Nicholas's firm control of her career and personal life in this popular film. In both *The Seventh Veil* and *The Man in Grey,* Mason inflicts physical damage on his women—beating Margaret Lockwood* to death in *The Man in Grey* and thrashing the delicate fingers of pianist Todd in *The Seventh Veil.* Mason's highwayman, Captain Jackson, opposite Lockwood, in *The Wicked Lady* (1945) was more of the same, the only difference is that this time Lockwood kills him.

A welcome change for Mason was his performance as the vulnerable Northern Irish gunman Johnny McQueen in Carol Reed's* *Odd Man Out* (1947). This critically celebrated film depicts the last hours in McQueen's life after he has been fatally wounded in a raid on a linen mill to obtain money for the Irish Republican Army. Before he left for Hollywood, following the success of the *Odd Man Out,* he gave a less showy, but equally impressive performance as a doctor avenging the death of his lover in Lawrence Huntington's superior psychological thriller *The Upturned Glass* (1947), where Mason co-starred with his wife, Pamela Kellino, whom he murders in the film.

Mason was voted as the number-one male star in Britain in the mid-1940s. It took time to establish himself in Hollywood—an early film role was as a sympathetic doctor with a working-class clientele in Max Ophul's melodrama *Caught* (1949) with Mason, now the hero, opposite the archetypal screen villain Robert Ryan. After essaying the famed German general Erwin Rommel in two films for Twentieth Century Fox, *The Desert Fox* (1951) and *The Desert Rats* (1953), and the notorious espionage agent Ulysses Diello ("Cicero") in *Five Fingers* (1952), he played Norman Maine, the fallen movie star, in the Technicolor remake of *A Star Is Born* (1954). This role earned him his first Academy Award nomination.

As Mason gradually moved into character parts in Hollywood in the 1950s, he produced a number of his films, including Nicholas Ray's bold melodrama *Bigger Than Life* (1956), a story of a teacher who terrorizes everyone around him after becoming a prescription drug addict. Later, he was cast as Professor Humbert Humbert, who becomes infatuated with underage Sue Lyon in Stanley Kubrick's *Lolita* (1962). In 1969, Mason came to Australia to portray a painter, loosely based on the activities of artist Norman Lindsay, who gains inspiration from young Helen Mirren in *Age of Consent* (Mason also produced this film, directed by Michael Powell*). The 1970s and early 1980s were less rewarding as he "walked" through numerous European coproductions, although he gave a strong performance as the cruel plantation owner in *Mandingo* (1975), and he was a fine Dr. Watson in *Murder by Decree* (1979). The standout performance by Mason in his final decade was as the amoral lawyer Edward Concannon in Sidney Lumet's courtroom drama *The Verdict* (1982). Mason's Concannon demonstrated in this role that when the script and direction were right, Mason was a fine actor. He died in Switzerland in 1984. Aside from his nomination for *A Star Is Born,* Mason also received Oscar nominations for *Georgy Girl** (1966) and *The Verdict.* Mason was nominated for Best British Actor at the 1963 BAFTA Film Awards for *Lolita* and the 1968 Awards for *The Deadly Affair* (1967).

FILMS: Late Extra (1935), Trouble Waters (1936), Twice Branded (1936), Blind Man's Bluff (1936), Prison Breaker (1936), The Secret of Stamboul (1936), Fire over England (1936), The Mill on the Floss (1937), The High Command (1937), Catch As Catch Can (1937), The Return of the Scarlet Pimpernel (1937), I Met a Murderer (1939), This Man Is Dangerous (1941), Hatter's Castle (1941), The Night Has Eyes (1942), Alibi (1942),

Secret Mission (1942), Thunder Rock (1942), The Bells Go Down (1943), The Man in Grey (1943), They Met in the Dark (1943), Candlelight in Algeria (1943), Fanny by Gaslight (1944), Hotel Reserve (1944), A Place of One's Own (1945), They Were Sisters (1945), The Seventh Veil (1945), The Wicked Lady (1945), Odd Man Out (1947), The Upturned Glass (1947), Caught (1949), Madame Bovary (1949), The Reckless Moment (1949), East Side, West Side (1949), One Way Street (1950), Pandora and the Flying Dutchman (1951), The Desert Fox (1951), Lady Possessed (1952), Five Fingers (1952), The Prisoner of Zenda (1952), Face to Face (1952), The Man Between (1953), Charade (1953), The Story of Three Loves (1953), The Desert Rats (1953), Julius Caesar (1953), Botany Bay (1953), Prince Valiant (1954), A Star Is Born (1954), 20,000 Leagues under the Sea (1954), Forever Darling (1956), Bigger Than Life (1956), Island in the Sun (1956), Cry Terror! (1956), The Decks Ran Red (1958), North by Northwest (1959), Journey to the Centre of the Earth (1959), A Touch of Larceny (1959), The Trials of Oscar Wilde (1960), The Marriage-Go-Round (1961), Escape from Zahrain (1961), Lolita (1962), Hero's Island (1962), Tiara Tahiti (1962), Torpedo Bay (1962), The Fall of the Roman Empire (1963), The Pumpkin Eater (1964), Lord Jim (1965), Genghis Khan (1965), Les Pianos Mecaniques (1965), The Blue Max (1965), Georgy Girl (1966), The Deadly Affair (1966), Stranger in the House (1967), Duffy (1968), Mayerling (1968), The London Nobody Knows (doc., 1968), The Age of Consent (1969), The Sea Gull (1969), Spring and Port Wine (1970), The Yin and Yang of Mr. Go (1970), Cold Sweat (1971), Bad Man's River (1971), Kill! Kill! Kill! (1972), Child's Play (1973), The Last of Sheila (1973), The Mackintosh Man (1973), 11 Harrowhouse (1974), The Marseille Contract (1974), Kidnap Syndicate (1974), Mandingo (1975), Inside Out (1975), Autobiography of a Princess (1975), The Flower in His Mouth (1975), The Schoolmistress and the Devil (1975), La Mano Sinistra Della Legge (1975), The Voyage of the Damned (1976), Homage to Chagall (voice, 1976), Cross of Iron (1977), Fear in the City (1977), Heaven Can Wait (1978), The Boys from Brazil (1978), Murder by Decree (1978), The Passage (1980), Bloodline (1980), The Water Babies (1980), North Sea Hijack (1980), A Dangerous Summer (1982), Evil under the Sun (1982), The Verdict (1982), Yellowbeard (1983), Alexandre (1983), The Assisi Underground (1984), and The Shooting Party (1984).

A MATTER OF LIFE AND DEATH (Archers/Rank, 1946)—Fantasy. *Directors:* Michael Powell and Emeric Pressburger; *Producers:* Michael Powell, Emeric Pressburger, and George Bushby; *Script:* Michael Powell and Emeric Pressburger; *Cinematography:* Jack Cardiff; *Music:* Allan Gray; *Cast:* David Niven (Peter Carter), Kim Hunter (June), Roger Livesey (Dr. Frank Reeves), Marius Goring (Conductor 71), Raymond Massey (Abraham Farlan), Robert Coote (Bob Trubshawe), Kathleen Byron (an Angel), Richard Attenborough (an English Pilot), Bonar Colleano (an American Pilot), Joan Maude (Chief Recorder), and Abraham Sofaer (the Judge).

Along with *A Canterbury Tale** (1944), *A Matter of Life and Death* is the most complex, multi-layered film produced by Michael Powell* and Emeric Pressburger.* As the film's prologue moves through outer space toward the earth, an omniscient narrator (John Longden) warns the audience that "this is a story of two worlds, the one we know and the other which exists only in the mind of a young airman whose life and imagination have been shaped by war. Any resemblance to any other world, known or unknown, is purely coincidental." Despite superficial similarities, the system of duality in Powell-Pressburger's world is not the same as the contrasting worlds established in Frank Capra's *It's a Wonderful Life,* released in the same year.

In *A Matter of Life and Death,* Powell and Pressburger move well beyond their initial brief from the British Ministry of Information to develop a film that would heal the deterioration in U.S.–British relations. This aspect is developed within the film, as one of many strands, but, as would be expected from the filmmakers who irritated Winston Churchill in 1943 with their presentation of British-German relations in *The Life and Death of Colonel Blimp,* (1943) their treatment is much more problematic than the British ministry had hoped. The film, combining comedy, romance, and fantasy within a potentially sentimental paradigm, refuses to be constrained by any genre or realist presentation.

The film opens as Peter Carter's plane is about to explode after a bombing mission over Germany. Carter establishes contact with a female American ground controller (June) and declares his love for her before falling from the plane without a parachute. Carter survives and, in one of many spectacular images in the film, wakes up on a semi-deserted beach where he meets June riding her bicycle home from duty. Heaven has made an error and Conductor 71, the angel who bungled Carter's case, is sent to earth to fetch him. Carter, however, in the twenty hours since leaving his plane, has fallen in love with June and refuses to go to Heaven without a trial. Meanwhile, June asks Frank Reeves, a local doctor and brain specialist, to treat Carter and he recommends an operation.

At this point, the playful aspects of the Pressburger-Powell narrative structure become apparent as Carter's trial in the heavenly High Court, attended by representations of every nationality throughout history, is paralleled by his brain operation on the earth—the surgeon carrying out the operation is played by the same actor (Abraham Sofaer) who is the judge in the celestial High Court. Carter, fortunately, is defended by Reeves, who, conveniently, dies just prior to the operation and trial. Reeves, assisted by June's determination to save Carter by, if necessary, replacing him in heaven, wins his case and Carter survives the brain operation.

Often, films produced by Powell and Pressburger, including *A Matter of Life and Death,* were criticized for the wrong reasons, such as their determination not to work in the favored realist mode of the 1940s. Both filmmakers, at times, display an overreliance on whimsy, shallow stereotypes and weak comedy—some of these faults are evident in *A Matter of Life and Death.* While they should be celebrated for their courage, innovation, and cinematic expertise, this film is not their best—despite the contribution of Alfred Junge's sumptuous production designs.

MATTHEWS, JESSIE (1907–1981). A great ambition of Jessie Matthews was to dance with Fred Astaire and this wish indicates the type of musicals she starred in during her peak years in the mid-1930s. Like Gracie Fields,* Matthews came from a working-class (Soho) family. She demonstrated talent as a dancer from a young age, working her way up from the chorus line, through stage revues, to the position of Britain's pre-eminent film star in the mid-1930s. Although Matthews made her first film in 1923, her first sound film was the unsuccessful *Out of the Blue* (1931). It was not until she teamed up with director Victor Saville* that her film career blossomed. Saville, an experienced director-producer, was shrewd enough to create a viable, consistent film persona for Matthews as the wide-eyed waif from Soho who exuded both vulnerability and sensuality through her revealing costumes and sinuous, high-kicking style of dancing. Saville was also proficient in utilizing the basic elements of the film musical, including popular songs, well-executed dance routines, romance, sentiment (*Evergreen* [1934]), fantasy, and frivolity within Art Deco settings—similar, in some ways, to the "escapist" Astaire-Rogers Hollywood musicals of the 1930s.

Beginning with *The Good Companions* (1933), Saville directed Matthews in five successive hit films, including her most popular film, *Evergreen,* an adaptation of her 1931 stage success. This was followed by *First a Girl* (1935), a British variation of the gender confusions developed in the German film *Viktor and Viktoria* (1934). A plot contrivance allows Matthews to play a woman playing a man playing a woman, a situation that begins when Matthews replaces a female impersonator (Sonnie Hale) and masquerades as a man. This allows the plot to move into predictable areas of sexual confusion, particularly after Matthews falls in love with Griffith Jones, who, for the greater part of the film, believes that she is a man. Unlike Gracie Fields, who remained, at least in her films, clearly associated with the working class, Matthews worked hard at removing her origins and, through careful diction, could, in films such as *It's Love Again* (1936), be convincing as a socialite.

The Saville-Matthews films were also popular in the United States, where Matthews was billed as "The Dancing Divinty," and *Evergreen* became the first British musical to open at the prestigious Radio City Music Hall. When Matthews left Gaumont-British and Saville, her husband Sonny Hale assumed direction of her musicals and the quality deteriorated. By the time of *Climbing High* in 1939, a non-musical directed by Carol Reed,* her film career was in trouble and she left the film industry until her appearance in *Forever and a Day,* the 1943 all-star fund-raiser for the British Relief Fund, which was filmed in the United States. This was followed by the thriller *Candles at Nine* (1944), which did little to help Matthews restore her film career. There were sporadic supporting film roles after 1944, such as the mother of *tom thumb* (1958) in George Pal's MGM musical filmed in London, but her main claim to fame during the 1960s and 1970s was the title role in the long-running BBC radio serial *Mrs. Dale's Diary.* Matthews, who suffered from emotional problems throughout most of her career, died in 1981. Her autobiography, *Over My Shoulder,* was published in 1974.

FILMS: The Beloved Vagabond (1923), This England (1924), Straws in the Wind (1924), Out of the Blue (1931), There Goes the Bride (1932), The Midshipmaid (1932), The Man from Toronto (1933), The Good Companions (1933), Friday the Thirteenth (1933), Waltzes from Vienna (1934), Evergreen (1934), First a Girl (1935), It's Love Again (1936), Head over Heels (1937), Gangway (1937), Sailing Along (1938), Climbing High

(1939), Forever and a Day (1943), Victory Wedding (dir., short, 1943), Candles at Nine (1944), Life Is Nothing without Music (short, 1947), Making the Grade (short, 1947), tom thumb (1958), A Hundred Years Underground (short, 1963), and The Hound of the Baskervilles (1977).

MILLS, JOHN (b. 1908). The career of John Mills almost spans the length of the British sound film industry in the twentieth century. Despite his prevailing image of decency, moral authority, and heroism, Mills's career is deceptively varied with greater diversity than is often appreciated. In the relatively short period from 1941 to 1952, Mills worked either sides of the law and was a convincing representation of both postwar optimism and the fears and anxieties of a changed society emerging from a devastating world war. For example, in his first film after his discharge from the army for medical reasons (duodenal ulcer), Mills was a Nazi spy posing as a member of the Royal Air Force in Anthony Asquith's* *Cottage to Let** (1941). This role was the antithesis of the patriotic values embedded in his celebrated performance as Ordinary Seamen "Shorty" Blake in Noël Coward's *In Which We Serve** (1942).

Later, toward the end of the war, Mills was the concerned husband Private Jim Colter, who goes AWOL to save his young wife from the temptations of black marketeer Stewart Granger* in *Waterloo Road* (1944). Yet, just after the war, Mills, seemingly, shed years for his role as Pip in David Lean's* magisterial interpretation of *Great Expectations** (1946). He followed this optimistic role with the darkly pessimistic, psychologically disturbed Jim Ackland, who contemplates suicide in Roy Ward Baker's* film noir *The October Man** (1947). Then there was the Antarctic explorer in *Scott of the Antarctic* (1948) and the heroic submarine commander who loses his life when his submarine strikes a mine in another Baker film, *Morning Departure* (1950). Mills was the working-class mentor to the tragic young boy in the bizarre melodrama *The Rocking Horse Winner** (1950), one of the two films he produced (the other was *The History of Mr. Polly* [1949]), and the embittered Phillip Davidson seeking revenge on an unfaithful girlfriend in *The Long Memory** (1952).

In the 1950s came more war films and police officers, interspersed by better opportunities, such as his performance as the officious martinet opposite Alec Guinness* in *Tunes of Glory* (1960). One of the few misfires of his career was as the priest Father Keogh, who becomes entangled with a bizarre bandit (Dirk Bogarde*) and a young woman (Mylene Demongeot) in the melodrama *The Singer Not the Song* (1961). In the same year, Mills appeared in another Baker film, *Flame in the Streets,* where he more than redeems himself as the working-class union official fighting to restore racial harmony on the shop floor while confronting his daughter's decision to marry a West Indian.

Mills entered the film industry in a Jessie Matthews'* musical, *The Midshipmaid* (1932). He worked as a chorus dancer in the late 1920s and did some stage work in the early 1930s. Mills then honed his film acting skills in a succession of "quota quickies" where there was little time for rehearsal and discussion before his elevation to the more conducive atmosphere of the lead role in *Forever England* (1935) and a strong supporting part in the MGM production of *Goodbye, Mr. Chips* (1939).

Throughout the 1940s and 1950s, Mills was a major British film star and leading man. He gradually moved into character parts during the 1960s, culminating in his Oscar for Best Supporting Actor as Michael, the retarded villager in *Ryan's Daughter* (1970). During the late 1950s and 1960s, he also acted opposite his talented daughter Hayley Mills in *Tiger Bay* (1959), *The Chalk Garden* (1963), *The Truth about Spring* (1964), and *The Family Way** (1966), with each film charting the maturation of Hayley, culminating in the sexual and domestic problems faced by newlyweds Hayley and Hywell Bennett in the last film. Mills also directed Hayley in *Gypsy Girl* in 1966. Mills continued to act in supporting parts and on television throughout the 1980s and 1990s. He was nominated for Best British Actor at the BAFTA Film Awards in 1955 for *Hobson's Choice* (1954), 1961 for *Tunes of Glory* (1960), and 1971 for Best Supporting Actor for *Ryan's Daughter,* for which he also won a Golden Globe Award. Mills won the Best Actor Award at the 1960 Venice Film Festival for *Tunes of Glory.* Mills was knighted in 1977.

FILMS: The Midshipmaid (1932), Words and Music (1932), Britannia of Billingsgate (1933), The Ghost Camera (1933), The River Wolves (1934), A Political Party (1934), The Lash (1934), Those Were the Days (1934), Blind Justice, Doctor's Orders (1934), Royal Cavalcade (1935), Forever England/Brown on Resolution (1935), Car of Dreams (1935), Charing Cross Road (1935), The First Offence (1936), Tudor Rose (1936), OHMS (1937), The Green Cockatoo (1937), Goodbye, Mr. Chips (1939), Old Bill and Son (1940), All Hands (doc., 1940), Cottage to Let (1941), The Black Sheep of Whitehall (1941), The Big Blockade (1942), The Young Mr. Pitt (1942), In Which We Serve (1942), We Dive at Dawn (1943), This Happy Breed (1944), Victory Wedding (doc., 1944), Waterloo Road (1944), The Way to the Stars (1945), The Sky's the Limit (doc., 1945), Total War in Britain (voice, 1945), Land of Promise (voice, 1946), Great Expectations (1946), So Well Remembered (1947), The October Man (1947), Scott of the Antarctic (1948), The History of Mr. Polly (1949), Friend of the Family (voice, 1949), The Flying Skyscraper (voice, 1949), The Rocking Horse Winner (1950), Morning Departure (1950), Mr. Denning Drives North (1951), The Gentle Gunman (1952), The Long Memory (1952), Hobson's Choice (1954), The Colditz Story (1954), The End of the Affair (1955), Above Us the Waves (1955), Escapade (1955), It's Great to Be Young (1956), War and Peace (1956), The Baby and the Battleship (1956), Around the World in Eighty Days (1956), Town on Trial (1956), The Vicious Circle (1956), Dunkirk (1958), Ice Cold in Alex (1958), I Was Monty's Double (1958), Tiger Bay (1959), Summer of the Seventeenth Doll (1959), Tunes of Glory (1960), The Swiss Family Robinson (1961), The Singer Not the Song (1961), Flame in the Streets (1961), The Valiant (1962), Tiara Tahiti (1962), the Chalk Garden (1963), The Truth about Spring (1965), Operation Crossbow (1965), King Rat (1965), The Wrong Box (1966), The Family Way (1966), Chuka (1967), Africa—Texas Style (1967), Lady Hamilton (1968), A Black Veil for Lisa (1968), Oh! What a Lovely War (1968), Run Wild, Run Free (1969), Adam's Woman (1969), Ryan's Daughter (1970), Dulcima (1971), Young Winston (1972), Lady Caroline Lamb (1972), Oklahoma Crude (1973), The Human Factor (1976), A Choice of Weapons (1976), The Devil's Advocate (1977), The Big Sleep (1978), The Thirty-Nine Steps (1979), Zulu Dawn (1979), Gandhi (1982), Sahara (1984),

Who's That Girl (1987), Deadly Advice (1994), The Grotesque (1995), Hamlet (1996), and Bean (1997).

MINE OWN EXECUTIONER (London Film Productions, 1947)—Psychological drama/film noir. *Director:* Anthony Kimmins; *Producers:* Anthony Kimmins and Jack Kitchin; *Script:* Nigel Balchin, based on his novel; *Cinematography:* Wilkie Cooper; *Music:* Benjamin Frankel; *Cast:* Burgess Meredith (Felix Milne), Dulcie Gray (Patricia Milne), Kieron Moore (Adam Lucian), Christine Norden (Barbara Edge), Barbara White (Molly Lucian), John Laurie (Dr. James Garsten), Michael Shepley (Peter Edge), Walter Fitzgerald (Dr. Norris Pile), and Edgar Norfolk (Sir George Freethorne).

After World War II, there was a cycle of films produced in Hollywood and London concerned with the psychological and physical effects of the war on the combatants. *Mine Own Executioner,* produced by Alexander Korda's* London Films, was a good example of this cycle and, despite overt signs of studio (and possibly censorship interference) affecting the character motivation and narrative coherence, the film retains its bitter, downbeat climax. After Adam Lucian tries to murder his wife, Molly, she approaches London psychoanalyst Felix Milne to treat her husband. Felix, reluctantly, accepts the case and quickly realizes that Adam is schizophrenic as a result of the torture and mental anguish inflicted on him by the Japanese during the war. Initially, Felix seemingly makes rapid progress with Adam, but the psychoanalyst realizes that this early success is misleading as Adam's problems are deep seated and will not respond easily to treatment.

There are a number of fascinating, if underdeveloped, subplots in *Mine Own Executioner.* These include the personal and professional tensions emanating from the fact that Felix is not a qualified doctor and only practices due to the support from the eminent Harley Street specialist Dr. James Garsten. Felix's lack of qualifications, in turn, threaten the funding of his institute. Felix also suffers from his own form of schizophrenic behavior with regard to his marriage. While Felix loves his long-suffering wife, Patricia, under pressure he is drawn to the sensual charms and forbidden excitement offered by Barbara Edge, a family friend. Patricia is aware of this relationship and, in an unlikely plot device, decides to accept Felix's relationship with Edge despite her anguish.

Most of these narrative threads come together when Felix, feeling poorly because of the flu, fails to follow his intuition and allow Adam to postpone treatment until the next day. Felix, realizing that Adam's mental condition represents an immediate threat to his wife, Molly, is distracted because of his own problems, including the news that the institute will be denied funding because of Felix's lack of formal qualifications. As the pressure on the psychoanalyst intensifies, Felix resumes his affair with Edge and just as they are about to sexually consummate the affair, Felix receives the news (from his wife, Patricia, who knows that he is spending the night with Edge) that Adam has fired four bullets into Molly. Felix tries to redeem himself by climbing a long fire ladder to speak to Adam, who is poised on the roof of a building, but this fails and Adam shoots himself in the head. Only the support of Dr. Garsten at the subsequent inquest saves Felix's position at the institute.

After Adam's death and Felix's humiliation at the inquest, the ending of the film is less than satisfactory. Although Felix has failed to heal Adam, which resolves the main narrative thread, other issues, notably the funding of the institute and, more importantly, Felix's relationship with Patricia and Edge are basically ignored. This, however, did not weaken support for the film, assisted by the casting of noted left-wing Hollywood actor Burgess Meredith in the central role as Felix Milne. This occurred because Meredith was in London with his wife, Paulette Goddard, who was shooting Oscar Wilde's *An Ideal Husband* for Alexander Korda.* Although the marriage soon collapsed, *Mine Own Executioner* was both a critical and commercial success.

MORE, KENNETH (1914–1982). In early 1960, Kenneth More was at the peak of his career, having starred in a succession of popular British films, a cycle that began with *Genevieve** in 1953, and continued through films such as *Doctor in the House** (1954), *Reach for the Sky* (1956), *The Admirable Crichton* (1957), *A Night to Remember* (1958), and *North West Frontier** (1959), co-starring Lauren Bacall. This last film, directed by J. Lee Thompson,* a late (superior) addition to the cycle of empire films, was a critical and commercial success and it was expected that More would be cast in the role of Sergeant Miller (eventually played by David Niven) in Lee Thompson's *The Guns of Navarone* (1961). However, More insulted Sir John Davis, the chairman of Rank, at a dinner and the studio refused permission for him to appear in the film.[4] While it is difficult to be sure exactly what effect this may have had on More's career, the international success of *The Guns of Navarone* proved to be Lee Thompson's "ticket" to Hollywood and the film was released just as More was about to be replaced as one of Britain's leading men by a different type of British actor in the early 1960s. *The Guns of Navarone* may have allowed More to extend his career at the top level in Hollywood whereas he was soon relegated to supporting roles in Britain. When More's part was cut from William Wyler's *The Collector* (1965), the chance of a second career in Hollywood was lost forever.

Before his breakthrough British film, *Genevieve,* More had played supporting roles in more than twenty films, including unbilled parts from 1935. In the 1930s, More supported himself for a while working in a comedy act at the Windmill Theatre, known more for its strippers than its comedic qualities. Yet, when his break came in 1953, when More was nearly forty years old, in *Genevieve,* this training must have served him well as More won many fans with his mildly lecherous Ambrose Claverhouse. This was followed by the equally worldly medical student in *Doctor in the House. Doctor in the House* was an important film for More as he now had co-starred in the top-grossing British film two years in a row (*Genevieve* the year before) and he more than held his own alongside Dirk Bogarde,* winning the 1955 BAFTA Best Actor Award for his role as Richard Grimsdyke, a perennial student living off his grandmother's £1,000 a year allowance. As the 1950s continued, this irresponsible "man about town" persona was replaced by a sense of dependability, exemplified by his resourceful butler (William Crichton), who rescues his aristocratic employers after they are shipwrecked, in *The Admirable Crichton,* and the Western hero who romances Jayne Mansfield in the spoof *The Sheriff of Fractured Jaw,* directed by veteran Hollywood director Raoul Walsh in London in 1958.

More's more lasting screen image as the determined, professional military figure culminated in his role as Douglas Bader in *Reach for the Sky.* This film was a major success for More even though many colleagues warned him of the danger of playing Bader, a pilot who continued to fly even though he lost his legs in a crash. More's popularity was enhanced as the heroic Second Officer Charles Lightoller, who keeps his head amid the panic when the Titanic begins to sink, in *A Night to Remember.* The only deviation in this pattern in the 1950s was his role as the troubled former fighter pilot, Freddie Page, who forms an uneasy relationship with an older woman (Vivien Leigh) in *The Deep Blue Sea* (1955).

After a curious role as the older man involved with young Susannah York in the bittersweet romantic drama *The Greengage Summer* in 1961, followed by a different kind of role for More as the second-rate repertory actor who briefly enjoys the transitory financial rewards of a successful television commercial, followed by growing disillusionment in the low-budget *The Comedy Man* (1963), More's status as a leading man disappeared in favor of Stanley Baker,* Albert Finney,* and more working-class figures. More returned to the stage and television (including the celebrated television adaptation of *The Forsyte Saga*), interspersed by supporting film roles and cameos in large-budget all-star films such as the *Battle of Britain* (1969) and *Oh! What a Lovely War* (1969). Aside from his 1955 BAFTA Best Actor Award for *Doctor in the House,* More was also nominated for *Genevieve, The Deep Blue Sea,* and *Reach for the Sky.* More died in 1982.

FILMS: Look up and Laugh (1935), Windmill Revels (1936), Carry on, London (1936), School for Secrets (1946), Scott of the Antarctic (1948), For Them That Trespass (1949), Man on the Run (1949), Now Barabbas Was a Robber (1949), Stop Press Girl (1949), Morning Departure (1950), Chance of a Lifetime (1950), The Clouded Yellow (1950), The Franchise Affair (1950), No Highway (1951), The Galloping Major (1951), Appointment with Venus (1951), Brandy for the Parson (1952), The Yellow Balloon (1952), Never Let Me Go (1953), Genevieve (1953), Our Girl Friday (1953), Doctor in the House (1954), The Man Who Loved Redheads (voice, 1955), Raising a Riot (1955), The Deep Blue Sea (1955), Reach for the Sky (1956), The Admirable Crichton (1957), A Night to Remember (1958), Next to No Time (1958), The Sheriff of Fractured Jaw (1958), Design for Living (short, 1958), The Thirty-Nine Steps (1958), North West Frontier (1959), Sink the Bismark! (1960), Man in the Moon (1960), Island of Surprise (narr., 1960), The Greengage Summer (1961), Some People (1962), The Longest Day (1962), We Joined the Navy (1962), The Comedy Man (1963), The Mercenaries (1967), Fraulein Doktor (1968), Oh! What a Lovely War (1969), Battle of Britain (1969), Scrooge (1970), Concorde—the 24-Hour World (narr., 1973), Look, No Hands (narr., 1973), Walking Wounded (narr., 1973), The Blind Shall Lead (short, 1975), The Slipper and the Rose (1976), Where Time Began

(1977), Leopard in the Snow (1977), The Silent Witness (narr., 1978), So Much to Offer (narr., 1978), and The Spaceman and King Arthur (1979).

MR. PERRIN AND MR. TRAILL (Two Cities, 1948)—Melodrama. *Director:* Lawrence Huntington; *Producer:* Alexander Galperson; *Script:* T. J. Morrison and L. A. G. Strong, based on the novel by Hugh Walpole; *Cinematography:* Erwin Hillier; *Music:* Allan Gray; *Cast:* David Farrar (David Traill), Marius Goring (Vincent Perrin), Greta Gynt (Isobel Lester), Raymond Huntley (Moy-Thompson), Mary Jerrold (Mrs. Perrin), Edward Chapman (Birkland), Finlay Currie (Sir Joshua Varley), Ralph Truman (Comber), Viola Lyel (Mrs. Comber), and Don Barclay (Rogers).

Although *Mr. Perrin and Mr. Traill* is largely forgotten today, it exemplifies many of the virtues of the British film industry in the 1940s and early 1950s. The story concerns a new teacher, David Traill, fresh from the army and successes on the rugby field, who fails to pay appropriate respect to the obsessive rituals of Vincent Perrin, a master in an elite private boarding school. The conflict between the two teachers escalates from small issues, such as Perrin's perceived right to the first reading of the daily newspaper and the sole occupancy of the communal bathroom, to larger issues, such as romancing local nurse Isobel Lester. The news of Traill and Lester's engagement results in the total breakdown of Perrin's fragile grasp on reality.

Another virtue in the characterizations in *Mr. Perrin and Mr. Traill,* which, thankfully, are far removed from the stereotypes found in *Goodbye, Mr. Chips* (1939), emanates from the film's determination not to polarize the conflict between absolute figures of virtue and evil. In fact, Traill, the film's "normal" character, gains most of his sympathy from the craven behavior of the other masters who, faced with a tyrannical headmaster, lack spirit. Similarly, Perrin's virtues, such as his dedication to the students and their education, is overwhelmed by his obsession with the trivialities of daily life until the climax of the film when circumstances transform him into a hero who saves Traill's life after he falls down the side of a cliff. After Perrin loses his life while rescuing his enemy, Traill accuses the real villain, the despotic headmaster Moy-Thompson, of sadistically breaking the spirit of Perrin and the other masters. Although the conclusion to the film is a somewhat perfunctory, *Mr. Perrin and Mr. Traill* provides another demonstration of the subtle skills of director Lawrence Huntington when working from a well-constructed script.

THE MUMMY (Hammer, 1959)—Horror. *Director:* Terence Fisher; *Producers:* Michael Carreras and Anthony Nelson Keys (associate); *Script:* Jimmy Sangster; *Cinematography:* Jack Asher; *Music:* Franz Reizenstein; *Cast:* Peter Cushing (John Banning), Christopher Lee (Kharis, the Mummy), Yvonne Furneaux (Isobel Banning/Princess Anaka), Felix Aylmer (Stephen Banning), Raymond Huntley (Joseph Whemple), George Pastell (Mehemet Bey, Priest of Karnack), Eddie Byrne (Inspector Mulrooney), Michael Ripper (Poacher), George Woodbridge (Police Constable Burke), and Gerald Lawson (Irish Customer).

Hammer's film production of *The Mummy* is the best "Mummy" film to date, largely owing to the visual skills of Terence Fisher* and his eerie use of Technicolor, particularly in the swamp scenes. *The Mummy* is perhaps the best-looking Hammer production of all time—due also to Bernard Robinson's production designs. After purchasing the rights to the Universal horror film in the mid-1950s, Hammer again underwent a major shift and abandoned ten of its planned films scheduled for release in 1956 in favor of horror films. This plan was successful and after the commercial success of *The Curse of Frankenstein** (1957), particularly in the United States, the studio embarked on a systematic reworking of the major horror figures developed by Universal Studios in the early 1930s. *The Curse of Frankenstein* was followed by *Dracula** (1958), again with Peter Cushing* and Christopher Lee,* and, after its success in the United States (it was estimated that the combined gross for *The Curse of Frankenstein* and *Dracula* was in excess of $4 million), another Universal monster, *The Mummy,* was put into production.

Hammer's production of *The Mummy,* however, did not follow the plot and characterizations of Universal's 1932 version, with Boris Karloff and directed by the German cinematographer Karl Freund. Instead they reworked plot details from two low-budget Universal films of the early 1940s (*The Mummy's Hand* [1940] and *The Mummy's Tomb* [1942]), which in turn were loosely influenced by the mysterious death of Lord Caernarvaon after he led an expedition to open up Tutankhamun's tomb in 1923. The film begins in 1895 when a British expedition breaks into the tomb of Queen Anaka, despite warnings from Mehemet Bey, an Egyptian nationalist, that disaster would befall all those who defile the tomb. This curse begins with Stephen Banning, the leader of the expedition, who lapses into incoherence after he witnesses events within the tomb. Later, after the expedition has returned to London, Bey summons the mummy Kharis from the tomb to kill Stephen, his son John, and Joseph Whemple, the other member of the expedition. Kharis kills Stephen and Whemple, but as he is about to kill John, the mummy hesitates when he sees John's wife, Isobel, who looks similar to Queen Anaka. Kharis, determined to take Isobel with him, is killed by the police in the swamp near John's house.

A significant difference between this production of *The Mummy* and earlier versions is the film's uneasy defense of British imperialistic behavior in raiding the artifacts of Egyptian culture. This narrative strand is foregrounded late in the film in a long conversation between Bey and John when the British archaeologist attempts to trap Bey and Kharis. The long conversation discussing the morality of British behavior in Egypt is shot by Fisher in a series of long takes as the camera carefully shifts its framing as John and Bey move around the spacious set. However, the demands of the genre for suspense and a violent closure push this discourse into the background in the last reel as Kharis and Bey invade John's house. As Kharis sinks below the murky waters of the swamp at the end of the film, and the figure of British imperialism (John) nervously regains his wife, the tone of the film is less triumphant, and more problematic, than earlier representations of this tale.

MY BROTHER'S KEEPER (Gainsborough, 1948)—Chase film/film noir. *Director:* Alfred Roome; *Producers:* Anthony Darnborough and Sidney Box (executive); *Script:* Frank Harvey, based on the story by Maurice Wiltshire; *Cinematography:* Gordon Lang; *Music:* Clifton Parker; *Cast:* Jack Warner (George Martin), Jane Hylton (Nora Lawrence), George Cole (Willie Stannard), David Tomlinson (Ronnie Waring), Yvonne Owen (Meg Waring), Raymond Lovell (Wainwright), Bill Owen (Syd Evans), Beatrice Varley (Mrs. Martin), Garry Marsh (Brewster), Wilfrid Hyde-White (Harding), Brenda Bruce (Winnie Forman), and Susan Shaw (Beryl).

Alfred Roome, one of Britain's top editors for more than forty years, directed only two films, *My Brother's Keeper* and *It's Not Cricket* (1948). Roome, uncomfortable directing the actors, was assisted by Roy Rich on both films. Although *My Brother's Keeper* is marred by a distracting subplot concerning a young journalist (Ronnie Waring) on his honeymoon, who is reluctantly dragged into the manhunt for escaped convicts George Martin and Willie Stannard by his tyrannical editor, the film is remarkably tough and unsentimental. *My Brother's Keeper* also provided Jack Warner* with his most complex and, arguably, his best screen performance as the hardened criminal George Martin.

My Brother's Keeper is a bleak film presenting a pessimistic image of a society devoid of compassion and the populist spirit of the war years. *My Brother's Keeper* is much closer to the nihilistic sentiments of film noir than the racial drama *The Defiant Ones* (1958), with which it is sometimes associated. Although both films share the basic premise of two contrasting convicts handcuffed together on the run, *My Brother's Keeper* has little in common with Stanley Kramer's 1958 Hollywood production. An almost complete absence of sentimentality in the British film is one distinguishing characteristic. Only with the offer of Martin's mistress Nora Lawrence to testify to the police on behalf of the hapless Stannard, and thereby incriminate herself, does the film display any sense of human generosity. In all other respects, the basic institutions of society, including the media and the police, lack compassion, as does Martin.

The dramatic focus in *My Brother's Keeper* is the complex character of Martin, a man who can use his literary knowledge and street cunning to charm most other people, notably the simple Stannard who initially idolizes Martin, his mistress Nora Lawrence, who assists the convict, and Martin's wife (Beatrice Varley), who tells Lawrence at the end of the film that in her twenty-two-year marriage to Martin she never really knew her husband as he spent fourteen years in jail, five in the army, and only three years with her (during which time she, presumably, shared Martin with Nora Lawrence). Both Stannard and Lawrence come to the realization that Martin cares for no one except himself (as Martin tells Stannard, "There's no such things as friends. People are either useful or useless. You're useless!").

The bulk of the film is taken up with Martin and Stannard's attempts to elude capture. After Martin is able to free himself from Stannard, who is presented as a basically innocent young man, the film focuses on Martin's flight from the police.

In this situation, audience sympathy normally gravitates toward the hunted, but Roome steadfastly refuses to present Martin as a victim—the closest we come to understanding his lack of compassion for other people comes from his wife's suggestion that the army, and his years in jail, played a part in molding his character. Essentially, the film is content to reinforce her conclusion that "there's something in his mind that's not quite right. He's just a misfit."

NOTES

1. See Slide, *"Banned in the USA,"* p. 101.
2. McFarlane, *An Autobiography of British Cinema,* p. 274.
3. McFarlane, *An Autobiography of British Cinema,* p. 274.
4. See Chibnall, *J. Lee Thompson,* p. 258.

N

NEAME, RONALD (b. 1911). British director Ronald Neame, like John Guillermin* (*The Towering Inferno* [1974]), enjoyed a spectacular commercial success with a Hollywood "blockbuster" (*The Poseidon Adventure* [1972]) relatively late in his career, after working productively in the British industry for many years. Neame, the son of photographer (and film director) Elwin Neame and actress Ivy Close, joined Elstree Studios in 1927, moving up to the position of assistant cameraman on Alfred Hitchcock's* *Blackmail* * in 1929. He photographed many "quota quickies" in the 1930s before forming a close working relationship with David Lean* and they, together with producer Anthony Havelock-Allan, reworked Noël Coward's script for *In Which We Serve* * (1942). Neame also photographed this film and the same partnership (Neame, Lean, and Havelock-Allan) co-scripted an adaptation of Coward's play *This Happy Breed* (1944), which they developed into a successful propaganda effort celebrating middle-class English values in the twenty-year period up to 1939. Neame was also cinematographer on this, his first color film.

After photographing *Blithe Spirit* (1945), which was his last film as cinematographer, Neame, Lean, and Havelock-Allan broke away from Coward and formed their own independent company, Cineguild, under the Rank umbrella. Neame, like Guillermin, visited Hollywood to study the studio production methods. This experience influenced both the type of material and the form of his films after this point. Neame began directing with one of his best films, the taut thriller *Take My Life* * (1947), based on the activities of a female protagonist (Greta Gynt*) forced to investigate the circumstances surrounding the death of her husband's ex-girlfriend. Neame's next film, *The Golden Salamander* (1950), has none of the "noirish" aspects of his previous film as it is an adventure film with Trevor Howard* and Anouk Amiée fighting smugglers in Tunisia.

After the successful comedy *The Card* (1952), with Alec Guinness,* Neame directed Gregory Peck in *The Million Pound Note* (1953), based on Mark Twain's story. The U.S. connection was tightened further with the Twentieth Century Fox film *The Man Who Never Was* (1956), with Clifton Webb and Gloria Grahame. This film was based on a true story detailing an elaborate hoax perpetuated by the Allies during World War II to deflect attention from their invasion of Sicily. Moving to MGM in Hollywood, Neame's next film, *The Seventh Sin* (1957), was a disaster for all concerned in its story of an adulterous woman (Eleanor Parker) who redeems herself during an epidemic in Hong Kong. Vincente Minnelli was forced to finish the film and Neame returned to England for *Windom's Way* (1957) with Peter Finch.*

The next period in Neame's career included the comedy *The Horse's Mouth* (1959), with Guinness as an eccentric artist, and *Tunes of Glory* (1960), Neame's best film. *Tunes of Glory* showcases the acting abilities of Guinness and John Mills* as the film traces the effect on a Scottish regiment when an easygoing officer (Guinness) is replaced by an officious martinet (Mills). These two films represent, creatively, the high point in Neame's career before moving to Hollywood for the efficient Middle Eastern thriller *Escape from Zahrain* (1961), starring Yul Brynner. Neame's output after this included a number of international coproductions. The quality was variable, ranging from soap opera stories such as *I Could Go On Singing* (1963), Judy Garland's last film, to very good soap opera such as *The Chalk Garden* (1964). There were also comedy-thrillers: *A Man Could Get Killed* (1966), with James Garner, and *Gambit* (1966), with Michael Caine.* His last good film was *The Prime of Miss Jean Brodie* (1969), with Maggie Smith in her Oscar-winning performance as the Edinburgh school teacher who exerts considerable influence over her female students.

The 1970s is notable for the commercial success of *The Poseidon Adventure,* an early example of the all-star bloated "disaster" cycle that occupied Hollywood for much of the 1970s with Neame also directing one of the last examples of the cycle, the even more dire *Meteor* (1979). Neame shared the 1947 and 1948 Oscar nominations for Best Screenplay for *Brief Encounter** (1945) and *Great Expectations** (1946), following an earlier Oscar nomination in 1943 for Best Effects for *One of Our Aircraft Is Missing* (1942). *Tunes of Glory* was nominated for Best Film at the 1961 BAFTA Film Awards and Neame won the New York Critics Circle Award for direction of this film.

FILMS (as director): Take My Life (1947), The Golden Salamander (1950), The Card (1952), The Million Pound Note (1953), The Man Who Never Was (1956), The Seventh Sin (1957), Windom's Way (1957), The Horse's Mouth (1959), Tunes of Glory (1960), Escape from Zahrain (1961), I Could Go Singing (1962), The Chalk Garden (1963), Mister Moses (1964), A Man Could Get Killed (1966), Gambit (1966), Prudence and the Pill (1968), The Prime of Miss Jean Brodie (1969), Scrooge (1970), The Poseidon Adventure (1972), The Odessa File (1974), Meteor (1979), Hopscotch (1980), First Monday in October (1981), Foreign Body (1986), and The Magic Balloon (1990).

NEWELL, MIKE (b. 1942). Television provided the base for the careers of many distinguished British directors, including Michael Apted, Stephen Frears, Ken

Loach,* and Mike Newell. Newell continued to produce and direct films for both U.S. and British television in the 1980s and 1990s after he had established himself with *Dance with a Stranger** in 1985. It is an indication of the quality of Newell's films made, initially, for television that some of them also received a theatrical release.

Granada Television provided Newell with his start as a trainee director in the early 1960s, after an education at Cambridge University. Newell also worked as a television news reporter before moving on to directing popular serials such as *Coronation Street.* A stirring version of the oft-filmed Alexandre Dumas's story *The Man in the Iron Mask* (1977), a U.S.–financed television movie with a cast that included Richard Chamberlain, Patrick McGoohan, Louis Jordan, and Ian Holm, was Newell's first film. It received some limited theatrical showings. This was followed by his first theatrical feature film, *The Awakening* (1980), an adaptation of "Jewel of the Seven Stars," one of Bram Stoker's lesser known stories, starring Charlton Heston and Stephanie Zimbalist, which had been made more successfully eight years earlier by British director Seth Holt as *Blood from the Mummy's Tomb** (1972).

An underrated factual study in paranoia and persecution, set in New Zealand during World War II, *Bad Blood* (1981), starring Australian actor Jack Thompson as the farmer who kills several people before the police hunt him down, provides an early indication of the type of material that best suited Newell. A dark, fatalistic strain that runs through many of his subsequent films was evident in his masterpiece *Donnie Brasco* (1997), scripted by Paul Attanasio (*Homicide: Life on the Streets* [1993]) and starring Al Pacino in one of his best performances as the low-level gangster who, fatally, forms a relationship with a Federal Bureau of Investigation undercover agent (Johnny Depp) in this morally problematic study of institutional, marital, and gang loyalties.

The most commercially successful film for Newell was *Four Weddings and a Funeral** (1994), which transformed Hugh Grant into a star after more than a decade honing his characteristic mixture of vulnerability and boyish charm. The real virtue of the film is the rich ensemble playing of Grant, Andie MacDowell, Kristin Scott Thomas, Simon Callow, John Hannah, James Fleet, and Charlotte Coleman. Surprisingly, Newell and Grant followed the enormous success of *Four Weddings and a Funeral* with the excellent, but commercially disastrous, sour comedy-fantasy *An Awfully Big Adventure* (1995), where Grant steps outside his usual screen persona to play a cruel theater director who mistreats his repertory talent in 1940s Liverpool.

Newell's most satisfying British film to date, *Dance with a Stranger,* features a stunning performance by Miranda Richardson as Ruth Ellis in this stylish film noir detailing, again, the self-destructive behavior of a woman who cannot relinquish her disturbed lover (Rupert Everett). *Dance with a Stranger* showcases Newell's best qualities that often emanate from a circumscribed, morally problematic world, inhabited by characters battling their own destructive inclinations. With *Pushing Tin* (1999), Newell transcribed this world to the hothouse milieu of

U.S. traffic controllers (John Cusack and Billy Bob Thornton) plagued by jealousy and marital problems. Yet, as Newell demonstrated with the television-produced film *The Good Father* (1987), which received a theatrical release in some markets, his mastery of melodrama was evident as Anthony Hopkins's bitterness over losing his child in a custody battle erupts in a series of escalating acts of irrationality. Only in the romantic *Enchanted April* (1992), with Miranda Richardson, Joan Plowright, Josie Lawrence, and Polly Walker as four women breaking from their traditional conformity while on vacation at the Italian Riviera, does Newell cast aside his customary sense of alienation and futility in this made-for-television film. It was also released theatrically in the United States.

In 2000, Newell was also executive producer on two very different, albeit successful, films, the award-winning Steven Soderberg film *Traffic* and the U.S. adaptation of Nick Hornsby's London-based story *High Fidelity,* which, coscripted by the film's star, John Cusack, the setting was moved from Britain to the United States. Newell won the David Lean Award for Direction for *Four Weddings and a Funeral* at the 1995 BAFTA Film Awards.

FILMS: The Awakening (1980), Bad Blood (1981), Dance with a Stranger (1985), The Good Father (1987), Amazing Grace and Chuck (1987), Soursweet (1988), Enchanted April (1992), Into the West (1992), Four Weddings and a Funeral (1994), An Awfully Big Adventure (1995), Donnie Brasco (1997), and Pushing Tin (1999).

NEWTON, ROBERT (1905–1956). The excessive image that characterized Robert Newton's performances in the latter part of his screen career overwhelms most critical evaluations of this actor's contribution to the cinema. A better indication of his talent can be found in his tragic patriarch in Lance Comfort's* *Hatter's Castle** (1941) and Frank Gibbons as the epitome of prewar British middle-class values in David Lean's* *This Happy Breed* (1944). Coming from a family of artists, Newton experienced success at a comparatively early age following his stage debut at fifteen and his Broadway debut when he replaced Laurence Olivier* in *Private Lives.* Newton, however, was not blessed with Olivier's leading-man physical features and his film roles in the 1930s were primarily character parts in films such as the Edgar Wallace's *The Squeaker* (1937), the popular historical drama *Fire over England** (1937), *Busman's Honeymoon* (1940), MGM's British version of the adventures of Dorothy Sayer's amateur criminologist Lord Pete Wimsey (played by Robert Montgomery), and Thorold Dickinson's* masterly version of *Gaslight** (1940). Leading roles and widespread critical approval followed *Hatter's Castle* and *This Happy Breed,* and by the late 1940s, after the excesses of his artist Lukey in *Odd Man Out* (1947), Bill Sykes in Lean's *Oliver Twist* (1948), and his even more excessive portrayal of Long John Silver in Disney's adaptation of Robert Louis Stevenson's *Treasure Island* (1950), Newton was elevated to the status of a major British film star.

In between these celebrated performances, Newton starred in two excellent film noirs. First, as the black marketeer Harry Carter who blackmails Burt Lancaster in *Kiss the Blood Off My Hands* (1948), and, even more successfully, as Dr.

Clive Riordan in Edward Dmytryk's *Obsession** (1949). In this latter film, a dark, perverse film noir, Riordan kidnaps his wife's American lover and imprisons him in a bomb site basement with a view to eventually murdering his rival and then disposing of the body in an acid bath. This would seem to provide Newton with the opportunity to ham it up, but his Riordan is basically a sane man with an insane desire and Newton contributes one of his most understated, and effective, performances. Each night Riordan transports acid to the bomb site in a hot water bottle before conversing with his victim in a civilized manner.

This was not, however, the dominant public image of Newton at this time and the eye-rolling excesses of Bill Sykes and Long John Silver remained in the public imagination to the extent that Newton was considered one of Britain's major cinema attractions in the late 1940s and early 1950s. His Long John Silver is normally considered the definitive interpretation despite numerous versions of this famous story. Newton's Long John Silver in *Treasure Island* deteriorated into broad caricature when he reprised the role in *Long John Silver* (1954), which formed the basis for a cheap television series shot in Australia in the mid-1950s. Newton applied the same excesses to his other pirate role as *Blackbeard the Pirate* (1952). Newton died soon after completing a cameo in Mike Todd's *Around the World in 80 Days* (1956).

FILMS: Reunion (1932), Fire over England (1937), Dark Journey (1937), The Squeaker (1937), Farewell Again (1937), The Green Cockatoo (1937), The Beachcomber (1938), Yellow Sands (1938), Jamaica Inn (1939), Poison Pen (1939), Dead Men Are Dangerous (1939), Hell's Cargo (1939), 21 Days (1940), Busman's Holiday (1940), Gaslight (1940), Channel Incident (1940), Bulldog Sees It Through (1940), Major Barbara (1941), They Flew Alone (1941), Hatter's Castle (1941), This Happy Breed (1944), Henry V (1944), Night Boat to Dublin (1945), Odd Man Out (1947), Temptation Harbour (1947), Snowbound (1947), Oliver Twist (1948), Kiss the Blood Off My Hands (1948), Obsession (1949), Treasure Island (1950), Waterfront (1950), Tom Brown's Schooldays (1951), Soldiers Three (1951), Les Miserables (1952), Blackbeard the Pirate (1952), Androcles and the Lion (1952), The Desert Rats (1953), The High and the Mighty (1954), Long John Silver (1954), The Beachcomber (1954), and Around the World in 80 Days (1956).

NIGHT AND THE CITY (Twentieth Century Fox, 1950)—Film noir. *Director:* Jules Dassin; *Producer:* Samuel G. Engel; *Script:* Jo Eisinger, based on the novel by Gerald Kersh; *Cinematography:* Max Greene; *Music:* Franz Waxman; *Cast:* Richard Widmark (Harry Fabian), Gene Tierney (Mary Bristol), Googie Withers (Helen Nosseross), Hugh Marlowe (Adam Dunne), Francis L. Sullivan (Phillip Nosseross), Herbert Lom (Kristo), Stanislaus Zbyszko (Gregorius), Mike Mazurki (the Strangler), Charles Farrell (Mickey Beer), Ada Reeve (Molly), Ken Richmond (Nikolas), Edward Chapman (Hoskins), Maureen Delaney (Anna O'Leary), James Hayter (Figler), and Gibb McLaughlin (Googin).

The political situation in the United States, specifically the investigations of the House Committee on Un-American Activities and the blacklisting of Hollywood actors and filmmakers, led Darryl F. Zanuck, head of production at Twentieth

Century Fox, to send French-born director Jules Dassin to London Film Studios at Shepperton with stars Richard Widmark and Gene Tierney, and supporting players Mike Mazurki and Hugh Marlowe, to film *Night and the City*. This expertise, in conjunction with cinematographer Max Greene (Mutz Greenbaum), composer Franz Waxman, and the talents of local actors such as Francis L. Sullivan, Googie Withers,* Herbert Lom, supported by an extensive list of British character players, including Maureen Delaney, James Hayter, and Gibb McLaughlin, produced not only one of the finest films made in London, but also one of the great film noirs. Never has London, including tourist landmarks such as Trafalgar Square and Piccadilly Circus, been transformed so effectively into an unrelenting vision of urban hell, a perfect encapsulation of a dark, threatening world permeated by betrayal, fall guys, and moral corruption.

The film begins with Harry Fabian, a cheap U.S.–born scam artist, running through the desolate streets of London, and the film ends in the same way with Fabian running for his life through the same wasteland until he is executed by his nemesis, the Strangler, with his body dumped into Thames at Hammersmith. In between these events, the film traces the downward spiral of Fabian as he tries to live down failed investments and "be somebody." In the past, Fabian's activities have caused suffering to his girlfriend, Mary Bristol. Now he is doomed. He overreaches himself and enters the world of large-scale corruption controlled by men such as Kristo. Fabian's problems intensify when he also threatens the fragile, perverse marital arrangement between Philip Nosseross, the owner of the Silver Fox nightclub, and his wife, Helen.

Fabian, striving to lift himself out of the world of small-time crime, manipulates himself into the position of wrestling promoter when Kristo's father, Gregorius, and his wrestling protégé, Nikolas, become disenchanted by Kristo's demeaning exploitation of the wrestling business in London. Fabian exploits this rift by promising Gregorius that he will promote classical Greco-Roman wrestling but, short of funds, Fabian gets caught between Helen Nosseross's desire to leave her husband and start up her own nightclub and Phil's jealousy and sexual frustration. Fabian accepts money from both parties and this, eventually, leads to his downfall when, in financial desperation, he tries to provoke Gregorius into fighting the Strangler. Fabian loses control of the situation and when Gregorius dies after subduing the Strangler, Kristo sets the London underworld onto Fabian with the promise of a bounty for his head.

At times, the doomed protagonists of film noir assume some of the dramatic characteristics of tragedy, particularly when they overstretch themselves. Similarly, Widmark's Harry Fabian, at times, assumes this tragic persona. At other times, he approximates his giggling psychopath persona from his trademark performance as Tommy Uddo in his debut film *Kiss of Death* (1947). Basically, he is a spiv, a con man sent out to "the American bar" to persuade gullible U.S. tourists to follow him back to Nosseross's Silver Fox club where "hostesses," trained and drilled by Helen Nosseross, can fleece their victims. He dies when he tries to move out of this limited sphere. In his attempt to "be somebody" and raise money to promote a legitimate wrestling match, Fabian takes the audience on a tour of London's underbelly as he visits, first, the Fiddler, who runs a scam involving beggars with fake disabilities (the Fiddler, who eventually betrays Fabian near the end of the film, offers to set Fabian up with his own operation involving "a few good beggars"), then Googin, who forges birth certificates, passports, and medical licenses, and finally Anna O'Leary, who deals in stolen nylons and cigarettes. This is a world devoid of "normal people."

Unfortunately, following hostile reviews from influential critics such as Dilys Powell, *Night and the City* performed poorly at the box office. The film was remade in 1992 with Robert DeNiro as the doomed protagonist, but the change of setting to New York, and a more sentimental perspective, severely weakened the film and it pales in comparison to the 1950 version.

THE NIGHT HAS EYES (Associated British Picture Corporation, 1942)— Gothic melodrama. *Director:* Leslie Arliss; *Producer:* John Argyle; *Script:* Leslie Arliss, based on the novel by Alan Kennington; *Cinematography:* Gunther Krampf; *Music:* Charles Williams; *Cast:* James Mason (Stephen Deremid), Wilfred Lawson (Jim Sturrock), Mary Clare (Mrs. Ranger), Joyce Howard (Marian Ives), Tucker McGuire (Doris), and John Fernald (Barry Randall).

The damaging social and/or psychological effects of war were utilized as a plot element in a number of films—such as *Mine Own Executioner** (1947) and *They Made Me a Fugitive** (1947). *The Night Has Eyes,* in this respect, is a rarity as the film was produced at a time (1942) when most British and U.S. films were focused not on the legacy, the harmful effects of past wars, but on the future and the need for communal solidarity to defeat the Axis powers. *The Night Has Eyes* is also significant in developing and reinforcing the distinctive screen persona of James Mason* within the British film industry as an authoritarian, dominant, morally problematic figure who is capable of dealing out rough treatment to the women he comes into contact with—a character trait that was exploited in subsequent films such as *The Man in Grey** (1943) and *The Seventh Veil** (1945).

Mason's Stephen Deremid in *The Night Has Eyes* is a tormented figure following his return from fighting for the Republican side in the Spanish Civil War. Deremid emerges as a shattered figure with his career as a composer and pianist in tatters. He is nursed back to a degree of health by his housekeeper, Mrs. Ranger, although he still fears that he has not conquered his murderous impulses completely. Consequently, Deremid lives an isolated existence on the Yorkshire moors and he is not amused when two schoolteachers on vacation, Marian Ives and her American friend Doris, seek the safety of his house during a storm.

Marian, however, has her own problems due to the loss of a close female friend who mysteriously disappeared in this area twelve months ago. Marian, who is presented as sexually repressed and introverted, and contrasted with the extroverted Doris, is immediately attracted to Deremid, especially after he explains to her what a "queer fascination cruelty has." He begins dressing her in his grandmother's clothes, carrying her around, and, on occasions, humiliating her with vicious taunts: "What've you got? No beauty. No brains. Just a lot of half-digested ideas about life picked up in a teachers' common room." Marian, however, rationalizes away Deremid's cruel behavior as a symptom of his wartime experiences.

Unfortunately, the climax to the film is a let down as a formulaic, rational explanation is produced to explain away the strange behavior of the characters. Deremid's mental problem, aggravated by the regular appearance of dead animals, was, it turns out, caused by his greedy housekeeper Mrs. Ranger and the handyman Jim Sturrock to keep Deremid dependent on them. They even killed Marian's friend when she threatened to upset their scheme by bringing in a medical specialist. Deremid, after saving Marian from Ranger and Sturrock, drives the crooked pair to their deaths on the moors.

The Night Has Eyes was released twice in the United States under two different titles. In 1943 the ultra low-budget studio and distributor PRC released the film as *Terror House.* In 1949, after Mason had left England and was working successfully for Hollywood studios, such as for MGM in *Madame Bovary* (1948), Cosmopolitan Pictures released the film again as *Moonlight Madness.*

NIL BY MOUTH (SE8 Group, 1997)—Social realism. *Director:* Gary Oldman; *Producers:* Luc Besson, Marc Frydman (associate), Hilary Heath, Gary Oldman, and Douglas Urbanski; *Script:* Gary Oldman; *Cinematography:* Ron Fortunato; *Music:* Eric Clapton; *Cast:* Ray Winstone (Ray), Kathy Burke (Valery), Charlie Creed-Miles (Billy), Laila Morse (Janet), Edna Dore (Kath), and Jamie Forman (Mark).

Toward the end of *Nil by Mouth,* Ray, alienated from his wife Valery and mother-in-law Janet, describes the lack of affection expressed by his father. This is the closest the film comes to explaining Ray's brutal behavior. The film provides a glimpse into the life of Ray, Valery, her brother Billy, and her mother Janet. It is a depressing world of domestic violence, poverty, drugs, and small-scale crime. Director, co-producer, and scriptwriter Gary Oldman, in his debut film, avoids moral judgments or simplistic solutions. His aim is to record a lifestyle that is familiar to him.[1]

Oldman does not provide a context, thematic or spatial, for many scenes in the film as he favors a style he describes as "early Ken Loach" and John Cassavetes. Most scenes are filmed with a hand-held camera and Oldman rarely pulls back to provide the viewer with a master shot. Thus, the viewing situation is always unstable and problematic. There is also the personal "Oldman factor," encapsulated in the dedication of the film to his father. Although Oldman admitted that Ray did not, literally, represent his dad, the film was a "love letter" to his father. Oldman, on the other hand, was pleased that his mother was captured in the film.

The film represents a continuation of Oldman's "confrontational" acting style found in performances in films such as *Sid and Nancy* (1986) and *Prick up Your Ears* (1987). *Nil by Mouth* is a brutal, engrossing film that terrifies, confuses, and at times borders on the self-indulgent by extending some scenes well past their usefulness. The film also contains many strong performances with both Ray Winstone* and Kathy Burke outstanding as the unhappily married couple.

The episodic story observes the world of Ray, Valery, and the drug-based culture of Billy. While Valery struggles with her pregnancy, Ray moves through the lower levels of petty crime, a world of strippers, drugs, and bashings. The only positive relationship is between Valery and Janet (Laila Morse, the real-life sister of Oldman). When Ray catches Billy stealing his drugs, he attacks the youth. Billy is later jailed. Ray erupts when he finds Valery playing pool in a pub with a man and the subsequent beating causes her to lose her baby. Ray is alienated from the family for a period. The film concludes with a "family get together," although there is no indication of any change in Ray's attitude or behavior.

Nil by Mouth won the Alexander Korda Award for Best British Film at the 1998 BAFTA Awards, and Oldman won Best Screenplay—Original. Burke won the Best Actress Award at the Cannes Film Festival in 1997, Oldman won the Channel 4 Director's Award at the 1997 Edinburgh International Film Festival, and Winstone and Burke won Best Performance Awards by a British Actor/Actress in a Independent Film. Morse won the Most Promising Newcomer at the 1998 British Independent Film awards.

NO LOVE FOR JOHNNIE (Embassy, 1960)—Political drama. *Director:* Ralph Thomas; *Producer:* Betty E. Box; *Script:* Nicholas Phipps and Mordecai Richler, based on a novel by Wilfred Fienburgh; *Cinematography:* Ernest Steward; *Music:* Malcolm Arnold; *Cast:* Peter Finch (Johnnie Byrne), Stanley Holloway (Fred Andrews), Mary Peach (Pauline West), Billie Whitelaw (Mary), Mervyn Johns (Charlie Young), Geoffrey Keen (Prime Minister), Donald Pleasance (Roger Renfrew), Rosalie Crutchley (Alice Byrne), Peter Barkworth (Henderson), Dennis Price (Flagg), Paul Rogers (Sydney Johnston), Michael Goodliffe (Dr. West), Gladys Hensen (Constituent), Hugh Burden (Tim Maxwell), Fenella Fielding (Sheilah), and Oliver Reed (Guest).

No Love for Johnnie was based on the 1959 novel by Labour politician Wilfred Fienburgh, who was killed driving home from the House of Commons just prior to the film going into production. Fienburgh's novel, and the film, pointed to the emergence of a new breed of "professional" Labour politicians in the 1950s. A breed that was less aligned with the traditional working-class values and more conscious of its image within the media. The film follows a period in the life of one of this new breed, Labour member of parliament Johnnie Byrne who ignores members of his electorate when they try to visit him at the House of Commons. Johnnie is more concerned with securing a cabinet post after winning his seat with an increased majority in the recent elections. However, the prime minister overlooks him while, at the same time, his wife, Alice, a member of the Communist Party, disillusioned with Johnnie's centrist policies, abandons their loveless marriage.

The film follows dual narrative strands as Johnnie, reluctantly, joins a left-wing splinter group determined to keep the Prime Minister "honest" to Labour policies.

The other strand is concerned with Johnnie's love life. After his wife leaves him, the film offers a frank depiction of middle-aged sexual despair as Johnnie wanders aimlessly, frustrated by his inability to satisfy his sexual needs. Johnnie watches a stripper and solicits a prostitute (without consummating the deal) before, drunkenly, groping Mary, a sad young woman in love with Johnnie who lives in a nearby apartment.

Johnnie's life regains some stability when he meets Pauline West, a young model, at a party. Their romance and the machinations within the Labour Party form the body of the film. The two strands intersect when Johnnie forgoes a promise to his splinter group to confront the prime minister in the House of Commons. Instead, he has sex with Pauline. As retribution, the left-wing group cause problems in Johnnie's electorate just as Pauline decides that Johnnie's lack of interest in children, together with their differing interests and experiences, renders him unacceptable as a husband. When Pauline leaves London, Johnnie follows her back to her provincial town where he discovers that Pauline's father is the same age and that the two men have more in common than he does with Pauline.

The film concludes on a suitably cynical note. Alice visits Johnnie and offers to resume their marriage while, at the same time, the Prime Minister offers Johnnie a minor cabinet position, based on the belief that Alice and Johnnie have permanently separated. However, if Johnnie resumes married life with Alice his cabinet post would be withdrawn due to the security risk caused by Alice's link to the Communist Party. Johnnie resolves this dilemma when he rips up Alice's contact phone number while sitting in the House of Commons listening to a boring speech, content that his political ambitions are now back on track.

Unfortunately, *No Love for Johnnie* was not well supported by either the public or the critics—perhaps because of the credentials of Betty E. Box and Ralph Thomas, who, in some people's eyes, were more associated with "light-weight comedies" such as *Doctor in the House* (1954). Peter Finch* won the Silver Berlin Bear Award for Best Actor at the 1961 Berlin International Film Festival and the Best British Actor Award at the 1962 BAFTA Film Awards.

NO ORCHIDS FOR MISS BLANDISH (Renown Pictures, 1948)—Gangster. *Director:* St. John Leigh Clowes; *Producers:* Oswald Mitchell and A. R. Shipman; *Script:* St. John Leigh Clowes; *Cinematography:* Gerald Gibbs; *Music:* George Melachrino; *Cast:* Jack La Rue (Slim Grisson), Linden Travers (Miss Blandish), Hugh McDermott (Fenner), Walter Crisham (Eddie), Danny Green (Flyn), Lila Molnar (Ma Grisson), Richard Nelson (Riley), Frances Marsden (Anna Borg), Percy Marmont (Mr. Blandish), Leslie Bradley (Bailey), Zoe Gail (Margo), and Charles Goldner (Louis).

Any film that could send the British critics in the late 1940s into a feeding frenzy of outrage and disgust cannot be all bad. The bad press that *No Orchids for Miss Blandish* received was surpassed only by the hostile critical reaction to Michael Powell's* *Peeping Tom** twelve years later. The film was little more than a low-budget gangster film that tried to replicate many of the conventions of this Hollywood genre. The weaknesses of the film are obvious—the phony U.S. dialogue and accents, the small budget that renders much of the film static by limiting the number of interior sets, mediocre nightclub acts, and variability of the performances, as some British actors, such as Sid James, struggle to duplicate the speech patterns of Hollywood gangsters. Perennial American B actor Jack La Rue, as the love-smitten gangster Slim Grisson, having spent the bulk of his career in such films, is excellent. Also notable is Linden Travers, repeating her 1942 stage role as the wealthy Miss Blandish, who prefers the masculine pleasures of gangster Slim Grisson rather than return to the bloodless respectability of life within the Blandish family.

What appeared, on the surface, to arouse the critics was the film's casual use of violence, especially early in the film, when Richard Nelson's Riley tries to maim most of the members of the cast, including the savage killing of Blandish's fiancé, Foster Harvey. However, the depiction of the violence is contained by its generic context. It is mainly implicit and conveyed by the reaction of the other actors. What may have really upset the British critics was the film's attempts to replicate a "low-brow" strand of U.S. popular culture. This is also evident in the controversial novel by James Hadley Chase, on which the film is based. Chase's 1939 novel tries to emulate the U.S. hard-boiled literary style.

Chase, in actuality Rene Raymond, a librarian and wholesale bookseller, wrote a more lurid story than the film focusing on the sexual harassment of an heiress who is kidnapped and repeatedly raped by gang members. Eventually, she falls prey to the attentions of Slim Grisson, a sexually disturbed member of the Grisson gang, headed by his mother, Ma Grisson. The novel concludes with Blandish's death. She kills herself because she feels degraded by the experience. The 1948 film changes the motivation for Blandish's suicide, a factor that may have inflamed the critics of the film even more. She chooses death in the film because she is separated from her lover. She would rather die than return to her family. Significantly, Travers's Blandish, after the initial violation from other gang members, is shown enjoying and soliciting Slim Grisson's attentions, even after he offers her the opportunity to escape.

NORTH WEST FRONTIER (Rank, 1959)—Empire film. *Director:* J. Lee Thompson; *Producer:* Marcel Hellman; *Script:* Robin Estridge, from a screenplay by Frank Nugent and based on a story by Patrick Ford and Will Price; *Cinematography:* Geoffrey Unsworth; *Music:* Mischa Spoliansky; *Cast:* Kenneth More (Captain William Scott), Lauren Bacall (Catherine Wyatt), Herbert Lom (Van Leyden), Wilfred Hyde-White (Bridie), Ursula Jeans (Lady Windham), Ian Hunter (Sir John Windham), I. S. Johar (Indian train engineer), and Eugene Deckers (Peters).

Although *North West Frontier* was described by Raymond Durgnat as an "elegiac farewell to [the] Empire" with its archetypal characters and, ultimately, its celebration of British imperialism in India, it also resembles a Hollywood Western in terms of narrative structure and imagery. This was especially evident in the scenes depicting the enemy on horseback attacking a British train as it travels across the barren Indian landscape. This visual debt to the Western, and especially the Westerns of John Ford, may be due, to some extent, to the fact that Hollywood scriptwriter Frank Nugent contributed to *North West Frontier.* Earlier, Nugent had worked on such Ford Westerns as *Fort Apache* (1948), *Three Godfathers* (1948), *She Wore a Yellow Ribbon* (1949), *Wagon Master* (1950), and *The Searchers* (1956). Or it may be more to do with J. Lee Thompson,* who, after two more films, fulfilled his desire to shift to Hollywood, where he worked on (mostly) genre films, including Westerns, for the rest of his career.

The film begins in the Northwest province of India in 1905 as Moslem rebels attack the palace of the Hindu maharajah. The maharajah's son, Prince Kishan, is transported from the palace after his father's death by his American governess, Catherine Wyatt, and a British military officer, Captain William Scott. They escort the child to the British base at Haserabad. Haserabad is also under attack and the British are determined to protect Prince Kishan as he is the spiritual leader of millions of Hindus. So they plan to transport him 300 miles across enemy territory to safety. To accomplish this, Captain Scott, Wyatt, Lady Windham, the wife of the British governor of Haserabad, Peters, a French-British armaments dealer who sold weapons to the Moslems, Bridie, a British civil servant, and Van Leyden, a Dutch Indian journalist, plus an Indian train engineer and a handful of Indian soldiers, commandeer an old shunting engine, *The Empress of India,* and set off on their perilous journey.

The small group encounters many obstacles along its way. These dangers function to highlight and celebrate such stereotypical attributes of the empire film such as self-sacrifice, devotion to duty, and resourcefulness. These traits combine with overt displays of paternalism with regard to the Indians. For example, the Hindu rebels, Captain Scott declares, are like children and there are, between the intermittent attacks, frequent discussions within the group regarding the British contribution in India. Van Leyden provides an alternative point of view. When, for example, the group encounters a refugee train with all of its inhabitants slaughtered, Scott tells Van Leyden, "You see what happens when the British aren't around to keep order." Van Leyden replies, "Divide and rule, the British policy is responsible for this." Scott counters by pointing out that the Moslems and Hindus were fighting each other for hundreds of years before the British arrived in India.

Gradually, the film subverts Van Leyden's assertion that the Moslems are only fighting for freedom. This point of view is associated with the half-caste Moslem journalist who is shown to be a sinister character, particularly after he tries to kill the young Indian prince. On the other hand, Wyatt initially functions as an "isolationist" with her independent, nonpartisan views. She represents a middle position between the more extreme supporters of the empire, such as Lady Windham ("Half the world mocks us and half the world is only civilized because we made it so."), and the nationalist Moslem position represented by Van Leyden. Gradually, Wyatt moves closer to Windham's imperial point of view and this affinity is reflected in her actions when she kills Van Leyden after he threatens Scott.

Despite its overt ideological context, *North West Frontier* is, ultimately, a rousing adventure film with superb action scenes and an effective musical score by Mischa Spoliansky, who also wrote the score twenty-four years earlier for another celebration of British imperialism, *Sanders of the River** (1935). *North West Frontier* is also one of the last effective films in this cycle. The end of colonial rule in India is acknowledged at the end of the film after Scott delivers Prince Kishan to safety. The young Indian child reluctantly tells the British officer that "my father says I must fight the British to make them go away. Will I have to fight you?" After Scott tells Kishan that he hopes not, Catherine retorts, "You see, you will have to fight Kishan. That's all the thanks you get." Scott's reply to this aptly sums up the self-serving, self-sacrificial ethos of this genre: "That's all the thanks we ever get."

NOTES

1. See G. Howell, "Gary Oldman: Soft Act to Follow," *The Australian Magazine,* April 14/15, 2001, p. 34.
2. Raymond Durgnat, *A Mirror for England: British Movies from Austerity to Affluence,* London, Faber, 1970, p. 82.

O

OBSESSION (An Independent Sovereign Film, 1949)—Crime/film noir. *Director:* Edward Dmytryk; *Producer:* N. A. Bronsten; *Script:* Alec Coppel, based on his novel *A Man about a Dog; Cinematography:* C. M. Pennington-Richards; *Music:* Nino Rota; *Cast:* Robert Newton (Dr. Clive Riordan), Sally Gray (Storm Riordan), Phil Brown (Bill Kronin), Naunton Wayne (Superintendent Finsbury), James Harcourt (Aitken), Ronald Adam (Clubman), and Michael Balfour (American Sailor).

In the late 1940s, Edward Dmytryk was forced out of Hollywood because of the blacklisting of communists, socialists, and fellow travellers. Dmytryk was a key figure during this period (he was eventually imprisoned for twelve months and then welcomed back into Hollywood when he supplied names to the House Committee on Un-American Activities) as his last Hollywood film before leaving for England was the controversial *Crossfire* (1947), a film that was singled out because of its overt anti-Semitism. Thus, for a director familiar with the world of film noir and the low-budget thriller (see *Murder, My Sweet* [1944] and *Cornered* [1946]), *Obsession* offered Dmytryk an opportunity to work within this type of film in Britain.

The outcome is a fascinating mixture of styles and narrative modes as U.S. film noir mutates into a different cultural context. Yet, despite the film's civilized tone, which emphasizes the superficial display of civility and manners between the three central characters (and a characteristically perceptive, if eccentric English police detective), *Obsession* still preserves a basic ingredient of film noir: the destructive power of sexual repression. The characters belong to the hard-boiled world of film noir—the bitter husband (Dr. Clive Riordan) who wants to preserve his marriage by killing his latest rival (Bill Kronin) despite the fact that his adulterous wife (Storm Riordan) despises him.

The basic dramatic situation in *Obsession* is a familiar one—Harley Street specialist Dr. Clive Riordan resents the succession of lovers attracted to his wife,

Storm. Thus, Riordan kidnaps Storm's latest lover, American Bill Kronin, and chains him to the wall in a bombed-out abandoned building. Riordan's plan is to keep Kronin alive so that if things go wrong he can produce him to the police. In the meantime, Riordan brings Kronin food, drinks (martinis), and the newspaper as he prepares to kill the American in an acid bath—in a characteristic English touch, each time Riordan visits Kronin with supplies, he also carries acid in a hot water bottle.

It is worth noting that the nationality of Storm's lover (American) is not an accident as early scenes involving Riordan at his private club show the elderly men discussing world politics where they bitterly resent the decline of the British Empire and the dependency of Britain on U.S. aid. This aspect is not fully developed as audience sympathy, almost by default, drifts toward the hapless American chained to the wall (symbolic revenge on the part of the British?) as Riordan's superior, calculating manner quickly destroys audience support for his situation, despite the callous treatment by his wife. Similarly, Storm is depicted as shallow and totally self-absorbed. At the end of the film when Storm visits Kronin in hospital, she tells him that she plans to recover from her ordeal with a South American vacation. Kronin, who is fortuitously saved by the actions of the Riordan family dog and an alert policeman, indicates to Storm that he prefers the family dog to her company. A satisfying end to a superior film noir.

THE OCTOBER MAN (Two Cities, 1947)—Film noir/melodrama. *Director:* Roy Ward Baker; *Producer:* Eric Ambler; *Script:* Eric Ambler; *Cinematography:* Erwin Hillier; *Music:* William Alwyn; *Cast:* John Mills (Jim Ackland), Joan Greenwood (Jenny Carden), Edward Chapman (Peachey), Kay Walsh (Molly Newman), Joyce Carey (Mrs. Vinton), Catherine Lacey (Miss Selby), Patrick Holt (Harry Carden), Jack Melford (Wilcox), Felix Aylmer (Dr. Martin), Frederick Piper (Detective Inspector Godby), James Hayter (Garage Man), and Juliet Mills (Child).

Jim Ackland, an industrial chemist, suffers both physically and mentally following a bus crash that kills a young child in his care. After spending a year in hospital recovering from the psychological trauma of the accident, Ackland, to the relief of his insurance company, is discharged and goes to live in a bleak boarding house on the edge of Clapham Common. Although Ackland still suffers from periodic bouts of depression and thoughts of suicide, his life gradually turns around, particularly after falling in love with Jenny Carden, the sister of a fellow worker (Harry Carden). However, when a resident of his boarding house, Molly Newman, is strangled on the common, the police, and a vindictive boarder (Mrs. Vinton), quickly assume that Ackland killed Newman. The film, however, points to another boarder, Peachey, although Roy Ward Baker* and scriptwriter Eric Ambler maintain a degree of ambiguity until Peachey reveals his guilt in a powerful scene as Edward Chapman, as the demented Peachey, points out to Ackland that he is trapped by circumstances. Prior to this confession, Ackland suffers regular bouts of self-doubt as no one, except Jenny, will believe him.

The basic story line of *The October Man* is relatively conventional, but Baker's direction transforms Ambler's story into a visually (and aurally) powerful drama that cleverly weaves the external elements, the crime, with the film's internalized (psychological) drama. Similarly, audience expectations are challenged by the casting of John Mills* as Ackland, whose disturbance is often conveyed by the alternate twisting of his handkerchief into the positive image of a rabbit or the more negative sign of a strangulation device. This motif is effectively used at the film's conclusion to signify Ackland's victory over his recurrent desire to kill himself.

The October Man was Baker's first film as director and although it was a somewhat troubled production, where producer and writer Ambler lost faith in Baker due to the slow pace of the production (the film was scheduled for twelve weeks and took seventeen),[1] it is a remarkably assured debut film. Baker's use of composition, lighting, and sound to advance the story is consistently employed, especially in the three scenes of Ackland contemplating suicide while standing on a railway bridge as a steam train passes below. Similarly, on a lighter note, Baker generates a degree of romantic warmth through his cutting and framing when Ackland first meets Jenny at a company dinner dance. While Jenny, the only person who supports Ackland throughout the film, is a relatively conventional character, Joan Greenwood* imbues the role with her customary sensuality and screen presence.

"Film noir," as a universal description, was, until recently, not used to describe films such *The October Man.* However, this film contains most of the basic characteristics generally associated with the U.S. cycle, with some local inflections. Such characteristics included the shift in focus to the insecure male protagonists who populated such films in the postwar period. In *The October Man,* these insecurities emerge through a combination of fate and a hostile environment that includes the vicious Mrs. Vinton and a police system eager to establish guilt. Equally importantly, the film blends the external problem, the death of the vulnerable Newman, with the internalized drama involving Ackland's suicidal tendencies. Both are shown to be related. Ackland's trauma is provoked by a hostile, arbitrary universe where fate works only in a negative fashion—Ackland happens to be walking alone on the common the night Newman is murdered carrying a check from him. Thus, *The October Man,* and other British films of the late 1940s (e.g., see *They Made Me a Fugitive** [1947], *Daybreak* [1948], *Mine Own Executioner** [1947], and *Dear Murderer** [1948]) signify a significant shift in the British crime film and melodrama. This shift is exposed by the prayer that Ackland reads on a plaque in his barren room: "From ghoulies, ghosties and short-legged beasts that go bump in the night, Good Lord deliver us." Unfortunately, *The October Man,* like other postwar British films, reveals a universe where such hopes for personal security are shown to be simplistic and obsolete.

OLIVIER, LAURENCE (1907–1989). In 1979, Laurence Olivier was seventy-two years old and no longer physically able to pursue his favorite craft: stage acting (and direction). Instead, he was now a feature film character actor, a phase that had begun, interspersed by occasional leading roles, in 1960 with *The Enter-tainer.* This stage in Olivier's career blossomed after his last stage performance in 1974. In 1978–1979, Olivier appeared in the crass melodrama *The Betsy* (1978), based on a Harold Robbins novel, the type of film where Olivier could always be counted on to produce an excessive performance; *The Boys from Brazil* (1978), with Olivier's Nazi-hunting protagonist combating Dr. Joseph Mengele's (Greg-ory Peck) plans to develop a breed of young Hitlers; *A Little Romance* (1979), with Olivier as the go-between in the romantic desires of a young American girl and a French youth; and the revisionist interpretation of Bram Stoker's *Dracula** (1979), with Frank Langella recreating his Broadway interpretation of Count Dracula as a romantic Gothic figure and Olivier as his nemesis, Professor Abra-ham Van Helsing. Although such films appear, at best, as a brief footnote to his career, the point is that within the limitations of each film Olivier demonstrated that he was a fine film actor—especially his Van Helsing in the underrated *Drac-ula.* For many, this period in Olivier's career was, unjustly, perceived as a sad phase—a period in which some saw his appearance in such films as "desperate" or "mercenary."

It is true that Olivier, like Gielgud* and some of his other British theatrical con-temporaries, despised film acting in the 1930s. It was not until his critically cele-brated performance as Heathcliff in the Hollywood production of *Wuthering Heights* (1939) that he expressed any interest in the aesthetics of screen acting, a change that he credits to William Wyler, the director of the film. In the early 1930s Olivier accompanied his actress-wife Jill Esmond to the United States for a Broadway production of *Private Live.* After signing a Hollywood contract with RKO he made little impression although he appeared in a number of American films during this period, such as *Friends and Lovers* (1931), *The Yellow Ticket* (1931) and *Westward Passage* (1932). After testing for the male lead in *Queen Christina* (1933), opposite Greta Garbo, he lost the part to John Gilbert and Olivier returned to the stage.

The stage occupied Olivier throughout the 1930s (and until the early 1970s, despite a prolonged period of "stage fright"). He was a romantic leading man in a few films in the second half of the decade, including the historical epic *Fire over England** (1937), opposite his soon-to-be second wife, Vivien Leigh; the lame screwball comedy *The Divorce of Lady X* (1938), opposite Merle Oberon; and the comedy-spy thriller *Q Planes* (1939). After this film, Olivier left England for Hollywood with Leigh, who (eventually) starred in *Gone with the Wind* (1939). Olivier followed with the successful Gothic melodrama *Rebecca* (1940), as Max-imillian de Winter, a role that suited his sensibility and screen image—his interest in Freudian psychology resulted in a penchant for psychologically disturbed, morally problematic characters (both on the stage and in the cinema).

Successful Hollywood productions of *Pride and Prejudice* (1940) and *Lady Hamilton* (1941), populated by U.S.–based British actors, cemented Olivier's reputation as a film actor but, after military service and a rousing cinematic production of *Henry V* (1944), which Olivier directed, produced, and starred, he returned to the stage. Olivier returned to film with his adaptations of *Hamlet* (1948) and *Richard III* (1955). A major disappointment in the 1950s was the British-based film version of Terence Rattigan's play *The Sleeping Prince*, retitled for the screen as *The Prince and the Showgirl* (1957), directed by Olivier and co-starring Marilyn Monroe. Olivier's seedy vaudevillian Archie Rice in *The Entertainer* marked the beginning of another phase in his career as he continued to apply himself to the stage with occasional cameo appearances in showy character roles on the screen—such as his bisexual Crassius in *Spartacus* (1960), Superintendent Newhouse in *Bunny Lake Is Missing* (1965), and the Mahdi in *Khartoum* (1966). In 1972, determined to arrest the public consideration of him as a "small-part actor" in films, he accepted the leading role, opposite Michael Caine,* in the film version of Anthony Shaffer's play *Sleuth* (1972). The success of this clever comedy-mystery rejuvenated his screen career and he continued to work regularly in both film and television productions until the mid-1980s.

Olivier was knighted in 1947 and made a life peer in 1970. He was the only person in the history of the Academy Awards to direct himself in an Oscar-winning role in *Hamlet (1948),* a film that won four Academy Awards. Earlier, Olivier starred in, and directed, the remarkable production of *Henry V* (1945), which won an Honorary Award at the 1947 Academy awards for Olivier for his "outstanding achievement" in bringing Shakespeare's play to the screen. Olivier was also nominated in successive years for the Best Actor Oscar for *Wuthering Heights* and *Rebecca* as well as nominations for *The Entertainer, Othello* (1965), *Sleuth, Marathon Man* (1976), and *The Boys from Brazil.* He was given an Honorary Award for his overall contribution to the cinema in 1979. Olivier was also nominated for *Carrie* (1952) at the 1953 BAFTA Film Awards, won Best British Actor for *Richard III* at the 1956 Awards, and was nominated for Best British Actor for *The Prince and the Showgirl, The Devil's Disciple* (1959), *The Entertainer,* and *Term of Trial* (1962). Olivier won the 1970 BAFTA Award for Best Supporting Actor for *Oh! What a Lovely War* (1969) and was nominated for Best Actor for *Sleuth.* Lord Olivier died in 1989. He published two autobiographical books: *Confessions of an Actor* (1984) and *On Acting* (1986).

FILMS: Too Many Crooks (1931), The Temporary Widow (1931), Friends and Lovers (1931), Potiphar's Wife (1931), The Yellow Ticket (1931), Westward Passage (1932), No Funny Business (1932), Perfect Understanding (1933), Moscow Nights (1935), As You Like It (1936), Fire over England (1936), Twenty-One Days (1937), The Divorce of Lady X (1938), Q Planes (1939), Wuthering Heights (1939), Rebecca (1940), Conquest of the Air (1940), Pride and Prejudice (1940), Words for Battle (voice, 1941), Lady Hamilton (1941), The 49th Parallel (1941), The Demi-Paradise (1943), The Volunteer (short, 1943), Malta GC (short, 1943), This Happy Breed (narr., 1944), Henry V (1945), Fighting Pilgrims (narr., 1945), Hamlet (1948), A Gift of Life (narr., 1949), Many Neighbours (narr., 1949), The Magic Box (1951), Carrie (1952), A Queen Is Crowned (narr., 1953), The Beggar's Opera (1953), The Drawings of Leonardo da Vinci (narr., 1953), Richard III (1955), The Prince and the Showgirl (1957), The Devil's Disciple (1959), The Entertainer (1960),

Spartacus (1960), The Power and the Glory (1961), Term of the Trial (1961), Bunny Lake Is Missing (1965), Othello (1965), Khartoum (1966), Romeo and Juliet (voice, 1968), The Shoes of the Fisherman (1968), The Dance of Death (1968), Oh! What a Lovely War (1969), Battle of Britain (1969), Three Sisters (1970), Nicholas and Alexander (1971), Tree of Life (narr., 1971), Lady Caroline Lamb (1972), Sleuth (1972), The Rehearsal (1974), Love among the Ruins (1975), The Gentleman Tramp (voice, 1975), The Seven-Per-Cent Solution (1976), Marathon Man (1976), A Bridge Too Far (1977), The Betsy (1978), The Boys from Brazil (1978), Dracula (1978), A Little Romance (1979), The Jazz Singer (1980), Inchon (1980), Clash of the Titans (1981), Wagner (1982), The Jigsaw Man (1983), The Bounty (1984), Wild Geese II (1985), and War Requiem (1988).

ONCE A JOLLY SWAGMAN (Wessex Films/Rank, 1948)—Motorcycle racing/ social problem. *Director:* Jack Lee; *Producer:* Ian Dalrymple; *Script:* William Rose and Jack Lee, based on the novel by Montagu Slater; *Cinematography:* H. E. Fowle; *Music:* Bernard Stevens; *Cast:* Dirk Bogarde (Bill Fox), Bonar Colleano (Tommy Possey), Renee Asherson (Pat), Bill Owen (Lag Gibbon), Moira Lister (Dorothy Elizabeth), Cyril Cusack (Duggie Lewis), Sid James (Rowton), James Hayter (Pa Fox), and Patric Doonan (Dick).

A left-wing sporting film such as *Once a Jolly Swagman* is a rarity in the British cinema. During the early sections, the film tries to link the exploitative conditions and audience appeal of motorcycle racing in the late 1930s with the rise of fascism. Once World War II begins, this theme is dropped as the film loses its dramatic focus. Also, the film's limited production values do not support its ambitious story line that extends from 1937 to 1947.

In 1937, working-class youth Bill Fox realizes that he can make more money as a speedway motorcycle racer than working in a dead-end factory job and he rises quickly to the top of his sport. In his first major race, he accidentally causes the reigning champion, Australian rider (hence the title of the film) Lag Gibbon, to fall and Gibbon never recovers from his injuries. During these early years, Fox is arrogant and ambitious, and he moves quickly into the fast lane with the assistance of a "society" woman, Dorothy Elizabeth ("Dotty Liz"). Dotty Liz is, essentially, a stereotype—blonde, permissive, and exploitative—with one added character trait—she is a fascist sympathizer who visited Germany in the years leading up to World War II.

This political strand is reinforced when Fox's brother leaves the family to fight on the Republican side in the Spanish Civil War. Both narrative strands, the political and the generic, come together, briefly, when Fox rejects Dotty Liz's nihilistic lifestyle. At this point, a parade of fighters returning from the Spanish conflict is shown as Fox walks away from Dotty. From this moment, Fox develops a social conscience, a character trait that is reinforced after a visit to Gibbon in hospital. Fox subsequently tries to organize the motorcycle riders into a union that will protect them and their families in case of injury or death.

Fox marries Gibbon's sister and uses his wedding reception as a political forum to criticize the exploitation of the riders by the owners of the speedway—this results in Fox's suspension and when he refuses to give up the sport his wife leaves him. The final section of the film is less successful as it tries to cover World War II and the postwar period, culminating in a conventional ending when Fox relinquishes the sport so that his wife will return to him. This ending is inconsistent with the film's dominant theme that there are few opportunities for working-class men like Fox—except dangerous sports such as motorcycle racing.

The best scenes in *Once a Jolly Swagman* occur the early part of the film. These scenes capture the atmosphere of motorcycle racing, with material shot at the New Cross Speedway stadium in South London. This material, combined with footage filmed in a field at night with Dirk Bogarde* strapped to the chassis of a truck to provide inserts for the racing scenes, is very effective.[2] Here the film captures the essence of the sport as it intercuts crowd reaction with the thrills and injuries suffered by the riders. The film is not reticent in exposing the (sexual) thrill enjoyed by young women as they anticipate the injuries that will be inflicted on the young riders. In these scenes, the film develops its bold thematic association between the exploitation of working-class males as they risk life and limb for thrill-seeking crowds, and the rise of fascism. At the end of the film, with the defeat of the fascists during World War II, the riders are now protected by adequate union coverage.

Once a Jolly Swagman was nominated for Best British Film at the 1949 BAFTA Film Awards.

O'TOOLE, PETER (b. 1932). Peter Seamus O'Toole, from County Galway, entered the British film industry from the theater as a classically trained actor. O'Toole studied at the Royal Academy of Dramatic Art, with Albert Finney,* Alan Bates,* and Richard Harris, before gaining stage experience at the Bristol Old Vic. He received critical acclaim in 1959 for his performance in *The Long, the Short and the Tall* (although he lost the lead in the film version to Laurence Harvey*). O'Toole's film debut in Nicholas Ray's Eskimo melodrama *The Savage Innocents* (1959) attracted little attention (with O'Toole's voice, one of his best assets, dubbed in post-production), as did his supporting role in the lackluster 1960 Disney version of Robert Louis Stevenson's *Kidnapped.* His next film, John Guillermin's* *The Day They Robbed the Bank of England* (1960), was at least an exciting crime film. These three films, however, did not prepare audiences and critics for the impact O'Toole would have around the world in his next film, David Lean's* *Lawrence of Arabia* (1962). O'Toole, who won the part after replacing Finney, appeared just right for the role of the dreamy, masochistic idealist T. E. Lawrence, and the role, a mixture of heroism, ego, savior, and madness, established character traits that were to permeate many of O'Toole's films over the next four decades.

Following his two years working with Lean on *Lawrence of Arabia,* a period that he later claimed taught him more than any other experience, the success of the film, and O'Toole's undoubted talent, resulted in many plum acting roles over the next few years—including his two interpretations of Henry II in *Becket* (1964), opposite Richard Burton as Becket, and *The Lion in Winter* (1968), with Katharine Hepburn as Eleanor of Aquitaine. These two films represent O'Toole at his peak in two highly disciplined performances where he more than held his own against his prestigious costars. O'Toole was a Nazi murderer (General Tanz) in Anatole Litvak's overblown World War II melodrama *The Night of the Generals* (1966), Lord Jim in Richard Brooks's equally overblown version of Joseph Conrad's novel by the same title (1965), and Arthur Chipping in the 1969 disastrous musical remake of the 1939 MGM hit *Goodbye, Mr. Chips.*

Although the 1960s was, to a degree, a productive period for O'Toole, with Oscar nominations for Best Actor for *Lawrence of Arabia, Becket, The Lion in Winter,* and *Goodbye, Mr. Chips,* heavy alcohol use and a poor selection of roles in the 1970s led to a relatively rapid decline in his career—with the best performance during this period as the British lord who thinks he is Jesus Christ in Peter Medak's irreverent comedy *The Ruling Class* (1972), a tailor-made role for the actor during this period of excess. In the early 1980s, O'Toole enjoyed a kind of "come back" following medical treatment and a period of abstinence, with critically celebrated performances in two Hollywood films: *The Stunt Man* (1980), with O'Toole as the film director who covers for Steve Railsback after he has accidentally killed his stunt man, and, in a funny impersonation of Errol Flynn in his final years, as the faded swashbuckler-actor, Alan Swann, in Richard Benjamin's comedy *My Favorite Year* (1982).

O'Toole received Academy Award nominations for both films and, later in the decade, he was nominated for the BAFTA Best Actor in a Supporting Role Award for his role as the English tutor of the last emperor of China in Bernardo Bertolucci's *The Last Emperor* (1987). O'Toole also appeared in numerous television productions in the 1980s and 1990s as prestigious film roles were sparse, although he did have a supporting role as a leper in Paul Cox's Australian-Dutch film that dramatized the role of a priest caring for people suffering from Hansen's Disease in *Molokai: The Story of Father Damian* (1999).

FILMS: The Savage Innocents (1959), Kidnapped (1960), The Day They Robbed the Bank of England (1960), Lawrence of Arabia (1962), Becket (1964), What's New Pussycat? (1965), Lord Jim (1965), The Sandpiper (voice, 1965), The Bible (1966), How to Steal a Million (1966), Night of the Generals (1966), Casino Royale (1967), The Lion in Winter (1968), Great Catherine (1968), Goodbye, Mr. Chips (1969), Country Dance (1969), Murphy's Law (1970), Under Milk Wood (1971), The Ruling Class (1972), Man of La Mancha (1972), Rosebud (1975), Man Friday (1975), Foxtrot (1976), Power Play (1978), Zulu Dawn (1979), Caligula (1979), The Stunt Man (1980), My Favorite Year (1982), Supergirl (1984), Creator (1985), Club Paradise (1986), The Last Emperor (1987), High Spirits (1988), In una Notte di Chiaro di Luna (1989), Wings of Fame (1990), The Rainbow Thief (1990), The Nutcracker Prince (voice, 1990), King Ralph (1991), Isabelle Eberhardt (1991), Worlds Apart (1992), Rebecca's Daughters (1992), The Seventh Coin (1993), Fairy Tale: A True Story (1997), Phantoms (1998), The Manor (1999), Molokai: The Story of Father Damian (1999), and Global Heresy (2001).

NOTES

1. See R. W. Baker, *The Director's Cut. A Memoir of 60 Years in Film and Television,* London, Reynolds and Hearn, 1999, p. 44.
2. McFarlane, *An Autobiography of British Cinema,* p. 356.

P

PARIS BY NIGHT (Film Four/Cineplex Odeon, 1988)—Political melodrama/
thriller. *Director:* David Hare; *Producers:* Edward Pressman and Patrick Cas-
savetti; *Script:* David Hare; *Cinematography:* Roger Pratt; *Music:* Georges
Delerue; *Cast:* Charlotte Rampling (Clara Paige), Michael Gambon (Gerald
Paige), Iain Glen (Wallace Sharp), Robert Hardy (Adam Gillvray), Jane Asher
(Pauline), Andrew Ray (Michael Swanson), Niamh Cusack (Jenny Swanton),
Linda Bassett (Janet Swanton), and Robert Flemying (Jack Sidmouth).

Celebrated British playwright David Hare wrote and directed this subversive
political thriller that works on many levels—as a straight thriller concerned with
Clara Paige's attempts to evade detection after killing a former business associate
in Paris and also as an effective metaphor for the changing social, economic, and
especially moral climate in Britain in the late 1980s. In this regard, Clara is
invested with sufficient recognizable traits, notably her emphasis on self-discipline
and accountability, to provide a link to the uncompromising characteristics celebrated in the early Margaret Thatcher years. Yet, the film is much more than a
reductionist, crude social parable and takes the viewer on an emotional ride,
beginning with a problematic presentation of Clara, who, at times, is invested with
a degree of sympathy and audience empathy as she faces a potential blackmailer.
This initial presentation only makes the final section of the film even more effective as Clara, metaphorically, removes her mask to reveal a self-interested, pragmatic, and hypocritical woman who publicly supports traditional values while
repudiating them through her actions. Ultimately, she represents the dark side of
entrepreneurial capitalism, the epitome of self-interested individualism.

Clara is a politically successful Conservative member of the European parliament, with a less successful marriage to aging British politician Gerald Paige.
The failure of the marriage does not unduly concern Clara, whose political star is
on the rise. The only cloud on her horizon is the repeated calls from a former business associate, Michael Swanson and, fearing blackmail, she has him removed

from a political meeting. While in Paris, however, she sees him again, and when she confronts him he falls to his death. Clara panics and runs away, leaving her handbag at the scene of the crime. After failing to retrieve it, she seeks sexual solace in the arms of young Wallace Sharp. When Wallace learns of Clara's actions, he is persuaded not to go to the police after she offers to divorce her husband and marry him. But Gerald, finally realizing the extent of his wife's deceit, has other ideas and kills her when she returns home.

The political ramifications of this film go beyond its literal subject matter and extend to the allegorical level based on a strong female politician at a time when Thatcher was in power. Importantly, the film systematically undermines the operation of traditional conservative values, based on the family, the need for self-discipline, and moral behavior.

Charlotte Rampling is riveting, as usual, as Clara Paige. The film exploits her cool beauty to gradually peel away the layers to reveal the monster lurking beneath this attractive facade. Her apparent vulnerability is interspersed with moments of ruthlessness early in the film, such as the brutal dressing-down of her distressed husband, and these early scenes foreshadow the revelation of her true character in the last part of the film when expediency and self-preservation overwhelm integrity. Hare's script skillfully probes Clara character, placing her in a series of morally problematic situations that reverse earlier expectations. For example, the film reveals that Michael Swanson, the potential blackmailer, was harmless and merely wanted financial assistance from his former business associates (Clare and Gerald Paige) as they had deceived him in a financial transaction. After his murder, Clare is forced to comfort Swanson's wife and daughter. Full of subtle ironies and dramatic twists, *Paris by Night* is one of the best films produced in Britain in the 1980s.

THE PASSIONATE FRIENDS (Cineguild Production, 1949)—Romance/melodrama. *Director:* David Lean; *Producers:* Ronald Neame and Eric Ambler; *Script:* Eric Ambler and Stanley Haynes, based on the novel by H. G. Wells; *Cinematography:* Guy Green; *Music:* Richard Addinsell; *Cast:* Ann Todd (Mary Justin), Claude Rains (Howard Justin), Trevor Howard (Steve Stratton), Isabel Dean (Pat), Betty Ann Davies (Miss Layton), Guido Lorraine (Hotel Manager), and Wilfred Hyde-White (Solicitor).

Much of the credit for *The Passionate Friends* must go to director David Lean,* art director John Bryan, and cinematographer Guy Green for the film's visual complexity, which rivals the best of the black and white melodramas from Warner Brothers in the 1940s. The script by Stanley Haynes and Eric Ambler, assisted by Bryan and Lean, is intensely emotional. This film could easily have been trite, overly sentimental, and utterly formulaic as it is based on one of the most familiar story lines—a wife (Mary Justin) torn between the romantic passion of her first love (Steven Stratton) and the security and affection offered by her husband (Howard Justin), who is both wealthier and older than she is. Some aspects of the film, as some critics noted, are similar to Lean's *Brief Encounter**

(1945). *The Passionate Friend* is more morally complex and, in its own way, as satisfying as *Brief Encounter.*

In 1948, Mary Justin arrives at a palatial Swiss hotel for a holiday—her husband, Howard, plans to join her in a few days. Unknown to Mary, her adjoining suite is, by chance, booked by her former lover, Steven Stratton. On the first night in the hotel, Mary remembers her last encounter with Steven at a New Year's Eve party in 1939, just after her marriage to Howard. At the New Year's Eve party, Mary's mind, in a "double" flashback, wanders back to her relationship with Steven prior to her marriage and she puzzles over the fact that although she tells Steven that she loves him, she cannot bring herself to marry him. When pressed by Steven for a reason, Mary tells him that she "wants to belong to myself," whereupon Steven tells her that her "life will be a failure." Herein lies the thematic crux of the film—a woman who, although attracted to the romantic notion of abandoning herself totally to wild, passionate love, cannot ultimately do it. Instead, she resigns herself to "love without all this clutching," a marriage not based on passion but affection and respect. Her choice was not at that time, and is not today, one favored by most films where "passion" and "love" are still equated.

This decision causes Mary great distress, a decision not helped by Fate in bringing Steven to an adjoining suite in her hotel. After nearly falling for him a second time, Mary discovers that not only is Steven married but that he has two young children. This assists her, and him, in keeping the relationship on a platonic basis. Howard fails to understand this and thinking that Mary has resumed her relationship with Steven, instigates divorce proceedings. In an emotionally powerful climax to the film, Howard provides a transparent explanation of the basis of his marriage to Mary—"I didn't expect love from you, or even great affection. I'd have been well satisfied with kindness and loyalty. You gave me love and kindness and loyalty. But it was the love you'd give a dog, and the kindness you'd give a beggar, and the loyalty of a bad servant." At the end of this tirade, delivered in characteristically powerful manner by Claude Rains, he turns and quietly apologizes by telling her that after all their years together, he finally realizes that he loves her. But Mary, distraught by this initial reaction, has run away to the London underground where she contemplates suicide. As she starts to fall onto the tracks, Howard clutches her and takes her home.

While this may seem a predictable, even banal, story, the execution is flawless as Lean is able to elicit tension from very familiar material. For example, Howard's suspicion that his wife is having an affair with Steven is confirmed when they inadvertently leave their theater tickets (for *First Love*) in the house. A close-up of these tickets, to show how this news is disturbing Howard, is inserted throughout the next scene as Howard dictates business material to his secretary (Miss Layton). This juxtaposition of images is followed by Howard strategically placing a theater program near Mary's cigarettes when she returns from her night out with Steven—to remind them that he knows they are deceiving him. There are many similar demonstrations of Lean's expertise throughout the film—particularly when Howard discovers his wife with Steven at the Swiss hotel. Here, Lean plays with the audience in a "Hitchcockian" manner as Howard casually fondles a pair of binoculars unaware that Steven and Mary are returning to the hotel from their trip into the mountains. Such sequences makes *The Passionate Friend* one of Lean's most masterly and underrated films.

PEEPING TOM (Anglo-Amalgamated, 1960)—Horror. *Director:* Michael Powell; *Producer:* Michael Powell; *Script:* Leo Marks; *Cinematography:* Otto Heller; *Music:* Brian Easdale; *Cast:* Carl Boehm (Mark Lewis), Moira Shearer (Vivian), Anna Massey (Helen Stephens), Maxine Audley (Mrs. Stephens), Brenda Bruce (Dora), Miles Malleson (Elderly Gentleman), Esmond Knight (Arthur Baden), Martin Miller (Doctor Rosan), Bartlett Mullins (Mr. Peters), Michael Goodliffe (Don Jarvis), Nigel Davenport (Sergeant Miller), Jack Watson (Inspector Gregg), Shirley Ann Field (Diane Ashley), and Pamela Green (Milly).

Before releasing *Peeping Tom,* Anglo-Amalgamated released *Horrors of the Black Museum* in 1959, directed by Arthur Crabtree. This film opened with a pair of trick binoculars that gouged out the eyes of a young woman. *Peeping Tom* soon followed with a more intelligent exploration of the sado-voyeuristic relationship between film and film viewer. The wrath of the British critics, naturally, was directed toward Michael Powell's* and Leo Marks's masterpiece rather than Crabtree's simple exploitation film. The extent of the critical reaction rendered *Peeping Tom* the most reviled film in British cinema history although the critical tide turned in the 1970s. Today, it is almost universally praised and even Dilys Powell revisited the film in 1994 and publicly retracted her scathing comments— unfortunately after Michael Powell's death.

Peeping Tom is a disturbing, confronting film, far from Powell's description of it as "a tender film, almost a romantic film." The troubling nature of the film is compounded when other factors are considered—such as the fact that Carl Boehm is dressed in Powell's old clothes and that the father who appears in the home movie made by Mark Lewis, and who is clearly the source of Lewis's murderous actions, was Powell himself as the scientist shown tormenting his young son, played by one of Powell's own children (Columba).

Peeping Tom, among other narrative strands, traces the effects of the scientist's experiments on Lewis, who works as a focus-puller in a film studio by day while moonlighting as a photographer of sex photos. These activities are interspersed with Lewis's real interest: his own movie that extends his father's research by capturing on film the fear expressed by young women in their final moments. The killings are carried out by Lewis's specially designed camera tripod that impales its victim just as the camera captures their final reaction. Powell's careful mixture of subjective and objective shots of the moments leading up to each killing involves the viewer—both as victim and killer. The result is an unsettling mixture of fetishistic voyeurism, sadism, and masochism. Powell cast Pamela Green, a popular nude model in the 1950s, as Milly, one of the models in the film. This serves to heighten his association between death, beauty, and voyeurism. On a less serious note, he also cast Esmond Knight, an actor blinded during World War II, as the director of the fictional film *The Walls Are Closing.*

Marks's script heightens the dramatic complexity of the film by presenting Lewis as a sympathetic figure, not the Jack-the-Ripper psychopath that would have provided the audience with a certain degree of "aesthetic distance" and emotional security. Instead, just as Alfred Hitchcock* cast young Anthony Perkins as the tormented Norman Bates in *Psycho* (1960), Lewis is a sympathetic figure. He tries to control his perverse impulses when he falls in love with Helen Stephens, the young woman who lives in a nearby apartment with her blind, whisky-drinking mother. The mother, played by Maxine Audley, who dyed her hair red to match the ill-fated Vivian's (Moira Shearer's) red hair, is a blind person who naturally intuits Lewis's disturbed nature.

Although Powell's contribution to the film has received significant critical attention, Marks's role should not be underestimated. The idea for the film came to Marks when he was working as a "codemaster" during World War II, when, he later pointed out, the fear within his unit was palpable. The agents were prepared by his team of women for service behind enemy lines, with the women knowing that many of them would be tortured and killed. This emphasis on fear and his fascination with Freudian psychology, combined with a love of intricate codes, provided the perfect template for Powell. In *Peeping Tom,* Powell continued to explore aspects of the cinema-going process, particularly the interrelationship between aesthetic experiences and life.

PINK STRING AND SEALING WAX (Ealing, 1945)—Period drama/film noir. *Director:* Robert Hamer; *Producers:* Michael Balcon and S. C. Balcon (associate); *Script:* Diana Morgan and Robert Hamer, based on the play by Roland Pertwee; *Cinematography:* Richard Pavey; *Music:* Norman Demuth; *Cast:* Mervyn Johns (Edward Sutton), Googie Withers (Pearl Bond), Gordon Jackson (David Sutton), Jean Ireland (Victoria Sutton), Sally Ann Howes (Peggy Sutton), Mary Merrall (Ellen Sutton), John Carol (Dan Powell), Catherine Lacey (Miss Porter), Garry Marsh (Joe Bond), Pauline Letts (Louise), and Maudie Edwards (Mrs. Webster).

This film is concerned with betrayal and domestic unhappiness, a theme that Robert Hamer* explored, in a contemporary setting, in *It Always Rains on Sunday** (1947). *Pink String and Sealing Wax,* set in 1890s Brighton, begins with members of the Sutton family anxiously waiting the return of Edward Sutton, the stern head of the family for his evening meal after testifying, in his capacity of consulting pharmacist, at the trial of a woman arrested for poisoning her husband. When Peggy Sutton notices her father's jaunty approach to the house, she realizes that the woman on trial has been condemned to death.

Patriarchal punishment of the "fallen woman" is a central motif in the film. Sutton's stern discipline of his family prohibits David's courtship of a young woman and Victoria's desire to train as an opera singer. Both desires, Edward Sutton tells his children, are immoral. He explains to his long-suffering wife, Ellen, his philosophical rationale for controlling the family in such a manner: "Love and fear are inseparable. God is love but we are taught to fear him." The film subjects this philosophy to a rigorous examination. Both David and Victoria disobey their father. David's rebellion, however, leads him to the marital problems of Pearl Bond. Her situation, in some way, parallels David's sense of entrapment with the Sutton family. Pearl suffers in a loveless marriage to Joe Bond, a drunken, abusive publican.

Pearl seeks solace with local womanizer Dan Powell. When David enters her world, she sees a means of escape from her intolerable situation. David takes Pearl back to the pharmacy to bandage her hand, after her husband accidentally strikes her, and Pearl steals poison to kill her husband. This action, eventually, implicates David after suspicions are raised about Joe's death. The situation becomes more complicated when Edward Sutton is commissioned to carry out the examination on the dead man. Edward resists Pearl's attempt to blackmail him into falsifying his report by threatening to implicate David. When this fails, and Dan abandons her, Pearl commits suicide.

Hamer is less concerned with the melodramatic details of the plot then with the dark ambience emanating from the repressive social context. Hence, the film concentrates on the ramification of Sutton's's unyielding control of his family. The film also consists of a series of failed love affairs—extending from David's disastrous infatuation with Pearl, to Pearl's betrayal by Dan, and minor figures, such as Louise's doomed love of Dan and, within the Sutton family, Victoria's rejection of Dan Bevan. Only a brief photograph at the end of the film, showing David's marriage to his first love, provides any semblance of a successful romance and a brief glimpse of "normality."

Hamer presents the restoration of "normality" in a cursory fashion. Instead, he emphasizes the cost of this restoration—the suicide of Pearl. This is presented as the major visual set piece in the film as a long track follows Pearl before she plunges to her death. The suicide of this strong, sensual woman, the film suggests, is a necessary precondition for the restoration of patriarchal rule. Googie Withers* is outstanding as the sensual, complex Pearl Bond and she is matched by Catherine Lacey as the cynical prostitute, Miss Porter. The overt references to Porter's profession, together with Pearl's suicide and the detailed poisoning of her husband, denied *Pink String and Sealing Wax* a Production Code Certificate in the United States.[1] The release of the film in the United States was delayed until 1950 when it was shown in New York without a certificate.

POOR COW (Anglo-Amalgamated, 1967)—Neorealist social drama. *Director:* Ken Loach; *Producers:* Joseph Janni and Edward Joseph (associate); *Script:* Nell Dunn and Ken Loach, based on the novel by Nell Dunn; *Cinematography:* Brian Probyn; *Music:* Donovan; *Cast:* Carol White (Joy), Terence Stamp (Dave), John Bindon (Tom), Kate Williams (Beryl), Queenie Watts (Aunt Emm), Ray Barron (Customer in Pub), and Ellis Dale (Solicitor).

Ken Loach* directed two critically celebrated television dramas in the 1960s, *Up the Junction* (written by Nell Dunn and adapted for the cinema by Peter

Collinson in 1967) and *Cathy Come Home,* starring Carol White as a homeless mother in London. After producer Joseph Janni purchased the rights to Dunn's novel *Poor Cow,* he invited Loach to direct the film with the small budget of £200,000. Although Loach subsequently described the film as "a mess,"[2] *Poor Cow,* scripted by Dunn from her novel, retains the stream-of-consciousness device used in the novel. This technique provides a fascinating opportunity to hear a working-class feminine voice—"I've always wanted, not power, but I've always wanted to have something that was mine. If I'd have been an old brass I'd have power." Similarly, Joy explains, to her friend Beryl, that she does not want to resort to full-time prostitution—her objection is not based on moral principles but on a fear that working as a prostitute might ruin the pleasure of sexual intercourse for her.

Loach, in his debut feature, utilizes a range of cinema techniques, including "cinema verité" documentary techniques, an ultra-naturalistic mode of acting, captions that interrupt the narrative, plus direct address to the camera from White. The film also expresses Loach's socialist beliefs, which did not waver over the years. This working-class empathy is evident right from the start with Joy giving birth to her son, who remains the only constant male figure in her life. After her husband Tom is sent to jail, following a botched robbery, Joy takes up with Dave, a criminal colleague of her husband. A brief, happy period, including a rural vacation in Wales, ends when Dave is sentenced to twelve years imprisonment. Although Joy feels nothing for her husband, the loss of Dave is keenly felt and she visits him frequently in jail.

Loach and Dunn refuse to express moral judgments on Joy's behavior while Dave is in jail. Even when she works as a semi-nude photographer's model for men who don't even bother to put film into their camera, Joy is more than just as a victim. Similarly, Joy refuses to deny herself sexual pleasure and she is shown to be an active sexual partner with many men—despite reassurances to Dave that she is going to remain celibate until he is released from prison. Thus, Loach, as in his subsequent films, eschews any hint of sentimentality and the associated conventions of melodrama, even though the basic story invites the use of simple stereotypes and a sentimental ending. The power of the film emanates from its refusal to resort to such practices.

PORTMAN, ERIC (1903–1969). Eric Portman was never comfortable playing conventional characters as he, generally, imbued his roles with a suggestion of perversity or other signs of emotional and/or psychological disturbance. He began on the stage in the mid-1920s, followed by a succession of minor film roles in the 1930s, including a brief, unsuccessful stint in Hollywood with a small role in *The Prince and the Pauper* (1937). Portman made a striking impression as the central character in Michael Powell's* *The 49th Parallel** (1941), the ruthless Nazi Lieutenant Hirth. In this film, Hirth is determined to let nothing interfere with his passage across Canada to the safety of the United States. Portman followed this with more humane haracterizations, such as the pilot in *One of Our*

Aircraft Is Missing (1942) and the factory foreman in *Millions Like Us* (1943). However, it was Lance Comfort's* moving melodrama *Great Day** (1945) that allowed Portman to display his acting range and talent as the tragic Captain John Ellis, a figure who lives only in the past "glories" of his military achievements in World War I and, with the changed circumstances of World War II, resists any attempt to subjugate his achievements in the past to the demands of the present. Ellis has little interest in communal village life and his reckless actions culminate in thoughts of suicide. Portman's Ellis, with his unrelenting focus on the past, is similar to his Thomas Colpepper in Powell's *A Canterbury Tale** (1944), a justice of the peace who diverts soldiers away from the local women and toward his lectures on his native Kent, by pouring glue on the hair of the local women.

The intensity of these performances, combined with his screen persona that perfected an unstable, brittle quality, characterized Portman's performances in the 1940s, especially from the period between 1945 and 1949—in films such as *Daybreak* (1948), as the hangman in a doomed love affair with Ann Todd,* as Paul Mangin, the artist living in the past and obsessed with the image of Edana Romney in Terence Young's visually splendid film noir *Corridor of Mirrors** (1948), and as the dangerously effete Richard Howard in *The Mark of Cain** (1948), Brian Desmond Hurst's melodrama of desire and sibling rivalry. This was followed by the husband driven to murder by his unfaithful wife (Greta Gynt*) in *Dear Murderer** (1947). Finally, in 1949 in Robert Hamer's* *The Spider and the Fly** (1949) Portman displayed a degree of sexual ambiguity as policeman Fernand Maubert, involved in a game of cat and mouse with thief Guy Rolfe, in this tale of a "strange friendship."

The 1950s and 1960s were less rewarding for Portman with less opportunity to essay his morally problematic characters, although there were a number of strong character parts, including the reliable Colonel Richmond in the popular prisoner-of-war film *The Colditz Story** (1954), the trade union leader turned governor in *His Excellency* (1952), Commodore Wolfgang Schrepke in the revisionist Cold War melodrama *The Bedford Incident* (1965), starring Richard Widmark* and Sidney Poitier, a supporting role in John Huston's *Freud* (1962), and, before his death in 1969, two films directed by Bryan Forbes,* *The Whisperers* (1966), opposite Edith Evans, and *Deadfall* (1967), where Portman played the homosexual father of the heroine.

FILMS: The Girl from Maxim's (1933), Maria Marten (1935), Abdul the Damned (1935), Old Roses (1935), Hyde Park Corner (1935), The Cardinal (1936), The Crimes of Stephen Hawke (1936), Hearts of Humanity (1936), The Prince and the Pauper (1937), The Singing Marine (1937), Moonlight Sonata (1937), The 49th Parallel (1941), One of Our Aircraft Is Missing (1942), Uncensored (1942), Squadron Leader X (1942), We Dive at Dawn (1943), Escape to Danger (1943), Millions Like Us (1943), A Canterbury Tale (1944), The Air Plan (short, 1945), Great Day (1945), Wanted for Murder (1946), Men of Two Worlds (1946), Dear Murderer (1947), The Mark of Cain (1947), Corridor of Mirrors (1948), Daybreak (1948), The Blind Goddess (1948), The Spider and the Fly (1949), Cairo Road (1950), The Magic Box (1951), His Excellency (1951), Painter and the Poet (1951), South of Algiers

(1952), The Colditz Story (1954), The Deep Blue Sea (1955), Child in the House (1956), The Good Companions (1957), The Naked Edge (1961), The Man Who Finally Died (1962), West 11 (1963), The Bedford Incident (1965), The Spy with a Cold Nose (1966), The Whisperers, (1966), Deadfall (1967), and Assignment to Kill (1968).

POWELL, MICHAEL (1905–1990)/**PRESSBURGER, EMERIC** (1902–1988). "I am simply cinema," one of Michael Powell's oft-quoted remarks, was used to differentiate him from the commercial pretensions of other British directors. This referred to Powell's commitment to the "art" of the cinema, and his opposition to the "realist" aesthetic that colored much of the British critical reaction to his films in the 1940s. Such cinematic sensibilities were developed by Powell over a long period, first as an assistant in Rex Ingram's studio in Nice in 1925 and then his long "apprenticeship," directing twenty-five low-budget films, some of which were "quota quickies," between 1931 and 1936. While Powell has mostly dismissed these films, academics and critics are now reassessing them for distinctive visual touches and thematic elements. For example, a superior example of Powell's work during this period was *The Fire Raisers,* co-scripted by Powell (with producer Jerome Jackson) in 1934 for Gaumont. *The Fire Raisers* starred Leslie Banks* as a ruthless insurance assessor who marries out of his class and, needing money, joins Francis L. Sullivan's criminal fire raising activities on behalf of owners who wish to fraudulently claim insurance money. This formulaic, low-budget film was, above all else, a melodrama, a mode that Powell subverted throughout the 1940s. Yet, without trying to resurrect *The Fire Raisers* to the status of a neglected "masterpiece," the film has sufficient distinctive qualities to differentiate it from the run-of-the-mill low-budget British crime film of the early 1930s—especially the way in which Powell allows Banks to occupy a different cinematic space than the other actors. There is, in other words, a kind of "strangeness" in this film that points to the offbeat qualities that characterize many of his films in the 1940s.

After directing *The Edge of the World* on the remote island of Foula in the Shetland archipelago in 1937, Powell vowed to devote himself to personal projects in the future and to abandon the formulaic films of the 1930s. In 1939, he was joined by Hungarian-born screenwriter Emeric Pressburger, at the instigation of Alexander Korda,* for *The Spy in Black* and the two men worked together for the next seventeen years, forming a production company, The Archers, in 1942. While Powell directed all of their films, the writing, directing, and producing credits were shared. More importantly, their films challenged many cinematic precepts, including traditional narrative structures and the conventions of melodrama, notably the polarization of the world into moral absolutes, while injecting liberal doses of mysticism into their stories. Powell also excelled at the purely cinematic elements—especially color and sound. For example, *Black Narcissus** (1947), a film shot almost entirely in the studio, conveys more effectively the sensuality of an abandoned palace in a remote Nepalese kingdom than any location shooting could have done.

Notable Powell-Pressburger films in the 1940s include *The 49th Parallel** (1941), which consolidated their reputation with nominations for Best Picture and Best Screenplay at the 1943 Academy awards. *The 49th Parallel,* unlike most propaganda films, placed the enemy at the center of the action and then proceeded, with one exception, to portray all Nazis as ruthless fanatics. *The Life and Death of Colonel Blimp* (1943) is an affectionate portrait of an anachronistic relic, Major-General Clive Wynne Candy, over three periods in his life. The film provided an insight into Powell's (and Pressburger's) largely romanticized view of England, a view that provoked considerable criticism from both the left, who objected to the film's (non-realist) style, and the British government, lead by Winston Churchill, who wanted to prevent the export of the film, fearing that it would reinforce a stereotype of the English as a nation of bumbling amateurs. *A Canterbury Tale** (1944) provides another metaphor, or interpretation, of "Englishness" through a modern pilgrimage to Canterbury by an assortment of (largely) troubled characters. The film also mystified some critics, especially with its depiction of the bizarre behavior of a local justice of the peace (Eric Portman*) who pours glue on the heads of young girls. *I Know Where I'm Going!** (1945) allowed Powell to return to the location of *The Edge of the World* for this romantic story of a young career woman who rejects her materialistic lifestyle and succumbs to the charms of the Laird of the Isle and the mysticism of his island. And finally, *A Matter of Life and Death** (1946), the antithesis of the prevailing "realist" aesthetic, based on the story of a pilot trying to convince a heavenly court that he should be allowed to live.

The use of time, space, color, and composition in *A Matter of Life and Death* was surpassed by their next film, *Black Narcissus,* which contained one of the cinema's most startling representation of sexual repression as Sister Ruth, mad with desire, abandons her white habit for a scarlet dress and red lipstick, captured by Powell in a "shocking" close-up. *The Red Shoes** (1948) was Powell and Pressburger's dedication to the primacy of art above all else as a young ballet dancer (Moira Shearer) commits suicide because of the pressures of domesticity and the threat to her artistic expression. Both Rank and its U.S. distributor, Universal, disliked *The Red Shoes,* although it became Britain's most commercially successful film, receiving an Academy Award nomination for Best Picture. *The Red Shoes* was the last Powell-Pressburger production for Rank. After this film, they took their production company to Korda for *The Small Back Room* (1949), a film that incorporated many elements of film noir in its story of male insecurity and self-loathing.

The 1950s were less successful for Powell and Pressburger, beginning with the deeply fatalistic *Gone to Earth* (1950), which reworked themes of sexual desire and repression, and the negative power of superstition, but it was poorly distributed and badly cut by its U.S. distributor. After Pressburger's departure in 1956, Powell ended the decade with another masterpiece, the intensely confronting *Peeping Tom** (1960), which he described as a "tender film." *Peeping Tom,* released prior to Alfred Hitchcock's* *Psycho,* attracted similar criticism because of the film's ability to expose the scopophilic relationship underpinning the cinematic experience, forcing the viewer to confront the inherent voyeurism of the filmic situation.

Powell's career was destroyed by the critical reaction to *Peeping Tom,* although he did direct a few more films, including two in Australia: the comedy of contrasting cultures *They're a Weird Mob* (1966) and the story of an aging artist (James Mason*) and his young model (Helen Mirren) in *Age of Consent* (1969). After the highs and lows of his peak years in the 1940s, Powell's reputation was at a low point after *Peeping Tom,* only to be resurrected by academics, critics (with frequent museum retrospectives throughout the 1970s and 1980s), and filmmakers (notably Francis Ford Coppola, who hired Powell late in his career to work at Coppola's ill-fated Zoetrope Studios, and Martin Scorsese). Unlike Hitchcock, who was knighted in 1969, and despite the fact that Hitchcock left Britain twenty years earlier and was a U.S. citizen, Powell and Pressburger remained undervalued in Britain, with few film awards to mark their contribution to the cinema—Powell and Pressburger did receive a Special Award from the BFI in 1978 and a Career Golden Lion Award at the 1982 Venice Film Festival. Powell married the celebrated film editor Thelma Schoonmaker in 1984 and he died in 1990. Pressburger made one attempt at directing (*Twice upon a Time* [1953]) and he produced *Miracle in Soho* in 1957. Pressburger died in 1988.

FILMS: Michael Powell (as director): Two Crowded Hours (1931), My Friend the King (1932), Rynox (1932), The Rasp (1932), The Star Reporter (1932), Hotel Splendide (1932), C.O.D. (1932), His Lordship (1932), Born Lucky (1933), The Fire Raisers (1934), The Night of the Party (1934), Red Ensign (1934), Something Always Happens (1934), The Girl in the Crowd (1935), Lazybones (1935), The Love Test (1935), The Phantom Light (1935), The Price of a Song (1935), Someday (1935), Her Last Affaire (1936), The Brown Wallet (1936), Crown vs Stevens (1936), The Man behind the Mask (1936), The Edge of the World (1937), The Lion Has Wings (codir., 1939), The Thief of Baghdad (codir., 1940), An Airman's Letter to His Mother (short, 1941), Honeymoon (1959), Peeping Tom (1960), The Queen's Guard (1961), Bluebeard's Castle (1964), They're a Weird Mob (1966), Age of Consent (1969), The Boy Who Turned Yellow (1972), and Return to the Edge of the World (1978).

Michael Powell (as director) and Emeric Pressburger (as screenwriter and/or producer): The Spy in Black (1939), Contraband (1940), The 49th Parallel (1941), One of Our Aircraft Is Missing (1942), The Life and Death of Colonel Blimp (1943), The Volunteer (short, 1943), A Canterbury Tale (1944), I Know Where I'm Going! (1945), A Matter of Life and Death (1946), Black Narcissus (1947), The Red Shoes (1948), The Small Back Room (1949), Gone to Earth (1950), The Elusive Pimpernel (1951), The Tales of Hoffman (1951), The Sorcerer's Apprentice (short, 1955), Oh Rosalinda! (1955), The Battle of the River Plate (1956), and Ill Met by Moonlight (1957).

THE PRIVATE LIFE OF HENRY VIII (London Films, 1933)—Historical drama. *Director:* Alexander Korda; *Producers:* Alexander Korda and Ludovico Toeplitz; *Script:* Lajos Biro and Arthur Wimperis; *Cinematography:* Georges Perinal; *Music:* Kurt Schroder; *Cast:* Charles Laughton (Henry VIII), Robert Donat (Thomas Culpepper), Franklin Dyall (Thomas Cromwell), Miles Mander

(Wriothesley), Lawrence Hanray (Archbishop Thomas Cranmer), William Austin (Duke of Cleves), John Loder (Thomas Peynell), Merle Oberon (Anne Boleyn), Wendy Barrie (Jane Seymour), Elsa Lanchester (Anne of Cleves), Binnie Barnes (Catherine Howard), Everley Gregg (Catherine Parr), and Lady Tree (Nurse).

The Private Life of Henry VIII premiered not in London but at the recently opened Radio City Music Hall in New York. Although it had a relatively high production budget by British standards (£93,710), it grossed more than £7,000 in its first week in New York, eventually grossing more than £500,000. This success encouraged investment in the British film industry and Alexander Korda,* with the financial support of the Prudential Assurance Company, completed a modern studio complex at Denham in Buckinghamshire and, in 1935, became a partner in United Artists with access to the U.S. market. Subsequent productions by Korda were less successful and he soon lost control of Denham. Nevertheless, *The Private Life of Henry VIII* deserves a prominent place in the history of the British film industry. Aesthetically, its status is less assured as the film is dated and Charles Laughton's Oscar-winning performance as the tyrannical, sad king now appears overly mannered and highly theatrical.

The film concentrates on the love life of Henry VIII. It begins with the beheading of Anne Boleyn, his second wife, and traces his marital misfortunes through the luckless Jane Seymour, who dies after giving birth to a son, followed by the amusing Anne of Cleves, the adulterous Catherine Howard (who has an affair with Henry's friend Thomas Culpepper), and the shrewd Catherine Parr. A rueful Henry confides to the audience at the end that although Catherine Parr is his best wife she is also the worst. The wide appeal of the film had much to do with the fact that it purported to present the sexual dalliances of one of Britain's most widely known monarchs while simultaneously "cutting him down to size" by showing how even the powerful can be bedevilled by matters of the heart.

The Private Life of Henry VIII was nominated for the Best Picture Award at the 1934 Academy Awards.

NOTES

1. See Slide, *"Banned in the USA,"* p. 196.
2. McFarlane, *An Autobiography of British Cinema,* p. 372.

Q

QUATERMASS II (Hammer, 1957)—Science fiction. *Director:* Val Guest; *Producer:* Anthony Hinds; *Script:* Nigel Kneale and Val Guest; *Cinematography:* Gerald Gibbs; *Cast:* Brian Donlevy (Quatermass), John Longdon (Lomax), Sidney James (Jimmy Hall), Bryan Forbes (Marsh), William Franklyn (Brand), Vera Day (Sheila), Percy Herbert (Gorman), Michael Ripper (Ernie), Tom Chatto (Broadhead), John Van Eyssen (PRO), and Charles Lloyd Pack (Dawson).

Hammer Studios produced the first Quatermass film, *The Quatermass Xperiment,* starring Brian Donlevy, in 1955 following the popularity of Nigel Kneale's television series. The success of this film prompted a sequel, *Quatermass II* (released in the United States as *Enemy from Space*), again starring Donlevy as the obdurate scientist Professor Quatermass. *Quatermass II* is an even better film and it shares many of the qualities of the 1956 Hollywood film *Invasion of the Body Snatchers,* especially the idea of an alien takeover of human bodies through the disbursement of foreign organisms. A more general influence on the film was the overall sense of paranoia embodied in George Orwell's *1984.*

When Quatermass's car nearly hits another car containing a distressed woman and her badly scarred boyfriend, he learns of a secret government project at Wynnerton Flats. The discovery of this enterprise, ostensibly to manufacture synthetic food, is accompanied by a mysterious meteorite shower. After one of Quatermass's scientists (Marsh) is scarred by the tiny living organisms inside one of the "rocks," security forces from the installation knock Quatermass over and take Marsh away. Despite warnings not to become involved, the obstinate scientist joins with a rebel politician (Broadhead) to investigate the project. During a supervised visit to the installation, the politician dies and Quatermass has to flee for his life. Faced with bureaucratic obstacles, Quatermass, with the assistance of a senior policeman (Lomax), penetrates a conspiracy that includes senior members of the government and the Commissioner of Scotland Yard. Quatermass, with the assistance of local villagers from Wynnerton, in an ending similar to the climax used in many of Hammer's subsequent horror films, storms the installation and takes over its operating center. Quatermass pumps oxygen into the pressure domes containing the aliens and destroys the invasion attempt.

This low-budget film benefits from the casting of Donlevy as the single-minded, humorless scientist who crashes through all obstacles, plus the effective use of the Shell Refinery at New Haven, whose contorted machinery and miles of pipes provides the requisite setting for an alien invasion. Kneale's paranoid screenplay, which suggests a massive conspiracy following the alien takeover of the security forces and the British establishment, is especially effective in showing those in power as a mindless group, devoid of initiative or independent thought. Hammer also produced the third film in the Quatermass series, *Quatermass and the Pit,* directed by Roy Ward Baker,* ten years later in 1967.

R

THE RED SHOES (The Archers/Rank, 1948)—Ballet/romantic melodrama. *Director:* Michael Powell; *Producers:* Michael Powell and Emeric Pressburger; *Script:* Emeric Pressburger and Michael Powell; *Cinematography:* Jack Cardiff; *Music:* Brian Easdale; *Cast:* Anton Walbrook (Boris Lermontov), Marius Goring (Julian Craster), Moira Shearer (Victoria Page), Robert Helpmann (Ivan Boleslawsky), Leonide Massine (Grischa Ljubov), and Albert Bassermann (Sergei Ratov).

Sir John Davis, the managing director of the Rank organization, stormed out of the preview screening of *The Red Shoes* after trying to stop production of the film midway through the shooting. Only Alexander Korda's* money and distribution contacts facilitated the release of the film. Also, Moira Shearer was less than delighted with the project as she was appalled by the original story ("a typical woman's magazine view of the theatre")[1] and the cruel behavior of Michael Powell* on the set. Nevertheless, *The Red Shoes* eventually became a major commercial success, particularly in the United States and, for many years, it was the top-grossing British film. It began its successful run in Manhattan, where it screened for nearly two years before a general release throughout the rest of the United States.

With *The Red Shoes*, Powell and Emeric Pressburger* extend their fascination with romantic expressionism, as opposed to the prevailing (1940s) emphasis on cinematic realism. They blend mythic elements from Hans Christian Anderson's story with a story that is essentially concerned with the clash between art and domesticity—a theme that interested Pressburger who wrote the first draft of the script in 1939 for a film with Merle Oberon. This aspect is developed in the film through the behavior of Anton Walbrook as the obsessive ballet company director Boris Lermontov. Lermontov believes, like Pressburger, that the restrictions imposed by a middle-class lifestyle destroys creativity: When his choreographer Grischa Ljubov tells Lermontov that "you can't alter human nature," the obsessive ballet manager replies, "You can do better than that, you can ignore it." This attitude is also expressed, in a different way, by Victoria Page. When questioned by Lermontov as to why she wants to dance, Page replies, "Why do you want to live?"

Lermontov's determination to develop Page into the best prima ballerina in the world is threatened when Page forms a relationship with composer Julian Craster. Lermontov dismisses Craster and forces Page to focus on her art. He urges her to reject the path followed by those dancers who are "imbecile enough to get married." This tension between the demands of "art" and "love" is central to *The Red Shoes*. However, the actual choice facing Page at the climax of the film is not whether she should give up dancing to support Craster's career, but whether she should heed Craster's demand not to dance *The Ballet of the Red Shoes* for the Lermontov Ballet Company.

Torn between her desire to continue with the best ballet company in the world and her love for Craster, the red shoes drive Page to suicide. Powell's presentation of the events leading to her death, with the dancer unable to control her body before throwing herself under a train in Monte Carlo, is skillfully executed. It is also one of the most bizarre resolutions in the cinema. This dilemma facing Page at the end is foreshadowed in the lengthy dance sequence, *The Ballet of the Red Shoes,* where images of Craster and Lermontov are superimposed on the screen. They emphasize not only a choice between men but a choice between lifestyles.

Hein Heckroth and Arthur Lawson won the 1949 Oscar for Best Art Direction—Set Direction for a Color Film and Brian Easdale won an Oscar for Best Music, while Pressburger was nominated for Best Story and Powell and Pressburger for Best Picture. *The Red Shoes* was nominated for Best Picture at the 1949 BAFTA Awards and won the Golden Globe Award for Best Motion Picture score. It was also the first British film to gross more than $5 million.

REDGRAVE, MICHAEL (1908–1985). The Redgrave family have, in various ways, contributed substantially to the British theater and the cinema. The Redgrave participation stretches from Roy Redgrave and Margaret Scudamore, Michael's father and mother, in the silent period, to Michael's grandchildren, Joely and Natasha Richardson and Gemma Redgrave. Although Michael Redgrave never quite secured a permanent position as a top-rank "film star," due to the nature of his roles, he began as an amiable hero in Alfred Hitchcock's* *The Lady Vanishes** (1938). He had an uncredited role in the earlier Hitchcock film *Secret Agent* (1936).

After a stint as a schoolteacher, Redgrave made his stage debut in 1934 and worked with most of the top British directors throughout the late 1930s, 1940s, and early 1950s. Redgrave made three films for Carol Reed* (*Climbing High* [1939], *The Stars Look Down* [1940], and *Kipps* [1941]) and three films for Anthony Asquith* (*The Way to the Stars* [1945], *The Browning Version* [1951], and *The Importance of Being Earnest* [1952]). After the disappointments of his sojourn in Hollywood, after World War II, *The Browning Version* was a significant film for Redgrave, winning him the Best Actor Award at the Cannes Film Festival. As the middle-aged school teacher Andrew Crocker-Harris, Redgrave skillfully captures the disappointments of a man who realizes that he is trapped in a less than fulfilling life with an unfaithful wife (Jean Kent) and a vocation he no longer enjoys. The screenplay is by Terence Rattigan and is based on his play. One of Redgrave's more heroic roles was in *The Captive Heart** (1946). Yet, even in this film the positive qualities are tinged with ambivalence and insecurity, traits that characterize many of his performances.

In one of his most famous roles, as the ventriloquist Maxwell Frere, who comes to be dominated by his dummy in *Dead of Night** (1945), Redgrave gives an intense performance as the demented victim. Redgrave made two films in the United States after World War II: *Mourning Becomes Electra* (1947), a lumbering 173-minute adaptation of the Eugene O'Neill play, which, perversely, resulted in Redgrave's only Oscar nomination, and the lead role in Fritz Lang's Gothic thriller *Secret beyond the Door* (1948), with Redgrave as the psychologically troubled husband of Joan Bennett. Unfortunately, the film received a poor critical response and dismal box office returns.

During the 1950s, Redgrave became more of a character actor. This change in his status was confirmed by roles such as inventor Barnes Wallis in *The Dam Busters** (1955), the ruthless inquisitor in *1984* (1956), and the alcoholic father who desperately tries to prevent his son's execution for a crime he did not commit in Joseph Losey's* *Time without Pity* (1957). This last film provided another opportunity for Redgrave to display the self-loathing and personal insecurities that characterized many of his roles on screen. He was nominated for a BAFTA Best British Actor Award for this performance. Later character parts for Redgrave, such as the weak medical examiner in *The Hill* (1965), became little more than extended cameos.

Redgrave, who suffered from Parkinson's Disease in his final years, wrote a number of books. One was concerned with the craft of acting (*The Actors Ways and Means* [1979]), two autobiographies, and a novel (*The Mountebank's Tale* [1959]). With actress-wife Rachel Kempson, who was his lover in *The Captive Heart,* he had three children who are all actors (Vanessa, Corin, and Lynn). Redgrave was knighted in 1959 and died in 1985.

FILMS: The Lady Vanishes (1938), Climbing High (1939), Stolen Life (1939), A Window in London (1939), The Stars Look Down (1940), Kipps (1941), Atlantic Ferry (1941), Jeannie (1941), The Big Blockade (1942), Thunder Rock (1942), The Way to the Stars (1945), Dead of Night (1945), The Captive Heart (1946), The Years Between (1946), The Man Within (1947), Fame Is the Spur (1947), Mourning Becomes Electra (1947), The Secret beyond the Door (1948), The Browning Version (1951), The Magic Box (1951), Winter Garden (short, voice, 1951), The Importance of Being Earnest (1952), The Green Scarf (1954), The Sea Shall Not Have Them (1954), The Night My Number Came Up (1955), The Dam Busters (1955), Oh Rosalinda! (1955), Confidential Report (1955), 1984 (1956), Kings and Queen (voice, 1956), The Happy Road (1957), Time without Pity (1957), Law and Disorder (1958), Behind the Mask (1958), The Immortal Land (voice,

1958), The Quiet American (1958), The Wreck of the Mary Deare (1959), Shake Hands with the Devil (1959), No, My Darling Daughter (1960), May Wedding (voice, 1960), The Innocents (1961), The Loneliness of the Long Distance Runner (1962), Young Cassidy (1965), The Hill (1965), The Heroes of Telemark (1965), Assignment K (1967), The 25th Hour (1967), Oh! What a Lovely War (1969), Battle of Britain (1969), Goodbye, Mr. Chips (1969), Connecting Rooms (1969), David Copperfield (1969), Goodbye Germini (1971), The Go-Between (1971), Nicholas and Alexandra (1971), The Last Target (1971), and A Christmas Carol (narr., 1972).

REED, CAROL (1906–1976). Although Carol Reed received the 1969 Academy Award for Best Direction for the musical *Oliver!,* it was not his best film and the 1960s was not his best decade. He was also removed from the disastrous remake of *The Mutiny on the Bounty* in 1963. Although Reed's best work came in the period after World War II, he directed a series of better than average films prior to the war, and one of Britain's most popular propaganda films during the war, *The Way Ahead** (1944). This film had its genesis as an Army Film Service short, *The New Lot,* directed by Reed in 1943, and it was concerned with the successful adjustment of civilians to army life.

Reed, the illegitimate son of theater manager Herbert Beerbohm, worked his way up the hierarchical structure of the British industry. Beginning as a stage actor and assistant to Edgar Wallace in the theater, a dialogue director, and assistant director in the early 1930s, he was the sole director on *Midshipman Easy* in 1935. This film initiated a prolific period for Reed, a man who had little interest in political or social issues outside of the cinema. This was a surprising fact considering his successful adaptation of A. J. Cronin's politically charged best seller *The Stars Look Down* (1940), starring Michael Redgrave.* Reed, however, admitted that he did not feel passionate about the film's subject matter, the nationalization of the mines, and that he "could just as easily make a picture on the opposite side."[2]

If politics and social justice did not move Reed, he was passionate about the cinema and when he formed a loose kind of collaboration with Graham Greene after World War II he directed two great British films. The most famous, *The Third Man** (1949), was based on a premise that intrigued Reed, the notion that a man did something wrong for the right reason. Reed's contribution to *The Third Man* has not always been fully appreciated. It was, undeniably, one of the most fortunate conjunctions of talent, with Orson Welles, Greene, Trevor Howard,* Alida Valli, Anton Karas's haunting zither music, and the special work of cinematographer Robert Krasker, who won an Oscar for this contribution to the film. However, it was Reed who devised the shot of Harry Lime's hands through the sewer gratings (the hands were actually Reed's as Welles had left the film by this stage). He also staged the unforgettable long, silent walk, filmed without a cut, by Valli at the end of the film past the love-stricken Joseph Cotton along a path lined by autumn trees shedding the last vestiges of their foliage.

The Odd Man Out (1947), detailing the last hours of a Northern Irish gunman, attracted universal critical acclaim for the director and a five-film contract with

Alexander Korda.* However, the film's manipulative "machinery" is more obvious and lacks the moral complexities of his next two films: *The Third Man* and *The Fallen Idol* (1948). Reed also directed a number of better than average films prior to *The Odd Man Out,* especially the assured propaganda thriller *Night Train to Munich* (1940). This benefited from a humorous script by Frank Launder* and Sidney Gilliat.*

There were also notable films after *The Third Man,* such as *The Man Between* (1953), a Cold War thriller starring James Mason* and Claire Bloom, and *Our Man in Havana* (1960), which reunited Reed with the jaundiced world of Greene. However, compared to their 1940s collaborations, *Our Man in Havana* was a lesser work and many of Reed's films of the 1950s and 1960s, especially *The Key* (1958), *The Mutiny on the Bounty, The Running Man* (1963), and *The Agony and the Ecstasy* (1965), were diluted by the compromises of "star vehicles" and lacked the dramatic energy of his earlier films. Reed's second last film, *The Last Warrior/Flap* (1971), concerning the victimization of a Native American (Anthony Quinn), was burdened by a poor script and it was a surprising project for director who expressed little interest in films with strong social messages. Reed was nominated for Best Director at the 1950 Academy Awards for *The Fallen Idol* and the following year for *The Third Man,* while *The Odd Man Out* won the 1947 BAFTA Best British Film Award, as did *The Fallen Idol* the next year. Reed, who was knighted in 1952, died in 1976.

FILMS: It Happened in Paris (codir., 1935), Midshipman Easy (1935), Laburnum Grove (1936), Talk of the Devil (1937), Who's Your Lady Friend? (1937), Bank Holiday (1938), Penny Paradise (1938), Climbing High (1939), A Girl Must Live (1939), The Stars Look Down (1940), Night Train to Munich (1940), The Girl in the News (1941), A Letter from Home (short, 1941), Kipps (1941), The Young Mr. Pitt (1942), The New Lot (short, 1943), The Way Ahead (1944), The True Glory (doc., 1945), Odd Man Out (1947), The Fallen Idol (1948), The Third Man (1949), Outcast of the Islands (1951), The Man Between (1953), A Kid for Two Farthings (1955), Trapeze (1956), The Key (1958), Our Man in Havana (1960), Mutiny on the Bounty (completed by Lewis Milestone, 1963), The Running Man (1963), The Agony and the Ecstasy (1965), Oliver! (1968), The Last Warrior/Flap (1971), and Follow Me (1972).

RICHARDSON, RALPH (1902–1983). It would be unfair to say that this brilliant stage actor only dabbled in films, but it is clear that his career was dominated by the stage with only sporadic forays into the cinema. Yet Richardson gave one of the very great film performances, albeit in his first Hollywood film, as the cruel patriarch in *The Heiress* (1949), a performance that was the antithesis of stage acting, and, correspondingly, captured the essence of film acting in the way he was able to clearly communicate every trait of his despicable character through the minimum of effort and expression. The greatness of this performance only magnified the cinema's loss in that he did not similarly "stretch" himself more often with full-length roles. Even his early film roles gravitated toward the eccentric, as in one of his favorite early performances as the obstinate aging

Colonel Winstanley in *The Man Who Work Miracles** (1936)—although Richardson was only thirty-four at the time—or as the befuddled Lord Mere in *The Divorce of Lady X* (1938).

Richardson made his stage debut in 1921 and acted with the Birmingham Rep in the 1920s and then with the Old Vic in the 1930s. His first film was *The Ghoul* (1933), starring Boris Karloff, an attempt by Gaumont-British to capture the mood and success of the Universal horror films of the early 1930s. This film provided him with another eccentric part as a phoney vicar. A major role as Bulldog Drummond in *The Return of Bulldog Drummond* (1934) followed, yet within a few months he was playing the master criminal (Morelle) in a spoof on the Drummond series in *Bulldog Jack** (1935). In this film, Jack Hulbert assumes the savior duties, fighting Morelle's machinations, when Drummond (Atholl Fleming) is incapacitated by a broken leg. However, Richardson's decision to participate in this film is further evidence that he never considered himself a "film star" as most Hollywood actors would not transfer so easily from hero to villain, especially when the same series character is involved.

Richardson was more prolific in the early years of World War II. Beginning with his role as Major Charles Hammond in *Q Planes* (1939), an excellent mixture of comedy and espionage, he followed with the heavy-handed propaganda film *The Lion Has Wings* (1939), which combined footage from *Fire over England** (1937), an illustrated lecture, and Richardson and Merle Oberon pontificating on those qualities that made Britain great. Later, Richardson was the owner of a Dutch shipyard in *The Silver Fleet* (1943) who sacrifices his life when he betrays the Germans by sabotaging a submarine built in his shipyards. However, his best role during this period was in the downbeat melodrama *On the Night of the Fire* (1940) as Will Kobling, a seemingly decent man tempted to steal to offset his wife's debts. This action leads to murder and Kobling's eventual suicide. Even Richardson expressed satisfaction with this film although some critics took issue with the casting of Richardson and Diana Wynward as the lower-middle-class cockney couple.

The 1940s produced one more masterly example of film acting with Richardson as Baines the butler in Carol Reed's* *The Fallen Idol* (1948), adapted by Graham Greene from his story "The Basement Room." The story involved the warm relationship between a butler and a young boy who, mistakenly, believes his mentor has murdered his wife. He was nominated for the Best Actor in a Supporting Role at the 1950 Academy Awards for *The Heiress,* and he won the Best British Actor Award at the 1953 BAFTA Awards for *The Sound Barrier* (1952), directed by David Lean* for Alexander Korda,* with Richardson as a designer determined to produce a supersonic aircraft whatever the cost to himself and his family. Korda was an influential figure in maintaining Richardson's film career and when Korda died in 1956 Richardson reduced his interest in the cinema.

In 1952, Richardson directed and starred in the efficient thriller *Home at Seven,* involving a club treasurer who cannot account for his movements on a day when a murder and robbery take place. Cameos dominated his filmography after 1960, although they were often fascinating filmic interludes, including his final role as Tarzan's grandfather in *Greystoke* (1984), a role for which he was nominated, posthumously, for the Best Supporting Actor Award at the 1985 Academy Awards and the 1985 BAFTA Awards. Richardson was knighted in 1947 and died in 1983.

FILMS: The Ghoul (1933), Friday the Thirteenth (1933), Java Head (1934), The Return of Bulldog Drummond (1934), The King of Paris (1934), Bulldog Jack (1935), Things to Come (1936), The Man Who Could Work Miracles (1937), Thunder in the City (1937), South Riding (1938), The Divorce of Lady X (1938), The Citadel (1938), Q Planes (1939), The Four Feathers (1939), The Lion Has Wings (1939), Health for a Nation (short, 1940), On the Night of the Fire (1940), The Day Will Dawn (1942), The Silver Fleet (1943), The Volunteer (short, 1943), School for Secrets (1946), Anna Karenina (1948), The Fallen Idol (1948), The Heiress (1949), Outcast of the Islands (1951), Home at Seven (also dir., 1952), The Sound Barrier (1952), The Holly and the Ivy (1952), Richard III (1955), Smiley (1956), The Passionate Stranger (1956), Our Man in Havana (1959), Oscar Wilde (1960), Exodus (1960), The 300 Spartans (1962), Long Day's Journey into Night (1962), Woman of Straw (1964), Doctor Zhivago (1965), The Wong Box (1966), Chimes at Midnight (voice, 1966), Khartoum (1966), The Midas Run (1969), The Bed-Sitting Room (1969), Oh! What a Lovely War (1969), The Looking Glass War (1969), Battle of Britain (1969), Eagle in a Cage (1971), Who Slew Auntie Roo? (1971), Tales from the Crypt (1972), Lady Caroline Lamb (1972), Alice's Adventures in Wonderland (1972), A Doll's House (1973), O, Lucky Man! (1973), Rollerball (1975), Watership Down (voice, 1978), Time Bandits (1980), Dragonslayer (1981), Invitation to a Wedding (1984), Give My Regards to Broad Street (1984), and Greystoke (1984).

RICHARDSON, TONY (1928–1991). After graduating from Oxford University, and participating in their dramatic society, Tony Richardson worked as a television director for the BBC in the early 1950s before co-directing a documentary with Karel Reisz (*Momma Don't Allow*) in 1955. This film was included in the influential *Free Cinema* season of films shown at the National Film Theatre between 1956 and 1959. After *Momma Don't Allow,* Richardson established the English Stage Company with George Devine at the Royal Court Theatre. In retrospect, Richardson can be seen as a major contributor to the development of the British New Wave although it came about due to a confluence of many factors. One significant factor, however, was Richardson's production of John Osborne's play *Look Back in Anger* in 1956.

The *Free Cinema* group, which included Lindsay Anderson* and Karel Reisz, challenged the basic tenets of British cinema by propagating a "poetry of everyday life" and a keen interest in many of the techniques of the European art cinema. Richardson was an adherent of this ethos and his entry into the film industry came at an opportune time. He established, with John Osborne and U.S. producer Harry Saltzman, Woodfall Productions in 1959. Richardson's first film for Woodfall, financed by Warner Brothers, was a film adaptation of *Look Back in Anger.* The timing of this film, starring Richard Burton, was a significant factor as it was released in the same year as Jack Clayton's* *Room at the Top** (1959).

Richardson's films for Woodfall, culminating in the highly successful *Tom Jones** (1963), guaranteed him a prominent place in the history of the British cinema—after Woodfall he directed few successful films. From the late 1950s, however, Richardson had an opportunity to develop and execute a number of key principles regarding filmmaking. For example, he espoused shooting on location[3] as allowing a "rougher," more experimental style that would provide a "different kind of authenticity" than was possible within a film studio. Richardson was hoping to duplicate in film the energy and innovations of the Royal Court Theatre by bringing a "sense of life" to the British cinema.

After the commercial and critical failure of his next film, *The Entertainer* (1960), with Laurence Olivier* as a faded music-hall comedian, Richardson postponed his planned adaptation of Shelagh Delaney's *A Taste of Honey* to supplement Woodfall's income by directing another adaptation, William Faulkner's *Sanctuary* (1961), for Twentieth Century Fox in Hollywood. Although Richardson did not enjoy the Hollywood experience, Reisz's *Saturday Night and Sunday Morning* (1960), produced by Richardson, restored Woodfall's fortunes. This provided Richardson the opportunity to put *A Taste of Honey* (1961) into production and he followed this with two of his best films, *The Loneliness of the Long Distance Runner** (1962) and *Tom Jones.*

Tom Jones was highly successful and influential and it won the Academy Award for Best Picture in 1964, with Richardson receiving an Oscar for Best Director—earlier he had won the 1962 BAFTA Award for Best British Film for *A Taste of Honey* and shared the screenwriting credit with Delaney. Financed by United Artists, the profits from *Tom Jones* not only bolstered Woodfall but encouraged the U.S. studios to finance numerous British films in the mid- to late 1960s. *Tom Jones* also signaled a profound change in Richardson's career—it was not only his last film for Woodfall, it was his last commercially successful film.

Most of Richardson's films after *Tom Jones* were produced in the United States, although notable exceptions included two (commercially unsuccessful) films with Jeanne Moreau, *Mademoiselle* (1965) and *The Sailor from Gibraltar* (1967), the big-budget, all-star, revisionist, anti-war historical epic *The Charge of the Light Brigade* (1968), an idiosyncratic interpretation of the life of Australia's most famous bushranger, *Ned Kelly* (1970), starring Mick Jagger, and an unprofitable return to Henry Fielding for *Joseph Andrews* (1977).

While *The Charge of the Light Brigade, Ned Kelly,* and *Joseph Andrews* at least enjoyed widespread distribution, the mystery thriller *Dead Cert* (1973) was shelved until it finally surfaced on pay television in recent years. Ironically, one of Richardson's better films, and his last, *Blue Sky,* also suffered a similar fate. It was filmed in 1990 but did not received a major release until 1994 when Jessica Lange won an Oscar for her performance as the troubled wife of a military man. Richardson, however, did not live to enjoy Lange's success as he died in 1991. Two of Richardson's children, Natasha and Joely, born while he was married to Vanessa Redgrave in the 1960s, are both actresses. His autobiography, *The Long Distance Runner,* was published posthumously in 1993.

FILMS: Momma Don't Allow (doc., 1955), Look Back in Anger (1959), The Entertainer (1960), Sanctuary (1961), A Taste of Honey (1961), The Loneliness of the Long Distance Runner (1962), Tom Jones (1963), The Loved One (1965), Mademoiselle (1965), The

Sailor from Gibraltar (1968), Red and Blue (1968), The Charge of the Light Brigade (1968), Laughter in the Dark (1969), Hamlet (1969), Ned Kelly (1970), A Delicate Balance (1973), Dead Cert (1973), Joseph Andrews (1977), The Border (1982), The Hotel New Hampshire (1984), Turning a Blind Eye (doc., 1985), and Blue Sky (1990).

ROBSON, FLORA (1902–1984). Considering the fact that Flora Robson's film career spanned fifty years, the cinema did not fully utilize the talent of this charismatic actress. Mostly, she was restricted to supporting roles of servants, spinsters, officials, and other women devoid of passion. Yet her talent was evident as early as 1934 when, as the empress in Alexander Korda's* production of *Catherine the Great* (1934), she dominated the film through her ability to express the inner turmoil of this powerful woman. Similar qualities, involving sexual longing and personal loneliness, coupled with a necessary display of external strength, characterized her Queen Elizabeth in *Fire over England** (1937). Elizabeth's address to the British soldiers as they prepare to combat the Spanish Armada was recycled in Korda's episodic propaganda film *The Lion Has Wings* (1939).

Robson enjoyed her role as Elizabeth I in *Fire over England* as it offered her a rare opportunity to portray a woman of action, not just a passive character or romantic appendage. However, after the 1930s she had few opportunities to essay similar roles. Warner Brothers, impressed by Robson's Elizabeth in *Fire over England,* invited her to Hollywood to portray her again in their Errol Flynn swashbuckler *The Sea Hawk* (1940), and a final scene was added allowing Elizabeth to offer a wartime message to British audiences. Thereafter, it was a long succession of secondary roles for Robson, as the efficient Liz Ellis who heads the organizing party for Eleanor Roosevelt's visit to the rural English village of Denley in *Great Day** (1945); as Sister Philippa, the gardener so seduced by the sensual atmosphere of the "House of Women" in *Black Narcissus** (1947) that she ignores the need of her community for food in favor of honeysuckle and forget-me-nots; as the chair of the juvenile court who recounts the fall of Jean Kent as a warning to Diana Dors in *The Good Time Girl* (1948); and as the Labour candidate who worries that her brother's marriage to a German woman will threaten her election prospects in *Frieda* (1947).

Robson's appearances in Hollywood films allowed only a slight variation as the housekeeper in *Wuthering Heights* (1939); as Angelique Buiton, Ingrid Bergman's overly protective servant, in the turgid *Saratoga Trunk* (1945), for which she won an Academy Award nomination; as the evil Dowager Empress Tzu-Hsi who incites the attack on the Westerners during the Chinese Boxer Rebellion in *55 Days at Peking* (1963); and as Miss Binns, one of the missionaries under siege in China, in John Ford's *Seven Women* (1966). Mostly, however, it was the stage that offered her the greatest opportunities and she was made a dame in 1960. Robson died in 1984.

FILMS: A Gentleman of Paris (1931), Dance Pretty Lady (1932), One Precious Year (1933), Catherine the Great (1934), Fire over England (1937), Farewell Again (1937), I, Claudius (never completed, 1937), Wuthering Heights (1939), The Lion Has Wings

(1939), Invisible Stripes (1939), We Are Not Alone (1939), Poison Pen (1939), The Sea Hawk (1940), Bahama Passage (1941), The Demi-Paradise (1943), 2,000 Women (1944), Saratoga Trunk (1945), Great Day (1945), The Years Between (1946), Caesar and Cleopatra (1946), Black Narcissus (1947), Frieda (1947), Saraband for Dead Lovers (1948), Holiday Camp (1948), The Good Time Girl (1949), The Frightened Bride (1953), The Malta Story (1953), Romeo and Juliet (1954), No Time for Tears (1957), High Tide at Noon (1957), The Gypsy and the Gentleman (1958), Innocent Sinners (1958), 55 Days at Peking (1963), Murder at the Gallop (1963), Guns at Batasi (1964), Those Magnificent Men in Their Flying Machines 1965), Young Cassidy (1965), Seven Women (1966), Eye of the Devil (1967), The Shuttered Room (1967), Fragment of Fear (1970), Sin (1970), The Beast in the Cellar (1971), Alice's Adventure in Wonderland (1972), Dominique (1978), and Clash of the Titans (1981).

ROC, PATRICIA (b. 1918). In the minor British comedy *The Perfect Woman* (1949), Patricia Roc provides the inspiration for a scientist to create the "perfect robot woman." The casting of Roc is indicative of the popularity, and beauty, of this British star in the 1940s. Roc made her film debut in 1938 (*The Rebel Son*), and her breakthrough role was in the Launder-Gilliat* wartime populist melodrama *Millions Like Us* (1943) as Celia Crowson, a young factory worker who forms a strong communal bond with her colleagues. This bond is strengthened following the death of her husband during the war. Roc followed this with her best films, including the Gainsborough melodramas *Madonna of the Seven Moons* (1944) and *Love Story* (1944), and the Launder comedy-propaganda film *2,000 Women* (1944). This latter film, set in an internment camp for women in France during the war, cast Roc as a nun, a role initially intended for Phyllis Calvert,* who turned it down in favor of another part in the film.

A supporting role to Margaret Lockwood* in the highly successful melodrama *The Wicked Lady* (1945) was followed by another film designed to boost morale during the war, *Johnny Frenchman* (1945), which emphasized the war-related goals shared by a Cornish fishing village and a Breton community. Roc went to Hollywood for Jacques Tourneur's magisterial Western *Canyon Passage* (1946), where she played the second female lead as Caroline Marsh, a young frontierswoman who cannot go with Dana Andrews when he decides to move on. Five years later, Tourneur gave Roc the lead role when he came to England to film *Circle of Danger* (1951), where she played an independent woaen torn between the traditional life offered by Hugh Sinclair and the excitement of Ray Milland's quest to find out why his brother was murdered by fellow soldiers during World War II. She chooses Milland.

In between the two Tourneur films, Roc starred in one of her best films, *The Brothers** (1947), as Mary Lawson, a young, beautiful woman who intensifies the rivalry between two warring clans on the Isle of Skye after she arrives on the island. In this intense melodrama, Mary's striking beauty and spirit of independence clashes with the repressive patriarchal traditions enforced on the island, resulting in violence and death, including her own. In Lawrence Huntington's *When the Bough Breaks* (1947), Roc was Lily, a working-class woman impregnated and abandoned by a bigamist. Forced by circumstances to give her baby up for adoption to an upper-middle-class woman, Lily comes to want her child back. However, the realities of postwar Britain convince her that his future resides with his foster mother.

A change of casting for Roc in the costume melodrama *Jassy* (1947), as the duplicitous Dilys Hatton, opposite Lockwood, was followed by a succession of less interesting roles in the late 1940s and throughout the 1950s, with one more Hollywood film, *The Man on the Eiffel Tower* in 1949. A couple of French films in the 1950s preceded her final film, *Bluebeard's Ten Honeymoons* (1960), a low-budget movie that unites Roc with Jean Kent (*2,000 Women, Madonna of the Seven Moons,* and *The Wicked Lady*) in this oft-told tale of a man (George Sanders) who marries and murders a series of women.

FILMS: The Rebel Son (1938), The Gaunt Stranger (1938), A Window in London (1939), The Mind of Mr. Reeder (1939), Dr. O'Dowd (1939), The Missing People (1940), Three Silent Men (1940), Pack up Your Troubles (1940), My Wife's Family (1941), It Happened to One Man (1941), The Farmer's Wife (1941), We'll Meet Again (1942), Let the People Sing (1942), Suspected Person (1943), Millions Like Us (1943), Madonna of the Seven Moons (1944), Love Story (1944), 2,000 Women (1944), The Wicked Lady (1945), Johnny Frenchman (1945), Canyon Passage (1946), The Brothers (1947), When the Bough Breaks (1947), So Well Remembered (1947), Jassy (1947), One Night with You (1948), Holiday Camp (1948), Return to Life (1949), The Perfect Woman (1949), The Man on the Eiffel Tower (1949), Fugitive from Montreal (1950), Black Jack (1950), Circle of Danger (1951), Something Money Can't Buy (1952), La Mia vita e tua (1953), The Widow (1954), Cartouche (1954), The Hypnotist (1957), The House in the Woods (1959), and Bluebeard's Ten Honeymoons (1960).

THE ROCKING HORSE WINNER (Two Cities/Rank, 1950)—Family drama. *Director:* Anthony Pelissier; *Producer:* John Mills; *Script:* Anthony Pelissier, based on the story by D. H. Lawrence; *Cinematography:* Desmond Dickinson; *Music:* William Alwyn; *Cast:* Valerie Hobson (Hester Grahame), John Howard Davies (Paul Grahame), Ronald Squire (Oscar Cresswell), John Mills (Bassett), Hugh Sinclair (Richard Grahame), Charles Goldner (Mr. Tsaldouris), Susan Richards (Nannie), and Cyril Smith (Bailiff).

John Mills* produced and acted in two films for Rank: *The History of Mr. Polly* (1949) and *The Rocking Horse Winner.* Based on a story by D. H. Lawrence, this cautionary fable warns of the dangers of greed and the disastrous effects it has on a family. Hester Grahame's constant demands on her family to support her affluent lifestyle not only emasculates her husband Richard, but also kills her son Paul. As her demands intensify, Paul begins hearing voices within the house and the only way he can silence them is to ride his rocking horse in a frenzied manner, whipping it as he throws himself about in the saddle. This behavior not only silences the voices (temporarily), but also enables Paul to pick the winner of forthcoming horse races. Eventually, his "riding" kills him.

The Rocking Horse Winner functions as a morality play, warning of the dangers of material excess by showing how maternal greed and family disharmony lead to the death of an innocent young boy. At this level, the meaning of the film is clear: Hester, whose affection for Paul and her other children is subsumed by her desire for wealth, realizes that she killed her son and refuses to touch Paul's winnings (£80,000). Anthony Pelissier closes the film in a redemptive manner showing the distressed Hester, dressed in black with her hair pulled tightly to her head, watching Paul's rocking horse burn. However, there is a symbolic dimension to the film, concerned with the financially and sexually impotent father, the frustrated mother—it is Hester's distorted voice within the house that disturbs Paul—and Paul's "masturbatory" riding of his rocking horse. It is only Paul's ability to produce wealth from his racing predictions, resulting from his frenzied riding, that can satisfy Hester—all of the other men in her life are symbolically impotent, due to financial weakness (her husband), age and kinship (her brother Oscar), or class differences (Bassett, the family handy man). In a period of strict censorship, *The Rocking Horse Winner* is a fascinating film that weaves its disturbing ramifications within a symbolic form not common in the British cinema in the late 1940s.

ROEG, NICHOLAS (b. 1928). Nicholas Roeg, like Peter Greenaway,* is not interested in making films within the strictures of classical filmmaking and the limitations imposed by a linear narrative structure and the tight cause-and-effect pattern of the Hollywood film. Before directing his first film in 1968, Roeg spent twenty-one years in the industry. He began as an apprentice editor at MGM British, and then second assistant cameraman on films such as *The Miniver Story* (1950). From 1961, he was director of photography on films such as *The Masque of the Red Death* (1964), with its dramatic use of color, *Fahrenheit 451* (1966), for François Truffaut, *Far from the Madding Crowd* (1967), for John Schlesinger,* and *Petulia* (1967), for Richard Lester. When friend, screenwriter, and painter Donald Cammell and producer Sandy Lieberson raised sufficient money to film Cammell's script for *Performance* (1970), Cammell invited Roeg to co-direct his screenplay concerning a criminal on the run (James Fox) who moves into the home of a rock star (Mick Jagger). However, the film's strained atmosphere of sexual and moral decadence, reinforced by representations of heterosexuality and homosexuality and the perverse transfer of power between the gangster and the rock star, horrified Warner Brothers, which was hoping for a light-hearted musical exploiting Jagger's popularity.

Although *Performance* was shelved by Warners for two years, this did not deter Roeg in *Walkabout* (1971), one of his best films (and his last as cinematographer) and his first as solo director. In this film, Roeg transformed a children's book into an adult tale of cultural dislocation mediated through temporal ellipses to fragment the story into carefully selected visual and thematic patterns. *Walkabout,* which was filmed in the Australian outback, used its distinctive setting to explore the physical and metaphorical notions of what constitutes being "lost," as two Europeans, a young woman (Jenny Agutter) and a boy (Lucien John), rely on an aboriginal youth (David Gulpilil) to save them. This journey has consequences for all concerned. Roeg followed with his most critically admired film *Don't*

Look Now* (1973), which again utilized a temporally fragmented story line to maximize the dramatic and emotional ramifications felt by Donald Sutherland and Julie Christie* after the loss of their daughter and their subsequent traumatic experiences in Venice.

The next few years were productive for Roeg, with *The Man Who Fell to Earth* (1976) and especially *Bad Timing* (1980). This latter film, which detailed the destructive relationship between a manipulative psychiatrist (Art Garfunkel) and a masochistic, sensual woman (Theresa Russell), failed to reach a wide audience and the critical response, due to the film's subject matter and Roeg's style, was mixed. Thereafter, Roeg's films have been plagued by distribution problems, especially *Eureka* (1982) and *Cold Heaven* (1992), and critical and commercial indifference, such as *Track 29,* a weird Dennis Potter story filmed in North Carolina in 1988, and *Two Deaths* (1995). During this period, however, Roeg directed his most commercially successful film, an excellent adaptation of Roald Dahl's children story *The Witches* (1990). After *Bad Timing,* Roeg married U.S. actress Theresa Russell, who also starred in *Eureka, Insignificance* (1985), *Aria* (1987), *Track 29,* and *Cold Heaven.* Roeg was nominated for Best Direction for *Don't Look Now* at the 1974 BAFTA Film Awards and for Best British Cinematography (Color) for *Nothing But the Best* in 1965 and *Far from the Madding Crowd* in 1968.

FILMS: Performance (codir., 1970), Walkabout (1971), Glastonbury Fayre (doc., 1971), Don't Look Now (1973), The Man Who Fell to Earth (1976), Bad Timing (1980), Eureka (1982), Insignificance (1985), Castaway (1987), Aria (one segment, 1987), Track 29 (1988), The Witches (1990), Cold Heaven (1992), Hotel Paradise (1995), and Two Deaths (1996).

ROOM AT THE TOP (Remus, 1958)—Drama. *Director:* Jack Clayton; *Producers:* James Woolf and John Woolf; *Script:* Neil Patterson, based on the novel by John Braine; *Photography:* Freddie Francis; *Music:* Mario Nascimbene; *Cast:* Laurence Harvey (Joe Lampton), Simone Signoret (Alice Aisgill), Heather Sears (Susan Brown), Donald Houston (Charles Soames), Donald Wolfit (Mr. Brown), Hermione Baddeley (Elspeth), Allan Cuthbertson (George Aisgill), Raymond Huntley (Mr. Hoylake), Beatrice Varley (Aunt), Wilfred Lawson (Uncle Nat), Ambrosine Phillpotts (Mrs. Brown) and Wendy Craig (Joan).

The status of *Room at the Top* as a seminal film in the British cinema, and one of the first New Wave films, has been a matter of conjecture for some years. Some argue that it, like other films of the British New Wave in the late 1950s and early 1960s (including *Saturday Night and Sunday Morning* [1960], *Look Back in Anger* [1959], and *This Sporting Life* [1963]), is thematically and formally conservative and should be seen as a continuation of the British studio tradition. Others maintain that films such as *Room at the Top* were part of a cinematic revolution that represented a significant rupture in the 1950s British cinema. The truth lies somewhere between these two positions.

Although John Trevelyan, the secretary of the British Board of Film Censors, admired the film, he gave it an X certificate that, in normal circumstances, would severely reduce its commercial chances. As a result, the film's producers marketed it as a "savage story of lust and ambition." Fortunately, the public flocked to the film and it was the fourth most popular film in 1958 as well as receiving recognition in the United States, winning two Academy Awards in 1960 for Best Actress (Simone Signoret) and Best Writing, Screenplay Based on Material from Another Medium (Neil Patterson). *Room at the Top* also won BAFTA Awards in 1959 for Best Film and Best Actress (Signoret) as well as the National Board of Review in the United States for Best Actress (Signoret). Laurence Harvey* was nominated for Best Actor, Jack Clayton* for Best Director, Hermione Baddeley for Best Supporting Actress, and the film for Best Picture at the 1960 Academy Awards.

The modernist style of the credits points to its desire to be seen as different from the run-of-the-mill British drama and for its period. The film achieves a remarkably frank examination of ambition, betrayal, and guilt. Joe Lampton, secure in his ambition and good looks, leaves his working-class origins in the industrial town of Dufton for an accountant's position in the council offices at Warnley. He wants to better himself through his relationship with Susan Brown, the daughter of a wealthy local industrialist. This desire is threatened by his affair with Alice Aisgill, a mature married French woman. Alice's husband threatens Lampton with exposure and legal action at the same time that Susan's father offers him a senior position in his company if he will marry Susan, now pregnant with Lampton's baby. After being told by Lampton that he cannot see her any more, Alice commits suicide, which inadvertently leaves him with feelings of guilt. Nevertheless, he marries Susan. In the final scene, Lampton cries in the car as it leaves the wedding ceremony. While Susan interprets his tears as a sign of his love for her, it is more an expression of self-pity and the price he has paid for his ambition. Not only has he lost Alice but he is trapped—a feeling conveyed by the barren images that close the film.

Room at the Top, based on John Braine's best-selling 1957 novel, is a powerful film and it provided Harvey with the breakthrough role he had sought for many years. The moral center of the film is Signoret's Alice, who is able to cut through Lampton's pretensions and self-delusions while still recognizing positive qualities in this angry young man. The film's sexual frankness, conveyed largely through Signoret's sensual performance, relies on pauses and facial reactions. A crucial factor was the fact that the film refuses to moralize about Alice's relationship with Lampton. This "casual" attitude to an extra-marital relationship and the calculating attitudes of the central character make it a landmark film within the British cinema. It captured Braine's central theme: The desire of the working class to leave their origins as quickly as possible for the pleasures of a "girl with a Riviera tan and the Lagonda."

A RUN FOR YOUR MONEY (Ealing, 1949)—Comedy. *Director:* Charles Frend; *Producers:* Michael Balcon and Leslie Norman (associate); *Script:* Charles Frend, Leslie Norman, and Richard Hughes, with additional dialogue by Diana Morgan; *Cinematography:* Douglas Slocombe; *Music:* Ernest Irving; *Cast:*

Donald Houston (David "Dai Number 9" Jones), Meredith Edwards (Thomas "Twm" Jones), Moira Lister (Jo), Alec Guinness (Whimple), Hugh Griffiths (Huw), Clive Morton (Editor), Julie Milton (Bronwen), Peter Edwards (Davies), and Joyce Grenfell (Mrs. Pargiter).

Although *A Run for Your Money* was nominated for the Best British Film Award at the 1950 BAFTA Film Awards, it was one of the weakest comedies released by Ealing at a time when the studio was producing *Passport to Pimlico* (1949), *Whisky Galore!* (1949), and *Kind Hearts and Coronets** (1949). The script, credited to Charles Frend, Welsh novelist Richard Hughes (*A High Wind in Jamaica*), and Leslie Norman, was largely written by Diana Morgan, although she only received an "additional dialogue" credit. The simple story concerns two Welsh miners, Dai and Thomas Jones, who win a trip to London, a rugby game, and £200 in a newspaper competition. However, when the brothers miss their newspaper contact at Paddington station, they are exposed to the dangers of the big city, particularly Jo (she is described as a "pro" by the police), who latches onto Dai and his money.

Although much of the film consists of heavy-handed situations based on the familiar premise of the "innocent abroad," the film, to its credit, refuses to sentimentalize Jo as the "whore with a heart of gold" and it makes clear that Dai's money is the only reason for her interest in such an insipid character. Thus, when she finally manages to inveigle Dai back to her apartment for a "cup of tea," the sexually excited Welshman is prepared to promise Jo anything to get what he wants (sex), including a promise to take her back to his Welsh village. However, after sex Dai withdraws his offer. Thus, the film's ending is disappointing—in a sentimental gesture Jo, having escaped with Dai's money, suddenly changes her mind and throws his money back to him as his train pulls out of the station.

A Run for Your Money provided Alec Guinness* with one of his less rewarding roles as the gardening correspondent charged with protecting the two miners. Henceforth, Guinness would refuse roles that he considered too close to his actual, real-life persona.

RUSSELL, KEN (b. 1927). Can a filmmaker who is responsible for a camp, incoherent film such as *The Lair of the White Worm* (1988), loosely based on the novel by Bram Stoker, be taken seriously? The film includes a scene where Amanda Donohue, in full fetish gear including black boots, drowns a young Boy Scout in her bath with the tip of her spiked heel! Such scenes became the norm in Ken Russell's films in the 1970s and beyond, as he allowed his predilection for sexual and religious symbolism to overwhelm his films at the expense of narrative and thematic coherence. Even when the material was conducive to his excessive style, as in *Crimes of Passion* (1984) and *Whore* (1991), Russell fails to fully explore the dramatic potential of each film beyond the damaging effects of sexual repression (*Crimes of Passion*) and the dangers to personal safety and emotional stability of a life on the street (*Whore*). These films, in effect, become little more than a pretext for his penchant for excessive visual symbolism.

After losing interest in a naval career, Russell tried ballet dancing, while dab-bling in photography and black and white silent films. When Russell submitted one of his films, *Amelia,* to the BBC's *Monitor* television program in the late 1950s, he was hired and began making short programs on the arts. Russell's repu-tation grew following his low-budget documentaries dramatizing the lives of famous composers and dancer Isadora Duncan. This series of films often posited a direct association between the lifestyle of an artist and his or her work. Following the unsuccessful *French Dressing* (1964) and an uneven third outing in the Harry Palmer series *Billion Dollar Brain* (1967), Russell's third film, *Women in Love* (1969), was his best and he was rewarded with both Academy Award and BAFTA nominations for Best Director. However, he still managed to outrage F. R. Leavis and other literary scholars with this adaptation of D. H. Lawrence's novel.

The six years following *Women in Love* was Russell's most creative and criti-cally appreciated period, although the critical storm clouds were gathering, espe-cially after the historically dubious *The Music Lovers* (1970), which suggested that Peter Tchaikovsky (Richard Chamberlain) was gay and his wife Nina (Glenda Jackson) a nymphomaniac, a theory that outraged many music lovers. Russell followed this with an even more scandalous film, *The Devils** (1971), complete with graphic depictions of religious and sexual deviations of church fig-ures in seventeenth-century France. The film's mixture of drama, comedy, and surreal imagery, plus scenes of deviant sexual behavior, repression, and violence extended it well beyond the taste, and capabilities, of many viewers. At this point, the consistently excessive nature of Russell's style worried many critics, although it did not deter the director from his pattern of (sometimes rich) visual symbolism that was often divorced from the narrative and thematic demands of the work.

In some films, the generic material disguised his shortcomings, as in Russell's adaptation of Sandy Wilson's spoof of the musical *The Boyfriend* (1971), which allowed Russell to return to his own passion for dancing while legitimizing his interpretation of the excesses of the equally excessive Busby Berkeley, and in *Tommy* (1975), which was adapted from The Who's rock opera. Such projects were compatible with his ability to contrive powerful visual images, often designed to shock. Subsequent films often failed to provide compensating dis-plays of nuance or moral complexity to match the dazzle of his imagery.

FILMS: French Dressing (1964), Billion Dollar Brain (1967), Women in Love (1969), The Music Lovers (1970), The Devils (1971), The Boyfriend (1971), Savage Messiah (1972), Mahler (1974), Tommy (1975), Lisztomania (1975), Valentino (1977), Altered States (1980), Crimes of Passion (1984), Gothic (1987), Aria (codir., 1987) The Lair of the White Worm (1988), Salome's Last Dance (1988), The Rainbow (1989), Whore (1991), The Insatiable Mrs. Kirsch (short, 1993), Erotic Tales (codir., 1994), URI (1995), and Mindbender (1995).

RUTHERFORD, MARGARET (1892–1972). The term "character actress" does not come close to describing the special talents of Margaret Rutherford. A skilled scene-stealer, in the nicest possible sense, Rutherford, after years as a speech and piano teacher, studied acting at the Old Vic and made her stage debut in 1925. Her film debut came in *Dusty Ermine* in 1936. One of her special qualities, despite her unique appearance, was that Rutherford rarely plundered a role for laughs ("I never intended to play for laughs. I am always surprised that the audience thinks me funny"),[4] yet with her characteristic tweeds, multiple chins, and ever-present earnestness, Rutherford injected humor and sparkle into the most mundane film.

Rutherford's most notable early role was the medium Madam Arcati in David Lean's* *Blithe Spirit* (1945), having first appeared in the role on the stage in 1941 with Noël Coward directing his own play. Lean's film, however, consolidated not only Rutherford's status in the film industry, but also her distinctive persona that, although tweaked over the years, remained basically intact. A special highlight in her film career was the casting of Rutherford opposite that other great eccentric of the British screen, Alastair Sim,* in Frank Launder's* *The Happiest Days of Your Life* (1950). Rutherford, as Muriel Whitchurch, the headmistress of St. Swithin's Girls School, is forced to deal with Wetherby Pond (Sim), headmaster of Nutbourne College, when, as a result of a bureaucratic mistake, St. Swithin's is located with the boys school.

Her best-known role in her later years was as Miss Jane Marple, Agatha Christie's spinster sleuth, a role she played in four films for MGM between *Murder, She Said* in 1961 and *Murder Ahoy* in 1964. Stringer Davis, Rutherford's husband, provided (limited) assistance to Miss Marple in her investigations. Rutherford reprised the character of Marple for a humorous cameo in *The Alphabet Murders* (1965), starring Tony Randall as Hercule Poirot.

Rutherford also appeared in a number of films directed by Anthony Asquith* over the years, including *The Demi-Paradise* (1943), *The Importance of Being Earnest* (1952), and *The VIPs* (1963). In the latter film, Rutherford provides the only highlight in an otherwise turgid film and she was rewarded with the 1964 Oscar for Best Actress in a Supporting Role and also a Golden Globe Award. In 1967, Rutherford became a dame of the British Empire, later publishing her autobiography in 1972, the year she died.

FILMS: Dusty Ermine (1936), Talk of the Devil (1936), Beauty and the Barge (1937), Catch As Catch Can (1937), Big Fella (1937), Missing Believed Married (1937), Spring Meeting (1940), Quiet Wedding (1941), The Yellow Canary (1943), The Demi-Paradise (1943), English without Tears (1944), Blithe Spirit (1945), While the Sun Shines (1947), Meet Me at Dawn (1947), Miranda (1948), Passport to Pimlico (1949), The Happiest Days of Your Life (1950), Her Favourite Husband (1950), The Magic Box (1951), Curtain Up (1952), The Importance of Being Earnest (1952), Castle in the Air (1952), Miss Robin Hood (1953), Innocents in Paris (1953), Trouble in Store (1953, The Runaway Bus (1954), Aunt Clara (1954), Mad about Men (1954), An Alligator Named Daisy (1956), The Smallest Show on Earth (1957), Just My Luck (1957), I'm All Right Jack (1959), On the Double (1961), Murder, She Said (1961), The Mouse on the Moon (1963), The VIPs (1963), Murder at the Gallop (1963), Murder Most Foul (1964), Murder Ahoy (1964), The Alphabet Murders (1965), A Countess from Hong Kong (1967), Chimes at Midnight (1967), The Wacky World of Mother Goose (voice, 1967), and Arabella (1969).

NOTES

1. McFarlane, *An Autobiography of British Cinema,* p. 532.
2. McFarlane, *An Autobiography of British Cinema,* p. 474.
3. See Murphy, *Sixties British Cinema,* p. 21.
4. McFarlane, *An Autobiography of British Cinema,* p. 506.

S

SANDERS OF THE RIVER (London Films, 1935)/Death Drums along the River (Big Ben Productions/Hallam, 1963)—Imperial adventure.

SANDERS OF THE RIVER
Director: Zoltan Korda; *Producer:* Alexander Korda; *Script:* Lajos Biro and Jeffrey Dell, based on the novel *Sanders of the River* by Edgar Wallace; *Cinematography:* Louis Page, Osmond H. Borradaile, and Georges Perinal; *Music:* Mischa Spoliansky; *Cast:* Paul Robeson (Bosambo), Leslie Banks (Commissioner R. G. Sanders), Nina Mae McKinney (Lilongo), Robert Cochrane (Tibbets), Martin Walker (Ferguson), and Richard Grey (Captain Hamilton).

DEATH DRUMS ALONG THE RIVER
Director: Lawrence Huntington; *Producer:* Peter Welbeck (Harry Alan Towers); *Script:* Kevin Kavanagh, Nicholas Roeg, Lawrence Huntington, and Harry Alan Towers, based on the novel *Sanders of the River* by Edgar Wallace; *Cinematography:* Bob Huke; *Cast:* Richard Todd (Inspector Harry Sanders), Marianne Koch (Dr. Inge Jung), Albert Lieven (Dr. Weiss), Walter Rilla (Dr. Schneider), Robert Arden (Hunter), Vivi Bach (Marlene), Bill Brewer (Pearson), Jeremy Lloyd (Hamilton).

The 1935 production of Edgar Wallace's novel was greeted at the time of its release as an effective endorsement of the British Empire in Africa and a celebration of the bravery and fortitude of those colonial administrators working in remote areas. Today, unless the film is carefully contextualized within the prevailing ethos at the time of its release, it is open to obvious charges of patronizing the Africans and elevating one culture, the British, above another. In this regard, the involvement of U.S. black singer and activist Paul Robeson, who is top billed in the film as Bosambo, is interesting as he was first attracted to the project after viewing documentary footage shot by Zoltan Korda in East and West Africa before principal photography took place in England. Robeson believed the film would legitimize aspects of African culture for European audiences and he sang four songs in the film that were adaptations of traditional tribal chants that had been modified ("Westernized") by Mischa Spoliansky, who received an award for Best Music at the 1935 Venice Film Festival. However, following its release, black organizations in Britain and the United States criticized the film for its representation of the natives as children, a charge supported by the film's reference to the relationship between Commissioner R. G. Sanders and the locals as a father-child relationship. Robeson subsequently disowned the film and regretted his involvement. He demanded greater creative control in the five films he made in Britain after *Sanders of the River.*

Leslie Banks* as Commissioner R. G. Sanders, on the other hand, established, in his superb performance as Sanders, the dominant traits of the archetypal colonial administrator for the next thirty years, traits that could be found in many British and Hollywood productions set in Africa and Asia. Banks's Sanders is humorous, authoritative, brave, and caring and treats the natives as would a kind, but firm parent. The force of Sanders's personality is an integral part of the plot (the natives refer to him as "Lord Sandi") as he has little military support—a few white officers and one regiment of native troops—to administer a large, unruly territory.

Sanders of the River polarizes the drama, as in virtually every Empire film, into the "good African" (Bosambo) and the "evil African" (Mofalaba). The story is careful not to allow Mofalaba's opposition to the British to be associated with any political program promoting independence or freedom from colonial authority (e.g., compared with the presentation of the conflict in Kenya in *Simba** [1955]). Instead, Mofalaba's actions are motivated by power, cruelty, and a wish to reinstate the slave-running activities that had been banned in the river region by Sanders. Yet, the film contains its own inherent criticism of colonial rule by pointing to the fragility of its power and its dependence on the strength and understanding of extraordinary men like Sanders. When he leaves the territory to marry his sweetheart back in England, everything disintegrates into violence and within one week of his departure, as Captain Grey remarks, all of Sanders's work over the past ten years has been brought down. His successor, Ferguson, is killed by Mofalaba. The situation gets so bad that the local priest, Father O'Leary, cables the colonial office to send "four battalions or Sanders."

Sanders returns by plane, flying godlike back into his territory and then takes a paddle steamer upriver to rescue Bosambo and his wife Lilonga, before killing Mofalaba. Sanders then bestows overall native control of the river district to Bosambo, subject, of course, to the absolute power of the British district commissioner (Sanders).

Death Drums along the River, released nearly thirty years after *Sanders of the River,* is less patronizing than the 1935 film, largely due to the fact that the story ignores the tribal issues raised in the earlier film. Instead, its plot concerns diamond smuggling and a series of murders. The most significant difference between the two films emanates from Richard Todd's* characterization of Sanders as a facsimile of the humorless, grimly determined, recessive officer class that characterized many British war films in the 1950s. This characterization compares poorly with Banks's flamboyant, effusive district commissioner. The plot of the 1963 film concerns the murder of a policeman that takes Sanders to a rural hospital that, we eventually learn, is positioned over a large diamond mine. A doctor at the hospital plots to keep the diamonds for himself. *Death Drums along the River* was commercially successful enough for Todd to return as Commissioner Sanders, with Marianne Koch, the following year in *Coast of Skeletons* (1964). However, despite the imperial propaganda that imbues much of *Sanders of the River,* the Alexander Korda* film was a more significant and emotionally compelling film than Lawrence Huntington's attempt, shot in South Africa, to revive the Sanders characterization.

SAVILLE, VICTOR (1897–1979). An important figure in the development of the British film industry prior to World War II, Victor Saville entered the British cinema in 1917 through the industrial and economic side, first as a theater manager, and then forming a small distribution company in Birmingham with Michael Balcon. Saville worked as a production manager in the 1920s, finally directing (and writing and producing) his first film, *The Arcadians,* in 1927. As a director, as opposed to his role as a specialist producer, Saville's most creative period was the 1930s—especially his assured remake of *Hindle Wakes* in 1931. However, Saville's most notable films were the series of musicals he directed for Jessie Matthews,* and he persuaded her that she would photograph well for the screen. She starred in *The Good Companions* (1933), which was followed by *Friday the Thirteenth* (1933), the enormously successful *Evergreen** (1934), which was adapted from the Richard Rodgers and Lorenz Hart musical, *First a Girl* (1935), and *It's Love Again* (1936).

One of Saville's best films as a director was *South Riding* (1938), an adaptation of Winifred Holtby's popular novel detailing the lives of a small group of people in the Yorkshire dales. The film gave Ralph Richardson* one of his best early film roles as the local squire who, depressed by the mental illness of his wife (Ann Todd*), is attracted to schoolmistress Edna Best. After this melodrama of domestic conflict and civic corruption, Saville, temporarily, abandoned directing and joined MGM as a producer. He excelled in this role, producing two highly successful MGM British films: *The Citadel* (1938) and especially *Goodbye, Mr. Chips** (1939). Both films received Academy Award nominations for Best Picture. After this success, Saville left Britain to work as a producer at MGM in Hollywood, where he produced a succession of glossy, commercially successful films, such as his 1940 remake of the 1933 Herbert Wilcox–Anna Neagle film version of Noël Coward's *Bitter Sweet.* Saville's followed this inferior remake, which starred Jeanette MacDonald and Nelson Eddy at their most sentimental, with another sentimental MacDonald vehicle, *Smilin' Through* (1941), a remake of Norma Shearer's 1932 film.

Saville resumed directing with the episodic *Forever and a Day* in 1943, a film in which many U.S. and British artists contributed their services to raise funds for British War Relief. Saville returned to Britain intermittently throughout the late 1940s and early 1950s to direct MGM productions such as *Conspirator* (1949), with Elizabeth Taylor discovering that husband Robert Taylor is a communist, and *Calling Bulldog Drummond* (1951), with Walter Pidgeon's Bulldog Drummond coming out of retirement to assist Scotland Yard. The last British film he directed was *24 Hours of a Woman's Life* (1952), a minor melodrama co-starring Merle Oberon and Richard Todd.*

Saville's last credited film as a director was the infamous *The Silver Chalice* (1955), a costume melodrama starring Paul Newman in his first film. Newman, however, was so embarrassed by the resultant film that he apologized in a Hollywood trade magazine. More importantly, Saville's production company Parklane secured the rights in the early 1950s to the novels of lurid hard-boiled crime writer Mickey Spillane. Saville produced the lackluster *I, the Jury* (1953), *The Long Wait* (1954), starring Anthony Quinn, and the magnificent Robert Aldrich directed *Kiss Me Deadly* (1955). While Saville's overall contribution to the British and U.S. cinemas was to supply a long series of well-crafted, genre films (such as the breezy Rex Harrison –Vivien Leigh social comedy *Storm in a Teacup [1937]),* it was ironic that his production of *Kiss Me Deadly,* near the end of his career, was one of the most radical and influential Hollywood films of the 1950s in terms of its style and politics. The last Spillane-based film produced by Saville was the low-budget *My Gun Is Quick* (1957). Saville's last two productions were British films, the bitter-sweet romance *The Greengage Summer* (1961), starring Kenneth More,* and the Adam Faith crime melodrama *Mix Me a Person* (1962). Saville died in 1979.

FILMS (as director): The Arcadians (1927), The Glad Eye (1927), Tesha (1927), Kitty (1929), Woman to Woman (1929), Me and the Boys (1929), The W Plan (1930), A Warm Corner (1930), The Sport of Kings (1930), Sunshine Susie (1931), Michael and Mary (1931), Hindle Wakes (1932), The Faithful Heart (1932), Love on Wheels (1932), The Good Companions (1933), I Was a Spy (1933), Friday the Thirteenth (1933), Evergreen (1934), Evensong (1934), The Iron Duke (1934), Me and Marlborough (1935), The Dictator (1935), First a Girl (1936), It's Love Again (1936), Storm in a Teacup (1937), Dark Journey (1937), Action for Slander (1938), South Riding (1938), Forever and a Day (1943), Tonight and Every Night (1945), The Green Years (1946), Green Dolphin Street (1947), If Winter Comes (1947), Conspirator (1949), Kim (1950), Calling Bulldog Drummond (1951), 24 Hours of a Woman's Life (1952), The Long Wait (1954), and The Silver Chalice (1955).

SCANDAL (British Screen/Palace Pictures, 1989)—Political melodrama. *Director:* Michael Caton-Jones; *Producers:* Stephen Woolley, Joe Boyd (executive), Redmond Morris (associate), Nik Powell (executive), Bob Weinstein (coexecutive), and Harvey Weinstein (coexecutive); *Script:* Michael Thomas; *Cinematography:* Mike Molloy; *Music:* Carl Davis; *Cast:* John Hurt (Stephen Ward), Joanne

Whalley-Kilmer (Christine Keeler), Bridget Fonda (Mandy Rice-Davies), Ian McKellen (John Profumo), Leslie Phillips (Lord Astor), Jeroen Krabbe (Eugene Ivanov), Britt Ekland (Mariella Novotny), Daniel Massey (Mervyn Griffith-Jones), Roland Gift (Johnnie Edgecomb), Jean Alexander (Mrs. Keeler), and Ronald Fraser (Justice Marshall).

When Stephen Frears (*Sammy and Rosie Get Laid* [1987] and *Dangerous Liaisons* [1988]) was asked to direct *Scandal,* he rejected the offer because he believed that the Profumo scandal (the basis of *Scandal*) in the early 1960s and the U.S. Watergate scandal of the early 1970s were the two great political events of his life. He felt his objectivity would be compromised and that he would get "trapped between fact and fiction." Instead, the much younger Michael Caton-Jones replaced him and, with Michael Thomas's script, the film focuses more on the relationship between Christine Keeler and Stephen Ward rather than the political and social ramifications of this tumultuous period. Only occasionally does the political and social significance of the events, which extended beyond Britain, emerge. One is left wondering how Frears, or some other filmmaker with a more intimate knowledge of the events, would have presented this period.

The affair between John Profumo, married to former British film star Valerie Hobson,* and Christine Keeler follows their initial meeting on July 8, 1961, at Lord Astor's Cliveden Estate. Captain Eugene Ivanov, naval attaché to the Soviet embassy in London, also attended this party. However, instead of the developing the ramifications of this issue, involving sex and political intrigue, the film touches on these issues only through its sympathetic presentation of the two key players: Stephen Ward and Christine Keeler. The film suggests that Ward and Keeler were in love although their relationship was platonic.

While focusing more on the personal relationship between Ward and Keeler, as opposed to the wider political machinations, the film provides a clear motivation for Ward's behavior. A London osteopath, he wants to mingle with people of power and he achieves this through his ability to supply his female "protégés" to men in positions of power and influence. Thus, Ward, superbly played by John Hurt,* is portrayed as essentially benign, a man who wanted merely to move with the rich and famous and the film repudiates the claim at his trial that he supplied prostitutes to people such as Lord Astor and John Profumo. The motivation for Keeler, however, is less clear—aside from the suggestion that, because of her youthful interest in all things new, she merely wanted to please Ward. The money and the trappings of Profumo's office, and the fact that he regularly met with the Queen, were, the film suggests, of little interest to her. Hence the two key players are presented as a libertine (Ward) and a gullible woman (Keeler)—both are presented as the victims of a pernicious Establishment that quickly closed ranks after the scandal broke with Ward and Keeler offered up as scapegoats to an unsympathetic judicial system and an exploitative press.

The film depicts the scandal as a combination of coincidence, lust, and the vindictive use of power. There are also insinuations that the British secret service, or another government agency, specifically cultivated Ward's association with Captain Ivanov, who was sleeping with Keeler at the same time she was having sex with Profumo, the Secretary of War in Harold Macmillan's government. As this event took place during the tensions of the Cold War, the potential for espionage was considerable. However, the film offers little in this regard. Instead, it is more concerned with emphasizing the destructive role of the tabloid press in targeting Ward and Keeler. Thus, Ward is shown to be a sad, expendable pawn caught between upper-class lust and the irresponsible, but essentially innocent, behavior of a young woman (Keeler). They were destroyed, the film suggests, because of guilt by association rather than any deep personal flaws. Teenager Mandy Rice Davies, on the other hand, is presented in a less favorable manner and depicted as more calculating compared to Keeler.

The film is vague as to the attraction between the young Keeler and the government minister. It appears that there are still too many legal and censurable obstacles to fully develop this fascinating story as character motivation and the political and international significance of the events are yet to be fully and frankly explored—who, for instance, was the infamous "man in the mask" in the "orgy" scene. There are currently three versions of *Scandal* available, including a 114-minute unrated version, although the widely distributed 105-minute version is, through heavy censorship, inadequate. For example, Britt Ekland as Mariella Novotny, a key figure in the sex scandal, is rarely seen in this version.

Bridget Fonda, as Mandy Rice Davies, was nominated for Best Performance by an Actress in a Supporting Role at the 1990 Golden Globes Awards.

SCHLESINGER, JOHN (b. 1926). An ability to adapt to institutional and cultural changes, plus a consistent ability to capture strong performances from his actors, are the reasons why John Schlesinger has been able to continue make feature films and prestigious television programs for more than four decades. After an Oxford education, where he joined the Oxford University Dramatic Society, Schlesinger acted (in small parts) in a number of British films in the 1950s (including playing a German officer in Michael Powell's* *Battle of the River Plate* [1956]). Later, while working on the *Monitor,* an arts program at the BBC, he made a brief segment on an Italian opera company coming to the Dury Lane Theatre. This program, together with his 1961 award-winning documentary on London Waterloo's station (*Terminus*), attracted the interest of producer Joe Janni and after Schlesinger completed some commercials for Janni's company, he was "tested" for a feature film by directing a test of Tom Courtenay for *Billy Liar** (1963). Consequently, Schlesinger was offered *A Kind of Loving** (1962).

A Kind of Loving, a key film in the New Wave, was a domestic drama with a dark side found in many of Schlesinger's films, especially *Day of the Locust* (1974). He also created the joyous "star-making" entrance of Julie Christie* in *Billy Liar*—a montage made up of images filmed in London, Bradford, and Manchester of her skipping happily along a busy street. Yet, the film closed on the ambiguously bleak image of Courtenay returning to his parent's semi-detached home, content to live a fantasy existence in "Ambrosia" rather than take a chance with Christie, and a new career, in London.

Schlesinger's third film, *Darling** (1965), was an international success for the director, although he claims it is one of his "least favourite films," feeling, in retrospect, that "it was too pleased with itself."[1] The idea for the script came from journalist Godrey Winn, who knew a woman who was the mistress of a number of prominent people. They supported her in various ways, including the provision of a flat. However, after initially cooperating with writer Frederic Raphael and Schlesinger, the woman changed her mind and issued an injunction against the film, forcing them to abandon many of the ideas they had developed. The resultant film, nevertheless, retains their central idea, attacking the superficiality of consumerist middle-class society in Britain in the 1960s.

Despite a visually splendid adaptation of Thomas Hardy's *Far from the Madding Crowd* (1967), aided by Richard Rodney Bennett's score, Frederic Raphael's script, Nicolas Roeg's camera, and strong performances from Peter Finch,* Christie, Alan Bates,* and Terence Stamp, the film failed to find an audience. Schlesinger left for Hollywood for his next film, his groundbreaking adaptation of James Leo Herlihy's novel *Midnight Cowboy* (1969). With its (for the time) explicit depiction of non-conventional sexual behavior, the film was awarded an X rating in the United States, which was later reduced to an R, and it was the first film with an X to win an Oscar for Best Film and an Oscar for Schlesinger for Best Direction (plus the 1970 BAFTA Film Award).

Schlesinger followed the success of *Midnight Cowboy* with his most personal film, *Sunday Bloody Sunday* (1971), where both Peter Finch and Glenda Jackson love Murray Head. The initial premise for the film came from Schlesinger's own experience of a two-year romance with a younger man and, while editing *Far from the Madding Crowd,* Schlesinger spent time with critic Penelope Gilliatt exchanging experiences from their personal lives. Out of this, Gilliatt developed the script that earned Schlesinger his third Oscar nomination for Best Director and a Best Direction Award at the 1972 BAFTA Film Awards.

After one of his best films, an adaptation of Nathanael West's surreal, bitter perception of the underbelly of Hollywood in *The Day of the Locust* (1974), his next film was a more conventional thriller, *The Marathon Man* (1976), with Dustin Hoffman accidentally caught up in international intrigue. This was followed by Schlesinger's return to Britain for the U.S.–financed epic *Yanks* (1978), detailing the romance between U.S. soldiers (including Richard Gere) and English women (including Lisa Eichhorn) in the period just prior to the D day invasion. With rising production costs, and the formal and ideological conservatism of the mainstream cinema in the 1980s and 1990s, Schlesinger found it increasingly difficult to get projects off the ground, although there were still moments of innovation and inspiration (*Cold Comfort Farm* [1994]). However, his output also included inferior films, such as *The Innocent* (1993), *Eye for an Eye* (1995), a hysterical revenge melodrama, and the abysmal *The Next Best*

Thing (2000). His television work during this period, such as *An Englishman Abroad* (1983), was more satisfying.

Schlesinger won a 1961 BAFTA Award for Best Short Film for *Terminus* and he was nominated for Best Direction at the 1966 Academy Awards and the 1966 BAFTA Awards for *Darling*. Schlesinger was nominated for Best Direction for *Yanks* at the 1980 BAFTA Film Awards.

FILMS: Horror (short, 1946), Black Legend (short, 1948), The Starfish (short, 1950), Sunday in the Park (short, 1956), Terminus (short, 1961), A Kind of Loving (1962), Billy Liar (1963), Darling (1965), Far from the Madding Crowd (1995), Midnight Cowboy (1969), Sunday Bloody Sunday (1971), Visions of Eight (the marathon segment from the 1972 Olympics titled "The Longest," 1973), The Day of the Locust (1974), Marathon Man (1976), Yanks (1978), Honky Tonk Freeway (1981), The Falcon and the Snowman (1985), The Believers (1987), Madame Sousatzka (1988), Pacific Heights (1990), The Innocent (1), (1993), Cold Comfort Farm (1994), Eye for an Eye (1995), and The Next Best Thing (2000).

SELLERS, PETER (1925–1980). There were two distinctive parts to Peter Sellers's film career. Throughout the 1950s, he enjoyed a growing reputation as a talented comedian with the ability to play varied roles. In the 1960s, Sellers was "elevated" to the position of "international" film star, a status that earned him a lot of money and few good films. Despite Sellers's oft-repeated claim that, off-screen, he had no personality of his own, his film performances were often larger than life and there was a fine line between his clever characterizations in films such as *Only Two Can Play* (1962) and *Waltz of the Toreadors* (1962), and the simplistic caricatures found in films such as *The Bobo* (1967). Often, in the British films of the late 1950s, Sellers was part of a team of scene-stealing actors, such as his role as the corrupt Prime Minister Amphibulos of Gaillardia in *Carlton-Brown of the F.O.* (1959) where he competed with Terry-Thomas,* and others, for laughs. Sometimes in his films it was difficult to distinguish between Sellers, the surreal *Goon Show* (the long-running BBC radio show) comedian capable of expert mimicry, and the film actor. Even his Fred Kite, the radical, pro-Russian trade union official in *I'm All Right Jack** (1959), which won Sellers Best British Actor at the 1959 BAFTA Film Awards, shares the same vocal qualities and mannerisms as the characters of *The Goon Show.*

The son of comedians, Sellers was on stage at an early age, including a period as an entertainer in the Royal Air Force, before joining Spike Milligan and Harry Secombe in 1949 in *The Goon Show.* Television appearances and small film roles, beginning with *Penny Points to Paradise* (1951), with Milligan and Secombe, accompanied the growing popularity of his radio program. A strong supporting role as a "Teddy Boy," one of the crooks who invade Katie Johnson's house in *The Ladykillers** (1955), was a key role for Sellers. This was followed by a succession of "showy" featured parts, such as his alcoholic projectionist in *The Smallest Show on Earth* (1957) and his murderous television comic Wee Sonny MacGregor in *The Naked Truth* (1957). The growing cynicism of British film comedy in the late

1950s assisted Sellers and by the end of the decade, with *I'm All Right Jack,* triple roles in *The Mouse That Roared* (1959), and a starring role in Charles Crichton's* *The Battle of the Sexes* (1959), he consolidated his position as Britain's preeminent comedic character actor. Only his role as a sadistic villain in John Guillermin's* *Never Let Go* (1960) deviated from this pattern. *Never Let Go* was not well received by the critics who objected to the film's "unpleasant tone." In 1962, he experimented again with his role as Quilty in Stanley Kubrick's *Lolita.*

After international success as the Indian doctor Dr. Ahmed el Kabir in Anthony Asquith's* *The Millionairess* (1961), co-starring Sophie Loren, *The Pink Panther* (1963), the first Inspector Clouseau film directed by Blake Edwards, and his triple role as the timid U.S. president, British soldier, and obsessed German scientist in Kubrick's *Dr. Strangelove* (1964), Sellers became an international film star. However, after 1963 there were few films worthy of note—some of the Inspector Clouseau films, especially *A Shot in the Dark* (1964) and the impeccably timed pratfalls and other disasters of *The Party* (1968), again directed by Edwards. Sellers's second last film, *Being There* (1979), was overlong, but "worthy," and gave him a final chance to demonstrate his talent as the childlike Chauncey Gardener.

Sellers, who long suffered from heart trouble, aggravated by hard living, died in 1980, after completing the dismal *The Fiendish Plot of Dr. Fu Manchu.* The sixth Inspector Clouseau film with Sellers, *The Trail of the Pink Panther,* using unseen footage and new linking material, was released two years after Sellers's death. Sellers received nominations from the U.S. Academy Awards for Best Actor and the BAFTA for Best British Actor for *Dr. Strangelove* and *Being There.* He also received nominations for Best British Actor from BAFTA for *Only Two Can Play* and *The Pink Panther.*

FILMS: Penny Points to Paradise (1951), London Entertains (1951), Let's Go Crazy (short, 1951), Down among the Z Men (1952), Super Secret Service (1953), Orders Are Orders (1954), John and Julie (1955), The Ladykillers (1955), The Case of the Mukkinese Battlehorn (1955), The Man Who Never Was (voice, 1955), The Smallest Show on Earth (1957), Dearth of a Salesman (short, 1957), Cold Comfort (1957), Insomnia Is Good for You (1957), The Naked Truth (1958), Up the Creek (1958), Tom Thumb (1958), Carlton-Browne of the F.O. (1958), The Mouse That Roared (1959), I'm All Right Jack (1959), Battle of the Sexes (1959), Two Way Stretch (1960), The Running, Jumping and Standing Still Film (short, 1960), Never Let Go (1960), The Millionairess (1961), The Road to Hong Kong (1961), Mr. Topaz (and dir., 1961), Only Two Can Play (1962), Waltz of the Toreadors (1962), Lolita (1962), Dock Brief (1963), Heavens Above! (1963), The Wrong Arm of the Law (1963), The Pink Panther (1963), Dr. Strangelove, or How I Learned to Stop Worrying and Love the Bomb (1964), The World of Henry Orient (1964), A Shot in the Dark (1964), What's New Pussycat? (1965), The Wrong Box (1966), After the Fox (1966), Casino Royale (1967), The Bobo (1967), Woman Times Seven (1967), The Party (1968), I Love You, Alice B. Toklas (1968), The Magic Christian (1969), Hoffman (1969), Hoffman (1971), There's a Girl in My Soup (1971), A Day at the Beach (1971), Simon, Simon (short, 1971), Where Does It Hurt? (1972), Alice's Adventures in Wonderland (1972), The Blockhouse (1973), The Optimists (1973), Soft Beds, Hard Battles (1973), Ghosts in the

Noonday Sun (1974), The Great McGonagall (1974), The Return of the Pink Panther (1974), Murder by Death (1976), The Pink Panther Strikes Again (1976), The Revenge of the Pink Panther (1978), The Prisoner of Zenda (1979), Being There (1979), The Fiendish Plot of Dr. Fu Manchu (1980), and Trail of the Pink Panther (1982).

THE SEVENTH VEIL (Ortus Films, 1945)—Psychological melodrama. *Director:* Compton Bennett; *Producer:* Sydney Box; *Script:* Muriel Box and Sydney Box; *Cinematography:* Reginald Wyer; *Music:* Benjamin Frankel; *Cast:* James Mason (Nicholas), Ann Todd (Francesca Cunningham), Herbert Lom (Dr. Larsen), Hugh McDermott (Peter Gay), Albert Lieven (Maxwell Leyden), and Yvonne Owen (Susan Brook).

The Seventh Veil was not only the most commercially successful British film of the mid-1940s, it was also one of the strangest. Perhaps its emphasis on the recuperative powers of psychology and the fact that the film's overall plot, the musical career and psychological "cure" of young, fragile, pianist Francesca Cunningham, "hides" the film's more disturbing elements. The film begins with a failed suicide attempt by Francesca who then relates her story, in flashback, to Doctor Larsen. After the death of her parents, Francesca, a shy schoolgirl, is sent to Nicholas, a relative. Nicholas, who suffered when his mother abandoned him in favor of a lover, shows little affection to Francesca and appears to have little interest in women in general (his home only has male servants). This, plus the film's emphasis on his crippled state, and his dependency on a cane, symbolizes a flaw in his "masculinity." His lack of interest in a "normal" sexual relationship is reiterated when Nicholas points out to Francesca that in devoting himself to her career he expects nothing in return.

Nicholas guides and shapes Francesca's career as a classical pianist while systematically removing her lovers along the way. Francesca's desire to marry musician Peter Gay is destroyed when Nicholas takes her to the Continent for seven years. Later, artist Maxwell Leyden's interest in Francesca provokes Nicholas's vicious attack on her hands with his cane while she is playing the piano. At the end of the film, a "cured" Francesca has the choice of three suitors—Peter Gay, Maxwell Leyden, and Nicholas. She chooses Nicholas, the man who has ruled her with strong discipline and the only one of the three men whom she has not slept with. Nicholas, unlike Gay and Leyden, has displayed little or no affection toward her—a truly perverse choice considering that the film provides little evidence of any substantial change in their relationship of guardian and ward. The film implies that Francesca is clearly comfortable occupying a submissive position and the repression of her sexual inclinations.

Francesca is one of the more overt masochistic heroines in the cinema and the film dramatizes numerous situations where she is powerless under the control of a dominant figure—beginning with her assertive girlfriend at school who leads Francesca into trouble and a caning from the headmistress. This causes Francesca to miss an opportunity for a musical scholarship. Subsequent (male) authority figures include conductors, lovers, doctors, and, of course, Nicholas. All exert control over Francesca. This quality is accentuated by her narration that approximates the quality long associated with the fragile heroines of Gothic fiction. At one point in the film, as Nicholas strikes Francesca across the face, director Compton Bennett presents this action via a subjective close-up, presumably to dramatize this display of female submissiveness and male sadism. This may have reinforced James Mason's* popularity in Britain in the mid-1940s following his brutality in *The Man in Grey** (1943).

SHALLOW GRAVE (Channel Four Films/The Glasgow Film Fund, 1994)— Film noir/black comedy. *Director:* Danny Boyle; *Producers:* Andrew Macdonald and Allan Scott (executive); *Script:* John Hodge; *Cinematography:* Brian Tufano; *Music:* Simon Boswell; *Cast:* Kerry Fox (Juliet Miller), Christopher Eccleston (David Stephens), Ewan McGregor (Alex Law), Ken Stott (Detective Inspector McCall), Keith Allen (Hugo), Colin McCredie (Cameron), and John Hodge (Detective Constable Mitchell).

Shallow Grave was Britain's most commercially successful film of 1995 and this success provided screenwriter John Hodge, director Danny Boyle, and producer Andrew Macdonald with the opportunity to make the even more commercially successful, and confronting, *Trainspotting* (1996) two years later. *Shallow Grave,* a surprising hit, was cleverly promoted and it tapped into a niche market of savvy filmgoers and young viewers. It also provided an effective launching pad for the career of Ewan McGregor. Overall, *Shallow Grave* received a positive critical reaction, especially in Britain, although some critics, notably in the United States, objected to the film's "mean-spirited" quality, unrelenting cynicism, and lack of sentiment. This aspect was most evident in the ending that was similar in tone (irony) to the closing moments in *The Treasure of the Sierra Madre* (1948).

Shallow Grave was celebrated by British critics for its effective use of local (Edinburgh and Glasgow) settings. It was presented as a successor to the dark strain of British comedy that seeped through the conventional surface of the British cinema in the late 1940s and 1950s in films such as Ealing's *Kind Hearts and Coronets** (1949) and *The Ladykillers** (1955). Yet, the story line and characterizations of this film, unlike the Ealing films, are more universal and could be found in any city, as David Stephens points out at the start of the film. This extends to the film's simple theme concerning the association between personal corruption and money, a theme found in many films.

Shallow Grave is impatient to show evidence of its mean-spirited tone right from the start as accountant David Stephens, doctor Juliet Miller, and journalist Alex Law humiliate a succession of applicants who subject themselves to ridicule in an effort to rent an empty room in their apartment. Juliet, who refuses to take phone calls from a former boyfriend (Brian) because he displays "certain personal weaknesses," is impressed by the worldly Hugo. Hugo tells Juliet that he is writing a novel about a priest who dies. However, it is Hugo who dies the next day with a large amount of money in a suitcase beside his body. Although Alex,

Juliet, and David agonize over whether to take the money to the police or keep it, there is little doubt what their decision will be. When David pulls the short straw, he is forced to mutilate Hugo's body so that it will not be recognized when discovered. This decision takes the occupants on a dark journey leading to death and betrayal as the initial skirmishes for power within the group blossom into full-blown paranoia.

Although Hodge, Macdonald, and Boyle keep pushing the darker elements of the story, they provide just enough character detail to make Alex, David, and Juliet interesting. Thus, Juliet, the doctor, smokes while David, the only member of the group to display remorse, cuts through tissue and bone in an effort to destroy Hugo's identity. Ironically, Alex, the journalist, receives the best break of his short career when he is assigned to investigate the discovery of three bodies in the countryside. These are the bodies they have tried to conceal. David, on the other hand, following the mutilation of Hugo, becomes mentally unhinged and moves into the small space between the ceiling and roof of their flat. This action proves useful when two criminals burst into the apartment and terrorize Juliet and Alex. When they enter David's domain, between the roof and ceiling, they die.

Juliet, the most calculating member of the group, fulfils the function of the femme fatale as she moves between David and Alex late in the film. However, Hodge and Boyle provide an early indication of her true nature when, during a charity function, Alex trips while dancing with Juliet. At this point Boyle, with a low-angle shot from Alex's point of view, emphasizes Juliet's power when she places her foot on Alex's chest as he licks it before she dances away. Later, Juliet betrays both men by purchasing a single plane ticket to South America and she reveals the extent of her corruption, and ruthlessness, when she takes the shoe off her foot and bangs at a knife impaled in Alex's shoulder in a scene reminiscent of the earlier episode on the dance floor. A final, and obvious, twist denies her the money she covets so badly and David's voice-over concludes the film, in a kind of homage to *Sunset Boulevard* (1950), as he laments the failure of their friendship, despite the fact that he is now dead, courtesy of a knife through his neck from Juliet.

Shallow Grave walks a fine line between cynicism and calculation, combining Grand Guignol moments, film noir sensibilities, and Boyle's showy visual style matched by a dramatic use of color and music. The discovery of Hugo's body draped over a red satin bed cover is accompanied by Nina Simone's *My Baby Just Cares for Me* on the sound track. *Shallow Grave* won the Alexander Korda Award for Best British Film at the 1995 BAFTA Film Awards and Boyle won the Best Newcomer Award from the 1996 London Film Critics Circle Award.

THE SILENT ENEMY (Romulus, 1958)—War. *Director:* William Fairchild; *Producers:* Bertram Ostrer, James Woolf (executive), and John Woolf (executive); *Script:* William Fairchild, based on a book by Marshall Pugh; *Cinematography:* Otto Heller; *Music:* William Alwyn; *Cast:* Laurence Harvey (Lieutenant Lionel Crabb), Dawn Adams (Third Officer Jill Masters) Masters), Michael Craig

(Leading Seaman Knowles), John Clements (Admiral), Gianna Maria Canale (Conchita), Sidney James (Chief petty Officer Thorpe), Alec McCowen (Able Seaman Morgan), and Howard Marion-Crawford (Wing Commander).

In 1941, Lieutenant ("Buster") Crabb arrives in Gibraltar and immediately becomes fascinated with a small British unit responsible for protecting British shipping in the harbor from Italian explosive devices, placed on the ships by enemy midget submarines. As the enemy is operating out of neutral Spain, the British are restricted in their response to this threat although Crabb pesters the admiral to build up his unit. This they do under the guidance of Chief Petty Officer Thorpe (Sidney James in a characteristically scene-stealing performance). Crabb then illegally infiltrates the enemy base and destroys its operation.

The Silent Enemy is a low-key film that benefits from the underwater sequences that are masterful and predate similar scenes in the James Bond adventure *Thunderball* by seven years. An implied love affair between Crab and Jill Masters goes nowhere as the film concentrates on the achievements of Crabb and his small unit. The film was directed and scripted by William Fairchild, better known as a British screenwriter responsible for another seagoing drama (*Passage Home* [1955]), as well as many other British film in the 1950s and 1960s. Most of *The Silent Enemy* was filmed in Malta and Gibraltar.

SIM, ALASTAIR (1900–1976). By the late 1930s and early 1940s, Alastair Sim had perfected a distinctive film persona—the eccentric, seemingly distracted policeman. This image began with his 1930s role as the comic sergeant in the Inspector Hornleigh series, starring Gordon Harker. Occasionally, Sim added a more sinister layer to this persona, a mixture that made him suitable for his role as Charles Dimble in *Cottage to Let** (1941), Anthony Asquith's* clever comedy-espionage film. For the greater part of this film, it appears that Sim may be an enemy spy trying to steal Leslie Banks's* secret invention, only to find out that clean-cut John Mills* is the traitor and Sim a policeman sent to protect the invention. An even better example was his Inspector Cockrill, who investigates the murder of the local postman in a military hospital in *Green for Danger** (1946). Unlike the Inspector Hornleigh series, where Sim was merely a buffoon, *Cottage for Let* and especially *Green for Danger* provided Sim with the opportunity to exploit his bumbling, inoffensive traits as a facade to cover up his inquisitive behavior and sharp mind.

Sim had an academic career as Fulton Lecturer in Elocution at Edinburgh University from 1925 to 1930, where he returned as rector from 1948 to 1951. In 1930, he made his stage debut and in 1935 his film debut, appearing in four films in his first year. However, it was in the 1940s that he made his greatest impression, and, aside from *Cottage for Let* and *Green for Danger,* he was the community doctor in *Waterloo Road* (1944), the sinister Henry Squales in *London Belongs to Me* (1948), and Felix H. Wilkinson, the comic strip writer, in *Hue and Cry** (1947). This last role consolidated his image as an eccentric, a quality reinforced by his role as an author of hard-boiled detective fiction in *Laughter in Paradise** (1951).

Many of Sim's performances in the 1950s would present a variation on this creation—including the seemingly inoffensive professional assassin in *The Green Man** (1956), Miss Fritton, the corrupt, pragmatic headmistress overseeing the anarchy in *The Belles of St. Trinian's** (1954), with Sim also appearing as Fritton's even more corrupt brother Clarence. Sim repeated this role in *Blue Murder at St. Trinian's** (1957), and his absence in the next two St. Trinian's films (*The Pure Hell of St. Trinian's* [1960] and *The Great St. Trinian's Train Robbery* [1966]) weakened the series. Sim was also the definitive Scrooge in *Scrooge* (1951) and Inspector Poole, in a rare dramatic role, in *An Inspector Calls* (1954). However, Sim's Wetherby Pond, the headmaster of Nutbourne College, and Margaret Rutherford's* Miss Whitchurch, the headmistress of St. Swithin's, in Frank Launder's* *The Happiest Days of Your Life* (1950), brought two of the funniest, most distinctive and bizarre British actors together in this wonderful farce. After the rich roles of the 1940s and 1950s, his performances were less memorable in the 1960s and 1970s, although he had one final chance to steal a film with an eccentric characterization as the clergyman in Peter Medak's black comedy *The Ruling Class* (1972). Sim studiously avoided publicity during his career in films, even to refusing to sign autographs. Sim died of cancer on August 19, 1976.

FILMS: The Case of Gabriel Perry (1935), The Riverside Murder (1935), The Private Secretary (1935), Late Extra (1935), A Fire Has Been Arranged (1935), Troubled Waters (1936), Wedding Group (1936), Wrath of Jealousy (1936), Keep Your Seats Please (1936), The Big Noise (1936), The Man in the Mirror (1936), Strange Experiment (1936), Clothes and the Woman (1937), Gangway (1937), A Romance in Flanders (1937), Sailing Along (1937), Melody and Romance (1937), The Squeaker (1938), Alf's Button Afloat (1938), The Terror (1938), This Man Is News (1938), Inspector Hornleigh (1939), Climbing High (1939), This Man in Paris (1939), Inspector Hornleigh on Holiday (1939), The Mysterious Mr. Davis (1940), Law and Disorder (1940), Inspector Hornleigh Goes to It (1941), Cottage to Let (1941), Her Father's Daughter (short, 1941), Let the People Sing (1942), Waterloo Road (1945), Green for Danger (1946), Hue and Cry (1947), Captain Boycott (1947), London Belongs to Me (1948), The Happiest Days of Your Life (1950), Stage Fright (1950), Laughter in Paradise (1951), Lady Godiva Rides Again (1951), Scrooge (1951), Folly to Be Wise (1952), Innocents in Paris (1953), An Inspector Calls (1954), The Belles of St. Trinian's (1954), Escapade (1955), Geordie (1955), The Green Man (1956), Blue Murder at St. Trinian's (1954), The Doctor's Dilemma (1959), Left Right and Centre (1959), School for Scoundrels (1960), The Millionairess (1960), The Anatomist (1961), The Ruling Class (1972), Royal Flash (1975), and Escape from the Dark (1976).

SIMBA (General Film Distributors, 1955)—Empire film. *Director:* Brian Desmond Hurst; *Producer:* Peter de Sarigny; *Script:* John Baines and Robin Estridge, based on a novel by Anthony Perry; *Cinematography:* Geoffrey Unsworth; *Music:* Frances Chagrin; *Cast:* Dirk Bogarde (Allan Howard), Donald

Sinden (Inspector Drummond), Virginia McKenna (Mary Crawford), Earl Cameron (Karanja), Basil Sydney (Mr. Crawford), Marie Ney (Mrs. Crawford), Joseph Tomelty (Dr. Hughes), and Ben Johnson (Kimani).

The pre-credit sequence in *Simba* shows a young black man gently singing as he cycles through the Kenyan bush in the 1950s. He pauses when he hears the cries of a man off the side of the track. The man then leaves his bicycle and walks toward the wounded white man, who anticipates help. However, the black man pulls a machete from his belt and savagely cuts into the wounded man, killing him before resuming his journey. The sudden brutality of this sequence serves both an ideological and narrative function in the film. Ideologically, this prologue establishes the extent of the hatred and anger between the white colonialists and the locals in Kenya during the Mau Mau uprising in the 1950s. The narrative function of the sequence reveals that the white community did not know who was to be trusted and who would turn on them during this period. This action also has an effect on Allan Howard, a new arrival in the territory, as the dead man was his brother who had been farming in the district for many years.

Allan's arrival also reunites him with a former girlfriend, Mary Crawford. Mary rejected Allan's offer of marriage years earlier because she thought he was too immature. Initially, Allan is hostile to the black community and, in particular, to an educated black doctor, Karanja, whom Allan suspects of being in league with the Mau Mau. Mary, on the other hand, assists Karanja at the local clinic as part of her desire to show that whites and blacks can work together. The film explores a range of positions as to this issue, including extreme white and black supremacist positions. Eventually, Allan comes to trust Karanja as the film appears to endorse Mary's desire for liberal coexistence. However, when Karanja is killed by supporters of his father, force is shown, by the film, to be the only effective form of response—compromise and reason prove inadequate.

Karanja, the symbol of co-existence and understanding, is rejected by everybody except Mary and Allan. He is disliked by the police, expelled by his father (and the black nationalists), and the local white community do not trust him—Mary's mother will not let Karanja treat her after she has been attacked. Karanja's death destroys the possibility of integration and cooperation, and the film concludes with a close-up of the face of a black child, Joshua, who has been taken in by Allan. Joshua is shown looking at the violence and the carnage caused by the Mau Mau and the police and while the destructive effects of imperialism are acknowledged, the film concludes on a pessimistic note emphasizing fear and distrust between blacks and whites in Kenya. Violence and bloodshed, and a general breakdown in communal goodwill, are the only possibilities suggested by the ending of the film. The nihilism and bleak outcome predicted in this film are contrasted by the sense of optimism found two decades earlier in films of the Empire such as *Sanders of the River** (1935).

Simba was nominated for Best Film from Any Source and Best British Film at the 1956 BAFTA Film Awards.

THE SKIN GAME (British International Pictures, 1931)—Family drama. *Director:* Alfred Hitchcock; *Producer:* John Maxwell; *Script:* Alfred Hitchcock and Alma Reville, based on the play by John Galsworthy; *Cinematography:* Jack. E. Cox; *Cast:* C. V. France (Mr. Hillcrest), Helen Haye (Mrs. Hillcrest), Jill Esmond (Jill Hillcrest), Edmund Gwenn (Mr. Hornblower), John Longden (Charles Hornblower), Phyllis Konstam (Chloe Hornblower), Frank Lawton (Rolf Hornblower), Edward Chapman (Dawker), Herbert Ross (Mr. Jackman), and Dora Gregory (Mrs. Jackman).

This little-known Alfred Hitchcock* film concerns the issue of change, represented by the Hornblower family, versus the virtues of tradition, represented by the Hillcrest family. After Mr. Hillcrest sells part of the family estate to Hornblower, he becomes agitated when he learns that Hornblower wishes to evict the Chapman family, who were long-established tenants. Hornblower wants to clear the land so that he can extend his pottery business. This raises the fear in Hillcrest that his beloved forest and meadows will become an industrial nightmare, a fear that Hitchcock dramatizes in one of the film's most stylized scenes.

Hillcrest subsequently confronts Hornblower at the auction but Hornblower, after paying more than he intended, acquires the land. However, Hillcrest's wife, in conjunction with a Hillcrest employee (Dawker), unearths scandal within the Hornblower family—Chloe Hornblower, married to Hornblower's son Charles, worked in a racket that took money from men wanting to divorce their wives prior to her marriage. As this information reflects badly on Chloe's reputation, Mrs. Hillcrest blackmails Hornblower into returning the land he acquired from Hillcrest. This represents a substantial monetary loss to Hornblower. It also does not prevent Chloe's secret from becoming public and she commits suicide.

The calculating, negative role of Mrs. Hillcrest in the film is an early example of a character, the malevolent matriarch, who would surface again in Hitchcock's films, such as *Notorious* (1946) and *Psycho* (1960). The determination of Mrs. Hillcrest to acquire the disputed land at all costs, including the use of blackmail, leads to an innocent woman's death.

The most striking image in the film highlights the consequence of Mrs. Hillcrest's action. As representatives of both families squabble in the background, Chloe's limp body is lifted from the family pool in the foreground. The film's final image, a severed tree trunk on the disputed land, symbolizes the consequences of Mrs. Hillcrest's actions and the fact that, in the long run, the Hillcrest family will not be able to impede progress despite the death of Chloe and the ruination of Hornblower.

SNATCH (Columbia, 2000)—Heist/comedy. *Director:* Guy Ritchie; *Producers:* Stephen Marks (executive), Peter Morton (executive), Angad Paul (executive), Trudie Styler (executive), and Steve Tisch (executive); *Script:* Guy Ritchie; *Cinematography:* Tim Maurice-Jones; *Music:* John Murphy; *Cast:* Benico Del Toro (Franky Four Fingers), Dennis Farina (Uncle Avi), Vinnie Jones (Bullet Tooth

Tony), Brad Pitt ("One Punch" Mickey O'Neil), Rade Serbedzija (Boris the Blade), Jason Statham (Turkish), Alan Ford (Brick Top), Mike Reid (Doug the Head), Robbie Gee (Vinny), Lennie James (Sol), Ewen Bremner (Mullet), Jason Flemying (Darren), Stephen Graham (Tommy), and Ade (Tyrone).

Snatch, with its obvious double entendre (despite the fact that the film is almost totally devoid of women), is Guy Ritchie's follow-up to the commercially successful *Lock, Stock and Two Smoking Barrels* (1998). *Snatch* is similar in style, tone, and humor to the first film. Borrowing the concept of the "McGuffin" from Alfred Hitchcock,* where the audience believes that the film is about one (story) thing, when in fact it is about another, Ritchie inveigles the audience into believing that it is about a diamond stolen from an Antwerp broker by criminals disguised as Hassidic Jews. Instead, this heist provides the pretext for Ritchie to play narrative "games" within his cynical view of the world.

The heist is led by Frankie Four Fingers who, on the way to New York to deliver the diamond to his boss Avi, is waylaid in London by Boris the Blade. Avi hires Tony the Tooth to retrieve the diamond. Meanwhile, the film's narrator, Turkish, and his mate Tommy, are reluctantly brought into the world of psychotic gambler Brick Top, who feeds his enemies to his pigs. They are forced to persuade Irish gypsy boxer "One Punch" Mickey to take a dive in the ring so that Brick Top and his gambling syndicate can collect. Meanwhile, black pawn-shop owners Vinny and Sol and their getaway driver Tyrone become involved after helping Boris the Blade. When their dog ingests the diamond, trouble ensues.

The plot eventually comes together but it is largely inconsequential in the over-all scheme of things. Ritchie further confuses matters by having Brad Pitt deliver his lines in a broad Irish accent that cannot be understood. Ritchie also utilizes rapid cutting, accelerated motion and slow motion, photomontage, and an arsenal of other visual and sound devices, including oddball musical tracks to attract attention to his story based on "who is going to get hurt next."

After a while, appreciation for Ritchie's manipulations, and his lack of interest in character development and story credibility, wears thin but for much of the time the film is a wild ride. While *Lock, Stock and Two Smoking Barrels* was followed by many inferior copies by other directors, *Snatch,* hopefully, will mark the end of this cycle. It is time for Ritchie, a talented filmmaker, to move on as this cinematic vein has been well and truly exploited.

SO EVIL MY LOVE (Paramount Pictures, 1948)—Film noir *Director:* Lewis Allen; *Producer:* Hal Wallis; *Script:* Ronald Miller and Leonard Spigelgass, based on the novel by Joseph Shearing; *Photography:* Max Greene; *Music:* William Alwyn (additional music by Victor Young); *Cast:* Ray Milland (Mark Bellis), Ann Todd (Olivia Harwood), Geraldine Fitzgerald (Susan Courtney), Leo G. Carroll (Jarvis), Raymond Huntley (Henry Courtney), Raymond Lovell (Edgar Bellamy), Martita Hunt (Mrs. Courtney), Moira Lister (Kitty Feathers),

Roderick Lovell (Sir John Curle), Muriel Aked (Miss Shoebridge), and Finlay Currie (Dr. Krylie).

So Evil My Love is a superior film noir. There was a Hollywood contribution with Ray Milland and director Lewis Allen learning their craft in the U.S. before returning to England for this film. *So Evil My Love* was produced by veteran Hollywood producer Hal Wallis for Paramount-British and it was filmed at the British D&P Studios. The focus of the film is Olivia Harwood, expertly played by Ann Todd.* While the other characters (skillfully) fulfill their conventional roles, the film focuses on the transformation in Harwood from her social status as a missionary's widow to the sensual, conniving mistress of a thief and murderer. This transformation is neither linear nor simplistic as her moral code clashes with her carnal desires throughout the film. A notable example of this occurs near the end of the film when distressed at the prospect that her friend Susan Courtney will hang (because of Harwood's actions), she is able to displace this guilt with lust at the prospect of a reunion with Mark Bellis.

On a boat returning to England from Jamaica, Harwood reluctantly nurses typhoid victim Mark Bellis back to health. Bellis, hiding from the police, takes a room in Harwood's house and gradually exploits the widow's desire for a fulfilling sexual relationship. He also convinces her that she has not fulfilled her ambitions in life (Harwood: "My life was to be rich and full and complete."). When a former school friend, Susan Courtney, makes contact with Harwood, Bellis encourages her to insinuate herself in Susan's household and exploit Susan's growing dependency on her. Susan is even more vulnerable because she is married to the tyrannical, impotent Henry Courtney, a wealthy barrister.

In a perverse way, Harwood begins to enjoy her power over Susan ("Poor Susan, so pampered, such a fool.") and when she believes that she also has control over Henry, due to incriminating letters in her possession, Harwood's transformation, and corruption, is complete. She tells Bellis after demanding $5,000 from Henry Courtney:

HARWOOD: I had the whip hand and he knew it. I was utterly in command.
BELLIS: You enjoyed yourself.
HARWOOD: Yes, the power of it. It was a wonderful sensation. I've never had it before. I was quite calm, my heart wasn't pounding and my mouth wasn't dry. I was utterly in possession.
BELLIS: I am beginning to know you Olivia.
HARWOOD: I am beginning to know myself.

When the blackmail scheme fails, and Henry has a heart attack, Harwood manipulates Susan so that she inadvertently kills her husband with poison. Harwood, however, discovers that Bellis has another mistress and despite his pledge that he loves her Harwood stabs him and gives herself up to the police.

So Evil My Love was one of four films in the 1940s based on the novels of Joseph Shearing, three British films including *Blanche Fury** (1947) and *The Mark of Cain** (1948) and the Hollywood production of *Moss Rose* (1947), with

Victor Mature and Peggy Cummins. Shearing was the pseudonym for Gabrielle Margaret Vere Long and her novel *For Her to See* was changed for the cinema to *So Evil My Love.*

THE SPIDER AND THE FLY (Mayflower/Setton-Baring/Rank, 1948)–Crime/ romance. *Director:* Robert Hamer; *Producer:* Aubrey Baring; *Script:* Robert Westerby; *Cinematography:* Geoffrey Unsworth; *Music:* Georges Auric; *Cast:* Eric Portman (Ferdinand Maubert), Guy Rolfe (Philippe de Ledocq), Nadia Gray (Madelaine Saincaize), George Cole (Marc), Edward Chapman (Minister for War), Maurice Denham (Colonel de la Roche), and John Carol (Jean Louis/Alfred Louis).

Robert Hamer* left Ealing Studios soon after the completion of *Kind Hearts and Coronets** (1949) and made *The Spider and the Fly* for an independent company. Both films were criticized, unfairly, as cold and remote. The basis for this reaction came from their less than optimistic presentation of human nature and morally problematic characters. Intelligence, not the law, becomes the prime determinant of human worth in *The Spider and the Fly,* which focuses on the powerful bond between three characters—Inspector Ferdinand Maubert, the criminal Phillipe de Ledocq, and Madelaine Saincaize, the woman they both desire. While Maubert's aim, initially, is to capture Ledocq, Ledocq's aim is to commit robberies. Both men wish to be friends as neither receives adequate stimulation or satisfaction from incompetent colleagues. Saincaize is in love with Ledocq but she is courted by Maubert. Because of circumstances beyond her control, she cannot form a lasting relationship with either man.

The film begins in France in 1913 as Ledocq uses Saincaize to commit a robbery. When it is completed, he rejects her offer to continue the relationship. Maubert, in turn, utilizes Saincaize in order to capture Ledocq. Faced with the choice between both men, she chooses the criminal by providing a false alibi for him. Thus, Maubert also rejects her. Saincaize, however, is a survivor and although both men come to love her, circumstances, Maubert's arrest of Ledocq, keep them all apart. However, in 1916 Maubert, now working for the military, needs Ledocq's criminal skills to break into the German legation in Bern to steal a list of enemy agents in France. After Ledocq acquires the list of names, they discover that Saincaize, in order to survive during the war years, worked as a German agent. Consequently, Saincaize is arrested in front of both men. Ledocq joins the French army and the film concludes as Maubert stands at the station to farewell his friend, and adversary. Ledocq is sent to the front and his probable death.

When Maubert tells an incompetent military officer, who objects to Ledocq working on behalf of the French government, that "better a knave than a fool," he exposes the film's main theme. *The Spider and the Fly* refuses to endorse conventional moral values or conventional presentations of sexual desire and attraction. The three central characters are presented as intelligent, flawed, and attracted to each other although circumstances conspire to keep them apart. The ending, with Saincaize's arrest, comes as a shock as it is likely that both Saincaize and Ledocq will die.

THE SQUARE PEG (Rank, 1958)/Follow a Star (Rank, 1959)—Comedy.

THE SQUARE PEG

Director: John Paddy Carstairs; *Producer:* Hugh Stewart; *Script:* Jack Davies, Henry Blyth, Eddie Leslie, and Norman Wisdom; *Cinematography:* Jack Cox; *Music:* Philip Green; *Cast:* Norman Wisdom (Norman Pitkin/General Schreiber), Honor Blackman (Lesley Cartland), Edward Chapman (Mr. Grimsdale), Campbell Singer (Sergeant Loder), Hattie Jacques (Gretchen), Brian Worth (Henri Le Blanc), Terence Alexander (Captain Wharton), and Eddie Leslie (Medical Officer).

FOLLOW A STAR

Director: Robert Asher; *Producer:* Hugh Stewart; *Script:* Jack Davies, Henry Blyth, and Norman Wisdom; *Cinematography:* Jack Asher; *Music:* Philip Green; *Cast:* Norman Wisdom (Norman Truscott), June Laverick (Judy), Jerry Desmonde (Vernon Carew), Hattie Jacques (Dymphna Dobson), Richard Wattis (Dr. Chatterway), Eddie Leslie (Harold Franklin), John Le Mesurier (Birkett), and Fenella Feilding (Lady Finchington).

John Paddy Carstairs directed the first six films Norman Wisdom* made for Rank in the 1950s, beginning with *Trouble in Store* in 1953. *The Square Peg* was Carstairs's last and most commercially successful film with Wisdom. In 1959, Robert Asher, the brother of cameraman Jack Asher, was elevated from the crew (Asher had been the floor manager for most of the Wisdom-Carstairs films) to direct the first of six films with Wisdom, beginning with *Follow a Star.* Thus, Carstairs and Asher directed most of Wisdom's films during his heyday. There are, of course, many similarities between these two groups of films—most notably Wisdom's character as the perennial good-hearted "little man," whom Wisdom labeled the "Gump," meaning a simple working-class man who responds to the world in a literal way without nuance. This causes him constant pain and humiliation although he never gives up.

A sense of continuity in Wisdom's films in the 1950s and early 1960s was also served by the casting of actors such as Hattie Jacques, Eddie Leslie, and Jerry Desmonde. However, the change in directors in 1959 also brought about a change in the formula with a stronger emphasis on pathos and sentimentality after *The Square Peg.* In *The Square Peg,* Norman Truscott is an assertive, confrontational character who is drafted into the army during World War II. Prior to this, as an officious council worker, he regularly disrupts the military training in a nearby base. After Truscott is drafted, he falls in love with Lesley Cartland, who is sent on a mission to France. When Truscott jumps onto the wrong military vehicle and has to parachute into France, he joins up with Lesley and the French resistance. After their capture by the Germans, Truscott facilitates their escape by impersonating a high-ranking Nazi officer. This allows Wisdom to play dual roles, a device he repeated in *On the Beat* (1962) and *A Stitch in Time* (1963).

There is a quintessential Wisdom moment in *The Square Peg* when Sergeant Loder, trying to transform the new recruits into "killing machines," so motivates Truscott that he runs through a wooden fence to "kill" the straw targets. The military hierarchy is so impressed by his violence that they immediately send him off to France. The humor in this scene comes from a characteristic Wisdom trait—his inability to separate reality from hyperbole. Similarly, when Gretchen (Hattie Jacques) tries to seduce General Schreiber, played by Wisdom, Truscott has dispatched Schreiber so that he can rescue Cartland. This provides an opportunity for Wisdom to demonstrate his best quality—his comic timing in physical routines.

In *Follow a Star,* however, the ever-present masochistic dimension in Wisdom's persona is intensified. In the film's simple story, Truscott is an aspiring singer with a great voice who cannot perform under pressure, especially when he is away from Judy, his crippled girlfriend. When Vernon Carew, a fading entertainer, learns of Norman's voice and his psychological problem, he exploits Truscott by taking him on as his student (and full-time servant and secretary). Carew secretly makes recordings of Truscott's voice and releases them under his own name. While the film includes many typical Wisdom sequences, particularly when Jacques takes a very physical approach to improving Truscott's diction, the relentless humiliation of Truscott contrasts with the feisty aggressiveness he displayed in *The Square Peg* and earlier films.

THE STORY OF ESTHER COSTELLO (Romulus, 1957)—Melodrama. *Director:* David Miller; *Producers:* Jack Clayton and David Miller; *Script:* Charles S. Kaufman; *Cinematography:* Robert Krasker; *Music:* Georges Auric; *Cast:* Joan Crawford (Margaret Landi), Rossano Brazzi (Carlo Landi), Heather Sears (Esther Costello), Lee Patterson (Harry Grant), Ron Randell (Frank Wenzel), Denis O'Dea (Father Devlin), John Loder (Paul Merchant), Robert Ayres (Mr. Wilson), Andrew Cruickshank (Dr. Stein), Sidney James (Ryan), Megs Jenkins (Nurse Evans), Bessie Love (Matron in Art Gallery), and Fay Compton (Mother Superior).

Joan Crawford's intense, florid acting style sets the overall dramatic tone for this melodrama of rehabilitation, rape, and betrayal. The film, in mood and style, is reminiscent of Sam Fuller's equally excessive melodrama *The Naked Kiss* (1964). The plot, on the other hand, is a hybrid of sentimental drama and domestic melodrama with a dash of the fundamentalist religious and charity campaigns dramatized in films such as *Meet John Doe* (1940) and *Elmer Gantry* (1960). A wealthy American woman, Margaret Landi, agrees to help in the rehabilitation of a blind, deaf, and mute young woman, Esther Costello. Costello was badly wounded as a child when a hand grenade exploded while she was playing near her Irish village. The grenade also killed her mother.

Margaret takes Costello back to the United States and with the help of a progressive therapist, Costello becomes the center of a large-scale charity campaign, masterminded by Margaret's estranged husband Carlo and a corrupt promoter Frank Wenzel. Margaret is unaware that the charity is a scam. However, a young reporter, Harry Grant, who falls in love with Costello, exposes the crooked operation.

The Story of Esther Costello is a representative example of the adaptation of the conventions of nineteenth-century melodrama to the cinema. The film can be stripped down to a story of Virtue (Costello) rendered blind, deaf, and mute. Partially restored (by Margaret and Wilson, a progressive therapist), she is violated by Evil (Carlo rapes Costello when Margaret is out of their apartment). Catharsis is achieved when Costello overcomes her disability and regains her sight and hearing. Retribution occurs when Margaret, learning of her husband's rape of Costello, kills him and herself by driving into a tree.

Although *The Story of Esther Costello* was mainly set in the United States, with some European, London, and Irish settings, it was shot entirely in England by a British company (Romulus). It had American (Joan Crawford) and Italian (Rossano Brazzi) stars and a Hollywood director (David Miller) and screenwriter (Charles Kaufman). *The Story of Esther Costello* is similar to the domestic melodramas produced in Hollywood in the mid-1950s (especially Douglas Sirk's *The Magnificent Obsession* [1954] and *All That Heaven Allows* [1955]).

NOTE

1. McFarlane, *An Autobiography of British Cinema,* p. 512.

T

TAKE MY LIFE (Cineguild, 1947)—Melodrama. *Director:* Ronald Neame; *Producer:* Anthony Havelock-Allan; *Script:* Winston Graham, Margaret Kennedy, and Valerie Taylor; *Cinematography:* Guy Green; *Music:* William Alwyn; *Cast:* Hugh Williams (Nicholas Talbot), Greta Gynt (Phillipa Shelley), Marius Goring (Sidney Fleming), Francis L. Sullivan (Prosecuting Counsel), Henry Edwards (Inspector Archer), Rosalie Crutchley (Elizabeth Rusman), Leo Bieber (Parone), Marjorie Mars (Mrs. Newcombe), David Walbridge (Leslie Newcombe), Maurice Denham (Defending Counsel), and Ronald Adam (Detective Sergeant Hawkins).

Within little more than twelve months, Marius Goring* starred in three very different films. In *The Red Shoes** (1948), he played the young composer in love with the tragic heroine, followed by the middle-aged school master who makes life difficult for David Farrar* in *Mr. Perrin and Mr. Traill** (1948). Goring, however, preceded these roles with a very different schoolmaster (Sidney Fleming) in *Take My Life* who murders his wife (Elizabeth Rusman) when she threatens to divorce him on the grounds of cruelty, thereby threatening his reputation and career as a the headmaster of an elite private boys school in Scotland.

Nicholas Talbot is charged with murdering Elizabeth Rusman because he was in the vicinity of the murder and that he had a relationship with her some years earlier (and, coincidentally, his forehead is injured following an argument with his wife). Talbot's wife, Phillipa, is forced to try and find evidence that will establish her husband's innocence. Phillipa's initial search proves fruitless until she discovers a piece of music that leads her to Fleming's school in Scotland. Here, a tense cat-and-mouse sequence follows, culminating in the deserted school as Fleming and Phillipa confront each other. The tension is carefully orchestrated during these scenes, especially when Phillipa plays the incriminating tune on the school's organ while Fleming moves closer and closer to her exposed back.

Although the basic narrative structure of the film is, by its very nature, based on coincidence and contrivances, it marks a smooth, skillful directorial debut for cinematographer Ronald Neame.* The film also gave Greta Gynt,* as the wife whose investigations finally establish her husband's innocence, one of her best dramatic roles. It is worth comparing *Take My Life* with the U.S. film noir *Phantom Lady* (1944) as both films share similar plots—a woman trying to establish the innocence of her lover who is in jail. While Ella Raines in *Phantom Lady* is forced to inhabit a succession of dives that reek of desperation and excessive sexuality, Phillipa in *Take My Life* moves through a different world of class, propriety, and repression. Thus, while these films share a similar premise, they also reflect differences between each country.

TARZAN'S GREATEST ADVENTURE (Paramount, 1959)—Adventure. *Director:* John Guillermin; *Producers:* Sy Weintraub and Harvey Hayutin; *Script:* Berne Giler and John Guillermin, based on the story by Les Crutchfield and the character created by Edgar Rice Burroughs; *Cinematography:* Edward Scaife; *Music:* Douglas Gamley; *Cast:* Gordon Scott (Tarzan), Anthony Quayle (Slade), Sara Shane (Angie), Niall MacGinnis (Kruger), Sean Connery (O'Bannion), Al Mulock (Dino), and Scilla Gabel (Toni).

After the poor commercial response to *Tarzan's Fight for Life* in 1958, veteran Hollywood producer Sol Lesser agreed to sell the franchise to producers Sy Weintraub and Harvey Hayutin for $2 million. The new owners decided to change the ape-man's image into something closer to Edgar Rice Burrough's original conception of the character. The producers also noted that the most successful recent Tarzan film, *Tarzan and the Lost Safari* (1957), had been shot on location in Africa with British technicians. Consequently, they employed British director John Guillermin* to direct and co-script *Tarzan's Greatest Adventure* with British actors (Anthony Quayle, Sean Connery,* and Niall MacGinnis) and technical staff and 60 percent of the film was shot in Kikuyu country in Kenya with the rest completed in the studio in London.

The most important change to the series was the alteration to Tarzan's character from the primitive, inarticulate figure popularized by Johnny Weissmuller, to a intelligent, literate man capable of savagery. Jane was deleted and Cheetah was relegated to one scene when Tarzan farewells him at the start of the film. In place of the increasingly juvenile stories that had marred the series since the censorship controversy that followed *Tarzan and His Mate* in 1934, *Tarzan's Greatest Adventure* had a strong plot, based on Tarzan's determination to seek revenge on an old enemy, Slade, who killed most of the inhabitants of a jungle outpost on his way to a diamond mine. The only concession in the tough-minded story was the inclusion of a blonde aviatrix (Angie) who accompanies Tarzan on his mission after her plane crashes in the jungle. There was no romance between Tarzan and Angie although a kissing scene was deleted from the release print.

In keeping with the changes to the series, the four criminals pursued by Tarzan were a perverse bunch, led by the sadist Slade (effectively played by Quayle), the greedy and lecherous Kruger (MacGinnis), and the brutal O'Bannion (Connery). Scilla Gabel (Toni) was also included as Slade's girlfriend and her presence provokes tension between Kruger and Slade. There is even a brief scene where Toni and Slade go off into the jungle for sex.

This transformation from the grunting ape-man of earlier films to the articulate protagonist of this film was matched by Gordon Scott's performance and while the ape-man is shown to be intelligent and literate, he is also capable of inflicting violence. At the climax of the film, Guillermin highlights Tarzan's thinly veiled savagery as he sheds his civilized veneer. Tarzan's primal excitement is matched by Slade, who also relishes the prospect of a violent confrontation. Only after Tarzan has killed Slade does he let forth his famous yell, a satisfying closure to the best Tarzan film of all time.

TERRY-THOMAS (1911–1990). Terry-Thomas's appearance in a series of popular British comedies in the mid-1950s established a distinctive screen persona for this comedian who had been working at the lower levels of the British entertainment industry for more than twenty years. In Boulting Brothers'* comedies such as *Private's Progress* (1956) and *I'm All Right Jack** (1959), Terry-Thomas played Major Hitchcock, a charlatan military officer on the take with a penchant for toothy insults to the hapless Ian Carmichael* ("You're an absolute shower."). He never entirely shed this image. Although there would be variations, he would remain the "rotter," a pretentious, elitist, seedy, sometimes lecherous cad with an eye for quick money and the easy life.

These traits were further refined, and often given a negative twist, when Terry-Thomas appeared in international productions and Hollywood films (and Hollywood productions shot in London) in the 1960s, beginning with *It's a Mad Mad Mad World* (1963) as J. Algernon Hawthorne, one of many greedy citizens desperately searching for stolen bank money. In two similar films, *Those Magnificent Men in Their Flying Machines* (1965), Terry-Thomas was the Victorian villain (Sir Percy Ware Armitage) constantly plotting to destroy Stuart Whitman, and *Monte Carlo or Bust/Those Daring Young Men in Their Jaunty Jalopies* (1969), as Sir Cuthbert Ware-Armitage, the sworn enemy of Tony Curtis. Terry-Thomas was also prominent in a number of Hollywood (soft) "sex" comedies during this period, including *Bachelor Flat* (1961), *Strange Bedfellows* (1964), *How to Murder Your Wife* (1965), with Terry-Thomas assisting Jack Lemmon's plans to dispose of his wife (Virna Lisi), *A Guide for the Married Man* (1967), and *Where Were You When the Lights Went Out?* (1968), a limp Doris Day comedy based on the New York City blackout on November 9, 1965.

International success, however, came late to Terry-Thomas and after uncredited bit parts in British films in the mid- to late 1930s, he served in the Royal Signal Corps in World War II before reviving his career as a comic. Supporting roles in a number of undistinguished British films, such as *Helter Skelter* (1949), in the late 1940s preceded his period of (British) popularity from the mid-1950s. Then came a series of popular Hollywood films in the 1960s. However, his creative period was confined primarily to the period between 1956 and 1960 (*Make Mine Mink* [1960]).

The Green Man* (1956), Terry-Thomas's first major role, cast him as Charles Boughtflower, a lecherous coward leaving his wife for a "dirty weekend" in a rural pub. Boughtflower, together with his next role as Major Hitchcock in *Private's Progress,* consolidated many of the "rotter" traits. These traits that were reinforced by his inappropriate clothes, outrageous moustache and cigarette holder, and the gap in his front teeth that assisted his distinctive voice. These qualities were on show in *Blue Murder at St. Trinians** (1957) when, as a shady con man, he tries to seduce Joyce Grenfell.

A variation of this image came in the Frank Launder* and Sidney Gilliat* comedy of the British Foreign Office (and the veiled references to the 1956 Suez campaign) in *Carlton-Browne of the F.O.* (1959). Terry-Thomas, as Cadogan deVere Carlton-Browne, is summoned from his bureaucratic hideaway at Miscellaneous Territories and appointed special ambassador to Gaillardia as he, mistakenly, appears to be the only bureaucrat who knows where Gaillardia is. On Gaillardia, Carlton-Browne, with the assistance of the equally inept Major Bellingham (Thorley Walters), becomes a pawn of the corrupt Prime Minister Amphibulos (Peter Sellers*), who covets the cobalt deposits on the island. Carlton-Browne's inability to understand, let alone control, the local politics produces a diplomatic disaster and a British military expedition is despatched to protect its "interests" in this former colony. However, the military expedition proves to be, in Carlton-Browne's words, an "utter shamble."

Terry-Thomas was diagnosed with Parkinson's Disease in the early 1970s. This reduced his film career to supporting roles and cameos in films such as *The Abominable Dr. Phibes* (1971) and *The Vault of Horror* (1973). Following Paul Morrisey's disastrous remake of *The Hound of the Baskervilles* (1978), he retired and moved to the Caribbean. Later, as his health deteriorated, he returned to London, where his financial plight received a good deal of publicity. Terry-Thomas, born Thomas Terry Hoar Stevens, died in 1990.

FILMS: When Knights Were Bold (1936), Things to Come (1936), This'll Make You Whistle (1936), Rhythm in the Air (1936), Once in a Million (1936), It's Love Again (1936), Rhythm Racketeer (1937), Climbing High (1939), Flying Fifty-Five (1939), Under Your Hat (1940), For Freedom (1940), A Date with a Dream (1948), Brass Monkey (1948), Melody Club (1949), Helter Skelter (1949), The Queen Steps Out (short, 1951), Cookery Nook (short, 1951), Private's Progress (1956), The Green Man (1956), The Naked Truth (1957), Lucky Jim (1957), Happy is the Bride (1957), Brothers in Law (1957), Blue Murder at St. Trinian's (1957), tom thumb (1958), Too Many Crooks (1958), I'm All Right Jack (1959), Carlton Browne of the F.O. (1959), School for Scoundrels (1960), Make Mine Mink (1960), A Matter of Who (1961), His and Hers (1961), Bachelor Flat (1961), The Wonderful World of the Brothers Grimm (1962), Kill or Cure (1962), Operation Snatch (1962), The Mouse on the Moon (1963), It's a Mad, Mad, Mad, Mad World (1963), The Wild Affair (1963), Strange Bedfellows (1964), How to Murder Your Wife (1965), Those Magnificent Men in Their Flying Machines (1965), You Must be Joking! (1965), Our Man in Marrekesh (1966), Kiss the Girls and Make Them Die (1966), Top Crack (1966), The Sandwich Man (1966), Munster, Go Home (1966), Don't Look Now, We're Being Shot At (1966), The Fantastic World of Dr. Coppelius (voice, 1966), The Daydreamer (voice,

1966), The Karate Killers (1967), Those Fantastic Flying Fools (1967), The Perils of Pauline (1967), Don't Raise the Bridge, Lower the River (1967), Arabella (1967), Diabolik (1968), Where Were You When the Lights Went Out? (1968), How Sweet It Is (1968), Seven Times Seven (1968), It's Your Move (1968), Monte Carlo: C'est La Rose (doc., 1968), How to Kill 400 Duponts (1968), Monte Carlo or Bust (1969), Twelve Plus One (1969), Arthur! Arthur! (1969), 2000 Years Later (1969), Atlantic Wall (1970), The Abominable Dr. Phibes (1971), Colpo grosso, grossissimo . . . anzi probabile (1972), Eroi, Gli (1972), Dr. Phibes Rises Again (1972), The Cherry Picker (1972), Robin Hood (voice, 1973), The Vault of Horror (1973), Chi ha rubato il tesoro della scia? (1974), Side by Side (1975), Spanish Fly (1975), The Bawdy Adventures of Tom Jones (1976), Happy Birthday, Harry (1976), The Last Remake of Beau Geste (1977), and The Hound of the Baskervilles (1978).

THEY CAN'T HANG ME (Vandyke Productions, 1954)—Crime/espionage. *Director:* Val Guest; *Producer:* Roger Proudlock; *Script:* Val Guest and Val Valentine, based on the story by Leonard Mosley; *Cinematography:* Stanley Pavey; *Cast:* Terence Morgan (Inspector Brown), Jill Wilson (Yolande Donlan), André Morell (Robert Pitt), Anthony Oliver (Inspector Newcomb), Guido Lorraine (Peter Revski), Reginald Beckwith (Harold), and John Horsley (Assistant Commissioner).

The opening minutes, prior to the credits, in *They Can't Hang Me,* directed by stalwart genre specialist Val Guest,* demonstrates some of the virtues of the British B crime film. The film begins at night in Soho as a middle-aged man enters an apartment with the words "Anglo-Slav Freedom League" on the door. In the foreground, a woman, watching the man go into the apartment, enters a phone box and makes a call. An upstairs window in the apartment shows a man and woman arguing and fighting, followed by her brief scream and the man running from the apartment into the street as the police arrive and take him into custody. This is presented without dialogue, just sounds and images, with a limited number of camera set-ups depicting a dark street with the apartment in the background and the phone box in the foreground. This is followed by the trial that is presented without dialogue until the last shot. The sequence culminates with the voice of the accused man screaming: "You can't hang me!" Newspaper reports reveal that the man sentenced to death, Robert Pitt, is a senior British public servant and after the trial we learn that he is part of an East European spy ring. In an attempt to save his life, Pitt offers to provide details of a plan to steal a British military invention in four days' time, as well as reveal the identity of the communist master spy operating in Britain, if the British government will repeal his death sentence.

The rest of the film is as economical as these opening minutes as Inspector Brown and his colleague Inspector Newcomb check out aspects of Pitt's story that lead the two detectives to a military base and four suspects who are involved in weapons development. Into the investigation Guest inserts a running comic interlude involving Brown and his long-suffering girlfriend (played by Yolande Donlan, the director's wife), who is continually stood up by her boyfriend because of the demands of the investigation. A further subplot involves Brown's servant Harold, played by another Guest regular, Reginald Beckwith. The film's short running time (seventy-five minutes) does not allow very much character development but the sheer pace of the film, and its professional execution, establishes *They Can't Hang Me* as superior example of the British B film.

THEY MADE ME A FUGITIVE (Alliance/Warner Brothers, 1947)—Film noir/gangster. *Director:* Alberto Cavalcanti; *Producer:* Nat Bronsten; *Script:* Noel Langley, based on the novel *A Convict Has Escaped* by Jackson Budd; *Cinematography:* Otto Heller; *Music:* Marius-Francois Gaillard; *Cast:* Sally Gray (Sally), Trevor Howard (Clem Morgan), Griffith Jones (Narcy), Rene Ray (Cora), Mary Merrall (Aggie), Charles Farrell (Curley), Michael Brennan (Jim), Jack McNaughton (Soapy), Cyril Smith (Bert), Eve Ashley (Ellen), Vida Hope (Mrs. Fenshaw), Maurice Denham (Mr. Fenshaw), Ballard Berkeley (Inspector Rockcliffe), Peter Bull (Fidgety Phil), Sebastian Cabot (Tiny), and Ida Patlanski (Soho Girl).

About a third of the way through *They Made Me a Fugitive,* Clem Morgan, recently demobbed Royal Air Force (RAF) pilot, escapes from jail and heads toward London in search of the criminal (Narcy—short for Narcissus) who framed him for the murder of a policeman and stole his girlfriend Ellen. After receiving a load of buckshot in his back, fired by an irate farmer, Morgan stumbles into the rural household of Mr. and Mrs. Fenshaw. Although Mrs. Fenshaw recognizes Morgan as the escaped convict, she offers him food, clothing, and a bathroom to shave and wash, in exchange for a small favor. Morgan readily agrees and after cleaning himself up and eating Fenshaw's food he learns the nature of the "favor." Mrs. Fenshaw wants Morgan to kill her husband. After Morgan refuses to cooperate, and leaves her house, Mrs. Fenshaw picks up the gun she offered to Morgan (with Morgan's finger prints on the barrel of the weapon), and fires six bullets into Mr. Fenshaw as he wanders down the stairs in search of a drink.

This incident encapsulates the film's abrasive tone, which is tinged with a lingering sense of melancholy. Mrs. Fenshaw, who only appears briefly in the film, wants her husband dead—other than the fact that he is drunk, the film is not interested in establishing the motivation for her action. Similarly, Morgan's refusal to participate, which is the moral decision, only causes him further trouble as Mrs. Fenshaw blames the killing on the escaped convict. The media readily accept her story. This is the arbitrary world of film noir where detailed motivation for perverse desires, such as killing one's spouse, is not necessary. In such a world, it comes as no surprise when Morgan is jailed for fifteen years for a crime he did not commit.

Morgan, a former RAF pilot who drifts into the world of crime in search of excitement in postwar Britain, is essentially a moral man. He is happy to participate in black market criminal behavior as long as it is restricted to items such as nylons, cigarettes, and bacon, but he draws the line at drugs ("sherbet"). Unfortunately, he finds out that it is impossible to make such as distinction. In this way, the film points to the problems of postwar adjustment for men such as Morgan. The special qualities of war, the socially sanctioned killings (Morgan kills a German after escaping from a prison camp), and the extraordinary situations are hard, the film suggests, to (legally) match in peacetime—a point made by Morgan when he explains that he "gave up [killing] when it went out of season."

The film establishes a link between the nature of postwar crime and specific social problems emanating from the difficulties of postwar adjustment by men such as Morgan. At the same time, Narcy is established as a new kind of criminal, identified by his sadism and perversities, qualities that emerged toward the end of World War II. This point is made by Sally when she describes Narcy as "not even a respectable crook, just cheap, rotten after-the-war trash." Narcy, unlike earlier criminals, does not just hunger for wealth and power, but wallows in the misery of others, particularly Morgan and the two women (Sally and Cora) he brutalizes during the film.

There are many fine moments in this film, including the final shootout in the Valhalla funeral parlor where Morgan, assisted by Sally, defeats Narcy's gang, forcing its leader onto the roof, where he falls to his death. However, the film maintains its bleak mood to the very end and resists a conventional, sentimental resolution. As Morgan and Sally plead with the dying Narcy to confess that he set Morgan up for the killing of the policeman, Narcy, true to form, dies cursing Morgan and Sally. The film ends with Morgan facing the resumption of his long prison sentence for a crime he did not commit (there is a small degree of hope as Inspector Rockcliffe tells Morgan that if new evidence comes to light he will reopen the case). The final image shows Sally alone on the dark, wet streets, watching the police car drive away. This is an appropriate ending to a strange love story where the most affectionate, and erotic, moment takes place when Sally removes the inflamed pellets from Morgan's back—a superbly realized sequence as Alberto Cavalcanti skillfully cuts from close-ups registering Sally's horror to the stoic reaction of Morgan as he is forced, finally, to trust someone other than himself.

THE THIRD MAN (London Films, 1949)—Film noir/postwar thriller. *Director:* Carol Reed; *Producers:* Carol Reed, David O. Selznick, and Alexander Korda; *Script:* Graham Greene; *Cinematography:* Robert Krasker; *Music:* Anton Karas; *Cast:* Joseph Cotton (Holly Martins), Alida Valli (Anna Schmidt), Orson Welles (Harry Lime), Trevor Howard (Major Calloway), Bernard Lee (Sergeant Paine), Wilfred Hyde-White (Crabbin), Ernst Deutsch ("Baron" Kurtz), Siegfried Breuer (Popescu), and Geoffrey Keen (British Policeman).

Graham Greene never intended *The Third Man* to be a "serious film," yet it remains one of the great films. There are numerous highlights, including the memorable first shot of Orson Welles, as Harry Lime, exposed in a doorway by an overhead light, together with the famous climax in the sewers beneath Vienna. But the film is also notable in its clever reworking of familiar narrative conventions to form a coherent, fatalistic mosaic that captures the despair, pain, and corruption of postwar Europe. The genesis for the film came from Greene's experiences in Vienna in the winter of 1948 where he was told of the enormous system of sewers beneath the city, which breached the national zones as the Russians refused to lock the thinly disguised advertisement kiosks that covered the various entrances.

U.S. pulp author Holly Martins arrives in Vienna at the invitation of Harry Lime only to find that his friend has been killed in an automobile accident. Once Martins discovers discrepancies in the eyewitness accounts, he behaves in a similar manner to the simple-minded heroes of his Western novels in their search for the "truth." Martins blunders toward the revelation that Lime is not dead and that his friend is living off the proceeds of his penicillin racket in the Russian sector— at the expense of children and adults deformed by his criminally adulterated medicine. Martins gradually realizes that the moral complexities of postwar Vienna cannot be equated to the simplicities of his pulp stories and he agrees to participate in Major Calloway's plan to lure Lime from the Russian zone where they trap and kill him in the sewers under Vienna.

The two American characters in the story occupy different positions in the film's moral spectrum. Lime's callous black market racketeer and Martins's naive "hero" (Anna Schmidt, in disgust at Martins's betrayal of Lime, tells him that "Holly" is such a "silly name"). The characterization of Martins as gullible and out of his depth also provides an indication of Greene's low opinion of postwar United States and its tendency to reduce complex world problems to simplistic platitudes. While Martins is, initially, only interested in finding the "truth," Major Calloway provides a more "realistic" view of the world that includes making deals with the Russians. He, unlike Schmidt or Martins, is aware of the ramifications of Lime's callous disregard for humanity.

The other major figure in the film, and perhaps the most enigmatic character of all, is Anna Schmidt. The film does not romanticize her but emphasizes her loyalty to Lime, whatever the cost. When she discovers the horrific nature of Lime's crimes, she cannot reject her former lover and align herself with Martins. Nor can she forgive Martins—even though he initially agrees to participate in Calloway's plan so that she will not be transported back to the Russian section. Schmidt not only rejects Martins in the film's famous last scene, where she walks past the American, but also refuses to avail herself of the protection of the British authorities as this protection caused Lime's death. Instead, she faces the prospect of deportation and possibly death.

Robert Krasker won the Academy Award for Best Cinematography, Black and White, at the 1951 Academy Awards, Carol Reed* was nominated as Best Director, and Oswald Hafenrichter for Best Film Editing. The film also won Best British Film at the 1950 BAFTA Awards and Reed won the Grand Prize of the Festival at the 1949 Cannes Film Festival. The memorable zither score of Anton Karas, whom Reed noticed playing in a Vienna club, was a sensation at the time of the film's release (the theme from the film was a major hit in the early 1950s) and added another original touch to a film that benefited from the collaboration of many artists—including Welles's contribution of his own dialogue during the Ferris wheel scene where he tries to rationalize Lime's callous behavior ("In Italy for thirty years under the Borgias they had warfare, terror, murder, and bloodshed, but they produced Michelangelo, Leonardo da Vinci, and the Renaissance. In Switzerland, they had brotherly love. They had 500 years of democracy and peace, and what did they produce? The cuckoo clock."). Yet it was Reed who opposed David O. Selznick's attempt to shoot the film in the studio and he also opposed the casting of Noël Coward as Harry Lime in line with Selznick's plan for a more upbeat, conventional story. Above all else, it was Reed who insisted on the despairing tone of the film's last scene, the long-held shot showing Schmidt's lengthy walk past Martins in the avenue near the cemetery.

THIS SPORTING LIFE (Independent Artists/Rank, 1963)—Drama. *Director:* Lindsay Anderson; *Producer:* Karel Reisz; *Script:* David Storey, based on his novel; *Cinematography:* Denys Coop; *Music:* Roberto Gerhard; *Cast:* Richard Harris (Frank Machin), Rachel Roberts (Mrs. Hammond), Alan Badel (Weaver), William Hartnell (Johnson), Colin Blakely (Maurice Braithwaite), Vanda Godsell (Mrs. Weaver), Arthur Lowe (Slomer), and Leonard Rossiter (Phillips).

The best, the most uncompromising, and one of the last New Wave films, *This Sporting Life* was important to the career of actor Richard Harris, who was nominated for an Academy Award for his role as the rugby playing ex-miner Frank Machin. When Lindsay Anderson* read David Storey's novel, he took it to Tony Richardson,* who advised Anderson that he (Anderson) was not the right person to make the film. Rank eventually purchased the rights from Storey and planned a film with Joseph Losey* directing and Stanley Baker* in the lead role. When the project was passed to Julian Wintle at Independent Artists, an organization with strong links to Rank, Wintle ruled out Losey and, as a consequence, Baker declined the part of Frank Machin. Wintle then selected Karel Reisz but he also declined an offer to direct, suggesting Anderson with himself (Reisz) producing and Storey scripting.

Although *This Sporting Life* is usually linked with the New Wave films, it is in many ways quite different from earlier films in the cycle such as *Room at the Top** (1959) and *Saturday Night and Sunday Morning* (1960). Basically, Anderson eschews the usual "regional naturalism" of this cycle for a very stylized expressionism, including a prolonged series of flashbacks interspersed with Frank Machin having surgical repairs to his mouth and teeth following a rugby clash. While the flashbacks establish the main characters and the regional setting, they also reiterate the film's prime focus—the troubled relationship between Machin, a young rugby player, and his landlady, Mrs. Hammond, a widow with two children. Although there are scenes showing the rough atmosphere of the sporting field and the rugby club, the social context is used primarily to reinforce the film's pervasive sense of futility and brutality.

The film presents Machin as a ruthless, brutal ex-miner, who, after assaulting one of his own players for refusing to pass the ball, wins a lucrative contract with a major rugby club. However, it is not the external drama, rugby and its world, but the internal drama, Machin's desire and problems, that interest Storey and Anderson. The film concentrates on the emotional pain of the relationship between Machin and Hammond, emanating from Machin's inability to comprehend his landlady's distress following the brutal death, and possible suicide, of her husband at the local factory. Although he tries to court Hammond, by taking her and the children to the countryside for an afternoon by a lake, by buying expensive presents, including a fur coat, and a disastrous night at an expensive restaurant, he never penetrates her resolve not to become emotionally involved. After a violent argument, where Machin raises the possibility that Hammond's husband killed himself so as to get away from her, she dies in a hospital following a brain hemorrhage. In this, the bleakest of all endings of the New Wave films, a desolate Machin is left only with the internal pain of Hammond's death and the external pain inflicted by a less than satisfying, and possibly short-lived, career as a professional rugby player.

Although Anderson captures the limitations of those who live their life through sport, and class divisions within sporting clubs, he is much more interested and intrigued by conflict within Machin and his desperate need for a maternal, as opposed to just a sexual, partner. Tormented by his inability to understand his landlady, Machin resorts to boorishness and confrontation, punctuated by moments of affection and sensitivity. Nothing alleviates Hammond's distress that is externalized in the film by her ritualized cleaning of her dead husband's work boots. Although there are sufficient subsidiary events to push the narrative along, including Machin's brittle relationship with Weaver and his duplicitous wife, the film never deviates from its real focus, which, given its uncompromising ending, probably contributed to its failure at the box office. The hostility expressed by Sir John Davis, the managing director at Rank, toward the film also did not help and Rank refused to finance any more films in this cycle.

Rachel Roberts was nominated for an Academy Award, and she won the Best Actress Award at the BAFTA Film Awards. Harris was nominated for an Academy Award and a BAFTA Award, along with writer Storey, and the film was nominated for Best Film at the BAFTA Film Awards. Harris won the Best Actor Award at Cannes.

THOMPSON, EMMA (b. 1959). One of the most talented and versatile British actresses to appear in recent years, Emma Thompson's career has traversed British and U.S. television and cinema. While her worldwide public image was established primarily in roles opposite then-husband Kenneth Branagh in two Shakespearian adaptations for the cinema, and a BBC production of *Look Back in Anger* (1993), it would be a mistake to limit appreciation of Thompson's acting skills to her multi-award-winning performances, including Oscar and BAFTA Best Actress Awards, in "quality" productions such as the Merchant-Ivory Films's *Howards End** (1992) and *The Remains of the Day* (1993).

In between these roles, Thompson appeared as the lascivious children's entertainer "Nanny Gee," who tries to seduce her ex-husband, Frasier Crane, away from his wife in an outrageous episode of *Cheers*. Thompson's "Nanny Gee" allowed audiences to see another side of her talent. This range was evident early in her career in British television productions, and most notably as the Glasgow waitress in the six-part television production *Tutti Frutti* (1987), for which Thompson won a BAFTA TV Award for Best Actress. Eleven years later Thompson repeated this television success with an Emmy for her guest role in *Ellen*.

Her parents, Phyllida Law and Eric Thompson, worked in show business and she quickly became involved at Cambridge University with the Cambridge University Footlights and Woman's Hour, an all-female troupe. After touring with the popular satire *Not the Nine O'Clock News* and appearing in the sketch comedy *Alfresco* with ex-Footlight members Hugh Laurie and Stephen Fry, Thompson met Branagh while working on the miniseries *Fortunes of War* (1988) and for the next few years Thompson's personal and professional fortunes were closely linked with Branagh. She appeared opposite him in William Shakespeare's *Henry V* (1989), the convoluted film noir *Dead Again* (1991), the bittersweet comedy *Peter's Friends* (1992), with Thompson's mother Phyllida Law in a supporting role as the housekeeper, and the Shakespearian comedy *Much Ado about Nothing* (1993).

For a brief period, Branagh and Thompson were celebrated in the popular British press as a reincarnation of earlier stage and screen favorites Laurence Olivier* and Vivien Leigh. However, Thompson's separation and divorce from Branagh in 1995 was accompanied by universal praise for her adaptation of Jane Austen's *Sense and Sensibility* (1995). For this film she won an Oscar for Best Screenplay, together with an Oscar nomination for Best Actress, a Golden Globe Award for Best Adapted Screenplay, a BAFTA Award for Best Actress, and a BAFTA nomination for Best Screenplay. The touching, sometimes painful, role of the Bloomsbury painter Dora Carrington and her relationship with homosexual writer Lytton Strachey in *Carrington* (1995) followed and Thompson appeared with her mother next in *The Winter's Guest* (1997).

Two radically different U.S. films allowed Thompson to further demonstrate her versatility, first as Susan Stanton in *Primary Colors* (1998), Mike Nichols excellent adaptation of Joe Klein's thinly disguised insider's interpretation of the rise of a southern governor to the White House with Thompson as his ambitious, periodically frustrated, wife. Second, Thompson's Federal Bureau of Investigation agent Sadie Hawkins, working with Alan Rickman's local investigator in Sebastian Gutierrez's knowing neo-noir *Judas Kiss* (1999), benefited from the casting of Thompson and Rickman against type. Thompson's range was again in evidence in the made-for-television film *Wit* (2001) as Vivian Bearing, a literature professor preparing for death after being diagnosed with ovarian cancer in the television adaptation of Margaret Edson's play.

FILMS: The Tall Guy (1989), Henry V (1989), Dead Again (1991), Impromptu (1991), Howards End (1992), Peter's Friend (1992), Much Ado about Nothing (1993), The Remains of the Day (1993), In the Name of the Father (1993), Junior (1994), My Father the Hero (1994), Carrington (1995), Sense and Sensibility (1995), The Winter Guest (1997), Primary Colors (1998), Judas Kiss (1998), and Maybe Baby (2000).

TIME IS MY ENEMY (Vandyke Productions, 1954)—Crime melodrama. *Director:* Don Chaffey; *Producer:* Roger Proudlock; *Script:* Allan MacKinnon, based on the play *Second Chance* by Ella Adkins; *Cinematography:* Geoffrey Faithfull; *Cast:* Dennis Price (Martin Radley), Renee Asherson (Barbara Everton), Patrick Barr (John Everton), Susan Shaw (Evelyn Grover), Duncan Lamont (Inspector Charles Wayne), Bonar Colleano (Harry Bond), Alfie Bass (Ernie Gordon), and Dandy Nicholls (Mrs. Budd).

Time Is My Enemy is another efficient B crime film from Vandyke Productions, a minor production company specializing in the low-budget end of the market in the 1950s. *Time Is My Enemy* begins with a botched robbery of a jewellery shop when Martin Radley kills the owner. Forced to flee England with his girlfriend Evelyn Grover, Radley blackmails his former wife Barbara Everton, who, believing that Radley died during World War II, married successful businessman John Everton.

Radley desperately tries to raise money to pay for this flight from Britain while Barbara tries to hide the fact that her first husband is still alive. *Time Is My Enemy* is an unpretentious film that contains an effective, if contrived, twist near the end. After a distraught Barbara shoots Radley with his own gun, a friend of the family, Inspector Charles Wayne, reveals that Radley filled the gun with blanks and then killed another man and substituted his body. In a more "civilized" climax, Wayne quietly arrests Radley at the airport where he expresses regret for the pain and angst he has caused Barbara.

TO THE DEVIL A DAUGHTER (Hammer, 1976)—Horror/occult. *Director:* Peter Sykes; *Producer:* Roy Skeggs; *Script:* Christopher Wicking, based on the novel by Dennis Wheatley; *Cinematographer:* David Watkin; *Music:* Paul Glass; *Cast:* Richard Widmark (John Verney), Christopher Lee (Father Michael Rayner), Honor Blackman (Anna Fountain), Denholm Elliott (Henry Beddows), Michael Goodliffe (George De Grass), Nastassja Kinski (Catherine Beddows), and Anthony Valentine (David Fountain).

As the traditional Hammer horror film was declining in production and popularity, *To the Devil a Daughter* indicates Hammer's approach to restoring support, largely through greater emphasis on sex, and spreading the financial risk with international partners. This latter development also weakened the film with extraneous Bavarian footage, which was included only to meet the requirements imposed by the film's co-producers. Also, the abrupt ending does not provide a satisfying climax as American novelist John Verney tries to save Catherine Beddows from the satanic control of Father Michael Rayner.

Director Peter Sykes and scriptwriter Christopher Wicking, exploiting themes established in *The Exorcist* (1973), generate an appropriate degree of tension as the Satanists close in on Catherine, who is being protected by Verney and a married couple, Anna and David Fountain. Father Rayner systematically removes all of the opposition to his control and possession of Catherine. *To the Devil a Daughter,* like many Hammer horror films, dramatizes the universal battle between innocence and evil culminating in the confrontation between the evil priest and the novelist.

TODD, ANN (1909–1993). Francesca Cunningham, the masochistic, tormented pianist played by Ann Todd in Compton Bennett's *The Seventh Veil** (1946), was not only Todd's breakthrough film to stardom, but also one of the most perverse love stories in the history of the British cinema. Cunningham, trained and molded (and disciplined) by her woman-hating uncle (James Mason*) into a world-renowned pianist, has a variety of lovers to choose from but, ultimately, returns to the controlling arms of her uncle. Todd reprised this role in a stage version with Leo Genn but failed to capture the powerful screen chemistry between Todd and Mason that elevated *The Seventh Veil* to the position of the most popular British film in 1946–1947. The relative failure of the play, compared with the film, may also had something to do with Todd's ease in front of the camera and her ability to suggest emotional turmoil within layers of repressions beneath her seemingly fragile beauty, a quality that was exploited over the next four years as Todd enjoyed her greatest film roles.

During this period, Todd essayed a series of emotionally and morally divided women who were unable to maintain "normal" relationships with their lovers or husbands. Beginning with Compton Bennett's bleak film noir *Daybreak* (1948), Todd is the vulnerable wife of Eric Portman* who, through circumstances and personal weakness, falls for the superficial sexual attentions of Maxwell Reed. This leads to murder suicide and murder. This was followed by another morally problematic role in Lewis Allen's superb film noir *So Evil My Love** (1948) with Todd as Olivia Harwood, the sexually repressed widow of a missionary, who is seduced by Ray Milland into blackmailing a vulnerable friend (Geraldine Fitzgerald), an action that also leads to murder.

In another U.S. film shot in London, Alfred Hitchcock's* *The Paradine Case* (1948), Todd is betrayed by her lawyer husband Gregory Peck, who becomes infatuated with murderess Alida Valli. This position is reversed in David Lean's* domestic melodrama *The Passionate Friends** (1949), with Todd, as Mary Justin, trapped in a compassionate, but sexless, marriage to Claude Rains. After betraying her husband with lover Trevor Howard,* Justin's equilibrium is disturbed years later when he reappears in her life, forcing her to contemplate suicide before an emotional reconciliation with Rains.

Aside from Francesca Cunningham in *The Seventh Veil,* Todd's best role was in the second of the three films directed by her husband David Lean. In *Madeleine** (1950), Todd was able to combine her characteristic sense of vulnerability with a series of less appealing character traits. However, the film's refusal to clarify her exact moral and criminal status (the jury at her trial for poisoning her lover eventually renders an inconclusive "not proven" verdict) probably cost it a large audience, although this morally complex tale of lust, betrayal, and class barriers is one of the best melodramas produced in Britain in the 1940s. A third film with Lean, *The Sound Barrier* (1952), followed and they ended their eight-year marriage in 1957.

The Green Scarf (1954), a courtroom thriller set in Paris involving a blind man (Kieron Moore) accused of murder, directed by George More O'Ferrall, marked the end of Todd's career as a major star and only Joseph Losey's* *Time without Pity* (1957) and Seth Holt's convoluted psychological thriller *Taste of Fear* (1960), written by Jimmy Sangster, were of interest in the final phase of Todd's film acting career as she moved into character roles. *Taste of Fear,* a film that Todd disliked, was commercially successful and it launched another phase in the development of Hammer Films as it tried to capitalize on the success of *Psycho* (1960). *The Son of Captain Blood* (1962), a Spanish–Italian–U.S. coproduction shot in Spain, saw Todd playing Sean Flynn's (son of Errol Flynn) mother in Casey Robinson's (who scripted *Captain Blood* in 1935) attempt to recapture the spirit of his original film. This lackluster pirate story presented Sean as following in his father's footsteps. After concentrating on the stage in the 1950s with the Old Vic, Todd returned to film in the 1960s, this time as the writer, producer, and director of travel documentaries. Todd's autobiography, *The Eighth Veil,* was published in 1980.

FILMS: Keepers of Youth (1931), These Charming People (1931), The Ghost Train (1931), The Water Gypsies (1932), The Return of Bulldog Drummond (1934), Things to Come (1936), Action for Slander (1937), The Squeaker (1937), South Riding (1938), Poison Pen (1939), Danny Boy (1941), Ships with Wings (1941), Perfect Strangers (1945), The Seventh Veil (1945), Gaiety George (1946), Daybreak (1948), So Evil My Love (1948), The Paradine Case (1948), The Passionate Friends (1949), Madeleine (1950), The Sound Barrier (1952), The Green Scarf (1954), Time without Pity (1956), Taste of Fear (1961), The Son of Captain Blood (1962), Thunder in Heaven (short, 1964), 90 Degrees in the Shade (1965), Thunder of the Gods (short, 1966), Thunder of the Kings (1967), The Fiend (1971), The Human Factor (1979), and The McGuffin (1985).

TODD, RICHARD (b. 1919). Most of Richard Todd's best films were in the decade after his film debut in 1948, especially after his rapid rise to stardom as Lachie, the prickly Scot who learns that he is dying, in the Warner Brothers production of *The Hasty Heart* (1949). This was filmed in London starring Ronald Reagan and Patricia Neal. The 1950s was a rich period for Todd, culminating in 1960 with one of his best, and least characteristic, roles as the perfume salesman who takes on the crooks and the police after his new car is stolen and the authorities don't seem to care very much in John Guillermin's* *Never Let Go* (1960).

Born in Ireland, Todd spent part of his childhood in India with his father who was an army physician. Following his training at the Italia Conta School in the late 1930s, Todd appeared in productions at the Dundee Repertory Company prior to World War II, where he returned after military service during the war. On the last day of shooting of his first film role, Alberto Cavalcanti's *For Them That Trespass* (1948), Todd was invited to a reception at Elstree Studios to welcome Jack Warner Jr. and director Vincent Sherman, who were in Britain to make *The Hasty Heart.* When Sherman spotted Todd, he asked him to test for the part of Corporal Lachlan MacLachlan (Lachie)[1] and this film gave his career an initial boost as he was nominated for Best Actor at the 1950 Academy Awards and he won the Most Promising Newcomer Award at the Golden Globes. Todd's second important break came when Alfred Hitchcock* cast him as the murderer in *Stage Fright* (1950), even before the release of *The Hasty Heart. Stage Fright,* a thriller with a duplicitous flashback, also provided Todd with widespread international exposure as he played opposite Marlene Dietrich, Jane Wyman, and Michael Wilding. In between *The Hasty Heart* and *Stage Fright,* Todd also starred in the clever film noir *The Interrupted Journey** (1949), opposite Valerie Hobson,* as a married man whose plans to run away with his mistress are disrupted by a train wreck near his home.

More international exposure for Todd came with his starring roles in three films made for Disney in Britain—*The Story of Robin Hood* (1952), energetically directed by Ken Annakin, with Todd in the title role and a cast that included Peter Finch* and James Robertson Justice; *The Sword and the Rose* (1953), another costume melodrama directed by Annakin, with Justice as Henry VIII and Todd romancing Mary Tudor (Glynis Johns); and *Rob Roy, The Highland Rogue* (1954), with Todd as the leader of the rebellious Scottish clan, and much the same cast as the previous film. These films elevated Todd's status in Hollywood and he went to the United States for his next two films, the sentimental *A Man Called Peter* (1955), with Todd in the starring role as the Reverend Peter Marshall, a Scotsman who became a U.S. Senate chaplain, and *The Virgin Queen* (1955), with Todd as Walter Raleigh opposite Bette Davis, who was reprising her role as Queen Elizabeth I.

While these international films were important to Todd's career, his British films in the mid- to late 1950s, especially three films for director Michael Anderson, were more interesting. The most commercially successful of these films, *The Dam Busters** (1955), cast Todd as Wing Commander Guy Gibson, who led the British raid to deliver a series of "bouncing bombs" to the Ruhr dams in Germany during World War II. The second Anderson-directed war film, also based on a true incident, was the *Yangtse Incident* (1956), with Todd commanding a British cruiser, the HMS *Amethyst,* which was trapped by Chinese communists on the Yangtse River in 1949. The third film was also good, an ingenious cat-and-mouse thriller, *Chase a Crooked Shadow** (1957), with Todd as a mysterious stranger who disrupts Ann Baxter's ordered life by reviving incidents from her past that she would prefer to ignore. Toward the end of the 1950s, Todd starred in *The Danger Within** (1958), one of the last, and best, of the popular prisoner of war dramas that reached a peak with *The Colditz Story** in 1955. *The Danger Within,* which was set in an Italian prison camp during the summer of 1943, details a successful mass escape and the unveiling of a traitor in the camp. Todd, in a film such as this, was almost an iconic presence having essayed similar roles throughout the decade.

After *Never Let Go* and *The Long and the Short and the Tall* (1961), a war film that Todd disliked due to the behavior of his co-star, Laurence Harvey,* Todd's film roles became less significant, with starring roles in pot-boilers such as *Death*

Drums Along the River* (1963), with Todd as Harry Sanders, a character made famous by Leslie Banks* in *Sanders of the River** (1935). Todd reprised the character in *Coast of Skeletons* (1964). Todd also appeared in a cameo role as Major Howard, a British glider infantry officer, in *The Longest Day* (1962), a role he requested as Howard was Todd's actual commanding officer during World War II. The theater, however, occupied much of Todd's attention in the 1960s and 1970s as his screen roles deteriorated even further, although there were a couple of interesting supporting parts, including an adulterous husband planning to murder his wife in Roy Ward Baker's* *Asylum** (1972).

FILMS: For Them That Trespass (1948), The Hasty Heart (1949), The Interrupted Journey (1949), Stage Fright (1950), Portrait of Clare (1950), Flesh and Blood (1951), Lightning Strikes Twice (1951), The Story of Robin Hood (1952), 24 Hours of a Woman's Life (1952), The Venetian Bird (1952), The Elstree Story (doc., 1952), The Sword and the Rose (1953), Rob Roy, The Highland Rogue (1953), The Bed (1954), A Man Called Peter (1955), The Virgin Queen (1955), The Dam Busters (1955), Marie Antoinette, Reine de France (1955), D-Day the 6th of June (1956), Saint Joan (1957), Yangtse Incident (1957), Chase a Crooked Shadow (1958), The Naked Earth (1958), Intent to Kill (1958), Danger Within (1958), Never Let Go (1960), The Long and the Short and the Tall (1961), Why Bother to Knock (1961), The Hellions (1961), Le Crime Ne Paie Pas (1961), The Boys (1962), The Longest Day (1962), The Very Edge (1963), Death Drums along the River (1963), Coast of Skeletons (1964), Operation Crossbow (1965), Battle of Villa Fiorita (1965), Blood-Bath (1966), The Love-Ins (1967), Subterfuge (1968), The Last of the Long-Haired Boys (1968), Dorian Gray (1970), Asylum (1972), The Acquarian (1972), Number One of the Secret Service (1977), The Big Sleep (1977), Home before Midnight (1979), House of the Long Shadows (1983), and Incident at Victoria Falls (1991).

TOM JONES (Woodfall Films, 1963)—Period comedy. *Director:* Tony Richardson; *Producers:* Michael Balcon (executive) and Tony Richardson; *Script:* John Osborne, based on the novel by Henry Fielding; *Cinematography:* Walter Lassally; *Music:* John Addison; *Cast:* Albert Finney (Tom Jones), Susannah York (Sophie Western), Hugh Griffith (Squire Western), Edith Evans (Miss Western), Joan Greenwood (Lady Bellaston), Diane Cilento (Molly Seagram), George Devine (Squire Allworthy), David Tomlinson (Lord Fellamar), Wilfred Lawson (Black George), Rosalind Knight (Mrs. Fitzpatrick), Jack MacGowran (Partridge), David Warner (Blifil), and Joyce Redman (Mrs. Waters).

Within the context of the British cinema, *Tom Jones* was a highly significant film. It marked the high point of Tony Richardson's* career and encouraged the U.S. studios to invest heavily into the "Swinging London" cycle of the 1960s. The film also provided a strong financial basis for Woodfall Films. The British company Bryanston, who had first call on financing, delayed so long that United Artists replaced it with Woodfall; Bryanston went bankrupt in 1965.

Despite the film's many virtues, it was also a film of missed chances, largely due to Richardson's panic in the editing room when he became depressed and felt that much of the comedy in the film did not work. He therefore speeded up sequences, such as the chase in the Upton Inn, and cut much of Diane Cilento's performance as Molly Seagram, thereby rendering her part nearly incoherent. Other sequences, on the other hand, such as the stag hunt, begin in an exhilarating fashion, with superb aerial photography, but carry on too long and labor their anti–blood sport point of view. Nevertheless, Richardson's decision to film entirely on location was a good one and the film, in part, captures the feel of the period, especially when his editing does not impede on Walter Lassally's photography and John Addison's score.

Loosely based on Henry Fielding's picaresque novel of life in eighteenth-century England, John Osborne's script and Richardson's direction emphasize the sexual adventures of Tom Jones, beginning in Somerset and, after his expulsion from Squire Allworthy's estate, on the road to London. The journey to London includes the film's most famous scene as Jones and Mrs. Waters bypass the relatively strict censorship restrictions of the early 1960s to suggest, with a combination of carefully selected foods (comprising mostly seafood that have to be sucked), what Jones and Waters are planning to do in bed after their meal.

The film's episodic plot, beginning with a pre-credit "silent cinema" sequence, (seemingly) establishes Jones's status as a bastard, a victimized state that allows the machinations of Blifil, Jones's rival for the hand of Sophie Western, to nearly destroy him. It is not only Blifil, and other adversaries, who threaten Jones's union with Sophie, as his own sexual appetite for Lady Bellaston (Joan Greenwood* in a scene-stealing performance) and other willing females that cause him problems. A last-minute rescue from the gallows and last-minute revelations about the true nature of his birthright see Jones returned to his rightful place with Sophie and the Allworthy estate. Yet, it is the "animal" behavior of Sophie's father (Hugh Griffith) that captures the tone of film, reinforced by the delightfully amoral, pragmatic advice of Lady Western (Edith Evans).

The film careers of Richardson and Albert Finney* should have received a great impetus from the film's immense popularity and numerous awards. Yet, both men refused to capitalize on their opportunities, at least in terms of the cinema. Finney went next to the commercially disastrous role of the psychopathic killer in Karel Reisz's remake of *Night Must Fall* (1964), and then back to the stage, returning only periodically to film while Richardson used his leverage from *Tom Jones* to undertake a long series of commercially and critically unsuccessful films. While Finney received a Best Actor nomination, with other nominations going to Griffith, Cilento, Evans, and Joyce Redman for Supporting Roles, John Osborne won the Best Screenplay Award, Richardson the Best Director Award, John Addison Best Score, and the film won the Best Picture at the 1964 Academy Awards as well as the 1964 BAFTA Film Award for Best Film, and Osborne for Best Screenplay.

TOPSY-TURVY (October Films, 1999)—Biographical musical/drama. *Director:* Mike Leigh; *Producers:* Simon Channing-Williams and Georgina Lowe (associate); *Script:* Mike Leigh; *Cinematography:* Dick Pope; *Music:* Carl Davis (from Arthur Sullivan); *Cast:* Jim Broadbent (William Schwenk Gilbert), Allan Corduner (Arthur Sullivan), Timothy Spall (Richard Temple), Lesley Manville (Lucy Gilbert), Eleanor David (Fanny Ronalds), Ron Cook (Richard D'Oyly Carte), Shirley Henderson (Leonora Braham), Martin Savage (George Grossmith), Wendy Nottingham (Helen Lenoir), and Kevin McKidd (Durward Lely).

Mike Leigh,* based on previous films such *Naked* (1993) and *Secrets and Lies* (1996), would not be an obvious name to be associated with a film depicting the genesis of Gilbert and Sullivan's *The Mikado.* This misconception is wrong on both accounts. Leigh demonstrates an affectionate affinity for the works of Gilbert and Sullivan, even daring to spend some time on *Princess Ida,* one of their less successful productions.

It would also be a mistake is to reduce *Topsy-Turvy* to the formulaic conventions associated with the backstage musical. Although the film does spend considerable time on the intricacies of the production of *The Mikado,* Leigh avoids, or side steps, the conventions of the genre, particularly the usual contrivances that threaten opening night. The one, minor, exception here is Gilbert's decision to delete veteran Richard Temple's musical number from the finished production, much to the distress of the performer. However, a last-minute confrontation between the cast and Gilbert sees the song restored. Otherwise, Leigh eschews melodrama in favor of backstage detail by showing extended rehearsals.

Topsy-Turvy covers the period from 1884, and the commercial and critical failure of *Princess Ida,* to the successful first night of *The Mikado* at the Savoy in 1885. At the start of the film, Sullivan, recently knighted by the queen after ten successful productions, is shown to be tired of Gilbert's "topsy-turvy" as he wants to be working on more serious music. After his trip through Europe, Sullivan tells Richard D'Oyly Carte that although he is under contract to produce a new work with Gilbert each year, he cannot work with the librettist's new material concerning magic and a Sicilian princess. Just as the partnership is about to be dissolved, Gilbert reluctantly accompanies his wife to an exhibition of Japanese culture in London that inspires *The Mikado.*

There are many narrative strands running through this long film (161 minutes) detailing aspects of the personal life of the two main protagonists and the members of the Savoy Theatre, including the touching, vulnerable Shirley Henderson, as Leonora Braham, a member of the troupe who is reminded of her "little secret," her alcoholism, by D'Oyly Carte at the time when her contract comes up for renewal—other performers have less public secrets, such as George Grossmith's drug addiction. The film ends on bitter-sweet note as it shifts from an intoxicated Braham singing to herself in the dressing room to her evocative performance on stage earlier that night.

Other narrative strands develop this recurring pattern of public success and private pain as Gilbert sits with his long-suffering wife Lucy, after *The Mikado*'s opening night, as she tries to explain, in metaphorical terms, her unhappiness with their marriage and the fact that they do not have children. Similarly, Sullivan's excitement is mitigated on the same night by the news from his mistress, Fanny Ronalds, that she is pregnant again and when he offers to make the "necessary arrangements" (for an abortion), Fanny tells him that she will look after it as, "after all, it is 1885." In this way, *Topsy-Turvy* is more than a beautifully crafted celebration of the music and theater of Gilbert and Sullivan as the film delineates between the magic on stage and the pain and insecurities of those involved in its creation.

Jim Broadbent won the Best Actor Award at the 1999 Venice Film Festival, Lindy Hemmings an Oscar at the 2000 Academy Awards for Best Costume Design, and Christine Blundell and Trefor Proud for Best Makeup, while Leigh was nominated for Best Writing and John Bush and Eve Stewart for Best Art Direction. *Topsy-Turvy* won the Alexander Korda Award for Best British Film at the 2000 BAFTA Film Awards where Broadbent, Timothy Spall, and Leigh were also nominated. Leigh won a Special Achievement at the London Critics Circle Awards and the Best Director Award at the National Society of Film Critics Awards where *Topsy-Turvy* won Best Film and this was repeated at the New York Critics Circle Awards.

TWENTY FOUR SEVEN (BBC/Scala Films, 1997)—Realist social drama. *Director:* Shane Meadows; *Producers:* Imogen West, George Faber (executive), Nik Powell (executive), David M. Thompson (executive), and Stephen Woolley (executive); *Script:* Paul Fraser and Shane Meadows; *Cinematography:* Ashley Rowe; *Music:* Boo Hewerdine and Neil MacColl; *Cast:* Bob Hoskins (Alan Darcy), Danny Nussbaum (Tim), Bruce Jones (Tim's Dad), Annette Badland (Pat, Tim's Mother), Justin Brady (Gadget), James Hooton (Knighty), Darren Campbell (Daz), Krisham Beresford (Young Darcy), Karl Collins (Stuart), Anthony Clarke (Youngy), Johann Myers (Benny), Jimmy Hynd (Meggy), Mat Hand (Fagash), James Corden (Tonka), Pamela Cundell (Auntie Iris), and Jo Bell (Jo).

"I was a forgotten thirtysomething in the eighties," burnt-out soccer coach Alan Darcy admits at the start of *Twenty Four Seven,* "everything was a boom, a transaction or a take-over. Our town was forgotten. I feel as though I am a casualty— but that's cool 'cause most of us feel that way." This prologue sets the tone for another rage against the economic and social effects of Thatcher's reforms in provincial cities such as Nottingham. Unlike other films that draw on these changes to celebrate the ability of the human spirit to cope with the devastating economic consequences, such as *The Full Monty** (1998), Shane Meadows's film never allows the viewer to forget the pain that these changes brought to many people in Great Britain.

The film is told through Darcy's flashback as he reads from his diary, recounting how a boxing club saved him when he was young and how he wants to revitalize the 101 Boxing Club to instil some meaning into the lives of the disenfranchised youths of his depressed East Midlands city who "have been the living the same day all of their lives." Hence the title of the film, twenty four hours a day, seven days a week. Darcy brings the two warring groups together in the boxing ring and begins the process of instilling self-control, both inside and outside the ring. The sense of community between all of the boys is fostered by a camping trip in Wales.

Darcy appears to have succeeded as the boys and their parents are brought together for a boxing competition with another club. Just as of the ingredients seem to come together for an upbeat ending, the film suddenly reverses the upbeat mood as Darcy loses his own self-control and badly beats up an abusive parent resulting in the destruction of the club and, ultimately, Darcy's death. The first fight staged by the 101 Boxing Club also turns out to be its last. However, Meadows is not content to end his film in this state of abject alienation and, at Darcy's funeral, he indicates that, ultimately, Darcy has been successful. It is a touching, powerful ending, without a hint of contrivance.

The ultra realist tone utilized in *Twenty Four Seven* is very much in the British film tradition and, in some ways, a legacy of the British realist dramas of the early 1960s. Meadows's film takes pride in its low budget and his determination to not follow conventional narrative patterns. As a consequence, the film is dependent on Bob Hoskins's* performance to hold audience attention and although the lives of each boy is sketched in, they are difficult to differentiate. There is also a comedic strand, especially Darcy's relationship with the local thug who finances the club. The most striking moment in the film has little to do with the boxing and the boys as it shows Darcy ballroom dancing with his Auntie Iris.

NOTE

1. See McFarlane, *An Autobiography of British Cinema,* p. 563.

U

UNMAN, WITTERING AND ZIGO (Hemmings/Mediarts, 1971)—Mystery. *Director:* John Mackenzie; *Producers:* Gareth Wigan, Stanley O'Toole (executive), and David Hemmings (executive); *Script:* Simon Raven, based on the play by Giles Cooper; *Cinematography:* Geoffrey Unsworth; *Music:* Michael J. Lewis; *Cast:* David Hemmings (John Ebony), Douglas Wilmer (Headmaster), Anthony Haygarth (Cary Farthingale), Carolyn Seymour (Silvie Ebony), Hamilton Dyce (Mr. Winstanley), Barbara Lott (Mrs. Winstanley), Donald Gee (Stretton), David Jackson (Clackworth), and Michael Kitchen (Bungabine).

This underrated British film is neither as ambitious nor as subversive as Lindsay Anderson's* *If . . .* (1968), released three years before *Unman, Wittering and Zigo.* However, it complements the theme of Anderson's film by highlighting the repressive and destructive aspects of elite British schools. When John Ebony joins the teaching staff of a private school for boys and is placed in charge of Lower 5B, he learns that his predecessor recently died when he fell from a cliff while walking at night. This death was not an accident, as Ebony learns while marking the roll call on his first day when his class informs him that they murdered their former teacher when he imposed detention on them on a Saturday afternoon. Ebony, slowly, discovers that the boys were telling the truth and when he tries to alert other people, such as his wife, Silvie, or the headmaster, they refuse to believe him.

Unman, Wittering and Zigo reverses traditional images of good and evil. Although *Lord of the Flies* (1963) and other films have explored this theme of murderous schoolchildren (see also the St. Trinian's films), there is something chilling in *Unman, Wittering and Zigo* when "innocent," polite, fresh-faced schoolboys are shown to be the source of evil, where manners and "breeding" mask thoughts of rape and murder.

When the headmaster tells Ebony that his teaching contract will not be renewed, productivity in the class comes to a halt as Ebony, disgusted with his treatment by both the school administration and the boys, refuses to teach and reads the paper during class time while the boys study the racing guide. An abortive attempt to rape Ebony's wife leads to the suicide of Wittering after the other boys taunt him when he refuses to participate. The discovery of Wittering's body is accompanied on the sound track by Wittering reading his suicide note confessing to the killing of Ebony's predecessor. The film concludes with a roll call on the sound track ending with Wittering and Zigo being marked absent (Zigo is absent throughout the film) and the realization that the boys have got away with murder and that the system has covered their sins.

V

VICTIM (Rank, 1961)—Social melodrama. *Director:* Basil Dearden; *Producer:* Michael Relph; *Script:* Janet Green and John McCormick; *Cinematography:* Otto Heller; *Music:* Philip Green; *Cast:* Dirk Bogarde (Melville Farr), Sylvia Syms (Laura Farr), Dennis Price (Calloway), Anthony Nicholls (Lord Fullbrook), Peter Copley (Paul Mandrake), Norman Bird (Harold Doe), Peter McEnery (Jack Barrett), Donald Churchill (Eddy Stone), Derren Nesbit (Sandy Youth), John Barrie (Detective Inspector Harris), John Cairney (Bridie), Alan MacNaughtan (Scott Hankin), Nigel Stock (Phip), and Noel Howlett (Patterson).

When Detective Inspector Harris tells embattled lawyer Melville Farr that the British law, which criminalizes male homosexuality, is the "blackmailer's charter," he is spelling out the central theme in *Victim*. The film is, paradoxically, both courageous and flawed. Brave in openly dramatizing the intolerable situation faced by homosexual men in Britain at that time through their vulnerability to blackmail. Flawed by depicting the central character, Melville Farr, as a married gay man and as a *nonpracticing* homosexual. Thus, the film compromises, or weakens, the injustice it seeks to expose by making Melville perform the function of the "hero" by investigating the death of Jack Barrett, a young man who was infatuated with him. While Barrett, and all of the other homosexuals shown in the film, remain at the level of victim, Melville, through his ability to deny his sexual impulses, is elevated to a different (higher?) status. In a crucial scene late in the film, Melville admits to his wife that although he desired Barrett, he did not act on it. Melville's denial of his sexual desires also makes possible a reconciliation between Laura and Melville—if he had sex with Barrett, this would not have been available as a viable ending.

Melville's heroic status is enhanced by his decision to destroy his legal career by testifying against the vicious blackmail ring, conducted by the psychotic Sandy Youth and Miss Benham (who is described in the film as "half avenging angel and half peeping tom"). Indeed, the film's depiction of Youth and Benham as demented grotesques serves to foreground its social message and reflects the intentions of scriptwriter Janet Green to assimilate a social message into the conventions of the crime film, a tactic endorsed by director Basil Dearden* and producer Basil Relph,* who had examined racial issues in much the same manner in *Sapphire* (1959).

Dirk Bogarde* was not the first actor offered the lead role in *Victim* and his decision to accept the role marks a seminal point in his career. In *Victim,* his character, for the first time on the British screen, confesses that he desires another man. This admission occurs late in the film in a scene specially written by Bogarde and this, in itself, makes *Victim* a significant film. As a result of the film's sympathetic depiction of homosexual desires, *Victim* was denied a certificate by the Production Code Administration in the United States although *Oscar Wilde* (1959) was granted one in the same year.[1]

While most critics have acknowledged the courage of *Victim* in its depiction of the male characters, the repressive characterization of Laura has been treated less charitably as some suggest that the film blames exploitation of homosexuals on two women in the film—the blackmailing hysterical spinster Benham and the repressed wife Laura, who, it has been suggested, sadistically pursues and interrogates her husband until he admits his "deviance." Yet, as actress Sylvia Syms points out, "In those days women of a certain class were very innocent. The wife's knowledge of sex would be very limited; she may have had her suspicions but I think that it was perfectly possible for her to love Dirk's character and have a reasonably happy marriage."[2] In fact, the relationship between Melville and Laura is one of the more complex aspects of the film with Dearden's emphasizing that their home is weakened by its lack of children, compensated for by her work with handicapped children. Yet, as Melville admits in the final scene, he needs her and she replies that need is a "bigger word than love." This suggests she will return to him. While, for some, this is a compromised ending, *Victim* paved the way for valid alternative representations of sexual desire that prior to 1961 were subject only to ridicule.

VILLAGE OF THE DAMNED (MGM Britain, 1960)—Science fiction. *Director:* Wolf Rilla; *Producer:* Ronald Kinnoch; *Script:* Stirling Silliphant, Wolf Rilla, and George Barclay (also known as Ronald Kinnoch), based on the novel *The Midwich Cuckoo* by John Wyndham; *Cinematography:* Geoffrey Faithfull; *Music:* Ron Goodwin; *Cast:* George Sanders (Gordon Zellaby), Barbara Shelley (Anthea Zellaby), Michael Gwynn (Major Alan Bernard), Martin Stephens (David Zellaby), Laurence Naismith (Dr. Willers), John Phillips (General Leighton), Richard Vernon (Sir Edgar Hargreaves) and Peter Vaughan (Police Constable Gobbey).

Long before the advent of the evil child in the horror genre (e.g., see *It's Alive!* [1974] and *The Omen* [1976]), *Village of the Damned,* based on John Wyndham's popular novel *The Midwich Cuckoo,* struck a chord with the viewing public with its disturbing characterization of twelve children born to the fertile women in a small English village after the entire inhabitants of the village fall asleep for twenty-four hours. David, the leader of the children, supposedly the child of formerly childless parents, Professor Gordon Zellaby and his wife Anthea, is chillingly portrayed by Martin Stephens, who was also effective in Jack Clayton's* *The Innocents** (1961).

Distinguished by their hair coloring and striking eyes, which blaze whenever their anger is aroused, the children quickly bond together into an exclusive group. They are also highly intelligent and share telepathic powers that they use against the villagers whenever they perceive a threat. The fact that they are (attractive) children and that most of the village, and society in general, is inherently hostile and narrow minded, produces a disturbing moral ambivalence in the viewer as the children also orchestrate a series of killings.

This moral disturbance is also reinforced by the rupture in the natural bond between parent and child and the fact that the children are unable to exhibit any degree of trust toward adults. Ironically, when they place their (slight) trust in one adult, Gordon Zellaby, this leads to their deaths as he uses this position of trust to secretly bring a bomb into the church where they are forced to protect themselves from society. Their isolation from "normality" is an integral aspect of the film's dramatic structure involving a growing polarization between the children and all adults, thus providing a clear social parable for the Cold War years in its depiction of a world based on suspicion and paranoia. This fact is referred to when it records the reaction of both the East and the West to the "threat" imposed by the children, a threat that is largely based on their failure to conform to the norm. This theme was also developed in the 1963 sequel *Children of the Damned.*

NOTES

1. See Slide, *"Banned in the USA,"* p. 115.
2. McFarlane, *An Autobiography of Britsh Cinema,* p. 550.

W

THE WAR ZONE (Channel Four Films, 1999)—Social realism. *Director:* Tim Roth; *Producers:* Eric Abraham (executive), Steve Butterworth (associate), Dixie Linder, and Sarah Radclyffe; *Script:* Alexander Stuart, based on his novel; *Cinematography:* Seamus McGarvey; *Music:* Simon Boswell; *Cast:* Ray Winstone (Dad), Lara Belmont (Jessie), Tilda Swinton (Mum), Freddie Cunliffe (Tom), Colin J. Farrell (Nick), Aisling O'Sullivan (Carol), Kate Ashfield (Lucy), and Annabelle Apsion (Nurse).

Incest is not an unknown topic in the contemporary cinema, but often it is reduced to morally simplistic presentations designed to provoke a sense of indignation, followed by catharsis and relief when the problem is resolved within the terms of the drama. The treatment of incest in this film, unlike other films and television movies, is not used merely as a narrative device to shock or to moralize, but to establish the film's emotional complexity and heighten the audience's horror at the deception in what is, otherwise, a loving, tight-knit family. Tim Roth's direction and Alexander Stuart's script, based on his novel, reject any simplistic rendering of this social taboo.

The film is presented largely through the eyes of fifteen-year-old Tom, who with his eighteen-year-old sister Jessie and parents move from London to a remote part of Devon. The family lives openly in its small cottage and nudity and shyness do not seem part of their ethos. Dad appears caring in a rough way, while Mom is happily pregnant. On the way to the hospital, the car overturns although the family, and new baby, survive with just a few scratches.

Returning home one afternoon after the birth, Tom looks through the kitchen window and sees his father and Jessie in a sexual embrace—as the viewer is denied his visual perspective, a sense of ambiguity is retained as Jessie denies Tom's accusations. This event changes Tom's carefree reaction to his sister although they remain close. His anger boils over and he attacks her after she spends a night on the beach with Nick, her occasional boyfriend. Later, Tom's suspicions are confirmed when he watches Dad sodomizing Jessie in an abandoned concrete bunker. Jessie's relationship with her brother deteriorates further, despite a trip to London where Jessie encourages her girlfriend to seduce Tom. This act, however, is not consummated as Jessie intervenes. When the baby is taken to the hospital, Tom confronts his mother and after returning home Tom stabs his father before retreating to the concrete bunker with Jessie.

Despite the subject matter, Roth employs a traditional art-cinema form of narration by refusing to knit the various plot aspects tightly together—there are numerous scenes that deliberately fail to move the plot forward in a coherent manner and Roth and Stuart force the viewer to work hard to form some semblance of narrative coherence from the seemingly discrete scenes. Roth does, of course, intrude on the material by subtly pointing the viewer in certain directions, but the film emphasizes mood and atmosphere at the expense of pace. Similarly, it refuses to provide pat answers or even address in detail many of the issues it raises—is Jessie having a lesbian affair with her girlfriend in London and why does she intrude on the girl's seduction of Tom, after seemingly setting it up? More importantly, Roth and Stuart refuse to present Jessie as just a victim—she is a victim but not *just a* victim and her attitude toward Tom is loving although she expresses a wish that he would not interfere in her relationship with her father. Dad is both villain and, seemingly, loving father. This creates a degree of emotional confusion in the viewer with regard to his character, which is superbly conveyed by Ray Winstone.*

This is a highly disciplined film and Roth strives to construct an emotionally neutral context to explore one the of the society's last sexual taboos. It is also a strong directing debut from one of Britain's most striking contemporary actors. *The War Zone* received a positive response from the 1999 Sundance Film Festival and was awarded Best New British Feature at the 1999 Edinburgh International Film Festival.

WARNER, JACK (1896–1981). In 1947 and 1948, Jack Warner had two strong supporting roles, and one starring role, that, from the perspective of his overall career, now appear aberrant, or at least inconsistent with his dominant film (and television) image. In the 1950s, Warner was primarily seen as a policeman and/or a representative member of working-class virtues with values rooted in a strong sense of community and family. These qualities were apparent in his long-running television character P. C. Dixon in the BBC series *Dixon of Dock Green* (1955–1976). Warner's Dixon was first seen in the cinema in *The Blue Lamp** (1950) and the fact that Dirk Bogarde* murdered him midway during the film did not hinder his resurrection for television. Therefore, in *Against the Wind** (1948), when Simone Signoret discovers that Warner is a spy who has infiltrated their SOE group in Belgium, and then executes him while he is shaving, is comparable in dramatic effect to John Wayne's psychotic killing of the buffalo in *The Searchers* (1956). Warner's Covent Green wholesaler, and criminal mastermind, in the Ealing comedy *Hue and Cry** (1947) comes as less of a shock as the film's genre (comedy) allows for greater flexibility of characterization.

My Brother's Keeper* (1948) gave Warner his least typical, and best, role as the escaped convict who callously uses his wife, mistress, and fellow escapee (George Cole). Instead, the public warmed much more to Warner's Joe Huggett in *Holiday Camp* (1948) and the popular series of films that followed (*Here Comes the Huggetts* [1948], *Vote for Huggett* [1949], and *The Huggetts Abroad* [1949]). These films, and *The Blue Lamp,* were more influential in establishing and consolidating his screen persona, both on film and television.

Warner's best films came in the first part of his film career, beginning with *The Captive Heart** (1946), where, as the paternal Corporal Ted Horsfall, he sacrifices his carefully self-carved wooden ship so that the men can fire up the stove for a brew in their prison hut. It was this film that first brought Warner and Jimmy Hanley together in their (surrogate) "father and son" relationship that extended beyond *The Captive Heart* to the reform school melodrama *The Boys in Brown* (1949), with Warner as the stern but fair governor and Hanley an inmate, and *The Blue Lamp.* In the Huggett series, they played father and son.

As his film career developed, Warner was often typecast as a policeman—Inspector Penbury in the well-crafted film noir *Dear Murderer** (1947), Detective Sergeant Fothergill in *It Always Rains on Sunday** (1948), and Inspector Peterson in the *Valley of the Eagles* (1951). Lance Comfort's* neglected 1954 thriller *Bang! You're Dead* offered Warner a variation on this authoritarian, but kindly image, as Perce Bonsell, the father of a young boy who accidentally kills a man when he finds a gun left behind by a U.S. soldier after the war. While the police suspect another man, the boy is ultimately exposed as the culprit. At the close of the film, Bonsell acknowledges that through parental negligence the man's death was really his fault, not his son's.

After 1955, Warner was occupied by his television series although he took time away from his television programs to appear as another policeman, Inspector Lomax, in Val Guest's* science fiction film *The Quatermass Xperiment* (1955) and again in a brief, but funny, appearance in the final scene of *The Ladykillers** (1955) when Mrs. Wilberforce fails to convince Warner, at the police desk, that she has been living with criminals and their stolen money. Warner continued as Dixon of Dock Green on television until he was eighty years of age. He died in 1981.

FILMS: The Dummy Talks (1943), The Captive Heart (1946), Hue and Cry (1947), Dear Murderer (1947), It Always Rains on Sunday (1948), My Brother's Keeper (1948), Holiday Camp (1948), Here Come the Huggetts (1948), Easy Money (1948), Against the Wind (1948), Vote for Huggett (1949), Train of Events (1949), The Huggetts Abroad (1949), Boys in Brown (1949), The Blue Lamp (1950), Valley of the Eagles (1951), Talk of a Million (1951), Scrooge (1951), Those People Next Door (1952), Meet Me Tonight (1952), Emergency Call (1952), The Square Ring (1953), The Final Test (1953), Albert R. N. (1953), Forbidden Cargo (1954), Bang! You're Dead (1954), Break to Freedom (1955), Quatermass Xperiment (1955), Now and Forever (1955), The Ladykillers (1955), Home and Away (1956), Carve Her Name with Pride (1958), Jigsaw (1962), and Dominique (1978).

THE WAY AHEAD (Two Cities Films, 1944)—War. *Director:* Carol Reed; *Producers:* Norman Walker and Stanley Haynes (associate); *Script:* Eric Ambler and Peter Ustinov, based on a story by Peter Ustinov; *Cinematography:* Guy Green; *Music:* William Alwyn; *Cast:* David Niven (Lieutenant Jim Perry), Stanley Holloway (Private Ted Brewer), James Donald (Private Lloyd), Raymond Huntley (Private Herbert Davenport), John Laurie (Private Luke), Leslie Dwyer (Private Sid Beck), Hugh Burden (Private Bill Parsons), Jimmie Hanley (Private Geoffrey Stainer), Billy Hartnell (Sergeant Ned Fletcher), Leo Genn (Captain Edwards), Renee Asherson (Marjorie Gillingham), Mary Jerrold (Mrs. Gillingham), Peter Ustinov (Rispoli), Raymond Lovell (Mr. Jackson), and Penelope Ward (Mrs. Perry).

At the time of its release in 1944, *The Way Ahead* was celebrated for its "documentary realism." The film documented the transformation of seven "ordinary" Englishmen into a cohesive fighting unit. It was similar, in some ways, to the cycle of combat films produced in Hollywood in 1942–1943 that showed how individualism had to be subsumed by collective social and military goals (e.g., see *Air Force* [1943] and *Cry Havoc* [1943]). While the Hollywood films focused more on ethnic and racial differences, *The Way Ahead* was more concerned with the "ordinariness" of the seven men and their ability to band together as a fighting unit. Each man "represents" a class or sectional interest. Herbert Davenport, the most elitist and class conscious character, initially demands attention from his junior employee but this relationship changes throughout the film as they adjust to demands of army life—although Bill Parsons goes AWOL when his wife gets into financial trouble. Working-class mannerisms and attitudes are encapsulated in Ted Brewer, the furnace stoker, the rural section is represented by Luke, the battling farmer, and Geoffrey Stainer is the angry working-class lad. Middle-class recruit Lloyd undergoes a transformation from embittered recruit to leadership potential, and the accommodating Sid Beck completes the unit.

It is necessary to consider *The Way Ahead* within its historical context. The polemical basis of the film is now transparent as "straw dogs" are set up within the narrative—that is, broad resentment against various rules and conditions pertaining to army life—before demonstrating the necessity for such regulations and practices. The film was released at the time of the Normandy landing and commitment to the war effort and the need for unity to defeat a common enemy was paramount. The film's claim to "documentary realism," with its focus on training and preparation, was more a product of its style and the period in which it was produced.

The ending to *The Way Ahead,* as the men disappear into the smoke and dust, almost breaches the film's "realist" tone as their deaths take on a mythic dimension. The men are elevated to the status of heroes, sacrificing themselves to the common good. This is acknowledged in the film's prologue where two old soldiers celebrate the continuation of the regiment's honorable reputation. This mythical dimension is accentuated by the film's refusal to show the actual deaths of the men, preferring to follow the pattern of many Hollywood combat films (e.g., see the end of *Wake Island* [1943] and *Bataan* [1943]) by closing with their show of defiance, not their deaths.

The film is also careful to include the role of the home front, represented by the Gillingham family who throw open their house to military men so that they can bathe, eat, and entertain themselves. It is at the Gillingham house where their leader, Lieutenant Jim Perry, is finally integrated into the group. Sergeant Ned Fletcher's relationship to the men is more problematic—resulting from a confrontation between Fletcher and Stainer on a railway station just prior to his arrival at the army camp. The film, however, quickly eradicates any real display of hostility between Fletcher and the men and shows him extolling the virtues of his unit, privately, to the other officers while publicly driving the seven recruits on to greater achievements. Thus, the historical context determines what actually constitutes "reality." The unity shown in *The Way Ahead* differs markedly from the ethos of division expressed in later films, such as *The Hill** (1965).

WEDDING REHEARSAL (London Films, 1932)—Comedy. *Director:* Alexander Korda; *Producer:* Alexander Korda; *Script:* Lajos Biró, George Grossmith, Helen Gardom, and Arthur Wimperis; *Cinematography:* Leslie Rowson; *Music:* Kurt Schroeder; *Cast:* Roland Young (Reggie, the Marquis of Buckminster), George Grossmith (Earl of Stokeshire), John Loder (John Hopkins, "Bimbo"), Wendy Barrie (Lady Mary Rose Wroxbury), Joan Gardner (Lady Rosemary Wroxbury), Merle Oberon (Miss Hutchinson), Maurice Evans (George Thompson, "Tootles"), Kate Cutler (Dowager Marchioness of Buckminster), Lady Tree (Countess of Stokeshire), Morton Selten (Major Harry Wroxbury), Edmund Breon (Lord Fleet), and Diane Napier (Mrs. Dryden).

Hungarian filmmaker Alexander Korda* came to England in 1931 and established the British film studio London Films. *Wedding Rehearsal* was its first production. Although the script is based on a clever premise, it is a patchy film with an overreliance on British class stereotypes for its humor. With Korda's characteristic emphasis on strong production values, it is a good-looking film with polished cinematography by Leslie Rowson, an above average musical score and a top cast. Reggie, the Marquis of Buckminster, is reluctant to give up his unencumbered lifestyle despite the pressure from a wealthy relative, and his benefactor, to marry and provide children. When this relative, the Dowager Marchioness of Buckminster, draws up a list of eligible women, Reggie sets about marrying them off to other men so that he can retain his independence. The film concentrates on the wedding preparations of two of the women on the Dowager's list, twin sisters Lady Rosemary Wroxbury and Lady Mary Rose Wroxbury. Reggie, however, is relieved when he learns that they wish to marry "Bimbo" and "Tootles." However, during the wedding rehearsal things start to go wrong when Tootles and Bimbo overhear comments from some of the wedding guests that they are a couple of fortune-hunters with little to offer the twins. Reggie has to repair both romances and, as a precaution, he arranges for the marriage of four other women selected by the dowager. However, having manipulated so many marriages, Reggie, unexpectedly, falls in love with Miss Hutchinson, the dowager's secretary.

Wedding Rehearsal benefits from the casting of Roland Young, as Reggie, whose excellent timing and distinctive delivery lifts the mediocre script. The film lags when the focus shifts from Young to the wedding preparations of the Wroxbury twins. Korda, however, has the commercial sense to populate this lightweight film with attractive young women, such as Wendy Barrie, Joan Gardner, and Merle Oberon. Barrie and, especially, Oberon went on to a much more successful film career in Hollywood, as did John Loder, who has little to do as Bimbo, Gardner's fiancé.

THE WICKER MAN (British Lion, 1973)—Thriller/mystery/occult. *Director:* Robin Hardy; *Producer:* Peter Snell; *Script:* Anthony Shaffer; *Cinematography:* Harry Waxman; *Music:* Paul Giovanni; *Cast:* Edward Woodward (Sergeant Howie), Christopher Lee (Lord Summerisle), Diane Cilento (Miss Rose), Britt Ekland (Willow), Ingrid Pitt (Librarian), Lindsay Kemp (Alder MacGregor), and Russell Waters (Harbor Master).

Prior to the credits for *The Wicker Man,* a brief title acknowledges the contributions of "Lord Summerisle and the people of his island off the west coast of Scotland for this privileged insight into their religious practices." A strange appreciation considering the film's subject matter that involves the investigation of Sergeant Howie, a virginal, God-fearing police officer, into the reported disappearance of a young girl on a remote island off the coast of Scotland. On Summerisle's island, Howie discovers an agricultural community able to produce apples and other produce that are inconsistent with climatic rigors of its North Sea setting. However, after many years of abundance, 1972 proved to be a barren year and the residents of the island, who worship ancient gods of nature, believe that only the sacrifice of a virginal adult will ensure the return of the crops. Howie discovers, too late, that the reported disappearance of the young girl was a ruse to get him to the island so that he could be sacrificed in a giant wicker man during their May Day Festival.

The dramatic power of *The Wicker Man* emanates largely from Anthony Shaffer's intricate script, which carefully builds its story from the familiar generic basis of a mystery surrounding the disappearance of young girl (Rowen Morrison) and the policeman who encounters hostility from the locals. Howie's investigation, initially, points to a conspiracy of silence among the islanders, including the girl's mother. However, as the story progresses Howie appears less and less sympathetic due to his rigid moral code and expressions of religious bigotry. The nudity and open sexual displays of the islanders disgust him and he reproaches the local teacher, Miss Rose, after her discussion of phallic symbols in her classroom. Howie realizes that the islanders live by different moral codes, which he considers pagan. This is confirmed when Willow, a woman who initiates young boys and rejuvenates older men, invites him to join her in an adjacent room by striking on his wall while performing a sensual song and dance. If he had gone to her he may have been saved.

Lord Summerisle, Christopher Lee* in a memorable performance, also fails to impress Howie when he tries to explain the basis of the islanders' beliefs. Howie, however, cannot comprehend anything that violates his fundamentalist Christian values. Ultimately, his unyielding bias and narrow perspective make him the ideal fool for their May Day ceremony. The ending, however, still comes as a shock as Summerisle, Willow, Miss Rose, the librarian, and others chant their songs while Howie, screaming his Christian mantra, perishes in a giant wicker man.

The distribution history of *The Wicker Man* in the early 1970s is an extreme example of ineptitude. After Shaffer's script was accepted by British Lion and Robin Hardy completed the filming in Scotland, British Lion, in financial trouble, was purchased and the new owners butchered the film by severely editing it and releasing it as a second-feature horror film (with the marketing based solely on the presence of Lee). After the distribution rights were sold to National General, the company was declared bankrupt and when Warner Brothers acquired the rights, it shelved the film. Over the years, faithful supporters have promoted its status.

WILCOX, HERBERT (1892–1977)/**NEAGLE, ANNA** (1904–1986). Herbert Wilcox entered the British film industry by establishing a film distribution company with his brother. Wilcox's ability to gauge public taste was a crucial factor in his longevity—until the commercial disasters of the 1950s. Wilcox was a significant factor in guiding the successful career of Anna Neagle, who became his wife in 1940. The Wilcox "formula," developed in the 1920s, was not unusual (the importance of a major star associated with a popular genre). But Wilcox was skilled in deciding which genre to utilize at different times. Although Neagle remarked that they preferred "films that were light and gay,"[1] not all of the Wilcox-Neagle films were optimistic and "escapist"—even one of the so-called London cycle, *Piccadilly Incident* (1946), ends on a downbeat note.

Wilcox enjoyed success in the 1920s, especially after he transferred the popular stage show *Chu Chin Chow* to the screen in 1923. This was followed by four films with imported American star Dorothy Gish (such as *Nell Gwyn* [1926]) and in the 1930s the Aldwych farces were also popular. However, it was his chance encounter with Neagle in 1932, when visiting the Hippodrome to meet Jack Buchanan, that changed the careers of both Wilcox and Neagle. Neagle, born Florence Marjorie Robertson, appeared in the Wilcox-directed musicals *The Little Damozel* (1933), *Bitter Sweet* (1933), and *The Queen's Affair* (1934), but it was *Nell Gwyn* 1934) and *Peg of Old Dury* (1935) that gave her career a boost as both films allowed Neagle a stronger sexual presence. Wilcox transformed Neagle yet again in one of their greatest film successes, *Victoria the Great* (1937), emphasizing a more conservative femininity.

Buoyed by the success of *Victoria the Great,* and its facsimile *Sixty Glorious Years* (1938), Wilcox and Neagle spent the early years of World War II in the

United States. The films they produced in Hollywood did not match their successes of the late 1930s so they returned to Britain and, after a couple of war-related films, such as the spy film *The Yellow Canary* (1943), they made the so-called London or Mayfair cycle, beginning with *I Live in Grosvenor Square* (1945). This film, starring Rex Harrison, Hollywood actor Dean Jagger, and Neagle, casts Jagger as an American serviceman in London who falls in love with Neagle (a member of the Women's Auxiliary Air Force). So that unity between the Allies would not be disturbed, Jagger, after enjoying the pleasures of the British aristocracy, dies in the war, thus allowing Harrison to marry Neagle. When Harrison was not available for the next film, *Piccadilly Incident,* Michael Wilding starred opposite Neagle and this romantic drama, based on lovers separated by the war, was followed by three more commercially successful films—*The Courtneys of Curzon Street* (1947), *Spring in Park Lane* (1948), and *Maytime in Mayfair* (1948), all costarring Neagle and Wilding. These lightweight films (Neagle described them as "pleasant films about pleasant people"),[2] were carefully controlled by Wilcox so as to present his wife in the best possible light and the glossy production values were helped by the fact that they were filmed at MGM's British studio. *The Courtneys of Curzon Street* and *Spring in Park Lane* were the top British box office successes of their respective years.

The 1950s for Wilcox and Neagle were less successful, although they did have some success with their "Great Woman" films: *Odette* (1950), the story of Frenchwoman Odette Churchill's torture and imprisonment by the Nazis during World War II, and *The Lady with a Lamp* (1951), based on Florence Nightingale's heroic deeds in the Crimea. Their other 1950s films were disappointing—two films co-starring a visibly aging Errol Flynn with Neagle (*Lilacs in the Spring* [1954] and *King's Rhapsody* [1956]) failed at the box office and a return to the Neagle-Wilding partnership in *Derby Day* (1952) proved to be a disaster. Similarly, their attempt to turn singer Frankie Vaughan into a film star in the late 1950s was also a failure with Neagle producing most of these films. Neagle returned to the stage for the remainder of her career and she was made a Dame of the British Empire in 1969. Wilcox, who co-founded Elstree Studios in 1926, and became head of production at British and Dominions in 1928, ended his career in bankruptcy in 1964.

FILMS: Herbert Wilcox (as director): Chu Chin Chow (1923), Southern Love (1924), Decameron Nights (1924), The Only Way (1925), Nell Gwyn (1926), London (1926), Tiptoes (1927), Mumsie (1927), Madame Pompadour (1927), Dawn (1928), The Bondman (1929), The Woman in White (1929), Rookery Nook (1930), The Loves of Robert Burns (1930), Wolves (1930), The Speckled Band (1931), Money Means Nothing (codir., 1931), The Chance of a Night Time (codir., 1931), Plunder (1931), Carnival (1931), Goodnight Vienna (1932), Yes, Mr. Brown (1932), The Blue Danube (1932), The Little Damozel (1933), The King's Cup (1933), Bitter Sweet (1933), The Queen's Affair (1934), Nell Gwyn (1934), Peg of Old Dury (1935), The Three Maxims (1936), This'll Make You Whistle (1936), Limelight (1936), Victoria the Great (1937), London Melody (1937), Sixty Glorious Years (1938), Nurse Edith Cavell (1939), Irene (1940), No, No, Nanette

(1940), They Flew Alone (1941), Sunny (1941), The Yellow Canary (1943), Forever and a Day (codir., 1943), I Live in Grosvenor Square (1945), Piccadilly Incident (1946), The Courtneys of Curzon Street (1947), Spring in Park Lane (1948), Maytime in Mayfair (1949), Elizabeth of Ladymead (1948), Into the Blue (1950), Odette (1951), The Lady with a Lamp (1951), Trent's Last Case (1952), Derby Day (1952), Trouble in the Glen (1953), Laughing Anne (1953), Lilacs in the Spring (1954), King's Rhapsody (1955), My Teenage Daughter (1956), These Dangerous Years (1957), Wonderful Things (1958), The Man Who Wouldn't Talk (1958), The Lady Is a Square (1959), and The Heart of a Man (1959).

   Anna Neagle: Should a Doctor Tell? (1931), The Chinese Bungalow (1931), Goodnight, Vienna (1932), The Flag Lieutenant (1933), The Little Damozel (1933), Bitter Sweet (1933), The Queen's Affair (1934), Nell Gwyn (1934), Peg of Old Dury (1935), The Three Maxims (1936), Limelight (1936), Victoria the Great (1937), London Melody (1937), Sixty Glorious Years (1938), Nurse Edith Cavell (1939), Irene (1940), No, No, Nanette (1940), They Flew Alone (1941), Sunny (1941), The Yellow Canary (1943), Forever and a Day (1943), I Live in Grosvenor Square (1945), Piccadilly Incident (1946), The Courtneys of Curzon Street (1947), Spring in Park Lane (1948), Maytime in Mayfair (1949), Elizabeth of Ladymead (1948), Odette (1951), The Lady with a Lamp (1951), Derby Day (1952), Lilacs in the Spring (1954), King's Rhapsody (1955), My Teenage Daughter (1956), No Time for Tears (1957), The Man Who Wouldn't Talk (1958), and The Lady Is a Square (1959).

THE WINGS OF THE DOVE (Miramax/Renaissance Dove, 1997)—Historical melodrama/tragedy. *Director:* Iain Softley; *Producers:* Stephen Evans and David Parfitt; *Script:* Hossein Amini, based on the novel by Henry James; *Cinematography:* Eduardo Serro; *Music:* Edward Shearmur; *Cast:* Helena Bonham Carter (Kate Croy), Linus Roache (Merton Densher), Alison Elliott (Milly Theale), Elizabeth McGovern (Susan), Michael Gambon (Mr. Croy), Alex Jennings (Lord Mark), and Charlotte Rampling (Aunt Maud).

   Arguably the best British film of the 1990s, *The Wings of the Dove* is that rare adaptation that captures the essence of its source while establishing its own status as a great film. In early twentieth-century London, Kate Croy lives with her wealthy Aunt Maud but loves (relatively) poor radical journalist Merton Densher. Maude, however, opposes this union and promotes Lord Mark as a more suitable partner for Kate. Kate, who is forced to meet Merton secretly, is dependent on Maud for the financial support of her drug-addicted father. Thus, while Kate wants financial security, she also wishes to retain Merton as her lover. To this end, Kate develops a diabolical plan to replace the patronage of Aunt Maud with the financial support of a wealthy American visitor Milly Theale ("the world's richest orphan").

   At the dinner party that reunites Kate with Merton, she also meets Milly and her companion Susan. They meet again in a London bookshop where Kate boldly leads Milly to the pornographic section at the rear of the shop where Kate picks up one of the books and opens it to the sexual image of two women sharing one man, a revealing image that foreshadows events in Venice when Merton joins

Kate and Milly. When Lord Mark tells Kate that Milly is dying, she devises her plan with Merton as the (romantic) bait.

In Venice, Kate brings Merton and Milly together, first in a gondola ride at night, and then at the night of carnival. In between these two events, Kate outlines aspects of her plan to Merton, after telling him that Milly is dying. When Merton asks is that why she wanted him to come to Venice, Kate replies, "For her. . . . And for us." However, the seeds of Kate's downfall also begin that night as she watches Milly and Merton dance together, followed by a kiss from the American. Confusion begins to erode her confidence as she fears that Merton may actually fall in love with the beautiful American. To reassure herself, Kate takes Merton into the darkness and encourages a sexual response from him. However, when Kate stops short of sexual intercourse, Merton "blackmails" her into sexually consummating their relationship as his price for participating in her scheme.

This troubling scene allows the audience an insight into another, less complimentary, aspect of Merton. Similarly, Kate's doubts concerning Milly and Merton begins her transformation from melodramatic villain to the tragic heroine. Eventually, Kate's fear that she will lose Merton overcomes her desire for financial security and this fear destroys not only her scheme, but also her relationship with Merton. In the film's final scene, she finds that, even after Milly's death, she cannot accept Merton unless he is able to convince her that he is not in love with Milly's memory. Merton is unable to answer this request from Kate, so she leaves him and he returns to Venice to assuage his guilt.

The three principals are totally convincing with Helena Bonham Carter* a standout as the complex Kate Croy. Bonham Carter was nominated for the Best Actress Award at the 1998 Academy Awards.

WINGS OF THE MORNING (New World/Twentieth Century Fox, 1937)— Melodrama. *Director:* Harold Schuster; *Producer:* Robert Kane; *Script:* Thomas J. Geraghty and Donn Byrne (story); *Cinematography:* Jack Cardiff and Ray Renahan; *Music:* Arthur Benjamin; *Cast:* Annabella (Marie, Maria), Henry Fonda (Kerry), Leslie Banks (Lord Clontarf), D. J. Williams (Marik), Stewart Rome (Sir Valentine), Irene Vanbrugh (Maria), Helen Haye (Jenepher), John McCormack (himself), Harry Tate (Paddy), and Phillip Frost (Valentine).

Wings of the Morning, Britain's first Technicolor film, utilizes many of the conventions of nineteenth-century melodrama, including an emphasis on bloodlines, both horse and human. The first part of the story provides a thematic context for the bulk of the film—the Earl of Clontarf (Leslie Banks*) falls in love with Maria (Annabella), a beautiful gypsy woman, and he agrees to protect the rights of gypsies on his land. Although Clontarf's relatives and friends treat Maria with disdain, except Clontarf's young cousin Valentine, the marriage between Clontarf and Maria is a happy one until Clontarf dies following a riding accident. Maria, pregnant, returns to the gypsies after a gypsy woman tells her that her blood will be cursed for three generations. Maria moves to Spain where, fifty years later, she is threatened by the Spanish Civil War. Maria's great-granddaughter, Marie (Annabella), engaged to an (impoverished) Spanish nobleman, flees the fighting in Spain dressed as a young boy and joins her great-grandmother in Ireland where she meets Kerry, a Canadian nephew of Valentine.

Kerry, a horse trainer, acquires Wings, a promising young horse, from Marie in exchange for five of his horses. When Maria points out to her great-granddaughter that this was a bad bargain, young Marie, still dressed as a boy, goes back to Kerry to regain Wings. When Wings escapes, Kerry and Marie pursue the horse and are forced to spend a night together in a barn. However, Kerry discovers that Marie is a woman, not a young boy, when he rips off her clothes in an attempt to throw her into a river. Soon, after seeing her in evening clothes, Kerry falls in love with Marie. Complications concerning her engagement to the Spanish nobleman are resolved at the English Derby when Wings wins the race, thereby restoring Maria, through Marie, to the Clontarf family. However, the film's ending does not signify Maria's return to the aristocracy as Kerry, with his U.S.–Canadian associations (reinforced by the casting of Henry Fonda), is decidedly middle class and democratic—unlike the more formal members of the Clontarf family.

Wings of the Morning is noteworthy because it was Britain's first color film with superb cinematography by Jack Cardiff and veteran Hollywood cinematographer Ray Rennehan, one of the pioneers of tricolor photography in the early 1930s. Fonda brings his easy manner to the film, which contrasts sharply with the stiff performance of Banks as Lord Clontarf and Annabella (in her first English language film after starring in French films since 1926) in a dual role as the young Maria and Marie.

Annabella is more at ease masquerading as a young boy, and her scenes flirting with Henry Fonda, where he mistakes her for a male, are the most interesting moments in the film as they exploit the "forbidden" concept of homosexual desire while also allowing sexual situations that would normally be heavily censored—such as Kerry's insistence that Marie bring him a towel when he is naked in the bathtub, despite the fact that she is clearly embarrassed by his open display of nudity. Similarly, their night together in the barn, within the rigid censorship context of the late 1930s, allows Annabella to stroke Fonda in a loving manner and these scenes, including the bathtub episode, caused Joseph Breen and the U.S. Production Code Administration concern, and some local censorship boards in the United States removed this material.[3]

THE WINSLOW BOY (British Lion Film Corporation, 1948)—Melodrama. *Director:* Anthony Asquith, *Producers:* Anatole de Grunwald, Teddy Baird (associate), *Script:* Terence Rattigan,Anatole de Grunwald, based on the play by Terence Rattigan, *Cinematography:* Freddie Young, *Music:* William Alwyn. *Cast:* Robert Donat (Sir Robert Morton), Cedric Hardwicke (Arthur Winslow), Basil Radford (Desmond Curry), Margaret Leighton (Catherine Winslow), Kathleen Harrison (Violet), Neil North (Ronnie Winslow), Frances L. Sullivan (Attorney General), Marie Lohr (Grace Winslow), Jack Watling (Dickie

Winslow), Walter Fitzgerald (First Lord of the Admiralty), Frank Lawton (John Watherstone).

THE WINSLOW BOY (Sony Picture Classics, 1999)—Melodrama. *Director:* David Mamet; *Producer:* Sarah Green; *Script:* David Mamet, based on the play by Terence Rattigan; *Cinematography:* Benoit Delhomme; *Music:* Alaric Jans; *Cast:* Nigel Hawthorne (Arthur Winslow), Jeremy Northam (Sir Robert Morton), Rebecca Pidgeon (Catherine Winslow), Gemma Jones (Grace Winslow), Guy Edwards (Ronnie Winslow), Matthew Pidgeon (Dickie Winslow), Colin Stinton (Desmond Curry), Aden Gillett (John Watherstone), Sarah Flind (Violet), and Neil North (First Lord of the Admiralty).

Both versions of *The Winslow Boy* (1948, 1999) are based on events surrounding the 1910 trial of George Archer-Shee, a thirteen-year-old cadet at the Osborne Naval Academy who was accused of stealing a five shilling postal order, and the determination of the boy's father, a Liverpool bank manager, to fight this accusation by enlisting the barrister who prosecuted Oscar Wilde in his famous libel suite. Both films follow Terence Rattigan's play, which altered the names and some of the facts (e.g., the date was changed to 1912 and the Winslow family home was relocated to South Kensington) for his 1946 play. The first film version appeared two years later with Rattigan adapting his play, in conjunction with director Anthony Asquith* and producer Anatole de Grunwald.

Ronnie Winslow returns home from the Royal Naval Academy in disgrace after his expulsion for allegedly stealing a five shilling postal note. Ronnie's arrival coincides with the family's celebration of Catherine Winslow's engagement to John Watherstone and only the maid's (Violet) mistake in providing an extra glass alerts the boy's father, Arthur Winslow, to his presence in the home. The rest of the family attempts to shield both father and son from the ramifications of the news until after the celebration. After questioning Ronnie, Arthur is convinced his son did not commit the theft and thereby embarks on an obsessive path to clear his name, a path that adversely affects all concerned.

Arthur selects the celebrated barrister and conservative politician Sir Robert Morton to fight his case and this imposes severe strain on the family's finances. The growing notoriety of the case, celebrated in music halls and in the popular media, destroys Catherine's engagement to Watherstone while Arthur is forced to terminate Dickie's candidature at Oxford University because of his son's poor academic record and the £200 required to maintain him at university. As the fight continues for many months, both the health of Arthur and Morton deteriorate. Morton also has to decline an offer to become the next chief justice so that he can continue the case.

Initially, Morton's appointment by Arthur to represent the family is opposed by Catherine because of his conservative social beliefs, including his opposition to the suffragette movement that Catherine actively supports. Catherine's perception that Morton's alliance with conservative legal causes will disrupt his active processing of the case proves to be incorrect as Morton's determination to "let right be done" overrides all other considerations. However, the costs—financial, vocational, health-wise, and emotional—on the Winslow family and their supporters are immense and both film versions emphasize that the key question was not Ronnie's guilt, or otherwise, but the right of every British citizen to a fair trial.

Both Asquith's 1948 film and American David Mamet's 1999 version replicate these events while sharing the prevailing discourse involving the principle of "let right be done." There are, however, significant differences between the two versions. While the 1948 film reenacts portions of the trial and, generally, provides more material so that the audience can more easily understand the motivation of the characters, Mamet strips the play back to an elemental level, resisting the temptation to exploit the high points of the trial, such as Morton's devastating cross-examination of the handwriting expert Ridgeley-Pearce (which is included in the 1948 version). Instead, Mamet compresses information into newspaper headlines and other sources, preferring to remain at the level of the family and focus on their reaction, especially Arthur's and Catherine's, to the various pieces of news as it reaches the family home.

The Winslow Boy (both versions) provides a celebration of the Edwardian patriarchy through the determination of Arthur to vindicate his son. Only when his daughter's happiness is jeopardized, by Watherstone's decision to break off the engagement, does his resolve weaken. In the years since World War II, such representations are rare. Similarly, while nuances of acting styles and character inflections reflect the period in which the films were made, as opposed to the period in which they were set, most notably in Rebecca Pidgeon's Catherine Winslow and her erotic sparring with Robert Morton, which essays a more spirited presentation of equality and defiance than Margaret Leighton's more subdued performance, both films are marked by superb performances with Nigel Hawthorne's Arthur Winslow supreme.

Jeremy Northam won Best British Performance at the 1999 Edinburgh International Film Festival and Mamet won the Los Charales Award for Best Studio Feature Film at the 1999 Ajijic International Film Festival. Neil North played Ronnie Winslow in the 1948 film and the First Lord of the Admiralty in Mamet's version.

WINSTONE, RAY (b. 1957). Both Gary Oldman (*Nil by Mouth** [1997]) and Tim Roth (*The War Zone** [1999]) cast Ray Winstone in lead roles in their debut films. While each role shares strong negative traits, as the brutal, wife-bashing foul-mouthed Ray in *Nil by Mouth,* and the psychologically disturbed father who regularly commits incest with his daughter in *The War Zone,* each role is also different in tone and performance. In *The War Zone,* for example, Winstone, despite committing one of society's gravest crimes, avoids the melodramatic trappings that often accompanies such material and his ability to present himself as a "normal," caring parent creates a disturbing moral dimension within the overall film.

Prominent influences on Winstone include his long stint as an amateur boxer, beginning when he was twelve and winning medals, trophies, and English representation. He also admired James Cagney. While both actors assume a street-wise aggressive image, they also share the ability to suggest danger and confrontation even in their tender scenes. Winstone studied acting as a teenager, before expulsion, at the Corona School. This did little for his employment prospects and he had decided to forgo acting when director Alan Clarke cast him as the lead role in *Scum,* a television film focusing on violence within a reform school. When the BBC shelved *Scum,* Winstone worked in a range of lowly paid jobs, such as selling fruit, before the decision to convert *Scum* into a feature film revived his acting ambitions. He followed it with other dramas involving teenage violence, such as *Quadrophenia* (1979) and *That Summer* (1979). This film consolidated his career with a BAFTA nomination for the Most Promising Newcomer to a Leading Film Role.

Winstone was prolific in television throughout the 1980s and early 1990s and in films from the mid-1990s, with a lead roles in Ken Loach's* *Ladybird, Ladybird* (1994), in the tough crime-revenge drama *Face* (1997), as Dave the robber who betrays fellow criminal Robert Carlyle, and in *Nil by Mouth,* winning international recognition and a BAFTA Best Actor nomination. Winstone also costarred with Ben Kingsley in *Sexy Beast* (2000) and, although Kingsley had the more extroverted role as the psychotic hit man, Winstone more than held his own as the ex-criminal retiring to Spain while trying to extricate himself from his criminal associates in Britain. Winstone contributed another strong performance as Michael Caine's adopted son in Fred Schepisi's bittersweet drama *Last Orders* (2002).

FILMS: Scum (1979), Quadrophenia (1979), That Summer (1979), All Washed Up (1981), Tank Malling (1989), Ladybird, Ladybird (1994), Nil by Mouth (1997), Face (1997), Our Boy (1997), Martha, Meet Frank, Daniel and Laurence (1998), The Sea Change (1998), Darkness Falls (1998), Woundings (1998), Final Cut (1998), The War Zone (1999), Agnes Browne (1999), Fanny and Elvis (1999), Five Seconds to Spare (1999), Love, Honour and Obey (2000), Sexy Beast (2000), There's Only One Jimmy Grimble (2001), Last Orders (2002), The Martins (2002), and Ripley's Game (2003).

WISDOM, NORMAN (b. 1917). The last great British comic to come out of the English music halls, Norman Wisdom's popularity increased due mainly to his television appearances from 1948. While appearing in *Paris to Piccadilly* at the Prince of Wales Theatre, Wisdom was signed to a seven-year film contract by Rank. After a false start, when he was pulled from his first film, the previews for his next film, *Trouble in Store* (1953) at the Odeon in Camden Town, showed Rank that they had a hit on their hands and a new film star. From 1953, until the series ended with *Press for Time* in 1966, Wisdom's low-budget films never failed at the box office and although they were less popular with the critics, they generated substantial revenue for Rank.

The formula for the Rank-Wisdom films was remarkably consistent, especially Wisdom's character, always called "Norman," the perennial good-hearted "little man," who Wisdom labeled the "Gump," meaning a simple, working-class man who failed to understand that evil and duplicity was ever present. This would bring him pain and humiliation although he would never give up. Wisdom's first six films were directed by John Paddy Carstairs, ending with one of his best and most commercially successful films: *The Square Peg** (1958). When Robert Asher, who had been working as the floor manager on most of the Carstairs-Wisdom films, was promoted to the position of director, which he occupied for six films with Wisdom, the ever-present pathos and sentimentality of the formula was intensified, beginning with the first Asher-directed film *Follow a Star** (1959). The relentless humiliation of Norman by Jerry Desmonde, a regular cast member in the Wisdom films, makes this film less enjoyable than the reactive aggressiveness demonstrated by Wisdom in his earlier films, especially *The Square Peg* where he has a dual role as an army private and a Nazi general—a technique repeated in *On the Beat* (1962) and *A Stitch in Time* (1963), where Wisdom also played a nurse.

Although Wisdom's style has often been associated with George Formby and other British music hall comics, the emphasis in his films on physical comedy, and his recurring characterization as a simple, disaster-prone victim, was similar to the early Jerry Lewis films. Rarely did he deviate from this formula and when he did, such as two films for United Artists in the early 1960s, *There Was a Crooked Man* (1960) and *The Girl on the Boat* (1961), the public was not enthusiastic. Wisdom returned to Rank, Asher, and his proven formula for the remaining films in the series, which concluded in 1966.

While starring on Broadway in a musical version of *Hobson's Choice,* called *Walking Happy,* in 1966, he was approached by Hollywood director William Friedkin for a prominent supporting role as burlesque comic Chick Williams in *The Night They Raided Minsky's* (1968). Wisdom then returned to London for *What's Good for the Goose* (1969), his last, and worst, film as a bank clerk involved with a girl (Sally Geeson) who was far different from the virtuous heroines of his 1950s films. This attempt to exploit the growing permissiveness of the cinema in the late 1960s failed, and Wisdom resented director Menahem Golan's attempt to change his character.

Wisdom won the Most Promising Newcomer Award at the 1954 BAFTA Film Awards for *Trouble in Store* (1953) and received a knighthood in 2001.

FILMS: A Date with a Dream (1948), Trouble in Store (1953), One Good Turn (1954), Man of the Moment (1955), As Long As They're Happy (1955), Up in the World (1956), Just My Luck (1957), The Square Peg (1958), Follow a Star (1959), There Was a Crooked Man (1960), The Bulldog Breed (1960), The Girl on the Boat (1961), On the Beat (1962), A Stitch in Time (1963), The Early Bird (1965), The Sandwich Man (1966), Press for Time (1966), The Night They Raided Minsky's (1968), What's Good for the Goose (1969) and Double X (1992).

WITCHFINDER GENERAL (Tigon, 1968)—Historical drama/horror. *Director:* Michael Reeves; *Producers:* Louis M. Heyward, Arnold L. Miller, and Phillip Waddilove; *Script:* Michael Reeves, Louis M. Heyward, and Tom Baker, from the novel by Ronald Bassett; *Cinematography:* John Coquillon; *Music:* Paul

Ferris; *Cast:* Vincent Price (Matthew Hopkins), Ian Oglivy (Richard Marshall), Rupert Davies (John Lowes), Hilary Dwyer (Sara), Robert Russell (John Stearne), and Nicky Henson (Trooper Swallow).

At the age of twenty-four, Michael Reeves directed and co-scripted his finest and last film: *Witchfinder General.* Within a few months of the film's release, Reeves had died of an overdose of sleeping pills and his meager film legacy consisted of two Italian co-productions: *The Sorcerers* (1967), starring Boris Karloff, and *Witchfinder General.* Reeves's film is set in the Civil War and follows the barbaric activities of Matthew Hopkins in torturing and murdering (mainly) women and some men. The film explores the problematic appeal of violence and the punitive role of the state. The parallel between the pernicious witch-hunting operations of Hopkins, sanctioned by the state, and the social divisions in contemporary (mid- to late 1960s) society is apparent.

Hopkins and his equally sadistic assistant John Stearne systematically violate the villages of East Anglia in the 1640s seeking out local nominations for the Devil's disciples. For every witch burned at the stake, Hopkins and Stearne receive a bounty, plus the opportunity to rape and humiliate numerous women. When they execute priest John Lowes, and rape his niece Sara, trooper Richard Marshall deserts from fighting the Royalists on behalf of Oliver Cromwell to avenge his fiancée and her uncle. Within this elemental premise, Reeves works effectively with a low budget and he carefully contrasts the tranquil scenes of the English countryside with the sordid violence inflicted by Hopkins and his followers. Reeves even uses the zoom judiciously.

In the film's morally problematic ending, Marshall traps Hopkins in a dungeon and hacks him to death in front of a distressed Sara. Only a bullet from a trooper puts Hopkins out of his misery while Marshall screams at the soldier: "You took him away, you took him away." Reeves, determined to leave the viewer with an unsettling ending, zooms in on the demented face of Sara as she cannot stop screaming. Thus, Reeves cleverly shifts the madness and violence from the sociopath Hopkins to the romantic couple, as the end credits appear over a close-up of Sara's distressed face.

Reeves wanted Donald Pleasance as Matthew Hopkins (which would have been more consistent with the film's U.S. release title *The Conqueror Worm* [1968], based on the Edgar Allan Poe poem), but the U.S. distributor insisted on Vincent Price because of the actor's association with Roger Corman's series of Poe-inspired horror films. This decision proved to be correct as Price dominates the screen with his chilling mixture of lechery and cruelty and provides one of the best performances of his long career.

WITHERS, GOOGIE (b. 1917). Born Georgette Withers in Karachi, India, Googie Withers acquired her nickname early in her professional career. After a succession of "quota quickies" in the 1930s, beginning with Michael Powell's* *The Girl in the Crowd* (1934), Withers was perceived within the industry as a comic actor due to her films with, among others, George Formby* and Will Hay,* and it was difficult for her to win "serious" dramatic roles. Her breakthrough came with Powell, who told her that because she was half-Dutch he wanted her for *One of Our Aircraft Is Missing* (1942).[4] This was quickly followed by *The Silver Fleet* (1942) with Ralph Richardson.* After these two successful films, she disappeared from the cinema for nearly two years to star in the play *They Came to a City,* which was made into a film by Ealing in 1944. Although Withers resisted pressure to change her name for the play, it was a success even though she had no formal stage training.

The mid- to late 1940s was Withers's golden period in the cinema, especially her Ealing films for Robert Hamer.* This period began with the "Haunted Mirror" episode in *Dead of Night** (1945), with Withers presenting husband Ralph Michael with a mirror that threatens their marriage and nearly causes her death. Her other films at Ealing emphasized an image of brazen sexuality combined with assertive characteristics. Often, in her films a tension is created due to the conflict between her desires and the expectations of society. This was evident in her best film, Hamer's *It Always Rains on Sunday** (1947), as Edward Chapman's wife Rose, who sees a way out of her mundane existence when her convict ex-boyfriend escapes jail and re-enters her life. This jeopardizes not only her marriage, but also her freedom when she shelters him from the law.

In Hamer's superb film noir *Pink String and Sealing Wax** (1945), Withers, as Pearl Bond, slowly poisons her publican husband (Garry Marsh) in a desperate attempt to win the love of a selfish lover. To assist in the murder, she seduces young Gordon Jackson, who has access to the ingredients necessary to carry out the deed. A more sympathetic figure, although equally determined and independent, was Withers as Joanna Godden in *The Loves of Joanna Godden* (1947), who inherits a struggling sheep farm on the Romney Marsh. Godden, despite the dire warnings of a childhood boyfriend (John McCallum), and with the assistance of Chips Rafferty, sets out to prove the men wrong while overcoming emotional and physical obstacles in the process.

After *It Always Rains on Sunday,* Withers's films were more conventional and an attempt to rework the dramatic intensity of her best film, *It Always Rains on Sunday,* in Herbert Wilcox's *Derby Day** (1952) was unsuccessful. Although she also starred in a series of comedies for Gainsborough—*Miranda* (1948), *Once upon a Dream* (1949), and *Traveller's Joy* (1949)—the only notable films for Withers after 1947 were the hospital melodrama *White Corridors* (1951) and Jules Dassin's masterly film noir *Night and the City** (1950). In this bleak, fatalistic film noir, co-starring Richard Widmark and Gene Tierney, Withers extended the ruthless strand of her screen persona as the calculating, adulterous wife of Francis L. Sullivan. In the mid-1950s, Withers and husband John McCallum emigrated to Australia, where they became formidable figures on the Australian stage and within the entertainment industry. This included an occasional sojourn into film, such as *Nickel Queen* (1971), and television production. Withers also had a prominent role in *Country Life* (1994) and a supporting role in the award-winning Australian film *Shine* (1996).

FILMS: The Girl in the Crowd (1934), The Love Test (1934), Windfall (1935), Her Last Affaire (1935), All at Sea (1935), Dark World (1935), Crown vs Stevens (1936), King of Hearts (1936), She Knew What She Wanted (1936), Accused (1936), Crime over London (1936), Pearls Bring Tears (1937), Paradise for Two (1937), Action for Slander (1938), Paid in Error (1938), If I Were Boss (1938), Kate Plus Ten (1938), Strange Boarders (1938), Convict 99 (1938), The Lady Vanishes (1938), You're the Doctor (1938), Murder in Soho (1939), Trouble Brewing (1939), Dead Men Are Dangerous (1939), The Gang's All Here (1939), She Couldn't Say No (1939), Bulldog Sees It Through (1939), Busman's Holiday (1940), Jeannie (1941), Back Room Boy (1942), One of Our Aircraft Is Missing (1942), The Silver Fleet (1942), On Approval (1944), They Came to a City (1944), Dead of Night (1945), Pink String and Sealing Wax (1945), The Loves of Joanna Godden (1947), It Always Rains on Sunday (1947), Miranda (1948), Once upon a Dream (1949), Traveller's Joy (1949), Night and the City (1950), White Corridors (1951), The Magic Box (1951), Derby Day (1952), Devil on Horseback (1954), Port of Escape (1956), Nickel Queen (1971), Country Life (1994), and Shine (1996).

NOTES

1. McFarlane, *An Autobiography of British Cinema,* p. 428.
2. McFarlane, *An Autobiography of British Cinema,* p. 428.
3. Slide, *"Banned In The USA,"* p. 146.
4. McFarlane, *An Autobiography of British Cinema,* p. 608.

Y

THE YOUNG LOVERS (General, 1954)—Political thriller/love story. *Director:* Anthony Asquith; *Producer:* Anthony Havelock-Allen; *Script:* George Tabori and Robin Estridge; *Cinematography:* Jack Asher; *Music:* Benjamin Frankel; *Cast:* Odile Versois (Anna Szobek), David Knight (Ted Hutchens), David Kossoff (Geza Szobek), Joseph Tomelty (Moffatt), Paul Carpenter (Gregg Pearson), Theodore Bikel (Joseph), and Betty Marsden (Mrs. Forrester).

Despite producer Anthony Havelock-Allen's lament that *The Young Lovers* could have been a much better film if Rank had allocated a larger budget to attract James Stewart to the film and selected a much tougher director (Havelock-Allen wanted Hollywood director Mark Robson) instead of Anthony Asquith,* *The Young Lovers* is both a fascinating historical document as well as a touching love story. At a time when Hollywood would not consider producing any (liberal) film that directly repudiated the anti-communist hysteria of the period, except in the form of disguised, generic metaphors such as *High Noon* (1952) and *Johnny Guitar* (1954), *The Young Lovers,* written by anti-Fascist author George Tabori, had the courage to criticize the obsessive, single-mindedness of both the East and the West in the early 1950s.

While attending a ballet performance of *Swan Lake,* young U.S. embassy official Ted Hutchens meets Anna Szobek, the daughter of a high-ranking official of an unnamed East European legation in London. Initially, both Anna and Ted are unaware of each other's background and they quickly fall in love. Although Ted works in a high-security area in the embassy, he fails to inform his employer of his romance with a communist. Similarly, Anna tries, unsuccessfully, to hide her relationship with Ted from her father, Geza Szobek. After learning of Anna's affair, Geza orders his daughter to stop all contact with Ted, despite her plea that she loves the American. Geza dismisses this by pointing out the harsh realities of the situation: "Anna, the world is divided into two and you cannot escape that fact by running away from it. And is there any place to which you could run?"

Anna tries to stay away from Ted, but when she learns that she is pregnant, she meets him for the one last time in a bookshop. Because of this indiscretion, her father decides to send her back home, but on the train from London to Newhaven Ted rescues her and they hide out from both sides in a boarding house in Brighton. As the British police close in, the lovers take a small boat out to sea in bad weather. However, before sailing away, Anna leaves a note for her father on a pier and, believing that his daughter is dead, Geza reads her words to representatives of both the East and West gathered on a lonely beach. Anna's note is a deliberate rejoinder to her father's earlier reference to the restrictions imposed on love in a polarized world: "Dear father, we are running away not because we are guilty but because you will not believe that we are innocent. You say that the world is divided into two, that we cannot escape that fact. We are going to try. You, who live in separate worlds, can no longer believe in innocence because you no longer believe in love. But without love you will destroy not, as you think, each other, but yourselves."

The romantic ending to the film shifts the tone away from the its semi-realist mode that dominates much of the production, reinforced by Jack Asher's low-key black and white photography, closer to romantic fantasy. Just prior to reading Anna's note, Ted and Anna appear doomed, as they battle the raging sea. However, after Geza finishes reading the note, the film cuts to Anna and Ted standing close together as their boat moves smoothly over the calm sea and beautiful weather. This is a reference to the miraculous "third place," that area between the East and West that Geza and the U.S. embassy officials would not acknowledge as existing in the polarized world of the Cold War.

Benjamin Frankel's musical adaptation of Peter Tchaikovsky's *Swan Lake* is used effectively through the film to reinforce the sense of desperation and longing between the two lovers. Fittingly, the dominant musical motif from *Swan Lake* is the last sound heard in the film. *The Young Lovers* is also enriched by the touching performance of Odile Versois as the vulnerable Anna Szobek.

Z

ZULU (Diamond Films, 1964)—Empire film. *Director:* Cy Endfield; *Producers:* Stanley Baker and Cy Endfield; *Script:* John Prebble and Cy Raker Endfield; *Cinematography:* Stephen Dade; *Music:* John Barry; *Cast:* Stanley Baker (Lieutenant John Chard), Jack Hawkins (Reverend Otto Witt), Ulla Jackobson (Margereta Witt), James Booth (Private Henry Hook), Michael Caine (Lieutenant Gonville Bromhead), Nigel Green (Color Sergeant Fred Bourne), Glynn Edwards (Corporal William Allen), Patrick Magee (Surgeon Major James Henry Reynolds), Richard Davies (Private William Jones), and Richard Burton (Narrator).

While John Barry's music is often associated with the James Bond series, his exciting, ominous score for *Zulu* is possibly his best as it perfectly captures the enormity of the challenge facing the 105 soldiers of the South Wales Borderers who successfully combated 4,000 Zulu warriors in January 1879 at Rorke's Drift in Natal, Africa. In this film, almost the last "celebration of the Empire" films, the "Welshness" of the soldiers is emphasized through their dedication to song, and the film includes a stirring rendition of "Men of Harlech" from the Welsh soldiers in response to the intimidating chant from the approaching Zulus.

The unit comprises standard British military archetypes—from the stolid bridge builder Lieutenant John Chard, thrusted into leadership when he is separated from his regiment after being despatched to build a bridge at Rorke's Drift; the aristocratic Lieutenant Gonville Bromhead, who is more concerned, initially, with a neat uniform and shooting impala than military matters; and the down-to-earth Color Sergeant Fred Bourne, who acts as a "fatherly" bridge between the officers and his more inexperienced soldiers; to the malingering Private Henry Hook, who redeems himself sufficiently in battle to win the Victoria Cross. Although the Zulus are not similarly differentiated, the film is careful not to depict them as savages but as warriors—the villain is the Reverend Otto Witt, who conspires to weaken the morale of the soldiers while lapsing into drunkenness as the battle approaches.

Cy R. Endfield* directed a number of fine genre British films, especially *Hell Drivers** with Stanley Baker* in 1956. As the bulk of the film is concerned with either the preparation for battle, or the battles themselves, Endfield prepares the audience by building tension and developing the characters in the early scenes. This includes the Zulu celebration of their slaughter of 1,300 British troops at Isandlwana prior to moving on to the small garrison at Rorke's Drift—the British disaster at Isandlwana was recreated in *Zulu Dawn,* scripted by Endfield, in 1979.

Zulu was Endfield's masterpiece and this film emulates some of visual characteristics of a John Ford cavalry film by placing the Zulus strategically on the hills surrounding the garrison as a menacing image prior to the carefully choreographed battle scenes. The ending recaps this pattern. Finally, after the remnants of the command congratulate themselves on surviving the ordeal, they witness massed Zulus massed on the hills above them. This time, however, the Zulus appear only to celebrate the courage of the soldiers before leaving the battlefield. Richard Burton's narration closes the film by pointing to the high number of Victoria Crosses awarded to the South Wales Borderers as a result of their bravery.

Much of the credit for the success of the film must also go to Baker, who not only starred, but also produced the film with Endfield. *Zulu* was Michael Caine's* first starring role after eight years of supporting roles and bit parts—although he was cast against type—Endfield was convinced that Caine's "horsy face" and blonde hair epitomized the British aristocrat. He was effective as the effete officer who ultimately redeems himself in battle and eventually forms an effective relationship with Lieutenant Chard.

APPENDIX: LIST OF FILMS, ACTORS, AND DIRECTORS, 1929–2000

Above Us the Waves
Accident
Aces High
Against the Wind
Alfie
All Night Long
And Now the Screaming Starts!
Anderson, Lindsay
Angels and Insects
Arsenal Stadium Mystery, The
Asquith, Anthony
Asylum
Attenborough, Richard
Back Room Boy
Baker, Roy Ward
Baker, Stanley
Banks, Leslie
Bates, Alan
Beauty Jungle, The
Belles of St. Trinian's, The
Billy Elliot
Billy Liar
Black Narcissus
Blackmail
Blanche Fury
Blood from the Mummy's Tomb

Blue Lamp, The
Blue Murder at St. Trinian's
Bogarde, Dirk
Bonham Carter, Helena
Boulting, Roy/Boulting, John
Box, Muriel
Boys Will Be Boys
Brassed Off
Brief Encounter
Brighton Rock
Brothers, The
Bulldog Jack
Byron, Kathleen
Caine, Michael
Calvert, Phyllis
Canterbury Tale, A
Captive Heart, The
Caravan
Carlyle, Robert
Carmichael, Ian
Carnival
Carry on Cleo
Carry on Sergeant
Cash on Demand
Challenge, The
Chance of a Lifetime

Chariots of Fire
Chase a Crooked Shadow
Chiltern Hundreds, The
Christie, Julie
Circus of Horrors
Clairvoyant, The
Clayton, Jack
Colditz Story, The
Comfort, Lance
Connery, Sean
Corpse, The
Corridor of Mirrors
Cosh Boy
Cottage to Let
Countess Dracula
Crichton, Charles
Criminal, The
Crooked Road, The
Croupier
Cruel Sea, The
Cummins, Peggy
Curse of Frankenstein, The
Cushing, Peter
Dam Busters, The
Dance with a Stranger
Danger Route
Danger Within
Darling
Daughter of Darkness
Davies, Terence
Day the Earth Caught Fire, The
Dead of Night
Dear Murderer
Dearden, Basil/Relph, Michael
Death Drums along the River (see
   Sanders of the River)
Defence of the Realm
Dench, Judi
Devil Rides Out, The
Devils, The
Dickinson, Thorold
Divorcing Jack
Doctor at Sea
Doctor in the House

Donat, Robert
Don't Look Now
Dors, Diana
Dr. No
Dracula
Drum, The
Embezzler, The
Emma
Endfield, Cy Raker
Esther Waters
Evergreen
Expresso Bongo
Family Way, The
Farrar, David
Father Brown
Fields, Gracie
Finch, Peter
Finney, Albert
Fire over England
Fish Called Wanda, A
Fisher, Terence
Follow a Star (see The Square Peg)
Forbes, Bryan
Formby, George
49th Parallel, The
Four Weddings and a Funeral
From Russia with Love
Full Monty, The
Gasbags
Gaslight
Genevieve
Georgy Girl
Get Carter
Gielgud, John
Gilbert, Lewis
Good Die Young, The
Goring, Marius
Governess, The
Granger, Stewart
Gray, Sally
Great Day
Great Expectations
Green for Danger
Green Man, The

Greenaway, Peter
Greenwood, Joan
Guest, Val
Guillermin, John
Guinness, Alec
Gynt, Greta
Hamer, Robert
Harvey, Laurence
Hatter's Castle
Hawkins, Jack
Hay, Will
Hell Drivers
Hilary and Jackie
Hill, The
Hindle Wakes
Hitchcock, Alfred
H.M.S. Defiant
Hobson, Valerie
Hopkins, Anthony
Hoskins, Bob
House across the Lake, The
House of Mirth, The
Howard, Trevor
Howards End
Hue and Cry
Hurt, John
I Am a Camera
I Know Where I'm Going!
I See a Dark Stranger
Ice Cold in Alex
Ideal Husband, An
I'm All Right Jack
In Which We Serve
Innocents, The
Interrupted Journey, The
It Always Rains on Sunday
It Started in Paradise
Jackson, Glenda
Jassy
Jet Storm
Joe Macbeth
Johnson, Celia
Kerr, Deborah
Kind Hearts and Coronets

Kind of Loving, A
Korda, Alexander
Lady Vanishes, The
Ladykillers, The
Last Holiday
Late Edwina Black, The
Laughter in Paradise
Launder, Frank/Gilliat, Sidney
Lavender Hill Mob, The
League of Gentlemen, The
Lean, David
Lee, Christopher
Lee Thompson, J.
Leigh, Mike
Little Friend
Little Voice
Loach, Ken
Lockwood, Margaret
Lodger, The
Loneliness of the Long Distance Runner, The
Long Memory, The
Losey, Joseph
Lost
Mackendrick, Alexander
Madeleine
Man in Grey, The
Man in the White Suit, The
Man Who Could Work Miracles, The
Manuela
Mark of Cain, The
Mason, James
Matter of Life and Death, A
Matthews, Jessie
Mills, John
Mine Own Executioner
More, Kenneth
Mr. Perrin and Mr. Traill
Mummy, The
My Brother's Keeper
Neame, Ronald
Newell, Mike
Newton, Robert
Night and the City

Night Has Eyes, The
Nil by Mouth
No Love for Johnnie
No Orchids for Miss Blandish
North West Frontier
Obsession
October Man, The
Olivier, Laurence
Once a Jolly Swagman
O'Toole, Peter
Paris by Night
Passionate Friends, The
Peeping Tom
Pink String and Sealing Wax
Poor Cow
Portman, Eric
Powell, Michael/Pressburger, Emeric
Private Life of Henry VIII
Quatermass II
Red Shoes, The
Redgrave, Michael
Reed, Carol
Richardson, Ralph
Richardson, Tony
Robson, Flora
Roc, Patricia
Rocking Horse Winner, The
Roeg, Nicholas
Room at the Top
Run for Your Money, A
Russell, Ken
Rutherford, Margaret
Sanders of the River/Death Drums along the River
Saville, Victor
Scandal
Schlesinger, John
Sellers, Peter
Seventh Veil, The
Shallow Grave
Silent Enemy, The

Sim, Alastair
Simba
Skin Game, The
Snatch
So Evil My Love
Spider and the Fly, The
Square Peg, The/Follow a Star
Story of Esther Costello, The
Take My Life
Tarzan's Greatest Adventure
Terry-Thomas
They Can't Hang Me
They Made Me a Fugitive
Third Man, The
This Sporting Life
Thompson, Emma
Time Is My Enemy
To the Devil a Daughter
Todd, Ann
Todd, Richard
Tom Jones
Topsy-Turvy
Twenty Four Seven
Unman, Wittering and Zigo
Victim
Village of the Damned
War Zone, The
Warner, Jack
Way Ahead, The
Wedding Rehearsal
Wicker Man, The
Wilcox, Herbert/Neagle, Anna
Wings of the Dove, The
Wings of the Morning
Winslow Boy, The (1948 and 1999)
Winstone, Ray
Wisdom, Norman
Witchfinder General, The
Withers, Googie
Young Lovers, The
Zulu

SELECTED BIBLIOGRAPHY

REFERENCE BOOKS

The British Film and Video Council. *The Researcher's Guide to British Film and TV Collection.* London: British Film and Video Council, 1997.

The British Film Institute (BFI). *BFI Film and Television Handbook.* London: BFI (annual from 1983).

Burrows, E., Moat., J., Sharp, D., and Wood, L. *The British Cinema Source Book: BFI Archive Viewing Copies and Library Materials.* London: BFI, 1995.

Caughie, J., with Rockett, K. *The Companion to British and Irish Cinema.* London: Cassell, 1996.

Gifford, D. *The British Film Catalogue, 1895–1970: A Guide to Entertainment Films.* London: David and Charles, 1986.

McFarlane, B., *Encyclopedia of British Film.* London: Methuen and the BFI, 2003.

Palmer, S. *A Who's Who of British Film Actors.* Metuchen, NJ: Scarecrow, 1981.

Quinlan, D. *British Sound Films: The Studio Years, 1928–1959.* London: Batsford, 1984.

GENERAL HISTORIES

Aldgate, A., and Richards, J. *Best of British: Cinema and Society from 1930 to the Present.* London: Tauris, 1999.

Armes, R. *A Critical History of the British Cinema.* London: Secker and Warburg, 1978.

Ashby, J., and Higson, A., eds. *British Cinema: Past and Present.* London: Routledge, 2000.

Barr, C., ed. *All Our Yesterdays: 90 Years of British Cinema.* London: BFI, 1986.

Curran, J., and Porter, V., eds. *British Cinema History.* London: Weidenfeld and Nicholson, 1983.

Dixon, W. W., ed. *Re-reviewing British Cinema, 1900–1992: Essay and Interviews.* New York: SUNY Press, 1994.

Harper, S. *Women in the British Cinema: Mad, Bad and Dangerous to Know.* London: Continuum, 2000.

Higson, A. *Waving the Flag: Constructing a National Cinema in Britain.* Oxford: Clarendon, 1995.

Murphy, R., ed. *The British Cinema Book.* London: BFI, 1997.

Richards, J. *Films and British National Identity: From Dickens to Dad's Army.* Manchester: Manchester University Press, 1997.

Street, S. *British National Cinema.* London: Routledge, 1997.

BRITISH CINEMA, 1930s–1990s

Adair, G., and Roddick, N. *A Night at the Pictures: Ten Decades of British Film.* Kent: Columbus, 1985.

Aldgate, A. *Censorship and the Permissive Society: British Cinema and Theatre 1955–1965.* Oxford: Clarendon, 1995.

Aldgate, A., and Richards, J. *Britain Can Take It: The British Cinema in the Second World War.* Edinburgh: Edinburgh University Press, 1994.

Arnold, K., and Onyekachi, W. *The Fuller Picture: The Commercial Impact of Six British Films with Black Themes in the 1990s.* London: BFI, 1999.

Auty, M., and Roddick, N., eds. *British Cinema Now.* London: BFI, 1985.

Barr, C. *Ealing Studios.* London: Studio Vista, 1993.

Bourne, S. *Black in the British Frame: Black People in British Film and Television, 1896–1996.* London: Cassell, 1998.

———. *Brief Encounters: Lesbians and Gays in British Cinema, 1930–1977.* London: Cassell, 1996.

Brooks, X. *Choose Life: Ewan McGregor and the British Film Revival.* London: Chamelon, 1998.

Chapman, J. *The British at War: Cinema, State and Propaganda, 1939–1945.* London: Tauris, 1998.

Cook, P., ed. *Gainsborough Pictures.* London: Cassell, 1997.

Coultass, C. *Images for Battle: British Film and the Second World War, 1939–1945.* London: Associated University Presses, 1989.

Drazin, C. *The Finest Years: British Cinema of the 1940s.* London: Andre Deutsch, 1998.

Durgnat, R. *A Mirror for England: British Movies from Austerity to Affluence.* London: Faber and Faber, 1970.

Falk, Q. *The Golden Gong: Fifty Years of the Rank Organisation, Its Films and Its Stars.* London: Columbus, 1987.

Friedman, L., ed. *British Cinema and Thatcherism: Fires Were Started.* London: UCL Press, 1993.

Geraghty, C. *British Cinema in the Fifties: Gender, Genre and the "New Look."* London: Routledge, 2000.

Gledhill, C., and Swanson, G., eds. *Nationalising Femininity: Culture, Sexuality and British Cinema in the Second World War.* Manchester: Manchester University Press, 1996.

Higson, A., ed. *Dissolving Views: Key Writings on British Cinema.* London: Cassell, 1996.

Hill, J. *British Cinema in the 1980s: Issues and Themes.* Oxford: Clarendon, 1999.

———. *Sex, Class and Realism: British Cinema 1956–1963.* London: BFI, 1986.

Hurd, G., ed. *National Fictions: World War Two in British Films and Television.* London: BFI, 1984.

Lant, A. *Blackout: Reinventing Women for Wartime British Cinema.* Princeton, NJ: Princeton University Press, 1991.

Low, R. *The History of the British Film, 1929–1939.* London: Allen and Unwin/BFI, 1985.

Macnab, G. *J. Arthur Rank and the British Film Industry.* London: Routledge, 1993.

Macpherson, D., ed. *Traditions of Independence: British Cinema in the Thirties.* London: BFI, 1980.

Murphy, R., ed. *British Cinema of the 90s.* London: BFI, 2000.

———. *Realism and Tinsel: Cinema and Society in Britain, 1939–1948.* London: Routledge, 1989.

———. *Sixties British Cinema.* London: BFI, 1992.

Park, J. *Learning to Dream: The New British Cinema.* London: BFI, 2000.

Petrie, D. *Creativity and Constraint: Contemporary British Cinema.* London: Macmillan, 1990.

———. *New Questions of British Cinema.* London: BFI, 1992.

Richards, J. *The Age of the Dream Palaces: Cinema and Society in Britain, 1930–1939.* London: Routledge and Kegan Paul, 1984.

———, ed. *The Unknown 1930s: An Alternative History of the British Cinema, 1929–1939.* London: Tauris, 1998.

———. *Visions of Yesterday.* London: Routledge and Kegan Paul, 1973.

Richards, J., and Aldgate, A. *Best of British Cinema and Society, 1930–1970.* Oxford: Basil Blackwell, 1983.

Sellar, M. *Best of British: A Celebration of Rank Film Classics.* London: Sphere, 1987.

Shafer, S. C. *British Popular Films, 1929–1939: The Cinema of Reassurance.* London: Routledge, 1997.

Slide, A. *"Banned in the USA": British Films in the United States and Their Censorship, 1933–1960.* London: Tauris, 1998.

Stead, P. *Film and the Working Class: The Feature Film in British and American Society.* London: Routledge, 1989.

Taylor, P.M., ed. *Britain and the Cinema in the Second World War.* London: Macmillan, 1988.

Threadgall, D. *Shepperton Studios.* London: BFI, 1994.

Walker, A. *Hollywood England: The British Film Industry in the Sixties.* London: Harrap, 1986.

———. *National Heroes: British Cinema in the Seventies and Eighties.* London: Methuen, 1985.

Warren, P. *British Film Studios: An Illustrated History.* London: Batsford, 1995.

———. *Elstree: The British Hollywood.* London: Elm Tree, 1983.

Williams, T. *Structures of Desire: British Cinema, 1939–1955.* New York: SUNY Press, 2000.

BRITISH FILM GENRES

Aspinall, S., and Murphy, R., eds. *Gainsborough Melodrama.* London: BFI, 1993.

Burton, A., and Petley. J., eds. *Journal of Popular British Cinema,* no. 1 (1998).

Chibnall, S., and Murphy, R., eds. *British Crime Cinema.* London: Routledge, 1999.

Eyles, A., Adkinson, R., and Fry, N., eds. *The House of Horror: The Complete Story of Hammer Films.* London: Lorrimer, 1984.

Hardy, P., ed. *The BFI Companion to Crime.* Berkeley: University of California Press, 1997.

Harper, S. *Picturing the Past: The Rise and Fall of the British Costume Film.* London: BFI, 1994.

Hearn, M., and Barnes, A. *The Hammer Story.* London: Titan, 1997.

Hunter, J., ed. *House of Horror: The Complete Hammer Films Story.* London: Creation, 1996.

Hutchings, P. *Hammer and Beyond.* Manchester: Manchester University Press, 1993.

Johnson, T., and Del Vecchio, D. *Hammer Films: An Exhaustive Filmography.* Jefferson, NJ: McFarland, 1996.

Landy, M. *British Genres: Cinema and Society, 1930–1960.* Princeton, NJ: Princeton University Press, 1991.

Meikle, D. *A History of Horrors: The Rise and Fall of the House of Hammer.* Lanham, MD: Scarecrow, 1996.

Petley, J., and Chibnall, S. *British Horror Cinema.* London: Routledge, 2002.

Pirie, D. *Heritage of Horror: The English Gothic Cinema, 1946–1972.* London: Gordon Fraser, 1973.

Ross, R. *The Carry on Companion.* London: Batsford, 1996.

ACTORS AND DIRECTORS

Anderegg, M. *David Lean.* New York: Twayne, 1984.

Atkins, T. R., ed. *Ken Russell.* New York: Monarch, 1976.

Baker, R. W. *The Director's Cut: A Memoir of 60 Sixty Years in Film and Television.* London: Reynolds and Hearn, 2000.

Barr, C. *English Hitchcock.* Moffat: Cameron and Hollis, 1999.

Box, M. *Odd Woman Out.* London: Leslie Frewin, 1974.

Brown, G. *Launder and Gilliat.* London: BFI, 1977.

Brown, G., and Kardish, L. *Michael Balcon: The Pursuit of British Cinema.* New York: Museum of Modern Art, 1984.

Brownlow, K. *David Lean.* London: Richard Cohen, 1996.

Burton, A., O'Sullivan, T., and Wells, P., eds. *The Family Way: The Boulting Brothers and British Film Culture.* Trowbridge: Flick, 1999.

———, eds. *Liberal Directions: Basil Dearden and Post-war British Film Culture.* Trowbridge: Flick, 1997.

Cardiff, J. *Magic Hour: The Life of a Cameraman.* London: Faber and Faber, 1996.

Caute, D. *Joseph Losey: A Revenge on Life.* London: Faber and Faber, 1994.

Chibnall, Steve. *J. Lee Thompson.* Manchester: Manchester University Press, 2000.

Christie, I. *Arrows of Desire: The Films of Michael Powell and Emeric Pressburger.* London: Waterstone, 1985.

———. *Powell, Pressburger and Others.* London: BFI, 1978.

Ciment, M. *Conversations with Losey.* London: Methuen, 1985.

Croall, J. *Gielgud.* London: Methuen, 2000.

Dixon, W. W. *The Charming Evil: The Life and Films of Terence Fisher.* Metuchen, NJ, The Scarecrow Press, 1991.

Dors, D. *Behind Closed Doors.* London: Allen, 1979.

———. *For Adults Only.* London: Allen, 1978.

———. *Swingin' Dors.* London: World Distributors, 1959.

Elliott, B., and Purdy, A. *Peter Greenaway: Architecture and Allegory.* London: Academy Editions, 1997.

Gaston, G. M. A. *Jack Clayton: A Guide to References and Resources.* Boston: Hall, 1981.

Gottlieb, S. *Hitchcock on Hitchcock: Selected Writings and Interviews.* London: Faber and Faber, 1995.

Gough-Yates, K. *Michael Powell in Collaboration with Emeric Pressburger.* London: BFI, 1971.

Hacker, J., and Price, D. *Take Ten: Contemporary British Film Directors.* Oxford: Clarendon, 1991.

Hanke, K. *Ken Russell's Films.* Metuchen, NJ: Scarecrow, 1984.

Hedling, E. *Lindsay Anderson: Maverick Film-Maker.* London: Cassell, 1998.

Johnson, L., ed. *Talking Pictures: Interviews with Contemporary British Film-Makers.* London: BFI, 1997.

Kemp, P. *Lethal Innocence: The Cinema of Alexander Mackendrick.* London: Methuen, 1991.

Kulik, K. *Alexander Korda.* London: Allen, 1975.

Lawrence, A. *The Films of Peter Greenaway.* Cambridge: Cambridge University Press, 1997.

Loach, K. *Loach on Loach.* London: Faber and Faber, 1998.

Macdonald, K. *Emeric Pressburger: The Life and Death of a Screenwriter.* London: Faber and Faber, 1994.

Macnab, G. *Searching for Stars: Stardom and Screen Acting in British Cinema.* London: Cassell, 1999.

Mason, J. *Before I Forget.* London: Hamilton, 1981.

McFarlane, B., ed. *An Autobiography of British Cinema by the Actors and Filmmakers Who Made It.* London: Methuen, 1997.

———. *Lance Comfort.* Manchester: Manchester University Press, 1999.

———, ed. *Sixty Voices: Celebrities Recall the Golden Age of British Cinema.* London: BFI, 1992.

McKnight, G., ed. *Agent of Challenge and Defiance: The Films of Ken Loach.* Trowbridge: Flick, 1997.

Minney, R. J. *The Films of Anthony Asquith.* South Brunswick: Barnes, 1976.

More, K. *More or Less.* London: Hodder and Stoughton, 1978.

Morley, S. *Odd Man Out: James Mason.* London: Weidenfeld and Nicholson, 1989.

———. *The Other Side of the Moon—David Niven: A Biography.* London: Coronet, 1986.

Moss, R. F. *The Films of Carol Reed.* London: Macmillan, 1987.

Niven, D. *The Moon's a Balloon.* London: Coronet, 1972.

Pascoe, D. *Peter Greenaway: Museums and Moving Images.* London: Reaktion, 1997.

Petrie, D., ed. *Inside Stories: Diaries of British Filmmakers at Work.* London: BFI, 1996.

Phillips, G. D. *Ken Russell.* Boston: Twayne, 1979.

Powell, M. *A Life in the Movies.* New York: Knopf, 1987.

———. *Million-Dollar Movie.* London: Heinemann, 1992.

Richards, J. *Thorold Dickinson and the British Cinema.* Lanham, MD: Scarecrow, 1997.

Ryall, T. *Alfred Hitchcock and the British Cinema.* London: Croom Helm, 1986.

Salwolke, S. *The Films of Michael Powell and the Archers.* Lanham, MD: Scarecrow, 1997.

Silver, A., and Ursini, J. *David Lean and His Films.* London: Frewin, 1974.

Silverman, S. *David Lean.* New York: Abrams, 1989.

Sinden, D. *A Touch of Memoirs.* London: Hodder and Stoughton, 1982.

Sinyard, N. *Jack Clayton.* Manchester: Manchester University Press, 2000.

Sussex, E. *Lindsay Anderson.* London: Studio Vista, 1969.

Truffaut, F. *Hitchcock.* London: Secker and Warburg, 1968.

Wapshott, N. *The Man Between: A Biography of Carol Reed.* London: Chatto and Windus, 1990.

Wood, R. *Hitchcock's Films Revisited.* London: Faber and Faber, 1989.

Yacowar, M. *Hitchcock's British Films.* Hamden, CT: Archon, 1977.

FILMS

Chapman, J. *Licensed to Thrill: A Cultural History of the James Bond Films.* London: Tauris, 1999.

Dyer, R. *Brief Encounter.* London: BFI, 1993.

Giles, J. *The Crying Game.* London: BFI, 1997.

Houston, P. *Went the Day Well?* London: BFI, 1992.

Kennedy, A. L. *The Life and Death of Colonel Blimp.* London: BFI, 1997.

MacCabe, C. *Performance.* London: BFI, 1998.

Ryall, T. *Blackmail.* London: BFI, 1993.

Vaughan, D. *Odd Man Out.* London: BFI, 1995.

Wood, R. *The Wings of the Dove.* London: BFI, 1999.

INDEX

Abbott and Costello Meet Frankenstein, 86
Abbott, Bud, 86
Abominable Dr. Phibes, The, 356
Above Us the Waves, 1–2
Accident, xiii, 2–3, 19, 34, 253, 254
Aces High, 3–4
Adams, Ken, 116
Addison, John, 369
Adler, Larry, 147
Admirable Crichton, 110, 152, 272, 273
Adventures of a Taxi Driver, 114
Adventures of the Scarlet Pimpernel, The, 154
Afterglow, 66
Against the Wind, 4–5,78, 379
Age of Consent, 309
Age of Innocence, 192
Age of Kings, The, 72
Agony and the Ecstacy, The, 317
Agutter, Jenny, 324
Ah, Wilderness, 13
Aimée, Anouk, 194
Air Force, 381
Airport, 215
Alamo, The, 175
Aldrich, Robert, 334
Alexander the Great, 87
Alexander, Terence, 234
Alfie, 5–6, 47, 132, 147, 152
Alfie Elkins and his Little Life, 5
Alfresco, 363

Alien, 198
All Creatures Great and Small, 188
All Night Long, 6–7
All That Heaven Allows, 352
All the Brothers Were Valiant, 157
All the President's Men, 103
All Through the Night, 76
Allan, Irving, 115
Allegret, Marc, 156
Allen, Chesney, 144
Allen, Lewis, 348, 365
Allied Film Makers, 137, 177, 235
Alligator Named Daisy, An, 113, 241
Allingham, Margery, 18
Alphabet Murders, The, 329
Altman, Robert, 21, 65
Always a Bride, 84
Always Tell Your Wife, 184
Ambler, Eric, 17, 84, 292, 293, 300
Amelia, 328
Amicus Productions, 7, 13, 18, 99
Amistad, 189
Among Vultures, 157
And Now the Screaming Starts, 7, 18, 88
Anderson, Lindsay, 8–9, 62, 108, 319, 361, 362, 373
Anderson, Michael, 63, 91, 367
Andress, Ursula, 19, 141
Andrews, Dana, 84, 322
Angel Street, 145
Angela's Ashes, 54

Angels and Insects, 9–10
Anglo-Amalgamated, 66, 302
Angry Silence, The, 13, 137
Anna Karenina (1948), 224
Anna Karenina (television), 72
Annabella, 387, 388
Annakin, Ken, 38, 367
Anniversary, The, 18
Another Time, Another Place, 72
Apted, Michael, 279
Arcadians, The, 333
Archers, The, 307
Arliss, Leslie, 11, 156
Arrangement, The, 219
Arrighi, Luciana, 196
Arsenal Stadium Mystery, The, 10–11, 20, 21, 108, 171
Arthur, 150
As Time Goes By, 105
Ashcroft, Peggy, 213
Asher, Jack, 116, 153, 350, 397
Asher, Robert, xiv, 350, 392
Ask a Policeman, 178
Askey, Arthur, 16, 166
Asquith, Anthony, 11–12, 20, 36, 37, 49, 156, 269, 314, 329, 339, 343, 389, 390, 396
Assam Garden, The, 219
Assignment Foreign Legion, 71
Associated British Pictures Corporation, 113
Astaire, Fred, 267, 268
Astonished Heart, The, 134
Asylum, 7, 12–13, 18, 368
Attanasio, Paul, 280
Attenborough, Richard, 13–14, 19, 37, 43, 44, 94, 100, 137, 168, 177, 188, 206, 234, 235
Au Pair Girls, 166
Audley, Maxine, 303
Auric, Georges, 209
Avengers, The, 78
Awakening, The, 31, 280
Awfully Big Adventure, An, 280

Bacall, Lauren, 272
Bacharach, Burt, 6
Bachelor Flat, 355

Back Room Boy, 16
Bad Blood, 280
Bad Timing, 325
Baddeley, Hermione, 326
Bader, Douglas, 110, 273
Baines, John, 99, 100
Baker, Robert S., 120, 229
Baker, Roy Ward, xii, 7, 13, 16–19, 35, 67, 88, 154, 165, 249, 262, 269, 292, 293, 312, 368
Baker, Stanley, 3, 19–20, 79, 108, 122, 153, 179, 253, 273, 361, 399
Balcon, Michael, 130, 146, 221, 233, 244, 333
Bancroft, Ann, 68, 188
Band Waggon, 16
Bang! You're Dead, 71, 380
Bank Holiday, 248
Banks, Leslie, 11, 20–21, 108, 258, 307, 332, 333, 343, 368, 387, 388
Bannen, Ian, 182
Bardot, Brigitte, 109
Barefoot Contessa, The, 154
Barker, Lex, 157
Barr, Charles, xii
Barrie, Amanda, 57
Barrie, Wendy, 383
Barry, Joan, 28
Barry, John, 141, 398
Baseheart, Richard, 153
Bataan, 382
Bateman, Colin, 109
Bates, Alan, 21–22, 137, 147, 223, 254, 297, 337
Bathory, Countess Elizabeth, 77
Battle of Britain, The, 273
Battle of the River Platte, 130, 336
Battle of the Sexes, The, 78, 339
Baxter, Anne, 212, 367
Be My Guest, 72
Beach, The, 55
Beat the Devil, 68
Beatty, Warren, 65
Beau Brummell, 157
Beaudine, William, 178
Beauty and the Beast, 75
Beauty Jungle, The, 22–23, 166, 212
Becket, 150, 297

Beckwith, Reginald, 358
Bedalia, 56, 71, 249
Bedford Incident, The, 306
Bennett, Joan, 315
Being There, 339
Belles of St. Trinian's, The, 23–24, 344
Bells Go Down, The, 102
Belly of Architect, The, 164
Ben-Hur (1959), 156, 177
Benjamin, Richard, 298
Bennett, Charles, 67
Bennett, Compton, 156, 211, 212, 365
Bennett, Hywel, 37
Bennett, Richard Rodney, 337
Benson, E.F., 99
Bergman, Ingmar, 9
Bergman, Ingrid, 50, 145
Berkeley Square, 17
Berkeley, Busby, 328
Berman, Monty, 120
Bernard, James, 116
Bertolucci, Bernardo, 298
Bespoke Overcoat, The, 68
Best, Edna, 124, 333
Betrayed, 55
Betsy, The, 294
Beyond Mombasa, 238
Beyond the Poseidon Adventure, 48
Bianchi, Daniela, 141
Big Fish, Little Fish, 150
Bigger Than Life, 265
Billion Dollar Brain, The, 47, 328
Billy Elliot, 24–25, 40, 41
Billy Liar, 25–26, 64, 65, 95, 336
Bird, Antonia, 54, 55
Bird, Norman, 234
Birdman of Alcatraz, 78
Birds, The, 185
Biró, Lajos, 224
Bitter Sweet (1933), 333, 384
Bitter Sweet (1940), 333
Bitter Victory, 238
Black Knight, The, 87, 137
Black Narcissus, 26–28, 45, 46, 127, 203, 218, 219, 307, 308, 321
Black Rose, The, 177
Black Sheep of Whitehall, 102, 178
Blackbeard the Pirate, 282

Blackmail, xiii, 28–29, 45, 184, 278
Blame It on Rio, 48
Blanche Fury, 29–30, 96–97, 156, 186, 187, 263, 264, 348
Blanchett, Cate, 205
Bleak Moments, 243
Blethyn, Brenda, 245, 246
Blind Corner, 72
Blind Date, 19, 79, 253
Blithe Spirit, 278, 329
Bloch, Robert, 13
Blood and Wine, 48
Blood from the Mummy's Tomb, 30–31, 88, 280
Blood of Fu-Manchu, The, 239
Bloody Countess, The, 77
Bloom, Claire, 317
Blue Lamp, The, 31–32, 34, 39, 44, 52, 84, 102, 233, 379, 380
Blue Max, The, 168
Blue Murder at St. Trinian's, 32–33, 344, 356
Blue Sky, 320
Bluebeard's Ten Honeymoons, 323
Blundell, Christine, 371
Blyth, Ann, 17, 127
Bobo, The, 338
Boehm, Carl, 302
Bogarde, Dirk, xii, 3, 12, 18, 32, 33–35, 78, 96, 102, 109, 110, 123, 134, 186, 253, 264, 269, 272, 297, 376, 379
Bonham Carter, Helena, 35–36, 104, 387
Bonham Carter, Lady Violet, 36
Bonjour Tristesse, 218
Boom, 252
Boone, Pat, 136
Born to Kill, 153
Bouchet, Barbara, 93
Boulting, John, 36–38, 55, 206, 231, 243, 355
Boulting, Roy, 36–38, 55, 126, 206, 231, 247, 355
Bounty, The, 188
Bowles, Sally, 174
Box, Betty, 39, 109, 231, 287
Box, Muriel, 38–39, 55, 175
Box, Sydney, 38
Boy with Green Hair, The, 252, 253

Boyd, Stephen, 104
Boyer, Charles, 145
Boyfriend, The, 213, 328
Boyle, Danny, 341, 342
Boys from Brazil, The, 294, 295
Boys in Brown, The, 380
Boys Will Be Boys, 39–40, 178
Boys Will Be Girls, 171
Bradbourne, John, 186
Bradley, Buddy, 124
Banks, Monty, 129
Bragg, Melvyn, 235
Braine, John, 68, 326
Bram Stoker's Dracula, 189
Branagh, Kenneth, 362, 363
Brand, Christianna, 162
Brassed Off, 25, 40–41, 143
Brazzi, Rossano, 352
Break, The, 70–71
Breaking the Sound Barrier, 224
Breen, Joseph, 123, 210, 200, 208, 221,
   259, 388
Brent, George, 191
Brickhill, Paul, 91
Bride of Frankenstein, The, 186
Brides of Dracula, The, 135
Brides of Fu-Manchu, The, 239
Bridge at Remagen, The, 168
Bridge on the River Kwai, The, 169, 170,
   177, 234, 235, 236
Bridge Too Far, A, 14
Brief Encounter, vii, 41–43, 194, 217,
   236, 257, 300, 301
Brighton Rock, xv, 13, 37, 43–44, 148
Britannia Hospital, 8, 9
British Instructional Films, 38
British International Pictures, 184, 232,
   241
British Lion, 37, 208, 224, 384
British New Wave. *See* New Wave
Britton, Tony, 213
Broadbent, Jim, 371
Broccoli, Albert, 115
Brooks, Richard, 298
Brother Rat, 153
Brothers, The, xv, 44–45, 322
Brothers-in-Law, 37, 55, 206
Brown, Jim, 168

Browning Version, The (1951), 11,
   314–315
Browning Version, The (1994), 132
Brubeck, Dave, 7
Bryan, John, 161, 300
Brynner, Yul, 279
Buchanan, Jack, 384
Bulldog Jack, 45, 232, 318
Bullet to Beijing, 47, 48
Bullets Over Broadway, 121
Bunker, The, 188
Bunny Lake Is Missing, 295
Burke, Kathy, 286
Burroughs, Edgar Rice, 354
Burton, Richard, 188, 217, 297, 319, 399
Burton, Tim, 239
Bush, John, 371
Busman's Holiday (*Haunted Honeymoon*),
   281
Byron, Kathleen, 45–46, 175

Cabaret, 174
Caffrey, David, 109
Cagney, James, 390
Caine, Michael, 5, 47–49, 132, 152, 245,
   246, 295, 391, 399
Caine Mutiny, The, 47
California Suite, 48
Calling Bulldog Drummond, 334
Callow, Simon, 140, 280
Calvert, Phyllis, 11, 49–50, 138, 258, 322
Cammell, Donald, 324
Campbell, Beatrice, 229
Campbell's Kingdom, 79
Campion, Gerald
Candles at Nine, 268
Canonero, Milena, 63
Canterbury Tale, A, 50–51, 201, 266, 306,
   308
Canyon Passage, 322
Cape Fear, 241, 242
Capra, Frank, 267
Captain Blood, 111, 366
Captain Horatio Hornblower, 237
Captain's Paradise, The, 217
Captain's Table, The, 84
Captive Heart, The, 51–52, 90, 102, 315,
   380

Caravan, 53, 156
Card, The, 278
Cardiff, Jack, 27, 28, 211, 388
Career Girls, 243
Carey, Harry, Jr., 8
Carey, Joyce, 43
Carla's Song, 55
Carlton-Browne of the F.O., 37, 206, 338, 356
Carlyle, Robert, 53–55, 391
Carmichael, Ian, 37, 39, 55–56, 70, 355
Carmilla, 18
Carnival, 56–57, 158
Caron, Leslie, 137
Carreras, Michael, 30
Carrie (1952), 295
Carrington, 363
Carroll, Madelaine, 171
Carry On Cleo, xv, 57–58
Carry On Columbus, 58
Carry On Sergeant, xv, 58
Carstairs, John Paddy, xv, 350, 392
Cartland, Barbara, 36
Cash on Demand, xiii, 58–59, 87
Cass, Henry, 228, 229
Cassavetes, John, 285
Cast a Dark Shadow, 249
Castle of Fu-Manchu, The, 239
Catch Me a Spy, 194
Catherine the Great, 321
Cathy Come Home, 247, 305
Caton-Jones, Michael, 198, 335
Caught, 265
Cavalcanti, Alberto, 21, 78, 100, 102, 127, 158, 359, 366
Cavani, Liliana, 35
Ceremony, The, 175
Chalk Garden, The, 270, 279
Challenge, The, 59–60
Chamberlain, Richard, 280, 328
Chance of a Lifetime, 61–62
Chandler, Raymond, 149
Chaplin, 14, 137
Chaplin, Charles, 223
Chapman, Edward, 394
Charge of the Light Brigade, The, 194, 320
Chariots of Fire, xiv, 9, 62–63

Charlie Bubbles, 132
Chase a Crooked Shadow, 63, 367
Chase, James Hadley, 288
Checkpoint, 79
Cheers, 363
Cher, 190
Cherry, Helen, 194
Children of the Damned, 377
Children, 97
Chiltern Hundreds, The, 64, 222
Chinatown Squad, 186
Chocolat, 105
Chorus Line, A, 14
Christiansen, Arthur, 99
Christie, Agatha, 329
Christie, Julie, 22, 35, 64–66, 95, 96, 113, 254, 325, 336, 337
Christmas Carol, A, xiii, 59
Chrystal, Belle, 183
Chu Chin Chow, 384
Chump at Oxford, A, 87
Churchill, Winston, 224, 267, 308
Cider House Rules, The, 48
Cilento, Diana, 17, 262, 368–369
Cimino, Michael, 188
Cineguild, 278
Cinematograph Films Act (1927), xiv
Circle of Danger, 322
Circus of Horrors, 66–67
Citadel, The, 111, 333
Clairvoyant, The, 67
Clark, Dane, 249
Clarke, Alan, 391
Clarke, T.E.B., 5, 78, 100, 102, 197, 233
Clayburgh, Jill, 22
Clayton, Jack, ix, 67–69, 175, 190, 209, 319, 326, 377
Cleef, Lee Van, 168
Cleese, John, 78, 134
Cleopatra, 57
Climbing High, 268, 314
Clive, Colin, 186
Clockwork Orange, A, 3, 8, 107
Close, Ivy, 278
Cloudburst, 191
Clowes, St. John, 100
Clueless, 121
Coast of Skeletons, 333, 368

Coates, John, 91
Cockleshell Heroes, The, 137
Cocteau, Jean, 75
Coen, Ethan, 132
Coen, Joel, 132
Cold Comfort Farm, 337
Cold Heaven, 325
Colditz Story, The, 1, 52, 69–70, 94, 136, 306, 367
Cole, George, 24, 33, 163, 380
Coleman, Charlotte, 280
Coleman, Ronald, 84
Collector, The, 272
Collette, Toni, 121
Collins, Pauline, 152
Collinson, Peter, 19, 304–305
Colonel March of Scotland Yard, 238
Coltrane, Robbie, 54
Come On George, 33
Comedy Man, The, 273
Comfort, Lance, xi, xii, 70–72, 75, 96, 97, 159, 176, 249, 281, 306, 380
Commissioner, The, 198
Confessions of a Window Cleaner, 166
Connell, Richard, 20
Connery, Sean, 72–73, 115, 141, 152, 167, 179, 181, 194, 264, 354
Connolly, Billy, 105
Connor, Kenneth, 57, 58
Conquering Worm, The. See Witchfinder General
Conquest of the Planet of the Apes, 242
Consider Your Verdict, 36
Conspirator, 334
Constant Husband, 232
Conversation, The, 104
Coppola, Francis Ford, 309
Corman, Roger, 393
Cornelius, Henry, 146–147, 200
Cornered, 292
Coronation Street, 280
Corpse, The, 31, 72–73
Corridor of Mirrors, xiii, 74–75, 237, 306
Cosh Boy, 75–76, 151, 153
Costello, Lou, 86
Cottage to Let, 20, 76, 269, 343
Cotton, Joseph, 194, 316
Count of Monte Cristo, The, 111

Countess Dracula, 31, 76–77
Country Life, 394
Courtenay, Tom, 251, 336
Courtneys of Curzon Street, The, 385
Coward, Nöel, 13, 42, 134, 208, 236, 269, 278, 329, 333, 361
Cox, Paul, 298
Crabtree, Arthur, 11, 70, 100, 156, 302
Cracker, 54
Craig, Michael, 120, 175
Crawford, Andrew, 45
Crawford, Joan, 351, 352
Crazy Gang, The, 144, 165
Creeping Flesh, The, 31
Crichton, Charles, 5, 77–79, 100, 104, 134, 233, 339
Crimes of Passion, 327
Criminal, The, 19, 79–80, 253
Crimson Pirate, The, 238
Cronin, A.J., 70, 111, 176, 316
Crooked Road, The, 80–81
Crooks Anonymous, 65
Crossfire, 153, 291
Croupier, 81–82
Crucible, The, 54
Cruel Sea, The, 82–83, 136, 177, 234
Cry Freedom, 14
Cry Havoc, 381
Cry the Beloved Country, 224
Cukor, George, 107
Cummins, Peggy, 84–85, 179, 349
Cure for Love, The, 111
Currie, Finlay, 45
Curse of Frankenstein, The, xiii, 85–86, 87, 116, 135, 166, 191, 238, 275
Curtis, Jamie Lee, 134
Curtis, Richard, 140
Curtis, Tony, 189, 256, 355
Cusack, Cyril, 123
Cusack, John, 281
Cushing, Peter, xii, xiii, 18, 59, 86–89, 135, 136, 189, 238, 239, 275

Dad and Dave Come to Town, 129
Daddy Nostalgia, 34
Dahl, Arlene, 171
Dale, Jim, 58
Dalrymple, Ian, 123

Dam Busters, The, 90–91, 315, 367
Dance Pretty Lady, 56
Dance with a Stranger, 91–92, 280
Dancing with Crime, 113
Dandy in Aspic, A, 175
Danger Route, 92–93
Danger Within, 93–94, 367
Dangerous Liaisons, 335
Dangerous Moonlight, 158
Dankworth, John, 7
Darby O'Gill and the Little People, 72
Darling, 35, 64, 65, 94–96, 147, 175, 337, 338
Darnborough, Anthony, 134
Darnell, Linda, 17, 84
Darwin, Charles, 9
Dassin, Jules, 283, 394
Daughter of Darkness, xiii, 71, 75, 96–97
Davenport, Nigel, 122
David, Hal, 6
Davies, Jack, 110
Davies, John Howard, 187
Davies, Terence, xiii, 97–98, 193
Davis, Bette, 8, 367
Davis, John, 14, 110, 272, 313, 362
Davis, Stringer, 329
Davy, 102
Dawker, Rob, 248
Dawn Patrol, The, 4
Day in the Life of Joe Egg, A, 22
Day of the Locust, 336
Day the Earth Caught Fire, 98–99, 166
Day They Robbed the Bank of England, The, 168, 297
Day, Doris, 355
Day, Robert, 163
Day, The, 130
Daybreak, xiii, 38, 293, 306, 365
De Sade, 122
Dead Again, 363
Dead Cert, 320
Dead of Night, 78, 99, 101–103, 173, 188, 315, 394
Deadly Affair, The, 265
Deadly Is the Female (Gun Crazy), 84
Dear Mr. Prohack, 136
Dear Murderer, xiii, 39, 100–101, 171, 293, 306, 380

Dearden, Basil, 6, 32, 137, 177, 231, 235, 376
Death and Transfiguration, 97
Death Drums along the River, 331–333, 367–368
Death in Venice, 34
Death Wish 4: The Crackdown, 242
Deep Blue Sea, The, 273
Defence of the Realm, 103–104
Defiant Ones, The, 276
Del Guidice, Filippo, 208, 237
Delaney, Maureen, 284
Delaney, Shelagh, 92, 320
Deliverance, 107
Demi-Paradise, The, 329
Demongeot, Myléne, 18, 269
Demons of the Mind, 31
Dench, Judi, 104–105
Denham Studios, 173, 223, 310
Denison, Michael, 11
Depp, Johnny, 280
Derby Day, 385, 394
Desert Fox, The, 265
Desert Rats, 265
Desert Victory, 37
Desmonde, Jerry, 350, 392
Despair, 34
Desperate Hours, The, 188
Destry Rides Again, 109
Devil and Daniel Webster, The, 189
Devil Is a Woman, The, 257
Devil Rides Out, The, 105–106, 136, 239
Devil-Ship Pirates, 238
Devils of Darkness, 72
Devils, The, 106–107, 328
Di Caprio, Leonardo, 55
Diaboliques, Les, 74
Diamond, Margaret, 123
Diamonds Are Forever, 72, 262
Dickens, Charles, xiii, 59,
Dickinson, Thorold, 10, 20, 70, 107–108, 145, 171, 281
Dietrich, Marlene, 257, 367
Diffring, Anton, 66
Dighton, John, 257, 260, 261
Dimes, Albert, 80
Distant Voices, Still Lives, 97, 98
Divorce of Lady X, The, 294, 318

Divorcing Jack, 108–109
Dixon of Dock Green, 379
Dmytryk, Edward, 282, 291
Doctor at Large, 34
Doctor at Sea, 34, 109–110
Doctor in Distress, 34
Doctor in the House, 34, 109, 110–111,
    272, 273, 287
Doctor Zhivago, 65, 170, 235
Doctor's Dilemma, The, 12
Don't Bother to Knock, 17
Don't Look Now, 65, 112–113, 324–325
Don't Make Waves, 257, 260
Donat, Robert, 111–112, 224
Donen, Stanley, 132
Donlan, Yolanda, 166, 357
Donnie Brasco, 140, 280
Donohue, Amanda, 327
Dors, Diana, 113–114, 321
Double Indemnity, 30, 191, 217
Douglas Fairbanks Presents, 71
Douglas, Paul, 216
Dr. Dolittle, 14
Dr. Jekyll and Sister Hyde, 18
Dr. No, 72, 114–116, 141, 179
Dr. Strangelove, 339
Dr. Terror's House of Horror, 238
Dracula (1958), 85, 86, 87, 116–118, 135,
    191, 238, 275
Dracula (1979), 294
Dracula A.D., 135
Dracula, Prince of Darkness, 135, 239
Draughtsman's Contract, The, 163
Dresser, The, 132
Driver, Minnie, 155, 205
Drowning by Numbers, 164
Drum, The, 118–119, 186, 223
Durgnat, Raymond, xii, 288
Dury, David, 104
Dusty Ermine, 329
Dwan, Allan, 127

Ealing Studios, xiii, 4, 5, 16, 30, 52, 77,
    78, 102, 111, 146, 164, 169, 173, 178,
    196–197, 210, 227, 233, 256, 260, 327,
    341, 349, 394
Earth Dies Screaming, The, 136
Easdale, Brian, 27, 28

Easy Rider, 235
Eaton, Shirley, 58
Eddy, Nelson, 333
Edgar Marriott, 178
Edge of the World, The, 70, 202, 307, 308
Edge, The, 189
Educating Rita, 48, 152
Edward My Son, 219
Edwards, Blake, 339
Efficiency Expert, The, 188
Egoyan, Atom, 190
Eichhorn, Lisa, 333
8 ½ Woman, 164
80,000 Suspects, 166
84 Charing Cross Road, 104, 105, 188
Ekland, Britt, 336
El Condor, 168
Elephant Boy, 77
Elephant Man, The, 197, 198
Elephant Walk, 130
Elizabeth, 151
Elizabeth R, 214
Ellen, 363
Elmer Gantry, 351
Elstree Studios, 63, 184, 224, 278, 366, 385
Elvey, Maurice, 182
Embezzler, The, 120, 229
Emery, Dick, 231
Emma, 46, 120–121,
Empire Films, 272, 118–119, 288–290,
    331–333, 345, 398
Enchanted April, 281
End of the Affair, The (1955), 87, 219
Endfield, Cy R., xii, 19, 47, 79, 84,
    121–122, 179, 399
Endless Night, 231
Enemy at the Gates, 190
Enemy Coast Ahead, 91
Enemy from Space. See Quatermass 11
English Patient, The, xiv
Englishman Abroad, An, 338
Entertainer, The, 21, 131, 294, 295, 320
Entrapment, 73
Ercole al centro della terra, 238
Erin Brockovich, 132
Escape from Zahrain, 279
Escape to Burma, 127
Escape, 84

Esther Waters, 34, 122–123, 156
Eureka, 325
Eva, 19, 253
Evans, Edith, 306, 369
Even Cowgirls Get the Blues, 198
Evensong, 161, 169
Everett, Rupert, 205, 280
Evergreen, 123–124, 268, 333
Exorcist, The, 364
Expert, The, 154
Expresso Bongo, 125, 166, 175
Eye for an Eye, 337

Face, 391
Face of Fu-Manchu, The, 239
Face, 55
Fahrenheit 451, 65, 324
Fairbanks, Douglas, 223
Fairchild, William, 343
Faith, Adam, 334
Faithful Heart, The, 124
Fallen Idol, The,71, 96, 224, 317, 318
Fame Is the Spur, 37, 38
Family Doctor, 153
Family Life, 247
Family Way, The, 37, 126–127, 222, 270
Fanny by Gaslight, 11, 49, 156
Far from the Madding Crowd, 22, 65,
  324, 325, 337
Farewell Again, 20
Farr, Derek, 159
Farrar, David, 78, 102, 127–128, 154, 353
Fassbinder, Rainer Werner, 34
Fast Lady, The, 65
Father Brown, 128–129, 130, 165, 174
Fear in the Night, 88
Fears, Stephen, 198
Felicia's Journey, 190
Fengriffen, 7, 18
Ferrer, José, 128, 137
Fields, Gracie, 129, 178, 267, 268
Fienburgh, Wilfred, 286
Fiendish Plot of Dr. Fu Manchu, The, 339
Fifty Days at Peking, 321
Fight Club, 36
Final Test, The, 11
Finch, Peter, 17, 39, 68, 129–132, 174,
  213, 279, 337, 367

Fine Madness, A, 73
Fine Romance, A, 105
Finney, Albert, 131–132, 273, 297, 369
Fire Over England, 132–133, 264, 281,
  294, 318, 321
Fire Raisers, The, 20, 307
First a Girl, 268, 333
Firth, Peter, 4
Fish Called Wanda, A, 77, 78, 133–134
Fisher, Gerry, 4
Fisher, Terence, 85, 88, 106, 116, 117,
  134–136, 238, 239, 275
Fitzgerald, F. Scott, 68
Fitzgerald, Geraldine, 365
Five Fingers, 265
Fixer, The, 22
Flame in the Streets, 18, 269
Flaming Frontier, 157
Flanagan, Bud, 144
Flap. See The Last Warrior/Flap
Fleet, James, 140, 280
Fleming, Atholl, 318
Fleming, Ian, 72, 115, 142, 152, 237
Flesh Gordon, 81
Floods of Fear, 78
Flynn, Errol, 111, 366, 385
Flynn, Sean, 366
Follow a Star, ix, 350–351, 392
Fonda, Bridget, 336
Fonda, Henry, 388
Footsteps in the Fog, 157
For Them That Trespass, 366
For Those in Peril, 78
Forbes, Bryan, 13, 136–138, 177, 234,
  235, 249, 306
Ford, John, 8, 177, 289, 321, 399
Foreman, Carl, 132
Forever Amber, 84
Forever and a Day, 268, 334
Forever England, 270
Formby, George, 49, 138, 178, 392, 393
Forsyte Saga, The, 273
Fort Apache, 289
Fortune Is a Woman, 171
Fortunes of War, 363
49th Parallel, 87, 138–140, 305, 308
Four Feathers, The, 118, 174, 224
Four in the Morning, 104

Four Weddings and a Funeral, xi, 140–141, 280, 281

Fox, James, 189, 236, 253, 324

Fraenkel, Heinrich, 244

Francis, Freddie, 209

Frank, Charles, 17

Frankel, Benjamin, 397

Frankenheimer, John, 22, 175

Frankenstein and the Monster from Hell, 86, 136

Frankenstein Must Be Destroyed, 88, 136

Fraser, Liz, 206

Frears, Stephen, 279, 335

Free Cinema, xv, 8, 319

French Dressing, 328

French Without Tears, 11

Frend, Charles, 327

Frenzy, 185

Freud, Sigmund, 306

Freund, Karl, 275

Friday the Thirteenth, 333

Frieda, 101, 321

Friedkin, William, 392

Friends and Lovers, 294

Frightened City, The, 72

From Here to Eternity, 218, 219

From Russia with Love, 141–142

Frozen Limits, The, 144

Fry, Stephen, 363

Full Monty, The, xi, 40, 41, 54, 55, 142–143, 371

Fuller, Sam, 351

Funeral in Berlin, 47

Fyffe, Will, 45

Gabel, Scilla, 354

Gable, Clark, 55

Gaffney, Marjorie, 124

Gainsborough Melodrama, xiii, 11, 156, 214, 215

Gainsborough Studios, 16, 17, 39, 166, 178, 184, 394

Gallipoli, 4

Gambit, 279

Gandhi, 14

Gandhi, Mohandas, 14

Gangster, The, 153

Garbo, Greta, 294

Gardner, Ava, 154

Gardner, Joan, 383

Garfunkel, Art, 324

Garland, Judy, 279

Garner, James, 279

Garnett, Tony, 247

Gasbags, 144–145

Gaslight (1940), 107, 145–146, 281

Gaslight (1944), 107, 145

Gastoni, Lisa, 153

Gaumont-British, 184, 236, 244, 268, 307, 318

Geeson, Sally, 392

Genevieve, 110, 146–147, 272, 273

Genn, Leo, 158, 162, 365

Gentle Gunman, The, 102

Gentle Sex, The, 164

Gentleman Joe Palooka, 123

George in Civvy Street, 138

Georgy Girl, xiii, xiv, 22, 147–148, 265

Gere, Richard, 337

Get Carter (1971), 48, 81, 148–150

Get Carter (2000), 150

Getting It Right, 36

Ghost of St. Michael's, 178

Ghost Train, 16

Ghoul, The, 318

Gibson, Mel, 188

Gideon's Day, 177, 234

Gielgud, John, 62, 150–151, 164, 169, 187, 243, 264, 294

Gold Diggers, The, 66

Gilbert, John, 294

Gilbert, Lewis, 151–152, 153

Gilliat, Sidney, 49, 162, 163, 202, 203, 219, 227, 231–232, 248, 317, 322, 356

Gilliatt, Penelope, 337

Gilling, John, 120

Girl from Maxim's, The, 200

Girl in the Crowd, The, 393

Girl on the Boat, The, 392

Girl with Green Eyes, 130

Gish, Dorothy, 384

Gish, Lillian, 8

Glory!Glory!, 9

Gobel, George, 114

Go-Between, The, 22, 65, 253, 254

Godard, Jean Luc, xii

Goddard, Paulette, 272
Golan, Menahem, 392
Gold, Jimmy, 144
Golden Horde, The, 127
Golden Salamander, The, 194, 278
GoldenEye, 105
Goldfinger, 73, 116, 141, 262
Gone to Earth (The Wild Heart), 127, 308
Gone With the Wind, 294
Good Companions, The, 150, 268, 333
Good Die Young, The, 19, 68, 79, 151, 152–153, 174
Good Father, The, 188, 281
Good Guys, The, 19
Good Time Girl, The, 321
Goodbye, Mr. Chipps (1939), 111, 270, 274, 333
Goodbye, Mr. Chipps (1969), 298
Goole by Numbers, 164
Goon Show, 338
Goose Steps Out, The, 178
Gordon, Colin, 163
Gorgon, The, 238
Goring, Marius, 153–155, 171, 353
Gosford Park, 21
Gough, Michael, 74
Governess, The, 155–156
Grahame, Gloria, 151, 153
Granger, Stewart, 11, 29, 49, 80, 81, 156–158, 159, 258, 269
Grant, Arthur, 23, 59
Grant, Cary, 55, 115
Grant, Hugh, 140, 141, 280
Grant, Richard, 36
Gray, Charles, 106, 177, 239
Gray, Sally, 57, 158–159, 162, 194, 264
Great Day, xi, xiv, 70, 71, 159–160, 306, 321
Great Expectations, xiii, 160–161, 169, 187, 235, 236, 254, 257, 269, 279
Great Gatsby, The, 67, 68, 69
Great St. Trinian's Train Robbery, The, 231, 344
Green, Pam, 302
Green for Danger, 158, 161–162, 194, 231, 343
Green Grass of Wyoming, 84
Green Man, The, 162–163, 232, 344, 356

Green Scarf, The, 366
Green, Danny, 228
Green, Guy, 161, 187, 254, 257, 300
Green, Janet, 254, 376
Greenaway, Peter, xii, 151, 163–164, 324
Greenbaum, Mutz (Max Greene), 183, 283
Greene, Graham, 37, 44, 144, 153, 316, 317, 318, 359, 360
Greene, Richard, 135
Greengage Summer, The, 152, 273, 334
Greenwood, Joan, 164, 186, 222, 293, 369
Greer, Jane, 194, 249
Gregson, John, 84, 110
Grenfell, Joyce, 24, 33, 356
Grey, Nadia, 80
Griffith, Hugh, 369
Griffiths, D.W., 9
Griffiths, Rachel, 180
Grunwald, Anatole de, 11, 37, 111, 389
Guest, Val, xii, 23, 98, 125, 165–167, 178, 357, 358, 380
Guide for the Married Man, A, 355
Guillermin, John, xii, 167–169, 241, 278, 297, 339, 354, 366
Guinness, Alec, 78, 134, 161, 169–170, 174, 186, 217, 222, 228, 229, 233, 235, 256, 259, 260, 269, 278, 279, 327
Gulpilil, David, 324
Gun Crazy, 84
Gun Glory, 157
Guns at Batasi, 14, 167, 168
Guns of Navarone, The, 242, 272
Gurney, Claude, 162
Gutierrez, Sebastian, 363
Gynt, Greta, 39, 100, 101, 158, 170–171, 278, 306, 354
Gypsy and the Gentleman, The, 253

H.M.S. Defiant, 34, 152, 185–186
Hackney, Alan, 38, 206
Hafenrichter, Oswald, 360
Hale, Sonny, 268
Halfway House, 102
Hall, Peter, 19
Hall, Willis, 223
Hallam Films, 239, 252, 260, 303, 304, 306, 349, 394

Hamer, Robert, xi, xii, 77, 99, 129, 130, 173–174, 186, 210, 220, 221, 222, 252, 260, 303, 304, 306, 349, 394
Hamilton, Guy, 136, 194, 262
Hamilton, Patrick, 134, 145
Hamish Macbeth, 54
Hamlet (1948), 71, 87, 96, 295
Hamlet (1990), 22, 36
Hammer Studios, xi, xii, xiii, 18, 30, 59, 77, 85, 86, 106, 116, 117, 134, 135, 136, 166, 191, 237, 238, 275, 311, 312, 364, 366
Hammett, Dashiell, 132
Hanbury, Victor, 127
Hand, The, 48
Handful of Dust, A, 105
Handl, Irene, 37
Hands of Orlac, The, 238
Hands of the Ripper, 31
Hanley, Jimmy, 52, 380
Hannah and Her Sisters, 48
Hannah, John, 141, 280
Hannibal, 189
Hannie Caulder, 239
Happiest Days of Your Life, The, 329, 344
Happy Family, The, 39
Hardy, Oliver, 87
Hardy, Robin, 384
Hardy, Thomas, 65
Harker, Gordon, 343
Harris, Julie, 201
Harris, Julie, 95
Harris, Richard, 8, 297, 361, 362
Harris, Vernon, 153
Harrison, Kathleen, 39
Harrison, Rex, 334, 385
Harvey, Frank, 38, 206
Harvey, Laurence, 68, 125, 166, 174–175, 297, 326, 367
Harwood, Johanna, 141
Hasty Heart, The, 209, 366
Hathaway, Henry, 157
Hatter's Castle, 70, 176–177, 218, 264, 281
Havelock-Allen, Anthony, 11, 187, 208, 236, 278, 396
Hawkins, Jack, 83, 84, 104
Hawks, Howard, 43, 177
Hawthorne, Nigel, 390

Hawtrey, Charles, 57, 58
Hay, Will, 16, 40, 102, 165, 178–179, 393
Haynes, Stanley, 158, 258, 300
Hayter, James, 283
Hare, David, 299–300
Hayutin, Harvey, 354
Hayward, Louis, 87
Hazard of Hearts, A, 36
He Who Rides the Tiger, 104
Head, Murray, 130, 213, 337
Hearts in Atlantis, 189
Heat and Dust, 68
Heaven Can Wait, 65
Heaven Knows Mr. Allison, 219
Heavens Above!, 37, 55, 206
Heckroth, Hein, 314
Heflin, Van, 253
Heiress, The, 317, 318
Hell Below Zero, 137
Hell Drivers, 19, 72, 79, 84, 122, 179–180, 399
Hell Is a City, 166
Helpmann, Robert, 53
Helter Skelter, 355
Hemmings, Lindy, 371
Henderson, Shirley, 370
Hendry, Ian, 23, 149, 182
Henreid, Paul, 191
Henry V (1989), 105, 363
Henry V (1944), 21, 295
Hepburn, Audrey, 132
Hepburn, Katharine, 236, 297
Here Comes Mr. Jordan, 65
Here Comes the Huggetts, 380
Herlithy, James Leo, 337
Herman, Mark, 41
Heston, Charlton, 280
Hidden Agenda, 247
Hidden Master, 87
Higgins, Jack, 81,
High and the Mighty, The, 215
High Command, 107
High Fidelity, 281
High Hopes, 243
High Jinks in Society, 167
High Noon, 396
High Treason, 37, 206
High Wind in Jamaica, 257, 327

Highly Dangerous, 154, 249
Hilary and Jackie, 180–181
Hill 24 Doesn't Answer, 108
Hill, The, 72, 73, 181–182, 315, 382
Hiller, Wendy, 202
Hillier, Erwin, 210, 263
Hindle Wakes (1931), xv, 182–183, 333
Hinds, Anthony, 116, 166
Hird, Thora, 223
His Excellency, 306
History of Mr. Polly, The, 269, 323
Hit Man, 149
Hit, The, 198
Hitchcock, Alfred, xi, xii, xiii, 13, 20, 28,
     29, 45, 52, 71, 73, 111, 150, 173,
     183–185, 226, 227, 231, 241, 248, 249,
     250, 302, 303, 309, 314, 346, 365, 367
Hobson, Valerie, 29, 156, 186–187, 210,
     335, 367
Hobson's Choice, 224, 236
Hodge, John, 341, 342
Hodges, Mike, 81, 82, 149
Hoffman, Dustin, 337
Holiday Camp, 39, 380
Holloway, Stanley, 43, 78, 134, 169, 233
Holly and the Ivy, The, 217
Holm, Ian, 63, 92, 105, 280
Holt, Seth, 30, 280, 366
Home at Seven, 177, 318
Home, Willam Douglas, 64
Homicide: Life on the Streets, 280
Hopkins, Anthony, 100, 104, 187–190, 196
Hornsby, Nick, 281
Horrocks, Jane, 245, 246
Horror of It All, The, 136
Horse's Mouth, The, 279
Hoskins, Bob, 190–191, 372
Houghton, Stanley, 182
Hound of the Baskervilles, The (1959),
     87, 135
House Across the Lake, The, 191–192, 217
House Committee on Un-American Activ-
     ities, 122, 253, 256, 291
House of Cards, 168
House of Darkness, 174
House of Mirth, The, 97, 98, 192–193
House on the Square, The, 17
Houston, Donald, 94

How the Grinch Stole Christmas, 189
How To Murder Your Wife, 355
Howard, Joyce, 264
Howard, Leslie, 150, 164
Howard, Trevor, 4, 37, 158, 162,
     193–195, 262, 263, 278, 316, 365
Howard, William, 133
Howards End, 36, 188, 195–196, 362
Howe, James Wong, 133
Hudis, Norman, 58
Hudson, Hugh, 63
Hue and Cry, 5, 78, 196–197, 343, 379
Huggetts Abroad, The, 380
Hughes, Ken, 191, 216, 217
Hughes, Richard, 327
Hulbert, Claude, 45
Hulbert, Jack, 45, 318
Hunt, Martita, 161, 212
Hunted, 78
Hunter, Ian, 249
Huntington, Lawrence, 70, 265, 322, 333
Huntley, Raymond, 163, 206
Hurry Sundown, 47
Hurst, Brian Desmond, 158, 264, 306
Hurt, John, 197–199, 335
Huston, John, 306
Huxley, Aldous, 106
Hylton, Jane, 212

I Accuse!, 128
I Am a Camera, 174, 200–201
I, Claudius, 198
I Could Go On Singing, 279
I Know Where I'm Going!, 201–202, 308
I Live in Grosvenor Square, 385
I Married a Woman, 114
I See a Dark Stranger, 194, 202–203, 219,
     232
I Was Monty's Double, 167
I, the Jury, 334
I'm All Right Jack, 37, 38, 55, 205–207,
     243, 338, 339, 355
Ice Cold in Alex, xv, 203–204, 242
Ideal Husband, An (1947), 68, 224, 272
Ideal Husband, An (1999), 204–205
If . . . , 3, 8, 9, 373
Importance of Being Earnest, The, 11, 12,
     314, 329

Impulse, 122
In Which We Serve, 13, 207–208, 217, 236, 269, 278
Indiscreet, 50
Inferno, 17
Ingram, Rex, 307
Inn of the Sixth Happiness, The, 111
Innocent Bystanders, 19–20
Innocent, The, 337
Innocents, The, 68, 69, 208–209, 219, 377
Inspector Calls, An, 136, 344
Inspector Hornleigh series, 343
International Velvet, 137
Interrupted Journey, 187, 209–210, 367
Ill Met by Moonlight, 154, 238
Intimate Stranger, 252
Invasion of the Body Snatchers, 311
Ipcress File, The, 47
Ireland, John, 153
Iris, 105
Isherwood, Christopher, 174, 244
Island of Terror, 136
It Always Rains on Sunday, 173, 210–211, 303, 380, 394
It Started in Paradise, 211
It's a Mad Mad Mad World, 355
It's a Wonderful Life, 267
It's Alive, 376
It's Love Again, 268, 333
It's Never Too Late, 50
It's Not Cricket, 276
Italian Job, The, 48
Ivanhoe, 71
Ivory, James, 189

Jackson, Freda, 153
Jackson, Glenda, 130, 213–214, 328, 337
Jackson, Gordon, 394
Jackson, Jerome, 307
Jacqueline, 17
Jacques, Hattie, 57, 58, 61, 350, 351
Jagger, Dean, 385
Jagger, Mick, 320
Jamaica Inn, 173, 185, 241
James, Henry, 68, 88, 192, 209
James, Sid, 57, 58, 229, 288, 343
Janni, Joseph, 305, 336
Jarman, Derek, 106

Jason, Rick, 153
Jassy, 214–215, 249, 323
Jaws: The Revenge (Jaws 4), 48
Jenkins, Megs, 162
Jennings, Humphrey, 26
Jet Over the Atlantic, 215
Jet Storm, 19, 215–216
Jewel of the Seven Stars, 30, 280
Jhabvala, Ruth Prawer, 196
Jigsaw, 166
Jinnah, 239
Joe Macbeth, 216–217
John, Lucien, 324
John, Rosamund, 162
Johnny Frenchman, 322
Johnny Guitar, 396
Johns, Glynis, 367
Johns, Mervyn, 173, 178
Johnson, Celia, 43, 113, 194, 217–218
Johnson, Katie, 169, 228, 338
Johnson, Richard, 4, 92
Johnston, Margaret, 71
Jones, Griffith, 158, 268
Jones, Peter, 33
Jordan, Louis, 280
Jordan, Neil, 190
Joseph Andrews, 320
Judas Kiss, 363
Judd, Edward, 98
Julius Caesar (1953), 150
Junge, Alfred, 27, 45, 67, 244, 267
Jurassic Park, 14
Justice, James Robertson, 110, 367
Jympson, John, 134

Kael, Pauline, 235
Karas, Anton, 316, 360
Karloff, Boris, 237, 238, 275, 318
Kaufman, Charles, 352
Kazan, Elia, 219
Keaton, Buster, 9
Keel, Howard, 78
Keeler, Christine, 335, 336
Keen, Geoffrey, 61
Keep It Up Downstairs, 114
Keep the Aspidistra Flying (A Merry War), 36
Kellino, Pamela, 265

Kempson, Rachel, 148, 315

Kendall, Kay, 39, 110, 146

Kenilworth Productions, 120

Kennedy, Margaret, 244

Kenney, James, 76, 151, 153

Kent, Jean, 53, 321, 323

Kerr, Deborah, 28, 46, 68, 158, 194, 203, 209, 218–219, 224

Kes, 247

Key, The, 194, 317

Khartoum, 295

Kid for Two Farthings, A, 113

Kidnapped (1960), 297

Kind Hearts and Coronets, 102, 165, 169, 173, 186, 187, 210, 219–222, 233, 260, 327, 341, 349

Kind of Loving, A, 21, 222–223, 336

King and Country, 253,

King and I, The, 218–219

King Kong (1976), 167

King Kong Lives, 167

King Rat, 137

King Richard and the Crusaders, 174

King Solomon's Mines (1950), 156, 218

King's Rhapsody, 385

Kingsley, Ben, 391

Kinnear, Roy, 182

Kipps, 314

Kiss Me Deadly, 334

Kiss of Death, 283

Kiss the Blood Off My Hands, 281

Kline, Kevin, 134

Knack, The, 147

Kneale, Nigel, 311, 312

Knight Without Armour, 111

Knight, Esmond, 303

Knight, Shirley, 65

Knowles, Bernard, 11, 46, 70

Knox, Alexander, 3, 253

Knox, Teddy, 144

Koch, Marianne, 333

Korda, Alexander, xi, 118, 133, 150, 176, 223–225, 261, 262, 271, 272, 307, 308, 310, 313, 317, 318, 321, 333, 382, 383

Korda, Vincent, 118, 224

Korda, Zoltan, 77, 118, 224, 331

Kramer, Stanley, 276

Krampf, Gunther, 244

Krasker, Robert, 80, 316, 360

Kristofferson, Kris, 168

Kruger, Hardy, 18

Kubrik, Stanley, 189, 339

La Rue, Jack, 288

Lacey, Catherine, 304

Ladd, Alan, 136, 137

Lady from Shanghai, The, 76

Lady Hamilton, 224, 294

Lady Jane, 35, 36

Lady Vanishes, The (1938), 100, 184, 185, 202, 203, 226–227, 231, 248, 314

Lady With a Lamp, The, 385

Ladybird, Ladybird, 391

Ladykillers, The, 30, 146, 169, 227–228, 256, 338, 341, 380

Lair of the White Worm, The, 288

Lancaster, Burt, 78, 238, 256, 281

Land and Freedom, 247

Land of the Pharaohs, 177

Landlady, The, 36

Lang, Fritz, 124, 210, 315

Lange, Jessica, 320

Langella, Frank, 294

Lassally, Walter, 251, 369

Last Emperor, The, 298

Last Grenade, The, 19

Last Holiday, 228–229

Last Hunt, The, 157

Last of the Blonde Bombshells, The, 105

Last Orders, 48, 191, 391

Last Page, The, 191

Last Safari, The, 157

Last Tango in Paris, 107

Last Warrior/Flap, The, 317

Late Edwina Black, The, 229–230

Late Extra, 264

Late George Apley, The, 84

Laughing Annie, 249

Laughter in Paradise, 230–231, 344

Laughton, Charles, 46, 236, 253, 310

Launder, Frank, 49, 163, 202, 203, 219, 227, 231–232, 248, 317, 322, 329, 344, 356

Laurel, Stan, 87

Laurie, Hugh, 363

Laurie, John, 45

Lavender Hill Mob, The, 78, 79, 134, 169, 170, 232–233

Law and Disorder, 78

Law, Phyllida, 121, 363

Lawless, The, 253

Lawrence of Arabia, 170, 177, 236, 297, 298

Lawrence, Josie, 281

Lawrence, Quentin, 59

Lawson, Arthur, 314

Le Carré, John, 170

Le Fanu, Sheridan, 17,18

League of Gentlemen, The, 137, 177, 234–235

Lean, David, xi, xii, 42, 43, 65, 160–161, 170, 177, 187, 208, 224, 235–237, 254, 257, 258, 269, 278, 281, 297, 300, 301, 302, 318, 329, 365

Lee Thompson, J., xi, xiii, xv, 113, 114, 204, 241–242, 272, 289

Lee, Bernard, 141

Lee, Christopher, xii, 18, 86, 87, 106, 117, 135, 136, 237–241, 275, 384

Lee, Mark, 4

Legend of the Seven Golden Vampires, The, 18

Leigh, Mike, 242–245, 370

Leigh, Vivien, 130, 224, 273, 294, 334, 363

Leighton, Margaret, 174, 390

Leland, David, 190

Lemmon, Jack, 355

Leslie, Eddie, 350

Lesser, Sol, 354

Lester, Richard, 65, 324

Let George Do It, 49

Lewis, Gary, 25

Lewis, Jerry, 392

Lewis, Ted, 149

Life and Death of Colonel Blimp, The, 267, 308

Life for Ruth, 102, 137

Lifeboat, 185

Lilacs in the Spring, 127, 385

Lindbergh Kidnapping Case, The, 188

Lion Has Wings, The, 318, 321

Lion in Winter, The, 189, 297, 298

Lisi, Virni, 253, 355

Listen to Britain, 26

Little Ballerina, The, 151

Little Damozel, 384

Little Dorrit, 170

Little Friend, 244–245

Little Hut, The, 157

Little Romance, A, 294

Little Voice, 48, 245–246

Litvak, Anatole, 298

Livesey, Roger, 137, 202, 234

Living Dangerously, 200

Llewelyn, Desmond, 141

Lloyd, Harold, 9

Loach, Ken, 53, 55, 243, 246–248, 279–280, 285, 304, 305, 391

Lock, Stock and Two Smoking Barrels, xiv, 347

Lockwood, Margaret, 49, 71, 214, 248–249, 258, 264, 265, 322, 323

Loder, John, 383

Lodger, The (1926), xiii, 184, 249–250

Lodger, The (1932), 176

Lolita, 265, 339

Lom, Herbert, 135, 228, 283

Lombard, Carole, 87

London Belongs to Me, 343

London Films, 77, 224, 261, 262, 271, 283, 382

Loneliness of the Long Distance Runner, The, 250–251, 320

Lonely Passion of Judith Hearne, The, 69, 190

Long and the Short and the Tall, The, 47, 297, 367

Long Arm, The, 177

Long Day Closes, The, 97, 98

Long Good Friday, The, 190, 191

Long John Silver, 282

Long Memory, The, 174, 251–252, 269

Long Wait, The, 334

Longden, John, 266

Longest Day, The, 368

Look Back in Anger (1959), 174, 222, 319, 325

Look Back in Anger (1993), 362

Look Back in Anger (play), xv, 21, 319

Looks and Smiles, 247

Lord of the Flies, 373

Lord of the Rings: The Fellowship of the Ring, 239
Lord of the Rings: The Return of the King, 240
Lord of the Rings: The Two Towers, 240
Loren, Sophia, 12, 217, 339
Lorna Doone, 248
Lorre, Peter, 150
Losey, Joseph, 2, 3, 19, 22, 34, 65, 79, 87, 252–254, 315, 361, 366
Lost Continent, The, 106, 239
Lost, 127–128, 254–255
Love and Death on Long Island, 198
Love Story, 156, 327
Lovell, Alan, xii, xv
Loves of Joanna Godden, The, 394
Low, Rachel, xii
L-Shaped Room, The, 137
Lucas, George, 170
Lucky Jim, 206
Lugosi, Bela, 85
Lumet, Sidney, 72, 182, 194, 265
Lust for a Vampire, 88
Lydecker, Howard, 186
Lynley, Carol, 87
Lyon, Bebe, 166
Lyon, Ben, 166
Lyons in Paris, 166
Lyons, Sue, 265

M (1951), 252
Macaulay, Richard, 153
Macaulay, Tom, 203
Macdonald, Andrew, 341, 342
MacDonald, Jeanette, 333
MacDougall, Roger, 257, 261
MacDowell, Andie, 280
MacGinnis, Niall, 354
Mackendrick, Alexander, xii, 50, 77, 169, 227, 256–257, 259–260, 261
Mackenzie, John, 190
MacPhail, Angus, 100
Macrae, Duncan, 45
MacWilliams, Glen, 67
Madame Bovary, 285
Madeleine, xii, 21, 236, 254, 257–258, 365
Mademoiselle, 320

Madison, Guy, 215
Madness of the Heart, 46, 249
Madonna and the Child, 97
Madonna of the Seven Moons, 49, 156, 322, 323
Magic Bow, The, 49, 156
Magic Box, The, 38, 188
Magic Christian, The, 239
Magic Fire, 87
Magic, 14, 100
Magnificent Obsession, The, 352
Mahoney, Jock, 168
Maibaum, Richard, 141
Major Barbara, 218
Make Mine Mink, 355
Mamet, David, 189, 390
Man Between, The, 317
Man Called Peter, A, 367
Man Could Get Killed, A, 279
Man in Grey, The, 49, 79, 156, 214, 248, 258–259, 264, 284, 341
Man in the Iron Mask, The (1939), 87
Man in the Iron Mask, The (1977), 280
Man in the White Suit, The, 165, 169, 206, 233, 256, 257, 259–261
Man of Two Worlds, 107
Man on the Eiffel Tower, The, 323
Man Who Could Work Miracles, The, 261–262, 318
Man Who Fell to Earth, The, 325
Man Who Knew Too Much, The (1934), 20, 31, 183
Man Who Never Was, The, 279
Man Who Would Be King, The, 48
Man with the Golden Gun, The, 239
Manchurian Candidate, The, 175
Mandingo, 265
Mandy, 49–50, 177, 257
Manhunter, 189
Mankiewicz, Joseph, 150, 211, 212
Mankowitz, Wolf, 125, 166
Mann, Anthony, 175
Mann, Michael, 189
Mansfield, Jayne, 273
Manuela, 194, 262–263
Marathon Man, 295, 337
Mark of Cain, The, xiii, 159, 263–264, 306, 348

Marks, Leo, 302, 303
Marlowe, Hugh, 283
Marnie, 73
Marriott, Moore, 16, 178
Marsh, Gary, 203, 394
Martinelli, Elsa, 194, 262
Mask of Zorro, The, 189
Masks of Death, The, 18
Mason, James, 49, 133, 150, 156, 158,
    258, 259, 264–266, 284, 285, 309, 317,
    341, 365
Masque of Red Death, The, 324
Master Plan, The, 122
Matter of Life and Death, A, 46, 154,
    266–267, 308
Matthews, A.E., 64
Matthews, Jessie, 124, 150, 267–269,
    333
Mature, Victor, 349
Maxwell, Lois, 141
Mayersburg, Paul, 81, 82
Maytime in Mayfair, 385
Mazurki, Mike, 283
Mazursky, Paul, 22
Mazzeti, Lorenza, 8
McCabe and Mrs. Miller, 65
McCallum, John, 49, 394
McCowen, Alec, 167
McDowell, Malcolm, 3, 8
McGoohan, Patrick, 6, 280
McGovern, Jimmy, 54
McGrath, Douglas, 121
McGregor, Ewan, 121, 341
McIlwraith, William, 18
McKenna, Siobhan, 71
McKinnal, Norman, 183
McLaglen, Victor, 122
McLaughlin, Gibb, 283
Meadows, Shane, 371, 372
Meantime, 243
Medak, Peter, 22, 177, 298, 344
Medicine Man, 73
Meet Joe Black, 189
Meet John Doe, 351
Meet Sexton Blake, 127
Melody in the Dark, 167
Melville, Alan, 39
Memento Mori, 69

Men of Sherwood Forest, 166
Men of Two Worlds, 107
Merchant, Vivien, 6
Merchant-Ivory Productions, 195, 196
Meredith, Burgess, 272
Merivale, John, 67
Mermaids, 190
Merrall, Mary, 230
Merrill, Gary, 17
*Merry War, A (Keep the Aspidistra Fly-
    ing),* 36
Meteor, 194, 279
Metropolis, 124
Miami Vice, 36
Michael, Ralph, 394
Middleton, Guy, 231
Midnight Cowboy, 337
Midnight Express, 198
Midnight in St. Petersburg, 47
Midshipmaid, The, 269
Midshipman Easy, 316
Mighty Aphrodite, 36
Miles, Bernard, 61, 158
Miles, Sarah, 253
Milland, Ray, 4, 322, 348, 365
Miller, Arthur, 54
Miller, David, 352
Miller's Crossing, 132
Milligan, Spike, 338
Million Dollar Note, The, 278
Millionairess, The, 12, 339
Millions Like Us, 232, 306, 322
Mills, Hayley, 37, 126, 137, 270
Mills, John, 2, 18, 20, 35, 94, 126, 127,
    156, 160, 165, 167, 204, 269–270, 279,
    293, 323, 343
Mine Own Executioner, 224, 271–272,
    284
Mingus, Charlie, 7
Miniver Story, The, 324
Minnelli, Liza, 132
Minnelli, Vincente, 279
Miracle in Soho, 309
Miranda, 394
Mirren, Helen, 265, 309
Miss London Ltd, 166
Miss Pilgrim's Progress, 166
Miss Robin Hood, 167

Mission: Impossible II, 189
Mitchell, Yvonne, 242
Mix Me a Person, 334
Modesty Blaise, 252
Moffat, Graham, 178
Molly Maguires, The, 73
Molokai: The Story of Father Damian, 298
Momma Don't Allow, 319
Mona Lisa, 48, 190, 191
Monkhouse, Bob, 58
MacGinnis, Niall, 61, 62, 167
Monroe, Marilyn, 17, 295
Monster Club, The, 18
Monte Carlo or Bust (Those Daring Young Men in Their Jaunty Jalopies), 355
Montgomery, Robert, 281
Moon Zero Two, 18
Moonlight Madness. See The Night Has Eyes
Moonraker, 152
Moore, Dudley, 150
Moore, Julianne, 104
Moore, Kieron, 234
Moore, Roger, 115, 152, 239
More, Kenneth, 14, 61, 110, 147, 152, 272–274, 334
Moreau, Jeanne, 19, 253, 320
Morell, Andre, xiii, 59, 165
Morgan, Diana, 327
Morgan, Terence, 84
Morley, Robert, 162
Morning Departure, 2, 17, 234, 269
Morris, Oswald, 182
Morrisey, Paul, 356
Morse, Laila, 286
Morse, Robert, 257
Moss Rose, 84, 263, 348
Most Dangerous Game, The, 20, 37
Mothman Prophecies, The, 22
Moulin Rouge, 68, 87
Mountain Eagle, The, 184
Mountbatten, Lord Louis, 208
Mourning Becomes Electra, 315
Mouse That Roared, The, 339
Mr. and Mrs. Edgehill, 105
Mr. Drake's Duck, 166

Mr. Klein, 254
Mr. Perrin and Mr. Traill, 127, 154, 171, 274, 353
Mrs. Brown, 104, 105
Mrs. Dale's Diary, 268
Much Ado About Nothing, 363
Mummy, The (1959), 86, 135, 238, 274–275
Mummy's Hand, The, 275
Mummy's Tomb, The, 275
Murder Ahoy, 329
Murder by Decree, 265
Murder on the Orient Express, 132
Murder Without Crime, 241
Murder, She Said, 329
Murder, My Sweet, 291
Muriel's Wedding, 121
Music Lovers, The, 213, 328
Mute Witness, 169
Mutiny on the Bounty, The (1963), 316, 317
My Brother's Keeper, 276, 380
My Favorite Year, 298
My Gal Sal, 166
My Gun Is Quick, 334
My Learned Friend, 178
My Name Is Joe, 247
Myers, Ruth, 121
Mystery of Marie Celeste, The, 85

Nabokov, Vladimir, 34
Naked Civil Servant, The, 197
Naked Kiss, The, 351
Naked Runner, The, 93
Naked Truth, The, 338
Naked, 243, 370
Name of the Roses, The, 73
National Velvet, 137
Naughton, Bill, 5,6
Naughton, Charlie, 144
Navigators, The, 247–248
Neagle, Anna, 333, 384–386
Neal, Patricia, 366
Neame, Elwin, 278
Neame, Ronald, xiv, 42, 154, 161, 208, 236, 278–279, 354
Ned Kelly (1970), 320
Neff, Hildegarde, 39

Nell Gwyn, 384

Nelson, Richard, 288

Neon Bible, 98

Nervo, Jimmy, 144

Network, 130

Never Let Go, 168, 339, 366, 367

New Lot, The, 316

New Wave, xiii, xiv, xv, 8, 21, 59, 80, 131, 147, 222, 223, 243, 247, 325, 336, 361, 362

Newell, Mike, 91, 92, 140, 141, 188, 279–281

Newman, Nanette, 137

Newman, Paul, 334

Newton, Robert, 70, 159, 176, 218, 281–282

Next Best Thing, The, 337–338

Next of Kin, 108

Nicholls, Mike, 363

Nickel Queen, 394

Nicol, Alex, 192

Night and the City, xiv, 282–284, 394

Night Has Eyes, The, 156, 259, 264, 284–285

Night Must Fall, 132, 369

Night of the Big Heat, The, 136

Night of the Demon, 84

Night of the Generals, The, 298

Night Porter, The, 34

Night They Raided Minsky's, The, 392

Night to Remember, A, 17, 18, 67, 272, 273

Night Train to Munich, 100, 203, 227, 232, 248, 317

Night Train, 198

Night Without Sleep, 17

Nightcomers, The, 209

Nil by Mouth, 97, 285–286, 390, 391

Niven, David, 272

Nixon, 189, 190

No Love for Johnnie, 120, 286–287

No Orchids for Miss Blandish, 287–288

Nolbandov, Sergei, 133

Nolte, Nick, 66

Norman, Leslie, 327

North by Northwest, 55

North to Alaska, 157

North West Frontier, 242, 272, 288–290

North, Neil, 390

Northam, Jeremy, 121, 390

Nose Has It, The, 166

Not the Nine O'Clock News, 363

Nothing But the Best, 325

Nothing But the Night, 239

Notorious, 184, 346

Nugent, Frank, 289

Number 13, 184

Nunn, Trevor, 36

O Lucky Man, 8,9

O'Ferrall, George More, 366

O'Toole, Peter, 47, 297–298

Oberon, Merle, 224, 294, 313, 318, 334, 383

Obsession, 159, 282, 291–292

October Man, The, 17, 165, 269, 292–293

Odd Man Out, 259, 265, 281, 316

Odette, 385

Offence, The, 72, 194

Oh Dad, Poor Dad, Mamma's Hung You in the Closet and I'm Feeling So Sad, 257

Oh! What a Lovely War, 14, 273, 295

Oh, Mr. Porter!, 178

Okay for Sound, 144

Old Mother Riley Detective, 84

Oldman, Gary, 97, 285, 286, 390

Oliver Twist, 71, 170, 236, 281

Oliver, 316

Olivier, Laurence, xii, 21, 88, 130, 133, 150, 187, 189, 224, 264, 281, 293–296, 320, 363

Omen, The 24, 31, 376

Ondra, Anny, 28

On Deadly Ground, 48

One of Our Aircraft Is Missing, 279, 305–306, 394

On the Beat, 350, 392

On the Night of the Fire, 318

Once a Jolly Swagman, 34, 296–297

Once Upon a Dream, 394

Ondricek, Miroslav, 8

One That Got Away, The, 18, 204,

Only Two Can Play, 232, 338, 339

Ooh, You Are Awful, 231

Ophuls, Max, 265

Orders to Kill, 11
Orwell, George, 86
Osborne, John, xv, 21, 319, 369
Oscar Wilde, 376
Othello (1965), 295
Our Gang series, 121
Our Man in Havana, 317
Our Mother's House, 68
Out of the Blue, 268
Out of the Clouds, 102
Overcoat, The, 68
Owen, Alun, 79
Owen, Clive, 82

P.J., 168
Pacino, Al, 280
Pal, George, 268
Palin, Michael, 134
Paltrow, Gwyneth, 121
Paluzzi, Luciana, 122
Paper Orchid, 17
Paradine Case, The, 365
Parallax View, The, 103
Paris by Night, 299–300
Parker, Alan, 132
Parker, Cecil, 228
Parker, Eleanor, 279
Parker, Oliver, 205
Party, The, 339
Passage Home, 17, 262, 343
Passage to India, A, 170, 235, 236
Passing of the Third Floor Back, The, 244
Passionate Adventurer, The, 184
Passionate Friends, xii, 194, 236, 254,
   257, 300–302, 365
Passport to Pimlico, 197, 327
Passport to Shame, 113
Patricia Neal Story, The, 214
Patrick, Nigel, 159, 234
Pavlow, Muriel, 110
Pearls of the Pacific, 127
Peck, Gregory, 278, 294, 365
Peeping Tom, xii, 66, 287, 302–303, 308,
   309
Peg of Old Dury, 384
Pelissier, Anthony, 324
Penn of Pennsylvania, 70, 176, 218
Penny and the Pownall Case, 237

Penny Points to Paradise, 338
Penny Princess, 166
Penrose, Valentine, 77
Peppard, George, 168
Perfect Friday, 19
Perfect Strangers, 224
Perfect Woman, The, 322
Performance, 324
Perkins, Anthony, 303
*Persecution and Assassination of Jean-
   Paul Marat,* 213
Peter's Friends, 363
Petley, Julian, xiv
Petulia, 65, 324
Phantom Lady, xiv, 354
Phantom of the Opera, The, 135
Phipps, Nicholas, 110, 258
Piccadilly Incident, 384, 385
Pickard, David, 115
Pickford, Mary, 223
Pidgeon, Rebecca, 390
Pidgeon, Walter, 334
Pilbeam, Nova, 244
Pinewood Studios, 27, 57, 146
Pink Panther, The, 339
Pink String and Sealing Wax, 173, 210,
   303–304, 394
Pinter, Harold, 2, 3, 253
Pirates of Blood River, The, 238
Pirie, David, xii
Pitt, Brad, 347
Pitt, Ingrid, 77
Pixérécourt, Guilbert de, 53
Planet of the Apes (2001), 36
Play Dirty, 48
Pleasance, Donald, 393
Pleasure Garden, The, 184
Plowright, Joan, 281
Plunkett and Macleane, 54
Poitier, Sidney, 306
Pommer, Erich, 133, 173
Pool of London, 233
Pooley, Olaf, 74
Poor Cow, 247, 304–305
Portman, Eric, xiii, 38, 39, 70, 94, 139,
   159, 160, 171, 174, 305, 308, 365
Portman, Rachel, 121
Portrait of an Artist As a Young Man, 150

Portrait of Clare, 71
Poseidon Adventure, The, 278, 279
Potter, Dennis, 325
Potter, Sally, 66
Powell, Columba, 302
Powell, Dilys, 284, 302
Powell, Michael, xii, 20, 27, 45, 46, 51,
    60, 66, 70, 87, 90, 127, 130, 136, 139,
    140, 154, 186, 201, 202, 203, 210, 224,
    265, 266, 267, 287, 302, 303, 305, 306,
    307–309, 313, 314, 336, 393, 394
Power and the Glory, 129
Power, Tyrone, 17, 177
Prayer for the Dying, A, 81
Press for Time, 391
Pressburger, Emeric, 51, 60, 87, 90, 127,
    139, 140, 154, 201, 202, 224, 266, 267,
    307–309, 313, 314
Preston, Robert, 191
Price, Dennis, 37, 53, 173, 220, 222
Price, Vincent, 8, 177, 393
Prick Up Your Ears, 285
Pride and Prejudice, 294
Priest, 55
Priestley, J.B., 33, 129, 136, 228, 229
Priestley, Jason, 198
Primary Colors, 363
Prime of Miss Jean Brodie, The, 217, 279
Primitive Peoples, 130
Prince and the Pauper, The, 305
Prince and the Showgirl, The, 295
Prisoner of Zenda (1952), 157, 218
Prisoner, The, 177
Private Life of Don Juan, The, 224
Private Life of Henry VIII, The, xi, 111,
    200, 223, 224, 309–310
Private Life of Sherlock Holmes, The, 239
Private's Progress, 37, 38, 55, 206, 243,
    355, 356
Production Code Administration, 109,
    123, 147, 183, 200, 208, 210, 221, 259,
    304, 376, 388
Professionals, The, 78
Profumo, John, 187, 335–336
Prospero's Books, 151, 164
Proud and the Profane, The, 218
Proud, Peter, 123
Proud, Trefor, 371

Providence, 150
Prowler, The, 253
Prude's Fall, The, 184
Psycho, 13, 184, 185, 303, 308, 346, 366
Puckoon, 14
Pulp, 81
Pumpkin Eater, The, 68, 69, 130
Purdom, Edmund, 23
Pure Hell of St. Trinian's, The, 344
Pushing Tin, 280–281
Putnam, David, 62
Pygmalion, 11

Q Planes, 294, 318
Qai des Brumes, 36
QBVII, 188
Quadrophenia, 391
Quatermass and the Pit, 18, 312
Quatermass Xperiment, 166, 380
Quatermass II, 166, 311–312
Quayle, Anthony, 167, 204, 354
Queen Christina, 294
Queen of Spades, The, 107
Queen's Affair, The, 384
Quiller Memorandum, The, 93
Quills, 48
Quinn, Anthony, 22, 257, 334
Quo Vadis?, 156

Radford, Basil, 61, 78, 100, 203
Rafferty, Chips, 394
Raggedy Rawney, The, 191
Railroaded, 153
Railsback, Steve, 298
Railway Station Man, The, 66
Rainbow, The, 214
Raines, Ella, 354
Raining Stones, 247
Rains, Claude, 67, 184, 301, 365
Raker, C. *See* Cy R. Endfield
Raker, Hugh. *See* Cy R. Endfield
Rampage at Apache Wells, 157
Rampling, Charlotte, 300
Randall, Tony, 329
Rank Organisation, 2, 12, 14, 23, 33, 39,
    61, 109, 110, 113, 134, 212, 235, 237,
    241, 253, 272, 278, 308, 323, 350, 361,
    362, 391, 396

Raphael, Frederic, 95, 96, 337
Rapture, 168
Rasputin, the Mad Monk, 239
Rather English Marriage, A, 132
Rats of Tobruk, The, 129
Ratsel der Roten Orchidee, Das, 238
Rattigan, Terence, 11, 12, 35, 37, 111,
   132, 295, 315, 389
Rattle of a Simple Man, The, 38
Ravenous, 54, 55
Raw Deal, 153
Rawlings, Terry, 63
Ray, Nicholas, 238, 265, 297
Ray, Satayit, xii
Reach for the Sky, 110, 151, 152, 272, 273
Reagan, Ronald, 366
Rear Window, 185
Rebecca, 185, 230, 294, 295
Rebel Son, The, 322
Red Beret, The, 137
Red Dragon, 189
Red Shoes, The, 127, 154, 308, 313–314,
   353
Redgrave, Corin, 315
Redgrave, Gemma, 314
Redgrave, Lynn, 148, 315
Redgrave, Michael, 52, 182, 248,
   314–316
Redgrave, Roy, 314
Redgrave, Vanessa, 196, 315, 320
Redman, Joyce, 369
Reed, Carol, xi, xii, 113, 224, 232, 248,
   265, 314, 316–317, 318, 360, 361
Reed, Maxwell, 365
Reed, Oliver, 22
Reeves, Michael, 393
Reisz, Karel, 8, 131, 132, 319, 320, 361,
   367
Relph, Michael, 101, 102, 137, 231, 235,
   376
Reluctant Widow, The, 46
Remains of the Day, The, 189, 362
Rembrandt, 224
Rennehan, Ray, 388
Requiem for a Heavyweight, 72
Return from the Ashes, The, 242
Return of Bulldog Drummond, The, 318
Return of the Saint, 78

Return of the Scarlet Pimpernel, The, 264
Return of the Soldier, The, 66
Reville, Alma, 184
Rhodes of Africa, 244
Rhodes, Marjorie, 127, 179, 255
Rich, Roy, 276
Richard III (1955), 224, 295
Richard, Cliff, 125, 166, 175
Richardson, Joely, 314
Richardson, Miranda, 92, 280, 281
Richardson, Natasha, 314
Richardson, Ralph, 21, 45, 150, 187, 217,
   243, 262, 264, 317–319, 333, 394
Richardson, Tony, 8, 21, 319–321, 361,
   368, 369
Rickman, Alan, 363
Ridley, Arnold, 16
Riefenstahl, Leni, 60
Riff Raff, 53, 54, 247
Rigby, Ray, 181, 182
Ring, The, 184
Ritchard, Cyril, 28
Ritchie, Guy, 347
Ritelis, Viktors, 74
Roache, Linus, 35
Road Safety for Children, 38
Roaring Twenties, The, 153
Rob Roy (1995), 198
Rob Roy, The Highland Rogue, 367
Robbery Under Arms, 130
Robbery, 19
Roberts, Julia, 132
Roberts, Rachel, 362
Robeson, Paul, 331, 332
Robin Hood, televisions series, 135
Robinson, Bernard, 116, 275
Robinson, Casey, 366
Robinson, Edward G., 13
Robson, Flora, 133, 321–322
Robson, Mark, 396
Roc, Patricia, 49, 322–323
Rock, The, 73
Rockets Galore, 102
Rocking Horse Winner, The, 187, 269, 323
Roeg, Nicholas, xii, 65, 112, 113,
   324–325, 337
Rolfe, Guy, 174, 306
Roman, Ruth, 216

Rome Express, 231
Romeo and Juliet (1936), 150
Romney, Edana, 75, 306
Romulus Films, 68, 174, 200, 352
Room at the Top, xiii, xv, 26, 68, 69, 174, 175, 319, 325–326, 361
Room with a View, A, 36, 104
Roome, Alfred, 276, 277
Root of All Evil, The, 49
Rope, 185
Rose, William, 146, 147, 227, 228
Rosenberg, Max, 7
Rosmer, Milton, 60
Rossington, Norman, 58
Roth, Tim, 378, 379, 390
Rowson, Leslie, 382
Rudolf, Alan, 66
Ruling Class, The, 177, 298, 344
Run for the Sun, 37, 194, 326–327
Run for Your Money, 169
Running Man, The, 317
Russell, Ken, 22, 106, 213, 327–328
Russell, Theresa, 324
Rutherford, Margaret, 167, 328–329
Ryan, Kathleen, 123
Ryan, Robert, 80, 81, 265
Ryan's Daughter, 235, 270

Sabotage, 184
Sabrina, 33, 113
Safe, 55
Sailor from Gibralter, The, 320
Saint in London, The, 158
Saint, The, 19
Saint's Vacation, The, 158
Sally in Our Alley, 129
Salome's Last Dance, 214
Saltzman, Harry, 115, 319
Sammy and Rosie Get Laid, 337
Sammy Going South, 257
Sanctuary, 320
Sand Pebbles, 14
Sanders of the River, 20, 21, 77, 118, 224, 290, 331–333, 345, 368
Sanders, George, 158, 323
Sands of the Kalahari, 19, 122
Sangster, Jimmy, 79, 116, 117, 366
Sapphire, 102, 103, 234, 376

Saraband for Dead Lovers, 102, 103
Saratoga Trunk, 321
Sasdy, Peter, 71
Saturday Night and Sunday Morning, xiii, 80, 131, 132, 320, 325, 361
Savage Innocents, The, 297
Saville, Victor, xv, 124, 182, 183, 268, 333–334
Saving Private Ryan, 46
Sayers, Dorothy L., 56
Scacchi, Greta, 121
Scandal, 198, 334–336
Scaramouche, 157
Scarlet Thread, The, 175
Scars of Dracula, 18
Schell, Maria, 154
Schepisi, Fred, 190–191, 391
Schickel, Richard, 235
Schlesinger, John, 26, 64, 65, 95, 96, 213, 222, 223, 324, 336–338
School for Scandal, 158
Schoonmaker, Thelma, 309
Scorsese, Martin, 192, 309
Scott of the Antarctic, 71, 269
Scott, George C., 65
Scott, Gordon, 167, 355
Scott, Janette, 23
Scott, Lizabeth, 191, 249
Scott-Thomas, Kristin, 140, 141, 280
Scrooge (1951), 344
Scrooge (1970), 132
Scudamore, Margaret, 314
Scum, 391
Sea Fury, 122
Sea Hawk, The, 321
Séance on a Wet Afternoon, 14, 137
Searchers, The, 289, 379
Searle, Ronald, 24
Sears, Heather, 135
Secombe, Harry, 216, 338
Secret Agent (1936), 150, 184, 314
Secret Agent (1996), 191
Secret Beyond the Door, The, 315
Secret Ceremony, 252
Secret Mission, 156
Secret People, 108
Secrets and Lies, 243, 370
Segal, George, 137, 213

Sellers, Peter, 12, 168, 206, 228, 338–340, 356

Selznik, David O., 183, 223, 361

Sense and Sensibility, 363

Separate Tables, 219

Servant, The, 34, 35, 253, 254

Seven Days to Noon, 38

Seven Sinners, 232

Seven Women, 321

Seventh Sin, The, 279

Seventh Veil, The, 38, 257, 264, 284, 340–341, 365

Sexton Blake and the Hooded Terror, 171

Sexy Beast, 391

Seyrig, Delphine, 253

Shadow of a Doubt, 185

Shadowlands, 14, 189

Shaffer, Anthony, 383, 384

Shakespeare in Love, 105

Shallow Grave, xiv, 341–342

Shamberg, Michael, 134

Shampoo, 65

Shaw, George Bernard, 12

Shaw, Susan, 153

She Wore a Yellow Ribbon, 289

Shearer, Moira, 303, 308, 313

Shearer, Norma, 150, 333

Shearing, Joseph (Gabrielle Margaret Vere Long), 29, 263, 348, 349

Sheena, 168

Sheepdog of the Hills, 127

Shelley, Elsa, 39

Shelley, Mary, 86

Shepperton Studios, 224, 283

Sheridan, Dinah, 110

Sheriff of Fractured Jaw, The, 273

Sheriff, R.C., 91

Sherlock Holmes and the Deadly Necklace, 238

Sherman, Vincent, 366

Shine, 151, 394

Shingleton, Wilfred, 161

Ship that Died of Shame, The, 102

Shipping News, The, 104

Ships with Wings, 20

Shiralee, The, 130

Shirley Valentine, 152

Shock Waves, 88

Shock to the System, A, 48

Shoot the Moon, 132

Shooting Stars, 11

Shot in the Dark, A, 339

Sid and Nancy, 285

Signoret, Simone, 326, 379

Silence of the Lambs, The, 188

Silent Dust, 159

Silent Enemy, The, 174, 175, 342–343

Silver Chalice, The, 334

Silver Fleet, The, 46, 318, 394

Sim, Alastair, 24, 33, 162, 163, 230, 231, 329, 343–344

Simba, 332, 344–345

Simmons, Jean, 134, 157, 161, 187

Simon and Laura, 39, 55

Sin of Esther Waters, The. See Esther Waters

Sinclair, Hugh, 158, 322

Sinden, Donald, 2, 110, 113

Sing As We Go, 129

Singer Not the Song, The, 18, 35, 269

Sink the Bismark!, 152

Siodmak, Robert, xiv

Sirk, Douglas, 352

Sixty Glorious Years, 384

Skin Game, The, 346

Sleeping Tiger, The, 34, 252, 253

Sleepy Hollow, 239

Sleuth, 48, 295

Slipper and the Rose, The, 249

Slocombe, Douglas, 197

Small Back Room, The, 21, 46, 90, 127, 136, 308

Smallest Show on Earth, The, 338

Smiley, 224

Smiley's People, 170

Smilin' Through (1941), 333

Smith, Alexis, 253

Smith, Herbert, 182

Smith, Maggie, 69, 190, 279

Snatch, 346–347

So Evil My Love, xiv, 56, 263, 264, 347–349, 365

So Little Time, 154

So Long at the Fair, 33, 134

Soderbergh, Steven, 132, 281

Sofaer, Abraham, 267

Softley, Iain, 192
Soldiers Three, 156, 171
Something Wicked This Way Comes,
   67–68, 69
Son of Captain Blood, The, 366
Son of Robin Hood, 128
Sons and Lovers, 194
Sorcerers, The, 391
Sothern, Ann, 8
Sound Barrier, The, 236, 365
Sound Barrier, The, 318
South Pacific, 72
South Riding, 333
Space 1999, 78
Spacey, Kevin, 104
Spall, Timothy, 371
Spartacus, 189, 295
Spellbound, 185
Spider and the Fly, The, xiii, 173, 210,
   306, 349
Spiegel, Sam, 236
Spielberg, Steven, 14
Spillane, Mickey, 334
Spoliansky, Mischa, 290, 332
Spotswood (The Efficiency Expert), 188
Spring in Park Lane, 385
Spy in Black, The, 60, 154, 186, 307
Spy Who Loved Me, The, 152
Squeaker, The, 281
Square Peg, The, xv, 350–351, 392
St. John, Earl, 39, 110
St. Martin's Lane, 173
Stage Fright, 367
Stallone, Sylvester, 150
Stamp, Terence, 198, 337
Stanley, Kim, 137
Stapenhorst, Gunther, 60
Star Is Born, A, 265
Star Wars, 88, 170
Stars Look Down, The, 248, 314, 316
Steaming, 254
Steele, Tommy, 19,
Stepford Wives, The, 137
Stephens, Martin, 377
Sternberg, Josef von, 257
Stevens, George, 87
Stevenson, Juliet, 121
Stevenson, Robert, 244

Stewart, Eve, 371
Stewart, James, 396
Still Life, 42
Stitch in Time, A, 350, 392
Stockwell, Dean, 253
Stoker, Bram, 30, 116, 117, 280, 294, 327
Stolen Face, 191
Stone, Oliver, 189, 190
Storey, David, 8, 361, 362
Storm in a Teacup, 334
Storm Over the Nile, 174
Storm, Lesley, 160
Story of Esther Costello, The, 352
Story of Robin Hood, The, 367
Strange Bedfellows, 355
Straw Dogs, 107
Street Corner, 39, 84
Stuart, Alexander, 378, 379
Study in Terror, A, 104
Stunt Man, The, 298
Subotsky, Milton, 7
Subway in the Sky, 39
Sullivan, Francis L., 20, 161, 283, 307, 394
Sum of All Fears, The, 22
Summer Madness, 236
Sunday Bloody Sunday, 130, 213
Sundowners, The, 218, 219
Sunset Boulevard, 342
Surviving Picasso, 189
Sutherland, Donald, 65, 66, 113, 324
Swarm, 48
Sweet Smell of Success, 256
Swinging London Films, xv, 26, 147, 148,
   368
Sword and the Rose, The, 367
Sykes, Peter, 364
Syms, Sylvia, 93, 102, 125, 376

Tabori, George, 396
Take My Life, xiv, 154, 171, 278, 353–354
Tale of Two Cities, A, 238
Tales of Hoffman, The, 224
Tarzan and His Mate, 354
Tarzan and the Lost Safari, 354
Tarzan Goes to India, 168
Tarzan's Fight for Life, 354
Tarzan's Greatest Adventures, 72, 167,
   354–355

Taste of Fear, 238, 366
Taste of Honey, A, xiii, 320
Taste the Blood of Dracula, 77
Tavernier, Bernard, 34
Tawny Pipit, 61
Taylor, Don, 166
Taylor, Elizabeth, 130, 334
Taylor, Robert, 157, 334
Taymor, Julie, 189
Tea and Sympathy, 218, 219
Tea with Mussolini, 105
Tempi Duri per I Vampiri, 135
Tempean Films, 122
Tempest, The, 150
Temple, Shirley, 244
Temptation Harbour, 71
10 Rillington Place, 14, 197
Tendre Dracula, 88
Term of Trial, 295
Terminal Man, The, 81
Terminus, 336, 338
Terror House. See The Night Has Eyes
Terror of the Tongs, 238
Terry-Thomas, 33, 37, 163, 338, 355–357
That Summer, 391
Theatre of Blood, 177
Theory of Flight, The, 36
There was a Crooked Man, 392
There's Only One Jimmy Gribble, 54
Thewliss, David, 109, 243
They Came to a City, 102
They Can't Hang Me, 166, 357–358
They Made Me a Fugitive, xiii, 148, 158, 194, 284, 293, 358–359
They Were Sisters, 49
They're a Weird Mob, 309
Thief of Baghdad, The, 78
Things to Come, 77, 261
Third Man, The, xv, 194, 223, 224, 316, 359–361
Third Secret, The, 104
Thirty-Nine Steps, The (1935), 111, 184
This Happy Breed, 217, 278, 281
This Man Is News, 186
This Sporting Life, xiii, 8, 222, 325, 361–362
300 Spartans, The, 128
Thomas, Andre, 75

Thomas, Michael, 335
Thomas, Ralph, 2, 111, 231, 287
Thompson, Emma, 121, 189, 196, 362–363
Thompson, Jack, 280
Thompson, Sophie, 121
Thorndike, Sybil, 183, 216
Thornton, Billy Bob, 281
Those Magnificent Men in Their Flying Machines, 355
Three Godfathers, 289
Three Men in a Boat, 68, 174
Three Musketeers, The (1973), 239
Thunder Rock, 38
Thunderball, 343
Thursday's Children, 9
Tierney, Gene, 283, 394
Tiger Bay, 270
Tiger in the Smoke, 17–18
Time Is My Enemy, 364
Time Without Pity, 87, 115, 366
Tinker, Tailor, Soldier, Spy, 170
Titus, 189
To Catch a Thief, 52
To Dorothy a Son, 39
To Paris with Love, 173
To Sir with Love, 147
To the Devil a Daughter, 364–365
To the Public Danger, 134, 153
Todd, Ann, 38, 194, 236, 257, 258, 264, 306, 333, 348, 365–366
Todd, Mike, 282
Todd, Richard, 71, 90, 94, 187, 209, 210, 333, 334
Tom Jones, xiv, 26, 131, 132, 165, 319, 320, 368
tom thumb, 268
Tomlinson, David, 134
Tommy, 328
Tomorrow at Ten, 71
Tomorrow Never Dies, 105
Too Late the Hero, 48
Too Young to Love, 39
Topsy-Turvy, 243, 369–371
Torment, 167
Touch of Class, A, 213
Touch of Death, 71
Tourneur, Jacques, 84, 322

Towering Inferno, The, 167, 278
Town Like Alice, A, 130
Town on Trial, 167
Townsend, Leo, 253
Track 29, 325
Tracker, The, 168
Traffic, 281
Trail of the Pink Panther, The, 339
Train of Events, 130
Trainspotting, xiv, 54, 341
Traitor, The, 238
Traveller's Joy, 394
Travers, Linden, 288
Treasure Island (1950), 281
Treasure of Silver Lake, The, 157
Treasure of the Sierra Madre, The, 341
Trenker, Luis, 60
Trevelyan, John (British Board of Film
    Censors), 325–326
Trials of Oscar Wilde, The, 130
Trinder, Tommy, 23
Trouble in Store, 350, 391, 392
Trouble in the Glen, 249
Truffaut, Francois, xii, 65, 324
Truman, Michael, 78
Truth About Spring, The, 270
Truth About Women, The, 175
Tunes of Glory, 169, 269, 279
Turn of the Screw, 68, 209
Turner, Lana, 55
Tushingham, Rita, 130
Tutti Frutti, 363
Twenty (Glory!Glory!), 9
24 Hours of a Woman's Life, 334
Twenty Four Seven, 190, 371–372
Twice Upon a Time, 309
Twins of Evil, 88
2000 Women, 49, 322, 323
Two Cities Films, 17, 237
Two Deaths, 325
Two for the Road, 132
Two Left Feet, 18
Tyson, Cathy, 190

Uncle Silas, 17, 53
Under Capricorn, 185
Under the Greenwood Tree, 231

Undercover, 19
Unman, Wittering and Zigo, 373–374
Unmarried Woman, An, 22
Unsworth, Geoffrey, 187
Untouchables, The, 72, 73
Up the Front, 190
Up the Junction, 247, 304
Upturned Glass, The, 265

V.I.P.s, 12, 329
Valentine, Val, 232
Valk, Frederick, 70
Valley of the Eagles, The, 237, 380
Valli, Alida, 316, 365
Value for Money, 113
Vampire Lovers, The, 18, 77, 88
Van Sant, Gus, 198
Vandyke Productions, 364
Varley, Beatrice, 179, 276
Varnel, Marcel, 165, 178
Vaughan, Frankie, 385
Vault of Horror, 7, 18, 356
Vengeance of Fu-Manchu, The, 239
Verdict, The, 265
Versois, Odile, 397
Vertigo, 75, 185
Vetchinsky, Alex, 263
Victim, 34, 102, 375–376
Victor, Charles, 120
Victoria the Great, 384
Victors, The, 132
Viertel, Berthold, 244–245
Vigil in the Night, 87
Viktor and Viktoria, 268
Village of the Damned, 376–377
Violent Playground, 19
Virgin Queen, The, 367
Visconti, Luchino, 34
Vote for Huggett, 380

Wagon Master, 289
Wake Island, 382
Walbrook, Anton, 145, 158, 313
Walkabout, 324
Walker, Polly, 281
Wallace, Edgar, 281, 316, 331
Waller, Anthony, 169

Wallis, Hal, 345

Walsh, Kay, 138, 161, 229

Walsh, Raoul, 273

Walters, Julie, 152

Walters, Thorley, 356

Walton, Joseph. *See* Joseph Losey

Waltz of the Toreadors, 168, 338

War and Peace (television miniseries), 189

War Zone, The, 378–379, 390

Ward, Stephen, 335–336

Warner, Jack, 5, 12, 31, 34, 39, 52, 78, 197, 211, 276, 379–380

Warwick Films, 115

Waterhouse, Keith, 223

Waterloo Road, 156, 269, 343

Watkin, David, 63

Watson, Emily, 180, 181

Watt, Harry, 130

Wattis, Richard, 33, 70

Waxman, Franz, 283

Way Ahead, The, 194, 316, 381–382

Way to the Stars, The, 11, 194, 314

Wayne, John, 157, 175, 215, 379

Wayne, Naunton, 78, 100, 203

Weak and the Wicked, The, 114

Weaker Sex, The, 17

Webb, Clifton, 279

Wedding Rehearsal, 382–383

Weintraub, Sy, 354

Weismuller, Johnny, 354

Welch, Raquel, 239

Welcome to Arrow Beach, 175

Welland, Colin, 62

Welles, Orson, 76, 168, 249, 316, 359, 361

Wells, H.G., 100, 261

Went the Day Well?, 21, 127

Werewolf of London, 186

West, Morris, 80

West, Nathanael, 337

Westward Passage, 294

Wetherby, 105

Whale, James, 85, 87

Whales of August, The, 8

Wharton, Edith, 97, 192

What's Good for the Goose, 392

Wheatley, Dennis, 106, 239

When the Bough Breaks, 322

When We Are Married, 33

Where Angels Fear to Tread, 36

Where Were You When the Lights Went Out?, 355

Where's Jack?, 19

Whisky Galore!, 78, 165, 256, 327

Whisperers, The, 306

Whistle Down the Wind, 21, 137, 235

White Buffalo, The, 242

White Bus, The, 188

White Corridors, 394

White Mischief, 198

White Shadow, The, 184

White Unicorn, The, 165

White, Carol, 305

Whiting, John, 107

Whitman, Stuart, 122, 355

Whittaker, Ian, 196

Whitty, Dame May, 248

Who Framed Roger Rabbit, 190

Whore, 327

Wicked Lady, The (1945), 248, 265, 322, 323

Wicker Man, The, 237, 383–384

Wicking, Christopher, 31, 364

Widmark, Richard, 17, 37, 194, 283, 306, 394

Wilcox, Herbert, 333, 384–386, 394

Wild and the Willing, The, 197

Wild Bill, 198

Wilde, Oscar, 12

Wilder, Billy, 239

Wilding, Michael, 94, 158, 367, 385

Williams, Hugh, 171

Williams, Kenneth, 57, 58

Willis, Ted, 102

Wilson, Josephine, 61

Wilson, Sandy, 328

Wimperis, Arthur, 224

Windbag the Sailor, 178

Windom's Way, 279

Windsor, Barbara, 57

Winger, Debra, 189

Wings of the Dove, The, 35, 192, 386–387

Wings of the Morning, 387–388

Winslow Boy, The (1948), 11, 71, 96, 111, 388–390
Winslow Boy, The (1999), 388–390
Winsor, Kathleen, 84
Winstone, Ray, xii, 286, 379, 390–391
Winter's Guest, The, 363
Wintle, Julian, 361
Wisdom, Norman, xv, 350, 351, 391–392
Wit, 363
Witches, The, 325
Witchfinder General, 392
Withers, Googie, 138, 173, 283, 304, 393–395
Witherstein, Frank, 238
Wodehouse, P.G., 56
Wolfit, Donald, 132
Woman in a Dressing Gown, 241
Woman in the Window, The, 120
Women in Love, 22, 213, 328
Women of Twilight, 174, 175
Wooden Horse, The, 136
Woodfall Films, 115, 319, 368
Woodward, Edward, 237
Woolf Brothers, 68, 174
Woolf, John, 39, 174
World Is Not Enough, The, 54, 105
Wright, Tony, 18
Wrong Box, The, 137
Wuthering Heights, 294, 321
Wyler, William, 272, 294
Wyman, Jane, 367
Wynyard, Diana, 145, 318
Yangtse Incident, 367

Yanks, 337, 338
Yellow Balloon, 241
Yellow Caesar, 78
Yellow Canary, The, 385
Yellow Rolls Royce, The, 12
Yellow Ticket, 294
Yesterday's Enemy, 19, 166
Yield to the Night, 113, 241
Yordan, Phillip, 216
York, Michael, 253
York, Susannah, 122, 152, 273
You Only Live Twice, 152
Young and Innocent, 184
Young Bess, 46, 157
Young Lovers, The, 11, 396–397
Young Mr. Pitt, 46
Young Scarface (Brighton Rock), 43
Young Veterans, The, 78
Young Winston, 14
Young, Roland, 383
Young, Terence, 75, 115, 141, 237, 306

Zanuck, Darryl F., 17, 84, 282
Zeffirelli, Franco, 22
Zemeckis, Robert, 190
Zero One, 19
Zetterling, Mai, 101
Zimbalist, Stephanie, 280
Zorba the Greek, 22
Zulu Dawn, 122, 399
Zulu, 19, 47, 398–399

About the Author

GEOFF MAYER is the Chair of the Cinema Studies Department and Deputy Chair of the School of Communication, Arts, and Critical Enquiry at Latrobe University in Melbourne, Australia. He co-edited *The Oxford Companion to Australian Film* and was the author of *New Australian Cinema and Film as Text.*